National Intelligencer Newspaper Abstracts 1850

Joan M. Dixon

HERITAGE BOOKS
2007

HERITAGE BOOKS
AN IMPRINT OF HERITAGE BOOKS, INC.

Books, CDs, and more—Worldwide

For our listing of thousands of titles see our website
at
www.HeritageBooks.com

Published 2007 by
HERITAGE BOOKS, INC.
Publishing Division
65 East Main Street
Westminster, Maryland 21157-5026

Copyright © 2007 Joan M. Dixon

All rights reserved. No part of this book may be reproduced or transmitted in any form or by any means, electronic or mechanical, including photocopying, recording or by any information storage and retrieval system without written permission from the author, except for the inclusion of brief quotations in a review.

International Standard Book Number: 978-0-7884-4183-7

NATIONAL INTELLIGENCER NEWSPAPER
WASHINGTON, D C
1850

TABLE OF CONTENTS

Daily National Intelligencer, Washington, D C, 1850: pg 1

Appointments by the Pres: see index pg 510
Arctic Expedition: 234
Battles of the Revolution: 419

Commencements: Columbian College: 296
              Nat'l Med College, D C: 155
              Visitation Academy, Gtwn: 302-304
              St Mary's, Chas Co, Md: 333

Continental money: 61
Court Martial of Capt Thos Ap Catesby Jones: 490

Death of Pres Zachary Taylor: 288
Deaths on the ship Lexington: 226-227
Deaths on the ship Sarah: 30
Funeral of Pres Zachary Taylor: 287-289

Government Bureau heads: 212-214
Heirs of Clement Wood: 161
Heirs of Kosciusko: 52
Licenses issued in Wash, D C: 4; 162; 243-249; 371-372

Monument of Baron DeKalb: 159-160
McDonogh estate: 429 & 489
Mechanics of Wash Navy Yard: 207
Military Academy Cadets: 186
Military Academy-Cadets appointed: 123; 198-199
Mount Alban, D C, students: 147
Mount Vernon: 276 & 426

Newspapers edited by Ladies: 181
Naval appointments: 404

Officers of the: Brandywine: 468
Marion: 56 & 482
Porpoise: 249
St Mary's: 255
Saranac: 217 & 469
Saratoga: 376

Officers of the War of 1812: 85; 197-198
Outrages on Swedish colony: 173
Packet ship Caleb Grinshaw disaster: 31-32

Sale of paintings: 156
Steamer Griffith disaster: 264
Steamer Troy disaster: 141
Steamboat Arkansas No 5 disaster: 464
Steamboat St John's disaster: 120
Steamship Southern disaster: 404
Stephen Decatur monument: 497

Trial of Capt Wm K Gardiner: 265
Victims of N Y disaster: 67

War Dept orders: 212-214; 325-329; 386; 399-400; 464; 482-485
Washington City: 97
Wash City officials: 266-267

Wash City tax sale: 501-508
Washington's farewell address sale: 73
Washington National Monument: see index pg 579
Yellow fever deaths on ship Ohio: 187 & 189
Yellow fever deaths on storeship Supply: 250

Index: 509

Dedicated to the memory of my Gr Gr Grandparents:
Geo W Keating, b. 1810-Va; died Jul 17, 1867-Wash, D C
Mrd: 1834 ca
Sarah A Jones, b. 1813, England; died Jul 8, 1883-Wash, D C

PREFACE
Daily National Intelligencer Newspaper Abstracts
1850
Joan M Dixon

The National Intelligencer & Washington Advertiser is hereafter the Daily National Intelligencer. It was the first newspaper printed in Washington, D C; Samuel H Smith, the originator. The same was transferred to Jos Gales, jr on Aug 31, 1810; on Nov 1, 1812, the paper was under the firm of Jos Gales, sr, & Wm W Seaton. The Library of Congress has microfilm of the paper from the first issue of Oct 31, 1800 thru Jan 8, 1870, the final paper. The Evening Star Newspaper of Jan 10, 1870 reports: The Intelligencer is discontinued: the proprietor, Mr Alex Delmar, says that having lost several thousand dollars, & being in poor health, he has resolved to discontinue its publication.

Included in the abstracts are advertisements; appointments by the President; Hse o/Rep petitions; passed Acts; legal notices; marriages; deaths; mscl notices; social events; tax lists; military promotions; court cases; deaths by accident; prisoners; & maritime information-crews. Items or events which might be a clue as to the location, age or relationship of an individual are copied.

No attempt has been made to correct the spelling. Due to the length of some articles, it was necessary to present only the highlights of same. Chancery and Equity records are copied as written.

The index contains <u>all</u> surnames and *tracts of lands/places*. **Maritime vessels** are found under barge, boat, brig, frig, schn'r, ship, sloop, steamboat, tugboat, yacht or vessel.

ABBREVIATIONS:

AA CO	ANNE ARUNDEL COUNTY
CO	COMPANY/COUNTY
CMDER	COMMANDER
CMDOR	COMMODOR
D C	DISTRICT OF COLUMBIA
ELIZ	ELIZABETH
ELIZA	ELIZA
MONTG CO	MONTGOMERY COUNTY
PG CO	PRINCE GEORGES CO
WASH	WASHINGTON
WASH, D C	WASHINGTON, DISTRICT OF COLUMBIA

BOOKS IN THE NATIONAL INTELLIGENCER NEWSPAPER SERIES: 1800-1805/1806-1810/1811-1813/1814-1817/1818-1820/1821-1823/1824-1826/1827-1829/1830-1831/1832-1833/1834-1835/1836-1837/1838-1839/1840/1841/1842/1843/1844/1845/1846/1847/1848/1849/1850 SPECIAL: CIVIL WAR 2 VOLS, 1861-1865

> **DAILY NATIONAL INTELLIGENCER NEWSPAPER**
> **WASHINGTON, D C**
> **1850**

TUE JAN 1, 1850
Senate: 1-Ptn of Caroline L Eustis, widow of the late Gov Eustis, of Mass. Her husband entered the army as a surgeon on the day of the battle of Bunker Hill, & continued to discharge the duties appertaining to a surgeon in the army through the whole war. Afterwards he became distinguished, politically & personally. During his life he applied for no pension or allowance of any kind, his circumstances not requiring that he should make a demand upon the country for an allowance. He was afterwards married, & his marriage was subsequent to the period fixed by law for authorizing widows of Revolutionary ofcrs to draw pension. Referred to the Cmte on Revolutionary Pensions. 2-Ptn of Eli R W Ross, asking the confirmation of his title to a tract of land in the State of Louisiana: referred to the Cmte on Private Land Claims. 3-Ptn of Morgan O Ross, asking the confirmation of his title to a tract of land: referred to the Cmte on Private Land Claims. 4-Ptn of Chas C Henderson & Wm T Remington, heirs of Jas L Henderson, asking confirmation to their title to a tract of land: referred to the Cmte on Private Land Claims. 5-Ptn of John Leroy, an express rider in the Mexican war, asking to be allowed a pension in consideration of a wound received while in the discharge of his duty: referred to the Cmte on Pensions. 6-Ptn of Harriet Pearce, widow of Dutee J Pearce, asking that the suit against the estate of her late husband may be discontinued: referred to the Cmte on the Judiciary. 7-Memorial of the heirs at law of Capt Wm Beatty, who entered the public service in the spring of 1776 as an ofcr in the Revolutionary army, & continued in the service until killed in the battle in the State of S C on Apr 25, 1781, prior to the passage of the resolution of Oct of 1781, promising half pay to the widow of ofcrs & soldiers who were killed in service. These memoralists also represent that this ofcr was unmarried, & died without leaving any children, & they think it just that some compensation should be made to his heirs for his 5 years' service & for losing his life in fighting the battles of the Revolution. 8-Memorial of Wm Smith & Isaac Sheen, representing themselves to be the legitimate Presidents of the Church of Jesus Christ or Latter Day Saints, & also 12 members of that church. More commonly known as Mormons. Referred to the Cmte on Territories. 9-Memorial of Hal J Kelley, asking to be allowed a grant of land in the Territory of Oregon, in consideration of services & sacrifices made in the exploration & settlement of that country: referred to the Cmte on Public Lands. 10-Memorial of Thos Arnold, & the memorial of the heirs of Nathan Lunt, asking indemnity for French spoliations prior to 1800: to lie on the table. 11-Memorial of the heirs of John Marrast, the heirs of John Smith, the heirs of John Guion, & the legal reps of John M Burt, asking indemnity for French spoliations prior to 1800.
12-Memorial of the heirs & legal reps of Otis Little, of the heirs of Mark Hatch, & the excs of Jas Crawford, asking indemnity for French spoliations prior to 1800: to lie on the table. 13-Ptn of David Gross, a soldier in the last war with Great Britian, asking to be allowed a pension: referred to the Cmte on Pensions. 14-Ptn of E P Hastings, asking

compensation for services as pension agent of the U S: referred to the Cmte on Pensions. 15-Memorials of the legal reps of T B Hathaway & Stephen Carpenter, & from the rep of Carrington Simpkins, asking indemnity for French spoliations prior to 1800: to lie on the table. 16-Additional documents were submitted in relation to the claim of Lewis Warrington: referred to the Cmte on Naval Affairs. 17-Memorial of the heirs of John Cameron, asking indemnity for French spoliations prior to 1800: to lie on the table. 18-Ptn of Thos & Eliz Armstrong, heirs of Josiah Fletcher, asking compensation for losses by depredations committed on his property by hostile Indians in the Creek war: referred to the Cmte of Claims. 19-Memorial of Benj E S Ely, proposing for the consideration of Congress a plan for maintaining a military force in the Territory of Calif: referred to the Cmte on Military Affairs. 20-Ptn of David McDuffie, a soldier in the last war with Great Britain, asking an increase of pension: referred to the Cmte on Pensions. 21-Memorial of the heirs of Edw Emerson, jr, asking indemnity for French spoliations prior to 1800: to lie on the table. 22-Ptn of Wm & Jno C Ribber, asking compensation for a vessel lost while in the employ of the U S as a transport during the Mexican war: referred to the Cmte of Claims. 23-Memorials of the heirs of Jas Williams, the heirs of Thos W Norman, & the heirs of the firm of Corringham & Nesbit, late merchants, asking indemnity for French spoliations: to lie on the table. 24-Two ptns of citizens of Lee Co, Iowa, asking an increase of the pension of Isaac W Griffith, a soldier in the Mexican war: referred to the Cmte on Pensions. 25-Ordered, that the ptns now on the files of the Senate in the several cases of Allen G Johnson, A H Cole, John M McIntosh, & Isaac Barnes, sen, be referred to the Cmte of Claims. 26-Ordered, that the documents on the files of the Senate relating to the claim of the heirs of Jas Rumsey be referred to the Cmte on Public Lands. 27-Ordered, that the ptn of Calvin Read, & the ptn of Geo W Walter, on file in the Senate, be referred to the Cmte of Claims. 28-Memorial of Wm H Burnes, an ofcr of the navy, which was referred to the Cmte on Naval Affairs: that the papers on file be withdrawn, that he may be enabled to carry his claim before the Dept. 29-Ordered, that W A Campbell, surviving partner of Jos C Watson, deceased, have leave to withdraw his memorial & papers. 30-Ordered, that Geo Poindexter have leave to withdraw his ptn & papers. 31-Bill for the relief of Cincinnatus Trousdale & John G Connelly: referred to the Cmte on Military Affairs. 32-The House passed a bill granting the franking privilege to Sarah Polk. 33-Resolved, that the Pres of the U S be requested to furnish the Senate with copies of all the papers on file relative to the removal or retention in ofc of Jesse B Clements, late marshal of the middle district of Tenn. 34-Cmte on Pensions: to inquire into granting to John Hinchell, the arrears of pension previous to Mar 7, 1834. 35-Cmte on Pensions: to inquire into granting to a pension to the widow of Dr Henry Lameke, late a surgeon in the U S army.

Commission on Claims against Mexico: Dec 31, 1849. 1-The case of Benj Holbrook, master of the ship **John**, claiming for the seizure of that vessel at Campeachy, in Jun 1835, as not having sufficient manifests, being taken up for consideration, the Board found the claim valid, & is allowed; the amount to be awarded subject to the future action of the Board. 2-The case of John Belden, claimant, for the forcible occupancy & use of certain real estate in the town of Matamoros, together with documents, the Board is of the opinion that the claim is valid, & is allowed; the amount to be awarded subject to the future action of the Board.

House of Reps: 1-Resolved, that the Pres be requested to inform this House whether Jas Collier, collector to the port of San Francisco, has received from the Gov't any appropriation in money or otherwise, as an outfit, or to defray the expenses of his journey to Calif; &, if so, how much, & by what authority of law. 2-Take from the files the papers of Robt Beach, Sylvester Blodget, & Jos Johnson, to be: referred to the Cmte on Pensions. 3-Bill for the relief of Jacob P Montgomery & other soldiers in the late Mexican war, introduced. 4-Bill for the relief of the assignees under the Baron De Ferriet: introduced. 5-Ptn of the heirs of Moses Van Campen. 6-Ptn of Jas Hamilton & Philip Schuyler. 7-Ptn of E Armstrong, for arrears of pension. 8-Ptn of T C Green, praying the restoration of his rights, lost in consequence of the negligence of the public ofcrs. 9-Ptn of B M Bouton, praying compensation for the use of his patent for the manufacture of percussion caps. 10-Ptn of Amaziah Ford, for arrears of pension. 11-Ptn of the heirs of John H Piatt, praying for the balance due him from the U S. 12-Ptn of John Hammond, Jos Sayward, & many others, for indemnity for spoliations by the French prior to 1800. 13-Ptn of Saml Cox, of Malden, & A T Goodwin, of Lynn, & others, last makers, using Blanchard's patented machine, asking protection of their rights against importers of lasts from the British provinces. 14-Memorial of Cmder T O Selfridge, of Boston, that his ptn herefore presented may be again considered. 15-Memorial of Jas W Wilkins, that he may receive the salary of a purser for the time he performed the duties of a purser during the war with Mexico. 16-Ptn of Susan Worth, mother-in-law of Gen Worth, for a pension. 17-Ptn of Nathan Corey, of Lake Co, Ill, soldier of Revolution-for a pension

For rent: a farm of 200 acres, 4 miles from Wash City. Apply on the premises to John F Clark.

Mrs M A Hamilton, from Balt, has constantly on hand a fresh supply of fancy Millinery & other fancy goods.

Henry Douglas, Florist & Seedsman, corner of 15th & G sts.

Orphans Court of Wash Co, D C. Letters of administration on the personal estate of Sam'l L Caldwell, late of Ala, deceased. -Chas H Stewart-adm, ofc 15th st, Wash, D C.

R H Fauntleroy, an assist in the Coast Survey, who arrived at Galveston on Dec 12, took suddenly sick & died the next day. His body was brought to New Orleans to be conveyed to his late residence, New Harmony, Indiana.

A little daughter of Hon Joel Jones, Mayor of Phil, died on Fri last from the effects of having swallowed a piece of ivory about the size of a button a few days previous.

Mrd: on Thu last, in Annapolis, by Rev Mr Nelson, Mr Robt F Bonsall to Miss Eliza Weems, both of Annapolis, Md.

Mrd: on Dec 27, at Balt, Pierre Della Torre, of Charleston, S C, to Mary Gordon Norris, of Balt, Md.

Died: on Fri last, in Phil, at the residence of his father-in-law, M Lewis, Sam'l Griffitts Fisher, age 40 years, atty at law, of Mobile. Lewis was a native of Phil.

WED JAN 2, 1850
Wash Corp: Condolences to the family of the late Wm Lloyd, a rep in the Councils of Wash City, from the 7th Ward, who died at his residence on Dec 27th, in their sudden bereavement of a husband, father & friend.

Rev Moses S Morris was shot dead recently, near Decatur, Ala, by Dr Delony. Difficulty appears to have been in family discords. Delony was committed to jail for trial.

Deliberately shot & killed: Mrs Lucinda Franklin, wife of Thos T Franklin, Dec 14, Owen Co, Indiana, by Martin Condor. Condor immediately fled.

Mrd: on Dec 23, by Rev Mr Mathias Alig, Marcus Claveleam & Mary Murray, both of Wash.

Died: on Dec 31, 1840, after a lingering illness, Ellen, consort of H G Korff, of Gtwn, D C, aged 31 years.

Died: on Mon, Laura Seymour, aged 7 years, 2nd daughter of Silas H & Mary B Hill. Her funeral is this day at 1 o'clock.

The gentleman who abstracted my wallet from my pocket yesterday, at the Presidential Mansion, will confer a favor by returning it to me. If desired, I will make a suitable reward. Leave at the letter-box of this newspaper. –Wm Cleary

THU JAN 3, 1850
A brutal attack was made on Mrs Fienfrutch, of Lancaster, Pa, on Fri last. Slight hopes of recovery. Suspicion rested strongly against a former husband of Mrs F from whom she was divorced on account of ill-treatment. The mother of the victim is missing.

Wm E Knowlton, who cut the throat of Prudence Arnold, age 12 years, at Uxbridge, Mass, in Jan last, had his trial last week, at Worcester, & was found guilty. The defence was insanity. He was sentenced to be hanged.

Mrd: on Jan 1, by Rev L F Morgan, John T Dennesson & Harriet H Hodgson.

Mrd: on Jan 1, by Rev F S Evans, Lewis Eyre to Mahala Eliz Smallwood.

Died: on Dec 31, in Wash, Chas Butt, youngest son of Solomon & Rebecca M Butt, age 5 months & 23 days.

Died: on Dec 28, in Phil, Saml Griffitts Fisher, atty, of Mobile; at residence of his father-in-law, M Lewis, age 40 years. Native of Phil, he studied law in Wash & moved to Mobile in early manhood.

Died: on Jan 2, in Wash, Helen, daughter of J C G & Cath Kennedy, late of Meadville, Pa, age 4 years, of scarlet fever.

New Boarding House, 11th & Pa ave, formerly occupied by J K Boyd.
-Robt B Hackney, late of Va.

FRI JAN 4, 1850
Senate: 1-Ptn & papers of Gen Roger Jones be withdrawn from the files & referred to the Cmte on Military Affairs. 2-Papers relating to the claim of Capt Gilbert Knapp be withdrawn from the files & referred to the Cmte on Commerce. 3-Bills introduced: relief of Jos P Williams. Relief of Miles Knowlton. 4-Cmte on Printing: to print the memorial of Hall J Kelley: which was agreed to. 5-Memorial of John N Buckhouse & John Simkins, adms of Covington Simkins; the memorial of John D Powell, citizens of Alexandria, Va; & the memorial of the heirs of Jas Miller: asking indemnity for French spoliations prior to 1800: ordered to lie on the table. 6-Memorial of Wm A Christian, a purser in the Navy, asking to be allowed a credit on his accounts made to certain warrant ofcrs on board the U S steamer **Princeton**: referred to the Cmte on Naval Affairs. 7-Memorial of Eliz B Lomax, widow of a deceased army ofcr, asking to be allowed a pension: referred to the Cmte on Pensions. 8-Ptn of J Downs, asking compensation for forage supplied by him to a company of mounted riflemen, in the Creek war of 1812: referred to the Cmte of Claims. 9-Memorial of the heirs of Joice Billups, deceased; memorial of the heirs of Ed Durant; memorial of the heirs of Philip Carr; memorial of the exc of Thos Edmonds; memorial of the heirs & reps of Alex'r Macauley; & memorial of the heirs of Jas Millar: asking indemnity for French spoliations prior to 1800: to lie on the table. 10-Ptn of Jas S Fowler, asking compensation for services rendered in the public stable by order of the Senate: referred to the Cmte on Public Bldgs. 11-Memorial of the heirs of Wm Melcher; memorial of the heirs of Wm Bartlett & John Storer, asking indemnity for French spoliations prior to 1800: to lie on the table. 12-Memorial of W S Coodery & John Drew, reps of the "old settlers" of the Cherokee Indians, asking that provision may be made for the adjustment of the debts due by that nation, under the treaty of Aug 6, 1846, which, with documents relating to the same subject, submitted by Mr Sturgeon, were referred to the Cmte on Indian Affairs. 13-Memorial of the heirs of Timothy Savage, deceased, asking indemnity for French spoliations prior to 1800: to lie on the table. 14-Memorial of the heirs of Robt Allyn, asking indemnity for French spoliations prior to 1800: to lie on the table. 15-Memorial of the legal reps of John Millikin, asking indemnity for French spoliations, prior to 1800: to lie on the table. 16-Memorial & additional evidence in relation to the claim of Geo Hervey, in behalf of the owners & consignees of the British ship **James Mitchell**, which, with the papers on file in the Senate, relating to the same: referred to the Cmte on Naval Affairs. 17-Memorial of the excxs of Robt Smith, deceased, asking indemnity for French spoliations prior to 1800: to lie on the table. 18-Ptn of W R Hallett, exc of Joshua Kennedy, asking compensation for the destruction of his property by hostile Indians in the Creek war of 1812: referred to the Cmte on Indian Affairs. 19-Ptn of Chas Brannan, John McCully, & the administrator of Francis McCully, asking compensation for a steamboat wrecked while employed by the Gov't as a transport in the Florida war: referred to the Cmte of Claims. 20-Ptn of John Mitchel, a naval pensioner, asking an

increase of his pension: referred to the Cmte on Naval Affairs. 21-Memorial of the heirs & legal reps of F W Geyer, asking indemnity for French spoliations prior to 1800: to lie on the table. 22-Ptn of Thos Johnson & John B Johnson, asking the reimbursement of expenses incurred in defending a defective title to certain lands derived from the Gov't: referred to the Cmte of Claims. 23-Memorial of the widow & heirs of Abraham Lasportas, asking indemnity for French spoliations prior to 1800: to lie on the table. 24-Ordered, that the ptn & papers of H L Kendrick, be taken from the files & referred to the Cmte of Claims. 25-Ordered, that the ptn of John S Devlin, adm of Elijah J Weed, late Quartermaster in the Marines, be withdrawn from the files & referred to the Cmte of Claims. 26-Ordered, that the ptn & papers of John Mackall be taken from the files & referred to the Cmte of Claims. 27-Ordered, that the papers in relation to the claims of Jos Watson be taken from the files & referred to the Cmte on Indian Affairs.

House of Reps: 1-Bill granting a pension to Danl Story, introduced. 2-Memorial of Isaac Everett, exc of Harriet Barney, widow of Com Barney, praying indemnity for French spoliations prior to 1800. 3-Memorial of Saml Chenowith, of Jefferson Co, Ky, with documents, praying extension of the pension & bounty laws to himself as a soldier in Wayne's Legion. 4-Memorial of Jos Fitzgerald, a soldier in Wayne's Legion, praying for arrears of pay, & to be placed on the pension roll, also for bounty land. 5-Memorial of A R Woolley & others, central cmte in behalf of the ofcrs of 1812, praying donations of land. 6-Memorial of F A Kounslar & others, praying indemnity for French spoliations prior to 1800. 7-Ptn of Capt Francis Cicott; also, of Geo Reynolds; also, of Hiram Moore & John Hascall; also, of Wm Woodbridge & Henry Chipman. 8-Memorial of David D Porter, of the U S Navy, praying that he may be remunerated for services as diplomatic agent to St Domingo.

M Verbeyst, the celebrated book collector, died lately in Brussels at an advanced age. He had built up his house several stories, almost as high as a church, & so arranged that it contained 300,000 volumes.

Tragic affair resulted in the death of both combatants, at Shreveport, La, on Dec 20, between 2 respectable citizens of that place, Dr Green & Mr D Hester, late a rep in the State Legislature for the parish of Caldo. Mr Hester went to the back door of Dr Green's room, pushed it open, & instantly fired twice at the Dr. Dr Green fired at Mr Hester. Both died. No cause for this melancholy affair is known.

N Y: On Jan 1, a sleigh with 2 men passing up Broadway, struck the curb, & both were thrown out. Mr F Luney, a master builder in 30th st, was instantly killed by breaking his neck. Mr J Shaw was badly injured, but will probably recover. Mr Luney leaves a wife & 5 children.

N Y: On Jan 1, as Mr Jos McClellan was bring up 2 passengers from Staten Island, when his boat was upset & Mr Wm Fream, a comparatively young man, who being inconvenienced by the water being blown upon him, rose suddenly from his seat, & caused the boat to capsize. The 2 passengers drowned. The other man was unknown.

Murder in Phil, on New Year's eve, at a social meting at the house of Mr Henry Hornkeith, a brickmaker, near Gray's Ferry road, Passayunk, a disturbance was created by some of the Schuylkill Rangers, who attacked the house. Mr Hornkeith, jr, was shot & died in half an hour. He was 32 years of age. Mr Hornkeith was stabbed, but the wounds were not of a dangerous character.
+
Killed: Henry Hornkeith, jr, son of Henry Hornkeith, a brick maker, shot to death in Phil, Dec 31, 1849, age 32 years.

Mrd: on Dec 31, 1849, by Rev Mr C M Butler, Geo G Cox to Miss Sophia W Purcell, daughter of Thos F Purcell, of St Louis, Mo.

Mrd: on Jan 2, by Rev Geo W Samson, at the residence of Mr Martin Johnson, Chas Simpson Heveningham, of Phil, & Sarah Cornelia Duckworth, formerly of Louisville, Ky.

Mrd: on Jan 3, by Rev C M Butler, Richard Moore to Miss Jane Lewis, both of Wash.

Criminal Court-Wash: 1-Wm Adams, free negro, guilty of grand larceny: sentenced to 1 year's imprisonment in the penitentiary. 2-Pink Coakley, colored man, convicted of 4 cases of outrageous assault, was sentenced, after a severe admonition, to be imprisoned 3 weeks for each offence. 3-Wm Hicks, Geo Ridgely, John Thruston, & Jos Jackson, free colored lads, were found guilty of an assault & riot: having been imprisoned for some time, the Court sentenced each prisoner to pay a fine of $8. 4-Wm A Webster, Robt Downing, & Alfred Ferguson, indicted & tried for a riot, & resisting ofcrs in the discharge of their duty, were found not guilty.

Commission on Claims against Mexico: 1-Memorial of Jas O'Flaherty, master of schnr **William A Turner**, claiming for 2 seizures of his vessel, & for imprisonment of himself, being once more taken up for consideration, together with the proofs & documents connected therewith, the Board came to an opinion that the claim is valid, & allowed accordingly: the amount of award to be subject to the future action of the Board. 2-Memorial of Robt J Clow, of La Vaca, Texas, claiming for the destruction of his goods at several mercantile establishments in Texas by the Mexican invading army in 1838, was submitted, but its reception for the present suspended.

Burglary yesterday in the bookstore of Mr Robt Farnham, & the millinery store of Miss Piling, on Pa ave. Mr Farnham's safe was broken open & Miss Pilling had sundry articles stolen.

For rent: large & commodious 3 story brick at 10th & F sts, at present occupied by the Sisters of Charity. The house is in perfect order. Possession on Jan 12: rent $600 per annum. Apply to J F Callan, E & 7th sts.

Household & kitchen furniture at auction: on Jan 10, at the residence of J E Kendall, E st, between 5th & 6th sts. –Green & Tastet, aucts

For sale: houses, lots, horses & carriages: having determined to move to the West on Mar 1 next, I offer the following for sale: house & lot adjoining McKendree Chapel, now occupied by me, on Mass ave, between 9th & 10th sts; one frame house & lot on north B st, between 10th & 11th sts; one vacant lot on Capitol Hill, across from Barney Parsons' residence; also, buggy wagons, carryall, & a pair of fine large bay match horses.
–T M Milburn

SAT JAN 5, 1850
Senate: 1-Ptn of Thoswell L Colet, late of Balt, Md, now of N J, trustee of Lemuel Taylor, late of Balt, asking indemnity for French spoliations prior to 1800: ordered to lie on the table. 2-Ptn of Fred'k Dawson, Jas Schott, & Elisha D Whitney, asking payment of certain bonds issued to them by the Gov't of Texas, previous to its annexation to the U S, under a contract furnishing that Republic with a naval armament, which, with the papers on the files of the Senate, were referred to the Cmte on the Judiciary. 3-Memorial of Fred'k Vincent, administrator of Jas Lecaze, late surviving partner of Lecaze & Mallet, asking the repayment of advances made during the Revolutionary war: with the papers on file: referred to the Cmte on Revolutionary Claims. 4-Ptn of Mark Bean & R H Bean, asking compensation for certain salt works of which they were dispossessed by the Cherokee treaty of 1828: referred to the Cmte on Public Lands. 5-Memorial of the administrator of Thos Vowell, deceased, asking indemnity for French spoliations prior to 1800: ordered to lie on the table. 6-Memorial of the heirs of Danl Hemtress & the memorial of the legal reps of T M Shaw, asking indemnity for French spoliations prior to 1800: ordered to lie on the table. 7-Ptn of Wm G Buckner, executor of John J Bulow, jr, asking compensation for property destroyed by the Seminole Indians in the Florida war: referred to the Cmte of Claims. 8-Memorial of Jos Kingsbury, asking indemnity for French spoliations prior to 1800: ordered to lie on the table. 9-Memorial of Peter Parker, asking the payment of a balance due him for diplomatic services near the Gov't of China: referred to the Cmte on Foreign Relations. 10-Memorial of the heirs of Gideon Leet, asking indemnity for French spoliations prior to 1800: ordered to lie on the table. 11-Memorial of Zebediah S Holt, heir of Ambrose Atkins, & the memorial of the heirs of Jos Christophers, asking indemnity for French spoliations prior to 1800: ordered to lie on the table. 12-Ptn of Jas C Wilson, a clerk on the ofc of the Chief Engineer of the Army, asking increase of compensation that he may be enabled to finish the education of his children & have something left to bury him when dead: referred to the Cmte on Military Affairs. 13-Ptn of the reps of Henry King, deceased, asking compensation for services in the Revolutionary war: referred to the Cmte on Pensions. 14-Ordered, that the ptn of Mary W Ketcham, on the files of the Senate, be referred to the Cmte on Pensions. 15-Ordered, that the ptn of Martin Dubois, on the files of the Senate, be referred to the Cmte on Pensions. 16-Ptn of the reps of John Hudry, on the files of the Senate, be referred to the Cmte on Military Affairs. 17-Ptn of the heirs of Wm Grayson, on the files of the Senate, be referred to the Cmte on Revolutionary Claims. 18-Ptn of Eliz Jones & the other heirs of John Carr, deceased, & the memorial of Thompson Hutchison, heir of Thos Hutchison, on the files of the Senate, be referred to the Cmte on Pensions. 19-Ordered, that the ptn of John Develin, on the files of the Senate, be referred to the Cmte of Claims. 20-Ordered, that Ezra Chapman have leave to withdraw his ptn & papers. 21-Ordered, that Demus Deming have leave to withdraw his ptn & papers.

22-Ordered, that Saml S Rind have leave to withdraw his ptn & papers. 23-Resolved, that the Sec of War communicate to the Senate a copy of a survey & examination of the river Savannah, made by Martin L Smith, Lt of Topographical Engineers, with a view to the improvement of the said river, & the estimates accompanying the same.

House of Reps: 1-Memorial of John S Littell, of Germantown, Phil Co, Pa, respectfully represents: that, on Oct 9, 1848, the time appointed by law for holding the general election in Pa, he was duly chosen to be a member, to represent the 4th district of Pa, by a majority of 88 legal votes over his competitor, John Robbins, jr, of Kensington: 6,318 for Littell; 6,230 for Robbins. 2-Memorial of Edw Sparrow, Lewis Selby, & J N T Richardson, to establish a term for the district court in certain parishes. 3-Ptn of E T Bussell, R Robbins, & others, citizens of Rush Co, Indiana, praying Congress to devise ways to suppress the African slave trade, by a vigorous colonization, & to this end, establish a line of transports to ply between this country & the western coast of Africa.

Ladies School, Providence, Fairfax Co, Va: will open on Jan 14, 1850. -Mrs Baker

Zachary Taylor, Pres of the U S of A, recognizes Cezar Henrique Stuart de la Figaniere as Consul Genr'l of the Portuguese nation in the U S of A, to reside in N Y. Also, recognizes Felix Lacoste, who has been appointed Consul Genr'l of the French Republic at N Y.

Mrd: on Jan 3, by Rev Mr Flannagan, John Alexander, of Wash, to Sallie E Pettit, daughter of Richard Pettit, of Gtwn.

Mrd: on Dec 27, 1849, by Rev Mr Lemuel Wilmer, Jas Ferguson & Amelia Matthews, 2nd daughter of Gen John Matthews, all of Chas Co, Md.

Died: on Jan 4, after a lingering & painful illness, Mrs Hannah Pettibone, in her 35th year, formerly of Phil, wife of John Pettibone. Her funeral is from residence of her husband, on 14th st, Island, on Jan 6, at 2 o'clock.

Died: on Dec 28, at his father's residence, in Chas Co, Md, Mitchell Freeman, in his 21st year.

Gen Rensselaer Van Rensselaer, son of Solomon Van Rensselaer, of Albany, died on Jan 1, at Syracuse, by inhaling charcoal gas.

Died: on Oct 11, 1849, at Port Grande, Island of St Vincent, Capt Alexander G Gordon, U S brig **Porpoise**. He had been in command of the African squadron since the return of Com Cooper. The squadron is now under the command of Cmder Marston, of Phil.

Trustee's sale: by deed of trust from Robt Rainey, dated Oct 1, 1847, recorded in Liber W B 139, folios 128 & 129, of the land records of Wash Co, D C: sale on Jan 16, at Pa ave & 3rd st, a 2nd hand coach & harness & one bay horse. –John McDermott, trustee

By writ of fieri facias, issued by Saml Drury, J P for Wash Co, D C: I will expose to public sale, on Fri next, 1 small frame house on square 120, lot 8, fronting on H st, between 19th & 20th sts, in Wash City, seized & taken as the property of Benj Thompson, to satisfy a judgment & execution in favor of Saml Stott. –John Dewdney, Constable

The fine ship **Caleb Grimshaw**, Capt Hoxie, lost at sea on Nov 12, was owned by S Thompson & Co, N Y, valued at $80,000, & her cargo over $200,000. She had 399 passengers, all of whom, except about 60, were rescued by the noble conduct of Capt David Cook, of the Nova Scotia ship **Yarmouth**, who came in sight after the crew had struggled 5 days & nights to extinguish the fire below in vain.

MON JAN 7, 1850
Destructive fire yesterday at the very large stable, on 14th st, near the Franklin engine house, occupied by Messrs A & T Nailor, which resulted in destruction of propery valued at $10,000, & the burning of 28 or 29 horses. The dwlg of Mr Philip Butler, & 2 small frame houses belonging to Mr A Nailor, were consumed. The pump shop of Mr Duff, & the wheelwright establishment of Mr A Joyce, was much damaged. Mr Albert Bell, a hackman, lost a fine carriage & a pair of matched horses. Mr Bell is a cripple, has a family, & this little property was his sole support.

Criminal Court-Wash, Fri: 1-John M Busher, a county constable & police ofcr, [tried with W A Mulloy & H T Wilson, constables, for an assault on Hugh Downey, also for riot,] found guilty of an assault on Downey. The jury acquitted Mulloy & Wilson of the assault. All were accused of riot. Verdict: guilty. Busher was fined $20. 2-Geo Henderson was found guilty of stealing at Gadsby's Hotel a cloak, the property of Wm M McPherson: sentenced to the penitentiary for 2 years & 6 months. 3-Edw Donelly was acquitted of the charge of picking the pocket of H McGarvey.

Athens [Ga] Banner announces the death of Mr Danl Hale, of Franklin Co, who died on Jul 2 last in his 119th year, leaving on the premises where he resided at the time of his death a son 76 years of age, a granddaughter 40 years of age, & a great granddaughter 22 years old.

The sugar-house of John C Preston, at Houma, La, was entirely destroyed by fire on Dec 24, with 350 hogsheads of sugar.

Died: on Jan 4, at Richmond, Minnie M Atwater, age 7 years, only child of G M Atwater, of Brooklyn, N Y.

Died: Jos Adams, of Roxbury, age 100 years, son of Rev Jos Adams. His father was a graduate of Harvard Univ in 1740 & for 45 years he was the respected Congregational minister of Strathan, N H. On Jan 1, 1775, at age 24 years, he mrd Mary Fosdick, age 19, a native of Boston. She died in 1845. For 69 years he lived in happiness with this excellent woman. She had born 10 sons & 1 daughter.

Valuable real estate for sale: by deed of trust, executed by Cornelius P Van Ness & Madalina his wife: part of lot 10 sq 454 in Wash, DC. Also, part of lot 12 in square that fronts on 7th st. -John H Saunders, trustee -Green & Tastet, aucts

Collision of the passenger train from Waynesburg to Phil on Thu, near Baileysville, caused the death of F Kurtz Heisley, a young gentleman of Harrisburg, who was supervisor on the road. Jos Hann, the conductor of the train, had a leg broken, & Henry Holt, engineer, was slightly injured.

Last Tue, at Charleston, S C, the 4 year old daughter & the 18 month old son of Mr & Mrs Leslie, were killed in a fire at their home, when Mr Leslie, a worthy Scotchman, had left home on business, & Mrs Leslie went to the market.

TUE JAN 8, 1850
Senate: 1-Memorial of the legal reps of Wm Ham; a memorial of John McClintock & others, of Portsmouth, N H; a memorial of the heirs at law of Saml Hill; & a memorial of Elis H Thacker: asking indemnity for French spoliations prior to 1800: ordered to lie on the table. 2-Ptn of Lois Brewster, widow of a Revolutionary soldier, asking to be allowed a pension: referred to the Cmte on Pensions. 3-Memorial of John D D Rosset, asking indemnity for French spoliations prior to 1800: ordered to lie on the table. 4-Memorial of Ether Shepley & others, citizens of Portland, Maine, asking that the Republic of Liberia, in Africa, be acknowledged as an independent nation. 5-Memorial of Wm C Gibbs, asking indemnity for French spoliations prior to 1800: ordered to lie on the table. 6-Memorial of the heirs of Andrew Glassell, & the memorial of the heirs of John Dunlop, asking indemnity for French spoliations prior to 1800: ordered to lie on the table. 7-Memorial of Thos Blanchard, inventor of a machine called Blanchard's self-directing machine, asking to be protected against violations of his patent right.
8-Memorial of Geo R Herrick, asking compensation for services as a clerk in the ofc of the Com'r of Indian Affairs: referred to the Cmte of Claims. 9-Ptn of Wm C Brown, U S marshal for the district of Georgia, asking an increase of compensation: referred to the Cmte on the Judiciary. 10-Ptn of Henry F Willink, asking permission to purchase a certain lot of ground belonging to the U S in Savannah, Ga: referred to the Cmte on the Judiciary. 11-Ptn of the heirs of Jas Chase, asking indemnity for French spoliations prior to 1800: ordered to lie on the table. 12-Memorial of Chas Byrne, asking to be allowed interest on money paid for lands & refunded to the U S on account of defective titles: referred to the Cmte on Public Lands. 13-Memorial of the administrator of Ambrose Vasse, the ptn of Geo Taylor, & the ptn of the legal reps of Alex'r McCauley, asking indemnity for French spoliations prior to 1800: ordered to lie on the table. 14-Ptn of Thos Dennis, late a seaman in the U S Navy, asking to be allowed a pension on account of injuries received in the discharge of his duty: referred to the Cmte on Naval Affairs.
15-Memorial of Henry Simpson, asking payment for a balance due for his services as appraiser for the port of Phil: referred to the Cmte on Finance. 16-Memorial of the heirs of Jas Vannuxen, memorial of the heirs of Em Duncan, deceased, memorial of Geo T Warfield, & the memorial of R O'Brien, asking indemnity for French spoliations prior to 1800: ordered to lie on the table. 17-Memorial of Wm H Marriott, asking compensation for extra services while Collector of the Customs for the port of Balt: referred to the

11

Cmte on Finance. 18-Ptn of B F Miller for compensation for medical services & losses in the late war with Mexico: referred to the Cmte of Claims. 19-Memorial of the heirs of Wm C Keene, an ofcr in the last war with Great Britain, asking to be allowed a pension for his services: referred to the Cmte on Pensions. 20-Documents submitted relating to the claim of the heirs of Wm Vawters, an ofcr in the Revolutionary army, for commutation pay: referred to the Cmte on Revolutionary Claims. 21-Memorial of the heirs of Robt Cunningham, asking the payment of certain promissory notes issued by the Continental Congress: referred to the Cmte on Finance. 22-Memorial of the heirs of John Ross, & the memorial of the widow of T Ring, asking indemnity for French spoliations prior to 1800: ordered to lie on the table. 23-Ptn of David P Barbydt, asking compensation for his services as an ofcr in the custom house at N Y: referred to the Cmte on Commerce. 24-Memorial of Thos R Johnson, administrator of Rinaldo Johnson, & Sarah A Nuthill, administratrix of Ann E Johnson, asking compensation for a quantity of tobacco destroyed by the British in 1814: referred to the Cmte of Claims. 25-Ordered, that the ptn of Wm H Topping, on files of the Senate, be referred to the Cmte of Claims. 26-Ordered, that the exc of Carlin Page have leave to withdraw his ptn & papers. 27-Ordered, that the ptn & papers on the files of the Senate in relation to the claim of Gad Humphreys, & also the claim of the legal reps of Moses Sheperd, be referred to the Cmte on Roads & Canals. 28-Ordered, that the papers on the files of the Senate relating to the claim of Thos Copperthwaite & Co, & the resolutions of the several State Legislatures on the subject of the distribution of the decisions of the Supreme Court, be referred to the Cmte on the Judiciary. 29-Ordered, that the papers of John Spencer, late Receiver of Public Moneys at **Fort Wayne**, on the files of the Senate, be referred to the Cmte on Private Claims. 30-Ordered, that the papers of Jos P Williams, now on the files of the Senate, be referred to the Cmte on Private Land Claims. 31-Ordered, that the ptn & papers of Mrs Emeline Porter, on the files of the Senate, be referred to the Cmte on Pensions. 32-Ordered, that David A Watson have leave to withdraw his ptn & papers. 33-Ordered, that the memorial of Luther Bradish & others, asking that certain statistics may be collected in connexion with the census, be referred to the Special Cmte on the Census. 34-Ordered, that Dr J Likins have leave to withdraw his ptn & papers. 35-Ordered, that the ptn & papers of Wm Miller, on the files of the Senate, be referred to the Cmte on Pensions. 36-Odered, that the ptn & papers on the files of the Senate, in relation to My Williams, for compensation for property destroyed by the Seminole Indians, be referred to the Cmte on Claims. 37-Cmte on Printing: was referred the motion to print the memorials of Fred'k Dawson, Jas Schott, & Elisha Dana Whitney, in relation to vessels furnished Texas before annexation to the U S, reported against printing the same; which was agreed to.

Died: on Jan 7, after a lingering illness, Mrs Mary Ann Hungerford, age 39 years, wife of Col Henry Hungerford. She possessed all the elements which give dignity to woman-the devotion which characterizes the wife & the affection which impresses upon the child that yearning for the mother which time can never obliterate. Her funeral is at her late residence on H st, between 12th & 13th sts, this afternoon, at 3 o'clock.

WED JAN 9, 1850
Senate: 1-Ptn of Eliza M Kiddal, Ann Wilder, & Mary Smith, asking indemnity for French spoliations prior to 1800: ordered to lie on the table. 2-Ptn of J Sidney Henshaw, late a professor of mathematics in the navy, asking to be allowed 3 months' pay granted discharged ofcrs: referred to Cmte on Naval Affairs. 3-Memorial of the heirs of Jos Mussi, asking indemnity for French spoliations prior to 1800: ordered to lie on the table. 4-Ptn of Marie Mason, widow of Milo Mason, late an ofcr in the U S army, asking to be allowed arrearages of pay due her late husband, & the reimbursement of money expended by him in the public service: referred to Cmte on Military Affairs. 5-Memorial of L E L A Lawson, daughter & heir of Eleazer W Ripley, asking the payment of a verdict rendered in favor of her late father in a suit instituted against him by the U S: referred to Cmte on the Judiciary. 6-Ptn of the legal reps of John M Buit, & memorial of Nathl Wattles, president of the Marine Ins Co, of Alexandria, asking indemnity for French spoliations prior to 1800: ordered to lie on the table. 7-Memorial of Sarah Snow, & the memorial of the heirs of Jabez Huntington, asking indemnity for French spoliations prior to 1800: ordered to lie on the table. 8-Memorial of Wm Woodworth, patentee of a planning machine, asking the renewal of his patent: referred to Cmte on Patents & the Patent Ofc. 9-Memorial of Jas Robertson, asking an investigation of certain charges made against him of threatening with violence a member of the U S Senate & redress for illegal imprisonment: referred to the Cmte of Claims. 10-Memorial of Gustavus A Parson, asking compensation for services in raising & organizing the volunteers furnished by the State of Missouri for the Mexican war: referred to the Cmte on Military Affairs. 11-Memorial of Nancy Kirkpatrick, widow of a Revolutionary soldier, asking to be allowed a back pension: referred to Cmte on Pensions. 12-Ptn of Francis A Stockton, purser in the navy, asking repayment of money expended by him on public account in the port of Southampton, Eng, while on board the U S ship **St Lawrence**: referred to Cmte on Naval Affairs. 13-Ptn of Frances P Gardiner, widow of an ofcr in the army, who was killed in battle, asking to be allowed a pension: referred to Cmte on Military Affairs. 14-Ptn of Frances Fowler, widow of an ofcr in the army, who died in service, asking a pension: referred to Cmte on Military Affairs. 15-Ordered, that the ptn of Nathl Kuykendall, on the files of the Senate, be referred to the Cmte on the Post Ofc & Post Roads. 16-Ordered, that the ptn of the heirs of Robt Jewell, on the files of the Senate, be referred to Cmte of Claims. 17-Ordered, that the ptn of Thos Allen, on the files of the Senate, be referred to Cmte of Claims. 18-Ordered, that the ptn of the legal reps of John Rice Jones, on the files of the Senate, be referred to Cmte on Private Land Claims. 19-Ordered, that the documents on the files of the Senate, relating to the claim of Gamaliel Taylor & his sureties, be referred to Cmte of Claims. 20-Ordered, that the memorial of the administrator of Wm A Slacum, on the files of the Senate, be referred to Cmte on Foreign Relations. 21-Papers relating to the claim of John L Russworm, on the files of the Senate, be referred to Cmte on Revolutionary Claims.

Died: on Jan 1, at Syracuse, N Y, Rensselaer Van Rensselaer, son of Gen Van Rensselaer, of Albany, & son-in-law of Maj S S Forman, of Syracuse. He was about 40 years old, & leaves his wife. He leaves a wife upon whom the sad occurrence has fallen with a severity which few are called to endure.

House of Reps: 1-Ptn of Cath Clark, widow of Jos Clark, a seaman, for a pension. 2-Ptn of Wm G Bucknor, exc of the estate of J J Bulow, jr, asking to be indemnified for the property destroyed by the Seminole Indians while in the occupancy of the U S troops. 3-Ptn & papers relating to the claim of Robt Roberts taken from the files: referred to the Cmte of Claims. 4-Ptn of Rulif Van Brunt. 5-Ptn of John C Hoyt & others, citizens of Key West, praying an increase of salary of the judge of the southern district of Florida. 6-Ptn of H H Booley, for a pension. 7-Ptn of Thos Dennis, asking for a pension, for loss of both arms while on duty board U S steamer **Princeton**. 8-Ptn of Linus Williams, of Warren Co, Ohio, praying to be enumerated for losses sustained while in service with the army in the war of 1812. 9-Memorial of Geo Hartwick, praying remuneration for damage done to the schnr **Robert Rennie**, while she was employed in Gov't service. 10-Memorial of Chas Mussey, jr, of Phil, for the repayment of an excess of duty erroneously exacted upon brown sugar from Canton. 11-Ptn of Eliz McDougal, of Phil, daughter of Saml Caustin, asking for a pension on account of the services of her father in the Revolutionary war. 12-Ptn of Godfrey Hager & other citizens of Phil, asking indemnity for French spoliations prior to 1800. 13-Ptn of Thos Flanagan, for a pension in consequence of sufferings & services in the army. 14-Ptn of Jos Roberts, of Ky, for scrip for 1,000 acres of land in lieu of 1,000 patented to Wm Armstead by the State of Ky on a land ofc military warrant, which said 1,000, embraced in the patent to Armstead, were covered by an older patent to Geo Rogers Clark. 15-Ptn of Geo F Warfield, asking indemnity for French spoliations prior to 1800. 16-Ptn of Mary Lee & others, asking indemnity for French spoliations prior to 1800. 17-Ptn of Wm D Shaw, for compensation for beef supplied to the U S troops at **Fort Gibson**, in the Creek Nation, in 1842. 18-Ptn of John Coltman, son of Capt Robt Coltman, of the Revolutionary army, for compensation for Revolutionary services. 19-Ptn of Mrs Hetty Jacobs, one of the heirs of Benj Norris, deceased, asking indemnity for French spoliations prior to 1800. 20-Memorial of Jas A Fawz, praying to be allowed the salary of Purser, while acting as such on board the U S brig **Bainbridge**. 21-Memorial of H N Crabb, Lt of the U S Marine Corps, for allowances withheld. 22-Memorial of Bernard Henry, for balance admitted to be due from the U S. 23-Ptn of Peter H Willitz, for increase of pension. 24-Memorial of Thos Blanchard, inventor, praying further protection for his patent right. 25-Ptn of Michl White, of Fred'k Co, Va, formerly a master's mate in the U S navy, praying to be placed on the roll of invalid pensioners. 26-Ptn of Saml Bodey, guardian of the minor children of John W Bush, deceased, late a soldier in the Mexican war, for a pension. 27-Ptn of John Moore White, of N J, son of Maj John White, asking a pension for services of his father during the Revolutionary war. 28-Ptns of Capt Wm Black & men, & of Capt J L Phillip's & men, for compensation for military services in Florida. 29-Ptn of T Hayward, asking remuneration for supplies furnished troops in Florida. 30-Ptn of John G Gamble, for compensation for hire of mules to the U S. 31-Ptn of Wynant Van Valdenburg. 32-Memorial & ptn of P F Schliecker, atty for John Vangevar, administrator de bonis non of the estate of John M Burt, deceased, asking indemnity for French spoliations prior to 1800. 33-Memorial of Mary Corby, widow of T M Corby, deceased, asking indemnity for French spoliations prior to 1800.

Died: a man named Raymond in Wheeling recently, at the advanced age of 110 years.

Postmaster Gen established the following new Post Ofcs for week ending Jan 5, 1850.

Ofc	County, State	Postmaster
East Auburn	Cumberland, Maine	John C Briggs
Lower Columbia	Coos, N H	Saml G Bishop
West Concord	Merrimack, N H	Nathl H Sanborn
Darien	Fairfield, Ct	Ira Scofield
East Suffield	Hartford, Ct	Francis A Sykes
Mansfield Depot	Tolland, N H	Enoch Hovey
Arkville	Delaware, N Y	Noah Dimmick
Moreau Station	Saratoga, N Y	Hiram Wilcox
Devereaux	Herkimer, N Y	P Goodwin
Cypress Grove	New Hanover, N C	Owen Bowden
Middle Ridge	Newton, Ga	Jas Riley
Payntersville	Jackson, Ia	C Dunham
Gallatin	Stark, Ill	Miles A Fuller
Montgomery	Kane, Ill	Ralph Gray
Goodman's Mills	Osage, Md	H W Neill
Cold Spring	Pottawatamie, Iowa	John Pettingal
Chariton C H	Lucas, Iowa	Wm H Moore
Centre Brook	Middlesex, Ct	Richd N Dowd
Marlbe Dale	Litchfield, Ct	W D Sperry
Hanover	Oxford, Maine	Phineas H Howe
Hales Eddy	Broome, N Y	Elisha Alexander
St Armand	Essex, N Y	Danl C Skiff
Cruso H	Lucas, Iowa	Wm H Moore
Green River	Rutherford, N C	Saml Stone
Lyon's Hollow	Steuben, N Y	Abner P Lyon
Roxana	Eaton, Mich	John Ewing
Three Springs	Wash, Va	Wm R Rhea
Pennsboro	Irvin, Ga	Jos Summer
Flat Berg	Irvin, Ga	Jas Hancock
Gin Town	Irvin, Ga	Allen Ratliff
Hearnville	Putnam, Ga	Wm Hearn
Oakland	Lauderdale, Ala	Saml Baughn
Davidsville	Franklin, Ten	John Atkins
Allison	Logan, Ky	F S Allison
Levee	Montgomery, Ky	V B Hainline
Taylorsburgh	Bartholomew, Ia	Cyrus Barlow
America	Wabach, Ia	Elijah Quick
Salt Ford	Vermillion, Ill	Saml Dougherty
May Hill	Lee, Ill	G S Morrison
Mud Creek	St Clair, Ill	Isaac Rainey
Banner	Kane, Ill	Melvin M Marsh
Mayberry	Lewis, Maine	W D Briscoe
Dixon's Mills	Buchanan, Maine	W H Finley

Elk Springs	Pike, Maine	Thos E Williams
Black River Falls	Crawford, Wis	Wm W Bennett
Lake Centre	Milwaukee, Wis	Israel B Cross
Kossuth	Racine, Wis	Robt Noxen
Fillmore	Dubuque, Iowa	Wm Haitchen
Cedar Falls	Black Hawk, Iowa	Demsey C Overman

Names Changed:
Monroe, Buck's Co, Pa, changed to Durham.
Greenvile, Luzerne Co, Pa, changed to Green Grove.
Van Buren, Lee Co, Iowa, changed to Warren.
Mendon, Clayton Co, Iowa, changed to Farmersburgh.
Darien, Fairfield Co, Conn, changed to Darien Depot.
Lexington Heights, Greene Co, N Y, changed to Jewett.
Coffee Creek, Porter Co, Indiana, changed to Claumet.

Mrs T L Ragsdale informs her friends & the public that she will give instruction on the Piano. Apply at her residence, 15th & Pa ave.

$10 reward for recovery of my Bay Horse & carriage, which was taken on 7th st from the corner of Garrison & Navy Yard, Wash. -Peter Francis, Bladensburg, Md

Orphans Court of Wash Co, D C. Letters of administration with the will annexed on the personal estate of John Evans, late of said county, deceased. –Susan Evans, admx W A

Mr Z Elliot, a brakeman on the New London & Willimantic road, was killed by striking his head against a bridge last week, while standing on the top of the cars. He leaves a wife & 2 children.

Mr Verbeyest, the most celebrated book collector in Europe, perhaps in the world, died lately at Brussels.

Geo Plowman, on trial at Portland, Maine, for the murder of his wife, has been found guilty & sentenced to be hung.

Mrd: on Jan 7, in Wash City, by Rev Mr Lynch, Wm Cameron, of Lockport, Ill, & Mrs Anna Maria Baldwin, formerly of Ohio.

Mrd: on Jan 4, at the Navy Yard, Wash, by Rev C W Denison, Thos E Rockett to Miss Mgt Staples, both of this District.

Died: Jan 8th, in Wash, after a long & painful illness, Mary Eleanor E R Ayton, in her 65th year, of Montgomery Co, Md. Her funeral is at the residence of Mr Abraham Cook, 3rd & G sts, this day, at 3 p m.

Died: on Dec 25, at the residence of Mrs E O Prather, near Rockville, Montg Co, Md, Elenora Ferguson, age 6 years, daughter of John W Ferguson.

Mr J H Kyan, who has been for some months a resident of N Y, died of apoplexy on Sat last, at his residence in that city. He was the inventor of much that is valuable in practical chemisty, especially by that process of preserving wood called after him kyanization. His papers have been taken charge of by the Coroner, for the benefit of his wife & children, now residents of London. –N Y Express

For rent: 3 story brick dwlg house on Pa ave, on square 762. Apply at Blagden's Wharf, to Geo Collard, Agent.

Pres Zachary Taylor recognizes Jas Dempsey who has been appointed Vice Consul of his Danish Majesty for the port of Alexandria, Va.

For sale: Houses, lots, & horses of T M Milburn, who is determined to move to the West.

THU JAN 10, 1850
Senate: 1-Ptn of John Thomas, inventor of the floating dry-dock, asking compensation for the use of his invention by the U S: referred to the Cmte on Naval Affairs. 2-Memorial of the heirs of Thos Fraser, asking indemnity for French spoliations prior to 1800: ordered to lie on the table. 3-Ptn of Edw Tracy & others, asking that the benefits of the act of Aug 11, 1848, for the relief of John P B Gratiot & the legal reps of Henry Gratiot may be extended to the lessees of lead mines lying in the lands of Ottawa & other tribes of Indians: referred to the Cmte of Claims. 4-Ptn of Benj Nones, asking indemnity for French spoliations prior to 1800: ordered to lie on the table. 5-Memorial of Jos Sims & others, of the heirs of Moses Gaylord, & the memorial of Prudence Doane, widow of Nathl Doane, asking indemnity for French spoliations prior to 1800. 6-Ordered, that the ptn of Chas F Gunter, on the files of the Senate, be referred to the Cmte on Private Land Claims. 7-Ordered, that the ptn of John B White, on the files of the Senate, be referred to the Cmte on Pensions. 8-Ordered the the ptn of Isaac P Simonton, on the files of the Senate, be referred to the Cmte on Indian Affairs. 9-Ordered, that Hugh Wallace Wormsley have permission to withdraw from the files of the Senate the papers relating to his claim.

Mrs J Lightelle informs the ladies of Wash that she is now prepared to receive all orders in the line of Dress & Habit Making: Pa ave, next door to Clagett's. Two apprentices wanted.

Wash Corp: 1-Ptn of Wm Furguson, of Jas Johnson, of Patrick Wilson, of Jos Swaggert, & of Wm W Davis, for the remission of fines: referred to the Cmte of Claims. 2-Ptn of John P Ingle & others, praying certain changes in the grade of part of N J ave: referred to the Cmte on Improvements. 3-Bill for the relief of Philip Mohum: passed. 4-Act for the relief of A Jackson: laid on the table.

Music. J K Foertsch, Prof of Music, lately removed his residence from 8th & E sts to Mrs Melillton's, on G st, for instructions on the Piano Forte & music instruments, generally.

Commission on Claims against Mexico: Memorial of Wm W Corcoran, of Wash City, as assignee of Bradford B Williams & Jos H Lord, claiming for illegal exaction of duties on the cargo of the ship **Henry Thompson**, & her detention in the port of Vera Cruz, in Jan, 1834, being taken under consideration, opinion of the Board that the claim is valid: amount to be awarded subject to the future action of the Board.

Mrd: on Jan 3, at N Y, Capt Chas Garnett, U S N, & Adelaide Smith, daughter of Col W P Smith, all of N Y, by Rev Dr Hone, of St Luke's Church.

Died: on Jan 3, in Fauquier Co, Va, [the residence of her mother,] Mrs Lucinda S Carr, in her 35th year, wife of Jas G Carr, & eldest daughter of late Gen W K Armistead, U S A.

Died: on Jan 8, at Balt, Catherine B Dobbin, age 18 years, daughter of Robt A Dobbin, of Balt.

Died: on Jan 8, Jas B Taggart, of the Treas Dept. His funeral is at St John's Church, this day, at 12 o'clock. .

St Louis Republican of Jan 1 announces the death of Mr Robt Rankin, one of the old & wealthy citizens of that city. He was a native of Ireland, & came to that city about 30 years ago. By his frugality & discretion he amassed a large fortune. He was at times eccentric in his manners, but had a heart open to generous impulses.

FRI JAN 11, 1850
Senate: 1-Ptn of Eleanor Ann Shaw, heir of Pelatiah Fitch, asking indemnity for French spoliations prior to 1800: referred. 2-Ptn of John O Harra, the heir of Danl O Harra, late of Charleston, S C, asking indemnity for French spoliations prior to 1800. 3-Memorial of Chas Evans & others, asking remuneration for losses occasioned by the operations of the American army in West Florida in 1814: referred to the Cmte on Foreign Relations. 4-Memorial of Benj Norris & others, asking indemnity for French spoliations prior to 1800: referred. 5-Memorial of the legal reps of John R Shaw, asking to be indemnified for losses of certain private stores on board the ship **Essex** at the time of her capture by the British squadron during the war with Great Britain: referred to the Cmte on Naval Affairs. 6-Ptn of Mary Farrer, asking a pension for the services of her husband as a chaplain during the Revolutionary war: referred to the Cmte on Pensions. 7-Ptn & papers of Conrad W Faber & Leopold Bieswirth, in relation to the war steamer **United States**: referred to the Cmte on Foreign Relations. 8-Ptn of Owen Connelly, asking remuneration for services & injuries sustained while in the employment of the Gov't at the Capitol: referred to the Cmte for D C. 9-Memorial of Jonathan Lewis, asking remuneration for losses sustained though depredations committed on his property by certain Cherokee Indians: referred to the Cmte on Indian Affairs. 10-Ptn of John Dawson, of Sangamon Co, Ill, asking compensation for his services as pension agent: referred to the Cmte on Claims. 11-Memorial of H M Breckenridge, asking a re-transfer of 20 acres, including his Orange Grove, embraced in certain lands containing live oak timber which had been sold by him to the U S: referred to the Cmte on Naval Affairs. 12-Ptn of F W Brune, acting exc of B J Von Kapff, last surviving trustee of R C

Boislandry, & as atty for Eleanor Clarke, admx of Ambrose Clarke, asking indemnity for French spoliations prior to 1800: referred. 13-Ptn of Wm Seeley, of N Y C: some 20 years ago the Prince & Princess of Orange lost from the palace in Brussels, belonging to the Gov't of Belgium, a large sum in value of crown jewels & some of the personal jewels of the princess. No trace for a long time; Mr Seeley, a professional gentleman, a lawyer of eminence, applied to aid in recovering this lost property. He dedicated nearly 3 years to its accomplishment. He recovered almost all the jewels, the detection & arrest of the thief; who was sent back to Europe. Application was made to Holland, but they were unwilling to make what he deemed to be an adequate compensation, or even to refer the matter to arbitration. Referred to the Cmte of Finance. 14-Ordered that the papers on file in the Senate relating to the claim of Thos P McBlair, be referred to the Cmte on Naval Affairs. 15-Ordered, that the Cmte on Pensions be discharged from further consideration of the claim of the rep of Wm King, & that it be referred to the Cmte on Revolutionary Claims. 16-Ptn of Wm Emmons, administrator of Uri Emmons, on the files of the Senate, be referred to the Cmte on Patents.

House of Reps: 1-Ptn of Lt Bartholomew Van Valkenburgh, for commutation pay. 2-Ptn of the heirs of Edw Durant, John Bell's administrator, Covington Simpkins' administrator, & John Burt's administration, asking indemnity for French spoliations prior to 1800. 3-Memorial of M X Harmony, in relation to his claim for losses sustained in the seizure of his property for the public service, by order of Col Doniphan, during the march of the U S forces in Chihuahua, in 1846. 4-Ptn of Eli Darling, praying for pecuniary aid in consideration of the loss of his eyes while in the service of the U S at the naval station of Brooklyn. 5-Ptn of Anna Giffin, the widow of a Revolutionary soldier, praying for a pension, under the act of Jul 4, 1836. 6-Ptn of Alanson Pool, of Murray, N Y, praying for a pension on account of disabilities incurred in the service of the U S in the war of 1812, with Great Britain; also for back pay & bounty land. 7-Ptn of Chas Stewart, praying for relief. 8-Ptn of the excs of the estate of Robt Smith, of Phil, asking indemnity for French spoliations prior to 1800. 8-Ptn of the heirs of Jas Vanuxen, asking indemnity for French spoliations prior to 1800. 9-Memorial of Thos C Wales, heir of B Holmes, late of the firm of Henry Bar & Co. 10-Ptn of Henry M Fleury & others, praying for the confirmation of a tract of land. 11-Ptn of the heirs of Robt Henry Dyer, deceased, late of Madison Co, Tenn, for a pension. 12-Ptn of Jas Somers, of Weakly Co, Tenn, for arrears of pension. 13-Ptn of John H B Rolls, of Gibson Co, Tenn, for compensation for his services as a surgeon in the late war with Mexico. 14-Ptn of John F Robertson, of Sevier Co, Tenn, for a pension on account of wounds received in the service of the U S. 15-Ptn of Robt James, of Blount Co, Tenn, for leave to import certain machinery free of duty.

Beautiful tribute of respect was presented to M A Tyson & Sisters by their Pupils: a Silver Fruit Basket, weighing 32 ounces. Signed: Ada B Campbell, Kate Mattingly, & Josepha Nourse.

Mrd: on Dec 24, 1849, by Rev Mr White, John L Hipkins & Martha, daughter of late Jas Compton, of Alexandria, Va, both of Wash.

Died: on Jan 4, Gen Daniel C Butts, a citizen of Petersburg, Va.

Sandwich [Mass] Observer: Mr Chas J Peterson was killed last week by following a deer which had taken to the ice in Waquoit bay & had broken through. Mr Jno Swift went to their assistance, & he & Peterson were immersed. Mrs Swift & an Indian took Swift out of the water, insensible, & revived him with difficulty. Mr Peterson perished.

From Calif: Elected Govn'r-Peter H Burnett; Lt Govn'r-John McDougall; Reps to Congress-Geo W Wright & Edw Gilbert.

SAT JAN 12, 1850
Phil newspaper announce the death of the eminent Divine Rev Dr Saml Miller, of Princeton. He was born near Dover, Dela, on Oct 31, 1769; graduated at the Univ in this city in 1789, &, as the oldest Alumnus, recently addressed his fellows on the centennial aniversary of that institution.

The Paris correspondent of the N Y Journal of Commerce announce the death, in Dec last, of Geo Washington Lafayette, son of the General of that name. On Jan 4 was the interment of Geo Wash Lafayette, son of the Gen, who accompanied his father in the final visit to the U S. His dissolution took place at *Lagrange*, the family seat.

Killed: W P Anderson, shot to death on Dec 26, in Van Buren, 10 miles from Bolivar, Tenn, age about 24 years. He had been paying attention to the daughter of Mr W A Moore, & was shot as he approached the residence of her father in Van Buren, with the intention of carrying her off to marry her. –Memphis [Tenn] Eagle, Dec 31.

Mr Thos Meacham, of Hopkinton, St Lawrence Co, N Y, died a few weeks ago, & for several years was a resident of Franklin Co, & was something of a hunter.

Murder near Paterson, N J, on Tue at the Goffie. The victims were an aged man & his wife, named Van Winkle, long residents in the county. The murderer is supposed to be a laborer, named John Johnson, who formerly worked on the farm. He was arrested. –N Y Mirror

House of Reps: 1-Ptn of Amos Armstrong, praying for a pension for injuries received while in the service of the U S in the last war with Great Britain. 2-Ptn of C Beatty & others, co-heirs of Jas Vanuxen, late of Phil, deceased, asking indemnity for French spoliations prior to 1800.

For sale: *Enfield Chase*, in PG Co, Md, 600 acres. Subscriber with view to other occupation. -N H Shipley.

Com'rs of Chas Co, Md, to meet at Dr Wm S Keechey's, to value & divide reaa estate of Priscilla E Keech, late of Chas Co. -Stouten W Dent, Josias H Hawkins, John Hamilton, Saml Core, Nicholas V Miles, com'rs.

Reward-$50 for return of Isaac, black, age 21. -Jas A Reid, Madison Co, Va.

Partnership formed called Havenner & bros: Thos H, Jno F, Chas W Havenner. Formerly, Thos Havenner & Son. Thos H, withdrew.

For sale: farm in Montgomery Co, Md, 300 acres, property of John A Carter, who removed to the West. Refer to my brother, Robt W Carter, residing near Rockville, Md.

For sale: *"Llewellyn"*, 416 acres, Clarke Co, Va; farm on which I reside, Franklin J Kerfoot, intending to move to the West.

Mrd: on Jan 8, at Phil, by Rev Dr Boardman, Edw B Dallam, of Balt, Md, & Henrietta J Mactier, daughter of late Henry Mactier.

Mrd: on Jan 3, by Rev Mr Peterken, at *Rose Hill*, Clarke Co, Va, C C McIntire, of Loudoun Co, Va & Harriet E, daughter of late Jacob Shively.

Died: on Jan 5, Mrs Charlotte Kirk, widow of late Henry N Kirk, & daughter of late Dr Benjamin Tabbs, of St Mary's Co, Md.

MON JAN 14, 1850
House of Reps: 1-Ptn of C A Trowbridge & 200 others, for the construction of a canal around the falls of St Marie. 2-Ptn of Sarah N Nickels, widow of John Nickels, Hannah Miller, widow of Thos Miller, & others of Maine, asking indemnity for French spoliations prior to 1800. 3-Ptn of Eliz Letting, heir of Jacob Letting, asking indemnity for French spoliations prior to 1800. 4-Ptn of Jonathan Holmes & others, of Carlisle, Pa, asking indemnity for French spoliations prior to 1800

Criminal Court-Wash. 1-Ofcr Hazard, tried for an assault on Justice Myers, was aquitted. 2-Thos Jones, alias Carpender, an old offender, well known for previous convictions, & who has been 12 years in the penitentiary, was again convicted of grand larceny, & sentenced by the Court to 4 years at labor in the penitentiary. 3-Caroline Johnson, free negress, indicted for theft, was acquitted. 4-John Casey, found guilty of common assault on Marcelus Wilson, & fined $5. 5-John Payne, found guilty of assault: sentenced to one month in jail. 6-Wm Webster found guilty of an assault & battery, & for breaking into a dwlg house.

Barnstable Patriot records the death of Benjamin Hallett, in his 90th year, father of Hon B F Hallett, of Boston. He was born in 1760, & leaves 78 lineal descendants alive at this period. He was for 15 years a subject of Geo III of England. In the revolution he served 3 years on board the frig **Dean**, & in the land forces. He was afterwards a member of the Mass Legislature & a magistrate in his county. He was 67 years a consistent Christian.

Capt R E Duvall, formerly of Gtwn, D C, now residing at *St George's island* near Piney Point, had his dwlg & furniture consumed by fire a few nights past, he & his family only escaping in their night clothes.

Died: on Jan 13, Vincent Massoletti, native of Genoa, in his 56th year; for the last 33 years he was a resident of Wash. His funeral at his late residence, Va Ave, near the Navy Yard, on Jan 15, at 2 o'clock.

TUE JAN 15, 1850
Senate: 1-Papers withdrawn from the files of the Senate: memorial of L Alexander & T Barnard: referred to the Cmte of Claims. Ptn of the legal reps of Nimrod Farrow & Richd Harris: referred to the Cmte of Claims. Ptn of the heirs of Wm Bowdon: referred to the Cmte on Pensions. Memorial of Foxall A Parker: referred to the Cmte on Naval Affairs. Ptn of Thos Snodgrass: referred to the Cmte on Indian Affairs. Ptn of Amaziah Goodwin: referred to the Cmte on Pensions. 2-Cmte of Claims: bill for the relief of Chas Reeder, Walter R Johnson, & the legal reps of Wm P Jones: to be printed. Same cmte: memorial of Jon M McIntosh: to be printed. 3-Memorial of John Trenchard, administrator of Saml Page, & the memorial of Lemuel Knal & others, asking indemnity for French spoliations prior to 1800: referred. 4-Cmte on Public Lands: reported a bill to provide for the final settlement of the accounts of Jonathan Kearsley, late receiver of the public moneys at Detroit, & John Biddle, late register of the land ofc at that place: to be printed. 5-Memorial of the widow of Henry Dashiell, deceased, asking indemnity for French spoliations prior to 1800. 6-Memorial of Isabella Coxe, excx of Wm Cole, asking indemnity for injuries to a vessel & cargo belonging to her late husband, by the authorities of the Peruvian Gov't, with the papers on file: referred to the Cmte of Claims. 7-Memorial of Anna McLean, widow of an ofcr who died in service during the last war with Great Britain: referred to the Cmte on Pensions. 8-Memorial of A R Woolley, late an ofcr of the army, representing that he has been unlawfully dismissed the service, & asking that he may be allowed his pay & emoluments from the date of his dismissal: referred to the Cmte on Military Affairs. 9-Memorial of the heirs & reps of John Chalmers, & the memorial of Hugh Auchincloss, exc of Barr & Stewart, asking indemnity for French spoliations prior to 1800: referred. 10-Ptn of Benj Wood, a Revolutionary soldier , asking to be allowed a pension: referred to the Cmte on Revolutionary Claims. 11-Memorial of W N, S H & H Dorsett; memorial of the legal reps of Paul Bentalou & Joshua Barney; memorial of the heirs at law of S G Kennard; memorial of the heirs of John Dumester, asking indemnity for French spoliations prior to 1800: referred. 12-Memorial of A M Dade, widow of a deceased army ofcr, asking a renewal of her pension: referred to the Cmte on Pensions. 13-Memorial of John S Knox, asking indemnity for losses sustained by the burning of a Gov't transport on the Mississippi river in 1848: referred to the Cmte on Military Affairs. 14-Memorial of Eleazer Williams, an Iroquois Indian, asking compensation for important services to the U S, rendered during the last war with Great Britain, & to be allowed a pension for a wound received in battle: referred to the Cmte on Pensions. 15-Resolved, that the account of Prosper M Wetmore, late navy agent at N Y, as remains unadjusted, with copies of all letters & papers pertaining to the account, be communicated to the Senate. 16-Resolved, that Rev Henry Slicer, be paid for his services at this & the special session

of Congress, the usual annual compensation paid to Chaplains. 17-Memorial of Hubert H Booly, wagon master in the army, asking to be allowed a pension: referred to the Cmte on Pensions. 18-Memorial of Chas Findlay, asking to be allowed interest on certain drafts paid by the U S out of the fund created for the benefit of the Shawnee Indians: referred to the Cmte on Indian Affairs. 19-Ptn of Stephen Colwell, administrator of Wm F Smith, asking the payment of certain outstanding loan ofc certificates: referred to the Cmte on Revolutionary Claims. 20-Ptn of Jas M Marsh, asking indemnity for depredations committed on his property while engaged in executing public surveys by a party of Sioux Indians: referred to the Cmte on Indian Affairs. 21-Memorial of the legal reps of J & E Gardner, asking indemnity for French spoliations prior to 1800: referred.

The Globe says Cmdor Conner, U S Navy, died on Sat at Erie, Pa. [Corr: Jan 16th newspaper: we should have said Capt Conner, of the Revenue service. –Globe of yesterday]

Mrd: on Jan 8, at **Mount Pleasant**, Chas Co, Md, by Rev W J Chiles, Franck Price to Miss Bettie M Barnes.

We are requested to state that the residence of the Hon Andre Stevenson, is **Blenehim**, Carter's Bridge Post Ofc, Albermarle Co, Va. The frequent misdirection of his letters to Charlottesville, & the reforwarding of them, occasions Mr S both inconvenience & double postage.

WED JAN 16, 1850
A late Thibodauxville paper: we surmised that out estimable fellow-citizen, Dr T M Williams, was one of the sufferers on the ill-fated steamer **Louisiana**. This conjecture has been but too sadly realized. His remains were brought to this place on the steamer **Hope**, on Sun last, & on the following day conveyed to their last resting place by a large concourse of mourners. Rt Rev Leonidas Polk performed an eloquent service.

Died: on Jan 10, Mr Chas Valentine, at his residence in Cambridgeport, Mass, of an apoplectic fit. He was of the firm of Chas Valentine & Co, wholesale Provision Dealers, 4 S Market st, Boston.

Drowned: a little daughter of Mr Chas Sneden, of Fairfax Co, Va, age about 2 years, on Jan 9, at residence of Levi Parker, near Fall's Church, Va.

Capt Alex'r G Gordon, of the U S brig **Porpoise**, died at Port Grande, Island of St Vincent, on Oct 11 last. He had been in command of the African squadron since the return of Cmdor Cooper.

The Coroner who held the inquest on the body of Gen R Van Rensselaer, at Syracuse, expressed the opinion that the death was accidental & not intentional. –Albany Evening Journal

Drowned: Mrs Robinson, wife of Mr Wm Robinson, of Bowling Green. Mr Robinson is a dealer in live stock, & was returning with his lady on the vessel **Alex Scott** from New Orleans. Mrs Robinson was sitting on the railing when she lost her balance & fell overboard. Mr Robinson & his brother-in-law were landed at a house close by where the accident occurred, to recover the lady if possible. Mrs Robinson had been married but about 6 months. Her maiden name was Whitesides. –Louisville Journal

House of Reps: 1-Ptn of John Russell, of Chautauque Co, N Y, praying for a pension for injuries received while in the service of his country in 1812 & 1813, in the war with Great Britain. 2-Ptn of Mary Cluss, formerly Mary Alexander, widow of Jas Alexander, a soldier in the Mexican war, praying Congress for a pension. 3-Ptn of F Gardere, for compensation for land taken by the Gov't for public purposes. 4-Memorial of David Montgomery, for an increase of pension. 5-Ptn of Buckingham Lockwood & others, asking indemnity for French spoliations prior to 1800. 6-Ptn of the heirs of Apollos Cooper, for such half-pay, as they are entitled to, in consequence of their ancestor having been killed in the battle of Brandywine. 7-Ptn of John G Wilkinson, praying compensation for his services as navy pension agent. 8-Ptn of Robt Owens, asking the difference of pay between that of chief boatswain's mate & a boatswain. 9-Memorial of Ann P Swift, A Jeffery, & others, asking indemnity for French spoliations prior to 1800.

On Jan 3 the extensive iron foundry of Mr A C Larring, at Wilkesbarre, Pa, was wholly consumed by fire, with all the stock, tools, & machinery. Loss estimated at $10,000.

Criminal Court-Wash, Mon: 1-Clinton Speiden, Gustavus Cozens, & Benj Baker, indicted & tried for riot, were acquitted of that charge, & Speiden & Cozens found guilty of assault & battery. 2-Henry Burke was found guilty of assault & fined $5. 3-Chas Matthews, free negro, found guilty for an assault, & for malicious mischief.

Mrd: on Jan 14, by Rev C M Butler, Mr Bushrod E Cockerill to Miss Eliza F Elgin, both of Loudoun Co, Va.

Mrd: on Jan 13, by Rev Mr McMullen, at Ellicott's Mills, Henry E Sengstack, of Wash, & Miss Eliz Isabel Riley, of Balt Co, Md.

Died: on Jan 15, in Wash City, Denis, youngest son of Timothy & Mgt Buckley. His funeral will take place at the residence of his father, Pa av bet 1st & 2nd sts, this afternoon, at 1 o'clock.

Died: on Mon last, Mrs Eliza, wife of Richard S Cox. Her funeral will be from the residence of her mother, Mrs Brook Williams, Heights of Gtwn, Jan 16, at 3 o'clock..

Died: on Oct 23, in Sacramento, Calf, after a brief illness of pulmonary consumption, Wm L Dixon, formerly of this city, in Sacramento, Calif, in his 28th year. Mild, amiable, generous, & self sacrificing, he left here just 12 months ago in hope to add to the comfort of friends whom he left behind. He yielded up his spirit into the hands of that God who gave it. -S

Senate: 1-Memorial of the exc of Cornelius Howland, asking indemnity for French spoliations prior to 1800: referred. 2-Memorial of Wm Rotch & others, asking indemnity for French spoliations prior to 1800: referred. 3-Memorial of Andrew A Jones, asking compensation for extra services in the N Y custom-house: referred to the Cmte of Claims. 4-Ptn from Geo W Billings, asking Congress to cause the proper ofcrs of the Navy Dept to complete a contract with him for water-rotted hemp according to his bid: referred to the Cmte on Naval Affairs. 5-Memorial of Capt Mansfield Lovell, of the artillery service of the U S: to improve the condition of the light artillery of the U S service: referred to the Cmte on Military Affairs. 6-Ptn of Mrs Cmdor DeKay, asking the payment of a balance that she alleges is due her late husband: referred to the Cmte on Naval Affairs. 7-Ptn of Saml McKenney & other trustees of the Methodist Episcopal Church in Gtwn, D C, asking the passage of a law authorizing them to sell & convey certain real estate, the propery of that church: referred to the Cmte on D C. 8-Ptn of the heirs of John Strykins, asking indemnity for French spoliations prior to 1800: referred. 9-Memorial of Walter Colton, a chaplain in the navy, asking compensation for services rendered while holding the ofc of alcalde & other judicial appointments in Monterey, during the military occupation of Calif by the U S: referred to the Cmte on the Judiciary. 10-Ptn of Albert Fitz, asking compensation for services as special agent of the U S to the British West Indies in 1841: referred to the Cmte on Foreign Relations. 11-Ordered, that the ptn of Nancy Haggard, heiress of Wm Grymes, have leave to withdraw her ptn & papers. 12-Cmte on Revolutionary Claims: ptn of the heirs of John Holden: ask to be discharged from the further consideration of the same. 13-Cmte of Claims: ptn of Jeremiah Downs, asking to be allowed a certain sum, made an adverse report on same.

Appointments by the Pres:
Alton Long, to be Register of the Land Ofc at St Louis, Mo, vice Thos Watson, whose term of service has expired.
Chas Noble, to be Surveyor Genr'l of the Public Lands in Ohio, Indiana, & Mich, vice Lucius Lyon, whose term of service has expired.
Saml C Major, to be Receiver of Public Moneys at Fayette, Mo, vice Alfred W Morrison, whose term of service has expired.
John L Allen, to be Register of the Land Ofc at Augusta, Miss, vice Woodson Wren, declined.
Ralph Guild, to be Receiver of Public Moneys at Jackson, Mo, vice Aaron Snider, whose term of service has expired.
Saml Cruse, to be Receiver of Public Moneys at Huntsville, Ala, his commission having expired.
Richd B Servant, to be Receiver of Public Moneys at Kaskaskia, Ill, vice John A Longlois, who term of service has expired.
Alex'r Irvin, to be U S Marshal for the western district of Pa, vice John Keatley, removed.
U S Patent ofc. Petition of Benjamin M Darling, for self, & as administrator of Barton Darling, deceased, of Cumberland, R I; for extension of patent granted Benjamin M & Barton Darling, improvement of pistols; for 7 years from the expiration of said patent, which takes place on Apr 13, 1850..

The ship **Catharine** sailed from Balt, Md on Jan 15, for San Francisco, taking the following passengers:

Jas T Shipp	Dr Wm Pannill	Jas Garde
Jas Clark	Jas O Miss	Lewis Brice
P Milholland	E Chenaulet	Henry L Drugnan
Mr Lynch	J C Share	Henry Stokes
Patrick Carroll		

U S Patent ofc. Petition of Thos D Dewey, of East Poultney, Vt, praying for the extension of a patent granted to Thos D Dewey, for an improvement in horse rakes for 7 years from the expiration of said patent; which takes place on Nov 23, 1851.

THU JAN 17, 1850
Senate: 1-Memorial of Harriet F Fisher, asking compensation for a machine invented by her late husband & used by the Gov't for charging percussion caps: referred to the Cmte on Military Affairs. 2-Memorial of J P K Henshaw, for himself & co-heirs of Danl Henshaw, late of Middlebury, Vt, asking indemnity for French spoliations prior to 1800: referred. 3-Ptn of Benj F Brooks, for himself & the co-heirs of Horace Hooker, late of Utica, N Y, asking indemnity for French spoliations prior to 1800: referred. 4-Ptn of the heirs of Henry Perrine, asking an extension of time for occupying a township of land granted for the cultivation of tropical fruits: referred to the Cmte on Public Lands.
5-Ptn of John Lee Jones, asking compensation for services rendered & expenses incurred in raising, organizing & subsisting volunteers for the service of the U S in the late war with Mexico: referred to the Cmte on Military Affairs. 6-Ordered, that the memorial of Jas McIntosh, on the files of the Senate be referred to the Cmte on Naval Affairs. 7-Ordered, that the memorial of Isaac W Griffith, on the files of the Senate, be referred to the Cmte on Pensions. 8-Ordered, that Frances C Elliot, widow of Jesse D Elliot, have leave to withdraw her ptn & papers. 9-Memorial of Wm Wood, in behalf of himself & a volunteer company of Texas riflemen, raised for service of the U S in the late war with Mexico, asking to be allowed extra pay & bounty land: referred to the Cmte on Military Affairs. 10-Resolved: that Wm D Bagnall be paid the sum of $100; to Pritchard the sum of $40; & to Moses M Myers the sum of $20, for services rendered by them in examining & stating accounts from the banks of Norfolk, Richmond, & Petersburg. 11-Cmte on the Judiciary, to which was referred the ptn of Thos Copperthwaite & Co, reported a bill providing for the purchase & distribution of the decisions of the U S Supreme Court among the several States & Territories: ordered to a second reading. 12-Cmte on Military Affairs: memorial of Gen Roger Jones: to be printed. 13-Cmte on Commerce: memorial of Horace Southmayde & Son, ask to be discharged from the further consideration of the ptn, & it be referred to the Cmte on Pensions. 14-Cmte on Printing: memorial of Wm A Seely: reported against printing the same: motion was agreed to.

The accounts from China are to Oct 29th. The death of Rear Admiral Sir Francis Collier is announced. He was cmder-in-chief of the naval forces in the East Indies.

Mrd: on Jan 15, at St Joseph's Church, Balt, Md, by Rev Wm F Clarke, S J, Geo B Clarke & Mgt Cecilia, daughter of John Fitzpatrick, of Balt, Md.

Mrd: on Jan 9, by Rev Mr McElfresh, John Henry Wilson & Marcelina Virginia Simms, both of Gtwn, D C.

Died: on Jan 6, Mrs Charlotte Tabbs Kirk, relict of late Henry N Kirk, of **Great Mills**, St Mary's Co, Md.

Died: on Dec 29, at Bethlehem, Pa, Mrs Rebecca Matilda Schultz, in her 42nd year, wife of Rev Henry A Schultz, & daughter of late Chas F Bagge, of Salem, N C. In the various relations of life, as daughter, mother & Matron of Bethlehem Female Brdg School, she manifested a character of consistent piety. .

I beg leave to inform my Md & Va friends, & the public in general, that I shall open, on Jan 16, a Farmers & Citizens' Refectory, on 9th st, Wash. –A N Clemants

By writ of fieri facias, at the suit of Jas Kennehan, against Dennis Woods, I shall sell one cart, the property of Dennis Woods, on Jan 24, in front of the Centre Market-house.
–H R Maryman, Constable

House of Reps: 1-Ptn of Danl Palmer, asking for a renewal of his pension: referred to the Cmte on Military Affairs. 2-Ptn of Eliz Patterson, widow of Jas Patterson, now on the files of the House: referred to the Cmte on Revolutionary Pensions.

Appointments by the Pres: 1-Alex'r Ramsey to be Govn'r of the Territory of Minnesota. 2-Edw Joy Morris, of Pa, to be Charge d'Affaires of the U S near his Majesty the King of the Kingdom of the Two Sicilies.

FRI JAN 18, 1850
Commission on Claims against Mexico: 1-Memorial of Elihu D Smith, of Reynoso, Tamaulipas, claiming for expulsion from that place on Apr 8, 1846, & damages thereon, was ordered to be received. 2-Memorial, as amended, of Wm S Parrot, claiming for injuries inflicted by a series of illegal prosecutions, & originally file on Apr 16 last, was ordered to be received.

Wash Corp: 1-Cmte of Claims: bill for the relief of Wm Cammack, jr: passed. 2-Ptn of Wm Matthews & others, owners of lots in square 376, praying the change of an alley in said square: referred to the Cmte on Improvements. 3-Cmte of Claims: bill for the relief of Jos Swaggert: passed. 4-Act for the relief of A Kliendenst: passed. 5-Cmte of Claims: ptn of J H Woodward & Wm Slade; & ptn of Jas A Wise: asking to be discharged from the further consideration of the same: cmte discharged accordingly. 6-Bill for the relief of A Jackson: passed.

The Caddo [La] Gaz says of the tragedy of that place, by which Dr Wm W Green & David Hester were killed, that the mournful catastrophe has given rise to no hot blood, no anger nor revengeful spirit. People mourn the unhappy end of their neighbors who have been cut off in the prime of manhood, loved & respected.

Postmaster General est'd the following new Post Ofcs for week ending Jan 12, 1850.

Ofc	County, State	Postmaster
Shanandoah	Richland, Ohio	Wm Hisey
Jerusalem	Monroe, Ohio	Isaac Brown
New Calif	Union, Ohio	Saml B Woodburn
Harshmansville	Montg, Ohio	Jonas Simmons
Effort	Monroe, Pa	Patrick Daily
Meredith	Lycoming, Pa	Jacob Rhoads
Ashland Furnace	Cambria, Pa	Jos A Conrad
Bently Crock	Bradford, Pa	Benj F Buck
Bridgeport	Gloucester, N J	Geo Fried
Arcadia	Wayne, N Y	Mather Scott
Ferrisburgh	Addison, Vt	Jas B Fraser
Squawbelty	Bristol Mass	Benj B Taylor
North Cohassett	Norfolk, Mass	Sol L Beal
North Jay	Franklin, Me	Elisha Keyes
East Sullivan	Cheshire, N H	Caleb Goodenow
Bakersville	Cochocton, Ohio	Andrew Hawk
Fleetwood Academy	King & Queen, Va	Oliver White
Guest Station	Russell, Va	Wm Gibson
Stewartstown	Onongalia, Va	Owen, John
Big Glades	Russell, Va	Danl Ramey
Alexander	Putnam, Va	Wm Alexander
Sarietta	Marion, Va	Danl H Phillips
Rich Fork	Davidson, N C	W D Wilson
Fryer's Pond	Burke, Geo	Franklin Godbee
Swan Lake	Carroll P, La	Lewis P Turner
Beech Bluff	Dallas, Ark	W R McKay
Gaines' Creek	Choctaw N, Ark	Henry Harder
Oakohay	Covington, Miss	Saml Croft
Pinnellville	Covington, Miss	Rich Pinnell
China Grove	Gonzales, Texas	Russell Jones
Grape Vine	Perry, Ky	Danl Duff
Volney	Logan, Ky	Geo A Williams
Oak Hill	Overton, Tenn	Adam Gardenhire
Fair Garden	Sevier, Tenn	Henry Harris
Pleasant Retreat	Scotland, Mo	John C Collins
Bethel	Wayne, Ia	Wm E Hindman
Pleasant Balley	Martin, Ia	Geo Snodgrass
Ferdinand	Dubois, Ia	G H Stiens
Melrose	Rush, Ia	John Abernathy
Jericho	Kane, Ill	Ira H Fitch
Jas' Mil	Monroe, Ill	Lewis James
Nancemont	Cass, Ill	O B Nance

Berryton	Cass, Ill	Keeling Berry
Martha Furnace	Hardin, Ill	Danl McCook
Kennebeck	Lee, Ill	Geo E Haskell
Billing's Grove	Livingston, Ill	B P Babcock
Eden	Fond du Lac, Wis	Peter Vandervoort
Dudley	Polk, Iowa	Jeremiah Church
Fort Atkinson	Clayton, Iowa	Alex Falconer
Monticello	Iones/Jones, Iowa	Danl Darrell
Avery's	Benton, O T	J C Avery
Skinner's	Benton, O T	Eugene F Skinner
Albany	Linn, O T	J Buckhart
Callapoosa	Linn, O T	H H Spaulding
Nisqually	Louis, O T	Simmons
O'Neal's Mills	Polk, O T	Jas A O'Neal
Vancouver	Vancouver, O T	Moses H Kellogg
Linn City	Wash, O T	Jas M Moore
Zam Hill Falls	Zam Hill, O T	Jacob House

Names Changed:
West Readsboro', Bennington Co, Vt, changed to Heartwellville.
Big Eddy, Sullivan Co, N Y, changed to Narrowsburgh.
Butternuts, Otsego Co, N Y, changed to Morris.
Eisenhart's, Lehigh Co, Pa, changed to Orefield.
Crittenden Springs, Crittenden Co, Ky, changed to Columbia Mines.
Greene, Grayson Co, Ky, changed to Rough Falls.
Williamsburg, Mason Co, Ky, changed to Orangeburg.
Hollinsworth, Habersham Co, Georgia, changed to Allandale.
Sweet Springs, Saline Co, Mo, changed to Brownsville.
Bullion, Waukesha Co, Wisc, changed to Eagle.
Crandall's Ferry, Whitesides Co, Ill, changed to Erie.
Eldorado, Mercer Co, Ill, changed to McAfee.

Died: on Jan 5, Wm Kinnell, Merchant of Cincinnati, formerly a resident of Balt. On Jan 1, in Cincinnati, he was assaulted in the street, knocked down with a colt, & robbed, by 2 persons unknown. Being thus found & taken home, he died of his injuries.

Mrd: on Jan 15, by Rev Mr Lanahan, Wm J McCormick & Miss Eliz B Martin, all of Wash City.

Mrd: on Jan 8, in Montgomery, Ala, by Rev Dr Ryden, Pres of Gtwn College, D C, Thos J Semmes, of Wash, & Myra Knox, daughter of Wm Knox, of the former place.

Died: on Jan 17, of scarlet fever, Mary Adeline, daughter of late Cosworth & Ann Maria Martin, in her 13th year. Her funeral is at residence of Wm A Griffith, 9th between G & H, at half past 2 o'clock, Jan 18.

Senate: 1-Ptn of Mary MacRae, widow of an army ofcr, asking a renewal of her pension: referred to the Cmte on Pensions. 2-Ptn of licenses, under the patent right of Thos Blanchard, of a machine for turning irregular forms, asking to be protected against foreign violations of said patent right: referred to the Cmte on the Judiciary. 3-Ptn of John Tettermay & others, asking indemnity for French spoliations prior to 1800: referred. 4-Memorial of Wm G Lockwood & others, asking indemnity for French spoliations prior to 1800: referred. 4-Ptn of Nancy G Van Rensselaer, widow of a Revolutionary ofcr, asking to be allowed an increase in pension: referred to the Cmte on Pensions. 5-Memorial of Wm E Asquith, asking to be restored to his rank in the army, from which he was dismissed under the sentence of a court-martial, which he alleges was rendered contrary to law: referred to the Cmte on the Judiciary. 6-Ordered, that the memorial of the legal reps of Wm Armstrong, on the files of the Senate, be referred to the Cmte on Indian Affairs. 7-Ordered, that the ptn of Martin Fenwick, on the files of the Senate, be referred to the Cmte on Private Land Claims. 8-Ordered, that the memorial of Mrs Carmick, widow of Danl Carmick, on the files of the Senate, be refered to the Cmte on Naval Affairs. 9-Ordered, that the ptn of Robt Butler, on the files of the Senate, be referred to the Cmte on Public Lands. 10-Ordered, that leave be granted to withdraw from the files the ptn of David McDuffie. 11-Ordered, that the reps of Francis Vigo, have leave to withdraw their ptn & papers.

House of Reps: 1-Ptn of Wm B Bingley & wife, asking additional compensation for 10 acres of land in Gosport, Va, sold to the U S as a site for the dry dock. 2-Ptn of Aaron Keeler, of N Y, a soldier of the Revolution, asking to be enrolled on the pension list. 3-Ptn of S J Bowen, asking pay for his services as clerk in the Second Auditor's Ofc; & as a clerk in the ofc of the Third Auditor. 4-Memorial of Joshua P Powers, of Brooklyn, asking to be indemnified for loss sustained in consequence of the illegal capture of the schnr **Mary Elizabeth** & cargo, by the Texan sloop of war **Washington**, in 1842. 5-Ptn of Jacob Shade, jr, were withdrawn from the files, & again presented & referred to the Cmte on Revolutionary Claims. 6-Memorial of the heirs of Richd Tittermary, late of Phil, asking indemnity for French spoliations prior to 1800. 7-Ptn & other papers of the widow & heirs of Fred'k Seigle, a surgeon in the Revolutionary war, were withdrawn from the files, & again presented, to the Cmte on Revolutionary Claims.

Boston Journal: drowned on Sat in a pond at Plymouth: Barnabas Churchill, jr, 16; Chas Bates, 15; & another named Leach, son of Capt P Leach, were skating when the ice broke through. Mr Asa Cook went to their aid, & reached Leach & saved him. Mr Geo Raymond hastened to their relief, & soon sank with Cook & Bates. Mr Cook was 28 years of age, & leaves a family. Mr Raymond was 45, a printer by trade, & leaves a family. The bodies were all recovered.

Died on board the ship **Sarah**, on the passage from Fayal to N Y: Michl Brown, infant; Nancy Dean, 60; Sophia Ellis, 45; one infant, name unknown. Left in the hosptal at Fayal, sick, & to be sent forward as soon as sufficiently recovered: Wm Gallagan, 14; Jas Gallaghan, 6; Patrick Rogers, 50; Jane Burns, 50; Patrick Burns, 30; Jas Daly, 40; Josiah Holand, 24.

By the arrival at N Y of the passengers who were taken from the burning packet-ship **Caleb Grinshaw**, the names of those supposed to have been lost have been ascertained. The figures denote their age.

Levi Cook	19
John Belamy	24
John Dove	21
John Braham	27
John Robinson	20
Geo Coy	24
Mary Cox	18
Chas Rowe	20
Bryan Murphy	20
Patrick Kernan	24
John Polland	26
Laura Fooley	27
Thos Welsh	27
Michl Farroll	16
Judy O'Connell	20
David Kidd	23
Bartel Finnegan	20
Francis Murphy	6
Ellen Morgan	4
Margaret Kidd	7
Jas Kidd	2
Francis McQuade	2
Ellen Farrall	5
Mary Farrall	8
Patrick Quinn	26
Mary Hickey	30
Wm Hickey	6
Bridget Flood	18
Susan Brogan	6
Jan Brogan	4
John Brogan	2
E W East	24
Philip Holland	22
John Tooney	24
Mary McAlaster	18
Michl Delany	20
Wm Barny	7
Henry Barny	5
Bridget Barny	2
Francis Mulvey	6
Mary Ann Trainer	6
Arthur Trainer	4

Catharine Grace	30
Mary Grace	6
John Rodgers	16
Ellen Calney	3
Ellen Wymbs	4
Jas O'Neil	1
Ann McGinn	26
Patrick Quinn	30
Maria Harken	8
Wm McKibber	2
Laura Gallagan	8
Ellen Dowd	25
Nicholas Connor	
Jas Connor	7
Owen Connor	5
Parick Connor	2
Philip Smith	28
Catharine Boyle	20
John Boyle	25
Eliza Rissity	6
Mary Rodgers	50
Thos Rodgers	16
Ellen Downey	19
Mary Welch	20
Biddy Spelman	26
John Gohan	18
Biddy Lynch	16
Thos Cain	1

Michl Riley, a laborer, resident at 11 Cross st, Boston, choked to death by a large piece of meat sticking in his throat. He leaves a wife & child with whom he has not lived for some time past.

For sale: ***Columbian Foundry***, [cannon foundry,] in D C, near Gtwn; sale by excx & excs of Gen John Mason, deceased, its late proprietor. 50 years in constant execution of contracts with the Gov't. -Jas M Mason, acting exc.

SAT JAN 19, 1850
Mr John Richards, the Superintendent of the Franklin Paper Mill in Richmond, was killed on Wed, by becoming accidently entangled in a part of the machinery of the mill.

Tornado struck on Jan 7 near Natchez, & Mr McCullen was killed.

Mrd: on Nov 27, at Clarksville, Tenn, by Bishop Henderick, Joshua Elder to Miss M M Martin, daughter of Hon M A Martin, all of the vicinity.

Circuit Sup Court of Law & Chancery of Loudoun Co, Va. Motion of John K Littleton, one exc of Enoch Furr, deceased, who presented a will of said Enoch Furr. To appear on the first day of the next term of this Court, to show cause if said will should not be admitted to probate: *Sam'l Berkeley & *Tacey his wife; Charity Wills, Newton Furr, Barsheba Morehead; *Sarah A Furr, *infant child of Edwin Furr deceased; *Mazariah Thomas & Eliz his wife; Hannah Littleton; Wm G Furr; *Jeremiah C Furr. [*Those with no known residence in Va] -Thos P Knox, clk crt.

House of Reps: 1-Memorial & papers of Wm B Muse were referred to the Cmte on Naval Affairs. 2-Ptn of Mgt Williams, for a pension as the heir & next of kin of Capt John Williams, who fell in an action in Sep, 1812, at Dan's Creek. 3-Ptn of Jos Wright, for an invalid pension. 4-Ptn of Mary Ruggles & Sally Parsons, widows of Revolutionary ofcrs, for a pension. 5-Ptn of Stephen Colville, of Phil, administrator of Wm F French, asking the payment of certain Loan ofc certificates. 6-Ptn of Winthrop S Harding, praying for certain relief. 7-Memorial of Eliz S Hill, Cyrus Rogers, & others, of Portsmouth, N H, asking indemnity for French spoliations prior to 1800. 8-Ptn of John McClintock, Saml Sheafe, & others, asking indemnity for French spoliations prior to 1800. Ptn of Margareta Bordley & others, asking indemnity for French spoliations. 9-Supplemental ptn of Delphine Isabella Trepagnier, widow of the late F B DeBellerne, praying for a pension.

SAT JAN 19, 1850
[Supplement with Post Ofc routes.]

MON JAN 21, 1850
Boarding: Mrs Jas France on E st, nearly opposite the old Medical College. Terms moderate.

The wife of Mr John B died in Leonox, Mass, on Oct 25, was buried on Oct 26, & her monument erected on Nov 3. On the same day, & by the same priest who was called to administer consolation to the deceased, the said inconsolable John was again married. [The B is not revealed.]

Dr John F Brooke, Fleet Surgeon to the U S Squadron in the Chinese seas, died at Macao on Oct 17.

Orphans Court of Wash Co, D C. Letters testamentary on the personal estate of Eliza Henning, late of said county, deceased.
-A Rothwell, exc

Mrd: on Jan 10, at Old Point Comfort, by Rt Rev John Johns, Bishop of Va, Maj Wm A Nichols, of 2nd Artl, U S Army, to Clara L, daughter of Lt Col R D De Russy, Corps of Engineers, U S Army.

Mr Isaac C Dunn, member of Va house of delegates, resigned Jan 8, intending to go to New Mexico, to rescue Mrs White, his sister, recently captured with her child, by Apaches, who killed her husband. [Jan 29th newspaper: Santa Fe, Nov 28. 10 days ago, when Maj Green came in sight of the Indian camp, they shot Mrs White & fled; no trace of her child].

Died: on Jan 20, in Gtwn, Mrs Mary M Cox, in her 47th year, relict of late Clement Cox. Her funeral is at her late residence on Gay st.

Died: Hon John Scott, of Genr'l Crt of Va, at residence of his son-in-law, Arthur Morson, in Richmond, Va, on Thu last.

Died: on Sat last, in Gtwn, D C, of scarlet fever, Saml, aged near 6 years, son of W H & Eliza Tenney. His funeral will be at residence of his parents, on Bridge st, this afternoon, at 3 o'clock.

Local News. Frank Nokes, a colored man, has been arrested under the charge of setting fire to the livery stable & coach factory of Mr Thompson Nailor.

City Ordinances-Wash: 1-Act for the relief of Philip Mohun: sum of $123.08 be paid to him for balance due for the grading & other work on Pa ave. 2-Act for the relief of Thos Lewis: fine imposed relative to grates placed over vaults, is remitted, provided Lewis pay the cost of prosecution. 3-Act for the relief of Wm Cammack: fine imposed in relation to hucksters, is remitted, provided Cammack pay the cost of prosecution.

Appointments by the Pres: 1-Henry D Maxwell, of Pa, to be U S Consul for the port of Triests, in Austria. 2-Jas Wright Gordon, of Mich, to be U S Consul for the port of Pernambusco, in Brazil.

Phil papers announce the death of Dr Saml Anderson, of Chester, Pa, who served as Rep in Congress in 1827 & for several years. He died at Chester, on Jan 17, in his 77th year.

TUE JAN 22, 1850
Congress-in Senate: 1-Memorial of Mrs Morris Foot, widow of Lyman Foot, late surgeon in the army, asking a pension, which, with the papers of Lymon Foot on the files of the Senate of the 23rd Congress, was referred to the Cmte on Military Affairs. 2-Memorial of the legal reps of Wm Carmichael, asking compensation for diplomatic services at the Court of Madrid: referred to the Cmte on Foreign Relations. 3-Ordered, that the ptn of Wm D & Julia Acken, reps of Wm Tool, deceased, be referred to Naval affairs cmte. 4-Sec of Interior, communicates papers in relation to the application of John A Rogers for a pension. 5-Memorial of Mary Smith Whetmore, widow of the late Maj Alphonso Whetmore, an ofcr in the war of 1812 with Great Britain, asking to be allowed a pension: referred to the Cmte on Pensions. 6-Statement & claims of Thos Allen against the U S for printing the compendium of the Sixth Census: referred to the Cmte of Claims. 7-Ordered, that the ptn of Adam D Stewart, on the files of the Senate, be referred to the Cmte of Claims. 8-Cmte of Printing: referred the motion to print the ptn of Chas L

Jones, for compensation for services in subsisting volunteers in the late war with Mexico, reported against the same: which report was concurred in. 9-Memorial of Wm Archer, of Wash City, asking for the survey & location of a railroad from the National metropolis to the Pacific Ocean: referred to the Cmte on Roads & Canals. 10-Ptn of Amelia Smith Catharine Whetmore, widow of Leonidas Whetmore, asking to be allowed a pension: referred to the Cmte on Military Affairs. 11-Memorial of John McCann & others, asking that diplomatic intercourse with the Gov't of Austria may be suspended: referred to the Cmte on Foreign Relations. 12-Memorial of the legal reps of John R Champagne, asking indemnity for French spoliations prior to 1800: referred to a select cmte. 13-Documents submitted relating to the claim of Absalom Hughes, a U S pensioner, for an increase of pension: referred to the Cmte on Pensions.

Balt Argus of Mon: In pursuance of a resolve of the present Legislature, Govn'r Thomas has appointed Hon Albert Constable to proceed to Pa as counsel for Mr Little, a citizen of Wash Co, Md, now confined in the jail of Huntingdon Co on a charge of kidnapping. A short time since a number of slaves, the property of our citizens, fled into Pa, & were caught & brought back by Mr Little. Mr Little later visited Huntingdon Co on business, & was arrested on the charge above referred to. Being a poor man, & unable to provide himself with counsel, he made application to our present Legislature for assistance, in which they promptly & cheerfully acquiesced.

Mr Michl Nourse has been appointed to act *ad interim* as Register of the Treasury, vice Mr Hall, until a successor be appointed.

Mr Jas Wickware, of Ogdensburg, N Y, was suddenly killed, at the barn of Mr J F Davies, near Black Lake, on Jan 9, by the bursting of the cylinder of a threshing machine.

$20 reward: the cellar of the subscribers was broken open on Jan 15, & a large number of trunks & valises taken. Reward for recovery of the property. –J Galligan & Son

The undersigned: practical mechanic, & bldg in Wash more than 16 years, will undertake the measuring of carpenter's work, & all other branches pertaining to bldg. Residence on H, between 8th & 9th sts, south of the Patent Ofc. –Jas Towles

For rent: new & commodious house, H & 15th sts. Apply to Dr Faley, Land Ofc, or to G Rodman, of the Treasury Dept.

Bouquest, wreaths, cut flowers, parlor & other plants: 12th & H sts.
-Geo McLeod

Commission on Claims against Mexico: 1-Memorial of Thos Morrison, surviving partner of Plumer & Morrison: claim is not valid: & accordingly not allowed. 2-Memorial of Dorcas Ann Plumer, admx of Robt Plumer: claim is valid: the amount to be awarded subject to the future action of the board. 3-Memorial of Patrick Hayes, of Phil: claim is valid, & is allowed: amount to be awarded subject to the future action of the Board.

Union Literary Debating Society meeting this evening at 7.
—D S G Cabell, Sec

Masonic regular meeting this evening at 7. —G A Schwarzman, Sec

On Sun week, Rev Mr Beecher, in a sermon at the new church in Orange st, Brooklyn, inveighed severely against the practice of spitting in churches. He said man had a right to snuff, & smoke, & chew as much as they pleased at home, but they had no right in introduce such profanity into the Church, destroying the carpets, & showing disrespect to the house of God. What would they think of him if he chewed in the pulpit & spat from it?

WED JAN 23, 1850
Commission on Claims against Mexico: 1-Memorial of Wm Homan, co-partner of Jas H Farrington, of the firm of Farrington & Homan, claiming for a forced loan in the city of Mexico, in 1836, being taken up for consideration together with the proofs & documents connected therewith: claim is valid: same is allowed accordingly to Wm Homan, to the extent of his interest therein: amount to be awarded subject to the future action of the Board. 2-Memorial of Mary Smith, of Galveston, Texas, claiming for supplies furnished to the garrison of Anahuac, with the proof & documents: claim is not valid: same is not allowed.

Richmond Whit: Died: on Jan 17, at the residence of Mr A A Morson, in Richmond, Va, Hon John Scott, age 69 years. He was a prominent member of the Senate of Va during 1811-12 & 1812-13. He contracted an illness in returning home from the last of these sessions which shattered his constitution for many years, & from which it never perhaps entirely recovered. He was a member of the convention in 1829, which assembled & formed the present Constitution of the State; & in a body composed of Madison, Monroe, Marshall, & a host of others.

N Y Journal of Commerce: Mr Jas M Forrester, a young gentleman, in the employ of Chas H Rogers & Co, 107 South st, N Y, was a member of engine company 2, of N Y C, & exerted himself so violently at the fire which destroyed the sugar refinery of Messrs Woolsey & others, in that city, that he died from the effects of his exertion. He leaves a widow, to whom he was recently married. The Messrs Woolsey sent to his widow a check for $500. Messrs Roger & Co have also made provision for his widow.

The trial of Capt Rynders, for participating in the Astor Place Opera Riot in N Y, has been acquitted.

Legislature of Va transacted no business on Fri. David Hargrave, the Delegate from Sussex Co, died on that morning, after an illness of several weeks' duration. He was a very amiable & estimable gentleman, highly respected & esteemed by his fellow-members.

Senate: 1-Memorial of the executors of John Mason, asking compensation for certain cannon manufactured for the naval service: referred to the Cmte of Claims. 2-Memorial of Sidney S Allcott, asking permission to correct an error in the entry of a quarter section of land: referred to the Cmte on Public Lands. 3-Ptn of N Lane, late a pension agent at Louisville, asking to be allowed a credit in the settlement of his accounts: referred to the Cmte on Pensions. 4-Ptn of Saml M Bootes, asking compensation for his services as book-keeper in the ofc of the Treasury of the U S: referred to the Cmte of Claims. 5-Ptn of Lemuel Vinal & others, asking indemnity for French spoliations prior to 1800: referred to the select cmte. 6-Ptn of Sarah Nicholls, widow of a Revolutionary soldier, asking to be allowed a pension: referred to the Cmte on Pensions. 7-Memorial from the executors of Wm Bartlett & others, asking indemnity for French spoliations prior to 1800: referred to the select cmte. 8-Memorial of Caleb D Owings & others, asking indemnity for French spoliations prior to 1800: referred to the select cmte. 9-Documents submitted relating to the claim of Wm S Waller for compensation for services in selling & disposing of Treasury notes for the U S during the last war with Great Britain: referred to the Cmte of Claims. 10-Memorial of the heirs of Jos Moosley, asking indemnity for French spoliations prior to 1800: referred to the select cmte. 11-Ptn of Joshua Follansbee & B F Isherwood, chief engineers in the navy, representing that they have been deprived of their promotion & pay in consequence of absence on foreign duty at the time they were entitled to examination, & asking for the passage of an act for their relief: referred to the Cmte on Military Affairs. 12-Memorial of Josiah Sturgis & other ofcrs & seaman of the U S revenue cutter **Hamilton**, on the Boston station, asking that the persons employed in that service may be placed on the footing, with reference to the pension laws, of the persons employed in the navy, & that the benefits & compensation of these laws may be entened to them. Capt Sturgis states that he has saved the lives of 11 persons, & boarded or spoken fifteen thousand & five vessels up to Dec 31, 1849. Referred to the Cmte on Pensions. 13-Ptn of Alex'r G P Garnett, on files of the Senate: referred to the Cmte of Claims. 14-Ptn of Danl G Garnsey, on the files of the Senate: referred to the Cmte on Military Affairs. 15-Ptn of John A Rogers, asking a pension: referred to the Cmte on Pensions. 16-Documents on the files of the Senate to the claim of Thos Rhodes: referred to the Cmte on Post Ofc & Post Roads. 17-Cmte on Military Affairs, asking to be discharged from the further consideration of the ptn of Mrs Frances Fowler & Mrs Frances P Gardiner, & that they be referred to the Cmte on Pensions: agreed to. 18-Cmte on the Public Lands: referred the ptn of Richd Chaney, reported a bill for the relief of the pre-emption claimants of the lands upon which the towns of ***Fort Madison*** & Burlington, in Iowa, are situated. 19-Cmte of Public Lands, to which was referred the ptn of citizens of the parish of Terrebonne, in La, asking the confirmation of a 16th section of land sold by the register at New Orleans, reported a bill to confirm the sale of school lands made to J B Gregoire & P Gregoire, in La: ordered to be printed. 20-Cmte of Claims: bill for the relief of Theodore Offutt & accompanying documents in relation to the same, reported it back without amendment, & recommended its passage.

Died: On Jan 1, at Holly Springs, Miss, Wm Anderson, age 21 years, son of late Henry Anderson, of that place.

Died: on Oct 17, Dr John F Brooke, Fleet surgeon of the E India Squadron at Macao; eldest son of Judge Brooke, Crt of Appeals, Va.

House of Reps: 1-Cmte of Claims: bill for the relief of Wm B Crews: committed. Same cmte: bill for the relief of Chas Ahrenfeldt & John H F Vogt: committed. 2-Cmte of Military Affairs: discharged from the further consideration of the ptns of Dr L K Hills, Dr Francis Drudy, Thos & Richd Hayward, & Augustus Buchell: laid upon the table. 3-Cmte on Naval Affairs: discharged from the further consideration of the ptn of A G Farragut: laid upon the table. 4-Cmte on the Post Ofc & Post Roads: ptn of Peter Kinney, laid on the table & to be printed. 5-Cmte on Revolutionary Pensions: discharged from the further consideration of the ptn of Henry Haines: laid on the table. 6-Cmte on Revolutionary Pensions: discharged from the further consideration of the ptns of Sarah Mandeville, legal rep oF John Mandeville & Saml Dewey: they were referred to the Cmte on Revolutionary Claims. 7-Resolved, that the Clerk furnish each member of the House with a copy of Joel B Sutherland's Congressional Manual, & to pay him $1 for each copy. 8-Ptn of Thos C Reed & others, praying that the soldiers of the war of 1812 may be placed by law on the same footing, with regard to pensions & pay, as the soldiers of the Revolution. 9-Ptn of Catherine J Claiborne, widow of Maj Richd Claiborne, an ofcr of the Revolution, praying for relief. 10-Ptn of Francis W Searing & 164 others, citizens of Pa, against liquor rations in the navy. 11-Ptn of Jacob Drinkhouse, a Revolutionary soldier, for aid. 12-Ptn of Mrs W W Drinker, for a pension, removed from the files: referred to the Cmte on Naval Affairs. 13-Ptn of Andrew A Jones taken from the files & referred to the Cmte on Commerce. 14-Memorial of Nathl Colton & a large number of others, of Cambridge, Mass, praying that a portion of the Western Territory may be set aside as a permanent home for the Indian tribes. 15-Ptn of Marinus M Perry, for a pension.

Zachary Taylor, Pres of the U S, recognizes G J Bechtel, who has been appointed Consul Gen of the Dukedon of Brunswick & Luneburg for the U S of America. Jan 22, 1850.

For rent: dwlg on **Mount Olivet**: lately occupied by Rev Mr Denison, midway between the Capitol & Garrison: contains in all 12 rooms, with all necessary out-bldgs. Rent $175. There are good pavements leading to the Capitol, [half a mile distant,] to Pa ave. This property can be purchased on reasonable terms. Apply to Mrs Geo Adams, near the Navy Yard gate, or J G Adams, Northern Liberties.

I certify that Thos B Goddard, of Wash Co, brought before me as an estray trespassing on his enclosure, a large red Steer. –J L Smith, J P

Wash Co, D C. To Jas W Osborn & Eliza Ann his wife, Chas S Matthews, Wm P Matthews, Ann Matthews, Benj H Dorsey & Henrietta his wife, Andrew S Matthews, Alex'r McD Matthews, & Richd S Matthews, heirs at law of Wm P Matthews, deceased. The undersigned, com'rs appointed by the Circuit Court of Wash Co, D C to value & divide lot 2 in square 488, in Wash City, late the property of Wm P Matthews, deceased, give notice we will meet on the said lot on Feb 28, for the purpose of making partition of the same. –H Naylor, Chas Pettit, Lewis Johnson, J F Callan, W Redin, Com'rs

Watches, clocks & spectacles for sale: 4½ & 6th sts. —Stephen Eddy

Sale of valuable property: by deed of trust from Richd G Briscoe to the subscribers, dated 22nd & recorded Feb 24, 1849, in Liber I A S 2, folios 304 to 310, land records of Wash Co, D C: public auction on Mar 6: lot 9 in square 382, in Wash City: with eight 3 story brick stores, with granite fronts & slate roofs. —John A Linton & others, trustees. —C W Boteler, Auct'r

THU JAN 24, 1850
House of Reps: 1-Bill to amend an act for the relief of Fred'k Durrine: introduced. 2-Moved to withdraw the papers of A Bandorim & A A Roberts from the files of the House, & have them referred to the Cmte of Claims. 3-Ptn of Geo Walter, asking compensation for services to the country rendered by his father, Michl Walters, in the Revolutionary war. 4-Ptn of Wm G Bucknor, executor of the estate of H Bulow, jr, to be indemnified for property destroyed by the Seminole Indians while in the occupancy of the U S troops. 5-Ptn of Catharine Clark, widow of Jos Clark, a seaman, for a pension. 6-Ptn & papers relating to the claim of Robt Roberts: referred to the Cmte of Claims. 7-Ptn of Rulif Van Brunt. 8-Ptn of H H Booley, for a pension. 8-Memorial of Mrs A Saunders, admx of the estate of Capt Wm Davis, praying compensation for services & reimbursement of the expenditures of said Davis whilst in command of the U S transport schnr **Eufaula**. 9-Ptn of Henry T Pairo, of Richmond, Va, administrator of John Lamb, deceased, late chief clerk in the ofc of the 1st Comptroller of the Treasury.

Senate: 1-Ordered, that the ptn of Eugene Van Ness, administrator of Nehemiah Brush, & ptn of Jas Edwards, administrator of Edw M Wanton, on the files of the Senate, be referred to the Cmte of Claims. 2-Ordered, that the ptn of Mangle M Quackenboss & others, sureties of Saml Swartwout, on the files of the Senate, be referred to the Cmte on Commerce. 3-Ordered, that the ptn of Bryan Callaghan, on the files of the Senate, be referred to the Cmte of Claims.

Some weeks ago, Wm Purcell, of Silver Creek, Pa, paid for the passages of his wife Mary & their 5 children from Ireland to N Y; at the same time Thos Purcell, of the same place, sent for his 2 sons-Margaret Purcell, of Minersville, sent for Mary Purcell, a little girl, & Jas Kain, of Valley Furnace, for his wife Margaret & their 7 children. Shortly after, they received intelligence that the little girl, Mary Purcell, died before the passage certificate reached her, & that the others named all sailed from Liverpool on Nov 28 in good health. Last week, on the arrival of the vessel at N Y, they learned that during the passage 26 of the passengers died of cholera, among whom were Mrs Mary Purcell, her 3 youngest children, & Mrs Mgt Kain, leaving the other 11 children helpless & unprotected, to make their way as best they might to this country. We will not attempt to depict the feelings of these bereaved familes on the reunion of the fathers with their motherless children, -Pottsville [Pa] Emporium

Orphans Court of Wash Co, D C. Letters of administration on the personal estate of Alfred Wallingsford, late of said county, deceased. -Eleanor Wallingsford, admx

Wash Corp: 1-Memorial of Geo Watterston & others, a cmte appointed on the subject of a free public library: referred. 2-Cmte on Police: ptn of Wm M Bayne, for relief: passed. 3-Cmte of Claims: bill for the relief of Thompson Nailor: passed. 4-Ptn from Elick H Woodward: referred to the Cmte of Claims. 5-Ptn of J C McKelden & others, master bakers, for a reduction in the scale of the assize of bread: referred to the Cmte on Police. 6-Bill for the relief of A Kliendenst was taken up & passed. 7-Bill for relief of Jos Swagert: referred to the Cmte of Claims. 8-Bill for the relief of A Jackson: referred to the Cmte on Police. 9-Ptn from A Simpson & others: referred to the Cmte on Improvements. 10-Ptn of B L Jackson & Brother, praying the payment of the balance due him as the assignee of P Crowley: referred to the Cmte on Improvements.
11-Ptn of W M Bayne, praying remission of a fine incurred for exhibiting his Panorama: referred to the Cmte of Police. 12-Ptn of John Bowen, praying remission of a fine: referred to the Cmte of Claims. 13-Cmte of Claims: bill for the relief of Christopher Cammack: read. Same cmte: asking to be discharged from the further consideration of the ptn of Jas Johnson: laid on the table. 14-Bill for the relief of Jas Crutchett: referred to the Cmte on Improvements. 15-Ptn of W A Evans & others, for a flag footway on 13th st west, at H & N Y ave: referred to the Cmte on Improvements. 16-Bill for the relief of Hanson Brown: passed.

Commission on Claims against Mexico: 1-Memorial of Patrick B Hayes & Chas B Jaudon, administrators of Thos Hayes, deceased, claiming for services in fitting for sea & navigating a Mexican public vessel **Tepeyac**, alias the vessel **Kensington**: claim not valid: not allowed. 2-Memorial of Jos W Wilson, claiming for money taken from him by the guard at Vera Cruz: with proofs & documents: claim not valid: not allowed. 3-The two several memorials of Roderick T Higginbotham & of David Hull, claiming for loss & imprisonment, the former as a passenger, the latter as a seaman on board the schnr **Champion**, captured by a Mexican squadron in Apr, 1837: claims are valid: amount to be awarded subject to the future action of the Board.

Mr Jas Denholn, of Quebec, who mysteriously disappeared on Jan 8, while on his way to Boston to take the steamer for England, was found on Sun in the woods near Great Falls, N H, covered with snow, having apparently fallen from cold & exhaustion, & frozen to death. On his person was found a gold watch & a number of sovereigns. He is supposed to have wandered off while under a fit of insanity. He leaves a wife & family at Quebec.

Died: On Tue, in Wash City, Myra Gaines Bowlin, aged 2 years 5 months, daughter of Hon Jas B & Mgt V Bowlin. Her funeral will be at Brown's Hotel, today, at 10 o'clock.

Died: on Jan 23, in Wash City, Jane Cunningham, age 2 years, 10 months & 12 days, daughter of Henry & Jannet West.

Postmaster General est'd the following new Post Ofcs for week ending Jan 19, 1850:

Ofc	County, State	Postmaster
Townsend	Lincoln, Me	Cyrus McKown
Houstonic	Berkshire, Mass	Jas C Hyde
No Bellingham	Norfolk, Mass	Milton Z Bulland

Long Ridge	Fairfield, Ct	Fred B Scofield
Owasco Lake	Cayuga, N Y	David Chamberlain
Laona	Chautauque, N Y	Jos B Hall
East Freetown	Courtland, N Y	John King
Barnes' Corners	Lewis, N Y	David Curtis
Brushville	Queens, N Y	Thos Brush
East Grafton	Rensselaer, N Y	John Tilley
Hart Lot	Onondaga, N Y	Elihu P Cornell
South Hartwick	Otsego, N Y	C W Rockwell
East Pitrairn	St Lawrence, N Y	Chas H Bowles
West Fowler	St Lawrence, N Y	Thos Mitchell
Wardboro	Warren, N Y	Wm H Ward
Kirk Wood	Broome, N Y	John F Weeks
Dannemora	Clinton, N Y	Jas H Gibson
De Lancey	Madison, N Y	Lewis C York
Temperanc'ville	Alleghany, Pa	Jas Richardson
West Dublin	Bedford, Pa	Jas G Lyon
Ogle	Butler, Pa	A Walker
Weatherby	Carbon, Pa	Richd D Stiles
Walnut Bottom	Cumberland, Pa	Jas H Wiley
Norritonville	Montg, Pa	Abrm Schwenck, jr
Andora	Phil, Pa	F W Hagy
Millview	Sullivan, Pa	John Holyneaux
Shirland	Wash, Pa	John Walker
McComb	Hancock, Ohio	Wm Mitchell
Ironton	Lawrence, Ohio	Caleb Briggs
Tabor	Tuscarawas, Ohio	Moses Wright
Woodhull	Shiawassee, Mich	D A Tower
California	Branch, Mich	Israel R Hall
Perry	Shiaeassa, Mich	Wm P Lang
McRea's Mills	Montg, N C	Jas W McRee
Kossuh	Cherokee, Geo	Jas Straine
Carlyle	Pickens, Ala	Robt Henry
Campbellton	Itawumba, Miss	Josiah Roberts
Pool's Mills	Jones, Miss	Alfred Pool
Gilead	Upshur, Texas	L B Camp
Sugar Hill	Panola, Texas	Ferrill Henson
Forrest Home	Cass, Texas	J W Moore
Cotland	Newton, Texas	S P McFarland
Manatee	Hillsboro, Fla	Henry S Clarke
Castor	Caldwell P, La	Asa Anderson
Dorsey	Woodford, Ky	John S Reardon
Lane	Elkhar, Ia	David Patterson
Fairland	Livingston, Mo	R R Mills

Lick Fork	Daviess, Mo	Elijah Foley
Brookline	Clarke, Mo	Saml Troxel
Fredonia	Wash, Wis	Wm Bell
Bluff	Sauk, Wis	Lewis B Smith
South English	Keokuk, Iowa	Robt Ardre

Names changed:
Prible's Mills, Wood Co, Va, changed to Newark.
Top Leve., Dallas Co, Ala, changed to Fulton
Baha'a, Lawrence Co, Miss, changed to Rayville
Fraziersville, Abbeville District, S C, changed to Harrisburg
Wood's Ferry, Green Co, Tenn, changed to Caney Braqnch.
Davy's Landing, Hardin Co, Tenn, changed to Saltillo.
Rock Springs, Saint Clair, Ill, changed to Shiloh.
Burton, Parke Co, Indiana, changed to Howard.
Beech Parke, Posey Co, Indiana, changed to Grafton Mills.
Darby, Adams Co, Indiana, changed to Pleasant Mills.
Jackson Prairie, Steuben Co, Indiana, changed to Flint.
Hickory Grove, Bond Co, Ill, changed to Pocahontas.
Plover Portage, Portage Co, Wisc, changed to Plover.
Dunn, Dane Co, Wisc, changed to Ancient.

Senate: 1-Memorial of Dudley Baldwin, Chas Stetson, & others, asking an extension of the admiralty & maritime jurisdiction of the district courts of the U S to all navigable waters: referred to the Cmte on the Judiciary. 2-Memorial of Geo Wright, asking compensation for the use by the U S of his invention for the manufacture of percussion caps: referred to the Cmte on Military Affairs. 3-Memorial of Wm Vernon & others, asking indemnity for French spoliations prior to 1800: referred to the select cmte. 4-Memorial of Robt Butler, late surveyor general of Florida, asking additional compensation, & the reimbursement of certain legal expenses incurred while in his official capacity: referred to the Cmte on Public Lands. 5-Memorial of the heirs of Henry Walker, asking compensation for property destroyed by the enemy in 1814: referred to the Cmte of Claims. 6-Memorial of A R Woolley, Chas J Nourse, & Geo A Bender, in behalf of the ofcrs of the war of 1812, asking that they be allowed bounty lands. 7-Additional document relating to the ptn of Geo R Herrick, submitted: & referred to the Cmte of Claims. 8-Memorial of Jos D Drinker & other heirs of John Skyrin, asking indemnity for French spoliations prior to 1800: referred to the select cmte. 9-Memorial of Susanna Rose, widow of a Revolutionary soldier, asking a pension: referred to the Cmte on Pensions. 10-Ptn of Jas Morrow, asking the payment of certain bills issued by the Continental Congress: referred to the Cmte of Claims. 11-Memorial of the legal reps of Robt & Alex'r McKim, asking indemnity for French spoliations prior to 1800: referred to the select cmte. 12-Cmte on Naval Affairs, to which was referred the ptn of John Mitchell, asking to be discharged from the further consideration of said ptn & that it be referred to the Cmte on Pensions. 13-Cmte on Revolutionary Claims, to which was referred the ptn of Benj Wood, a Revolutionary soldier, asked to be discharged from the further consideration of the same, & that it be referred to the Cmte on Pensions.

14-Cmte on Foreign Relations, was referred the memorial of Ladislas Wankowicz & G Tochman, heirs of Kosciusko, asking to be protected in certain rights; asking to be discharged from the further consideration of the same.

FRI JAN 25, 1850
Senate: 1-Memorial of the legal reps of John Bell, asking indemnity for French spoliations prior to 1800: referred to the select cmte. 2-Additional documents in the case of Rufus Dwinnell: referred to the Cmte on Post Ofc & Post Roads. 3-Documents submitted in relation to the claim of the administrator of Darius Garrason for compensation for furnishing supplies to the army during the Florida war: referred to the Cmte of Claims. 4-Memorial of the heirs of Woodbury S Nichols, asking indemnity for French spoliations prior to 1800: referred to the select cmte. 5-Ptn of Mrs Merebah Chandler, of N Y, a widow of a Revolutionary ofcr, stating her destitute condition, her poverty, & want, call for means of subsistence. She states that her late husband, a Revolutionary soldier, being entitled to a pension by the act of 1818, died not having received that pension, because his pride restrained him from taking the oath required by that act. But he is dead, & his widow is left with 2 daughters; & she prays that the arrears of pension due to her husband may now be paid her: referred to the Cmte on Pensions. Memorial states that her husband served 6 years as a soldier & petty ofcr in the war of the Revolution, & was honorably discharged by Gen Washington; that he received little or no pay for his services, save the satisfaction of having served his country faithfully; that he never held ofc & received no pension under the act of 1818, because unwilling to swear himself a pauper, nor until the change of the law in 1826, from which time he drew a pension until his death, in 1836, 10 years after. She says she is infirm as to be unable to walk; that she is dependent on her pension of $80 a year as a Revolutionary soldier's widow; that her daughters, both widows like herself, are destitute of property; & that her pension is utterly inadequate to provide her with the barest necessities of life. She asks Congress to grant her the 8 years' pension payable to her husband under the act of 1818, which he failed to receive through his irresistible repugnance to swearing himself a beggar: referred to the Cmte of Claims. 6-Ptn from John McAvoy, a soldier, who served in the Mexican war, for 4 or 5 years in the U S Army. He claims that he was compelled to pay $20 to Capt Ford, master of a vessel chartered, as he believed, to carry sick & wounded soldiers to New Orleans; that the payment has been proved by his affidavits filed in the Second Auditor's ofc; that his case was rejected on May 17, 1849, on account of Gen Worth's order not being produced, & which cannot now be done, & because his wife was not mentioned in the quartermaster's affidavit, though she was one of the 13 women allowed each company; that he appeals to Congress, hoping, in consequence of his services, [having been at the battle of Okechubbe under Col Taylor, & having been honorably discharged from 2 enlistments, as appears in the records of the War Dept,] a deaf ear will not be turned to a poor old soldier whose prime of life has been spent in fighting the battles of his country: referred to the Cmte of Claims. 7-Memorial of Ed Hill & others, asking indemnity for French spoliations prior to 1800: referred to the select cmte. 8-Documents in relation to the claim of the heirs of Wm Woodworth to the renewal of his patent right: referred to the Cmte on Patents & the Patent Ofc. 9-Resolved, the Sec of State to audit the claims of John Hogan, for his services & losses incurred as a confidential agent of the U S in St

Domingo, & pay the balance found due. 10-Cmte of Commerce: to report on the propriety of giving to Capt David Cook, of the British barque **Sarah**, some suitable token of the approbation of Congress of his gallant & humane conduct in rescuing the passengers, ofcrs, & crew of the American ship **Caleb Grimshaw**, destroyed by fire on the Atlantic ocean, & bring them in safety to the port of N Y. 11-Memorial of Elisha Munroe, on the files of the Senate: referred to the Cmte on Pensions. 12-Ptn of Peter Greer, on the files of the Senate: referred to the Cmte on Pensions. 13-Ptn of Geo S Gaines, on the files of the Senate: referred to the Cmte on Indian Affairs. 14-Ptn of Ann Dodd, on the files of the Senate: referred to the Cmte on Pensions. 15-Cmte on Commerce: memorial of P Pavenstedt & Schumacker, reported a bill for their relief. 16-Cmte on the Judiciary: was referred sundry memorials relating to the patent of Thos Blanchard, reported a bill giving further remedies to patentees. 17-Cmte on Private Land Claims:on the claim of Chas Gunter, reported a bill to relinquish the reversionary interest of the U S to a certain reservation in the State of Alabama, & to confirm the title of C G Gunter thereto: bill engrossed. 18-Cmte on Revolutionary Claims: resolved, that the claim of the legal reps of Wm Vawters, being, as appears, for half pay, & there being law for the settlement of such claims, the memorial & documents be referred to the Sec of the Interior for settlement. 19-Cmte on the Judiciary: on the memorial of Wm E Aisquith: asking to be discharged from the further consideration of the same. 20-Cmte on Private Land Claims: asking to be discharged from the further consideration of the ptn of Jos P Williams, & that it be referred to the Cmte on Public Lands. 21-Mr Clay: I have a ptn from Pa, numerously signed, requesting Congress to purchase **Mount Vernon**. 22-Mr Clay. Gen Washington selected the Daily Advertiser for the publication of his Farewell Address; after it was committed to print, Mr Claypoole proposed to return the original document to Gen Washington, but being extremely desirous to posses it, he expressed his wish, if the general did not wish it himself, he would like to retain it as a memorial. Gen Washington assented to the request; & that paper from that day to this has been in the hands of either Mr Claypoole or some of his descendants. But I was struck by an advertisement which I saw some short time ago, in one of the Phil papers. "The original manuscript of General Washington's valedictory address to the people of the U S will be sold on Feb 12, 1850. This paper, in the handwriting & bearing the signature of Gen Washington, was presented by him to Mr Claypoole, the then editor & proprietor of the Daily Advertiser-the paper which Gen Washington had selected for its publication. The sale will be premptory." Sir, in my own humble parlor at *Ashland*, I have at this moment a broken goblet which was used by Gen Washington, during almost the whole of the Revolutionary war. It was in his camp, confided to me by an old lady some 80 years of age; & that is nothing in that parlor so revered, or whichis an object of greater admiration to the stranger who comes to see me. Mr Pearce: the Library Cmte do not think they are authorized to purchase manscripts, which are valuable as relics merely. Resolved: that the Library Cmte be authorized to purchase the manuscript, provided it can be purchased on fair terms: passed.

Appointment by the Pres: Justin Butterfield, of Ill, to be Com'r of the Gen Land Ofc, vice Richd M Young, resigned.

Rololph Carnatz & his wife lately recovered $4,000 damages against the Mexican Gulf Railway Co, at New Orleans, for injuries received by them in consequence of the carelessness of the engineer.

House of Reps: 1-Ptn of Wm Gale & others, for the removal of rocks from Hurlgate Channel. 2-Nominations for the ofc of Chaplain:

L F Morgan, Meth Episcopal Church
Robt W Cushman, Baptist
Levi S Beebe, Presby
Ralph R Gurley, Presby
Levi R Reese, Methodist Episcopal
H S Porter, Presby
Orville Dewey, Unitarian
Wm F Bogakin, Baptist
Henry Slicer, Methodist Episcopal
J P Donelan, Roman Catholic
Wm Crew, Baptist
C C Conner, Baptist
Henry Neal, Congregational
John Brooks, Soc of Friends
Geo H Coff, Methodist Episcopal

Mrs Henry Wall still has some hours in the week unoccupied for lessons on the Piano Forte. Her residence is at 22nd & F sts.

House of Reps: 1-Cmte of Ways & Means: discharged from the further consideration of the memorial of Wm Archer, of Wash, D C, praying for a survey & location of a railroad from Wash to the Pacific Ocean: laid on the table. 2-Cmte on Revolutionary Claims: discharged from the further consideration of the ptn of Lawrence Vandyke, & others, heirs of Joachim Van Valkenbrugh, deceased: referred to the Cmte on Revolutionary Pensions. Same cmte: discharged from the further consideration of the memorial of L C Duncan: referred to the Cmte on Military Affairs. Same cmte: bill for the relief of the legal reps of Thos Jett: committed. 3-Cmte on Invalid Pensions: adverse report on the ptn of Sarah Worth: laid on the table. Same cmte: bill for the relief of Wm Paddy: committed. 4-Com't of Patents: bill for the relief of Hiram Moore & John Haskell: committed.

Commission on Claims against Mexico: 1-Memorial of Geo S Miller, of N Y, claiming for expulsion from Matamoros, on Apr 12, 1846, was submitted & ordered to be received. 2-Mr Jas H Causten submitted a motion for leave to withdraw the memorial of Danl Davis [#29] with a view to establish identity of said memorialist: leave granted. 3-Mr Jas J Dickins offered a paper, with accompanying documents, numbered 1 thru 5, purporting to be a reply to the answer of Richd S Coxe, & the affidavit of Jas Prentis & G L Thompson, filed in the case of the Union Land Co, Jan 14, 1850: ordered to be filed.

Mrd: on Jan 12, by Rev Mr Hodges, Francis S Hayn to Miss Jane T Swain, both of Wash.

Mrd: on Jan 20, by Rev Mr Hodges, Francis L Guy, of Chas Co, Md, to Miss Eliz E Howell, of Wash.

Mrd: on Jan 22, at St Peter's Church, Phil, by Rev Wm H Odenheimer, Saml Cooper, of Wash, & Rebecca H Roach, daughter of the late Maj Isaac Roach, of Phil.

Died: on Jan 23, in Wash City, Willie Fitzgerald Harris, age 13 months; & on Jan 24, Chas Edw, aged 7 years & 8 months, children of Saml L & Abba C Harris.

SAT JAN 26, 1850
Wilkesbarre [Pa] Advocate of Wed: on Sat last in Plymouth township, Miss Ellen, aged 15, eldest daughter of Hon Geo W Woodward, Miss Ann, aged 20 years, daughter of Mr Wm B Butler, who from her childhood had resided in the family of Judge Woodward, & Miss Benner, aged 17 years, a young lady from Centre Co, a visiter at Judge Woodward's, went out for recreation, & while amusing themselves by sliding on ice formed upon a pool on the flats near Judge Woodward's residence, the ice breaking, they all drowned. All the bodies have been recovered. The remains of Miss Benner have been sent to her widowed & now doubly bereaved mother, in Beelefont, Centre Co. On Mon the remains of Miss Butler & Miss Woodward were carried to the old burying ground in this borough.

Commission on Claims against Mexico: 1-Memorial of Ebenezer D Brockway, executor, & of Jos S & Mary S Brockway, legatees, of Geo Brockway, claiming for plunder of his effects & imprisonment, as one of the crew of the schnr **Julius Caesar**, seized by a Mexican brig of war in 1839, together with the proofs & documents connected therewith; & came to the opinion that the claim was not valid: same is accordingly not allowed.

Mrd: John Linthicum, of A A Co, Md, & Ann M Dare, daughter of Nath'l Dare, of Locust Grove, Calvert Co, Md, Jan 18, by Rev Mr Dashiell, at *Locust Grove*.

Mrd: On Jan 24, in Balt, by Rev Mr Fuller, Thos Stockdale to Miss Merab Neving, all of Balt.

Mrd: on Jan 24, at St John's Church, in Wash City, by Rev Mr Pyne, Lt Jas M Watson, U S Navy, & Therese R, daughter of late A D Crosby, Purser-U S N.

A rencontre at Galveston, Texas, on Jan 10, between Dr Robt Neill & Lawyer J J Mills, resulting in the death of the latter.

MON JAN 28, 1850
The Wash Republican announces the death of Philip Pendleton Cooke, of Clark Co, aged about 35. He was a native of Winchester, & a son of John R Cooke, now of Richmond. Mr Cooke was endowed with rare poetic talent. His "Florence Vane" has been placed by British critics among the finest poems of its class produced during the century.

Obit: died: a few days ago, in his 20th year, Mr Philemon Chew. He had been at the Infirmary, prosecuting his studies for the medical profession, but, alas! death has laid him in the cold grave. He was a devoted son & brother.

Mr John E Ricard, professional French cook, will be happy to be employed in the preparation of dinners for private parties, balls, or public assemblies. Apply to Mr J H Eberbach, E & 8th sts.

Orphans Court of Wash Co, D C. Letters of administration with the will annexed on the personal estate of Adam Bailey, late of Wash Co, deceased. -Jos Borrows, adm, w a.

Gtwn: we are gratified at the improvements in our sister city, Gtwn. A bldg styled "Forrest Hall," stands conspicuous among the improvements of the town. This hall is of the Ionic & Composite, fronting 66 feet on High st, & running back 73 feet. The first floor is intended for the Mayor's Ofc, Post Ofc, Board of Aldermen & Common Council, & Custom-house. The second floor has an elegant ball room. The basement is intended for a restaurant & ten-pin alleys. Persons employed in the bldg of this hall, viz: King & Chapin, Carpenters; Francis Hutchins, Bricklayer; Wm Ross, Plasterer; Z Offutt, Painter; ___ Exler, fresco Painter.

Lost: on Thu, a pocket wallet, containing about $150. A reward of $20 will be given for its recovery, if left at his ofc. –John Callow

TUE JAN 29, 1850
Senate: 1-Ptn of Phoebe & Sylvia Ann Wood, daughters of the late Jethro Wood, asking that the heirs of said Wood may be remunerated for the benefits conferred on the people of the U S by his improvements in the plough: referred to the Cmte on Patents & the Patent Ofc. 2-Memorial from Theophilus Hardenbrook, asking to be remunerated for losses & sufferings while a prisoner of war in Dartmoor prison, England, during the war with Great Britain: referred to the Cmte on Military Affairs. 3-Ptn of J R Creecy, asking compensation for his services & re-imbursement of his expenses in raising & subsisting volunteers for the service of the U S in the late war with Mexico: referred to the Cmte on Military Affairs. 4-Additional documents submitted in relation to the claim of John Mason, deceased: referred to the Cmte of Claims. 5-Memorial of Josiah Barker, Thos W Chinn, Micajah Courtney, & the reps of John Davenport, sureties of Thos Gibbs Morgan, late collector of the port of New Orleans, asking to be released from a judgment obtained against them by the U S: referred to the Cmte on the Judiciary. 6-Memorial of E L Blackburn, late the widow of Felix Boswell, asking that the estate of her late husband may be released from liabilities. Judge Felix Bosworth died while acting as paymaster in the U S army in the late war with Mexico. Three weeks after his arrival at Vera Cruz he was taken sick with the yellow fever & died. A clerk living with him died 3 days later. Of the 2 servants whom he had with him, one was taken sick with the fever, but recovered. His brother was attacked & has since died. An ofcr of the army, Capt Page, who attended him in his last moments, has also since died. His papers & money were put in a truck & dispatched to his widow at her residence. The trunk was robbed. Ptn was referred to the Cmte on Military Affairs. 7-Ptn of John Hollohan, asking compensation for his services as messenger & watchmen in the Patent Ofc: referred to the Cmte of Claims. 8-Ptn of Asenath M Elliott, widow of an army ofcr, asking a pension: referred to the Cmte on Military Affairs. 9-Additional documents submitted in relation of the claim of Edw Buncombe: referred to the Cmte on Revolutionary Claims. 10-Ptn of Lucius B Allyn, a clerk in the Bureau of Provisions & Clothing of the Navy Dept, asking additional compensation: referred to the Cmte of Claims. 11-Memorial of the heirs of Stephen Griffith & others; the memorial of the heirs of Saml Stone: asking indemnity for French spoliations prior to 1800: referred to the select cmte. 12-Ptn of Geo F De la

Roche, of D C, as the rep of the firm of Wm Lewis Sontag & Co, of Phil; the ptn of Catharine Wilson, of Balt City, in behalf of the heirs of David Wilson: asking indemnity for French spoliations prior to 1800: referred to the select cmte. 13-Ptn of Nathl Champ, asking a new land warrant in lieu of one supposed to be destroyed: referred to the Cmte on Public Lands. 14-Ptn of Stanton Wales, a capt during the war with Great Britain, asking remuneration for private property destroyed by the enemy in the public storehouse at Buffalo: referred to the Cmte of Claims. 15-Memorial, numerously signed by citizens of Wash Co, Pa, asking that Eliz Porter, widow of Jos Porter, may be allowed a pension: referred to the Cmte on Pensions. 16-Memorial of the heirs of Alex'r Mactire: asking indemnity for French spoliations prior to 1800: referred to the select cmte. 17-Ptn of Jas Wilson, surviving partner of Wm Wilson & Sons, & the ptn of Benj N Hodges, surviving partner of Hodges & Lansdale, asking compensation for tobacco destroyed by the enemy in 1814: referred to the Cmte of Claims. 18-Ptn of Jas A Goff, asking compensation for horses impressed into public service during the Seminole war: referred to the Cmte of Claims. 19-Additional documents submitted in relation to the claim of Robt Butler: referred to the Cmte on Public Lands. 20-Ptn of Moses Carlton: asking indemnity for French spoliations prior to 1800: referred to the select cmte. 21-Ptn of Sarah Ladd, mother of Jas M Ladd, late an ofcr in the navy, asking to be allowed a pension: referred to the Cmte on Pensions. 22-Ptn of Lewis Ralston, head of the Cherokee family, asking to be remunerated for the loss of his improvements, of which he was disposed contrary to the treaty of 1835: referred to the Cmte on Indian Affairs. 23-Ptns to be taken from the files of the Senate & referred: ptn of Lewis Morris, referred to the Cmte on Military Affairs. Ptn of John H Eastin: referred to the Cmte of Claims. Ptn of A Cowen, & other heirs of Robt Lilly: referred to the Cmte on Pensions. Ptn of Oliver Tucker: referred to the Cmte on Pensions. 24-Cmte of Claims: bill for the relief of Allen G Johnson: ordered to be printed. 25-Cmte of Claims: ptn of H L Kendrick, a major in the army, asking to be allowed a credit for public money stolen while in his possession, in Mexico, reported a bill for his relief: ordered to be printed. 26-Cmte on Private Land Claims: ptn of Geo W Jones, as atty for certain heirs, reported a bill for the relief of the legal reps of John Rice Jones, deceased: ordered to a second reading. 27-Cmte on Foreign Relation: memorial of Conrad W Faver, Leopold Bierwith, & Theodore Victor, asking to be released from bonds given by them, not to carry out of the port of N Y the steamship **United States**, have instructed me to present a report. It appears the steamship had been built under a contract of the Confederated Gov't of the German Empire. Cmte: it is now proper that the memorialists should be released from bonds; the ship is gone. 28-Cmte on Naval Affairs: adverse report on the ptn of Geo Harvey. 29-Cmte on Indian Affairs: memorial of Lewis A Thomas & Thos Rogers, reported a bill for their relief: ordered to be printed. 30-Bill introduced for the relief of Margaret E Carnes, widow of Peter A Carnes: referred to the Cmte on Pensions.

Commission on Claims against Mexico: 1-Memorial of Sidney Udall, a resident of Tampico, claiming for expulsion from that place on Jun 9, 1846, & losses consequent thereon, was submitted, examined, & ordered to be received. 2-The Board took up the 2 memorials of John Hartshoren & of Richd Harding, claiming for damages resulting from the detention of the ship **Henry Thompson**, & the seizure of her cargo: same was allowed: amount to be awarded subject to the future action of the Board.

House of Reps: 1-Ptn of Capt Josiah Sturgis & other ofcrs, that the pension laws may be applicable to the revenue service. 2-Ptn of Edw Thwing & other ofcrs of volunteers in the late Mexican war, praying additional remuneration for their services by a grant of land. 3-Ptn of J H Williams & 40 others, citizens of Erie Co, Pa, asking Congress to pass a law for the relief of Marcus Spalding, a soldier of the late war with Great Britain. 4-Ptn of Wm G Maupin & John F C Potts, second & third clerks in the Naval Store at Portsmouth, Va, asking an increase of compensation.

Santa Fe, Nov 28. 1-Ten days ago, Maj Green, with a military force, went in pursuit of the band of Utah Indians who had Mrs White a prisoner. When Maj Green came in sight of the Indian camp they shot Mrs White & fled. Her body was recovered, but no trace of her child. It will be recollected that her husband & 8 others were killed & Mrs White was taken prisoner, some time ago, while they were crossing the plains. 2-Capt Alex'r Papin was recently killed in a quarrel at Santa Fe. 3-John Adams was lately murdered at Pena Blanche by Mexicans. 4-Col Calhoun, Indian Agent, has failed to make a treaty with the Indians in Mexico.

Mrd: Jan 27, by Rev Mr Slattery, Jos Beckert to Miss Rosanna E Gallant, all of Wash.

Mrd: on Jan 27, by Rev Mr Roszell, R T McLain, formerly of Frederick Co, Md, to Eliza S, daughter of Jas Lawrenson, of Wash.

Died: on Jan 28, in Wash City, Lelia Payson, age 3 years, 7 months & 17 days, of scarlet fever, only daughter of Saml L & Abba C Harris.

Died: on Jan 27, at Concord, N H, suddenly, Mrs Hannah Ralston Whipple, wife of John Whipple, & sister of Hon Salmon P Chase, Sen of Ohio.

WED JAN 30, 1850
Senate: 1-Ptn of A W Starks, asking compensation for his services in carrying the mail: referred to Cmte on Post Ofc & Post Roads. 2-Documents submitted in relation to claim of Anthony Rankin, ensign in the late war with Great Britian, to reimbursement of money paid for medical attendance during an illness contracted prior to his discharge from the army: referred to Cmte of Claims. 3-Documents submitted in relation to claim of Wm Blake for a pension: referred to Cmte on Pensions. 4-Ptn of Peter Grover, with additional documents: referred to Cmte on Pensions. 5-Ordered: ptn of John T Sullivan, in files of the Senate, be referred to Cmte on Post Ofc & Post Roads. 6-Cmte on Finance: ptn of Jas Cunningham, of Adams Co, Pa, asking Congress to redeem certain notes issued by the Continental Congress, ask to be discharged from the further consideration of same: which was agreed to. Same cmte: memorial of Henry Simpson, formerly appraiser in the custom-house at Phil, asking to be paid for the entire year, he having been removed when only 2 months of the year had expired, made an adverse report on the same: which was agreed to. 7-Cmte on Foreign Relations: memorial of Abigail Shaler Stilwell, legal rep of Wm Shaler, deceased, submitted an adverse report on same: ordered to be printed. 8-Cmte of Claims: ask to be discharged from the further consideration of ptn of Jas Robertson: ordered to be printed.

The ship **Monterey**, Capt McManus, sailed from Balt on Sun for San Francisco, having on board Co I, of the 1st Regt of Artl, lately stationed at *Fort McHenry*, & a large quantity of Gov't stores. Ofcrs of the company: 1st Lt A R Eddy, commanding; 1st Lt F E Patterson, 2nd Lt D M Belzhoover; Assist Surgeon, R O Abbott; Sutler, Frank Eddy. The company is composed of 84 non-commissioned ofcrs & privates.

Mobile Advertiser: S Griffitts Fisher died at Phil on Dec 28, attended by his father, Redwood Fisher, & the family of his affectionate wife, & surrounded by numerous sympathizing friends. Mr Fisher has been long in feeble health, but was able to attend to business until about 2 weeks before his death. He had resided in Mobile for the last 12 or 15 years, & in the pursuit of his profession, the Law, attained a very high rank.

Hon John Reed, for 20 years President Judge of Cumberland district, died at his residence in Carlisle, Pa, on Jan 19, aged 64 years.

The friends of missions in this country will be pained by the intelligence, received by the vessel **Niagara**, that Mrs Harriet Scudder, wife of Rev John Scudder, M D, & for more than 30 years a missionary of the American Board, died at Madras on Nov 19, after an illness of 4 days. She was a woman of great excellence of character.

Return of sick seamen. N Y, Jan 29. The ship **Erie**, from Spezzia, has arrived at N Y. She brings 50 seamen & marines belonging to the squadron. Those who died since leaving the U S were Geo Downing, John Hewett, & Thos Jones.

Extensive sale of clothing, at auction, on Feb 1, at the store of Wm Marshall, next door to Mr Gilman's drug store, on Pa ave, between 6th & 7th sts. –Green & Tastet, aucts

Commission on Claims against Mexico: 1-Memorial of Wm H Freeman, administrator of Edmund B Freeman, deceased, claiming for losses by the seizure & condemnation of the schnr **Gardiner**, at Tabasco, in 1837: claim is valid: same to be allowed: amount to be awarded subject to the future action of the board. 2-Memorial of Wm S Henry & Arietta L Henry, his wife, by Cyrus Lawton, their atty, & M M Thompson, for himself, in the cases of the Union Land Co. Ordered that it be filed with the papers of the cases to which it relates.

Mrd: on Jan 28, by Rev C M Butler, D D, Mr Alex'r Johnson & Miss Sarah Coomes, both of Chas Co, Md.

City Ordinances-Wash: 1-Act for relief of A Kleindenst: to be paid $60, a refund, for the payment of a shop license, said Kleindenst having declined to open such establishment. 2-Act for the relief of Thompson Nailor: to be reimbursed $60, the amount paid for omnibus licenses & for stable license, the said property having been entirely destroyed in the recent fire. 3-Act for the relief of W M Bayne: that the fine imposed for the exhibition of his panorama view of a voyage to Europe, together with costs of prosecution: to be remitted, it being an exhibition of art & the product of his own labor.

Died: on Jan 28, after an illness of 8½ hours, Robt Winfield, son of R W & S R Bates, age 2 years, 7 months & 5 days. His funeral will be from the residence of his father, Pa av, between 17th & 18th sts, this afternoon at 2 o'clock.

Wanted immediately: a wet nurse, for 4 month old baby, Mrs J McClelland, 6th & D.

THU JAN 31, 1850
House of Reps: 1-Cmte on Foreign Affairs: discharged from further consideration of the ptn of Henry W Turner, heirs, assignee, & rep of Henry W Turner: referred to the Cmte on the Judiciary. Same cmte: ptn of Eustace Barrow & others, praying compensation for the schnr **William** & her cargo, which were captured & confiscated as lawful prize, at Monterey, Calif, during the Mexican war, made an adverse report thereon: laid on the table to be printed. 2-Cmte on Revolutionary Pensions: adverse report on the ptns of Mary Woods, widow of Hugh Woods, Henry Johnson, & Nathan Corey: to be printed. Same cmte: adverse report on the ptns of Abigail Fanning, widow of John Fanning, & Robt Beach: ordered to be printed. 3-Cmte on Revolutionary Pensions: discharged from the further consideration of the ptn of David Bell, heir of Jesse Bell: laid upon the table. 4-Cmte on Indian Affairs: bill for the relief of Jesse Sutton: committed. 5-Cmte on Invalid Pensions: adverse report on the ptn of Chas Allen: ordered to be printed. Same cmte: discharged from the further consideration of the ptn of Lot Davis: referred to the Cmte on Naval Affairs. 6-Cmte on the Judiciary: bill to refund the fine imposed on the late Dr Thos Cooper, under the sedition law, to his legal reps: committed. 7-Cmte of Claims: bill for the relief of Gideon Walker: committed. 8-Cmte of Claims: discharged from the further consideration of the ptn of Elisha Taylor & I B Mizner: referred to Cmte on Public Lands. 9-Cmte of Claims: adverse report on ptn of Wm S Osborne: ordered to be printed. 10-Cmte on Military Affairs: discharged from the further consideration of the ptn of Jno A King: laid on the table. 11-Cmte on Naval Affairs: bill for relief of Joshua Follansbee & B F Isherwood, & for other purposes: committed. 12-Cmte on Commerce: discharged from the further consideration of ptn of Robt James: laid on the table. 12-Ordered that the ptn & papers of Jacob Sagethy be withdrawn from the files & referred to Cmte on Invalid Pensions. Also, the ptn & papers of Saml Graves, & referred to Cmte on Naval Affairs. Also, the ptn & papers of Mrs Priscilla Decatur Twiggs, & referred to Cmte on Naval Affairs. 13-Ptn of Josiah Hooker & others, of Springfield, Mass, asking for cheap postage. 14-Ptn of Thos B Clarke, of Detroit, praying for a land patent to be issued to him. 15-Ptn of Geo Cassiday, an invalid soldier of the Mexican war, for a pension. 16-Ptn of Seth Adams, of Zanesville, Ohio: asking indemnity for French spoliations prior to 1800. 17-Ptn of Mrs Lucy Clark, widow of the late Rev John Clark, of King & Queen Cos, Va, praying for additional allowance on account of the Revolutionary services of her husband. 18-Ptn of Chas H Lee & other heirs of Oliver Lee, deceased, citizens of Chautauque Co, N Y, praying Congress for compensation for damages in relation to the schnr **Savannah**, at the mouth of Buffalo Creek.

N Y papers record the death of Wm A Colman, a virtuoso, who has been for a number of years a man of mark in his way, & extensively known as a collector of & dealer in pictures, engravings, works of art generally, & rare books. He was many years ago a faithful traveling collector of newspaper accounts for this & other ofcs.

Case of the heirs of Kosciusko. Circuit Court of Wash Co, D C-in Chancery. John F Ennis, adm de bonis non of Jos Zolkowski et al, vs Jonathan B H Smith, adm & trustee of the late Geo Bomford et al. On Sep 26, 1848, a bill was filed in this Court, having for its object to obtain discovery, account, & distribution of the personal estate of Gen Thaddeus Kosciusko, deceased. Said bill charges that Gen Kosciusko made & executed 4 wills-one of May 5, 1798, by which he disposed of his property left in this country for certain charitable purposes; another, on Jun 28, 1806, by which he bequeathed to Kosciusko Armstrong, $3,704, out of the same property; third, on Jun 4, 1816, by which he disposed of to sundry persons a portion of his property left in Europe, & then revoked all the wills & codicils made previously; fourth, on Oct 10, 1817, by which he disposed of the residue of his property left in Europe, leaving unrevoked the revoking clause of the will of Jun 4, 1816. Said bill further charges that, by reason of the revoking clause aforesaid, the wills of 1798 & 1806 became a nullity, & cannot take effect, & prays that the estate of Kosciusko, left in this country, may be distributed among his next of kin. The said bill was demurred to be Jonathan B H Smith, adm & trustee of Geo Bomford, the deceased administrator of Kosciusko's estate, & also by the sureties to the probate bonds of said Bomford, from & against whom discovery & relief is sought. The Court, by a decision given on Dec 11, 1849, overruled their several demurrers, & suggested that it may perhaps be necessary that Kosciusko Armstrong should be made a party before final decree can be made in this case. An amended bill making said Kosciusko Armstrong a party to the original bill was filed, praying, that said Armstrong be ordered to answer the premises thereof relating to the will dated Jun 28, 1806, & charging that it is a nullity in consequence of its having been revoked as aforesaid. The said amemded bill further charges that subsequent to the filing of the original bill, to wit, on Feb 6, 1849, the probates of the wills of 1798 & 1806 have been revoked by the Orphans Court of Wash Co, D C. It appearing to the Court that said Kosciusko Armstrong does not reside within the jurisdiction of this Court, it is, on motion of the solicitor of the cmplnts, [G Tochman,] this Dec 28, 1849, ordered that said dfndnt Kosciusko Armstrong appear on or before the 1st Mon of May, 1850.

Senate: 1-Memorial of Sylvester Churchill, asking to be allowed certain arrearages of pay due him as an inspector general of the army: referred to the cmte on Military Affairs. 2-Ptn of Evans & Churchman, & Jos R Evans, merchants of Phil, asking that certain duties illegally exacted may be refunded: referred to the Cmte on Commerce. 3-Memorial of Wm A Duer, adm of Wm Duer, asking the payment of a balance standing to the credit of said Wm Duer on the books of the Treasury: referred to the Cmte of Claims. 4-Memorial of the heirs of Stephen Griffith: asking indemnity for French spoliations prior to 1800: referred to the select cmte. 5-Memorial of Isabel Le Leon, for herself & co-heirs of Benj Nones, late of Phil: asking indemnity for French spoliations prior to 1800: referred to the select cmte. 6-Ordered, that the papers on the files of the Senate, relating to the claim of Orville B Dibble & Geo C Bates, be referred to the Cmte on Public Lands. 7-Cmte on the Post Ofc & Post Roads: ptn of Ira Day, of Vt, submitted a report, with a bill for his relief: to be printed. 8-Cmte on Commerce: referred the memorial of the sureties of Saml Swartwout, asking to be discharged from the further consideration of the same: to be referred to the Cmte on the Judiciary.

Died: on Jan 23, at St Louis, Hon Nathaniel Pope, Judge of U S Dist Crt of Ill, at St Louis, age 66 years.

Sudden death: Mr Thos Weatherhead, an old resident of the city of Richmond, Va, died last Sat, at the residence of Mr John D Quarles. He was there to revise accounts, & after seating himself, he appeared to be paralyzed, fell back in his chair, & expired.
-Republican

Died: on Jan 30, Frances Marion Sutton, wife of Jas Sutton, age 21 years. Her funeral will be at residence of her parents, 4th st near I this afternoon, at 3 o'clock.

Died: on Jan 29, in Gtwn, of scarlet fever, George, age 22 months, son of Wm H & Eliza Tenney.

By order of distrain, for house rent due John Grinder by Saml Entrisell, I will expose at public sale on Feb 7, 1850, sundry furniture & articles, of said Entrisell.
--H R Maryman, bailiff

U S Patent ofc-Petition of Jeremiah Myers, of Meredith Village, N H for extension of patent that expires May 8, 1851: <u>improvement in turn-about for railroads</u>.
--Dewitt C Lawrence, acting Com'r of Patents.

FRI FEB 1, 1850
House of Reps: 1-Ptn of Edmund Dexter, for cancellation of transportation bond. 2-Ptn of Eli Penny & other citizens of Missouri, praying the abolition of the ofc of chaplain.

Wash Corp: 1-Ptn of Wm B Lewis, praying remission of a fine: referred to the Cmte of Claims. 2-Cmte of Claims: bill for the relief of Jas A Wise: passed. 3-Cmte on Improvements: ptn of Jas B Greenwell & others, for a gravel foot-walk in the 7th Ward: passed. 4-Cmte of Claims: bill for the relief of Alfred Bell: passed. 5-Bill for the relief of Jas H Shreeve & Harrison Taylor: passed. 6-Ptn from F S Walsh: referred to the Cmte on the Asylum. 7-Cmte of Claims: bill for the relief of Jos Swagert: passed. Same cmte: asking to be discharged from the further consideration of the ptns of John H Woodward, Ezra Phelps, & Michl Duffy: discharged accordingly. 8-Bill for the relief of Hanson Brown: referred to the Cmte on Police. 9-Ptn of R W Latham: ordered to lie on the table.

College of St James, Wash Co, Md, will resume its 2nd term of the 8th session, on Mar 4.
--John B Kerfoot, Rector, College of St James Post Ofc, Md.

Mrd: on Jan 24, at the residence of Jas Wm Foster, Fauquier Co, Va, by Rev Mr Norton, Wm H Gaines, of Warrenton, to Mary Mildred, daughter of Jas Foster, of Pr Wm Co, Va. [Union & Alex. Gazette Copy]

Mrd: on Jan 30, by Rev John C Smith, Saml Barron to Miss Mary Ann Williamson, all of Wash City.

Coal & seasoned lumber for sale. --John Purdy [Local ad.]

Senate: 1-Ordered that the memorial of John Tucker, on the files of the Senate, be referred to the Cmte of Claims. 2-Ordered, that the papers on file in the Senate in the case of Caleb Swann be referred to the Cmte of Claims. 3-Memorial of F W Jobson, asking compensation for his services in carrying the mail: referred to the Cmte on the Post Ofc & Post Roads. 4-Cmte on Public Lands: bill for the relief of Jos P Williams, reported back with an amendment: ordered to be printed. Same cmte: memorial of Chas Byrne, praying interest on money paid to the U S for land to which the Gov't could give him no title, submitted an adverse report: ordered to be printed. 5-Cmte on the Post Ofc & Post Roads: ptn of Nathl Kuykendall, reported a bill for his relief. 6-Announcement of the death of Hon Rudolphus Dickinson, a rep from the 6th District of the State of Ohio, departed in this city, on Mar 20 last. He was born at Whately, Mass, on Dec 8, 1789; graduated at Williamstown College, & soon after emigrated to Ohio. He established himself in the practice of law, at Lower Sandusky, now Fremont; which continued to be his residence until his decease. In 1827 he married Miss Margarette Beaugrand , of Lower Dandusky, the daughter of a highly respectable French gentlemen, who settled there several years previous to the extinction of the Indian title in that country. He leaves an affectionate wife & devoted mother, & his orphan children.

Commission on Claims against Mexico: 1-Application from G R J Bowdoin, counsel of Francis Arenas, for a requistion on the Mexican Gov't for certain documents, as necessary evidence in the claim of said Arenas. Ordered that the application be transmitted to the Sec of State that it may be forwarded.

Henry Cook, editor of the Rochester Daily Democrat, died at his residence on Sat, in his 37th year. He has been connected with the Democrat since 1840, & for the last 3 years its principal editor.

Messrs Benj Marshall, L McIntosh, G W Stedham, & David Burnett, delegates from the Creek Nation west of the Mississippi, have arrived in town on their way to Wash. An old friend, Edw Harnick, of Montg, who has spent the past 5 months among the Indians, came in company with the delegates. --Mobile Tribune

103 soldiers of the British war of 1812 held a public meeting in Fayette Co, Pa, court-house, on Jan 21, at which, an eloquent address was given by Hon Andrew Stewart.

Annual meeting of the stockholders of the steamboat **Phenix** will be held on Feb 4 at the ofc of the company. --S Shinn, treasurer

Dissolution of the partnership under the firm of Newton & Lewis, Bookbinders, by mutual consent. The business will be continued at the old stand, Pa ave, next to the Odeon, by Harrison P Lewis.

Mrs Kilroy, aged 80, & her sister [mother & aunt of Rev Mr Kilroy] were burnt, with the Catholic Church & their residence, at Grand Rapids, Mich, on Dec 14.

Postmaster Gen has est'd the following new Post Ofcs for week ending Jan 26, 1850

Ruckerville	Clark, Ky	Wm Ritchie
Fryville	Clark, Ky	David H Butler
Ashland	Union, Ky	Union T Bray
New Durham Ctre	Strafford, N H	Jona H Downing
Durham Ctre	Middlesex, Ct	David Smith
Hartfield	Chautauque, N Y	D M Boyd
Wheatville	Genesee, N Y	Hiram Duel
Liberty Falls	Sullivan, N Y	Webb Horton
Shanesville	Berks, Pa	Peter J Hill
Upr Cross Roads	Harford, Md	Wm Wood
Cline's Mill	Augusta, Va	S W Bolen
Lindsay's Turnout	Albemarle, Va	Benj F Cosby
Worthington	Marion, Va	Wm Lucas
Newell	Anderson dist, S C	J C Smith
Hollidaysville	Dooley, Geo	Robt McCombs
Beard's Bluff	Marshall, Ala	Thos C Barclay
Rose Hill	Amite, Miss	G P Farwell
Hooker	Hunt, Texas	Jas Hooker
Fourche Dumas	Randolph, Ark	Jas G Russell
Shop Springs	Wilson, Ten	Thos Waters
Poplar Corner	Madison, Ten	Jas B Dawson
Hamilton's Landing	Jackson, Ten	O P Hamilton
South Boston	Wash, Ia	N E Rodman
Houston	Jackson, Ia	Hiram Noe
Fuldo	Spencer, Ia	Wm M Hammond
Medina	Winnebago, Ill	Price B Webster
Wantoma	Marquetto, Wis	John P Shumway

Names Changed:
Jefferson's Corner, Somerset Co, Md, changed to Bell Mount.
Mount Moriah, Butler Co, Ala, changed to Monterey.
Lower Blue Lick, Nicholas Co, Ky, changed to Blue Lick Springs.
Lake St Croix, St Croix Co, Wisc, changed to Point Douglas.
Nelson's Landing, Chippewa Co, Wisc, changed to Wabashaw, Minnesota Territory.

The barque **Sarah** sailed from N Y on Tue last, for her original destination, & while going down the bay the testimonial prepared by the Merchants of N Y to Capt Cook & his crew, was presented on their behalf, by Mr Jas H Braine. The Capt received $5,000, the first Mate $700, & each seaman $100 in gold. The sailors had no idea of the gift coming to them.

Household & kitchen furniture at auction: on Feb 5, at the house lately occupied by Dr Dubarry, on G st. –Dyer & Bro, auctioneers

SAT FEB 2, 1850
Windfall. The family of the late Mr Chas Frick, of Hagerstown, Md, have recently fallen heirs to an estate worth $40,000 or $50,000, by the death of an uncle in Illinois. They are at present in indigent circumstances.

House of Reps: 1-Rev R R Gurley received a majority of the whole number of votes given on the 3rd vote, for Chaplain of the 31st Congress. Gurley-110 votes; R W Cushman, 41 votes; L F Morgan, 30 votes; & Orville Dewey, 3 votes.

Died: Mrs Affa Miner, of Springfield, Mass, recently, from the effects of a pin scratch, received in washing some bandages which had been used for dressing abscissa on the person of her son, a physician. Dr Miner has wounded his hand during a post mortem examination of a child who had died from inflammatin of the bowels, & this resulted in the abscissa, which was the remote cause of his mother's death.

Mrd: on Jan 31, by Rev L F Morgan, Wm C Fisher & Mgt Ann Jacobs.

Mrd: on Feb 1, by Rev L F Morgan, Wm Hyde & Anna Hekroth.

Mrd: on Jan 31, by Rev L F Morgan, Wm Walker & Juliette Keith.

On Jan 23, when crossing Potomac River in a canoe with 2 other men, it upset & John Ginn was drowned..

Died: on Jan 30, in Gtwn, Eliza Page, relict of the late Peyton R Page, of Va, in her 58th year.

Died: on Jan 18, Harriet Silliman, wife of Prof of Benjamin Silliman, sr, at New Haven Conn.

The sloop of war **Marion**, bound to the East Indies, sailed from Boston on Tue. List of her ofcrs: Wm M Glendy, Cmder; Alex'r M Pennock, Geo L Selden, Benj S Gantt, & Andrew Weir, Lts; John A Lockwood, Surgeon; Edw Shippen, Assist Surgeon; Nixon White, Purser; Richd Aulick, Master; John P Jones, Wm D Whiting, John Wilkes, jr, Passed Midshipmen; Henry Wilson, N P Prickett, A J Dallas, Chas B Smith, John J Laughlin, Midshipmen; Wm H Macauley, Capt's Clerk; Wm Burditt, Boatswain; R M Stocking, Gunner; John T Rustic, Carpenter; Wm N Maul, Sailmaker; Guy C Underwood, Purser's Steward; Simson A Whittier, Surgeon's Steward. John L Broome, 2nd Lt, commanding marines.

MON FEB 4, 1850
At Brooklyn, N Y, a stagemen, Jas Daley, is under examination on a charge of manslaughter, in causing the death of Wm Jameson, one of his passengers, by leaving his horses insecure in Chatham square on Jan 11 last. The horses got frightened & ran, by which Jameson received such injuries that he died. Examination has not been finished.

Ladies with letters in the Post Ofc, Wash, Feb 1, 1850:

Albertson, Miss E-2
Ashley, Mrs Eliz
Adhby, Mrs John R
Adler, Mrs Mary
Ahern, Mgt
Ashton, Miss R D-2
Adkins, Miss Mgt
Burnes, Miss Mary
Baget, Mrs Ann M
Buchanon, Miss C
Brown, Miss C
Belt, Mrs E
Boston, Miss H
Butler, Miss Anna
Bothe, Mrs Johanna
Brown, Milley
Bennett, Miss Mary
Bosworth, Mrs M
Butler, Miss M A
Brooks, Miss Mary
Bonn, Mary
Brannon, Mrs M M
Barkett, Miss
Bowling, Miss E
Batemen, Mrs Sarah
Boynton, Mrs S L
Brown, Mrs Adelaide
Bowie, Miss Martha
Bloxham, Miss M T
Colelaser, Mrs E
Coners, Mrs Sarah
Cooper, Mrs M F
Coe, Miss Mary
Cheseline, Mrs M
Cox, Mrs M J
Cox, Miss M E
Colson, Mrs
Curley, Mary
Campbell, Mrs M
Compton, Miss M
Conlay, Mrs Provia
Campbell, Miss Jane
Dade, Mrs Sarah A
Duvall, Mrs A M
Dawes, Miss A E
Davis, Miss Ann
Davis, Mrs B G
Doiscroux, Mrs K
Dix, Miss D L
Delany, Mrs E
Donathien, Mrs E
Dines, Mrs Mary
Dunlap, Mrs Gen R G
Duvall, Miss Susanna
Duvall, Mrs S E
Dowling, Mrs Mgt
Dean, Miss Cathrine
Edwards, Miss S-3
Fowler, Mrs E
Fairall, Mrs E A
Fess, Mrs Harriet
Faussett, Miss
Fletcher, Mrs Sarah
Graham, Mrs E W
Green, Miss I F
Goldin, Miss Mary
Gaiones, Mrs Mira
Gaskins, Miss P
Greene, Mrs Sarah
Gamble, Sarah-2
Henderson, Mrs A
Hamilton, Mrs A L
Hume, Mrs B E
How, Miss Calra T
Hoover, Eliz A
Hurley, Mrs
Harwood, Mrs R L
Harding, Sarah J
Jones, Mrs Ann
Johnson, Miss C M
Jay, Mrs Nancy A
Johnson, Miss P
Kidwell, Miss A
Kennedy, Miss C
Karl, Margaretta
Kerr, Miss Henrieta
Lee, Miss Ann
Lyles, Miss Mary
Lawrence, Mrs N
Lusby, Mrs Susan

Morton, Mrs M-2
Monroe, Miss A E
Mattingly, Miss L
Milligan, Miss E or S
Mar, Helen
Moore, Mrs John
Mason, Miss M E
Mohon, Mrs Mary
Mullikin, Mrs M A
Martin, Miss Maria
Murray, Mrs M T
Mason, Miss Marg
Moore, Mary R
Monday, Mrs M
Morrison, Mrs M
Miller, Miss Lizze
Murphy, Mrs P
Milligan, Miss S B-2
Morgan, Mrs S A
McLaughlin, Mrs S
Magruder, Mrs
McDonnell, Mrs M C
McSpadden, Mrs J-2
McClellan, Miss F
McGregor, Mrs E
McLane, Mrs C E
Nally, Mrs Charity
Newman, Mrs E H
Neville, Miss Mary
Nally, Mrs M A
Newton, Miss V
O'Neil, Mrs Eliza-2
Pettitt, Miss A V
Pane, Hannah
Pearle, Miss M
Pleasants, Miss M C
Prall, Miss V-2
Robertson, Mrs A
Robb, Miss Ann E
Robertson, Miss E W
Robinson, Miss G
Rodier, Miss L
Richardson, Miss S
Rowan, Miss S T
Simms, Mrs Delilah
Smith, Mrs Lydia-3
Smith, Mrs M A
Sherwood, Miss M E
Simmons, Miss J
Stepney, Mrs Selina
Smith, Miss V-2
Sausser, Miss S A
Rillman, Miss M
Thocmorton, Mrs M
Taylor, Mrs M E
Thompson, Miss M
Turner, Miss V C
West, Mrs Anne E
Ward, Miss Ann R
Woolsey, Mrs B
Wilkerson, Miss E
Webster, Mrs C A
Watson, Mrs H
Ward, Miss L L-2
Wright, Miss M A-2
Wilcox, Miss M J
Wilson, Miss S C
Young, Miss S T
-Wm A Bradley, P M

Huntingdon Globe of Tue: the Govn'r of Md has taken in hand the case of Jonathan Little, who was arrested & imprisoned in our county jail in Oct last, on a charge of kidnapping. Hon Albert constable, appointed by the Govn'r of Md as counsel for Mr Little, & his witnesses, arrived on on Sat & Sun last, under the impression that our Jan term of court would commence on yesterday. Yesterday $1,000 bail was entered for the appearance of Mr Little at the Apr term. Mr Little is now at liberty.

The Hon Nathl Pope, Judge of the U S District Court for the District of Illinois, died at St Louis on Jan 23, aged 66 years. More than 30 years ago he served as a Delegate to Congress from the then Territory of Illinois.

Pres Zachary Taylor recognizes that B H Dixon, of Boston, has been appointed Consul of Netherlands for Mass, Maine, N H, & R I. Feb 2. 1850

The Mexican papers, received on Jan 22, announce the death of Pena Y Pena; a most eminent lawyer of his country. New Orleans Delta

On Mon last, Mr Jas Begley & his brother, went to work in the North American Mines, near this borough, but in a short time in the mines, the 2 brothers were suffocated by black damp, & fell. Begley leaves a young wife; his brother was single.
–Pottsville [Pa] Emporium

St Louis Republican: Mrs Geo A Sherman, formerly from Janesville, Wisc, on her way with her husband, to New Orleans, on board the steamer **North River**, on Dec 28, while walking on the hurricane deck with her husband, tripped in her dress, & was instantly precipitated 25 feet into the river. She was not seen afterwards. She left Janesville for Calif, where her husband was intending to reside.

Camp, near Edisto Base, Jan, 1850. The undersigned, Ofcrs of the Coast Survey, have learned with heartfelt regret of the decease of their associate, R H Fauntleroy, Assist in the Survey, while in the discharge of his duty in Texas, on Jan 13. He was a excellent husband, father, & brother. –A D Bache, C O Boutelle, Chas P Bolles

Mrd: on Jan 7, near Tuscumbia, Ala, at the residence of Geo W Carroll, by Rev Mr Brown, pastor of Roman Catholic Church, Nashville, Tenn, Wm Pinkney Brooke, of PG Co, to Martha Gabriella Adair, daughter of late Gen Wm Adair, of Franklin Co, Ala.

Mrd: on Jan 10, near Guyandotte, by Rev J B Poage, Mr Jas H Buffington to Miss Columbia L Nicholas, all of Cabell Co, Va.

Died: on Feb 3, Mrs Ann W Benning, age 72 years, relict of late Wm Benning. Her funeral is on Tue at 11 o'clock, from the residence of C S Fowler, **Union Row**, F St.

Died: on Jan 29, at the Rectory of St Andrew's Church, Springville, Susquehanna Co, Pa, Mrs Matilda T Bean, wife of Rev Henry H Bean, after a protracted illness of nearly 8 months.

TUE FEB 5, 1850
The rumor of Mr Bodisco's recall, [from the post of Minister of his Gov't to the U S,] which has been circulated by the employed agents of interested parties, & by Swiss mercenaries, who have malicious purposes, is unfounded. No foreign Minister has ever resided at Washington who has attracted to himself so much of the good feeling & respect of the citizens of the metropolis, or obtained such unlimited popularity with the public men of all parties. I know him to be a far worthier citizen, than the pack of brutal calumniators who have been let loose to torture his American wife & children, in the absence of their natural protector, by every kind of mischievous fabrications.

Senate: 1-Memorial of Mgt Hetzel, widow of A R Hetzel, late an assistant quartermaster in the army, asking to be allowed a commission upon the disbursements made by her late husband of the appropriation for the removal of the Cherokee Indians: referred to the Cmte on Military Affairs. 2-Memorial of Chas F Sibbald, of Phil, Pa, asking indemnity for losses sustained in consequence of the illegal & forcible entry & detaining of his property by agents acting under the authority of the U S: referred to the Cmte on the Judiciary. 3-Memorial of Josiah Sturgis, an ofcr in the revenue cutter service, asking that the benefits of the naval pension laws may be extended to the ofcrs & seamen engaged in the revenue service: referred to the Cmte on Naval Affairs. 4-Documents were presented relating to the claims of J McClintock, Harrison Gill, & Mansfield Carter, for services rendered at the Great Nemehaw sub-agency for the Sac & Fox Indians: referred to the Cmte on Indian Affairs. 5-Ptn of C W Fitch, asking indemnity for French spoliations prior to 1800: referred to the select cmte. 6-Memorial of Geo C Johnson, a licensed trader with the Indians, asking the payment fo a debt due him by the Shawnee Indians: referred to the Cmte on Indian Affirs. 7-Memorial of the heirs of Richd Barry, asking indemnity for French spoliations prior to 1800: referred to the select cmte. 8-Ordered that the ptn of the heirs of David Noble, on the files of the Senate, be referred to the Cmte of Claims. Same for the memorial of Hector St John Beetley: be referred to the Cmte on Pensions. Same for the ptn of Caleb Greene: be referred to the Cmte on Claims. Same for the ptn of Obed Hussey: be referred to the Cmte on Patents & the Patent Ofc. Same for the ptn of Wm Marvin: be referred to the Cmte on Public Lands. 9-Ordered, that Richd M Livingston, heir of Jas Livingston, having leave to withdraw his ptn.
10-Cmte on Pensions: ptn of John Mitchell for an increase of pension, with a bill for the further relief of John Mitchell, ordered to a second reading. Same cmte: ptn of Eliz Jones, with a bill for the relief of Eliz Jones & children [if any] of John Carr, ordered to a second reading. 11-Cmte on Pensions: ptn of Hubert H Booley, with a bill for his relief: ordered to a second reading. Same cmte: memorial of Thompson Hutchinson, asking arrears of pension: ordered to a second reading. Same cmte: memorial of Eliz Munroe, widow of a surgeon in the army, asking a pension: ordered to a second reading. 12-Cmte on Commerce: ptn of John A McGaw, of N Y, ordered to be printed, with a bill for his relief. 13-Cmte of Claims: adverse report on the papers of Dr B F Mullen: ordered to be printed. Same cmte: memorial of John Dawson, late pension agent at Ill: asking to be discharged from the further consideration of the same: which was agreed to. 14-Cmte on Foreign Relations: ptn of Alpheus Alga, Bazil Bumah, Chas Chartae, & others, asking to be placed on the same footing with the Hungarians in the distribution of public lands: asking to be discharged from the further consideration of the same: referred to the Cmte on Public Lands: agreed to. 15-Cmte on Public Lands: ptn of Robt Butler, asking compensation for his property taken for public use: ordered to be printed. 16-Memorial of Orville B Deeble & Geo C Bates, asking a grant of land & the right of way to aid in the construction of a canal around the Falls of St Mary's: ordered to a second reading. 17-Bill introduced for the relief of Wm L Cazeneau, of Texas: referred to the Cmte of Claims.

Five persons in the family of Mr J C W Talleson, residing about 4 miles from Helena, Ark, died on Jan 10 of cholera. Among them were Mr T's wife & daughter & his wife's sister.

Old Continental Money: extract from the account of Maj Garland, paymaster in a regt of the Va State line on the Continental establishment in 1781, will serve to illustrate the evil of a depraved irredeemable currency:

Hiram Conyers in account with the State of Va. Cr Jun, 1781. To 22 weeks' work in making coats, cloaks, waistcoats, & stable jackets, at $1,000 paper per week: $22,000.

John Griffin in account with the State of Va. Cr Jul, 1781. To repairing bugle horns & trumpets for the 1st Regt Dragoons: $13,203.

To making 4 dozen shirts, at $200 per shirt: $9,600.

To 40 pair of boots, at $2,000 per pair: $80,000.

To 10 cuts thread, at $150 per cut: $2,000.

Col White, Capt Belfield, Capt Watt, Capt Hill, & Dr Rose, having called on us to value their horses, taken & lost it, the service of the army of the U S, we do therefore value, to the best of our judgment, in the following manner:

Col White's bay gelding, at $23,000.

Capt Belfield's sorrel gelding: $20,000.

Capt Watts, a bay gelding: $20,000.

Capt Hill's, a bay gelding: $20,000.

Dr Rose's, a bay gelding: $25,000.

-Boston Journal

Digging Gold: Mr Geo S Kimberly, now in Calif, writes home recounting the success of he has met in procuring gold from the beds of the rivers by means of J E Cowen & Co's submarine armor. On one occasion he bagged $800 in 5 hours, at the depth of 25 feet, in 6 weeks he realized the handsome sum of $18,500. He has been offered $5,000 for the armor & had refused it. –New Bedford Mercury

House of Reps: 1-Bill for the relief of Alex'r Lea. 2-Ptn of Hannah Avery was withdrawn from the files & referred to the Cmte of Claims.

Died: on Feb 2, Thos Altemus, son of Thos & Mary Altemus, aged 13 months & 19 days.

WED FEB 6, 1850

Cmdor Danl Turner, of the U S Navy, died suddenly at Phil on Mon, where he had just arrived with a view to spend the winter.

Mrd: on Jan 30, in Fayetteville, by Rev Mr Buxton, Seaton Gales, editor of Raleigh Register, to Miss Mary A Cameron, eldest daughter of Dr T N Cameron, of Fayetteville.

Mrd: on Feb 5, in Wash City, in Trinity Church, by Rev C M Butler, John W Gibbons, of Miss, to Mrs Mary Anna Sturgeon, of Wash.

Died: yesterday, Mr Saml T Scott, in his 25th year. His funeral will take place this afternoon, at 2½ o'clock, from the residence of his brother-in-law, 7th st east.

Died: on Jan 2, at his residence in Alexandria Co, Va, Benj F Werdon, aged 30 years. He leaves a disconsolate widow & 4 children to mourn their bereavement.

Senate: 1-Memorial of Benj E S Ely, proposing for the consideration of Congress a plan for maintaining a military force in Calif: referred to the Cmte on Military Affairs. 2-Memorial of Central Bank of Ga, assignees of Henry W Jernigan, asking indemnity for Indian depredations during the Creek war: referred to the Cmte on Indian Affairs. 3-Ptn of David Humphreys, a soldier in the war of 1812, asking a pension: referred to the Cmte on Pensions. 4-Memorial of Richd North & Gaylord Griswold, asking indemnity for French spoliations prior to 1800: referred to the select cmte. 5-Memorial of Ezra Williams, asking compensation for services rendered as a clerk in the Gen Land Ofc: referred to the Cmte of Claims. 6-Documents submitted in relation to the claim of Nancy A Dewitt to the reissue of a military bounty land warrant: referred to the Cmte on Public Lands. 7-Cmte on Indian Affairs: ptn of the reps of Jos Watson, with a bill for their relief: ordered to a second reading. 8-Cmte on Public Lands: ptn of Hal J Kelly: adverse report on the same: ordered to be printed. 9-Cmte of Claims: memorial of John H Eaton, asking to be reimbursed the cost of a certain Arabian horse purchased of the U S that was afterwards found to be impotent, submitted an adverse report on the same: ordered to be printed. 10-Cmte of Claims: memorial of Jas Watson, surviving partner of Wm Wilson & Sons: adverse report on the same: ordered to be printed.

Died: on Feb 4, at the residence of her daughter, on H st, in Wash City, Mrs Eve Knowles, in her 79th year. She was left alone in the house for a short time, & by some means unknown her clothes took fire, & when found life was extinct. Her funeral will take place at the Presbyterian Church, 4½ st, at 3 o'clock, today.

Died: on Tue, in Wash City, after a lingering illness, Mrs Anne Williams, in her 25th year, relict of John Williams, late of Wash City. Her funeral is on Thu, at 3½ o'clock, from her late residence, on 8th st, between Pa ave & D st.

Died: on Feb 5, Esther Ann Stoops, age 2 years & 3 months, daughter of Richard & Lucretia Ann Stoops. Her funeral is this afternoon, at half-past 3 o'clock, from the residence of the family, 12th & N Y.

House of Reps: 1-Died: Hon Alexander Newman, July last, in Pittsburg; victim of Asiatic cholera; [while visiting;] born 1806 in Orange Co, Va; settled in Marshall Co, Va shortly after he married. He left a wife & numerous children. 2-Ptn of Gershom Manchester, of Windham, Maine, a Revolutionary soldier, 90 years old, praying for an alteration of the pension laws. 3-Ptn of W Lynch, of Butler Co, Pa, praying Congress to grant him a pension on account of wounds received in the last war with Great Britain. 4-Memorial of S Clayton, Peter J Walker, H P Caperton, J F Bradford, John G Winston, & Levi W Lawler, asking for additional compensation for their services as ofcrs in the land ofce at Lebanon, Ala, in the location of the military bounty land warrants. 5-Ptn of Mrs Mary W Thompson, widow of the late Lt Col Alex'r R Thompson, asking to be allowed a pension for the services of her husband.

Interments in Washington for month of Jan 1850 - 66. Thos Miller, Pres, Board of Health.

Sale: by deed of trust dated Jan 7, 1846, duly recorded, executed by Wm H Ward to the subscriber: public auction of lots 7 thru 12 & 42, in square 502, in Wash City, with the frame dwlg-house on the same, on *Greenleaf's Point*. –D A Hall, trustee
-Green & Tastet, aucts

THU FEB 7, 1850
Mrd: in Balt, by most Rev Archbishop there, Wm J Edelen, M D to Ellen, daughter of late Peter Gough, of St Mary's Co, Md. [No date-recent item.]

Mrd: on Jan 26, by Rev M Alig, Geo R Hooper & Miss Jane C Staples, all of Wash City.

Mrd: on Feb 5, at *Neosho*, near Bladensburg, PG Co, Md, by Rev John Decker, Wm H Thompson, of Annapolis, & Maria Louisa, youngest daughter of late Wm Ross, of *Neosho*.

Died: on Jan 25, at his mother's residence in Dallas Co, Ala, in his 21st year, John Archer Lewis, 2nd son of late Dixon H Lewis. He had just finished his collegiate course at Alexandria College, D C.

Late from Calif: Peter H Burnett was on Nov 21 inaugurated as Govn'r of the State. John C Fremont & Wm M Gwin are next named in our dispatch, for what purpose we are unable to say. It is probably that they have been chosen to represent the new State in the Senate of the U S.

Died: Cmdor Turner, native of N Y, citizen of R I at time of entering Navy; arrived in Phil, with his family in Nov last from Portsmouth, N H; died of affection of the heart. [no date] [Feb 9th newspaper: Cmdor Turner was a native of N Y, but a citizen of R I at the time of his entering the Navy: his rank as Capt was gained Mar 3, 1835. During the battle of Lake Erie, in 1814, he commanded the ship **Caledonia**, & aided the gallant Perry very materially in gaining the decisive victory.]

Commission on Claims against Mexico: 1-Memorial of Mary Hughes, admx of Geo Hughes, deceased, late of brig **John**, claiming for his seizure, imprisonment, the plunder of his property, & fatal ill-usage at Tabasco, in 1832, was submitted, & ordered to be received. 2-Memorial of Jas Cochrane, steam engineer, claiming for his forced service as such on board the steamer **Bellona**, alias **Hidalgo**, in the river Tabasco in 1832: claim is valid: amount to be awarded subject to the future action of the Board. 3-Memorial of Philo B Johnson, late master of the schnr **Consolation**, claiming for personal ill-usage & spoliation of property on board the same, while in the river Tabasco, in 1832: claim is valid, & allowed: the amount to be awarded subject to the future action of the Board.

John Steele, a German, was killed at Rochester last week, when shot by a gun which had not fired previously. He told the men to "Fire at me." The gun went off & Steele was killed almost instantly.

Some 40 years since the family of Dr Denormandie, formerly of Attleborough, Bucks Co, Pa, received a paper written in a language they did not understand. It was lately translated & found to be a will, leaving the family an immense estate. Dr Denormandie left 3 sons, & perhaps other children. Two of his sons went to Ky, about 1818, where one of them died; the other, it is believed, are still living. They were worthy men, & many friends will rejoice to learn that the long neglected bequest may yet be realized. –Trenton [N J] Gaz

The undersigned will practice Law in partnership, under the name of Ogden & Duncan, in New Orleans, & in the Dist Court of the parish of Jefferson. –Robt N Ogden, Garnett Duncan Ofc: 3 St Chas st.

Senate: 1-Ptn of Thos Flanagan, a Revolutionary soldier , asking to be allowed a pension: referred to the Cmte on Pensions. 2-Memorial of the heirs of Wm F Megee, asking indemnity for French spoliations prior to 1800: referred to the select cmte. 3-Memorial of Benj Kingsbury & others citizens of Portland, Maine, asking that a pension be allowed to Jas Wright, for injuries received while acting as chief engineer on board a revenue cutter: referred to the Cmte on Pensions. 4-Bill for the relief of Lewis Morris & others: referred to the Cmte on Military Affairs. 5-Resolved, that the Pres of the U S be requested to transmit to the Senate copies of all charges or cmplnts made for or exhibited for the removal of J D G Nelson from the ofc which he recently held of receiver of public moneys at **Fort Wayne**, Ind.

Household & kitchen furniture at auction: on Feb 13, at the residence of Jas A Kennedy, on E, near 7th st. –Green & Tastet, aucts

Rare chance for good bargains in real estate. Ground & improvements belonging to a gentleman who will leave this city in the spring for the West, viz: lots 1 thru 20 in square 244, being the whole of said square. Lots 2 & 9 in square 702, fronting on South Capitol st. Lots 8 thru 13 in square 846, fronting on 5th st east & south E st. Lot 11 in square 881, on south K, near 7th st, with a comfortable brick dwlg. Lot 21 in square 1020, fronting on south G st, between 12th & 13th sts, with 2 comfortable & nearly new frame dwlg-houses. Apply to Jas T Small, Navy Yard, or to S S Williams, Ofc-C st.

Trustee's sale of valuable improved property: by deed of trust, executed & recorded in Liber W B 137, folios 114 thru 118: public sale on Feb 28: parts of lots 17 & 18 in square 496, fronting on south F st, between 4½ & 6th sts, with improvements.
–Thos M Milburn, trustee -Dyer & Brother, aucts

FRI FEB 8, 1850
Commission on Claims against Mexico: 1-Memorial from Wm S Parrott, a claimant now before the Board, asking that an application in conformity with the 15th article of the treaty of Feb 2, 1848, be made to the Mexican Gov't for certain papers & documents, as necessary to the just decision of his claim. Ordered, thereon, that such an application be made & sent forward in the usual form.

Senate: 1-Memorial of Susan Decatur, widow of the late Cmdor Decatur, asking that the prize money due for the capture & destruction of the frig **Philadelphia** in the harbor of Tripoli may be distributed among the captors, & protesting against any portion of it being paid to Priscilla Decatur Twiggs or her sisters: referred to the Cmte on Naval Affairs. 2-Memorial of Henry A Wright, asking indemnity for French spoliations prior to 1800: referred to the select cmte. 3-Presented: additional documents in relation to the claim of Wm H Francis to compensation for services as a Lt in the late war with Mexico: referred to the Cmte on Military Affairs.

House of Reps: 1-Cmte on the Post Ofc & Post Roads: bill to pay Jas S Graham & Walter H Finnall the sum therein named: committed. 2-Cmte on Revolutionary Claims: bill for the relief of the heirs of Gen Thos Sumter, late of S C, deceased: committed. Same cmte: adverse report on the ptn of Sarah Bowler: laid on the table. 3-Cmte on Revolutionary Claims: bill for the relief of the legal reps of John H Stone: committed. Same cmte: bill for the relief of the legal reps of Willis Riddick, deceased: committed. Same cmte: adverse report on the ptn of the heirs of Moses Matthews: laid on the table. Same cmte: adverse report on the ptn of Gideon Bentley: laid on the table. 4-Leave was granted to withdraw the papers of John P Warnock. 5-Cmte of Claims: discharged from the further consideration of the ptn of Geo S Claflin: referred to the Cmte on Invalid Pensions. Same cmte: bill for the relief of John Dickson, surviving partner of Lambert & Dickson: committed. Same cmte: adverse reports on the ptns of Geo Hartwick, Saml S Rind, Lerias King, & Thos Jarrett: all laid on the table. Same cmte: bill for the relief of John Glenn, administrator of Richd Barry, deceased, & Washington Hall: committed. Same cmte: adverse report on the ptn of Wm D Shaw: laid on the table. 6-Cmte of Claims: discharged from the further consideration of the ptn of Eliz Ring, widow of Capt Thos Ring: laid on the table. Same cmte: discharged from the further consideration of the ptns of the heirs of Manuel Howe & of Wm Hudson: laid on the table. 7-Cmte on Naval Affairs: bill for the relief of John G Wilkinson: committed. Same cmte: adverse report on the ptn of Janet H De Kay, widow of Geo De Kay: laid on the table. Same cmte: discharged from the further consideration of the ptn of Jas W Low: referred to the Cmte on Commerce. 8-Cmte on Revolutionary Pensions: discharged from the further consideration of the ptn of David Belding: referred to the Cmte on Revolutionary Claims. 9-Cmte on Revolutionary Pensions: adverse reports on the ptns of Danl Story, John Euleck, Meribah Chandler, widow of Martin Chandler, & Catharine T Claiborne, widow of Maj Richd Claiborne: laid on the table. Same cmte: bill granting a pension to Avery Downer: committed. Same cmte: bill for the relief of Saml Dewey: committed. 10-The ptn & papers of Hector St John Beatty were withdrawn from the files, & referred to the Cmte on Invalid Pensions. 11-Cmte on Invalid Pensions, reported bills for the relief of: Henry F Evans; of Geo Cassidy; of Benj P Smith, & of Benj F Wesley: committed. Same cmte: adverse report on the ptn of Abijah T Bolton: laid on the table. Same cmte: bills for the relief of : Lewis Hastings; of Eliphas C Brown; & of Carafield Averitt: committed. 12-Cmte on Invalid Pensions: discharged from the further consideration of the ptns of Martin Hatch, Wm Roberts, Marcus Spalding, & Aaron Hoyt: laid on the table. Same cmte: bill for the relief of Wm Slocum, of N Y: committed. Same cmte: adverse reports on the ptns of March Farrington & Saml S Winslow: laid on the table. 13-Act for the relief of Nathl Kuykendall: referred to the Cmte on the Post Ofc & Post

Roads. 14-Cmte on Naval Affairs: bill directing the Sec of the Navy to purchase from Jas P Espey his patent right for the conical ventilator for the U S Navy: committed. 15-Cmte on Invalid Pensions: bill for the relief of Jos D Ward: committed. Same cmte: bill for the relief of Skelton Felton: committed. Same cmte: adverse report on the ptn of John Forrest: laid on the table. 16-Ptn, affidavits, & papers of Gideon A Perry for a pension were withdrawn from the files of the House, & returned to the petitioner. 17-The papers of Aaron Stafford, Pamelia Slavin, Henry N Halstead, & Warren Raymond, were withdrawn from the files of the House, & referred to the Cmte on Invalid Pensions. 18-Resolved, that the Cmte on Invalid Pensions inquire into the right of Hamilton Carroll, of S C, to an increase of pension, & to call for the declaration & proof in the Pension Ofc. 19-Resolved that the Cmte on Revolutionary Pensions inquire upon the right of Capt Robt Wilson, of S C, to an increase of pension for services rendered as Lt after the fall of Charleston in May, 1780, & to call for the declaration & proof in the Pension Ofc. 20-Introduced: bill for the payment of a debt due to the heirs of Antoine Peltier. Also, a bill for the payment of a debt due Nicholas Lachance et al. Both referred to the Cmte on Revolutionary Claims.

On Wed a thief entered the dwlg of Thos C Donn, on H st, & stole a gold pen & cloak, while Mr Donn lay asleep.

Died: on Wed, at the residence of Cmdor Jones, in Fairfax Co, Va, after a short illness, Mrs Joanna Christian, wife of Rev Levi H Christian, co-pastor of F St Church of Wash City. Her funeral will take place at the church this afternoon at 3 o'clock.

Wash Corp: 1-Mayor nominating Henry O Bowen, as superintendent of sweeps in 7th Ward, in the place of John Davis, resigned: confirmed. 2-Ptn of Wm H Yates, praying remission of a fine: referred to the Cmte of Claims. Same cmte: act for the relief of Wm P Howell: which was read. Same cmte: ptn of Patrick Wilson, reported a bill for his relief. 3-Cmte on Improvements: bill for the relief of Jas Crutchett: without amendment. Same cmte: asked to be discharged from the further consideration of the ptn of Elias Barnes: which was agreed to. Same cmte: recommitted the ptn of Jas Johnson, asked to be discharged from its further consideration. 4-Cmte of Claims: recommitted the ptn of Jas Johnson, with a bill for his relief.

Telegraph Reports: Balt, Feb 7. The family of Mr E W Robinson, of this city, has been seriously afflicted from the effects of scarlet fever. On Fri he lost his eldest daughter, Matilda, age 9 years; on Sat his son Frederick, aged 4 years; & on Mon his youngest daughter, Grace, aged 13 months. They were all carried out of the house & buried at the same time. Mrs Robinson is now very ill from the same disease, & almost broken-hearted.

On Tue, the lumber yard of Mr Lenman, on 12th st, near the canal, was set on fire, & lumber to the value of $1,500 was totally destroyed.

Public sale of the House-furnishing & Variety Store of Geo Morris, on Pa ave, between 17th & 18th sts, on Feb 8. –Green & Tastet, aucts

Victims of the disaster at N Y, who have been identified:
Peter Hyde, aged 18, resided in East Brooklyn
Geo Hyde, aged 28, resided in East Brooklyn
Adam Nealey, aged 33, resided in 6th ave, between 32nd & 33rd sts.
Levi Hall, aged 23
Isaiah Marks, colored man
Leonard Brooks, aged 30, resided 54 Oliver st
Alex'r Dixon, aged 23, resided 29 Front st, Brooklyn
Henry N Reed, aged 29, resided 328 9th st
Richd E Egbert, aged 30
Rufus Whiting, aged 30, resided in Wmsburg
John Dougherty, aged 19, resided in Brooklyn
Jas Brooks, aged 20, resided 54 Oliver st
Abraham C Kelsey, aged 31, resided in Rivington st
Robt Heslip, aged 27, resided 412 Pearl st
Patrick Burn, aged 29, resided in Division av, Brooklyn
John Rodgers, aged 34, resided 88 Mott st
Danl Dougherty, aged 16, resided in Brooklyn
Geo T Worrall, aged 17, resided 686 4th st
Lemuel B Whiting, aged 27, resided in Brooklyn
Lorin King, aged 22, resided 63 Oliver st
Jesse Haughton, aged 14, resided 87 Beekman st
Frank P Bartlett, aged 14, resided 74 Franklin st
Owen Brady, aged 14, resided 115 Willet st
Jas Zueile, aged 38, resided 84 Frankfort st
Geo Havest, aged 25, resided 223 8th st
Seneca Lake, aged 27
Jos Lockwood, aged 45, resided in Beekman st
Saml Tindale, aged 15, resided 84 Beekman st
Many were burned to death, rather than killed by the explosion or falling timbers. [Feb 6 newspaper: yesterday the boiler connected with the large printing-press manufactory of Alva B Taylor, 7 Hague st, adjoining Hull & Son's Soap Factory, exploded at 25 minutes before 8 o'clock this morning, with most disastrous effect. The entire bldg, which was of brick, & 7 stories high, was instantly razed to its foundation, burying in the ruins a large number of workmen.]

Postmaster Gen has est'd the following new Post Ofcs for the week ending Feb 2, 1850.

Ofc	County, State	Postmaster
Hunter's Creek	Greene, Pa	Wm Paul
Brownington	Butler, Pa	Wm P McKee
Terre Hill	Lancaster, Pa	Simon N Klauser
Buckstown	Butler, Pa	Wm P McKee
Ennisville	Huntingdon, Pa	Alex'r Stewart
Peru Mills	Juniata, Pa	Jas Mather
Reaville	Hunterdon, N J	Runkle Rea
Hawleyton	Broome, N Y	Jas S Hawley

West Cameron	Steuben, N Y	Wm Miles
West Camp	Ulster, N Y	Wm Adams
South Warsaw	Wyoming, N Y	Alonzo Choat
Cotuit	Barnstable, Mass	P Fish
Cochesett	Plymouth, Mass	Martin Alger
West Concord	Essex, Vt	Chas Chase
West Braintree	Orange, Vt	Albert Hawes
East Hampden	Penobscot, Maine	Wm Carey
West Enfield	Penobscot, Maine	Nathl Jones
Dover	Balt, Md	Wm L Nace
Pleasant Grove	Alleghany, Md	[no name]
Champion	Trumbull, Ohio	Jacob H Baldwin
Vanlue	Hancock, Ohio	Wm P Wilson
De la Palma	Brown, Ohio	Wm Weeks
New Princeton	Coshocton, Ohio	Wm Whinery
Kossuth	Anglaise, Ohio	Saml Dillinger
Manistee	Manistee, Mich	Stephen Batchelder
Le Roy	Ingham, Mich	Perry Henderson
Cedar Mount	Wythe, Va	Chas L Fox
Graham, C H	Allamance, N C	Jas S Scott
Institute	Randolph, N C	John L Brown
Warwick	Dooly, Geo	Wm Posey
Opalika	Walker, Geo	Henry Fisher
Kingsville	Talladega, Ala	Jesse Calhoun
Coldwater	Marshall, Miss	Thos Wilson
Rabbit Creek	Rusk, Texas	Wm P Chisum
Barren Ridge	Van Zant, Texas	Jas Bundy
Gustavus	Greene, Ten	Lemuel Gooden
Steamport	Henderson, Ky	Thos Gates
Larkinsburg	Clay, Ill	J W Murray
Washburn	Winnebago, Ill	Wm A Foster
Carrsville	Cooper, Mo	Mead Carr
West Union	Fayette, Iowa	Jacob W Rogers
Butler	Keotuck, Iowa	Wm Waugh
Tualatin	Washington, O T	David Hill
Milwaukee	Clackamas, O T	Lot Whitcomb

Names Changed:
Culbertson, Mercer Co, Pa, changed to Exchangeville.
Fulton, Dallas Co, Ala, changed to Orrville.
Loweville, Madison Co, Ala, changed to Maysville.
Chilesburg, Fayette Co, Ky, changed to Pine Grove.
Foster's Landing, Bracken Co, Ky, changed to Foster.
Vermillionville, La Salle Co, Ill, changed to Lowell.

SAT FEB 9, 1850
Senate: 1-Cmte on the Post Ofc & Post Roads: referred the ptn of Thos Rhodes: bill for his relief: passed to a second reading. 2-Ptn of Isaac F Miller, a soldier in the late war with Mexico, asking an increase of pension: referred to the Cmte on Pensions. 3-Addition documents relative to the claims of John Hogan: referred to the Cmte on Foreign Relations. 4-Ptn of Thos Webb & John Cokern, register & receiver of the land ofc at Greenburg, La, asking an increase in compensation.

Chancery sale-Circuit Court of Wash Co, D C, in Chancery, dated Dec 22, 1849: Henry Young, cmplnt, vs Ed Hart et al dfndnts. Public auction on Mar 13, of that piece or parcel of land called "*Alliance*" in Gtwn: containing 60 acres, more or less. -Walter D Davidge, trustee, La ave & 6th St. -Edw S Wright, auct. [Feb 12th paper: Hart is Hurt]

House of Reps: 1-Ptn of Cmder John L Saunders, U S Navy, asking to be reimbursed for certain expenses incurred while in command of the U S ship **St Mary's**. 2-Memorial of Wm N Dorsett & others, heirs of Fielder Dorsett, asking indemnity for French spoliations prior to 1800. 3-Memorial of Geo F Warfield & others, asking indemnity for French spoliations prior to 1800. 4-Ptn of Seth Adams, of Zanesville, Ohio, asking indemnity for French spoliations prior to 1800. 5-Ptn of Henry Allen Wright, asking indemnity for French spoliations prior to 1800. 6-Ptn of the heirs of Capt John McAdams, of Northumberland Co, Va, asking commutation pay.

Mrd: on Feb 7, by Rev Mr Plunkett, of Martinsburg, Va, Mr Wm Carroll, of Bolington, Loudoun Co, Va, to Miss Emily Augusta, daughter of Dr Tilghman Biser, of Burkittsville, Frederick Co, Md.

Mrd: on Feb 7, by Rev Mr Hodges, Jonathan Turner Padgett, of Port Tobacco, Md to Miss Adelaide R Richards, of Wash.

Mrd: on Feb 7, by Rev Mr Hodges, John Frederick Spicer to Mary Ellen Bryan, all of Wash.

Mrd: on Feb 5, in Wash City, by Rev Dr Johns, of Balt, Chas F Stansbury to Ellen R, daughter of late Thos R Riley, all of Wash City.

Died: on Feb 7, at Gtwn, N Thos Browning, age 27, of hemorrhage from the lungs. His funeral will be at his mother's residence, Jefferson st, on Sun, at 3 o'clock. [I O O F: Notice of the funeral of N T Browning. -F H Collier, N G; J H Craig, F A Lutz, J T Bangs, Cmte of Arrangements.

Died: on Feb 8, Benj Burns, sen, in his 71st year. His funeral will be tomorrow, from his late residence on B, bet 10th & 11th sts.

Died: on Feb 8, at her residence on the Heights of Gtwn, D C, Eliza Davidson, relict of late Lewis G Davidson. Her funeral is on Sun at 3 o'clock.

Yesterday as the train of cars was passing through our boroughs on its way to Balt, Mr Thos McNulty, a respectable citizen of York, had his leg crushed when he fell under the cars endeavoring to jump from the train. We learn that he died this morning.
–York Gaz, Feb 5

Organization of the State Gov't of Calif. On Dec 15, the following were in their seats: Senate-John McDougall, Lt Govn'r, Pres ex official; J F Howe, Sec; Mr Olds, Assist Sec; A W Luckett, Enrolling Clerk; Bela Dexter, Engrossing Clerk; Thos J Austin, Sgt-at-Arms; Eugene Russell, Doorkeeper. Assembly-J T White, Speaker; E H Tharp, Clerk; F H Sanford, Assist Clerk; A D Ohr, Enrolling Clerk; C Mitchell, Engrossing Clerk; S Houston, Sgt-at-Arms; J Warrenton, Doorkeeper.

By virtue of 4 writs of fieri facias issued by Saml Grubb, J P for Wash Co, D C, at the suits of A Nailor, C Cammack, Parker & Spalding, & A J Joyce, vs the goods & chattels of Thos Dumphrey, dated Feb 8, 1850, I have seized & levied on one frame house, at 10th & Va ave, in square 383 [Island,] & give notice of the sale to be Mar 15.
–O E P Hazard, Constable for Wash Co.

MON FEB 11, 1850
House of Reps: 1-Debate on the purchase of the manuscript Farewell Address of Gen Washington, came up in its regular order.

Dr Jno F Brooke, fleet surgeon of the East India squadron, a well known & valuable ofcr, died at Macao, on Oct 17 last. He was the eldest son of Judge Brooke, of the Court of Appeals of Va.

The Richmond Times states that on Sat last Rev Joel W Jones, who officiated at a Methodist chapel on Oregon Hill, in that city, suddenly took his departure, leaving his board & other bills unpaid. Rumors from Syracuse, N Y, where he formerly resided, led to a call for his credentials. He was engaged to be married to a lady of his congregation, &, it is said, he already has 2 wives in the State of N Y.

Walter Corcoran, a fine boy 12 years of age, was killed at Canandaigua on Sat, when he jumped on the cars as they started, & in trying to get off was thrown under one of the wheels, & killed.

City Ordinance-Wash. 1-Act for the relief of Jos Swagert: penalty imposed upon him for an alleged violation of an act in relation to wagons & carts, is remitted, together with the costs of prosecution.

For sale: Deed of trust from Dolly Ann Patten, dated Sep 2, 1848; recorded in Liber J A S, #1, folios 369, et seq, of the land records for Wash Co, D C: public auction of all that part of lot 20 sq 293, in Wash City, so described, with improvements. This property lies on 12th st west, between C & D sts, near the avenue. -Dickerson Nailor, trustee
-Dyer & Brother, aucts

Died: on Jan 17, 1850, at Gnadenhuetten, Ohio, Rev Chas A Bleck, Pastor of Moravian Brethren's Chrurch at Gnadenhuetten & Sharon, aged nearly 46 years. He leaves his wife & children to mourn their irreparable loss. While at his post & engaged in the services of the sanctuary, on Jan 16, he was seized with violent pains, & the next day he had fell asleep in Jesus. –H A S

H Berlyn, from Germany, Prof of Music, Vocal, Instrumental, & Organist. Residence at Mrs Ceare's, above the Bank of Washington.

TUE FEB 12, 1850
On Fri of last week Owen Murphy & Jas Johnson were killed at Gen Dickerson's Mines, at Succasunny, by the falling of a piece of large rock, which crushed & killed them.

Commission on Claims against Mexico: 1-Memorial of Hezekiah Child & of Chauncey Child, of Hallam, Conn, claiming for losses & damages ensuing by reason of the seizure of the schnr **Carnelion**, of Hallam, Conn, at Brasos Santiago, in Mar, 1843, by the Mexican authorities, being taken up for consideration: claim is valid, & the same is allowed: the amount to be awarded subject to the future action of the Board. 2-Memorial of John Smith, of Hallam, Conn, claiming for damages suffered by him while master of the schnr **Carnelion**, of the same place, by reason fo the seizure of the said schnr & prosecution of the claimant by the Mexican authorities, at Matamaras, in 1843: claim is valid, & the same is allowed: amount to be awarded subject to the future action of the Board. 3-The Sec submitted to the Board the memorial of Andrew Wylie, jr, administrator of Saml Baldwin, deceased, a claimant now before the Board, asking that an application, in conformity with the 15th article of the treaty of Feb 2, 1848, be made to the Mexican Gov't for a certain document, as necessary to the just decision of his claim. To be sent in the usual form.

House of Reps: 1-Ptn of the heirs of John Emerson, praying an allowance of interest on commutation pay allowed for services in the Revolutionary war. 2-Ptn of Wm Bartoll & 296 other citizens of Marblehead, for cheap postage.

Bldg lots on Pres' Square for sale. For terms apply to J S Gunnell, Pres' Square.

J S Gunnell, M D, Dentist: charges very moderate. [Local ad.]

Furniture, hardware, cutlery, & baskets at auction: on Feb 14, at the residence of Mr Norris, on Pa ave, between 17th & 18th sts. -Green & Tastet, aucts

U S Patent ofc-Petition of Nathan Lockling, of North Dansville, N Y, extension of patent that expires Apr 28, 1850: <u>improvement in ploughs</u>. –Dewitt Lawrence, Acting Com'r of Patents

Mrd: on Feb 6, at St Mary's Church, by Rev Mr Alig, Thos Conner to Miss Mary A Christell, all of Wash City.

Mrd: on Feb 6, at St Mary's Church, by Rev Mr Alig, Geo Bergling to Miss Josephine Barber, all of Wash City.

Mrd: on Feb 11, by Rev Mr Hodges, Mr Wm Turton, of Md, to Miss Rachel E, daughter of R Arnold, of Wash Co, D C.

Mrd: on Feb 10, at the Church of the Ascension, by Rev L J Gilliss, John F Crampton to Catharine V Offutt, all of Wash City.

Mrd: on Feb 11, in Wash City, by Rev L F Morgan, Wm P Hutchinson to Frances Palmer, all of Va.

Mrd: on Feb 10, in Wash, by Rev Mr Slattery, John Johnson, of Va, & Mrs Ann Eliott Wheeler, formerly of Balt City.

Died: on Feb 6, of pneumonia, in his 4th year, Lambert Wells, youngest son of Thos C & Jane R Wells, of Wash City.

Died: recently in Calif Mines, Alexander Garrett, late of Wash & formerly of Rockville, Md, age about 22 years.

Died: on Feb 9, Mrs Eliz Schneider, wife of L H Schneider, in her 28th year.

WED FEB 13, 1850
Senate: 1-Memorial of John S Van Dyke, legal rep of Henry Van Dyke, late a lt in the navy, asking the payment of certain prize money to which he claims to be entitled: referred to the Cmte on Naval Affairs. 2-Communication from Robt W Patterson, director of the U S Mint at Phil, in relation to the capacity of the mint, & in relation to the establishment of a branch mint at N Y: referred to the Cmte on Finance. 3-Additional documents submitted relating to the ptn of Lois Brewster, late Lois Drew: referred to the Cmte on Pensions. 4-Memorial of the heirs of Perez Morton, asking indemnity for French spoliations prior to 1800: ordered to lie on the table. 5-Ptn from Garret Burns, asking to be allowed a pension in consideration of wounds received in the military service of the U S: referred to the Cmte on Pensions. 6-Memorial from Franklin Drury & other citizens of Mass, engaged in the manufacture of shoe lasts, asking that the patent-right of Thos Blanchard may be protected from violation: ordered to lie on the table. 7-Memorial from the heirs of Ebenezer Harrington, a Revolutionary ofcr, asking to be allowed half-pay: referred to the Cmte on Military Affairs. 8-Memorial of Haym M Salomon, heir of Haym Salomon, asking the repayment of advances made by his father during the Revolutionary war: referred to the Cmte on Revolutionary Claims.
9-Memorial of Wm E McMaster, asking that he may be authorized to execute for the Gov't portraits of Presidents. This young gentleman is of high promise, not unknown in the galleries or art. 10-Additional documents submitted relative to the claim of Jas Wright for a pension: referred to the Cmte on Pensions. 11-Memorial of John O Means, asking compensation for services as acting Purser in the Navy: referred to the Cmte on Naval Affairs. 12-Ptn of Nancy Bowen, widow of a deceased naval seaman, asking to be

placed on the pension roll: referred to the Cmte on Pensions. 13-Memorial of Danl V Quenandon, in behalf of himself & the volunteers who served in the Seminole war, asking to be allowed bounty lands: referred to the Cmte on Public Lands. 14-Ordered, that the ptn of Saml D Davis, on the files of the Senate, be referred to the Cmte on Revolutionary Claims. 15-Ordered, that the ptn of Robt Armstrong, on the files of the Senate, be referred to the Cmte on Pensions. 16-Ordered, that the ptn of Bancroft Woodcock, on the files of the Senate, be referred to the Cmte on Patents & the Patent Ofc. 17-Ordered, that the ptn of Peter A Morgan, administrator of John Arnold & Geo G Bishop, on the files of the Senate, be referred to the Cmte on Patents & the Patent Ofc. 18-Ordered, that the memorial of Robt Pratt, on the files of the Senate, be referred to the Cmte on Revolutionary Claims. 19-Ordered, that I P Sanger & Frink Hadduck, severally have leave to withdraw their ptns & papers. 20-Ptn of the heirs of Casper Rouse, deceased, for remuneration for losses sustained by said Rouse in the Revolutionary war. 21-Ptn of Jos Trosklamski, praying compensation for services rendered as deputy surveyor. 22-Ptn of Thos Webb, register of the land ofc at Greensburg, La, & of John Cockern, receiver of public moneys in said district, praying compensation for extra services rendered by them. 23-Memorial of Mrs Nancy Haggard, asking the allowance of interest on commutation pay granted for the services of her father, Wm Grimes, in the war of the Revolution. 24-Ptn & papers of Wm Tee were ordered to be withdrawn from the files of the House & referred to the Cmte on Invalid Pensions.

Washington's Farewell Address was sold in Phil yesterday, at auction: at the enormous price of $20,300. The Rev Dr Boardman was the purchaser, for a gentleman at a distance. [Feb 14th newspaper: the document ran up to $2,300, & was knocked down to the Rev Dr Boardman, for a gentleman living at a distance. The original Portrait of Washington, by Jas Peale, painted for Mr Claypoole in 1778, was also bought by Dr Boardman, for the same gentleman.]

$5 reward for return of a sorrel Horse, stolen from the store of Jackson & Brother, on Pa ave, on Feb 11. -John H Loveless, near Queen Ann

Wash Corp: 1-Ptn of J A F Tottchinder, praying remission of a fine: referred to the Cmte of Claims. 2-Ptn of Richd Cruit, praying remission of a fine: referred to the Cmte of Claims. 3-Ptn of Henry Janney & others for the extension of the pavement from Pa ave to the Centre Market: referred to the Cmte on Police. 4-Ptn of Jas Williams & others, remonstrating against the occupancy of certain premises on 7th st, between D & E sts, as a woodyard: referred to the Cmte on Police. Same was passed. 5-Bills for the relief of Wm P Howell & for the relief of Jas Johnson: passed. 6-Ptn from Alex'r Bowland, agent for Jas Moore: referred to the Cmte of Claims. 7-Ptn of Pringle Sleight: referred to the Cmte on Police. 8-Act for the relief of Jos Swaggart & Thos Lewis: passed. 9-Ptn of Mrs Jane A Taylor: referred to the Cmte of Claims. 10-Bill for the relief of Philip Ennis: ordered to lie on the table. 11-Cmte of Claims: bill for the relief of Bazil Simms: passed.

Orphans Court of Wash Co, D C. In the case of Leonard Storm, exc of Henry Boose, deceased, has appointed Mar 9, for settlement, of the assets in his hands as executor. -Ed N Roach, Reg/o wills

Orphans Court of Wash Co, D C. Letters of administration on the personal estate of Ann W Benning, late of Wash Co, deceased. -Moses Poor, adm

Orphans Court of Wash Co, D C. Letters testamentary on the personal estate of Dr Nathaniel Pope Causin, late of Wash Co, deceased. -Nathaniel Pope Causin, exc

Died: on Feb 11, at the Naval Hospital in Brooklyn, Lt Thos T Sloan, of the U S M C. He entered the Marine Corps in 1834 & served with distinguished bravery throughout the Florida campaign. During the past 3 years he has been at the African station, where he probably contracted the disease of which he died.

Mrd: on Feb 12, by Rev Mr Hodges, John Goddard to Harriet Lindsay, both of Md.

THU FEB 14, 1850
Senate: 1-Memorial of Wm S Wetmore, of N Y C, & Jas Hamilton, of S C, a cmte of the revenue bond-holders in the late Republic of Texas, praying for the payment or adjustment of the bonds which they hold. 2-Ptn of the heirs & reps of Justus Riley, asking indemnity for French spoliations prior to 1800: ordered to lie on the table. 3-Memorial from Chas Colburn, asking compensation for his services as a yeoman in the Navy: referred to the Cmte on Naval Affairs. 4-Memorial from John Pierce, jr, late a Prof of Mathematics in the Navy, asking to be restored to his rank, & allowed back pay: referred to the Cmte on Naval Affairs. 5-Memorial from Josiah Sturgis & others, of the revenue service, asking that the benefits of the naval pension law may be extended to that service: referred to the Cmte on Commerce. 6-Ptn of Danl Nippes, asking compensation for certain arms manufactured for the War Dept: referred to the Cmte on Military Affairs. 7-Ptn of the heirs of Manuel Sulano, asking the confirmation of their title to a tract of land: referred to the Cmte on Private Land Claims. 8-Ptn of P E Thomas, Phineas Janney, & Benj Ferris, in behalf of the Seneca nation of Indians, asking the payment of certain moneys due & wrongfully withheld from them by a sub-agent of the U S: referred to the Cmte on Indian Affairs. 9-Ordered, that the ptn of Henry W Barnes & Randolph M Cooley, on the files of the Senate, be referred to the Cmte on Military Affairs. 10-Ordered, that the executrix of Conrad Ten Eyck have leave to withdraw her ptn & papers. 11-Cmte of Claims: memorial of Isabella Cole, excx of Wm Cole, asking indemnity for injuries done to a vessel & cargo by the authorities in Peru, submitted an adverse report: ordered to be printed. Same cmte was referred the ptn of Jno Spencer, late receiver of public moneys at **Fort Wayne**, Ind, asking to be discharged from the further consideration of the same, & that it be referred to the Cmte on Public Lands: which was concurred in. 12-Cmte on Public Lands: memorial of Nathl Champ, asking the renewal of a military bounty land warrant, odered to be printed, with a bill for the relief of John Camp & others: ordered to a second reading. 13-Cmte on Indian Affairs: ptn of the heirs of Joshua Kennedy, with a bill for the relief of the legal reps of Joshua Kennedy, deceased: ordered to a second reading.

Orphans Court of Wash Co, D C. Letters of administration on the personal estate of Warren Riggs, late of Wash Co, deceased. -J B Edelin, adm

House of Reps: 1-Cmte of Claims: bill for the relief of Geo Collier & Wm G Pettus: committed. Same cmte: asking to be discharged from the further consideration of the ptns of W N Dorsett & others, heirs of Fielder Dorsett, & of Geo F Warfield: referred to the Cmte on Foreign Affairs. Same cmte: asking to be discharged from the further consideration of the ptn of John Lee: referred to the Cmte on Accounts. Same cmte: adverse reports on the ptns of John G Gamble & of Henry D Johnson: ordered to be printed. Same cmte: bill for the relief of John Plunkett: committed. 2-Cmte of Claims: bill for the relief of A Bandouin & A D Roberts, of New Orleans; & a bill for the relief of S J Bowen: committed. 3-Cmte on Commerce: bill for the relief of Williams, Staples & Williams: committed. 4-Cmte of Claims: bill for the relief of Winthrop S Harding, & a bill for the relief of Danl Steenrod: committed. 5-Cmte on Commerce: bill for the relief of Smith & Hersey: committed. 6-Cmte on the Judiciary: discharged from the further consideration of the ptn of E R Rogers & wife: referred to the Cmte on Foreign Affairs. Same cmte: bill for the relief of Christophe H Bix: committed. Same cmte: adverse report on the ptn of the heirs of Wm Sterrett: ordered to lie on the table. 7-Cmte on Private Land Claims: bill for the relief of Jos Richards: committed. Same cmte: bill for the relief of Robt Davidson: committed. 8-Cmte on Indian Affairs: adverse report on the ptn of Israel Johnson: ordered to lie on the table. Same cmte: adverse report on the ptn of E D McKinny, R J McElhany, & N R Smith, securities of Saml H Bunch, Indian agent: ordered to lie on the table. 9-Cmte for the District of Columbia: bill for the relief of Jas Dixon: committed. 10-Cmte on Military Affairs: discharged from the further consideration of the ptns of A Hickman & other citizens of Ohio; of John Hughey & others, of **Fort Gallion**, Fla; of the adm of J A D Lawrence, of Geo Lendrum, & the ptn of Capt Wm Black's company of mounted Florida volunteers: ordered to lie on the table. Same cmte: bill for the relief of Manuel X Harmony: committed. Same cmte: discharged from the further consideration of the memorial R S Ely: ordered to lie on the table. Same cmte: discharged from the further consideration of the ptn of Eliz M Churchill: ordered to lie on the table. Same cmte: asking to be discharged from the further consideration of the ptn of Baptiste Klein: ordered to lie on the table. Same cmte: bill for the relief of Edw Everett: committed. 11-Cmte on Naval Affairs: bill for the relief of Thos O Selfridge: committed. Same cmte: bill for the relief of Saml Graves: committed. Same cmte: discharged from the further consideration of the ptn of Marinas W Piercy: referred to the Cmte on Invalid Pensions. 12-Cmte on Revolutionary Pensions: adverse report on the ptn of Zachariah Barber, for a pension: ordered to lie on the table. 13-Ptn of papers in the case of Lt E Steen were withdrawn from the files of the House & referred to the Cmte on Revolutionary Pensions. 14-Cmte on Revolutionary Pensions: bill for the relief of Jacob Drinkhouse; a bill for the relief of Anna Giffin: committed. Same cmte: adverse report on the ptn of Eliz McDougal: ordered to lie on the table. 15-Cmte on Invalid Pensions: bill for the relief of Jesse Doane; relief of Hubert H Booly; relief of Jacob Zimmerman; & for relief of Wm Whieher: committed. Same cmte: adverse report on the ptn of Eliz Armstrong; on the ptn of Amaziah Ford: ordered to lie on the table. 16-Ptn of Maria Hill, of Chautauque Co, N Y, praying Congress to order her name placed on the pension list as a widow of a Revolutionary soldier.

Mrd: on Feb 12, by Rev Mr Donelan, Mr Daniel Barren to Miss Emily Allen, all of Wash City.

Mrd: on Feb 12, by Rev Mr Donelan, Mr Edw M Boteler to Miss Mary Jane Davis, all of Wash City.

Mrd: on Feb 7, in Balt, by Rev H V D Johns, Dr Alex'r Matthews, of Gtwn, D C, to Miss Nannie E Spencer, of Talbot Co, Md.

Mrd: on Feb 11, in Richmond, by Rev Dr McCabe, of Smithfield, Va, Wm Q Force, of Wash City, toMiss Eliz A Stewart, of Richmond.

Maj Oscar E Edwards, who commanded a company of Voltigeurs in the various battles which proceeded the capture of Mexico, died at San Francisco in Dec last. His home was in Norfolk, where he has left a wife & young family to mourn his decease in a far distant land. -Herald

Official: Mr Lewis Cass, jr, Charge d'Affaires of the U S at Rome, has, under date of Dec 28, 1849, informed the Dept of State of the decease of Mr Chas Haviland Carter, who died at Viterbo, in the Papal States, on Dec 19 last. Mr Carter is supposed to have been a citizen of the State of N Y. His effects were to be transmitted to Mr Cass.

Commission on Claims against Mexico: 1-Memorial of Ann B Cox, excx of Nathl Cox, deceased, & that of Calvin J Keith, adm of Saml *E kins, deceased, claiming, severally, for certain advances of money & of supplies, made in 1816 to the early Revolutionary Gov't of Mexico, being taking up for consideration: claims are valid, & allowed accordingly: the amount to be awarded subject to the future action of the Board. [Space between the E & k—could be Elkins.]

FRI FEB 15, 1850
Sea Horse at auction: on Feb 16, in front of the Centre Market, a great curiosity, caught in the Potomac river by Capt Treakle, Oct, 1849. –John Robinson, auct

Land Warrants wanted, for which the highest market price will be paid. –J W Simonton, Pa ave, opposite Brown's Hotel.

Walker Sharpshooters, Birth Night Bal, Feb 22, 1850. No hats will be allowed in the room. Tickets $1, admitting a gentleman & ladies. Managers:

Capt J Y Bryan	Corp E G Evans
Lt M Birkhead	Corp J Lewis
Lt W J McCollam	Corp W H Padjet
Lt Jas Ward	P Dowling
Ensign W Gallant	W A Sommers
Serg H Curtis	J H Godard, jr
Serg P Harbam	T Galiger
Serg E C Eckloff	R G Hyatt
Serg J Foxwell	N Kelly
Band Serg R Downing	C Kaufman
Capr W Pumphrey	J H Glick

C Bell
J Willson
A Humes
O J Collins
A J Stewart
D Barns
F A Birch
W Ross
W T Broke
J Houck
Chas Stewart
L Curtis
J Suite
J Hodson
W D Leasus
J Rollins
B Bell
C Kloman

G Bremmer
F German
P Mitchell
J Moran
W Jones
P C Fischer
J S Esputua
J Nevins
C Klingler
C V Walter
F S Giger
P N Schroeder
G W Norbeck
D F Grindle
B T Esputua
O P Dickel
M Eagerton

Senate: 1-Memorial of R Bissell for self & the heirs of Nathl C Bissell, asking indemnity for French spoliations prior to 1800: ordered to lie on the table.

SAT FEB 16, 1850
Postmaster Genr'l established the following new Post Ofcs for week ending Feb 9, 1850:

Ofc	County, State	Postmaster
Tapleyville	Essex, Mass	Geo W French
Rainbow	Harford, Ct	Saml T McKenney
South Windham	Windham, Ct	Merrill Ladd
Mercereau's Ferry	Richmond, N Y	L Hillyer
West Ashford	Windham, Ct	E Knowlton
East German	Chenango, N Y	Luke Carr
Chittenango Falls	Madison, N Y	Orrin Ransom
Twelve Mile Creek	Steuben, N Y	Smith Tucker
So Candor	Tioga, N Y	Ebenezer Daniels
West Fort Run	Wash, N Y	Hiram Everest
Paulina	Warren, N J	Ira C Moore
Hainesburgh	Warren, N J	Jacob W Blair
Laurel Run	Cambra, Pa	Alex M White
Mapletown	Greene, Pa	Jas S Craig
Black Lick	Indiana, Pa	Geo W Campbell
Coopersburg	Lehigh, Pa	Edw Seider
Gen'l Wayne	Montg, Pa	David Young
Aldenbille	Wayne, Pa	Julius T Alden
Huntingdon Valley	Montg, Pa	Chas B Rankin
Bright Seat	Anne Arundel, Md	M Linthicum
Bloomfield	Balt, Md	J S Lemmon

Paradise	Rockingham, Va	Jas Bolton
Alum Rock	Alleghany, Va	Sampson Karnes
Govnr's Island	Macon, N C	Mark Coleman
Edito	Lexington D, S C	Jas E Coleman
Berkshire	Gwinnet, Geo	Wm J Nash
Pea Vine	Walker, Geo	A J Leet
Meadville	Jackson, Ala	L G Mead
Edenburgh	Cameron, Texas	John Conway
Jacksonport	Jackson, Ark	R L Vanmeter
Tullahoma	Franklin, Ten	N W Williams
Springvale	Jefferson, Ten	Wm McFarland
Longview	Morgan, Ten	Jesse Adkins
Rough & Ready	Anderson, Ky	E O Hawkins
Locust Spring	Cumberland, Ky	John M Price
Hunter	Belmont, Ohio	David S White
Ewington	Gallia, Ohio	Geo W Thompson
Gibsonville	Hocking, Ohio	J L Williams
Lyra	Sciota, Ohio	David Boye
Feed Spring	Harrison, Ohio	Jas M Glandon
Two Mile Prairie	Pulaski, Ia	Andrew Wirick
Cloverland	Clay, Ia	Jas M Lucas
Greentown	Howard, Ia	L W Bacon
New Richmond	Montg, Ia	Saml McComas
Jalapa	Greene, Ill	Franklin Witt
Ontario	Knox, Ill	Edw Hollister
Twelve Mile Prairie	St Clair, Ill	Thos Temple
Hollis	Peoria, Ill	Sanford H White
Lancaster	Cass, Ill	M S Marsh
Pleasantville	Marion, Iowa	Wesley Jordan
Thompsonville	Racine, Wis	Emerson Lombard

Mrd: on Jan 31, at Cherry Grove, near Terre-Haute, Ind, by Rev A M Freeman, of Covington, Louis M Cook to Miss Phebe Ann Dowling, only daughter of Thos Dowling, all of Vigo Co.

Mrd: on Feb 14, by Rev J W French, Rector, Church of Epiphany, Jos B Tate to Miss Mary A S Mills.

Mrd: on Feb 14, by Rev G W Samson, J B Tree to Fanny L Evans, all of Wash Coty.

Mrd: Rezin C Smith & Martha Olive, on Jan 31, by Rev J W French.

Died: Mr O Rich, Jan 20, at his residence in London, formerly a resident of Wash, DC.

MON FEB 18, 1850
Wash City Ordinance: 1-Act for the relief of Bazil Simms: fine for an alleged violation relative to runaway horses in the streets, is hereby remitted: provided Simms pay the costs of prosecution.

For rent: new 3 story dwlg on the south side of Pa ave, on square 762. Apply at Blagden's Wharf, to Geo Collard, agent.

Wanted: a respectable youth, about 17 years of age, to attend in a store. Apply to Wm Marshall, Clothing Store, Pa ave.

$30 reward for runaway mulatto man, Tom Wood. –Barbary Lowe

A young man, Henry Perrine, son of Enoch Perrine, residing near Half Acre, Middlesex Co, about a year ago swallowed a nut shell, which lodged in his wind pipe, & gradually worked down & settled in his right lung. A few days since, while in a fit of coughing, the shell came up. It is now thought he will recover his health. –Hightstown Record

Mrd: on Feb 15, in Wash City, by Rev G W Samson, Mr Jas Randolph West to Miss Johanna Kingsbury, all of Wash City.

Killed: Mrs Adams, whose husband runs the Adams Coal Bank, was killed lately at Portage, Pa, when powder exploded. Her husband & child both survived.

Hon Edw A Hannegan, late Minister of the U S to Prussia, arrived in Wash City on Sat last.

For Liberia: 164 negroes, belonging to the estate of the late Jacob Wood, & liberated at his death by his will, arrived at Savannah, Geo, on Feb 12 in the steamer **Robert Collins**. They were to sail in a few days for Liberia on board the barque **Chieftain**, Capt Drinkwater.

Died: on Feb 17, aged 43 years, Louis A Fleury. His funeral will be at his late residence on 19th st near K, at 4 o'clock, this afternoon.

Died: on Feb 15, in Wash City, Fred'k Harlowe, only child of Saml L & Abba C Harris, age 5 years 3 months.

Died: on Jan 27, at Waterford, Erie Co, Pa, Wm Benson, after a protracted illness, aged 63 years.

Orphans Court of Wash Co, D C. Letters of administration on the personal estate of N Thos Browning, late of Wash Co, deceased. -P F Berry, adm

TUE FEB 19, 1850
J Atwood, Portrait Painter, from Phil, will remain in Washington during the session of Congress. His Studio is in room 47, basement of the Capitol.

Trespassing upon the premises of the subscriber, an estray cow. Owner is to come forward, prove property, pay charges, & take her away. —W Linkins, E st, between 21st & 22nd sts

Wanted to rent about Mar 15 next, a comfortable 2 story frame or brick house, containing from 6 to 8 rooms, not more than 5 minutes' walk from Pa ave. Apply to Jno W Baden & Bro, Pa ave.

Arrest of counterfeiter. St Louis papers of Feb 8 brings accounts of the arrest at Alton, Ill, by ofcrs from St Louis, of a man named E W Dunn, in whose house was found a large amount of counterfeit money, & a complete bogus manufactory. Mrs Dunn was in the house at the time of the arrest & upbraided him for being taken.

Died: on Feb 14, at ***Belle Air***, D C, Louis, son of Col Jehiel Brooks, age 1 year, 7 months & 21 days.

The Mirimichient [N B] Gleaner contains an account of the burning of the house of Mr Geo Drysdale, at Big Tracedie, on Jan 22, when his eldest son, 18 years, a daughter 8 years, a son 6 years, & a grand-daughter, 2 years, were all burnt to death. Mr Drysdale was absent at the time, & Mrs Drysdale, in endeavoring to rescue one of the children, was badly burnt. One child was saved, when a daughter broke in a window.

Official appointments by the Pres: to be U S Consul:
Benj Everett Smith, of Md, for Turk's Island.
Alfred Mitchell, of N J, for the port of Cork, in Ireland.
Harvey Gleason, of Louisiana, for the port of Chagres, New Grenada.
Thos Turner, of N Y, for Bahia de San Salvador, Brazil.
Saml Simpson, of Va, for Bombay.
Wm P Rogers, of Mississippi, for Vera Cruz, Mexico.
Amos B Corwine, of Ohio, for Panama, in New Grenada.
Horace Smith, of Pa, for Portugal.
Danl Le Roy, of N Y, for the port of Genoa, in Sardinia.
Chas L Fleischmann, of D C, for Studtgardt, in Wurtemberg.

Senate: 1-Ptn of Jos Farrant, heir of a Revolutionary Ofcr, asking to be allowed a pension: referred to the Cmte on Pensions. 2-Memorial of the heir of Benj Montange, asking compensation for his services as a bearer of dispatches in the Revolutionary war: referred to the Cmte on Revolutionary Claims. 3-Memorial of Benj E S Ely, with a plan for maintaining a military post in Calif: referred to the Cmte on Military Affairs. 4-Joint resolution passed by the Legislature of Indiana, in favor of the claim of the reps of Col Francis Vigo, for advances made to the troops commanded by Gen Geo Rogers Clark in 1778-9: referred to the Cmte on Revolutionary Claims. 5-Report of Lt M L Smith upon the improvement & drainage of the Valley of Mexico: referred to the Cmte on Printing. 6-Ptn of Ezekiel Jones, an ofcr in the revenue cutter service, asking that the spirit ration may be abolished. 7-Ptn of Cyrus Wheelock, asking a pension for injuries sustained in the war of 1812: referred to the Cmte on Pensions. 8-Ordered, that the ptn of John Madlan, on the files of the Senate, be referred to the Cmte on Public Lands. 9-Ordered, that the ptn of Foxall A Parker be withdrawn from the files & referred to the Cmte on Naval Affairs. 10-Cmte on Naval Affairs: ptn of Em B Thompson, asking for compensation for diplomatic services performed by her husband: ask to be discharged from the further consideration of the ptn, & that it be referred to the Cmte on Foreign Relations: concurred in. 11-Same cmte: referred the memorial of Wm D & Julia Aiken, with a bill for her relief: passed to a second reading. Same cmte: the case of Cmder Jas McIntosh, with a bill for his relief: passed to a second reading. Same cmte: ptn of Chas Colburn: adverse report: ordered to be printed. Same cmte: ptn of John Pierce: adverse report: ordered to be printed. 12-Cmte on Printing: referred the motion to print the memorial of Chas Barrell & Wilder, in behalf of the heirs of the widow of Capt Robt Gray, asking confirmation of their title to the lands purchased of Indian tribes in 1791 in the n w coast of American, reported against printing the same: which was concurred in. 13-Cmte on Public Lands: ptn of Thos Webb & John Cookern, register & receiver of the land ofc at Greenboro', La, submitted an adverse report on the same: ordered to be printed. 14-Ptn of Lewis B Willis, formerly a paymaster in the army, asking an equitable settlement of his accounts: referred to the Cmte of Claims. 15-Memorial of the heirs of Chas Lewis, deceased, a Revolutionary ofcr, asking to be allowed 7 years' half pay: referred to the Cmte on Revolutionary Claims. 16-Memorial of Robt Ferguson, a memorial of Sarah G Besse, a memorial of Peregrine Shanks, & a memorial of Fred'k Kounig, all asking indemnity for French spoliations prior to 1800: referred to the select cmte. 17-Cmte on the Judiciary: memorial of Thos W Chinn & others, asking to be relieved from a judgment against them as sureties of Thos G Morgan, late collector of New Orleans: asked to be discharged from the further consideration of the same: referred to the Cmte of Claims. 18-Cmte on Foreign Relations: memorial of the reps of Wm A Slacum, asking compensation for his services in obtaining information in relation to settlements on the Oregon river: bill for his reps: passed to a second reading. 19-Memorial of Henry R Schoolcraft, asking compensation for his services as a disbursing agent of the Indian bureau between the years 1822 & 1841: referred to the Cmte on Indian Affairs. 20-Additional documents submitted relating to the memorial of the legal reps of John Anderson: referred to the Cmte of Claims. 21-Additional documents submitted relating to the ptn of Ezra Williams: referred to the Cmte of Claims. 22-Memorial of Peter M Paillet asking indemnity for losses sustained by the destruction of his property during the attack of the U S army on Tabasco, in Mexico: referred to the Cmte of Claims.

WED FEB 20, 1850
Wash Corp: 1-Bill for the relief of Christopher Cammack: rejected. 2-Cmte of Claims: act for the relief of A F Tottchender: was read twice. 3-Ptn of R Wimsatt & others, for the repair of the sea wall on the Potomac: referred to the Cmte on Improvements. 4-Cmte on Police: bill for the relief of Hanson Brown: passed. 5-Bills for the relief of Jas Johnson; relief of Jas H Shreves & Harrison Taylor; relief of W P Howell; & relief of

Jas A Wise: referred to the Cmte of Claims. 6-Bill for the relief of Edw Hammersley: rejected. 7-Cmte of Claims: ask to be discharged from the further consideration of the ptn of Mrs Jane A Taylor: recommitted to Cmte of Claims. 8-Cmte of Claims: ask to be discharged from the further consideration of the ptn of Henry Miller: discharged accordingly. 9-Bills for the relief of John Crome; of Patrick Wilson; & of Wm Cammack, jr: referred to the Cmte of Claims. 10-Cmte of Claims: ask to be discharged from the further consideration of the ptn of Alex'r Borland, agent for Jas Moore: ordered to lie on the table. 11-Cmte of Claims: bill for the relief of Wm B Lewis: read twice. Same cmte: bill for the relief of E W Hall: read twice. 12-Bill for the relief of Jos Swaggert & Thos Lewis: referred to the Cmte of Claims. 13-Ptn of Jas Caden, praying remission of a fine & complaining of the conduct of certain ofcrs of the Corp: referred to the Cmte of Claims. 14-Cmte of Claims: ptn of Richd Cruit: ask to be discharged from the further consideration of the same: discharged accordingly.

On Sat week, at Concord, N H, as Peter Jenness, of Chichester, was crossing the railroad track, his young horse became frightened by the whistle, & darted upon the track in time for the engine to strike the sleigh, missing the horse, killing Mr Jenness instantly. Mr Jenness was a respectable citizen, aged 54.

N Y papers: Mr Henry Grinnell, of N Y C, & not Mr Moses H Grinnell, makes the offer to the Gov't of 2 ships to go in search of Sir John Franklin.

House of Reps: 1-Ptn of Geo W Bush & 38 others, against the election of a chaplain to the House. 2-Ptn of John Bates, asking compensation for his services as acting boatswain. 3-Ptn of Ira T Horton, for compensation as a witness in the U S Court in a case of mutiny on board of ship **Meteor**. 4-Memorial & ptn of Geo R Herrick, asking an appropriation of the amount of the balance due him for services in the business of reservation; & grants under Indian treaties, under the act of May 9, 1836. 5-Ptn of Sherman Pierce for an invalid pension. 6-Ptn of Richd Robinson, of Dutchess Co, N Y, praying for relief for wounds received in the naval service in the war of 1812, '13, & '14. 7-Ptn of Jeptha L Heminger, for a pension for services in the U S army, from 1808 to 1812, & for loss of health in consequence of said service.

Superior Court, at Hartford, Ct, last week: verdict was rendered against Lyman B Marks for damages to the amount of $1,572, for having slandered Miss Ruth Chase, & thus causing her removal from a school which she taught in Hartland.

Commission on Claims against Mexico: 1-Memorial of John Bensley, claiming for the detention of a circus company, for 4 days, at Dolores, in Guanajunto, was presented, examined, & suspended. 2-Memorial of Danl Collins, claiming for damages by the seizure & condemnation of the brig **Splendid**, at Tobasco in 1835, was presented, examined, & ordered to be received.

Mrd: on Feb 18, by Rev Dr Butler, Jos Jesse to Mary M Jesse, both of Caroline Co, Va.

Senate: 1-Memorial of the heirs of Danl Francis: asking indemnity for French spoliations prior to 1800: referred to the select cmte. 2-Ptn from the heirs at law of Isaac White, asking permission to locate a bounty land warrant issued for his services as a soldier in the last war with Great Britian: referred to the Cmte on the Public Lands. 3-Memorial of C Bradbury: asking indemnity for French spoliations prior to 1800: referred to the select cmte. 4-Cmte on Naval Affairs: memorial of Lewis Warrington for himself & others, asking the payment of the balance of the prize money due them for the capture of the sloop-of-war **Epervier**, submitted a report, which was ordered to be printed, with a bill for the relief of Capt Lewis Warrington & others: passed to a second reading. 5-Cmte on Military Affairs: memorial of Chas Lee Jones, asking compensation for expenses incurred & services rendered in raising, organizing, & subsisting volunteers in the war with Mexico, submitted a report on the same, which was ordered to be printed, accompanied by a bill for the relief of Chas Lee Jones: passed to a second reading. 6-Mr Borland gave notice of his intention to ask leave to introduce a bill for the relief of the widow of the late Maj Gen Worth. 7-Joint resolution for the relief of John Hogan: ordered to a 3rd reading.

Died: on Mon, in Wash City, Mrs Eliza Hamilton O'Neale, of Montg Co, Md, in her 55th year. Her funeral will be at residence of her sons-in-law, R Greenhow & J M Cutts, & at St Patrick's Church, this afternoon, at half past 4 o'clock.

Died: on Feb 13, at **Fort Constitution**, Portsmouth, N H, Brevet Lt Col Richard D A Wade, of 3rd Regt of U S A; a brave ofcr, whose gallantry in the Florida & Mexican wars gained for him a brevet in each. He was badly wounded in the latter at the battle of Churubusco.

U S Patent ofc-Petition of Jas Criswell, of Pittsburg, Pa, extension of patent to expire Jul 31, 1851: improvement in preparing oleaginous seeds for pressing. –Thos Ewbank, Com'r of Patents

Furniture Store: having taken the large store-room formerly occupied by Mr N McGregor, on 7th st: I have a large & handsome assortment of house-furnishings articles. –C O Wall

THU FEB 21, 1850
Trustee's sale-lots in Wash, DC; case of Lewis G Davidson's heirs.
-Saml G Davidson, trustee.

Trustee's sale: on Mar 12 next: by virtue of an act of Congress, passed, Jul, 1840, & of the decree of the Circuit Court of Wash D C , & the Orphans Court of Wash Co, D C, made in the case of Lewis G Davidson's heirs, & by authority from the heirs, sale of the following lots, in Wash City: lots 6, 7, & 8 in square 168, on G st, between 17th & 18th sts. Lot 11 in square 168, on 18th st. Lots 3 & 4 in square 126, lying between the residences of Col Abert & Mrs Macomb. –Saml G Davidson, trustee -Dyer & Bro, aucts

Senate: 1-Cmte on the Judiciary: memorial of M M Quackenboss, reported a bill to authorize the Sec of the Treasury to make an arrangment or compromise with Mangle M Quackenboss & his co-obligors, or any of them, for claims or bonds given by them as sureties to the U S. Bill was read a third time & passed. 2-Documents relating to the claim of Danl D T Benedict, to pay & allowances as a soldier in the army for the full period of his enlistment: referred to the Cmte of Claims. 3-Ptn of Jno P Andrews, asking the adoption of measures for the settlement of international difficulties by arbitration: referred to the Cmte on Foreign Relations. 4-Memorial of Titian R Peale, asking compensation for his services as a member of the scientific corps attached to the Exploring Expedition: referred to the Cmte on the Library. 5-Ptn of Chambers C Mullin, a volunteer in the late war with Mexico, praying to be allowed an increase of pension: referred to the Cmte on Pensions. 6-Memorial of Henry R Schoolcraft, asking the payment of a balance due him on a settlement of his accounts as Indian agent: referred to the Cmte on Indian Affairs. 7-Memorial of the heirs at law of Wm W Chapman, asking to be indemnified against loss of the amount of a forged Treasury note which he received with other public moneys, while acting as an assist quartermaster in the army, in the late war with Mexico: referred to the Cmte of Claims. 8-Memorial of Jas Higginbotham, asking permission to correct an error in the entry of certain bounty land warrants: referred to the Cmte on Public Lands. 9-Ordered, that the documents on the files of the Senate relating to the claim of Elisha Hampton & others, be referred to the Cmte on Public Lands. 10-Cmte on Patents: ptn of Peter U Morgan, administrator of John Arnold & Geo G Bishop, made an adverse report on the same: ordered to be printed. 11-Cmte on Public Lands: memorial of John Baptist Valle, submitted an adverse report on the same, which was ordered to be printed.
Rev John L Reese, of Balt.

House of Reps: 1-Cmte on Public Lands: asked to be discharged from the further consideration of the ptn of W R W Cobb, of Alabama: referred to the Cmte on Invalid Pensions. 2-Ptn of Capt A H Hanscom, 1st Regt Michigan Volunteers, asking for additional remuneration. 3-Cmte on the Post Ofc & Post Roads: adverse report on the ptn of Jos F Caldwell: ordered to lie on the table. Same cmte: adverse report on the ptn of Lewis Trapp & John Howell: ordered to lie on the table. 4-Cmte of Claims: adverse report on the ptn of Wm Gibbons: ordered to lie on the table. Same cmte: reported bills for the following titles: relief of the legal reps of Jas C Watson, of Georgia, & a bill for the relief of Chas Stuart: committed. 5-Cmte on Commerce: bill to provide for the settlement of a claim of Henry Leef & John McKee: committed. 6-Cmte of Claims: bills of the following titles: for the relief of Sarah Jane West; & relief of Indiana Shoemaker: committed. 7-Ptn of Jas Lewis, asking compensation for attendance on the district court of the U S at Norfolk. 8-Memorial of Caleb J Good, exc of Lt John E Bispham, late of the U S Navy. 9-Ptn of Edw Ellis, of Brooklyn, N Y, praying for an increase of pension. 10-Ptn of John Shafer, of the city of Dayton, Ohio, praying for arrears of pay & bounty land due him as a soldier in the war of 1812.

Mrd: on Feb 20, in Church of the Epiphany, by Rev Mr French, Mr John C Engelbrecht, of Staunton, Va, to Miss Caroline E Ball, of Wash City.

Mrd: on Feb 20, in Eutaw st Methodist Episcopal Church, Balt, by Rev Mr Aquilla A Reese, Rev Wm H Pitcher, of Balt Annual Conference, to Miss Mary Jane, daughter of Rev John L Reese, of Balt.

Household & kitchen furniture at auction: on Feb 25, at the residence of Mrs Bancroft, on I, between 8th & 9th sts. –Green & Tastet, aucts

$25 reward for return of negro woman, Mary Ann Allen, about 27 years old. –Mary Jones, Bladensburg, PG Co, Md

Commission on Claims against Mexico: 1-Memorial of John Bensley being again taken up for examination, the Board came to an opinion that it dose not set forth a valid claim against the republic of Mexico, & it was rejected accordingly. 2-Memorial of F M Dimond, U S Consul at Vera Cruz, claiming for wages of certain American seamen employed in the Mexican navy discharged unpaid, in 1843, & 1844, was submitted, examined, & suspended.

Meeting in Wash, Mar 3, 1849 of the Ofcrs of War of 1812:

Maj Gen Wm O Butler	Col Gilbert C Rupell
Gen Chas Gratiot	Maj Chas J Nourse
Col Chas S Todd	Capt Henry S Geyer
Maj John G Camp	Maj Thos Harrison
Col John A Rogers	Maj Nath'l Nye Hall
Dr Adam Hays	Col John O'Fallan
Col Chas K Gardner	Capt Wm C Willis
Col Abram R Woolley	Col John McIlvain
Maj Geo Bender	Capt O C Merrill
Col Robt W Alston	Capt Rufus McIntyre
Dr Richmond Johnston	Gen John McNeil
Capt Boyd Reilly	Col John G Watmough
Capt Leonard Adams	Gen Cromwell Pierce
Capt Thos R Sanders	Col David Campbell
Maj D E Dunscomb	Col J P McDowel
Capt Henry Robertson	Col John Darrington
Capt Peter Douglass	Col Jos Phillips
Maj Chas Mullegan	Col Bernard Peyton
Maj J N Barker	

On Sat, a daughter of Mr Rufus S King, about 16 years of age, residing near Abingdon Square, N Y, was so dreadfully burnt upon her arms & chest that her life is in jeopardy. She was in a neighbor's house, where the lady was cleaning a pair of soiled gloves with camphine. She too decided to clean her gloves, & told to use caution, she went to the fire to dry them. The flames at once caught her dress. Last evening, Dr Kingsland, the physician, thought her life might be preserved, but it is doubtful if her arms or hands will ever be capable of use.

Law School, Harvard College, Cambridge, Mass. Instructors are Hon Joel Parker, LL D, Royall Prof; Hon Fred'k H Allen, Univ Prof: & Hon Luther S Cushing, Lecturer upon Parliamentary, Civil, & Criminal Law. –Jared Sparks, Pres

The subscriber offers for rent *Evermay*, the residence of the late Lewis Grant Davidson, on the extreme right of the Heights of Gtwn: dwlg house built of brick & is 2 stories high; with all out-bldgs & ofcs: lot covers an area of 20 acres & more. Inquire of the subscriber, Saml G Davidson, Agent & Trustee for Proprietors.

FRI FEB 22, 1850
We learn with regret that Baron Roenne, the highly esteemed rep at Wash of the German Confederation, has been recalled. He first came to this country in 1834, as the Charge d'Affaires of Prussia, & was soon after made Minister resident. –Republic

House of Reps: 1-Ptn of Col Jas T Swearingen, Col John McDonald, & W Marshal Anderson, for himself & other heirs of the late Duncan McArthur, Brig Gen of the U S Army, praying Congress to grant them so much of the public lands for services performed by them & those whom they represent in the war of 1812 & 1813 as may be right & proper. 2-Ptn of the heirs & distributes of Col Wm Nelson, for commutation of half pay. 3-Cmte on Revolutionary Claims: discharged from the further consideration of the ptn of Susan Tarn, widow of John Tarn, & it was referred to the Cmte on Invalid Pensions. Same cmte: discharged from the further consideration of the memorial of the legal reps of John Jackson, & it was referred to the Cmte on Naval Affairs. Same cmte: bill for the relief of the heirs of Joshua Eddy, deceased: committed. Same cmte: discharged from the further consideration of the ptn of Jos Carter, & it was referred to the Cmte on Revolutionary Pensions. 4-Cmte on Revolutionary Pensions: bills for the relief of the heirs of Larkin Smith, & for the relief of the heirs of Lt Bartlett Hinds: committed. 5-Cmte on Private Land Claims: adverse report on the ptn of Marcus Spalding: ordered to lie on the table.

The death of W P Brobson, late collector of the port of Wilmington, Dela, & for many years editor of the Deleware State Journal, is announced in the Phil papers.

Female Doctors: Two young ladies, Miss Almira Fraim & Miss Mary Ward, have become regular students in the medical dept of the Memphis Institute.

Mrd: on Feb 14, by Rev J G Hening, Mr Reuben Brown of Wash, to Miss Jemima P King, eldest daughter of Middleton King, of Montg Co, Md.

Mrd: on Feb 19, by Rev Mr Hodges, Peter M Dubant to Miss Delila Mead, all of Wash.

Mrd: on Feb 20, by Rev John C Smith, Daniel H Seybolt, of N Y, to Miss Eliza C Jones, of Wash City.

$100 for runaway mulatto woman named Judy, about 26 years of age. –Wm Major, near Culpeper Court House, Va

Senate: 1-Memorial of the legal reps of Wm Jamesville, asking compensation for property destroyed by the enemy during the last war with Great Britain: referred to the Cmte of Claims. 2-Ptn of Ephraim Larrabee & others, of Balt, engagd in the manufacture of shoe lasts, asking that the patent right under which they manufacture may be protected from foreign violation: referred to the Cmte on the Judiciary. 3-Memorial of Seth Adams, of Zanesville, Ohio, who says he is now 83 years of age, & was among the early settlers in Ohio, before it was a State, asking indemnity for French spoliations prior to 1800: referred to the select cmte. 4-Cmte on Naval Affairs: claim of Francis B Stockton, for allowance of expense incurred in going to London by order of the commanding ofcr, made an adverse report on the same: ordered to be printed. Same cmte: claim of Purser Francis B Stockton, for the allowance of expenses of a ball given on board the U S frig **St Lawrence**, made an adverse report on the same: ordered to be printed. Same cmte: memorial of Mgt Carmick, widow of Maj Carmick, late of the U S marine corps, submitted an adverse report on the same: ordered to be printed.
5-Memorial of D Hartwell Carvers, asking of Congress the confirmation of his title to a large tract of land, 100 miles in every direction from the Falls of St Anthony, on the Mississippi, purchased by his grandfather of the Indians before the Revolutionary war, & now in the Territory of Minnesota, the title confirmed & the deed recorded at London, in the Plantation Ofc, in the year 1768: referred to the Cmte on Public Lands. 6-Memorial of Edw Everett, of Ill, asking an appropriation for testing certain improvements which he claims to have made in the modes of constructing & working telegraphs. 7-Cmte of Claims: adverse reports on the ptn of J Downs, on the memorial of Jas Robertson, on the memorial of Jas Wilson, surviving partner of Wm Wilson & Sons, the memorial of John H Eaton, & on the claim of Dr B F Mullen. 8-Cmte on Public Lands: adverse report on the memorial of Chas Byrne, on the ptn of Robt Butler, on the memorial of citizens of Kaneville, Iowa, asking a grant of land, & on the memorial of Hall J Kelly. 9-Cmte on the Judiciary: adverse report on the memorial of Caleb Green, clerk of the district court of western Louisiana. 10-Cmte on Naval Affairs: adverse report on the memorial of Geo Hervey, on behalf of the owners & consignees of the British ship **James Mitchell**. 11-Cmte on Foreign Relations: adverse report on the memorial of Abigail Shaler Stillwell. 12-Cmte on Printing: adverse report on the memorial of Wendell & Van Benthuysen.

In Wisconsin, Mrs Lovicy Keyser has recovered $100 damages of Jos Heath for selling rum to her husband. Liquor dealers in that State have to give bonds to pay for all injury growing out of their traffic.

Died: on Feb 20, Mary Eliz Prity, age 1 year & 5 days, daughter of John G & Ann H Hobbs. Her funeral will be from the residence of Mrs N Wilson's on D st, between 9th & 10th, tomorrow at 4 o'clock.

Died: on Feb 21, Wm Henry, age 18 months, son of Jas L & Eliz F Tibbs. His funeral will be from the residence of his parents, on I st, between 9th & 10th sts, this afternoon.

For sale: about 65,000 square fetts of ground with a good 2 story brick house, near the Twenty Bldgs. –N Young, near Navy Yard

A modest Prussian mechanic, by the name of Chas Hartung, now in this city, invented a new style of rifle, known by the name of Lund Nadel, [darting needle,] which is attracting much attention. It loads at the breech; & it is discharged by a darting needle, which pierces the bottom of the cartridge & ignites the powder by friction.
–N Y Post

SAT FEB 23, 1850
Postmaster Gen established the following new Post Ofcs for week ending Feb 16, 1850:

Ofc	County, State	Postmaster
Mast Yard	Merrimack, N H	Marshall B Colby
Campbello	Plymouth, Mass	Nelson J Foss
Ercildown	Chester, Pa	Gideon Pearce
Camargo	Lancaster, Pa	H H Breneman
Scrantonia	Luzerne, Pa	John W Moore
Brush Run	Wash, Pa	Jas Clarke
Taylor Hall	Balt, Md	John Bond
Ocmulgee	Perry, Geo	Jesse McCraw
Wesley	Monroe, Miss	W Smith
Koshuh	Jackson, Tenn	F M Davis
Delphton	Fayette, Ky	O Nunnelley
Williamson	Jefferson, Ky	J B O'Bannon
Story	Ogle, Ill	H P Spaulding
Wester Saratoga	Union, Ill	Jas L Wallace
Kingston Mines	Peoria, Ill	Saml Hutchison
Buffalo Heart	Sangamon, Ill	Robt Cast

Names changed:
Carter Camp, Lycoming Co, Pa, change to Haneyville.
Haskellville, Lawrence Co, Oho, changed to Millers.
Bethpage, Harrison Co, Missouri, changed to Bethany.
Hamar, Wash Co, Wisc, changed to Addison.

Mrd: on Feb 13, by Rev L F Morgan, Mr Jos A Burch to Miss Sarah Jane Fridley; all of Wash City.

Died: on Feb 22, Archibald Thompson, in his 75th year, a native of county Down, Ire, but for the last 30 years a resident of Wash. His funeral will be at his residence on F st, between 13th & 14th sts, tomorrow, precisely at 2 o'clock.

Died: on Feb 22, Mr John Green, of **Rosedale**, near Gtwn. His funeral will take place from his late residence, on Mon, at 10 o'clock.

MON FEB 25, 1850
City Ordinance-Wash: 1-Act for the relief of Hanson Brown: the Mayor is to pay to Brown, late Police ofcr of the 5th Ward, the sum of $56.32, said amount being the balance found due him on the settlement of his police accounts up to Jun 30, 1849.

Geo Cortell died at his residence in Lambertville [formerly Coryell's Ferry,] on Feb 16, in his 91st year. Immediately after the close of the war in which he served, having participated amongst other services in the battle of Monmouth, he removed to Alexandria, near Mount Vernon, at the instance of Gen Washington, where he continued to reside until within a few years, when he returned to his native State. He was a confidential friend of Washington during his life, belonged to the same masonic lodge, a correspondent assures us, the last one of the six who bore the body of the Father of his Country to the tomb. -Newark Advertiser

We perceive by the last Maysville Eagle that Thos B Stevenson, of Cincinnati, has purchased that establishment, & will after Mar 1 assume the editorial direction of the paper.

St Louis Republican: on Feb 10: Gonsalve & Raymond de Montesqion were in court & entered a plea of not guilty of the murder of Theron K Barnum & Albert Jones, on Oct 19 last. The prisoners were then remanded to jail to await their trial.

Accident on Feb 11 on the 14th section of the Balt & Ohio Railroad, above Cresaptown, when a boat upset, & Patrick Caray & John Dooley, laborers, were drowned. –Cumberland Civilian

John H Barber, for many years editor & proprietor of the Newport [R I] Mercury, a journal now in its 89th year, is dead. Mr Barber has been connected with the Mercury for the last 60 years. It was begun by Jas Franklin, brother of the Dr, & by him sold to Mr Barber's father, & is now the oldest paper in the country-the Hartford Courant being the next oldest. [No death date-current item.]

Mrd: On Feb 19, by Rev A Colton, Robt W Smoot, of Gtwn, to Margaret A, daughter of Dr S N C White, of Montg Co, Md.

Died: on Feb 22, Ann Cath Bartley, wife of Isaiah Bartley, of paralysis.

Died: on Feb 9, at his residence in Louisville, Rt Rev Benedict Jos Flaget, 1st Roman Catholic Bishop of Louisville, in his 87th year.

Died: on Feb 8, at the Great Crossings, Scott Co, Ky, Mrs Nancy Johnson, the esteemed relict of Col Jas Johnson, in her 73rd year.

Died: on Sat last, at the Irving Hotel, in Wash City, Gen John McNeil, a distinguished ofcr of the war of 1812. His arrival from Boston, where he is Surveyor of the Port, was but just announced to us when we were apprized of his sudden & unexpected death, though we since learn that he has long been declining, & suffered much from a painful & protracted illness. He was born in Hillsborough, N H, & was in his 66th year. His funeral will take place on Tue. To be interred in <u>Congressional Burying Ground</u>.

Mr Jenkins, conductor of the Houstonic freight car, when near the Pittsfield Branch, coming down to Boston Wed, fell off, & the cars passed over him, killing him instantly.

Household & kitchen furniture at auction: on Mar 1, at the large Grocery Store of J H Kidwell, on High st, Gtwn. –Green & Tastet, aucts

Household & kitchen furniture at auction: on Feb 26, at the residence of Mrs Tompkins, at the corner of Gay & Montg sts, Gtwn. –E S Wright, auct -A Green, Crier, whith whom all accounts will be settled.

Circuit Court of Wash Co, D C-in Chancery, Oct Term, 1849. Wm Dowling & John Maguire, against John, Jas, Mary Ann, & Bernard Kelly, heirs at law of Bernard Kelly, deceased, & John F Ennis, adm. The trustee in this case reported that on Nov 27, 1848, the premises mentioned in the decree of sale made by the Court in the above cause were sold to Patrick McGarvey for the sum of $2,100. –Jno A Smith, clerk

TUE FEB 26, 1850
Commission on Claims against Mexico: 1-Memorial of John Bensley, of N Y, claiming for damages by seizure & detention of apprentice circus rider Anderson Farrington, in Guanajuato, in 1842, was submitted, examined, & suspended. Memorial of the same, claiming for damages by seizure & detention of the same boy at San Luis Potosi in 1844, submitted & also suspended. 2-That of Alex'r M Bouton & Matthew Armstrong, adms of John Blackburn, deceased, claiming for seizure of the cargo of the schnr **Rebecca Eliza** at Tampico in 1829: submitted & suspended. 3-That of John Haggerty, Thos E Davis, & Alex'r H Dana, claiming for the destruction of their property at New Wash, Texas, in 1836: submitted & suspended.

City Ordinance-Wash. 1-Act for the relief of Alfred Bell: to pay to him the sum of $10, to reimburse him for a license paid by him for running a hack, the said hack having been destroyed by fire. Approved, Feb 21, 1850.

Died: on Feb 17, Geo Washington, infant son of John C & Martha E Campbell, age 1 month & 20 days.

Household & kitchen furniture at auction: on Mar 5, by order of the Orphans Court of Wash Co, D C, at the residence of the late Geo Sweeny, on 7th st, between D & E Sts. –Dyer & Bro, aucts

Household & kitchen furniture at auction: on Mar 1, at the residence of Miss Ball, on G between 8th & 9th sts. –Green & Tastet, aucts

Senate: 1-Memorial of Salvador Pinistri, proposing to erect a national monument in front of the Capitol: referred to the Cmte on the Public Bldgs. 2-Memorial of Geo Dennett, asking compensation for services performed while naval ofcr at Portsmouth, N H: referred to the Cmte on Naval Affairs. 3-Cmte on Military Affairs: ptn of Mgt Hetzel, admx of the estate of Assist Quartermaster Hetzel, submitted a report, which was ordered to be printed, with a bill for the relief of Mrs Mgt Hetzel, widow & admx of A R Hetzel, last Assist Quartermaster in the U S Army: passed to a second reading. 4-Cmte on Naval Affairs: adverse report on the ptn of John S Van Dyke: ordered to be printed. Same cmte: memorial of Mrs Cmdor McKay, & the ptn of J Sydney Henshaw: asked to be discharged from the further consideration of the same: agreed to. 5-Ptn of Julius Meiere, late professor of mathematics in the navy, asking that certain allowances may be made for quarters & furniture: referred to the Cmte on Naval Affairs. 6-Memorial of M J Hill, asking an appropriation for the purpose of testing by experiments the value of certain improvements in the science of naval gunnery: referred to the Cmte on Naval Affairs. 7-Cmte on Public Lands: ptns of John Madlam & of citizens of Phil, moved to be discharged from the further consideration of the same: referred to the Cmte on Military Affairs. 8-Memorial of Sophia Davenport, heir of Ed James, asking indemnity for French spoliations prior to 1800: ordered to lie on the table. 9-Ptn from Lazarus Knapp, a soldier in the war with Mexico, asking to be allowed bounty land: referred to the Cmte on Pensions. 10-Memorial of J K Rodgers, legal rep of the widow & children of a Cherokee Indian, asking compensation for an Indian reservation of which he was dispossessed by the authorities of the State of Georgia: referred to the Cmte on Indian Affairs. 11-Ordered, that the ptn of Cyrus H McCormick, on the files of the Senate, be referred to the Cmte on Patents & the Patent Ofc. 12-Ordered, that the ptn of Jas Chapman, on the files of the Senate, be referred to the Cmte on the Judiciary. 13-Cmte on Indian Affairs, reported a joint resolution for the settlement of accounts with the heirs & legal reps of Col Pierce M Butler, late agent for the Cherokee Indians: passed to a second reading. Same cmte: joint resolution to extend the provisions of a joint resolution for the benefit of Frances Slocum & her children & grand-children, of the Miami tribe of Indians, approved Mar 3, 1845, to certain other individuals of the same tribe.

WED FEB 27, 1850
Senate: 1-Ordered, that the papers of the heirs of Thos West, now on the files of the Senate, be withdrawn therefrom. 2-Cmte on Military Affairs: discharged from the further consideration of the ptn of Zelotes Fuller & others, citizens of Pa, praying for the passage of law granting bounty lands to the army & volunteers who served in the Seminole war in Florida: referred to the Cmte on Public Lands. Same cmte: bill for the relief of Chas Lee Jones: committed. 3-Cmte on Naval Affairs: discharged from the further consideration of the ptn of Richd Robinson: referred to the Cmte on Invalid Pensions. Same cmte: discharged from the further consideration of the memorial of the legal reps of John Jackson: referred to the Cmte on Invalid Pensions. Same cmte: bill for the relief of Horatio M Crabb; relief of Mrs Sarah Duncan, widow of Silas Duncan, late master commandant in the U S Navy; & relief of the sureties of Benj M Hart, late purser in the U S Navy.

Phototypes on Paper. Mrs Bertha Wehnert Beekmann, from Leipzig, has opened her studio on Pa ave, between 10th & 11th sts, in the house of Mr J F Kahl, where a gallery of Phototyphic Pictures is opened for inspection. Mrs Wehnert will remain in Wash City until Mar 1.

Commission on Claims against Mexico: 1-Memorial of Bouton & Armstrong, adms of John Blackburn, deceased: rejected.

Orphans Court of Wash Co, D C. Letters of administration on the personal estate of Wm Lloyd, late of said county, deceased. –Matilda Lloyd, Saml E Douglass, admx

House of Reps: 1-Memorial of Kah-ge-ga-gah-baugh, or Geo Copway, asking for the organization of an Indian territory east of the Missouri river. 2-Ptn of Nathl White, asking payment of a reward due to his father for information leading to the conviction of counterfeiters. 3-Ptn of Jonathan Hutchins, of Randolph Co, Indiana, praying Congress to give him bounty land & a pension for services rendered in the Revolutionary war. 4-Ptn & other papers of Lucinda Washington, Louisa Meade, & Eliz C Turner, heirs of Dr John Nelson, a Surgeon in the Revolutionary war, praying compensation for services rendered by him during that war, & for which he received no pay. 5-Memorial & ptn of Isaac Hill, of N H, in relation to libel suits instituted against him in N Y C. 6-Ptn of Elisha Morrill, atty for the heirs of Jeremiah Prescott & Thos Canny, deceased, soldiers of Capt Elisha Smith's company of 12 months' volunteers in the war of 1812, for the passage of an act granting 160 acres of land to the heirs or legal reps of said soldiers.

Died: on Feb 9, at his residence near Fairfield, Rockbridge Co, Va, Mr John Hughes, soldier of the Revolution, aged 107 years.

Died: on Feb 26, Mrs Eliz Schofield, formerly of Shropshire, England, for last 25 years a resident of Wash, age 71 years & 8 months. Her funeral is today, at half past 11 o'clock, from her late residence on F st, between 8th & 9th sts.

Died: on Feb 26, after an illness of 4 days, Frances Eliot, youngest daughter of Capt Noah & Mary R Wilson, age 3 years, 7 months & 2 days. Her funeral will be at her mother's residence on D st, between 9th & 10th sts, on Wed at 3 o'clock.

Died: on Feb 12, in Rochester, N Y, John T Talman, aged 56, after a week's illness.

THU FEB 28, 1850
House of Reps: 1-Ptn of Abigail Davis for a pension. 2-Ptn of the heirs of Jas Conway, praying for the allowance of 7 years' half pay, under the resolution of Congress, of Aug 1780. 3-Ptn of Moses W Hunt, praying Congress to grant him an increase of pension. 4-Memorial of John Harper, remonstrating against the occupancy by agents of the U S of land claimed by him. 5-Memorial of John D Sloat & other ofcrs of the navy, asking bounty lands for the seamen engaged in the late war with Mexico. 6-Memorial of Winslow Lamer & Co, & 473 citizens of the U S, in favor of granting to P & F Degrand, Wm Ingalls, E H Derby, & others, a charter to construct a railroad & establish a line of telegraph from St Louis to San Francisco, with a capital of one hundred millions of dollars. [$100,000,000.00]

$100 reward for runaway negro boy Semon, about 19 or 20 years of age.
–Wm Clark living near Queen Anne, PG Co, Md.

The Telegraph brings news of the death of Geo W Weissinger, associate proprietor & editor of the Louisville Journal, who died on Feb 25, of congestion of the brain, after an illness of only 2 days. He was a native of Alabama, where most of his family yet reside. He went to Ky aout 25 years ago to enter Transylvania Univ as a student. -Republic

Senate: 1-Cmte on Military Affairs: asked to be discharged from the further consideration of the ptn of C L Harrington, & it be referred to the Cmte on Revolutionary Claims. 2-Resolved, that there be paid to Owen Connolly, a sum equal to the amount of his pay from the time of his removal as one of the police of the Capitol, on Apr 30, 1842, to the present time, in consideration of injuries sustained by him in the discharge of his public duties, & which have disabled him for life. 3-Cmte on the Judiciary: ptn of Jas Chapman, administrator of Thos Chapman, submitted a report with a bill for the relief of the legal reps of the late Thos Chapman, formerly collector of the port of Gtwn, S C, which was ordered to be printed. 4-Ptn of Thos R Joynes, asking indemnity for French spoliations prior to 1800: ordered to lie on the table. 5-Ptn of Jas Wright, asking to be allowed a pension in consequence of disease contracted while serving as engineer on board of a revenue cutter in the Gulf of Mexico during the Mexican war: referred to the Cmte on Pensions. 6-Cmte of Claims: ptn of Wm A Duer: ordered to be printed. 7-Memorial of W K Inglish & John C Douglas, volunteer ofcrs in the late war with Mexico, asking an allowance of bounty lands: referred to the Cmte on Military Affairs. 8-Cmte on Pensions: to inquire into allowing Caty Blevins, wife of Henry Blevins, deceased, who was a soldier of the Revolution: a pension. 9-Ptn of Freeman Blakely, a pensioner of the U S, asking an increase of pension: referred to the Cmte on Pensions.

For sale: farm on which I reside, "**Pomonkey Farm**", Chas Co, Md, 650 acres. Improvements: spacious & commodious dwlg, barns, & every necessary farm-house, in good repair. Address Wm H Plowden, Pomonkey Post Ofc, Chas Co, Md.

Chancery sale-Circuit Court of Wash Co, D C: Edw Hamilton, Josiah Hamilton & Francis Hamilton, cmplnts, & Mathew Hamilton, infant & heir at law of *Mathew, deceased, dfndnt. Public auction on Mar 30 of lot 3 in square 293, Wash, D C. Also, three undivided sixths of all that part of said lot 3 in square 293, in Wash City, so described in said decree. -Richd R Crawford, trustee, Greene St, Gtwn, D C. Dyer & Bro, aucts [Mar 5th newspaper: *Mathew, deceased, is Mathew Hamilton, deceased]

Died: on Feb 26, Mgt Chambers, wife of Patrick Dowling, age 32 years. Her funeral will be from their residence on 7th near L st, this afternoon at half-past 2 o'clock.

Died: on Tue last, Mildred H, wife of John P Ingle, in her 44th year. Her funeral is this afternoon at half past 3 o'clock.

Copartnership notice: S *S Wall & Z Brown have this day purchased of O P Donn his interest in the firm of Wall & Donn. The business will hereafter be conducted under the title of Wall & Brown. –S *T Wall, Z Brown [Note different initials.] [Mar 1st newspaper: S T correct initials.]

FRI MAR 1, 1850
Suicide: Capt Chas Peternell, of Cleveland, Ohio, on Feb 23rd, by cutting his throat. He was on parade the preceding day, & attended the Ball at night, appearing to be in good health. He was with Gen Scott's army in Mexico during the last war, & was in nearly every battle from the storming of Vera Cruz to the capture of the city of Mexico.

House of Reps: 1-Memorial of John Grayson & others, ofcrs & soldiers in the war of 1812, praying bounty land.

Postmaster Gen established the following new Post Ofcs for week ending Feb 23, 1850.

Ofc	County, State	Postmaster
Allenton	Wash, R I	H Allen
Hockanum	Hartford, Ct	Geo A Hall
East Canaan	Litchfield, Ct	E D Lawrence
Waterville	New Haven, Ct	Wm Pickett
Messina Springs	Onondaga, N Y	Miles Benham
Union Society	Greene, N Y	Lemuel Parsons
Middle Village	Queen's, N Y	Jona F Latham
Tranquillity	Sussex, N J	Geo W Steele
Millbuck	Lebanon, Pa	John B Walter
Nescopeck	Luzerne, Pa	Wm Schuyler
Zollersville	Wash, Pa	Thos Odbert
Halcyon	Westmoreland, Pa	Jacob Newmyer
Jeddo	Luzerne, Pa	Jacob S Yost
Maxwell	Delaware, Ohio	Walker L Nutt
East Clarksield	Huron, Ohio	H W Cunningham
Johnson's Corner	Summet, Ohio	Wm Hays
Oak's Shop	Pittsylvania, Va	Joab Oaks
Jim Town	Monongalia, Va	Wm P Williams
Jonathan's Creek	Maywood, N C	G B Garrett
Crawfordsville	Spartansburg, S C	Jas D Bivings
Miami	Dallas, Fla	Robt Fletcher
Indian River	St Lucia, Fla	Wm H Holden
Centrefield	Oldham, Ky	Martin Demoss
Bainbridge	Robertson, Ten	John Bainbridge
Kosuth	Wash, Ind	Wm Scarborough
Dolson	Clark, Ill	John B Beadle

Names Changed:
East Harrington, Wash Co, Maine, changed to Harrington.
New Castine, Dark Co, Ohio, changed to Castine.
Young's Mills, Knox Co, Ohio, changed to Lucerne.
Cobb's Corners, Portage Co, Ohio, changed to Mantua Centre.
Union Society, Greene Co, N Y, changed to Bailey's Four Corners.
Wellington, Desha Co, Ark, changed to Bellville.

English papers: Lord Jeffrey, long eminent as a Judge of the Supreme Court of Scotland, but more famous for his editorship of the Edinburgh Review, died on Jan 26, having been born in Oct, 1773.

Mrd: on Jan 21, at Spring Dale, Nelson Co, Va, by Rev Wm Pinkerton, Rev Ben M Wales, of Charlottesville, to Miss Constance C Paul, daughter of late Rev Isaac Paul, of Va.

Senate: 1-Ptn of Michl R Boos for a pension, on account of services in the U S army during the last war with Great Britain: referred to the Cmte on Pensions. 2-Memorial of Chas Findlay, in behalf of the chiefs, headmen, & counselors of the Delaware tribe of Indians, asking the balance of pay due for services in the Seminole war: referred to the Cmte on Indian Affairs. 3-Memorial of Edw Storer, a purser in the navy, asking the allowance of certain items in his accounts, rejected by the accounting ofcrs of the Treasury: referred to the Cmte of Claims. 4-Ordered, that the papers in the case of D W Nye be taken from the files & referred to the Cmte of Claims. 5-Cmte of Naval Affairs: asked to be discharged from the further consideration of the ptn of Geo Dennett: was referred to the Cmte on Commerce. 6-Cmte on Pensions: ask to be discharged from the further consideration of the ptn of Chas Larabbe: case will be provided for in a general bill: agreed to. 7-Cmte on Pensions: ask to be discharged from the further consideration of the ptn of David Humphries, as his case will be embraced in a general bill: agreed to.

Zachary Taylor, Pres of the U S, recognizes Jules Lombard as Consular Agent of the French Republic for Monterey, Calif. -Feb 28, 1850

Commission on Claims against Mexico: 1-Memorial of Fred'k Freeman, claiming for seizure & imprisonment at Frontera & Tabasco, in 1832, was submitted & examined, but not conforming to the rules of the Board, was ordered not to be received. 2-That of Robt T Brent, claiming for duties paid at Santa Fe, detention at Chihuahua, & loses thereby, in Jul, 1846, was examined, & suspended.

SAT MAR 2, 1850
The Rev Mr Leahy, ex-monk of La Trappe, delivered a series of lectures in St Louis highly abusive of Roman Catholicism, the result of which was that on Feb 16 a serious riot ensued, & Leahy was forced to take flight, narrowly escaping with his life.

Senate: 1-Ptn of Chas Larabee, asking to be allowed arrearages of pension: referred to the Cmte on Pensions. 2-Memorial of the heirs of F Skipwith, asking indemnity for French spoliations prior to 1800: ordered to lie on the table. 3-Odered, that the papers of Sarah Coodey be taken from the files & referred to the Cmte on Indian Affairs. 4-Ordered, that Wm L Cazeau have leave to withdraw his pen & papers. 5-Resolves, that the Pres of the U S send to the Senate a copy of all the charges which have been preferred against John H McKenney, late sutler at ***Fort Gaines***, Minnesota Territory; together with all the papers touching the removal of said McKenney.

Mrd: on Feb 28, by Rev Mr Lannahan, Mrs Isaac Leeds, of Phil, to Miss Marion Virginia, daughter of Robt T Thompson, of Fairfax Co, Va.

Died: on Fri, Sophia Wright, eldest daughter of Lewis & Sarah Wright. Her funeral is on Sunday at 2 o'clock, from her father's residence 4½ st, near F st.

House of Reps: 1-To be reported to the House without amendment: bill for the relief of:
Wm B Crews
Wm Paddy
Gideon Walker
Jesse Sutton
Richd H Barrett
Avery Downer
Capt Henry F Evans
Geo Cassady
Benj P Smith
Lewis Hastings
Chas Ahrenfeldt &
John F H Voght
E Paven Stadt & F A Schumacher
Ferguson & Milhardo

2-Bills being objected to, were laid over: relief of:
legal reps of Thos Jett, deceased, objected to by Mr Thompson, of Mississippi.
Relief of Hiram Moore & John Hascall, objected to by Mr Carter.
Bill to refund the fine imposed on the late Dr Thos Cooper, deceased, under the sedition law, to his legal reps, was objected to by Mr Evans, of Md. Subsequently, Mr Evans desired to withdraw his objection to this bill, he having objected under misapprehension; but such a proceeding was declared to be out of order, as the bill was disposed of.
Bill for relief of Joshua Follansbee & B F Isherwood, on motion of Mr Thomas, laid aside with the recommendation that it be committed to the Cmte of the Whole on the state of the Union.
Bill for relief of the captors of the frig **Philadelphia** was objected to by Mr Duncan.
Bill for relief of John Dickson, surviving partner of Lambert & Dickson, was objected to by Mr Carter.
Bill for relief of S T Nicoll & Jas Clinch, of N Y C, was objected to by Mr Thomas.
Bill for relief of John Glenn, adm of Robt Barry, deceased, & Washington Hall, was, on motion of Mr Thomas, laid aside, with recommendation that it be referred to Cmte of Claims.
Bill for relief of Brown & Tarbox, objected to by Mr Brown, of Indiana.
Bill for relief of the heirs of Gen Thos Sumter, late of S C, was proposed to be amended by Mr Thomas, by striking out the interest in the sum proposed to be given, &, this amendment failing, he objected to the bill.
Bill for relief of the legal reps of John H Stone was objected to by Mr Carter.
Bill for relief of the legal reps of Willis Reddick, deceased, was objected to by Mr Thomas.
Bill for relief of John G Wilkinson was objected to by Mr Crowell.
Bill for relief of Benj F Wesley was objected to by Messrs Brown, of Indiana, & Carter.
3-Memorial of Maj Logan & others, ofcrs & soldiers of the war of 1812, praying bounty lands.

The Boonsboro' Odd Fellows states that on Sat last, at Antietam iron Works, near Sharpsburg, Mr Earlanger, greaser of the rolling mill, was caught in the fly-wheel & forced through a narrow space, crushing him & causing instant death.

Sir Francis Jeffrey, recently deceased, married as his 2nd wife, a daughter of late Chas Wilkes, of the Bank of N Y. He was consequently the brother-in-law of D C Colden, of N Y. Lady Jeffrey survives & her only child is now the wife of Prof Empson, Editor of Edinburgh Review. -N Y paper.

When the city of Washington was laid off, it has been said that lots were designated for each of the great European nations then in amity with our youthful Republic. Various land records of Wash Co, for the year 1798, per Liber 3, folio 474 do testify. That on May 25, 1798, the Comer's of Wash City did grant by deed, duly executed under their hands & seals: "To her most faithful Majesty the Queen of Portugal, her heirs & successors forever, all that square in the city of Washington situated, lying, & being on the Pres's square east of square 171. –Gustavus Scott, W Thornton, A White, Com'rs. Appended: approval of the grant of land-John Adams; T Pickering, Sec of State. [The land in the foregoing deed granted forms, I believe, what is now regarded as part of the Pres' square, lying south of the Executive Mansion & the outlet of the Washington Canal. It has been recently enclosed, with other portions of the square, by a picket wooden fence, built not by order of the Queen of Portugal, but in derogation, as I greatly fear, of her legal vested rights. –Regia Jus

Zachary Taylor, Pres of the U S, recognizes Chas Fred'k Adae, appointed Consul of Bavaria in the city of Cincinnati. Mar 1, 1850. Also, recognizes Hermann Gustav Adolph Heymann, appointed Consul of the Free Hanseatic city of Bremen for the port of San Francisco, Calif. Mar 1, 1850

MON MAR 4, 1850
Mark Fisher, the engineer, & Jas Steward, an engineer of another train, killed last Fri, on the Camden & Amboy Railroad at Whitehills, N J, when the boiler exploded. Wm Greenleaf, another fireman, was severely, if not mortally injured.
–Commercial Advertiser

On Fri last the family of Mr John N Trook, clerk in the City Post Ofc, residing near the corner of 7th st & Md ave, was taken with alarming sickness soon after breakfast. Dr Morgan being sent for, & satisfied that poison had been mixed with the coffee drank by every member of the family, administered the proper remedies, which proved successful. Mrs Trook has not recovered, & was still suffering the effect of the poison. Nothing has transpired to fix the guilt of this diabolical act.

Mr C L Colman's carpenter shop, near his dwlg, was on fire on Fri; about the same time a stable occupied by Mr Parris, near the Six Bldgs, was also in flames. The latter bldg was totally consumed.

Died: on Mar 2, Patrick Luby. His funeral will be at residence of Patrick McGarvey, 27th & K, this afternoon, at 3 o'clock.

Died: on Feb 14, in Culpeper Co, Va, John P Fant, age 74 years, leaving a large family of sons & daughters.

Died: on Mar 2, in Wash City, Rebecca Morris, daughter of Chas W & Louisa Pemberton Forrest, age 1 year & 6 months.

Household & kitchen furniture at auction: on Mar 6, by order of the Orphans Court of Wash Co, D C, at the late residence of Basil Sems, deceased. –Green & Tastet, aucts

Groceries for sale: the undersigned, having bought out the stock of Jacob Keobel, in the store formerly occupied by the late Wm Allen. -Jas A Brown, La ave, between 6 & 7 sts

Co-partnership has been formed between Wm H Berry, of Balt, & Jas W Berry, of Wash, under the name of Berry & Brother: general Grocery & Commission Business in Balt, have taken one of the new spacious warehouses in Exchange Pl.
-Wm H Berry, Jas W Berry.

Notice: the subscribers have sold their entire stock of Lumber & Fixtures at the corner of 14th st & the Canal to Messrs Wm I Sibley & Co. Please call & settle accounts, as we expect to leave the city on Apr 1 for Calif. –O J Preston & Co

TUE MAR 5, 1850
Hon C A Wickliffe, who filled the ofc of Postmaster Gen under Pres Tyler, is in imminent danger of becoming blind, a disease having fastened upon his eyes which apparently defies medical skill.

Senate: 1-Ordered that the ptn of John Mounts, on the files of the Senate, be referred to the Cmte on Pensions. 2-Ordered, that leave be granted to withdraw the documents on the files of the Senate relating to the claim of N G Hamilton. 3-Cmte on Military Affairs: bill to authorize the Sec of War to cause to be paid to Capt Geo E McClellan, his ofcrs, & men composing his company of mounted volunteers full pay for services rendered, subsistence & forage furnished in East Florida, in 1840: passed to a second reading. 4-Cmte on Patents: ptn of Peter U Morgan: to lie on the table. 5-Cmte on Naval Affairs: claim of Francis B Stockton, for payment of certain traveling expenses: to lie on the table. 6-Several adverse reports on the memorial of Isabella Cole, excx of Wm Cole, the memorial of John Pearce, jr, the memorial of Chas Colburn, the ptn of Thos Webb, & John Cookern, & the memorial of Mgt Carmick, were taken up & concurred in. 7-Memorial of Benj Tatham & Henry B Tatham, asking an extension of their patent for an invention for manufacturing lead pipes: referred to the Cmte on Patents & the Patent Ofc. 8-Memorial of John Mercer: asking indemnity for French spoliations prior to 1800: ordered to lie on the table. 9-Ptn of Fred'k Dixon, asking compensation for services rendered, wounds received, & property sacrificed in the military service of the U S: referred to the Cmte on Pensions. 10-Ptn from Patrick Conway, a soldier in the late war with Great Britain, asking to be allowed bounty land: referred to the Cmte on Military Affairs. 11-Ptn of Horace H Day, Henry R Dunham, Jas Renwick, & Jas Stimson, a sub cmte on behalf of Convention of Inventors, & others interested in patent property, which was held at Balt in Sep last. Ptn referred to the Cmte on the Judiciary, & the motion to print was referred to the Cmte on Printing.

Mrd: on Feb 28, at the English Lutheran Church, by Rev J G Butler, Mr Fred S Kern to Miss Mary Ann Miles, all of Wash City.

John S Gallaher has disposed of his interest in the Winchester Republican to Messrs Geo E Senseney & C A Coffroth. The paper will be devoted to the interest of the Whig party.

Balt Co Court: in the case of Henry Suissman & wife vs Caspar Falch & wife, an action of damages for slander in charging the wife of the dfndnt with adultery, the Court [Judge Purviance on the bench] decided that adultery not being under the law of Md an infamous crime, or punishable except by fine, the charging of a person with being guilty of it was not of itself slander & not actionable. Under the decision of the Court on this & other points the plntf withdrew his case with leave to amend so as to claim special damages.

Jas G Berret, late Chief Clerk of the Pension Ofc, offers his services as Agent for the prosecution of Pensions on account of services in the Revolutionary war, under the various acts & resolutions of Congress. Ofc & dwlg on F st, between 9th & 10th sts.

Criminal Court-Wash. The following gentlemen were summoned to serve upon the Grand Inquest:

John P Ingle, Foreman
Geo Watterston
Edw M Linthicum
Jonathan Seaver
Saml Drury
Andrew Coyle
Jeremiah Orme
Wm Wilson
Willard Drake
Jesse E Dow
Harvey Cruttenden
Saml Kirby
Bushrod W Reed
Jas B Phillips
Danl Campbell
Thos Thornley
Geo H Fulmer
Ephraim Wheeler
Elias A Eliason
Judson Mitchell
Wm T Compton
Wm H Tenney
Zachariah Walker
Chas R Belt

Stock of Groceries, store fixtures, at public auction on Mar 12, at the Grocery Store of Geo A Lane, on the west side of Market Space, Gtwn, D C. –Edw S Wright, auct

WED MAR 6, 1850
Appointments by the Pres: 1-Fletcher Webster, Surveyor of Customs, Boston, Mass, vice John McNeil, deceased. 2-Chas Polk, Collector of the Customs for the District of Delaware, vice Wm P Brobston, deceased.

Mrd: on Mar 5, in Bladensburg, Mr Peter Francis to Miss Matilda Suit, daughter of Edw Suit, all of Bladensburg.

Died: on Feb 21, at Sonyea, Livington Co, N Y, after a short & severe illness, Ann Dana, wife of Dr D H Fitzhugh.

Died: on Mon, John Simpson, in his 70th year. His funeral will be at his residence, High & West sts, Gtwn, this afternoon, at 3 o'clock.

Notice: members of Columbia Fire Company: meet to attend the funeral of Wm Jones, deceased, this afternoon, at 1 o'clock.

The Union Literary Society will meet at McLeod Academy this evening at 7:30 p m. –D S G Cabell, sec

Palm-leaf mattresses for sale: also on hand, mahogany chairs with hair seats, well made & cheap. –N M McGregor

Missing: on Jan 28, Dr J C Rising, of this city, left home for Wash, intending to be absent only a few days. He went on business & had a considerable sum of money with him. His wife was on a visit to her father in Massachusetts, & his absence was not the cause of public attention till about 2 weeks ago, when it was found that she had not heard from him since he had left Hartford. He was a young man, about 30 years old, & sustained an excellent character. -Hartford Courant.

For sale: valuable Bldg Lots, with a small frame House, on north B, next to the corner of Second st west. Inquire of H M Morfit, Agent for owner, ofc 4½ st, near Pa ave.

Wash Corp: 1-Bill for the relief of Wm B Wilson: reported without amendment. 2-Cmte on Improvements: ptn of E A Evans & others, for a flag footway across 7th st & N Y ave: passed. 3-Act for the relief of John Dewdney: referred to the Cmte of Claims. 4-Cmte of Improvements: ptn of J S Gunnell & others, for grading & gravelling Vt ave: passed. 5-Act for the relief of Wm H Yates: read twice. 6-Bills for the relief of F S Walsh & for the relief of Jane A Taylor: referred to the Cmte of Claims.

House of Reps: 1-Ptn of the heirs of Nathan Beard, together with other papers in the case: referred to the Cmte on Revolutionary Claims. 2-Ptn of A A Dexter, of Alabama, praying the passage of an act compensating American citizens for French spoliations on their commerce. 3-Memorial of Benj Rush, of Pa, asking compensation for services as Charge d'Affaires at London. 4-Sec of the Navy to inter into a contract with Geo W Billings for furnishing 300 tons of American water-rotted hemp per annum for 5 years, according to the terms & conditions of the bid made by Billings.

Commission on Claims against Mexico: 1-Memorial of Robt T Brent, submitted on Feb 28, & suspended, against taken up & the Board came to an opinion that it does not set forth a valid claim against the Republic of Mexico: memorial was rejected.

Criminal Court-Wash. 1-Richd Walker & Chas Bridget were yesterday found guilty of refusing to aid constables, when legally called upon, to assist the latter in the arrest of prisoners. David Wentsril, charged with the same offence, was acquitted. 2-Fred'k Shotherd, free negro, convicted of aiding in the escape of a prisoner.

Valuable bldg lots at auction: recorder in Liber J A S, #1, folios 250 thru 253, one of the land records of Wash Co, D C: auction on Mar 18, of the following: lot 4 in square 295; lot 12 in square 454; part of lot 16 in square 455; lot 4 in square 492: lots front on 7th st, between F & G sts; one on F & one on G st, between 6th & 7th sts west; one on Canal st, between 12th & 13th sts; one on South C st, between 4½ & 6th sts. –W H English, trustee -Green & Tastet, aucts

Household & kitchen furniture at auction: Mar 8, at the residence of Jas P McLean, on H st, between 7th & 8th sts. –J Martin & Co, aucts

The steamship **Baltic** was launched at N Y on Sat, from the foot of Houston st, in the presence of nearly 10,000 spectators. She is rated at 3,000 tons, & Jacob Bell had the honor of bldg this gigantic specimen of marine architecture. The **Baltic** is 285 feet long, her breadth of beam is 46 feet, & her tonnage 3,000.

THU MAR 7, 1850
Lawrence B Taylor was elected Mayor of Alexandria, Va, on Mar 5.

Mrd: on Feb 28, by Rev Stephen Gassaway, Mr Uriah Wise to Miss Sarah Jane Doswell, of Fairfax Co, Va.

Commission on Claims against Mexico: 1-Memorial of Robt J Clow, of Texas, filed on Jan 3 & then suspended, which claims for the destruction of his goods at several mercantile establishments in Texas by the Mexican invading army in 1836: rejected. 2-Memorial of John Baldwin, claiming for losses by the confiscation of the cargo of the schnr **Orient**, at Vera Cruz, in 1837: opinion that the claim is valid: amount to be awarded subject to the future action of the Board.

Senate: 1-Ptn of Pamelia Reswick, in behalf of herself & other heirs of Wm Wigton, asking compensation for his services as an ofcr in the last war with Great Britian: referred to the Cmte on Military Affairs. 2-Ordered, that the ptn of Nathl Lewis, on the files of the Senate, be referred to the Cmte of Claims. 3-Ordered, that the ptn of the heirs of Gustavus Horner, on the files of the Senate, be referred to the Cmte on Revolutionary Claims. 4-Ordered, that the ptn of Miss M Alexander, only heir to Geo Madison, on the files of the Senate, be referred to the Cmte on Military Affairs. 5-Cmte on Public Lands: memorial & documents relating to the claim of Anthony Rankin: passed to a second reading.

Public sale of valuable improved property in Wash City: by deed of trust, dated May 15, 1831, recorded in Liber W B 37, pages 27 thru 32, of the land records of Wash Co: sale on Apr 8, all the lot numbered 4, of the subdivision of lots 1 & 2, is erected a 3 story brick dwlg, together with all the rights & privileges thereto belonging.
-C H Wiltberger, trustee -Green & Tastet, aucts

Mrd: on Feb 26, in Fredericksburg, Va, by Rev E C Maguire, Joshua T Taylor, of Wash, to Maria Louise Long, eldest daughter of Mr Anthony Kale, of the former place.

House of Reps: 1-Ptn of Child Farr & Co, merchants of St Louis, praying Congress for remission of duties paid on goods destroyed by fire on board of the steamer **Marshall Ney** at New Orleans. 2-Cmte of Naval Affairs: bill for the relief of Thos Dennis: passed. 3-Leave was granted to withdraw from the files of the House the ptn & papers of John Kendrick. 4-Cmte on Foreign Affairs: bill for the relief of Thos Ryder, a British subject: committed. Same cmte: adverse report on the ptn of Henry La Reintree: laid on the table. 5-Cmte on Revolutionary Pensions: adverse reports on the ptns of the heirs of Peter & Winifred Ashby; Mgt Williams; the heirs of Jas Broadus; Rosa Clarke; Roseman Porter, widow of John Brady; & Sarah Knight: laid on the table. Same cmte: bill for the relief of Eleanor Davidson, widow of Henry Davidson: committed. Same cmte: adverse report on the ptn of Catharine Michael: laid on the table. 6-Cmte on Revolutionary Pensions: discharged from the further consideration of the ptn of Caleb Dustin, praying for the redemption of Continental scrip: laid on the table. Same cmte: bill granting a pension to Sarah A Bush, & a bill for the relief of the heirs of Lt Col Henry Miller, deceased: committed. Same cmte: bill granting a pension to Mary Pike, widow of Ezra Pike: committed.

Interesting ceremony took place at the Pres' Mansion yesterday-the presentation of the Gold Medal voted by the Legislature of N Y some time since to Col W W S Bliss, of the Army, as a testimony of its respect for his distinguished service. The medal was presented Col Claxton, Aid-de-camp of Govn'r Fish, on behalf of the State of N Y.

FRI MAR 8, 1850
Register's Ofc Wash: Feb 26, 1850: list of persons who have taken out licenses under the laws of the Corp during the months of Nov & Dec, 1849 & 1850:

Animal: Hoyt, Otis-2, [1 week]; & Price, Saml

Auction:
Boteler, Chas W
Green & Tastet

Billard table:
Harrison, Jos
Morse, Jno E

Cart:
Buete, Henry
Barnett, Geo
Evans, Geo
Fisher, A
Goherns, J T
Jackson & Smith
Kimball, Alex
Lane, Jos
Milburn, Thos M

Morgan, Thos P
Newton, Benj
Pumphrey, John-2
Ritter, Wm
Smith, Reuben
Stansbury, J
Ward, W H
Wise, Uriah-2

Chinese Lady: Tweedy & Riley-[1 week]

Commission: Green & Tastet; Murray & Co Stan; Shanks & Wall

Concert: Nightingale Sere'rs-3; Wash'n Euterpeans-2

Dog:

Ayler & Thyson-3
Atkins, D-3
Abbot, Jos
Adams, Wash
Bowman, S B
Brown, Saml
Bogan, B S
Black, Jane
Bowie, A
Brady, P
Bock, M
Benter, W F
Byrne, C R
Bowie, Jas
Brooks, T J
Barcroft, Maria
Berkley, J W
Browning, P W
Bestor, C
Bradley, Chas
Butler, A
Brooks, Basil
Brown, A
Bower, John
Barr, H A
Bell, Eliza
Beachlin, Jno
Bully, A F
Briel, C
Beckett, W
Evans, Henry
Evans, F S
Earl, Robt
Ennis, Philip
Edelin, Jas-2
Eichorn, G
Eaton, J H
Emmert, H
Ehlen, J F
Ford, J N
Ford, Jas
Ford, Wm
Follansbee, Jos

Fairfax, Wilson-2
Fitton, W
Fearson, J C
Frees, J
Forrest, S
Farquhar, A M
Fletcher, John
Fink, J
Fox, Grace
Fraser, Jas
Fester, John
Ferguson, Wm
Goolsach, J C
Green, M
Griffith, W A
Gray, Thos K
Griffith, W T
Goddard, Thos
Grimes, M H
Grupe, Wm
Greason, W
Glick, J H
Gardner, J B
Garner, G W
Gautier, C-2
Grimes, J F
Hickman, A
Hanley, Jane
Honsthamp, H
Herrity, J
Heitmuller, A-2
Hiss, Paul-2
Hitz, J
Hamersley, E
Hobbie, S R
Herold, a G
Hess, Jacob
Howard, John-2
Howle, P G
Horning, G D
Hollidge, J
Harris, Warner
Jacob, G

103

Johnson, Richmond-2
Jones, Alfred-3
Jackson & Bro, B L
Jones, Jas
Jameson, J M
Johnson, Richd
Jesup, Thos S
Jackson, Susan
Knight, C
Kirby, Saml
Kepler, H
Krober, W
Killian, Laneheart
Krafft, J M-2
Kingman, E
Killian, John
Kuhl, H
Keyworth, Robt
Liomin, E
Lawson, Thos
Little, Peter
Landrick, Ann
Landrick, J
Lewis, J E
Lindsly, H
Ledever, C
Lord, jr, F B
Law, Jno Geo-2
Latham & Co, R W
Lambell, K H
Lavender, J
Lee, Michl
Magruder, R
Mustin, M
Mahar, J
Mason, Jos
McIntire, Alex
Mure, L
Mechlin, J P
Middleton, C H
Marks, S A H
Mankin, J
Meehan, C W H
McDonald, Wm J-2
Mount, J
Moore, J H

McClery, E J
Miller, Isaac S
Murray & Semmes
McNorton, Geo
Munch, C H
Murphy, Jno
Miller, Jos
McQuay, B
Miller, Chs-2
McPherson, J
Mullen, Basil
Mason, E
Newton, B
Nokes, Jas-2
Nugent, E E
Noble, Martha-2
Owens, B
O'Neale, H G
Otterback, Philip-2
Peterson, Jas
Page, W H
Parke, W
Pulizzi, V
Pleasants, S
Page, Y P
Peel, Rezin
Plant, N
Pettibone, N
Peterson, W
Poston, F B
Peck, Jos-2
Pursell, Thos
Ricker, L
Rice, E V
Rupp, W
Redfern
Roth, A
Rutter, A A
Rhodes, Jas
Roberts, J M-2
Ray, Alex
Riordan, J
Seldner & Co, L
Shields, Thos
Stutz, Geo
Saur, Lewis

Simms, A
Simms, Ann
Schwitzer, Adam-2
Sweeny, H B
Steiger, W T
Sanderson, Thos
Shaw, Alex
Seifferle, J
Slight, J
Sengstack, C P
Saunders, H
Scott, S
Sioussa, J
Sioussa, F
Shorter, Basil
Smith, Jno C
Semmes, J M
Sewall, Richd
Sutton, Robt
Spignall, W B
Smith, Wm
Shreve, Saml
Smith, J C
Sprigg, Thos
Shedd, J J
Tastett, N

Tanner, Lethe
Turpin, Thos
Todschnider, T
Tench, T P
Thomas, Chas-2
Taylor, Robt
Towling, E
Taggart, Jane L
Tarlton, L A
Tinney, Pompey
Twine, D
Visser, J
Winter, W H
Williams, Thos J
Watterston, Geo
Wilson, J M
Weber, Jos
Whitlock, W D
Walker, D
Wadsworth, A
Warner, Henry
Wheeler, E
Wheat, W
Weber, C
Watson, A J
Wagner, W

Dray: Wise, Uriah-2

Hack:
Anderson, Wm
Burrill, Jno
Bush, Thos
Braxton, Mary-2
Boyle, Christopher
Beasley, Jos-3
Bush, Jas
Butler, Jas
Bell, Alfred
Brown, Jas A
Boteler, P
Beckett, Wm
Beckett, Lemuel
Busha, Wm
Beasley, Jos
Begnam, Wm

Bowen, J A
Buete, Henry
Earle, Robt-4
Fletcher, W A-2
Fisher, David
Flemming, Pat
Flemming, Jno-2
Foote, Andrew
Fisher, H
Golden, Singleton-2
Golding, Fred'k
Goatherd, Saml
Gray, John
Grimes, C W
Golding, Singleton-2
Golding, Fred'k

Goatherd, Saml
Gray, John
Grimes, C W
Haggerty, Danl
Harris, Warner
Hartshorn, Geo
Hickerson, W
Hurley, John
Horner, Wm
Hobbs, Wm
Jeffers, Wm J
Jamieson, Elias
Jasper, Wm
Jameson, E
Kiger, A
King, Isaiah
Kitcher, Jas-3
Kendrick, Ann L
Kinsley, Henry
Kendrick, G H-2
Lewis, John
Looby, Terrence-2
Lee, Wm
McNamara, John
Mullen, John H
Mullen, Basil-2
Magee, R F
Martin, Hamilton
Mason, Henry
Mercer, Jas
Nailor, Wm-2

Page, L S-2
Powell, Abm
Pywell, R R
Powell, A
Ross, Danl
Smallwood, Dennis-3
Smith, Richd
Smithson, J H
Sheets, John-3
Sutton, Robt
Shorter, C W
Shannon, John
Smith, Wm
Sutton, Robt
Smith, Thos-5
Turner, H-2
Twine, D
Turner, Thos
Turner, Henry
Valentine, Wm
Von Essen, Peter
West, John
Wright, J H
Walker & Kimmell
Williams, Sol
Welsh, Thos
Wormley, Andrew
Wormley, J
Welsh, Thos
Yates, W H
Young, J M

Hats, Caps, etc

Brown, Jas
Barry, sen, Fras
Brown, T B
Bayne, Thos
Bergman, S M
Egan & Son, Wm
Emerick, P
Harvey & Co, J S
Hoover & Son, A
Hall, Raymond B
Harris, J C
Hall, E W
Johnson & Co, T W

Killian, John
King, Z M P
Mattingly, F
Magruder, T J
Marshall-3
McLean, R T
Mann, Chs
Mills, John
McDevitt, John
Maguire, John
O'Donoghue, J P
Perkins & Dyer
Randall, G A W

Ruff, John A
Rosenstock, Jos
Rosenstock, M
Rosenstock, S
Staffan, Geo
Seldner & Co, L-2
Stevens, M H
Sinsheimer & Co, L-3
Shanks & Wall-2

Sengstack & Clark
Todd, Wm B
Willson, John J
Wilson, Wm
Westcott, Jas
Wheatley, Wm J
Williams, Zadock
Young & Orem

Hawk'g & Peddl'g: Herst & Sons, H B

Huckster:
Barton, R C
Bohrer, Geo
Burns, P W
Borrows & Burns
Brown, Reuben
Brown, Chas
Bradley, J T
Bayliss & Skidmore
Eichorn, G
Eichorn, R
Fearson, J C
Fowler, W R
Frank, Jacob
Gordon, D S
Goldin, R R
Hughes, Elisha
Hill, Jno S
Hughes, Thos
Hough, W H
Haynes, W
Hawkins, P
Johnson, Jas
Jones, Alfred
Jones, Noah
Johnson, W C
Lauck, R M
Lacy, E
Lewis & Elisha
Lavender, J
Lowe, M
Maddox, A

MacDaniel, E S
McQuay, B
Murray, Wm A
Moore & Adamson
Nicholson, John
Oyster, G M
Pence, Richd
Palmer, John
Peddicord, J
Paine, Chas
Richardson, C T A
Sanders, Alex
Stunt, w H
Sheid, E T
Sis, John
Studds, Henry
Spignall, W B
Shreve, John
Shreve, Saml
Sis, John
Triplett, T J
Thompson, Wm
Visser, J & J
Wallace, Ellen
Ward & Hughes
Williams, Harrison
Wallingsford, W
Wallace, J E
Young, J W
Yeatman, Thos J
Yeatman, Jno H

Ins Agency: Lewis, J C

Livery-stable:
Boteler, P
Brown, John
Earl, Robt
Nailor, T
Pumphrey, Dennis
Pumphrey, L
Merchandise:
Addison & Cockrell-2
Adam, Wm
Aigler, Jacob
Aimey, Fred'k
Allen, G F
Aiglet, Christop'r
Bates, John E
Berry, W O
Barber, Jos & C
Brown, T B
Broadbeck, Jacob
Bayly, Wm F
Brenner, P
Barnes & Mitchell
Borremans, Chas
Brower, Geo
Boone, John B
Bradley & Son, H
Baden & Bro, J W
Bright, R
Burns, G
Briscoe & Clarke
Brereton, John
Bishop, D J
Bean, Geo
Bastianelli & Co, T
Browning, P W
Boteler, C W
Bird, Wm
Beven, Thos
Berry, jr, E D-transfer
Bartlett, Isaac C
Butt, Saml
Ellis, Hannah
Eberling, Henry
Egan & Son, Wm
Edmonston, Elijah
Eliot, Wallace

Shreve, J H
Smithia & Birch
Smith, Thos
Walker & Kimmell
Williams, J A

Eddy, Stephen
Fugitt, Jos
Flenner, Wm
Fischer, Wm
Funk, Nicholas
Feeney, Wm
Fowler, C S
Fitnam & Son, Th
Farnham, Robt
Fowler, Saml
Franklin, Stephen
Ford, Thos G
Fanning, W H
Futnam & Co, L
Greer, Henry
Galt & Bro, M W
Gray, A
Grupe, Wm
Guttenshu, John
Guiton, Ophelia
Gilman, Z D & W H
Garretson, Nimrod
Gautier, C
Green, Owen
Gardner, J B
Gibbs, J H-2
Grinder, H
Garner, Cath W
Grunebaum, M
Grimes, P H
Galligan & Son, J
Griffin, T B
Hazard, Robt R
Hatch, jr, & Co, A
Hammack, J C
Huggins, Jos
Hyde, T A
Hammond, Nathan

Harper & Co, W
Henning, Stephen
Huggins, Fras B
Hall & Dunn
Harvey & Co, J S
Hall & Bro
Hyatt & Frazier
Harbaugh, V
Hall, John
Hitz, John
Hill, Isaac
Howard, Jos
Haislep, H
Hall, Raymond B
Hamersley, Edw
Harvey & Lloyd
Horning, John
Holmead, J B
Hines, C & M
Hooe & Co, P H
Heydon, C W
Handley, Jas
Hall, J B
Harrover, Wm H
Hamilton, M A
Huginin, A C
Jones, Jas H
Jolly, John
Jillard & Son, J
Johnson & Co, T W
Jackson & Smith
Knott, G A
Kibbey, W B
Keyworth, Robt
Keys & Co, C M
Krafft, Jno
Lawrence, Jas
Letmate, C
Lenman & Bro
Lundy, E K
Lindsley, E
Lusby & Davall
Lane & Tucker
Lewis, Saml
Liphard, Jno H
McPherson, jr, H H

McCutchen, Jas
Miller, R E
Morrison, Grace
Moore, Jos B
Murtagh, Mary E
Magle, Jacob
Mitchell, Henry C
McCarthy, Winifred
Magruder, F
McLean, R T
Masi & Co, F
Mothershead, John
McClery, E J
Mortimer, J T
Miller, John
Masi, S
Maxwell & Sears
McGregor, N M
Morrison, Wm M
Miller, Jas
Martin & Co, John
Mitchell, Wm
McDevitt, John
Moore, Douglass
Martin, A W
McKean, Jas P
Morris, Geo
Morley, H L
Nairn, J W
Norbeck, Geo
Noyes, Wm
Nailor, D
Noell, Wm
Naylor, F Y
Nottingham, Wm
O'Dell, T T
Owen & Son, E
Powell, J E
Perry & Bro
Pearson, P M
Parke, W P
Perkins & Dyer
Preston & Co, O J
Pursell, Thos
Parker, M T
Phillips, J B

Pettibone, John
Parker, S
Purdy, John
Patterson, R S
Pulvermaker, Frs
O'Donnell, John
Riley, W R
Reed, Andrew
Rollins, Wash
Rigdon, E
Ridgely & Co
Robinson, J
Riley, Wm R
Ritter, W H
Steer, P J
Stone, Woodford
Stott & Co, Chs
Stevens, M H
Sellhausen, F W
Skriving, Jas
Stevens & Peaco
Shadd, B
Stewart, Geo W
Schwartz, jr, A J
Shuster & Co, W M
Stewart, W M
Shillington, J
Shanks & Wall
Savage, Geo
Savage & Co, J L
Stott & Co, S
Seifferle, J
Shaffer & Son, J
Stoops, Richd
Thompson & Broadbent
Tucker & Co, F A
Tyson, S E

Taylor & Maury
Travers & Son, J
Thompson, Henry
Tate, J B & A
Taylor, Franck
Thorn, Henry
Visser, J
Vansant, R
Visser, J & J
Venable, Wm S
Van Reswick, J
Westerfield, Jas
Warriner, Chaun'y
Walsh, Francis S
Waters, Elkanah
Wheeler & Co, W A
Ward. K B
Woodward, C
Warder, Wm
Westcott, Jas
Wall, Columbus O
Watson, Benj T
White & Bro
Waters, Gustavus
Williams, Zadock
Wheeler, E
Wilner, Geo
Welchmann, J C
Wilson, John
Wall & Donn
Whittlesey, O
Winter, Wm H
Wilkins, John L
Wonderlick, John
Wannall, Chas P
Yerby & Bro

Non-res Merch't: Pouder, W P

Retail:
Adams, Wash'n
Ailer & Thyson
Adams, John G
Adams, Alex'r
Armistead, Saml

Aylmer, R R
Brown, W T & R T
Boscoe, Arthur
Bower, John
Brereton, Wm H
Bacon & Co, Saml

Bevan, Thos
Brasnahan, Cor
Brashears, W B
Buthmann, J H
Boyd, Robt
Barr, J R
Bayliss, Collin
Bean, Geo
Bell, John
Ellis, Henry
Evans, J D
Foller, D
Fugett, F J
Frailer & Son, Ch
Frank, Jacob
Freeman, John
Fletcher, John
Guzenback, Dor
Goddard, Isaac
Green, Jas
Grimes, P H
Greenfield, H C
Harvey & Co, J S
Hitz, F
Haggerty, Danl
Huscamp, H
Hercus, Geo
Haggerty, Wm
Henning, Jas
Harper, W C
Hall, Edw
Handy, S W
Holmead, Anthony
Hughes, Wm
Hillyard, O
Hines, David
Hodge, Mary
Howell, jr, W P
Hinge, Lewis
Jackson, Susan
Joyce, John J
Jeffers, Wm J
Joyce, Michl
Jones, Raphael
Jackson & Bro, B L
Johnson, J H

Knott, J H
Kelly, John
Keobel, Jacob
King, V E
King, Z M P
Kane, Patrick
Kibby & Co, J B
Killmon, J T
King, Martin
Leddy, Owen
Lepreux, L & A
Leddy, Hugh
Lockney, Hugh
Lord, Wm
Lord, jr, F B
Laub, Eliz A
McGarvey, John
Myers, Benj
Magee, Patrick-2
Murray, Owen
Marceron, John L
Murray, Mary
Morsell & Wilson
Magee, Owen
McPherson, W S
McChesny & Co, J H
Milstead, Thos
Mills, Robt T
Murray & Semmes
McGanley, Patrick
McBlair, J H
McNeal, Mark
Mackey, Philip
Middleton & Beall
O'Hare, C S
Ober, S J
Orme, Wm
O'Leary, John
Parsons, Mary L
Pilling, jr, Jas
Peerce, J M
Pegg, Wm
Peters, J A
Parker & Co, G & T
Pumphrey, S
Powell, J E

Perry & Bro
Pearson, P M
Parke, W P
Perkins & Dyer
Preston & Co, O J
Pursell, Thos
Parker, M T
Phillips, J B
Pettibone, John
Parker, S
Purdy, John
Patterson, R S
Pulvermaker, Frs
Reed, B M
Randall, G A W
Redstrate, W J
Roberts, John
Roemmly, Jno C
Ryon, J T
Rice, Edmund V
Rigdon, E
Ryon, Richd J
Storm, Leonard
Shekells, jr, Thos
Semmes & Bro, B I
Simms, Ann
Simms, Elexius

Stoops, Richd
Simms & Son
Smith Stewart
Stewart, Wm E
Sothern, W B
Shadd, C
Sengstack & Clark
Semmes, T F
Semmes & Co, J H
Simmes, J M
Taylor, J H
Trimble, Matthew
Thornley, Thos
Tench, T P
Tench, Ann
Travers, E
Talbot, Wm
Thompson, Robt
Usher, J
Upperman, Wm H
Wroe, Saml
Wilson, Alfred
Welsh, Cath
Wimsatt, Richd
Webb, A J
Wheatley, Geo
Wilson, Patrick

Shop:
Bulley, Alex F
Brown, Jno
Buete, Henry
Boclanger, J
Bekert, Jos
Buckly, Timothy
Buete, Henry-transfer
Barnes, Danl-transfer
Ehrmanntrant, Jos
Fisher, Geo A
Fitzgerald, D
Fitch, H S
Greason, Wm
Hoffman, Henry-2
Heisler, John
Houn, Jas G
Harrison, Jos

Kuhl, Henry
Lehmah, Anton
Looby, Terrence
McGrann, Jas
Noble, John
Parker, Nathl
Quigley, Wm
Ruppell, G
Ready, John
Rollins, Joshua
Ritter, H G
Riley, John
Swearing, Fred'k
Stutz, Fred'k
Shadd, John
Totchnider, J E F
Thomas, Jos

Varden, Edmund
Williams, Fred H
Williams, Z

West, John D
Young, jr, E

Slave:
Eversfield, E
Eversfield, E
Early, L H
Fish, Nancy
Gunnell, Jas S for
R M Scott
Holliday, J E S

Harding, H
Mattingly, F
Middleton, C S-2
Nelson, E-2
Noland, C
Thompson, C F

Slut:
Dyvernois, G E
Shaw, Richd

Stage:
Bohrer, B
Brown, John-2
Fowler, Sol
Fitnam, jr, T-2
Ford, Wm
Nailor, Thompson-4

Rythers, E A-2
Stages:
Brown, John-2
Sebastine, C
Turner, Henry
Williams, Jos

Store:
Bradley, Mary
Braddock, John
Biscoe, G W-2

Tavern:
Brown, T P & M
Baker, Thos
Brady, Michl
Butler, Abm
Benter, Wm T
Benter, Wm
Finkman, Conrad
Foy, John
Fitzgerald, Jas
Fuller, E H
Gross, Andrew
Golden, Jno A
Harrington, R H
Howard, Geo T
Hendley, J R

Howison, W G
Hancock, Andrew
Jones, Peter
Jost, B
Klomann, Chas
King, P H
Maher, Jas
Mil, Andrew
Riley, John
Rupp, Wm
Ridgway, H
Stutz, Geo
Sweeting, Ellen
Shadd, B
St Clair, Geo

Talty, Michl
Topham, Geo
Thomas, J
Wingenroth, Fred

West, John
Willard, H A
Ward, Francis

Ten-pin alley:
Farrar, Jno M-5
Jost, Benedict-2

Topham, Geo-3

Theatrical:
Adelphi Theatre-11

Wagon:
Beachlin, Jno
Bradley & Son, H
Green, G
McGarvey, John

Pywell, R R
Ramsburg & Ebert
Shadd, A W
Stewart, Chs H

Senate: 1-Senate called to order; devotional exercises performed by the Chaplain, Rev C M Butler.

The following is a list of the persons fined during the months of Nov & Dec, 1849, & Jan, 1850. [Names & for what license fined.]
Boltzer, Mary Ann: liquors
Bute, Henry: liquors on Sunday
Ball, John: merchandise
Bergman, Wm: hack
Benter, Wm T: liquors on Sunday
Brashears, T N: merchandise
Berry, Jas W: merchandise
Bicknell & Co, Jas: exhibition without license
Bayne, Wm: exhibition painting
Bower, Jas: merchandise
Bower, Jas: liquor
Brown, Jas: liquor
Casparis, Jas: liquor without license
Davis, W W: keeping coal-yard without license
Davis, Jas: selling liquors on Sunday
Duffy, Michl: liquors
DeNeale K: hack
Eddy, Saml: merchandise
Fowler, Saml: merchandise
Fillens, Thos: liquor less than a pint
Hall, E W: merchandise
Hoover, Saml: shoes
Howell, Thos: omnibus

Howell, Wm P: merchandise
Hows, Jas: hack
Hartshorn, G W: hack
Hendley, J R: liquor after 12 o'clock
Jost, Benedict: tenpin alley-3
Jennings & Co: merchandise
Knowman, G C: liquors after 12 o'clock
Lehman, A: liquors
Lindsly, Harvey: dog
Lee, Wm: hack
Malone, L: liquor
Mason, Henry: hack
Moore, D: merchandise
Moran, P: hack
Maguire, John: merchandise
Mitchell, Wm: merchandise
Mackey, Philip: merchandise
McNeill, M: liquors
Murphy, Cornelius: selling without license
Murphy, Cornelius: liquor on Sunday
Murphy, Cornelius: selling without license
Mercer, Jas: hack
Rowland, Danl: dealing in exchanges
Ruppell, G: keeping bar open at night
Robinson, John: merchandise
Simms, Sampson: groceries
Selden, F: liquors
Stultz, Geo: selling liquors after 12 o'clock
Smith, Geo: dog
Tweedy, J H: public exhibition
Taverring, A L: merchandise
Todshinder, Fred: selling liquor without license
Van Reswick, Wm: dog
Wright, Jos: liquor
Wren, G W: liquor
Wilson, Patrick: fire-crackers
Wilson, Patrick: liquor
Wormly, Jas: hack
Wilson, Patrick: selling liquor by the mall
West, John: keeping bar open on Sunday
Wheatley, Geo: liquor
Yeates, Wm H: hack
Young, Ezekiel: liquor without license
Young, Ezekiel: liquor & open bar at night
-Wm J McCormick, Register

Appointments by the Pres: 1-Danl McCallum, of Tenn, to be U S Marshal for the eastern district of Tenn. 2-Wm M Brown, of Tenn, to be U S Marshal for the middle district of Tenn. 3-Andrew Guthrie, of Tenn, to be U S Marshal for the western district of Tenn. 4-Benj Bond, of Ill, to be U S Marshal for the district of Ill. 5-Z Collins Lee, of Md, to be U S Atty for the district of Md.

Died: on Feb 16, at Camden, Ark, in his 71st year, Rev Porter Clay, the last surviving full brother of Hon H Clay. Also, like his distinguished brother, he lived to witness the departure for a better world of many of his descendants. One of these, a most lovely & interesting grand-daughter, in the prime of life, preceded him only a few months.

Died: on Feb 14, in Phil, Chandler P McCorkle, formerly of Wash City.

SAT MAR 9, 1850
Bath fixtures, water closets, & plumbing: south side of Pa ave, near 3rd st. All work entrusted to the subscriber warranted to give satisfaction. –F Y Naylor

Senate: 1-Legislature of N Y requesting the Senators & Reps of that State in inquire whether the act of Feb 26, 1845, to extend a patent heretofore granted to Wm Woodworth, was not procured through misrepresentation & misunderstanding: &, if so, to use their efforts to procure its immediate repeal; which, without reading, was referred to the Cmte on Patents & the Patent Ofc. 2-Memorial of Wm Seely, asking to be remunerated for the sacrifices & losses of his father in the Revolutionay war, & for the services of his 2 sons in the last war with Great Britain: referred to the Cmte of Claims. 3-Memorial from Abraham L Knickerbocker, asking compensation for an injury caused by the explosion of the laboratory of the U S Arsenal at Watervliet whilst employed therein: referred to the Cmte on Pensions. 4-Ptn of Hannibal Faulk, asking the confirmation of his title to a tract of land within the limits of the Bastrop grant, in Louisiana: referred to the Cmte on Private Land Claims. 5-Memorial of Ambrose T Hatch, asking compensation for his services as a quartermaster & interpreter in the Indian Sioux war in 1832: referred to the Cmte on Military Affairs. 6-Memorial from Meigs D Benjamin, merchant in N Y C, asking the payment of certain import duties illegally exacted of him: referred to the Cmte on Finance. 7-Memorial of Thos Blanchard, inventor & patentee of a certain machine for turning irregular forms, asking an appropriation for the purchase of his patent oar machine for the use of the Navy: referred to the Cmte on Naval Affairs. 8-Memorial of Geo Copway, a chief of the Chippewa Indians, proposing a plan of organization for a new Indian territory east of the Missouri river: referred to the Cmte on Indian Affairs. 9-Memorial of Catharine B Turner, widow & admx of Danl Turner, late a capt in the U S Navy, asking the reimbursement of expenses incurred by her husband, in receiving & entertaining on board of the vessels under his command certain public functionaries of the U S in foreign countries, while on foreign stations, from the year 1841 to 1844: referred to the Cmte on Foreign Relations. 10-Ordered, that leave be granted to withdraw from the files of the Senate the ptn & papers of R K Meade. 11-Cmte on Revolutionary Claims: in the case of the rep of Henry King: passed to a second reading. 12-Resolved, that the Sec of War cause the report & maps of the exploration in the Territory of Minnesota, by Brevet Capt John Pope, be laid before the Senate. 13-Resolved, that the ptn & papers of Gen John McNeil, deceased, be taken from the files of the Senate & referred to the Cmte on Pensions; & said cmte inquire into the expediency of granting to his widow or legal reps the arrears of pension prayed for in said ptn; & also to inquire into the expediency of granting his said widow a pension. 14-Referred to the Cmte of Claims: bill for the relief of Wm B Crews; relief of Chas Ahrenfeldt & John F H Voght; & relief of Gideon Walker. 15-Bills referred to the Cmte on Pensions: relief of: Lewis Hastings; Benj P Smith; Geo Cassady; Henry F Evans; Saml Dewey; & Wm Paddy. Also, granting a pension to Avery Downer. 16-Bills referred to the Cmte on Finance: relief of Ferguson & Milhado. Relief of E Pavenstedt & Schumacher. 17-Bill for the relief of Jesse Sutton: referred to the Cmte on Indian Affairs. 18-Bill for relief of Thos Dennis: referred to the Cmte on Naval Affairs. 19-Bill for relief of Richd H Barrett: referred to Cmte on Private Land Claims.

Geo J Bullock, the cashier of the Central Railroad & Banking Co at Savannah, Ga, has absconded, taking with him about $100,000 in notes of the bank. It is understood that he sailed from Savannah on Feb 28 in a British schnr **Abel**, Capt Hicks, bound to Rotterdam, touching at Truro, in Cornwall, Eng. He is the only passenger.

Postmaster Genl established the following new Post Ofcs for week ending Mar 2, 1850:

Ofc	County, State	Postmaster
So Oxford	Chenango, N Y	Ebenezer Park
Moss Haven	West Chester, N Y	Henry H Roberts
Elwood's Bridge	Delaware, N Y	Geo H Phelps
Sharon Springs	Schoharie, N Y	Kneeland Eldridge
Golden's Bridge	W Chester, N Y	Orin P Frost
Big Spring	Cumberland, Pa	Philip Brown
Beaver Springs	Union, Pa	Geo Miller
Scott	Wayne, Pa	Henry D Williams
Franklin Corers	Erie, Pa	Alex Russell
Duquesne	Alleghany, Pa	Wm McConnell
Hibernia	Butler, Pa	Jos Coulter
Redstone	Fayette, Pa	D J Smith
Liberty Square	Lancaster, Pa	Jos P Hutton
Old Forge	Luzerne, Pa	Ebenezer, Drake
Cresent	Lycoming, Pa	Henry D Heylman
Chesterville	Kent, Md	J E Roberts
Pylesville	Harford, Md	Nathan Pyle, jr
St Augustine	Cecil, Md	John Mears
Keezletown	Rockingham, Va	Geo M Hosler
Miller's Mill	Bath, Va	Josiah C Loury
Sago	Lewis, Va	Alfred Morgan
Claysville	Wood, Va	Chas Drake
Lenn's Creek	Kanawha, Va	H M Onderdock
Buffalo Ford	Randolph, N C	John Pope
Chinkepin	Duplin, N C	Jas Lamb
Lovelace	Wilkes, N C	Larkin J Bicknall

Catharine Lake	Onslow, N C	John A Avirett
Falling Creek	Wayne, N E	M Cox
Mineral Springs	Anderson D, S C	Wm Milwee
Bear Creek	Pickens, Ala	Z D Carroll
Polk	Monroe, Ala	H B McDonald
Dantom	Tishamingo, Miss	John Robinson
Woodlawn	Itawamba, Miss	Swopson Tayloy
Austin C H	Tunica, Miss	Absalom S Nail
Rocky Comfort	Sevier, Ark	Ruston V R Green
Lamartime	Giles, Ten	Neill L Smith
Woodland	Barren, Ky	Wilson Ritter
Stratford	Delaware, Ohio	Norman D Perry
Nebo	Jefferson, Ohio	Wm Allman
Beaver Dam	Allen, Ohio	F Shull
Evansburgh	Coshocton, Ohio	Thos Watkins
Ridge	Coshocton, Ohio	John Brillhart
Tyrone	Coshocton, Ohio	Jas L Smith
Williamsville	Delaware, Ohio	Henry Jarvis
Montra	Shelby, Ohio	Jonas Mahurin
Cedar Creek	Barry, Mich	Isaac La Grange
Ronald	Ionia, Mich	Freedom Gates
Handy	Livingston, Mich	John T Watson
Grubb's Mills	Putnam, Ind	C C Grubb
Green Bush	Grant, Ind	Wm Hays
Yellow Creek	Stephenson, Ill	Geo W Andrews
Peoriaville	Peoria, Ill	Madison L K Hues
Williamsburg	De Kalb, Ill	John F Snow
Adams	Adams, Ill	Henry Wells
Armington	Tazewell, Ill	Jerome B Tenny
Poplar Bluff	Butler, Mo	Jesse A Gilley
Splice Creek	Maneteau, Mo	Green Clay
New Castle	Gentry, Mo	Wm H Waters
Durango	Dubuque, Iowa	Presly Samuel
Deep River	Poweshick, Iowa	Robt Taylor
Smeltyer's Grove	Grant, Wis	Geo Wineman
Winnicounce	Winnebago, Wis	Jos Edwards
West Rosendale	Fond du Lac, Wis	Chas F Hammond
Richland City	Richland, Wis	Chas C C Berry
Reed's Landing	Wabashaw, Min T	Chas Reed

Names Changed:
Palmer, Hampden Co, Mass, changed to Thorndike.
Palmer Depot, Hampden Co, Mass, changed to Palmer.
Prospect Hill, Jefferson Co, Pa, changed to Reynoldsville.
Andrew's Bridge, Lancaster Co, Pa, changed to Octorato.
Cane Point, Troupe Co, Georgia, changed to O'Neal's Mills.

Oakmulgee, Telfair Co, Georgia, changed to McRae's Store.
Woodardsville, Marengo Co, Ala, changed to Clay Hill.
The Meadows, Bedford Co, Va, changed to Fancy Grove.
Clinch River, Russell Co, Va, changed to Nash's Ford.
Shelburne, Lee Co, Ill, changed to Binghamton.
Swan, Winnebago Co, Ill, changed to Elida.
Orange, Cook Co, Ill, changed to Trenton.
Kewance, Waukesha Co, Wisc, changed to South Gene_ee.
Eagle, Waukesha Co, Wisc, changed to Bullion.
Juan, Wash Co, Iowa, changed to Marcellus.

Trustee's sale: by decree of Circuit Court of Wash Co, D C, passed in a cause wherein Jacob Snider is cmplnt, & the heirs of the late John Vaughan are dfndnts. Public auction on Mar 23, of: lots 14, 16, & 17 in square 585. Lots 6, 11, & 16 in square 585. Lots 14 thru 18 in square 589. Lots 5, 7, 8, 9, 10, 11, & 16 in square 643. –D A Hall, trustee -Green & Tastet, aucts

House of Reps: 1-Bills passed last Fri from the Cmte of the Whole: relief of: Wm B Crews; Chas Ahrenfeldt & John F H Voght; Wm Paddy; Gideon Walker; Jesse Sutton; E Pavenstadt & F A Schumacher; Ferguson & Milhardo; Richd H Barrett; Capt Henry F Evans; Geo Cassady; Benj P Smith; & Lewis Hastings. Also, a pension to Avery Downer. 2-Bill for the relief of Saml Dewey, proposing that the pension therein provided for should commence in 1849 instead of 1840. 3-Bill for the relief of Joshua Follansbee & B F Isherwood: referred to the Cmte of the Whole. 4-Bill for the relief of John Glenn, administrator of Robt Barry, deceased: referred to the Cmte of Claims. 5-Bill for the relief of the legal reps of Thos Jett, deceased: recommended that it do not pass. 6-Ptn of Edw Tilghman & others, praying the improvement of Queenstown creek, Md. 7-Ptn of Susan Spalding, widow of Gen Spalding, a Revolutionary soldier, praying for a pension.

By writ of fieri facias: sale on Apr 6, of part of lot 29 sq 517 in Wash City, the property of Thos Welsh, to satisfy judgment due John Robinson. -A E L Keese, cnstbl.

Commission on Claims against Mexico: 1-Memorial of John A Robinson, American Consul at Guaymas, claiming for losses by seizure & detention of property at that place in 1843; as also that of the same, claiming for a forced loan, at Hermosillo in 1847; as also that of Wm S Messervey, claiming for losses consequent on his expulsion from Chihuahua in 1846, were submitted, examined, & suspended.

Mr Robt Mills, architect of Wash City, appointed by the Govn'r of Va architect & superintendent of the Washington Monument about to be erected at Richmond. Mr Crawford, the eminent sculptor, & author of the design of the Monument, is about to proceed in Italy to execute the statues for the work.

For rent: 2 story brick residence on G st, lately occupied by Dr Dubarry, U S Navy. Apply to L Vivans, or J P Keller. The key may be had of Mr Dorsett, adjoining, who will state the terms.

Mrd: on Mar 7, by Rev Mr Flannegan, Mr Jas Wm Coombs, of Gtwn, to Miss Mary Eliz Mickum, of Wash City.

Mrd: on Mar 7, by Rev Mr Hodges, Jos H O'Brien to Sarah J Amstiad, all of Wash.

MON MAR 11, 1850
Dreadful steamboat disaster: Montg, Ala, Mar 7, 1850. The steamer **St John's** was burnt to the water's edge on Tue last, near Bridgeport, Dallas Co. About 30 persons, including 7 or 8 ladies, perished in the flames or were drowned. Lt Rice, of the U S army, lost $250,000. Many other Californians, who had just returned home, lost their all.
[Mar 14th newspaper: the Montg Journal gives the subjoined list of the person lost, as far as ascertained: Lost: Mrs Hall & daughter, supposed to be of Augusta, Ga; Mrs Vaughan, Miss Vaughan, Mrs McCain, Mrs Haley, Mrs Wright; Messrs McCain, of S C; T B Carson & son, of Dallas Co; Judge Lindsay, of Mobile; Thos Stephens, [printer,] of Camden; Hugh Hughs, second mate; Peter, [steward;] Easter, [chambermaid;] second cook; & 8 negroes. Saved: all the crew, with the exception of the second mate. The clerk, Mr Meaher, made strenuous exertions to save Mrs Hall & her daughter, but the powerful current made it impossible. He was only saved by the efforts of his brother. The only article saved was a trunk of Col Preston's, secured by his servant. Col Price, U S agent from Calif, lost $250,000 belonging to the Gov't.] [Mar 20th newspaper: Among the bodies recently found are those of Mrs Haley, Dr Smith, of S C, & young Carson, of Dallas. This is a severe blow to the family of Carson, the mother having gone deranged at the double loss of husband & son in this fearful visitation.]

Naval: Cmder Josiah Tatnall ordered to take command of the steam frig **Saranac**, at Portsmouth, N H, with a commission as Post-Capt. Destination is understood to be the East Indies.

On Fri, Mr Karr, toll-gatherer on Mayor's bridge, Richmond, while attempting to rescue his little daughter, who had fallen from the bridge into the river, was carried beyond his depth by the current & both father & child were drowned.

John Downs, for more than 20 years gardener in D C, invites public attention. His nursery & garden are at N & 3rd sts, Greenleaf's Point.

Wanted immediately: a competent Nurse. Apply to Mrs W C Zantzinger, s e corner of E & 10th sts, opposite the Masonic Hall.

Died: on Mar 5, in Southampton Co, Va, Hon Geo B Cary. In 1841 he was Rep in the U S Congress from Petersburg District, & served for 2 years. .

Mrd: on Mar 5, at Alexandria, by Rev C B Dana, Dennis R Blacklock to Sarah Ann, eldest daughter of late Thos Swann.

Trustee's sale of valuable lot: by deed of trust, from E H Roper, recorded in Liber W B 83, folio 1: public auction on Apr 15, of lot 9 in square 31, fronting on K st, between 11th & 12th sts. By order of the trustee. -Dyer & Brother, aucts

City Ordinances-Wash. 1-Act for the relief of Jas Johnson: fine imposed for firing a gun in violation of an ordinance, is remitted, provided Johnson pay the costs or prosecution. 2-Act for the relief of Wm Cammack, jr: sum of $10 to be refunded to Cammack, the amount of a fine paid by him, as per certificate of the register of Feb 8, 1850. 3-Act for the relief of Jane A Taylor: fine imposed for a violation of an ordinance relative to license law, be remitted; provided, Taylor pay the costs or prosecution. 4-Act for the relief of Jos Swaggard & Thos Lewis: refund Swaggard $5.58; Lewis $10: fines remitted by the Councils of Wash City.

Country seat for sale: my dwlg house & 80 acres of land in Fairfax Co, Va, adjoins the plantation of Com Thos Ap Catesby Jones, of which it formerly formed a part. The premises will be sold for $3,000 in cash, or $3,200 on a credit of not more than 5 years. Inquire of N Loomis, jr, on the premises, Mark Ap Catesby Jones, Sharon, or of the subscriber, Sec's ofc, Albany, N Y. -S S Randall, Secretary's ofc, Albany, N Y

Trustee's sale: by deed of trust: public auction on Mar 14, of parts of lots 6 & 7 in square 370, with a good 2 story frame house. –Geo Barber, trustee -Dyer & Brother, aucts

Household & kitchen furniture at auction: on Mar 14, by deed of trust from T M McIlhaney, executed to the subscriber on Aug 6, 1849: all the furniture in the 2 houses of the Exchange Hotel. –S S Williams, trustee -Green & Tastet, aucts

TUE MAR 12, 1850
New Music: Mrs Garret Anderson: Music & Fancy Store, Pa ave, 2 doors east of the Irving Hotel

For rent: large 3 story brick house ccupied at present by Robt Mills, on C st, between 4½ & 3rd sts. Inquire of J P Pepper, agent, adjoining the premises.

Orphans Court of Wash Co, D C. Letters of administration on the personal estate of Basil Sims, late of Wash Co, deceased. -John T Costin, exc.

From the Sandwich Islands: "The Polynesian" of Dec 15. On Dec 10, the King gave a special audience to Cmdor Voorhees, Cmder-in-Chief of the Naval Forces of the U S in the China & East India Seas. He was presented to the King by the Minister of Foreign Relations. He then presented the following ofcrs: Maj C A Ogden, U S Engineers; Cmder T M Goldsborough, U S Navy; Cmder G J Van Brunt, S R Addison, Surgeon; Cmder S K Knox; D B Phillips, Assist Surgeon; F B McNeill, 1s Lt Marines; U E Boudinot, Master; D L Braine, Midshipman; D Ochiltree, Acting Master; Cameron Anderson, Purser; D C Wirt, Sec to the Cmdor.

Senate: 1-Memorial of T P McBlair, a purser in the navy, asking to be allowed a credit in the settlement of his accounts for payment to certain warrant ofcrs holding appointments in the navy: referred to the Cmte on Naval Affairs. 2-Ptn of the heirs of Mary Jimeson, a Seneca Indian, asking the payment, with interest, of a sum of money deposited for the purpose of investment with a U S sub-agent: referred to the Cmte on Indian Affairs. 3-Cmte on Indian Affairs: bill for the relief of Jesse Sutton, reported without amendment. 4-Cmte on Private Land Claims: bill for the relief of Richd H Barrett, reported back without amendment, & recommended its passage. 5-Cmte on Public Lands: memorial of Dr Hartwell Carver, asking the confirmation of his title to a tract of land around the Falls of St Anthony, on the Mississippi river, purchased by his grandfather before the Revolutionary war, asked to be discharged from the further consideration of the ptn: ordered to lie on the table. 6-Memorial of Simeon Greenleaf, asking an extension of his copy right: referred to the Cmte on the Judiciary. 7-Ptn of Jacob Hickman, asking the confirmation of title to certain lands lying in the Bastrop grant, in Louisiana: referred to the Cmte on Private Land Claims. 8-Ptn of Willis Stephens, asking the confirmation of his claim to an Indian reservation: referred to the Cmte on Private Land Claims. 9-Ptn of Wm Ferguson, a pensioner of the U S, asking to be allowed a back pension: referred to the Cmte on Pensions. 10-Ptn from the heirs of Jonathan Patch, a Revolutionary soldier, asking to be allowed a pension to which their father was entitled: referred to the Cmte on Revolutionary Claims. 11-Ptn fom O Horward Wilson & others, asking a reduction of the rates of postage: referred to the Cmte on the Post Ofc & Post Roads. 12-Memorial of Leslie Combs, asking the payment of a debt due him by the late Republic of Texas, for which the public faith & revenues of that republic were pledged, which, together with his papers on the files, was referred to the Cmte on the Judiciary. 13-Memorial of Geo C Goss, asking that a burial ground may be purchased in the vicinity of the city of Mexico, which was used for the interment of American citizens during the occupation of that city by the U S army: referred to the Cmte on Military Affairs.

Mr Edwin Bell, so long editor of Hagerstown Torchlight, has permanently settled in Calif. His mother, Mrs Susan Bell, has associated with Mr Otis W Marsh, who will hereafter edit the paper, & conduct its business.

Mrd: on Mar 6, at *Hopeton*, residence of J C Lewis, by Rev S D Finckel, Sam'l H Platt, of N Y, to Miss Julia R Lewis, of Ohio.

Died: on Mar 7, in Detroit, Mich, very suddenly, of congestion of the brain, Mrs Martha R Joy, age 31 years, wife of J F Joy, & daughter of Rev John Reed, of Mass.

Rev J M P Atkinson, of Fredericktown, Md, will be installed as pastor of Bridge St Church, Gtwn, Mar 12th, by Presbytery of Balt.

The partnership existing between the subscribers, in the lumber business, is this day dissolved by mutual consent, John Pickrell having sold his entire interest therein to Jos Libbey. –Jos Libbey, John Pickrell

Military academy: following young men have been appointed Cadets by the Pres of U S, for this year, from the list at large:
Wm Croghan Jesup, son of Maj Gen Jesup, of the Army.
Wm C Nicholson, son of late Cmdor Jos J Nicholson, Navy.
Geo A Gordon, son of late Cmder Gordon, of the Navy, who died in service on coast of Africa.
Geo W C Lee, son of Col R E Lee, of the Corps of Engineers.
___ McKee, son of Col McKee, of the Ky volunteers, killed at Buena Vista.
Robt C Wood, son of Dr Wood, of the Army.
Wm F Drum, son of late Capt Drum, killed in front of the gates of the city of Mexico.
John R Smead, son of late Capt Smead, of the Army, who died of disease contracted in Mexico.
Maunsel White, Jr, of Louisiana.
_____ Hilliard, of Alabama.

House of Reps: 1-Ptn & papers of the heirs of Philip R Rice, deceased, formerly of King Wm Co, Va, & late of Bracken Co, Ky, praying compensation for a vessel lost in the service of the U S in the war of the Revolution. 2-Ptn of Wm Ferguson, for back pension. 3-Memorial of Wm H Simmons, praying Congress to pass an act for his relief. 4-Memorial of the Genr'l Assembly of Alabama, for the relief of John Scott.

Commission on Claims against Mexico: 1-Memorial of Elisha Copeland, for himself & as one of the assignees of Henry Price & Co, & of Wm Fowle, as one of the assignees of the same Price & Co, claiming payment of a draft given for supplies furnished in 1828, at Loretto, in Calif, to it Gov't, was submitted, examined, & ordered to be received. 2-Memorials of Stephen Morgan, & of Asa Fish, Stephen Morgan, Chas Mallory & others, claiming for seizure of the schnr **Orient** & her cargo, at Guasacualco in Mar, 1837: claim is valid for the vessel aforesaid, & the same is allowed accordingly; the amount to be awarded subject to the future action of the Board.

J Riggle, Merchant Tailor, 7th st, below the Patriotic Bank, Wash. [Local ad.]

WED MAR 13, 1850
Senate: 1-Memorial of Wm S McPherson, trustee of Lewis North, asking indemnity for French spoliations prior to 1800: referred to the select cmte. 2-Memorial of Benj Moore, late master armorer of the U S armory at Harper's Ferry, asking compensation for his services & for improvements made by him in machines & tools used in the manufacture & repair of firearms: referred to the Cmte on Military Affairs.

Commission on Claims against Mexico: 1-Memorial of Isaac D Marks, claiming for duties illegally exacted on specie at Matamoros, in 1838 & 1839, was ordered to be received. 2-Memorial of Geo A Gardiner, claiming for losses of property in certain silver mines, in consequence of his expulsion from the State of San Luis Potosi, in 1846: opinion is that the claim is valid: it was allowed accordingly: the amount to be awarded subject to the future action of the Board.

Freeman H Morse, was re-elected Mayor of Bath, Me, on Mon week, without opposition.

Scarlet fever prevails to an alarming extant in Lancaster Co, Pa. In 7 days, Mr John Loventy, of East Hempfield township, lost 6 children.

Wash City News: Criminal Court: Lewis Carley, a U S seaman, was yesterday put on trial under the charge of murdering a marine, Wm Brown, on board the U S steamer **Alleghany**, on the high seas, on Dec 2, 1848, while the steamer, under the command of Capt Hunter, was on her passage from Rio de Janeiro to Lisbon. The prisoner, about 30 years of age, is defended by Messrs Calisle, Ratcliff, & Decker. [Aug 21st newspaper: the court had jurisdiction in the case of Lewis Carley, & that he, having once been put in jeopardy before said court, cannot be lawfully tried therein again for the same offence. Judge Cranch: the case ended in the discharge of the prisoner.]

Died: on Mar 6, Chas Woolley, infant son of Eliza W & late Geo Clark.

Died: on Mar 11, at her residence, in Wash City, after a lingering illness, Mrs Ann Maria Minor, relict of late Hugh Minor, in her 63rd year.

Died: on Mar 10, at the Highlands, Maria L Nourse, widow of Jos Nourse, formerly Register of the U S Treasury. Her funeral will take place at Rock Creek Church, on Wed, at 1 o'clock.

For rent: 2 story brick house, H & 18th sts, containing 9 rooms. Apply to J M Krafft, F & 12th sts, or to a G Southall, adjoining.

Orphans Court of Wash Co, D C. Letters of administration on the personal estate of Vincent Massoletti, late of Wash Co, deceased.   -Sarah M Massoletti, admx

THU MAR 14, 1850
A lady who has much experience in teaching wishes to obtain a situation as a Governess. Address, post paid, Mrs Mary Alencon, St Clement's Bay, St Mary's Co, Md.

Died: on Fri last, at Orange Co, Va, after a very short illness, Mary Hill, wife of Lt Wm Lewis Maury, of the U S Navy.

Died: on Mar 13, at the **Highlands**, near Gtwn, Phoebe Pemberton Norris, daughter of Maj Chas Nourse. Her funeral will take place at Rock Creek Church, today, at 4 o'clock.

Died: on Fri, in Balt, Md, Henrietta R Stewart, wife of John Stewart, & daughter of Geo R Gaither.

Mrd: on Tue last, in Wash City, by Rev John C Smith, Mr Luther Osborn Parsons to Miss Mary Ann Lendorff, both of this place.

Mrd: on Mar 7, in Winchester, Va, by Rev Dr Hill, Geo A Thruston, of Cumberland, Md, & Bessie, only daughter of Thos A Tidball, of Winchester, Va.

House of Reps: 1-Cmte on Invalid Pensions: bill for the relief of Anthony Walton Bayard, & a bill for the relief of Jos Johnson: committed. Same cmte: bills for the relief of Jos M Rosebury; Geo Keller, of Missouri; & Thos R Saunders, of Va: committed. Same cmte: bill for the relief of Henry Click, of Cocke Co, Tenn; & a bill for the relief of Thos Coats: committed. Same cmte: bill for the relief of Pamelia Slavin, & a bill for the relief of Warren Raymond: committed. Same cmte: bill for the relief of Wm Sparks, & a bill for the relief of Geo S Claflin: committed. Same cmte: discharged from the further consideration of the ptn of Ursula E Cobb: referred to the Cmte on Naval Affairs. 2-Cmte on Patents: bill for the relief of Geo G Bishop, & the legal reps of John Arnold, deceased: committed. 3-Cmte of Claims: discharged from the further consideration of the ptn of the widow of Hubert Lacroix: laid on the table. 4-Cmte of Claims: adverse reports on the ptns of John Jardine, John P Converse, Ira Carpenter, Henry T Pairo, adm of John Laub, deceased, & of Nimrod Farrow & Richd Harris: laid on the table. Same cmte: bill for the relief of Polly Carver, excx of Nathan Carver, deceased, & a bill for the relief of Watson, Chabot & Co: committed. 5-Cmte of Claims: bill for the relief of John Poe, of Louisville, Ky: committed. Same cmte: J W Nye, to receive $525, on his executing a release, under his hand & seal, to the U S, of all claims against the U S or the Postmaster of the House, in respect to the several matters set forth in his ptns. 6-Cmte of Claims: bill for the relief of Capt Wm Duerson: committed. Same cmte: bill for the relief of the heirs of Geo B Reed, deceased; & a bill for the relief of the heirs of Bernard Todd, deceased: committed. 7-Cmte on Commerce: bills for the relief of Edmund Dexter, of Cincinnati, & for the relief of Adolphus Meier & Co, of St Louis. 8-Cmte on Commerce: discharged from the further consideration of the ptn of Andrew J Clifton: referred to the Cmte of Claims. Also, discharged from the further consideration of the memorial of Jas B Moore & Co: referred to the Cmte on Naval Affairs. 9-Cmte on the Post Ofc & Post Roads: discharged from the further consideration of the ptns of J M Gardner & of H H Hobbs: ordered to lie on the table. Same cmte: bill for the relief of John Deamit: committed. Same cmte: adverse report on the ptn of Wm Baker: laid on the table. 10-Cmte on the Judiciary: bill for the relief of the legal reps of Benj Fry, deceased: committed. Same cmte: adverse report on the ptn of Nathl White: laid on the table. 11-Ptn of Elnathan Phelps, an invalid pensioner, asking for bounty land. 12-Ptn of H A King, clerk to the naval constructor at the Gosport navy yard, asking an increase of pay.

Boarding: Miss McJilton, G st, near 15th. [Local ad.]

Zachary Taylor, Pres of the U S, recognizes Saml Price, appointed Consul of the Republic of Chili for Calif. Mar 13, 1850

Balt: fire destroyed the shoe store of Mr Jacob Link, Eutaw & Donovan sts, this morning. The adjoining store of Mr Martin Bragden was also destroyed.

Commission on Claims against Mexico: 1-Memorial of Asahel P Brittingham, claiming for damages sustained by the seizure of the brig **Ophir**, of which he was master & part owner, was submitted, examined, & suspended.

FRI MAR 15, 1850
Valuable real estate at public auction: by decree of Fred'k Co Court, in Equity: sale on Mar 26, at Ijamsville, all the real estate of which the late Plummer Ijams, deceased, was possessed. The *Homestead Farm*, containing 200 acres: with a 2 story brick dwlg-house, with 7 rooms, slate roofed, & good kitchen attached. The *Davis Farm*, of about 80 acres, adjoining the *Homestead*: with a log dwlg, kitchen, barn, & out-bldgs, & spring of pure water. The *Mill property*, of about 20 acres, with a dwlg-house, saw mill, & merchant mill 3 stories high. The Ijamsville property, of about 20 acres, adjoining the *Homestead & Mill property*, with store house, depot house, blacksmith shop, & other out-bldgs. Also, at the same time, by another decree of Fred'k Co Court of Equity, all the real estate bequeathed to the heirs of Mary Ann Ijams, deceased, by John Montgomery, deceased, about 206 acres, with Bush creek passing through it.
–Jas Ijams, Richd Ijams, trustees

For rent: brick dwlg, with 12 rooms, west side of 10th st, between Pa ave & E st, now occupied by Mr Henry Carter. Possession on Apr 1. Apply to F Masi & Co, between 9th & 10th sts, & Pa ave.

Hon Elijah Riley, member of Congress from the Chatanque district, has recovered from his recent accident near Binghampton, & is now in Rochester with his son-in-law, & will proceed to Washington in a few days. -Albany Even Jour

Natchez Free Trader of Feb 27. The awful scourge, the Asiatic cholera has descended upon the population with a fatality almost unheard of. Mr Snyder, formerly a resident of Natchez, kept a boarding house there, with 25 or 30 boarders, all of whom, who did not run away, died. Mr Snyder stayed & took care of them until the last one died; then he descended to the mouth of the Red River, & died on the steamer **Cincinnati** going to Natchez.

Zachary Taylor, Pres of the U S, recognizes Henry Winsor, who was appointed Consul of his Majesty the King of the Belgians, for Boston. -Mar 14. '50

The trial of Lewis Carley, charged with the murder of Wm Brown, was resumed yesterday. The jury returned a verdict of guilty of manslaughter.

For Boston: the fast sailing packet brig **Andover**, A Hardy, master, is now loading, & will be promptly dispatched on Mar 18. –John A Grimes, Commercial Wharf, Gtwn

Mrd: on Mar 14, in Wash City, by Rev G W Samson, Mr Calvin S McDaniel, of Greensborough, N C, to Miss Sarah A Beach, of Occoquan, Va.

Died: on Thu, after a long & painful illness, Thomas, son of Thos & Matilda Bayne, aged 20 years. His funeral will be from the residence of his father, 8th st, near the Navy Yard, this afternoon, at 3 o'clock.

Died: yesterday, at the village of Bladensburg, Md, Wm T Brown, late of Wash City. He was a young man, who was esteemed & beloved by all who knew him.

Died: yesterday, Mr John Howard, in his 55th year, late of Alexandria, where he resided for 25 years. His funeral is on Sat at 10 o'clock, at his late residence, Steamboat Wharf Hotel.

Died: on Mar 8, Hon Chas A Barnitz, of York, Pa, age 62 years. In 1815 he was elected to the Senate of Pa: in 1832 he was sent to the House of Reps of the U S by York Co; in 1837 selected as a Senatorial delegate to the Convention for the amemdment of the Constitution of Pa. For many years he was Pres of the York Bank. He was an accomplished scholar & able lawyer. –York [Pa] Gaz

SAT MAR 16, 1850

Postmaster General est'd the following new Post Ofcs for the week ending Mar 9, 1850:

Ofc	County, State	Postmaster
Red Beach	Wash, Maine	Jos Y Burgin
So Newburg	Merrimack, N H	Josiah Morse
Pleasant Brook	Otsego, N Y	Sawyer F Pearsons
N'th Broadalbin	Fulton, N Y	Roland E Ash
Alfred Centre	Alleghany, N Y	David C Green
West Kendall	Orleans, N Y	Delevan A Taft
Rose Hill	Seneca, N Y	Wm Herriess
Frantzdate	Ulster, N Y	Wm Kuykendall
West Aurora	Erie, N Y	Orin Thompson
Clark's Green	Luzerne, Pa	S A Northup
Y'k South Ridge	Sanduskey, Ohio	Jas C Wales
Wilow Dale	Trumbull, Ohio	Nicholas Depew
Medina	Lenawee, Mich	Ebenezer Daniels
Highland	Ritchie, Pa	John McGregor
Willard's	Wood, Pa	Benj Willard
Cataula	Harris, Ga	Wm Hartsfield
Tilton	Murray, Ga	John Howard
Shelby Springs	Shelby, Ala	Jas Gorge
Muckalusky	Neshoba, Miss	H M Walsh
Roesfield	Catahoula P, La	John Stapleton
Titer Creek	Claiborne P, La	John J Wise
Jatt	Rapides P, La	Thos F Swafford
Brownsville	Johnson, Ark	R H Brown
Palmer's Mills	Henry, Ten	E M Palmer
Halt's Hill	Rutherford, Ten	John W Hall

Oakville	Madison, Ten	John B Boykin
Boston	Williamson, Ten	Seth Sparkman
Julian's Gap	Hamilton, Ten	Jesse S Regan
Rose Hill	Robertson, Ten	Wm C Pepper
Carmargo	Lincoln, Ten	John Caughran
Prospect Hill	Lincoln, Ten	W H L Moore
Pucheon	Allen, Ky	A Hammett
Old Whitey	Graves, Ky	L R Wortham
Sank Village	Laporte, Ind	Thos Fisher
Sandwich	De Kalb, Ill	A L Merriam
Angola	Lake, Ill	Amaziah Smith
Carnents Prairie	Perry, Ill	Jas Cunningham
Louisa	Stephenson, Ill	John Roger
Pleasant Grove	Macoupin, Ill	Henry Begges
Lauretta	Sauk, Wis	Jared Fox

Names Changed: Willink, Erie Co, N Y, changed to East Aurora.
Medina, Lenawee Co, Mich, changed to Canandaigua.
Shuford's Ferry, Catauba Co, Maine, changed to Bunker's Hill.
Rice's X Roads, Panola Co, Miss, changed to Armuchee.
Beattie's Prairie, Benton Co, Ark, changed to Maysville.
Bath Springs, Perry Co, Tenn, changed to Shannonsville, Decatur Co.
Pleasant Ridge, Rock Island Co, Ill, changed to Andalusia.
Rives, C N, Henry Co, Missouri, changed to Clinton.
Southport, Racine Co, Wisc, changed to Kenozha, Kenozha Co.

Senate: 1-Recommended these bills pass: relief of Hiram Moore & John Hascall; relief of the captors of the frig **Philadelphia**; & relief of John Dickson, surviving partner of Lambert & Dickson. Also, bill to refund the fine imposed on the late Dr Thos Cooper, deceased, under the sedition law, to his legal reps. [To be refunded $400, being the fine imposed, together with interest thereon, at the rate of 6% per annum, from Nov 1, 1800, until paid.] 2-Cmte of the Whole House: discharged from the further consideration of the bill for the relief of S T Nicoll & Jas Clinch, of N Y C. It was not acted on. 3-Bill for the relief of Hiram Moore & John Hascall: passed. [See #1] 4-Cmte on Commerce: ptn of David P Barhydt was taken up & concurred in. 5-Cmte of Claims: adverse report on the ptn of sundry citizens of Michigan in favor of Hubert La Croix, was taken up & concurred in.

For sale: 4 small frame houses, on N st, in Gassawaytown, which will be sold very cheap for cash, if application be made immediately to E D Berry, jr, 8th st, one door from Pa ave, west side.

Died: on Mar 15, in Wash City, William, infant son of Lt R J H & Virginia Handy.

Died: on Thu, after a painful illness, Mrs Arabella Virginia Hurdle, youngest daughter of Wm Young, of Wash City, in the 23rd year of her age. Her funeral will be from the residence of Wm Tucker, C st, between 4½ & 6th st, on Sat, at 11 o'clock.

Zachary Taylor, Pres of the U S, recognizes Alfred Godeffroy, who has been appointed Consul of the Free & Hanseatic city of Hamburg, for Calif. –Mar 15, 1850

Constable's sale: by 3 writs of fieri facias: for cash, on the premises of John Schaub, near Corporation line & Mr Gilman's, on Mar 18, the following: 8 cows & 2 calves, 1 bay mare, 1 carryall & harness, cart & harness, ploughs, cultivator, harrow, shovels & tools, & some furniture, taken at the 2 suits of Dorothea Gengenbach & one of Chas Gengenbach. –A E L Keese, Constable

MON MAR 18, 1850

Henry H Hardy, a colored man, was sentenced on Wed, at Boston, to 4 months' immediate solitary confinement, & 4 years' additional imprisonment after the expiration of his former sentence, for an assault on the warden & 2 keepers of the jail.

On Wed, acting Sgt Jas Montgomery, of Marines, deliberately shot himself through the head with a musket. He was Sgt Major to the Marine regt, serving with the army at Chapultepec & other places, before entering the city of Mexico; but the severe campaign, with attendant illness, had rendered him weak & despondent.

Died: on Mar 15, in PG Co, Md, at the residence of her son-in-law, Thos H Osborne, after a few days illness, Mrs Maria Scott, wife of Mr S E Scott, of Wash City.

Drowned: on Sat last, at Pt Pleasant, Va, two gentlemen, one a son the other a son-in-law of Gen Beale, [Rep in Congress, we believe] & a young lady, had been taking an excursion in a skiff. The skiff capsized by the swells of a steamboat & Gen Beale's son was drowned. A faithful negro plunged into the river to rescue him, but he too drowned. A sister of Mr Beale's, who was on the shore, was restrained from plunging in by some by-standers. -Wheeling Gazette.

House of Reps: 1-Memorial of Jas R Howison, praying compensation for services as disbursing agent. 2-Ptn of Edw Wilbur & others, citizens of Orleans Co, N Y, praying for the repeal of an act approved Feb 26, 1845, entitled "an act to extend a patent heretofore granted to Wm Woodworth."

Destructive fire yesterday in Washington: the coach shop on 13½ st was found enveloped in flames; the wooden stable adjoining, occupied by Mr Jno Brown as a livery took fire; a large brick stable occupied by Mr Green, granite cutter, was destroyed. Several of the outbldgs belonged to Mr Allison Naylor, proprietor of one of the omnibus lines. Mr Naylor estimates his loss at between $10,000 & $15,000. The brick stable destroyed belonged to Mr Ogle Tayloe. The heat peeled the side of Maher's Hotel, leaving it well browned by the flames. The fire must have originated by the hand of an incendiary. A carriage was filled with straw which was partially burnt, it having been placed in the vehicle since the evening before. Another fire, near the northern boundary of the city, was seen yesterday on the farm formerly known as the residence of the late Jesse Brown, now in the occupancy of Dr Haw. A large valuable barn was burned.

For sale: sale for fisheries; Shenandoah flour; & rye flour. –I D Read, Water st, Gtwn

Orphans Court of Wash Co, D C. Ratification of sale of real estate of Lewis G Davidson, deceased : lot 6 to Louis Vivan; lots 7 & 8 to Jane L Graham; lot 11, to Chas H Winder, in square 168, for $1,435,78½; lot 3 to Alex'r H Mechlin; lot 4 to John H King, in square 126, for $1,064.60. -Wm F Purcell, Ed N Roach, Reg/o wills.

Died: on Mar 11, Hon Jas J Caldwell, Chancellor of S C, at his residence, near Columbia, S C.

Circuit Court of Wash Co, D C-in Chancery. Wm Peterson vs Geo Stroble & Eliz Stroble his wife. Geo Stroble is indebted to Wm Peterson for $250 with interest from Jun 20, 1848, that being the date the indebtedness was created; no payment ever made. Geo Stroble is residing in Calif Terr. Warning that the said Geo Stroble to be & appear in the Clerk's ofc of this county on the first Monday in August next, & answer said bill.
-W Cranch -Jno A Smith, clk

TUE MAR 19, 1850
Senate: 1-Ptn of Priscilla Prewett, asking the confirmation of her title to a tract of land: referred to the Cmte on Private Land Claims. 2-Memorial of the members of 2 companies of mounted volunteers, commanded by S L Sparkman & John Parker, asking compensation for their military services in a recent outbreak of the Indians in Florida. 3-Ptn of Jos Anderson, asking the repayment of a sum of money, advanced to a destitute volunteer in the late war with Mexico: referred to the Cmte on Military Affairs. 4-Ptn of John Cummins, asking compensation for his services as acting commissary of subsistence & acting assistant quartermaster in the army: referred to the Cmte on Military Affairs. 5-Ptn of Nathan Stanley, an ofcr in the last war with Great Britian, asking to be allowed a grant of bounty land: referred to the Cmte on Military Affairs. 6-Memorial of Thos O Leroy & David Smith, remonstrating against the extension of the patent of Tatum & others for a machine for making lead pipes: referred to the Cmte on Patents & the Patent Ofc. 7-Ptn of Jas H Robinson, a pensioner of the U S, asking to be allowed an increase of pension: referred to the Cmte on Pensions.

Orphans Court of Wash Co, D C. Case of Sarah Washington, admx-with the will annexed, of Martha Morgan, deceased. Settlement Apr 9, with the assets in the hands of said admx, so far as the same has been collected & turned into money.
-Ed N Roach, Reg/o wills

For rent & possession on May 1: 2 story frame tenement, on 19th st, between G & H sts. Rent $180 per annum. Inquire of S C Davison, at the Dept of the Interior.

House of Reps: 1-Ptn of Abagail Stafford, for a pension for the services of her father, Henry Smith, of Mass, during the Revolutionary war. 2-Ptn of Francis D P Leonard, son & heir of John Leonard: asking indemnity for French spoliations between 1795 & 1800. 3-Ptn of Geo C Thomas, for a pension for disability contracted whilst in the service of the U S.

Methodist Annual Conference: appointments for the Potomac District made at the late Conference: W Hamilton, Presiding Elder
Alexandria: Norval Wilson, A J Myers
Washington: Foundry & Asbury, L Morgan, F Job Guest; Wesley Chapel, Wm B Edwards; McKendree Chapel, S Asbury Roszel; Ebenezer, Thos Myers, M A Turner, sup; Ryland Chapel, J S Gorsuch, J M Hanson, sup; Union Chapel, D McElfresh.
Emory: Jas Bunting, sup
Gtwn: John Lanahan, Saml Rodgers
Fairfax: W Prettymen, John H Ryland
Stafford: John M Green
Fredericksburg: Benj N Brown
St Mary's: Thos Cornelius
Charles: Thos McGee, D Castleman
Bladensburg: J Smith, J Landstreet, J Turner, sup
Rockville: R Brown, J S Deal, B Barry, sup
Agent American Bible Society: John Poisal

Commission on Claims against Mexico: 1-Memorial of John Claiborne, administrator of Thos Hasam, claiming for the loss of the schnr **Hannah Elizabeth**, chased ashore near Matagorda, by the Mexican war schnr **Bravo**, in 1835: ordered to be received. 2-On the motion of John R Rockwell, atty in the case of Haggerty, Davis & Dana, the examination of their memorial, suspended on Feb 22 last, was further suspended until the first Mon in Nov next. 3-The Board resumed the examination of the memorial of Wm S Messervey, filed on Mar 8 & then suspended, finding it not to conform to the rules, ordered that it be not received. 4-Memorials of John A Robinson, severally claiming for seizure & detention of property in Guayamas in 1832, & for a forced loan at Hermosillo in 1847, which were filed on Mar 8, & then suspended, were again taken up: ordered to be received.

Died: on Mar 18, after a short illness, Mr Wm Cockrell, in his 44th year, leaving a large family & circle of friends to mourn his loss. His funeral will take place at his late residence near Blagden's Wharf, on Wed, at 3 o'clock.

Balt, Mar 18. Annual commencement took place at Wash Univ on Sat: among the students who graduated was Dr John R Dillard, of Va, who was awarded the gold medal.

WED MAR 20, 1850
From Texas: 1-Mr Nugent, formerly a Washington correspondent of a N Y paper, was supposed to be killed. 2-In San Antonio, on Feb 18, a Mexican named Marcelino Martinas, was shot by another Mexican. 3-Mr Wm L Dortch, [says the State Gaz] was killed in Hays Co on Feb 22, by the accidental discharge of a gun in the hands of Col Durham. Both gentlemen were hunting when the accident occurred. Mr Dortch was a native of Mecklenburg Co, Va, & had recently arrived in Western Texas, with the intention of making it his permanent residence. 4-Outrages committed by the Apaches & Comanches: David Torrey killed a little east of Presidio; 7 or 8 Americans had been massacred on the Gila.

Postmaster Genl established the following new Post Ofcs for week ending Mar 16, 1850:

Ofc	County, State	Postmaster
West Danville	Cumberland, Maine	Jos S Foster
Otter Creek	Addison, Vt	Eenezer B Jenney
Arcadia	Wash, R I	Jas T Harris
East Thompson	Windham, Conn	H N Tourtelotte
Pine Woods	Madison, N Y	Wm F Bonney
East Clarkson	Monroe, N Y	Isaac E Hoyt
Grosvenor's Corners	Schoharie, N Y	Jeremiah McCulloch
Arnoldton	Ulster, N Y	Benj C Arnold
Belcher	Wash, N Y	Warren Cleveland
Morrisania	West Chester, N Y	John M Myrick
Ryland's Depot	Greenville, Va	Wm Ryland
Falling Mill	Moore, N C	Hugh Black
Fountain Hill	Green, N C	Willis Dixon
Reedy Branch	Moore, N C	Jno M N Ferguson
Cane Point	Troup, Ga	Wm G Marcus
Long Street	Pulaski, Ga	Chas Walker
Glen Grove	Fayette, Ga	Jas E May
Fulton	Dallas, Ala	John Askew
Cato Springs	Rankin, Miss	C Moyers
Pitt's Point	Bullitt, Ky	John Greenwell
Puebla	Brown, Ohio	Geo W Day
Ridgeland	Henry, Ohio	Saml A Warwick
Reserve	St Joseph's, Mich	Heman Huntley
Sanilac Mills	Sanilac, Mich	Isaac Lentz
Port English	Carroll, Ind	Wm J Sayre
Jefferson Mills	Jefferson, Mo	Henry D Evan
White Sulphur	St Clair, Mo	John L Traham
Reindeer	Noddaway, Mo	J N Prather
Elizabeth	Andrew, Mo	Edw Wand
Macedonia	Pottawatamie, Iowa	Calvin A Beebee
Hardin	Olamkse, Iowa	Leonard B Hedges
Hurrican Grove	Grant, Wis	Thos Chandler
Hampden	Columbia, Wis	Nelson B Lloyd

Names Changed
Belvidere, Chester Co, Pa, changed to West Whiteland.
Moore's Iron Works, Johnson Co, Tenn, changed to Pandora.
Twelve Mile, Sangamon Co, Ill, changed to Nestor.

McCaffrey, the supposed murderer of Chas Smith & his wife, at East Rock, near New Haven, has been delivered to the authorities of Connecticut by Lord Elgin, & is now in their custody. The murdered persons were an old infirm couple, supposed to be wealthy, & the deed was committed under circumstances of unusual atrocity.

Foreign papers state that at the funeral of the Danish poet, Oerlenschlager, who expired lately of apoplexy, in his 81st year, upwards of 20,000 persons were present.

Senate: 1-Ptn of the heir-at-law of Solomon Parsons, asking compensation for the services of said Parsons as a soldier in the Revolutionary war: referred to the Cmte on Revolutionary Claims. 2-Memorial of J B Toby & Co & Lewis Kenney & Co, asking that certain duties illegally exacted of them on a cargo of coal, may be refunded: referred to the Cmte on Finance. 3-Submitted: the documents in relation to the claim of Robt Abbot for compensation for losses by Indian depredations: referred to the Cmte of Claims. 4-Ptn of Wm R Nevin, of N Y C, for a renewal or extension of his patent right. 5-Papers withdrawn & referred: ptn of Asa Andrews: referred to the Cmte of Claims. Ptn of the heirs of Jno Ramsay: referred to the Cmte on Revolutionary Claims. Ptn of Enoch Baldwin: referred to the Cmte on Commerce. Memorial of Lavinia Taylor, widow of Isaac Taylor: referred to the Cmte on Pensions. Memorial of John McColgan: referred to the Cmte on Commerce. 6-Cmte on Military Affairs: memorial of Gad Humphreys, asking compensation for property destroyed in Florida by order of the U S ofcrs during the Seminole war, reported a bill for his relief: ordered to a second reading. Same cmte: bill for the relief of Lewis Morris & others, without amendment. Same cmte: memorial of Danl G Garnsey, an ofcr in the last war with Great Britain, asking compensation for his military services, asked to be discharged from the further consideration of the same: which was concurred in. 7-Cmte of Claims: ptn of Thos Allen, asking an appropriation in fulfillment of a contract for printing the compendium of the 6th census: bill for his relief was ordered to a second reading. 8-Bill for the relief of Elisha Hampton & others, of Iowa: introduced.

Sale of U S land above Gtwn, D C: Ordnance Dept, Wash, Mar 19, 1850. Piece of land near the Little Falls of the river Potomac, which has been occupied as a U S magazine lot, together with the bldgs thereon. This land was conveyed to the U S by deed dated Sep 9, 1815. [Detailed description followed.] -Geo Talcott, Bt Brig Gen, & Col of Ordnance

Marshal's sale: by writ of venditioni exponas, on judgment of condemnation, issued from the Clerk's ofc of the Circuit Court of Wash Co, D C : public sale on Mar 30, of the Canal boat **James Rumsey,** property of Edw & Henry Wail, to satisfy debt due John D W & John Moore. –Richd Wallach, Marshal of D C

House of Reps: 1-Ptn & papers of Benj Moore, of Harper's Ferry, Va, praying compensation for his improved method of percussioning flintlock arms, which has been adopted by the ordnance board. 2-Ptn of Isaac Weaver & 66 other citizens of Delaware Co, Pa, asking the establishment of an agricultural bureau. 3-Cmte of Claims: discharged from the further consideration of the ptn of Wm Hardin: leave was granted to withdraw the papers in said case from the files of the House. 4-Remonstrance of David Dawson & others, against the extension of Woolworth's patent.

Commission on Claims against Mexico: 1-Memorial of Henry May, administrator of Ann P Boulden, claiming for pension granted to David H Porter, by special act of the Mexican Congress of 27th ___, 1828, was submitted, examined, & ordered to be received.

THU MAR 21, 1850
Appointments by the Pres:
Ephraim Geo Squier, of N Y, to be Charge d'Affaires of the U S to the Republic of Guatemala, vice Elijah Hise.
Thos M Foote, of N Y, to be Charge d'Affaires of the U S to the Republic of New Grenada, vice Benj A Bidlack, deceased.
Wm C Rives, of Va, to be Envoy Extra & Minister Pleni of the U S to the French Republic, vice Richd Rush, recalled.
Henry S Sandford, of Conn, to the Sec of the Legation of the U S to the French Republic, vice Stephen K Stanton.
Alex'r K McClung, of Mississippi, to be Charge d'Affaires of the U S to the Republic of Bolivia, vice John Appleton, resigned.
L W Jerome, of N Y, to be Consul of the U S for the city of Ravenna, in Italy, vice Henry J Brent.

Mrd: on Mar 19, by Rev J E Weems, Hazeal Benezette to Mrs Lana Mari Decover, all of Wash.

Mrd: on Mar 20, in Gtwn, D C, by Rev Mr Tillinghast, Saml B Paul, of Petersburg, Va, to Sophronia W, youngest daughter of John Pickrell, of Gtwn, DC,

Senate: 1-Ptn from John Frazer & Wm Lindlay, in behalf of the heirs of John G Clendenin, asking re-payment, with interest, of the purchase money of land by the U S, the title to which is defective: referred to the Cmte on Public Lands. 2-Ptn from Mariba Fairservice, asking to be allowed the right of pre-emption to an island lying in Lake Nemarbin, in Wisc: referred to the Cmte on Public Lands. 3-Cmte on Military Affairs: memorial of Col John C Hays, asking compensation for services in raising & organizing a regt of Texas mounted volunteers, reported a bill for the relief of Col Hays: passed to a second reading.

Died: on Mar 20, after a long & painful illness, Miss Harriet Hawke, in her 62nd year. Her funeral will be from the residence of her nephew, R A Hawke, on M st, between 7th & 8th sts, this afternoon, at 4 o'clock.

Died: on Mar 19, Mrs Amelia Sewall, in her 53rd year. Her funeral will be from the residence of her son-in-law, on D st, between 6th & 7th sts, this afternoon, at 4 o'clock.

Died: on Mar 20, Elizabeth, aged 9 years, youngest daughter of late John Daly. Her funeral will take place tomorrow at 3 o'clock.

Valuable woodland at auction on Apr 1 next: 38 acres on the new road to Bladensburg, adjoining the lands of Messrs Burr, Scott, Calvert, & Burrows. –Dyer & Bro, aucts

FRI MAR 22, 1850
Wash Corp: 1-Nomination from the Mayor of Dr T B J Frye, as a member of the Board of Health for the 4th Ward, in place of Dr W H Saunders, resigned: ordered to lie on the table. 2-Ptn of Wm W McCreery, praying indemnity for injuries sustained & damages incurred from falling into an uncovered culvert: referred to the Cmte on Police. 3-Cmte of Claims: bill for the relief of John Maguire: passed. Same cmte: bill for the relief of Elias Barnes: passed. Same cmte: asked to be discharged from the further consideration of the ptn of Geo Stewart: agreed to. Same cmte: ptn of Leonard S Roby, for remission of a fine: asked to be discharged from the further consideration of the same: agreed to. Same cmte: bill for the relief of F S Walsh: passed. Same cmte: asked to be discharged from the further consideration of the ptn of John Dewdny: agreed to. Same cmte: discharged from the further consideration of the ptn of Jas Caden: referred to the Mayor. 4-Bill for the relief of A F Tottchinder: passed. 5-Bill for the relief of E W Hall: passed. 5-Bill for the relief of Wm B Lewis: referred to the Cmte on Police. 6-Bill for the relief of John E Little: passed. 7-Ptn of Bernard Mulreny, praying remission of a fine: referred to the Cmte of Claims. 8-Bill for the relief of Wm H Fletcher: passed.

Criminal Court-Wash-Wed. John McMonegle [not McMullen, as erroneously published,] was found guilty of making & passing counterfeit money.

Commission on Claims against Mexico: 1-Memorial of Franklin Chase, & of Ann Chase his wife, claiming for losses by his expulsion from Tampico on Jun 6, 1846, being taken up for consideration: claim is valid: same was allowed accordingly: amount to be awarded subject to the future action of the Board.

The St Martinsville [La] Courier of Mar 2 says that, when the steamer **Dove** reached that place, on her previous trip, 8 of her passengers had died; of those who landed at St Martinsville, 13 have since died. Among them are 4 ladies: Mrs Ann Eliza Young, wife of Mr Smith Young, of Clarksville, Tenn; Mrs Martha Tucker, wife of Rev Robt Tucker of Christian Co, & her 2 daughters, Miss Mary Jane & Miss Virginia J Tucker.

At Richmond, on Wed, a horse attached to a butcher's wagon at the market, broke away & dashed up Main st, & ran over Mrs Francis Regnault & a servant woman, who were both instantly killed. Mrs Regnault is of a large family & a fond & attentive parent. –Whig

Senate: 1-Ptn of Elisha Wm Budd Moody, of Yarmouth, in the province of Nova Scotia, merchant: owner of the ship **Sarah**, sailed from London, Great Britain, on Oct 26 past, commanded by David Cook, & bound to the port of St John, New Brunswick, that on Nov 17 last, a ship was discovered in distress, the American ship **Caleb Grimshaw**, of N Y, with 420 passengers on board, & that she was on fire. The Sarah rescued 399 human beings & proceeded to Fayal, at which place she was quarantined, & heavy port charges there incurred. The petitioner has never received any remuneration from any person for port charges, nor for the loss of time of said ship caused by saving the 399 persons, the loss of freight, the provisions consumed, the extra wages paid the crew, or the wear & tear on the ship: prays that Congress will take this case into consideration.

House of Reps: 1-Ptn of W F Manly & 146 other citizens of Pittsford, Vt, that persons claimed as fugitive slaves may be entitiled to a trial by jury. 2-Ptn of J L P McCane & 14 others, & the ptn of Jos Perry & 25 others, citizens of Indiana, & ofcrs & soldiers of the last war with Great Britain or of the Indian wars, praying a grant of bounty lands. 3-Ptn of Saml Campbell, a citizen of Jennings Co, Indiana, asking to be placed on the invalid pension roll. Ptn of Hiram Prather & 130 others, praying the same thing in behalf of said Campbell. 3-Memorial of the widow & heirs of Fulwar Skipwith, deceased, praying for the passage of a law to indemnify them for losses sustained by French spoliations. 4-Memorial of Miss H H A Glavarry, sole heir of Cap Francis Glavarry, deceased, for passage of a law to indemnify them for losses sustained by French spoliations. 5-Ptn of Nicholas Grensel, one of the ofcrs of the volunteers in the late war with Mexico, praying additional remuneration for his services by grant of land. 6-Ptn of Saml Spaulding for increase of pension. 7-Claim of Francis Cuott for pay for his services as a capt of a company of Michigan militia in the war of 1812: submitted

Ptn of Geo S Griggs, of Roxbury, Mass, praying for the extension of a patent granted him for the improvement in railroad frogs, which expires on Jul 31, 1851.
–Thos Ewbank, Com'r of Patents.

Appointments by the Pres: 1-Wm P Ballinger, of Texas, to be U S Atty for the District of Texas. 2-John T Myrick, of Florida, to be U S Marshal for the Northern District of Florida. 3-Robt S Kennedy, of N J, to be U S Marshal for the District of N J. 4-Fielding Davis, of Mississippi, to be U S Marshal for the Southern District of Mississippi. 5-Jos Bates, of Texas, to be U S Marshal for the District of Texas. 6-Andrew J Jay, of Alabama, to be Receiver of Public Moneys at Sparta, Ala. 7-Chas F M Noland, of Arkansas, to be Receiver of Public Moneys at Batesville, Ark.

Sailing of Missionaries: the ship **Tartar** sailed on Sat, from N Y for Canton, with the following Missionaries: Rev Mr Talmage & wife, missionaries of the American board of Com'rs of Foreign Missions; Miss C Tenney, missionary of the Protestant Episcopal Board; Miss Sperry, missionary of the Methodist Board; Miss Baker, missionary of the Southern Baptist Board; Mr Gilbert, of Utica, N Y; Mr L N Hitchcock, of N Y; Mr Bradley, of New Haven, Conn; Mr Beyland, of Phil; Chun, a Chinese.

Mrd: on Mar 20, by Rev G Samson, Mr Robt Y Knight to Miss Mary Reill, of N Y.

Died: on Mar 17, in Centreville, Fairfax Co, Va, after a long & painful illness, Mr Worden Grigsby, in the 47th year of his age.

Died: on Thu, after a painful & lingering illness, Sarah Liedberg, aged 38 years. Her friends, & those of the family of her sister, Mrs E O Harrison, are invited to attend her funeral from her late residence on Pa ave, tomorrow, at 12 o'clock.

Died: on Mar 1, at her residence in Loudoun Co, Va, in her 57th year, Mrs Sarah McCarthy Throckmorton, relict of late Mordecai Throckmorton, & daughter of late Bernard Hooe, of Pr Wm Co, Va.

Died: on Mar 18, near Richmond, Va, Jas M Wickham, in his 48th year, son of late John Wickham, of Richmond.

SAT MAR 23, 1850
Senate: 1-Cmte on Pensions: reported a bill for the relief of Mrs A M Dade, widow of the late Maj F L Dade: ordered to a second reading. 2-Cmte on the Judiciary: memorial of Chas F Sibbald, asking indemnity for injuries sustained by being deprived of the possession of his property: submitted a report with a joint resolution for his relief: passed to a second reading. 3-Cmte on Pensions: bill for the relief of Margaret L Worth, widow of the late Gen Worth, of the army of the U S. He, with his wife & children, at the head of his column, [where he ever was when duty was to be done, or danger encounted,] was approaching San Antonio, Texas. He knew that the cholera was there, & death & desolation were its attendants; & yet he pressed forward. He wrote a letter on Apr 30, 1849, 20 miles from San Antonio to Maj L S Capers, that he will leave the ladies behind. On May 7, just one week afterwards, he was buried.

Mrd: on Mar 12, by Rev Mr Hodges, Richd Burch to Georgiana Myers, all of Wash City.

Mrd: on Mar 21, by Rev Mr Hodges, Christopher C Stone to Ann M Anderson, both of PG Co, Md.

Died: on Mar 22, in Wash City, in his 59th year, Mr Stanislaus Edelin. His funeral will be from his late residence, 3rd st, between L & N sts, on Sun at 3 o'clock.

Died: on Mar 16, in Fredericksburg, Va, Mrs Mary G Noyes, formerly resident of Alexandria, in her 54th year.

Died: on Mar 22, Julia Wood Whiting, youngest daughter of Lt Wm B Whiting, U S Navy, & his wife, Mary Lee Whiting, aged 1 year & 6 months. Her funeral will be from the residence of Lt Whiting, Six Buildings, this afternoon, at 4 o'clock.

School for Young Ladies: Miss Mary P Middleton will open on Apr 1, in the Lecture Room of St Paul's [English Lutheran] Church, corner of H & 11th sts. References: Hon Jas Cooper, U S Senate; Hon Thaddeus Stevens, House of Reps; & Ref J G Butler, Pastor of the Church. Call at the School Room or at her father's residence on G st, between 8th & 9th sts.

Commission on Claims against Mexico: 1-Memorial of Hezekiah D Maulsby, administrator of Geo G Alford, deceased, claiming for seizure of her person on board the schnr **Julius Caesar**, off the mouth of the Sabine in 1837, by a Mexican brig-of-war; for subsequent personal ill usage, imprisonment, & robbery of effects, was submitted, examined, & ordered to be received. 2-Memorial of Abner Woodworth, claiming for expulsion from Parras in 1846, & for losses arising thereby, was submitted, examined, & ordered to be received.

MON MAR 25, 1850
The polar expedition now fitting out by Henry Grennell, of N Y, for the search of Sir John Franklin will be ready to sail by May 1. It consists of the 2 vessels **Advance** & the **Rescue**. Lts DeHaven & Griffin are to command the expedition.

Dr Wm A Newell, a Rep from N J, has again been called home by severe illness of a member of his family.

Judge Ogden, in the Passaic [N J] Oyer & Terminer, on Tue, pronounced the sentence of the law upon John Johnstan, convicted of the murder of Judge Van Winkle & his wife. He is to be executed Apr 30.

The trial of Dr John W Webster, on a charge of having murdered Dr Parkman in Nov last, commenced at Boston on Mar 19. [Mar 31st newspaper: Prof Webster found guilty of murder in the first degree. On the rendition of the verdict Dr Webster fainted, & remained insensible for 10 minutes. He was then conveyed to jail, to await his sentence.]

F J Mills, postmaster at Hogansburg, Franklin Co, N Y, has been re-arrested at Kingston, Canada, & brought to Utica, where he was committed for trial in default of $1,500 bail. He is charged with robbing the mail, & has made a full confession.

Mrd: on Mar 21, at the Church of the Epiphany, by Rev Mr French, N B Harrison, U S Navy, to Maria P, daughter of late Dr Horace Wellford, of Fredericksburg, Va.

Died: on Mar 23, Parke Bailey France, infant son of Thos E & Annabella France, age 7 months & 27 days.

Died: on Mar 23, at the residence of Mrs L B Sheriff, Mr Wm Young, in his 74th year.

Died: on Mar 23, after a protacted illness, Capt Philo B Johnson.

Commission on Claims against Mexico: 1-Memorial of Mgt Ward, widow & admx of Capt Elliott Ward, deceased, master of the schnr **St Croix**, claiming for losses by seizure of that vessel & of his person, at the port of Arkansas in 1834, submitted, examined, & ordered to be received. 2-Memorial of Hezekiah D Maulsby, adm of Geo G Alford, deceased: claim is valid: amount to be awarded subject to the future action of the Board.

Wash City: Criminal Court: 1-Hubert H Booly, a man with one arm, charged with a violent assault on a female, resulted in his conviction: sentenced to 3 years' imprisonment in the penitentiary. 2-The court, in the case of Lewis Carley, the U S seaman convicted of manslaughter, on Sat delivered an opinion, disaffirming the jurisdiction & remanding the prisoner to jail to await such other proceedings as the U S Gov't may think proper to institute in the premises. The counsel for the prisoner entered an application for a writ of error, which was granted.

City Ordinances-Wash: 1-Act for the relief of Walker & Peck: that the fine imposed for an alleged violation relative to butchers' licenses, be remitted, provided that Walker & Peck pay the cost of prosecution. 2-Act for the relief of F S Walsh: that the sum of $6.64 be paid to F S Walsh, for medicines furnished, the out-door poor in the years 1845, 1846, & 1847, the same not having been previously paid.

TUE MAR 26, 1850
Senate:-the Territorial question. 1-A city meeting at New Haven, Conn, was held Sep 10, 1831, called by Dennis Kemberly, Mayor of New Haven, to consider a plan for the establishment in that city of a college for the education of colored youths; at which meeting it was-"Resolved by the Mayor, Alderman, Common Council, & freemen of the city of New Haven, in city meeting assembled, that we will resist the establishment of the proposed college in this place by every lawful means."
Mar, 1833; Town meeting at Canterbury, Conn, in reference to Miss Crandall's school for females of color. Resolutions passed that the school should not be established in that town.
May 24, 1833: Act passed by the Leg of Conn prohibiting schools for colored persons from other States. [In 1835 a petition of the Leg for the repeal of this act was rejected.]
Jun 27, 1833: Miss Crandall was imprisoned in Brooklyn, Conn, on charge of having taught persons of color from out of State
Sep 30, 1835: An assault was made on Miss Crandall's house while a clergyman was holding a religious meeting there. Rotten eggs & other missles were thrown at the windows. The well of the house on another occasion was filled with offal.
May 27: the Mayor & Aldermen of Boston rejected an application of 125 citizens for the use of Faneuil Hall for the purpose of holding a meeting to plead the cause of the slaves.
Aug 10, 1835: Canaan Academy, N H, was driven off by a mob for the crime of admitting colored youths.
Aug 10, 1835: Disturbance at Worcester, Mass, while the Rev Orange Scott was lecturing on slavery, some individuals tore up his notes, & offered violence to his person.
Jul 4, 9, 10, & 11, 1835, the abolitionists were mobbed in N Y.
2-The Senate proceeded to the consideration of the Pres' message transmitting the constitution of the State of Calif. 3-Memorial from Jas J Stark, a settler under the act of 1842, for the armed occupation of East Florida, asking that a patent may be issued for the lands settled by him: referred to the Cmte on Public Lands.

Mrd: on Mon, by Rev John C Smith, Mr Jas W French to Miss Harriet Dawson, all of Wash City..

Mrd: on Mar 20, by Rev G W Samson, Robt T Knight, of Wash, to Miss Harriet, daughter of Henry E Riell, of N Y.

Died: on Feb 13, near Jacksonville, Ala, John Chandler, aged 104 years. He was "better known as grandsire Chandler." He was a native of Va, & served 7 years in the Revolutionary war under Gen Greene & Gen Sumter. He was in the battles of Eutaw, Camden & Cowpens.

Died: on Mar 20, at the residence of his son, in Jefferson Co, Va, David English, sen, aged 81 years. He was a native of Monmouth Co, N J, but for the greater part of his life a resident of Gtwn, D C. He edited "The Sentinel of Liberty, or Gtwn & Wash Advertiser." From 1810 to 1838, he was Cashier of the Union Bank of Gtwn.

Died: on Mar 25, at the residence of Dr Maxwell, U S N, Mrs M Slaymaker, wife of Henry Y Slaymaker, of Cincinnati, & daughter of the late Robt Maxwell, of Delaware.

Zachary Taylor, Pres of the U S, recognizes Vittorio Sartori, who has been appointed Vice-Consul of Sardinia for the State of Pa, to reside at the city of Phil. Mar 25, 1850

Household & kitchen furniture at auction: on Mar 29, at the residence of Henry Carter, 10th st, between D & E sts. –Dyer & Bro, aucts

Commission on Claims against Mexico: 1-Memorial of Pierre Chouteau, jr, administrator of Chouteau & De Mun, & surviving partner of the persons trading under the firm & style of Augustus P Chouteau & Co, claiming the seizure, imprisonment, & confiscation in 1817, was taken up for consideration, together with the proofs & documents connected therewith; when the Board came to an opinion that the claim is a valid one against the Republic of Mexico, & the same was allowed accordingly; the amount to be awarded, subject to the future action of the Board. 2-Memorial of John W Simonton & John A Heath, claiming for a compulsory sale of cargo of provisions, on board the schnr **Dream**, at Lerma, in 1843, & for non-payment of a draft given for the same, was taken up for consideration, when the Board came to an opinion that is was a valid claim against the Republic of Mexico, & the same was allowed; the amount to be awarded subject to the future action of the Board. 3-Memorial of Henry May, administrator of Wm A Slacum, deceased, claiming for unpaid Treasury notes of the State of Sonora, [then independent,] taken at Guaymas, in 1835, in payment for a cargo of goods sold to a private person, was submitted, examined, & suspended.

WED MAR 27, 1850
Senate: 1-Cmte on Indian Affairs: referred the documents relating to the claim of H I McClintock, Harrison Gill, & Mansfield Carter, for services at the Nemeshaw agency for the Sac & Fox Indians, submitted a report, with a bill for their relief: ordered to a second reading.

House of Reps: 1-Ptn of Henry Kemper, of Madison Co, Mo, praying for an act for the relief of the heirs of Andrew O'Bannon, a soldier in the Revolution. 2-Ptn of Benj Lincoln Meade & Wm F Meade, residuary legatees of the late Gen Everard Meade, for arrears of interest. 3-Ptn of Mrs Mary Baury, of Boston, for relief.

Appointment by the Govn'r of Va: Saml L Lewis, of Wash, D C, to be com'r to take acknowledgments & proof of deeds.

Died: on Mar 9, of scarlet fever, Catherine, daughter of Eliz Smith & late Jos Smith, aged 3 years, 4 months & 11 days.

Died: on Mar 26, Mrs Jane Stone, wife of late Jos Stone, in her 50th year. Her funeral will be from her residence on G St, between 12th & 13th sts, today, at 3:30 o'clock.

Walker Sharpshooters meeting this evening, 7:30. –E C Eckloff, sec

Masonic, Columbia R A Chapter, #15, meeting this evening at 7 o'clock. -Pollard Webb, sec

For sale of exchange for city property: a farm in Illinois, containing 170 acres, in Vermilion Co. Apply to Wm H Ward, H st, near 6th.

Wanted to employ one or 2 sober & industrious drivers; white men would be preferred, & constant employment. Apply at the Lumber Yard on 1st st, where the undersigned keeps on hand a large supply of all kinds of seasoned lumber. –John Purdy

Commission on Claims against Mexico: 1-Memorial of Jas Taylor White, claiming for supplies by him furnished in 1832 to the Mexican garrison at Anahuac, being taken up for consideration: claim is not a valid one against the Republic of Mexico: same was not allowed.

Criminal Court-Wash. The trial of E H Fuller, charged with assault: verdict of guilty, & fined $10 & costs. [Mar 28th newspaper: Fuller was acquitted.]

THU MAR 28, 1850
Mrd: on Mar 26, by Rev Mr Moore, Mr John Small to Miss Mary Ann Cunningham, all of Gtwn.

Died: on Mar 20, at *Cedar Grove*, the residence of Dr R H Stuart, in King Do Co, Va, Francis Key, aged 9 months, son of Lt Francis K & Anna Murray, of Elk Ridge Md.

Dreadful steamboat disaster at Buffalo, on last Sat, the steamer **Troy**, Capt Wilkins, from Sandusky & other ports on Lake Erie, attempted to enter Buffalo harbor, but the ice preventing, she steered for Black Rock: her boiler exploded. Passengers blown overboard. Twelve persons are known to have lost their lives-7 passengers & 5 of the crew. Five in the water were rescued. [Mar 30th newspaper: cabin passengers saved: Messrs Reed, Miller, Menell & his wife, Pragoff & 2 boys, Secor & 2 sisters & child, Sertwell, Norton, Knapp, Miss Scott, Sizer & mother, Hutchinson, & Manahan. Mr Manahan is badly scalded, as is Mr Hutchinson. The cabin passengers, from whom nothing has been learned, are Messrs Brown, Faxon, Dr Wright, [who is believed to be drowned,] Curtis, Willis, Howe, Grant, Baily, Vesey, Bowen, & Arnold. The steerage passengers not heard from are Messrs Brandt, Irwin, Knight, & 18, mostly Irish & German, whose names were not taken.] [Apr 1: the explosion was occasioned by a lack of water in the boilers, owing to the omission of Levi L Post, the deceased engineer. Thos Wilkins, master, & his ofcrs are not responsible.]

For rent: 2 story brick dwlg on Gay st, for the last 2 years occupied by Rev Henry Slicer. Possession given immediately. Apply to D English, jr, Gtwn.

Commission on Claims against Mexico: 1-Memorial of Jonas P Levy, claiming for illegal duties exacted, corrupt judicial decisions, in 1843, & down to 1846, was submitted, & ordered to be received. 2-Memorail of Andrew Fenton, claiming for demurrage of brigantine **Ada Eliza**, & for loss of a chain cable, was examined & rejected, as not conforming to the rules of the Board. 3-Memorial of Sanforth Kidder, claiming for a forced loan of $20, at Matamoros, in 1836, was submitted: ordered to the received. 4-Ordered, that leave be given to withdraw the memorial & papers of Wm S Messervey, in order that they may be made to conform to the rules of the Board.

Senate: 1-Memorial of Jos Parks, a Shawnee Indian, asking compensation for a slave forcibly taken from his possession by persons in Illinois: referred to the Cmte on Indian Affairs. 2-Memorial of Henry Williams, U S Atty for the District of Georgia, asking an increase of his compensation: referred to the Cmte on the Judiciary. 3-Cmte on Patents, to which were referred the petition & papers of Benj Tatham & brothers, submitted an adverse report on the same: ordered to be printed. Same cmte: petition of Wm R Nevins, asking a renewal of his patent for a machine for cutting & rolling dough for crackers & biscuits: asked to be discharged from the further consideration of the same: which was ordered to be printed.

FRI MAR 29, 1850
Appointments by the Pres:
Jas Brown Clay, of Ky, to be Charge d'Affaires of the U S at the Court of her Most Faithful Majesty.
Chas B Wells, of Vt, to be U S Consul for Batavia, Island of Java.
Geo V Brown, of N Y, to be U S Consul for the Empire of Morocco.
Henry Naylor, John L Smith, Jas Crandell, Henry Howison, Saml Smoot, Chas J Nourse, Joshua Pierce, & Henry Addison, to be Justices of the Peace for Wash Co, D C.

House of Reps: 1-Cmte on the Judiciary: bill for the relief of Andrew Smith: committed. Same cmte: discharged from the further consideration of the claim of Saml & Jas Smith, of Indiana: referred to the Cmte of Claims. Same cmte: discharged from the further consideration of the ptn of Robt Graham: referred to the Cmte on Private Land Claims. Same cmte: discharged from the further consideration of the memorial of Henry Acker & Andrew Backus, praying a change of law providing for their pay for locating military bounty land warrants: referred to the Cmte on Public Lands. Same cmte: bill to provide compensation to Wm Woodbridge & Henry Chipman for services in adjusting titles to land in Michigan & for other purposes: committed. 2-Cmte on Commerce: bill to compensate & reimburse the owners & crew of the whaling ship **Chandler Price**, the losses & expenses in ransoming the crew of the ship **Columbia**; & a bill supplementary to an act for the relief of sick & disabled seamen: committed. 3-Cmte on Revolutionary Claims: bill for the relief of Nicholas Lachance, & a bill for the relief of Antoine Peltier & others: committed. Same cmte: adverse report on the memorial of Jonathan Hoge. Same cmte: adverse reports on the ptns of the heirs of Wm Hixt, deceased, of S C

continental line, & of the heirs at law of Capt Wm Davenport: laid on the table. Same cmte: bill for the relief of the heirs of Thos Wishart; bill for the relief of the grandchildren of Maj Gen Baron De Kalb; bill for the relief of the heirs of Capt Saml Rawson, an ofcr of the Revolutionary war, killed at the battle of Wyoming: committed. Same cmte: adverse reports on the ptn of the heirs of Lt Rignal, alias Nick Hilliary, & of Catharine N Van Rensselaer, only child & heir at law of Nicholas N Bogart: laid on the table. Same cmte: bill for the relief of Jos Savage, deceased; bill for the relief of Stephen Colwell, of Phil, administrator, with the will annexed, of Wm T Smith, deceased, late of Phil, in behalf of the distributes to said estate; bill for the relief of Ezra Chapman: committed. Same cmte: adverse reports on the ptns of March Farrington & of Wm R Johnston, executor of Geo Evans, deceased: laid on the table. Same cmte: bill for the relief of the heirs at law of Col David Hopkins, & a bill for the relief of the heirs at law of Dennis Purcell: committed. Same cmte: adverse report on the ptn of John Coltman, son of Capt Robt Coltman, deceased: laid on the table. 4-Cmte on Revolutionary Claims: discharged from the further consideration of the ptns of the heirs of Robt Kirk, deceased, & Thos A Baird, administrator of Dr Absalom Baird, deceased: laid on the table. 5-Cmte on Private Land Claims: bill for the relief of the heirs of Semoice, a friendly Creek Indian, & a bill further to amend an act, approved Jul 22, 1836, for the relief of Saml Smith, Linn McGhee, & Semoice, Creek Indians, & also an act passed Jul, 1836, for the relief of Susan Marlow: committed. Same cmte: adverse report on the petition of Jas Wood: laid on the table. Same cmte: bill to amend an act entitled, "an act for the relief of Fred'k Durrive," passed Aug 13, 1848: committed. 6-Cmte on Military Affairs: bill for the payment of the volunteers of the State of Vt for services at the battle of Plattsburg, & a bill for the relief of B M Bonton, Harriet F Fisher, & Geo Wright: committed. Same cmte: adverse reports upon the petitions of L C Duncan, Thos McDonald, & Ruth Freeman: laid on the table. Same cmte: adverse report on the petition of John Culp, administrator of Saml Dixon: laid on the table. 7-Cmte on Naval Affairs: bill for the relief of Capt Lewis Warrington & others: committed. Same cmte: bill for the relief of Gustavus A de Russe, late an acting Purser in the Navy; & a bill for the relief of David Myerle: committed. Same cmte: adverse report on the petition of Jonathan Gardner: laid on the table. Same cmte: bill for the relief of Dr Edmund L Du Barry, a Surgeon in the U S Navy: committed. 8-Cmte on Revolutionary Pensions: bill for the relief of Mary Kirby Smith: committed. Same cmte: discharged from the further consideration of the memorial of Nancy Haggard: & it was referred to the Cmte on Revolutionary Claims. 9-Cmte on Revolutionary Pensions: discharged from the further consideration of the ptns of Johnston Shrum, Wm Neal, Henry McKeavie, Henry Knoffenberger, Jas H Byersly, Wm Stevens, John Payne, John Henow, & others: laid on the table. Same cmte: adverse report on the petition of Mary Chess, widow of Jas Alexander: laid on the table.
10-Submitted: ptn of Mary Coil, of Crawford Co, Pa, widow of Patrick Coil, late of said county, praying Congress to grant her a pension, or an annuity, on account of the services rendered by said Coil, & sickness & disease contracted [from which he never recovered,] while in the service of the U S during the war of 1812.

In consequence of the sudden decease of his father-in-law, in Boston, Rev C W Denison has resigned his situation in the Navy Dept-the resignation to take effect on Jun 1 next. Mr Denison returns to Boston, to be connected with the "Olive Branch" of that city.

Lawsuit settled at New Orleans a few days ago, in the case of Eliz Hubgh vs Carrollton Railroad Co, in which the plntf sued for $10,000 damages for the killing of her husband by the explosion of a locomotive on the Carrollton railroad. Evidence showed that the locomotive was very old & the boilers were worn thin. It was also proved that Jacob Hubgh, the deceased, was an excellent engineer, experienced, skilful, & very prudent. The jury returned, after retiring 10 minutes, with a verdict for the plntf of $5,000.

The English papers announce the death of Sir Wm Allen, at the age of 68, Pres of the Royal Academy in Scotland. He was one of the most celebrated historical painters of the age. –Boston Journal

Hon John Maynard, a Judge of the Supreme Court of the State of N Y, died at his residence in Auburn on Sunday. He had been in feeble health for several years.

Mrd: on Mar 21, in N Y, by Rev Mr Stores, Mr Wm H Bassett, of Bridgeport, to Miss Adela, daughter of Philip Saunders of New Haven.

Mrd: on Mar 23, at the South Presbyterian Church, Brooklyn, N Y, by Rev Mr Spear, Geo Chapman, of N Y, to Miss Mary E, daughter of Saml B Deming, Brooklyn.

Mrd: on Mar 5, at Great Mills, St Mary's Co, Md, by Rev Mr Stanley, Dr A McWilliams, jr to Charlotte T Kirk, eldest daughter of late Henry N Kirk.

Mrd: on Mar 21, by Rev Mr French, N B Harrison, U S Navy, to Maria, youngest daughter of late Dr Horace Wellford, of Fredericksburg, Va.

Drowned: Capt Wm Clark, of Phil, on Mar 24, in Chesapeake Bay, off Chester River, 3 miles from Love Point, when the schnr **Tippecanoe** capsized during a snow squall. Four were on the boat, & two others also drowned.

Circuit Court of Wash Co-in Chancery: Edw Coles, cmplnt, against Wm H Deitz & Eliz C, his wife, dfndnts. The above cause states that to secure the sum of $1,200 with interest, payable annually from Nov 30, 1842, & the principal on Nov 30, 1852, the said Wm H Deitz executed his bond for the same, & the said dfndnts mortgaged lots 5, 6, & 10 in square 212 in Wash City; to be void if the said principal should be paid at the time mentioned above, & the interest annually, or upon demand after becoming due; but if the interest should not be paid as aforesaid, then the whole principal & interest should be & become due & payable; that the interest has not been paid since Nov 30, 1847, & that the said dfndnts have refused to pay the same; the object of the bill is to foreclose the said mortgage & to obtain a sale of the said premises for payment of the said principal & interest money. Wm H Deitz does not reside in this District, it is ordered, that the said complnt give notice to the said absent dfndnt of the substance & object of said bill: & said dfndnt to appear in this Court in person or by solicitor, on the first Mon of Sept next. –Jno A Smith, clerk

Senate: 1-Cmte on Pensions: bill for the relief of Geo Cassady, reported back the same without amendment & recommended its passage. Also, same cmte, bill for the relief of Wm Paddy, reported back the same without amendment & recommended its passage. Same cmte: bill for the relief of Lt Henry F Evans, reported back the same without amendment & recommended its passage. 2-Cmte on Private Land Claims: ptn of the heirs of Paschal Detchmendy, asking the confirmation of their title to a tract of land in Missouri, made an adverse report on the same. 3-Cmte on Contingent Expenses: resolution into making remuneration to J Robertson, made an adverse report thereon. 4-Cmte on Pensions: to inquire into granting a pension to the widow of Gen John McNeil: it is proposed to place Mrs McNeil on the pension roll for 5 years, at the rate of $50 per month. Mr Underwood: I wish to have time to consider this subject. The bill was not therefore considered at this time.

Valuable farm for sale: one on which the subscriber now resides: **Woodburn** in Fred'k Co: contains 415 acres, stone dwlg-house 2 stories high, plastered, containing 8 rooms & kitchen, & all necessary out-bldgs. Address by letter to J G Gray, Winchester, Va.

Criminal Court-Wash: 1-Wm S Mullin guilty, charging him with disabling the eye of Capt P Jones, in an affray, several weeks ago. The accused, who is a hack-driver, inflicted severe personal injury on Mr Jones, in an attempt to gouge him. 2-Chas Madden guilty of stealing 2 coats of the value of $30: to suffer 18 months' imprisonment in the penitentiary. 3-A true bill was found against David Little, charged with libel in vending & circulating the newspaper called the <u>Viper's Sting</u>. [Apr 2nd newspaper: David Little found guilty: sentenced to suffer 6 months imprisonment in jail & fined $50.]

Wet nurse wanted: she must be a young healthy free colored woman, with good recommendations. Apply to De Thos Miller.

Cigar stand for sale: subscriber desirous of entering into other business.
–E D Berry, jr, 8th st, 1 door from Pa ave

SAT MAR 30, 1850
The Phil papers record the death, at Naples, on Feb 22, of Chas Carroll Bayard, a Passed Midshipman in the U S Navy, son of the Hon Richd H Bayard, formerly U S Senator from the State of Delaware. Being on a cruise in the Mediterranean the vessel he was attached to stopped at Naples, & he obtained permission to visit Mount Vesuvius. While at the crater of the volcano an eruption suddenly took place, & some of the stones thrown out by the convulsion fell upon Mr Bayard's right arm, shattering it so badly as to cause his death.

The Richmond Whig records the death of Chas L Price, a tobacconist, who on Sunday, with a severe contusion over the right eye, from the effects of which, died on Tue. Mr Price said he fell on some steps, but blood being traceable on the street, & his hat found there also, the impression is that he was waylaid & bludgeoned.

Mr & Mrs Archer's Academy for Young Ladies, #40 Lexington st, Balt, Md. Its patronage extends through Mississippi, Alabama, Louisiana, & Va. The Principals refer to the Hon W L Sharkey, David Hunt, of Mississippi; Dr H W Tabb, Gen Rust, John H Bernard, of Va; Com Geisenger, U S Navy; Rev Thos Atkinson, Rev J G Hamner, Balt; & others whose daughters have been educated in this Academy. Annual examination was conducted through the past week of Jul 9. The gold medal for French was awarded to Miss Hollingsworth, of Elkton, Md; that for Music to Miss Sharkey, of Miss. The ceremony of closing took place in as private manner as possible, due to the recent death of the father of Mrs Archer, the late distinguished Chief Justice of Md. Diplomas were awarded to Misses S E Hopkins, O J Hamner, E B C Maddox, M H Alexander, M Gilman, M C Coakley, & E G Torrence, all of Balt City, & Misses J V Stone, of Louisiana, S W Dorsey, of Elkridge, Md, & E M Poindexter, of Halifax Co, Va. Diplomas were also awarded to Miss Bernard, of Miss, Miss Bailey & Miss Symington, of Balt, & Miss Warner, of Mass. [Mr Archer is a graduate of the West Point Academy.]

The Boston papers record the death of ex-Govn'r Saml T Armstrong, at his residence in that city, on Tue. He was in his usual health during the day, & expired almost immediately when he returned home. He was about 66 years of age.

Official: Zachary Taylor, Pres of the U S, recognizes Jas Grignon who has been appointed Consul of Her Britannic Majesty for the States of Maine & N H, to reside at Portland. Mar 28, 1850

Mrd: on Mar 28, by Rev Mr Edwards, J M Jesurun, of Curacoa, So America, to Ann Maria Johnson, of Colerain, Ireland.

Died: on Mar 23, at **Locust Hill**, Caroline Co, Va, Maria, consort of John Baylor, & youngest daughter of late Mungo Roy, in her 60th year.

For rent: desirable residence on the Anacostia, with 30 or 40 acres of land attached. Inquire of Mr Thos R Brightwell on the adjoining farm.

Appointments by the Pres: 1-Wm J B White, to be Deputy Postmaster at Phil. 2-Wm T Purnell, of Mississippi, to be U S Consul for the port of Bahia, in Brazil.

Notice-I O O F: Brothers of Anacostia Tribe, #3, are to meet at their Wigwan on Sun for the purpose of paying the last tribute of respect to our deceased brother, Wm H Page, deceased. –John H Russel, K of R

For sale: **Mondawmin**: the beautiful residence of the late Dr Patrick Macaulay, near the western verge of the city of Balt, offered by the trustees in chancery: 73 acres of land; dwlg is a modern structure of great elegance, 85 feet by 40, 2 stories, with porticoes; & all necessary out bldgs. The title is perfect, & all liens & taxes will be paid up to the day of sale. –J J Speed, Henry Webster, trustees

In Chancery: Wm Holmead & others, creditors of Patrick Moran, against Gregory Ennis, exc, & Mary Ann, Michael, John Thomas, & Rosa Moran, heirs of said Patrick Moran. Creditors of Patrick Moran, deceased, are to file their claims, properly vouched, with me, at my ofc, in the City Hall, Wash, or in Gtwn, before May 1. –W Redin, auditor

In Chancery: Circuit Court of Wash Co, D C. Sarah Craven et al vs Wm Craven. Trustees report sale, at public auction: French Forrest became the purchaser of the premises described in said decree & notice, for $1,075. The purchaser complied with the terms of the sale. –Jno A Smith, clerk

Mount Alban, D C: public examination, testimonials were awarded to:
Dennis B Lynes, of PG Co, Md
Jas Cortlandt Parker, jr, of N Y C
Ignatius Thos Davis, of Gtwn, D C
John Watts Kearny, of N Y C
Henry Warrington, of Wash, D C
Wm Pray Ten Broeck, of Mount Alban, D C
John Hobart Brown, of Newburgh, N Y
John Taylor, of Chas Co, Md
John W Lyons, of Gtwn, D C
Wm M Graham, of Wash, D C
Chas L Ellison, of New Windsor, N Y
Chas A Conrad, of New Orleans, La
L Lewis Conrad, of New Orleans, La
J Pemberton Nourse, of Highlands, D C
Wm Orton Williams, Gtwn, D C
Henry H Ten Broeck, Hudson, N Y
John G McBlair, Wash, D C
R Hilton Offley, of Gtwn, D C
Wm Henry Coles, jr, N Y
Walter H S Taylor, jr, Gtwn, D C
R W Meade Graham, Wash, D C
Wm Berrian Dayton, Wash, D C
Howard Parker, Wash, D C
Dallas Bache, Wash, D C
Robt W W Bowie, PG Co, Md
H Hobart Ten Broeck, Mount Alban, D C

MON APR 1, 1850
Died: on Fri last, Wm Page, while at work on a scaffold inside the Smithsonian Bldg, fell from the same, & fractured his skull as to cause his instant death. He was interred yesterday by the Society of Odd Fellows.

Public sale: writ of fieri facias: sale on May 2, all the right, title, & interest of Wm Hamilton in & to lot 3 in square 837; seized & taken as the property of said Hamilton, & will be sold to satisfy a debt due to the Corp of Wash –Jas M Bosher, Police Cnstbl

The Postmaster General has established the following new Post Ofcs for the week ending Mar 23, 1850.

Ofc	County, State	Postmaster
Ross Corner	York, Maine	Otis R Ross
West Groton	Middlesex, Mass	Adam Archibald
Oakdale	Worcester, Mass	E Clark, jr
West Bethany	Genesee, N Y	Heman Brown
Waverley	Tioga, N Y	B H Davis
Little Rest	Dutchess, N Y	B Humeston
Oswego Village	Dutchess, N Y	Robt Bennett
Cameron Mills	Steuben, N Y	Danl S Hubbard
Eatontown Landing	Monmoutn, N J	Wm Haynes
Jamesburgh	Middlesex, N J	Jas Redmond
Colesville	Sussex, N J	Wm J Owen
Pleasant Valley	Sussex, N J	Robt Lewis
Swartswood	Sussex, N J	Jos McDanolds
Coyleville	Butler, Pa	Francis Specht
Binkley's Bridge	Lancaster, Pa	T Brubaker
Greene	Lancaster, Pa	Wm P Pusey
Wheatland	Lancaster, Pa	Jacob Martin
Prentiss Vale	McKean, Pa	J W Prentiss
New Lexington	Somerset, Pa	Jacob R McMillen
Kentuckyville	Susquehannah, Pa	S S Chandler
Weisport	Carbon, Pa	Alex'r Lentz
Pleasant Hill	Wash, Pa	John McAdams
Mannis Choice	Bedford, Pa	V V Wertz
Tulpchocean	Berks, Pa	Moses Schock
Three Roads	Cambria, Pa	John Zerbee
Emigsville	York, Pa	J Blizzard
Little Creek Landing	Kent, Del	C H Heverin
Ringold	Wash, Md	Jos H Besore
Lacey Spring	Rochingham, Va	W H Barley
Sir John's Ruin	Morgan, Va	M P Higgins
Sleepy Creek Village	Moran, Va	Wm Rockwell
Erin Shades	Henrico, Va	Sol Lovenstine
Clover Creek	Highland, Va	C Carlisle
Patten's Home	Rutherford, N C	Elisha Banter
Bullock Creek	York D, S C	Danl Hamilton
Snapping Shoals	Newton, Ga	Jas W Hester
Yellow Creek	Lumpkin, Ga	Benj Jones
Fort Harley	Alachua, Fla	John P Weeks
Cedar Tree	Talladega, Ala	John Hubbard
Wilkesburg	Covington, Miss	S H Wilkes
Moon Lake	Coahoma, Miss	D D Thompson
Abbeville	Vermillion, La	Valsaint Veasy

Navarro	Leon, Texas	John J McBride
Minden	Rusk, Texas	Wm H Pate
Elkheart	Anderson, Texas	Jos Kennedy
Como	Henry, Tenn	A J Thomas
Stony Point	Bradley, Tenn	John Chilcutt
Chicamoga	Hamilton, Tenn	Smith Finley
Black Oak Grove	Hardeman, Tenn	John Miller
Big Ready	Edmondson, Ky	A B Mash
Cross Roads	Jefferson, Ky	Alex'r Sayres
Winton	Butler, Ohio	R T Butler
Lavona	Lucas, Ohio	P Robeson
Apple Grove	Meigs, Ohio	S H Hayman
Elliott's Cross Roads	Morgan, Ohio	Elliott
Marengo	Morrow, Ohio	Isaac Freeman
Vail's Cross Roads	Morrow, Ohio	Eli Dix
Winfield	Tuscarawas, Ohio	C C Correll
Herring	Allen, Ohio	Saml G Heath
East Exeter	Monroe, Mich	Peter Partland
Exeter	Monroe, Mich	Amos A Palmer
Grafton	Monroe, Mich	Josiah Littlefield
Millersville	Marion, Ia	Wm Winpenny
Vera Cruz	Wells, Ia	Jacob Filman
Sylvania	Parke, Ia	Jesse T Turner
Big Bend	Whitesides, Ill	Alfred A Higley
Killbuck	Ogle, Ill	Henry Hill
Bushy Ford	Coles, Ill	Benj Maddox
Prairie Bird	Shelby, Ill	Lawrence Walker
Hallsas	Noddaway, Mo	Amos Hallsa
Bagdad	Lafayette, Mo	Danl F Greenwood
Ringgold	Platte, Mo	Jas N Burnes
New Market	Van Buren, Iowa	N J Davis
Channingsville	Dubuque, Iowa	John C Hauley
Bennington	Marion, Iowa	Ezra H Baker
Oshaukuta	Columbia, Wis	Lafayette Hill
Fort Laramie	Oregon Terr	John S Turt

Names Changed:
Ireland Depot, Hampden Co, Mass, changed to Holyoke.
East Bradford, Essex Co, Mass, changed to Groveland.
Hart's Cross Roads, Crawford Co, Pa, changed to Hartstown.
State Ridge, York Co, Pa, changed to Bryansville.
Hynemansvilte, Lehigh Co, Pa, changed to Weisenburgh.
West Moriah, Essex Co, N Y, changed to North Hudson.
Salmonville, Oglethorpe Co, Ga, changed to Maxey.
Buena Vista, Henry Co, Ga, changed to Pittsburgh.
Dade Court-house, Dade Co, Missouri, changed to Greenfield.

Greenfield, Shelby Co, Missouri, changed to West Greenfield.
Bluff, Holt Co, Missouri, changed to Jackson Point.
Annsville, Pontotoc Co, Miss, changed to Harrisburgh.
Milton Mills, Ohio Co, Ind, changed to Guionsville.
St John's, Lake Co, Ill, changed to Port Clinton.

Died: yesterday, at his lodgings in Wash City, John Caldwell Calhoun. He was born Mar 18, 1782, & was therefore 68 years of age. He was more than 40 years with Genr'l Gov't. He was from S C. Buried in <u>Congressional Cemetery</u> then removed to his native S C for permanent interment. [Apr 3rd & 23rd] [Apr 2nd paper: John C Calhoun died of pulmonary; he was a native of S C; son of Patrick Calhoun who was born in Ire & came to Pa at an early age, moved to Va then to S C in 1756; John C's mother was born in Charlotte Co, Va.]

Orphans Court of Wash Co, D C. Letters testamentary on the personal estate of Philo B Johnson, late of said county, deceased. -Henry Johnson, exc

The steamer **Wilson G Hunt**, Capt Spall, from N Y for Calif, put into Bermuda on Mar 11 in a most deplorable condition, leaking badly, having narrowly escaped foundering at sea during a violent gale of wind on Mar 9. Thos Blackney, a fireman, was killed. A seaman, Richards, was put in a boat for safety, but the boat went adrift, & it was found impossible to save him. $10,000 in gold, belonging to the ship, accidentally fell into the sea & was lost.

Gtwn Dyeing Establishment: Old stand, west side of Jefferson st.
-F Wheatly, John T Berkley.

The house of Mr Jas Rouse, of French Creek, N Y, was consumed by fire on Mar 17, & 4 of his children perished in the flames. The fifth child was badly burnt. The parents were attending a meeting at a considerable distance from home, leaving the children to take care of the house.

TUE APR 2, 1850
Appointment by the Pres: 1-Jacob S Schriver, to be Deputy Postmaster at Wheeling, Va.

The trial of Albert G Gaskins, the young man who was arrested in Jan last, charged with robbing the U S mail, took place on Mon last before the Circuit Court of Charleston, S C, & resulted in his conviction on 4 separate indictments. He was sentenced to 40 years imprisonment at hard labor at Edgefield jail; 10 years for each offence.

Mrd: on Mar 6, in Atlanta, Ga, by Rev Ulzley G Parks, Mr J G U Mills, son of Gen E R Mills, of Marietta, & Miss Sarah E Payne, daughter of Edwin Payne, of Atlanta.

Died: on Mar 29, in Wash City, at the residence of her sister, Mrs Potter, Miss Mary Ellen Ford, of Balt.

Died: on Sun, Dr Alex'r McWilliams, in his 76th year, born in St Mary's Co, Md. He entered the Navy in 1801, & having served during the Tripolitan war, resigned in 1806 to practice medicine. He was the oldest living practitioner of medicine in Wash, as he would have been the oldest surgeon in the Navy, had he remained in that service. He was one of the founders of the Columbian Institute as well as of the Nat'l Institute. His funeral will be from his residence near the Navy Yard, at 4 o'clock, today.

Died: on Mar 23, Mrs Elvira Sedwick, consort of Mr Benj Sedwick, of Rappahannock Co, Va.

House of Reps: 1-Ptn of A P Brittingham, respecting his claims against Mexico: presented. 2-Ptn of the heirs of Peter Randon, for Creek depredations: presented.

WED APR 3, 1850
Destructive fire yesterday in a blacksmith's shop occupied by Mr Snyder, at C & 10th sts.

Yesterday the corner-stone of Trinity Church, 3rd & C sts, was laid by Rev Mr Butler, pastor of the Church: address delivered by Rev Mr Tillinghast. Rev Mr Gilliss read the prayers, & Hon Mr Berrien made an excellent address.

City Ordinance-Wash. 1-Act for the relief of Elias Barnes: the sum of $40 be paid to him being a balance due him for grading & gravelling B st, between N J & 2nd sts, per certificate of the Surveyor.

A costly dwlg house in Duxbury, Mass, was destroyed by fire last night, at the house of Hon G B Weston. The house was built about 6 years ago, cost about $40,000. The fire is supposed to have originated in the nursery. –Boston Traveller of Sat

Gershom Broadbent, #18 North Chas st, Balt, Md, has closed his store in Washington for the purpose of concentrating his business. He returns his sincere thanks to the ladies of that city for the kind patronage extended to him.

$30 reward for apprehension & conviction of the thief who entered my stable last Mon, & stole a valuable bay Horse. –Jas H Shreve, Livery Stable, 7th st, Wash

Silver & Brass Plating Manufactory, Wash, D C. Apply at 14, Pa ave, near 4½ st, at Mr Stephen Eddy's Watch & Jewelry Establishment.

I O O F members to attend funeral of David R Bell, late of Cross Creek Lodge, # 4, Fayetteville, N C. -Chas Calvert, rec sec

THU APR 4, 1850
Freehold Institute is situated in a retired part of the pleasant village of Freehold, Monmouth Co, N J. –Oliver Willis, A M, Principal

Senate: 1-Memorial of Wm H Chase, praying to be released from 2 judgments obtained against him by the U S on certain bonds, as given by him as Pres of the Alabama, Florida, & Georgia Railroad Co, for the payment of duties on railroad iron imported for the use of that company: referred to the Cmte on Commerce. 2-Memorial of P A S Dearborn, widow of Greenleaf Dearborn, late an ofcr in the army, asking to be allowed a pension: referred to the Cmte on Pensions. 3-Mr Foote presented documents relating to the claim of the widow of Leslie Chase, late an ofcr in the army, to a pension: referred to the Cmte on Pensions. 4-Ordered, that the ptn of Wm Wallis, on the files of the Senate, be referred to the Cmte on Public Lands.

I certify that John Nally, living near the Middle or Old Eastern Branch Bridge, brought before me as an estray, a bay roan mare. –Jas Crandell, J P [Owner is to prove property, pay charges, & take her away. –John Nally]

The steamer **H S Smith** took fire on Mar 17, while on her passage from Columbus to Apalachicola. Two of the passengers & 2 negro hands belonging to the boat were drowned. Gen Irwin, one of the passengers lost, was a wealthy planter, residing near Gainesville, & was returning home with the proceeds of his crop, $8,000 in gold. When the alarm of fire was given, he hastily seized the bag of gold, rushed to the side of the vessel, & jumped overboard, & almost instantly sunk

Boston Telegraph: Dr Webster's family were totally unprepared for the terrible result of his trial. The have all along had the strongest persuasion of his innocence. The character of the paper is to assure the afflicted family that, not withstanding the sad fate of the husband & father, the wife & daughters will continue as ever to be esteemed, respected, & beloved by their friends. [See Mar 25th newspaper.]

Naval. The sloop-of-war **St Louis**, Cmder Cocke, from Montevideo, arrived at Buenos Ayres Jas 8, & was to sail on the 21st for Rio Janeiro, with the remains of Com Rodgers, where they were to be conveyed to the U S in the U S frig **Brandywine**, it is believed. The ship **Albany**, Cmder Randolph, was below Para, Feb 21, bound to Barbadoes. Lt Washington Reid, of the **Albany**, died on board the 19th, & was buried in the village of Colares.

By order of the Orphans Court of Wash Co, D C. Sale of the personal effects of the late Geo Oyster deceased, at his late residence on Balt & Wash Turnpike: on Apr 11. –Green & Tastet, aucts

Mrd: on Apr 2, in Wash City, by Rev L F Morgan, Mr Jos Follansbee & Sarah Catharine Schwrar.

Mrd: on Apr 2, in Wash City, by Rev Mr Pyne, Lt John Navarre Macomb, of the Corps of Topographical Engineers, U S Army, to Miss Nannie Rodgers, daughter of late Cmdor John Rodgers, U S Navy.

Died: on Mar 19, in Dubuque, Iowa, Mr Wm A Nutt, of Alex, Va, in his 24th year.

FRI APR 5, 1850
The Portsmouth Pilot announces the arrival in Hampton Roads, on Tue, of the U S brig **Porpoise**. She sailed from Porto Praya on Feb 28, & St Thomas on Mar 21. List of her ofcrs & passengers: Lt Com'g Benj F Sands; Act Lt, J S Taylor, bearer of dispatches; Actg Master, Jas Armstrong; Asst Surgeon, Wm T Babb; Passed Midshipmen, Chas Gray & Jos E Seawell; Midshipmen, Geo E Belknap & John E Johnston; Capt's Clerk, Saml Harrison. Passengers, John D Parker, U S Consul, Capt de Verde Islands; Lt E S West, U S Marines, from U S ship **Portsmouth**; Actg Lt J C Wait, invalid, from U S ship **Portsmouth**; Passed Midshipman, Chas W Woolley, U S schnr **Taney**; J S Milligan, late Midshipman, from the U S ship **John Adams**.

Senate: 1-Memorial of Eliza Kirby, of Brownsville, N Y, widow of the late Edw Kirby, an ofcr in the U S army. Maj Kirby entered the army as an ensign in 1812, & served during the war with Great Britain. He continued until the close of the war; remained on the peace establishment till 1819, when he joined the staff of Maj Gen Brown as an aid de camp, & remained in his military family until 1824, when he was promoted to a captaincy. Soon afterwards he was appointed paymaster general, & continued in that ofc until his death. He was in the Black Hawk war & in the Creek campaigns; & on the breaking out of the war with Mexico, he joined Gen Taylor at Matamoros, & remained with him until he was ordered to join Gen Scott at Tampico, & served with him in all the battles which resulted in the conquest of the city of Mexico. In that campaign he contracted a disease of which he languished & died in Aug of last year. His widow, Eliza Kirby, daughter of Maj Gen Brown, brings before the Senate this memorial in a manner equally modest & touching. Memorial referred to the Cmte on Pensions. 2-Memorial of Jas Holford, a subject of Great Britain, & holder of some certain State bonds & securities, invoking the adoption of some measures by the Genr'l Gov't for their payment: referred to the Cmte on the Judiciary. 3-Memorial from the citizens of Cayuga Co, N Y, in behalf of the widow & heirs of Robt H Morris, an ofcr in the last war with Great Britain, asking that she be allowed a pension: referred to the Cmte on Pensions. 4-Ptn from Frances C Baden, widow of Maj Nehemiah Baden, late of the U S Army, asking that she may be placed on the pension roll. The ptn states that her husband's constitution was impaired by diseases incident to our Southern climate, & particularly at Ogelthorpe barracks, where he lost many of his men, & only escaped with his own life after a long & dangerous illness. Ptn referred to the Cmte on Pensions. 5-Memorial from Saml M Clendenin, asking compensation for clerical services rendered to an agent of the Gov't: referred to the Cmte of Claims.

Indian depredations in Texas. A party of 6 Indians killed a Mexican near Laredo, on Feb 23. Lt Viele started in pursuit, but was unable to come up with the marauders. About the same time Lt Hudson pursued a party of Indians at **Fort McIntosh**, & had a running fight with them for several miles. He rescued a Mexican boy. An escort returning from Eagle Pass was attacked by Indians 25 miles west of Leons. One of the soldiers was killed. A soldier's wife, in company, & the driver of the carriage, are supposed to have fallen into the hands of the Indians. There are now 4 scouts out in hot pursuit of the savages.

Died: on Apr 3, of lung fever, Wilfred M Grey, infant & only son of J W & Eliza J Grey, aged 2 years, 2 months & 19 days. His funeral will be at his parents' residence, 8th st, between L & M sts, Apr 5, at 2 o'clock.

Mrs Ann Clarke will open French Millinery on Apr 6, at her Fashionable Millinery Saloon. All repairing done at her store, Bridge st, Gtwn, opposite Mr H E Berry's store.

House of Reps: 1-Ptn of A G Penn, for advances made while postmaster at New Orleans. 2-Ptn of Nathan Lee, for compensation for carrying the mail; also, of Nathan Lee, Wm King, & Saml W Wickmine, for compensation as witnesses in the U S court; memorial of the widow & heirs of Fulmer S Skipworth. 3-Ptn of Jas Porterfield & other heirs of Jas Young, late of Bristol, Maine, deceased, asking indemnity for French spoliations prior to 1800. 4-Ptn of Edw L Young, praying pecuniary relief for the loss of his right eye, occasioned by the performance of public duties while in the naval service. Ptn of various citizens of Norfolk & Portsmouth, praying pecuniary relief for Edw L Young, for the same.

SAT APR 6, 1850
Senate: 1-Cmte on Indian Affairs: memorial of Wm Harding, asking remuneration of certain expenses incurred while U S agent among the Cherokees, submitted a report, which was ordered to be printed, accompanied by a bill for his relief, & recommending its passage. 2-Cmte of Claims: the case of Gamaliel Taylor, asking to be released from certain liabilities, submitted a report, which was ordered to be printed, accompanies with a bill for his relief, & recommending its passage. 3-Cmte of Claims: memorial & documents relating to the claim of Ezra Williams, a clerk in the Gen Land Ofc, asking compensation for extra services: passed to a 2nd reading. 4-Memorial from Geo Watterston, & other citizens of D C, asking the establishment of an Agricultural College in that District: referred to the Cmte on Agriculture. 5-The claim of John Hollahan: referred to the Cmte of Claims. 6-Motion was agreed to for the relief of Jas Robertson. 7-Memorial of Henry Grinnell, a merchant, who is now fitting out in the port of N Y 2 or 3 vessels, which he purposes to send out in search of Sir John Franklin & his companions.

The remains of late Cmdor Geo Washington Rodgers, U S Navy, were removed on 22nd, from old Protestant Cemetery, Buenos Aires, where they rested nearly 18 years, to the U S corvette **St Louis**, in order to be conveyed to the U S.

Two members of the late House of Reps of Louisiana, Mr McCranie, of Jackson, & Mr Livingston, of Morehouse, were seized with cholera on their way home after the adjournment of that body, & both died before they reached their residence.

Mrd: on Apr 4, at St John's Church, by Rev Smith Pyne, Chas St John Chubb to Eliza Crane, daughter of Cmdor Warrington, both of Wash City.

Mrd: on Apr 4, at St Peter's Church, by Rev Mr Lanaghan, Mr Jos Lowe to Mgt A Field, both of Wash City.

House of Reps: 1-Mr Stanton, of Tenn, asked the unanimous consent of the House to withdraw from its files the papers of Jos K Boyd, connected with the frig **Philadelphia**. 2-Bill for the relief of John Dickson, surviving partner of the firm of Lambert & Dickson: from the Cmte of the Whole House: recommended that it do not pass.
3-The following bills had no objections & were laid aside to be reported to the House- relief of: Eliphas C Brown; Skelton Felton; Geo Collier & Wm G Pettus; John Plunkett; Williams, Staples & Williams; Smith & Hersey; Jos Richards; Edw Everett, late a sgt of the U S army; Anna Giffin; Jacob Zimmerman; Wm Whicher; Chas Stuart; Sarah Jane West; & the legal reps of Capt Geo R Shoemaker, deceased. 4-Bills which were objected to, & therefore laid over-relief of: Wm Slocum, of N Y; Jos D Ward; A Baudouin & A D Roberts, of New Orleans; Sayles J Cowen; Winthrop S Harding; Danl Steenrod; Wm J Price; Christopher H Pix; Jas Dixon; Manuel X Harmony; Thos O Selfridge; Saml Graves; Jacob Drinkhouse; Jesse Doane; Hubert H Booly; legal reps of Jas C Watson, of Georgia; settlement of the claim of Henry Leef & John McKee; relief of the heirs of Joshua Eddy, deceased; relief of the heirs of Larkin Smith; relief of the heirs of Lt Barlett Hinds.

Died: on Mar 5, in Wash City, at the residence of his daughter, Mrs Louisa Collins, on G st, between 2nd & 3rd sts, Mr Jas Avery, a very respectable & venerable citizen, aged 74 years. His disease was most painful & lingering. His death was most peaceful & happy. His funeral sermon will be preached on Sabbath morning, at half past 9 o'clock, at the above place. After services at the house the remains will be conveyed to Alexandria for interment.

Died: on Mar 21, in Huntsville, Ala, the residence of Geo P Beirne, Mrs S Carter Gray, late of Charlottesville, Va, in her 66th year.

Mrd: on Apr 4, by Rev Mr Marks, Mr Levi Hazel to Miss Rebecca Little.

Died: on Mar 24, at Parkersburg, Va, Mr Jas H Neal, for many years Clerk of the Circuit & Superior & County Courts at that place.

Board of Health Report: interments in Wash, DC, for month ending Mar 31: total 70. –Thos Miller, M D, Pres

MON APR 8, 1850
An old & respectable citizen of N Y, Abraham Lockwood, committed suicide on Fri, by cutting his throat. He was a wealthy man, but the perplexities of business pressed upon him, depressed his spirits, & even deranged his mind. He was 51 years of age.

Wm A Coit, of Brooklyn, having been convicted of an assault upon his mother, Emily Coit, in Jun last, by a threat to shoot her if she did not sign & acknowledge a certain mortgage, was sentenced on Fri to 6 months in the county jail & fined $250, & to stand committed till paid.

Sale of paintings in N Y on Wed last:
The City of Edinburgh, by Naysmith: $525.
Madona, by Sirani: $220.
Madona, by Parmegiano: $240.
Angel's Visit, by Stella: $205.
Madona & St Elizabeth: $400
Sheep & Goats, by Rosa du Tivoli: $150.
Portrait of Mrs Robt Morris, by Stuart: $300.
A beautiful Landscape, by Fabricus: $170.
Beggar Boy, Murillo: $175.
Boy Firing a Pistol, $100.
Canal at Venice, $105.
Head of a Cow: $100.
Holy Family, by Battoni: $170.
Madonna, on copper: $150.
View in Holland, by Brakelenkay: $280.

The Cleveland Herald mentions the death of Dr Saml Strong, of Elyria, after a short illness, the exciting cause of which arose from an attack upon his character in the Courier newspaper, published there.

Jas M Davis, one of the principal merchants in Phil, died suddenly last evening, in the store of Mr Durand. –North Amer

Mrd: on Mar 19, by Rev Mr Blox, Mr Enoch Zell, of Balt, Md, to Miss Mary H Kirk, of Wash City.

House of Reps: 1-Ptn of Francis B Crump, of Va, for allowance of a claim based on the services of his ancestor, Benj Crump, in the war of the Revolution. 2-Memorial of Elisha Ques, for compensation for his boat captured in the war of 1812, while in Gov't service.

Graduates of the Nat'l Medical College, D C: annual Commencement held last Sat in the lecture room of the Smithsonian Institution.

Jas S Gunnell, jr, of D C
J M Adler, of D C
Ruel Keith Compton, of D C
Euserius Lee Jones, of D C
Wm A Williams, of D C
Alexander X Young, of D C
Wm A Douglass, of Va

Powhatan Jordan, of Va
Frisby R Smith, of Md
Wm B Butt, of Wash
S Blanchard, of N H
J Edw Chase, of Ohio
Leopold Dovilliers, of France

The honorary degree of Dr of Medicine was conferred upon Thos Ballamy, Surgeon, Isle of Guernsey, Great Britain.

Died: on Sun, at the U S Hotel, Mrs Henrietta M Dawson, wife of Hon Sen Wm C Dawson, Senator from Ga.

Died: on Apr 6, Mrs Mary Ann Ridgeway, wife of Mr Enoch Ridgeway, of Wash City. Her many virtues endeared her to a large family & friendly circle. Her funeral will take place today, at 3 o'clock.

Died: on Apr 6, after a short but painful illness, at the residence of Mr Jno R Murray, Richmond, Cornet Thompson, formerly of Culpeper Court House, Va, in her 20th year

TUE APR 9, 1850
House of Reps: 1-Ptn of Thos B Harvey, of Clarke Co, Va, praying for a pension. 2-Ptn of Thos S Winslow for a register for the British barque **Cornwallis**. 3-Ptn of Robt Milligan, a soldier of the war of 1812, for an increase of pension. 4-Ptn of Hugh Cosgrove & 26 others, for trial by jury for alleged fugitive slaves.

Senate: 1-Ptn from citizens of Cayuga Co, N Y, asking that a pension may be allowed to Mary Ingersoll, widow of a Revolutionary soldier: referred to the Cmte on Pensions. 2-Memorial of W W Loring & other ofcrs of the army stationed in the Oregon Territory, asking an increase of pay. 3-Cmte on Indian Affairs: ptn of Jos Parks, a member of the Shawnee tribe of Indians, asking compensation for a negro slave rescued from his possession by a mob of persons of the State of Illinois: asked to be discharged from the further consideration of the same: referred to the Cmte on the Judiciary. 4-Cmte on Indian Affairs: memorial of the chiefs of the Menominee Indians, asking payment of a debt due by them to Robt Grignon, made an adverse report on the same. 5-Cmte on the Judiciary: bill from the House of Reps: to refund the fine imposed on the late Dr Thos Cooper under the sedition law to his heirs, reported the same without amendment, & recommend its passage. 6-Ptn of Jas W Robinson, asking to be allowed an increase of pension: referred to the Cmte on Pensions.

Circuit Court of Wash Co, D C. Court of Chancery. Francis Dodge, jr, & A Hamilton Dodge, cmplnts, vs Geo Krafft & John M Krafft, dfndnts. Geo Krafft, late of said county, being indebted to cmplnts. Geo Krafft owned part of lot 16 square 141, in Wash City, D C, with a valuable dwlg, store-house & bakery; sold same to his brother, John M, for $3,000. Geo Krafft absconded from the district, concealing himself in some place unknown to the cmplnt. The object of the bill is to have the said deed vacated & annulled by a decree of said court, & the premises sold for the payment of the cmplnts' said debt, interest, & cost of suit. Geo Krafft, in person or by atty, to appear in this court on or before the third Mon in Oct next. -Jno A Smith, clk

Orphans Court of Wash Co, D C: sale of all the personal effects of the late Mrs Ann W Benning. –Dyer & Bro, aucts

Killed: on Mar 28, Mrs Ashworth, wife of Mr Ashworth, from Ky, who was crushed to death leaving a train, at Scipio, Indiana. She was with her husband on the train. Her infant was with her at the time of the accident. [No word about the condition of the infant.]

Died: on Apr 7, Miss Sarah McDermott, in her 19th year. Her funeral will be at residence of Mr Thos C Wilson, 14th & L sts, this afternoon at 4 o'clock.

WED APR 10, 1850
Senate: 1-Memorial of the heirs of Jas Young: asking indemnity for French spoliations prior to 1800: ordered to lie on the table. 2-Memorial of Howell R Robards, asking compensation for his services as surgeon to the regt of Tenn volunteers in the late war with Mexico: referred to the Cmte on Military Affairs. 3-Ptn of Wm A Adams & others, citizens of Hamilton Co, Ohio, asking indemnity for French spoliations prior to 1800: ordered to lie on the table. 4-Cmte of Claims: memorial of John S Develin, administrator of Elijah J Weed, late quartermaster of marines, asking that the accounts of said Weed be settled: passed to a 2nd reading. 5-Bills from the House of Reps: referred to the Cmte of Claims-relief of: John Dickson, surviving partner of the firm of Lambert & Dickson; Geo Collier & Wm G Pettus; legal rep of Capt Geo R Shoemaker, deceased; Sarah Jane West; John Plunkett; & Chas Stuart. 6-Bill from the House of Reps: referred to the Cmte on Pensions: relief of-Camfield Averill; Jacob Zimmerman; Anna Giffin; Skelton Felton; Eliphas C Brown; & Wm Whicher. 7-Bill for the relief of Edw Everett, late a sgt in the U S army: referred to the Cmte on Military Affairs. 8-Bill for the relief of Jos Richards: referred to the Cmte on Private Land Claims. 9-Congress of the U S, in Oct, 1780, passed the following: Resolved, that a monument be erected to the memory of the late Maj Gen the Baron DeKalb, at the city of Annapolis, in the State of Md, with the following inscription:
Sacred to the memory of the
BARON DE KALB,
Knight of the royal order of military merit,
Bigadier of the armies of France
And
Major General
In the service of the United States of America
Having served with honor and reputation
For three years
He gave a last and glorious proof of his
Attachment to the liberties of mankind
And the cause of America,
In the action near Camden, in the State of South Carolina,
On the 16th day of August, 1780,
When, in leading on the troops of the
Maryland and Delaware lines
Against superior numbers,
And animating them by his example
To deeds of valor,
He was pierced with many wounds,
And on the nineteenth following expired,
In the 48th year of his age.
The Congress

Of the United States of America,
In gratitude to his zeal, services, and merit,
Have erected this monument.
[And whereas, from some cause unknown to this Legislature, the resolution has never been carried into effect by the erection of a monument to the illustrious champion of liberty whose memory it was designed to perpetuate: referred to the Cmte on Military Affairs.]

Maj Gen Sir Hercules Pakenham, G C B, brother of Sir Edw Pakenham, who fell at New Orleans, died in Antoin, Ireland, Mar 7.

The U S mail steamer **Hermann**, Capt E Crabtree, has arrived at N Y, bringing the usual mail. She left Bremen on the 15th ult, arrived at Southampton on the 17th, in 48 hours, & sailed from the latter port at 4 p m on the 20th. She brings about 70 passengers & a valuable freight.

Naval: the U S storeship **Relief**, Lt Totten, was at Gibraltar on Mar 3.

Valuable improved property at auction: on Apr 17: lots 6 & 7, & part of lot 8, in square 118, with a 3 story brick house, formerly occupied by Mr Crampton, British Charge, situated at the corner of I & 20th sts. -Dyer & Brother, aucts

House of Reps: 1-The case of E D McKinney was recommitted: referred to the Cmte on Indian Affairs. 2-Select cmte to investigate the conduct & relation of the Sec of War, Geo W Crawford, to the claim of the reps of Geo Galphin, lately adjudicated & paid at one of the Depts of the Govn't.

Mrd: on Apr 2, by Rev Thos Myers, Mr Wm H Pritchett to Miss Mary J Marche.

Mrd: on Apr 9, at Christ Church, Gtwn, D C, by Rev Mr Gassaway, Robt H Watkins, of Norfolk, Va, to Sarah E, daughter of late Alex Suter, of Gtwn, D C.

Died: on Apr 9, in Wash, Mrs Maria Marceron, wife of Louis Marceron, in her 50th year, formerly of Chas Co Md. She leaves her husband & 7 children. Her funeral will be from her residence on Pa av, between 6th & 7th sts, near the Navy Yard, tomorrow, at 4 o'clock.

Died: on Mar 14, in Germantown, Pa, Mrs Susan K M Haverstick, wife of Prof H Haverstick, of Phil, & 2nd daughter of Robt Polk, deceased, of Wash, D C.

Died: The body of Peter Carrigan, U S Marine, was found in the Wash Canal Apr 8. He'd been missing from Marine Barracks for 18 days. Verdict of the inquest, accidentally drowned.

Loudoun land for sale: the undersigned, excs of the late Cuthbert Powell, by authority derived from his will, & by the desire of the heirs, will offer at public sale, on Jun 19, on the premises, *Llangollen*, the late residence of said Powell. It is about 2½ miles from Blue Ridge & contains about 762 acres: the dwlg is of brick, rough-cast, large & commodious. –Wm H Gray, Chas L Powell, excs

Public sale: on Apr 12, by order of the Orphans Court of Wash Co, D C, for cash, at the Wash Scales Hotel, 7th st west, the goods & chattels of the late Philo B Johnson, deceased: watch, clothing, trunks, axe, shaving implements, umbrella, & 5 shares of stock of the Smithfield Co, $200 each share. –Henry Johnson, exc

Household & kitchen furniture at auction: on Apr 16, at the residence of Lt Holcomb, on C st, near 3rd st. –Green & Tastet, aucts

THU APR 11, 1850
Brakeman, John Kearney, was instantly killed on Mon, as the steamboat train from the east, on the Boston & Worcester railroad, when crossing the Willkinson bridge, the bridge broke down and one passenger car was precipitated through the opening.

Senate: 1-Memorial of Gilbert Cameron, asking that a contract be made with him to complete the wings of the Patent Ofc, on the ground of his having been the lowest bidder under the advertisement: referred to the Cmte on Patents & the Patent Ofc. 2-Ptn of John S Gibson, asking the remission of a fine imposed on him for the non-performance of service on route 6,012: referred to the Cmte on the Post Ofc & Post Roads.

The Postmaster General has established the following new Post Ofcs for the week ending Apr 6, 1850:

Ofc	County, State	Postmaster
Yellow Mount'n	Yancy, N C	Alex Erwin
Childsville	Yancy, N C	A D Childs
Canberry Forge	Watauga, N C	John H Dunn
Roan Mountain	Carter, Tenn	Nicholas Smith
Zimmerman	Greene, Ohio	Alex Coy

Julius A Fay's Boarding School for Boys, Elizabethtown, N J: summer session will commence on the first Mon in May.

Mrd: on Apr 3, at Rochester, N Y, Henry J Brent, to Weltha, only daughter of Dr Fred'k F Backus.

Mrd: on Apr 10, by Rev J S Gorsuch, Job P McIntosh to Miss Angeline Hinton, both of Wash.

Delaware College will begin on Apr 24. Apply to W A Norton, Pres.

The heirs of Clement Wood, a native of Lincoln, England, & only son of Mgt & Cary Wood, of the Parish of St Michael, in that city, emigrated to the then British colonies in North America, about 1784. It is not known to what part of the said colonies he emigrated, nor has he been heard of since he left England. Should he or any of his descendants be now residing in the U S, he or they, by applying to Wm B Webb, Atty at Law, of Wash City, or Mr Pishey Thompson, 5, Bank Chambers, Lothbury, London, will hear something very much to his or their advantage. An ancestor of the said Clement Wood was named Bononi Wood; this was a family name, & very likely to be continued among the descendants of the said Clement Wood. Isaac & Mgt are also names which frequently occurred in the said family. All letters to London must be post paid to England. [May 7th newspaper: to the Editors of the Nat'l Intelligencer. Old Clem Wood, as he was usually called, kept the county jail in Lincoln about 1784, & died leaving a large property, said to have been obtained unlawfully, by taking the prisoners from the jail & working them on his farm. He left 2 sons, Isaac & Robt, & a daughter, I think, who all died unmarried. Isaac, a lunatic, & Robt not much better. These Woods were related to Benj Hyde, who was born near Lincoln, & came to the U S in 1784, & settled near to Fredericksburg, Spottsylvania Co, Va, & carried on a business, in connexion with his relations, named Young & Smith; & some of the descendants are now residing in that county & other places in the U S. The celebrated Richd Parkinson, who came to **Mount Vernon** about 1795, & afterwards settled at the Orange farm, near to Balt, & published his travels in the U S, was a relation of these Woods, Hydes, & Youngs. The gentlemen likely to know something of this Clement Wood are, perhaps, Wm Benton, near to Middleburg, Loudoun Co, Va, & John Yates, residing near to Charlestown, Jefferson Co, Va; or the heirs of Basil Gordon, or of Thos Goodwin, of Fredericksurg. –S S]

Things in Phil. 1-Henry Horst, whilst on a visit to his brother-in-law on Sunday, was seized with an illness & died in a few minutes, of an affection of the heart. 2-Albert Campbell aged 16 years, fell from a swing on Sunday, Apr 7, & was instantly killed. 3-Henry Jones, a musician, put an end to his life on Monday, by cutting his throat.

Mrs Webster, wife of Dr Webster, now under sentence of death, accompanied by her 3 daughters, called upon Govn'r Briggs, on Sun last, & presented a petition for the commutation of the penalty which now awaits their relative.

For sale: a likely negro boy, to serve 10 years, worth $6 per month, but the owner wishes to raise $200, which amount he is willing to take for him. Also, has a negro man to hire. Apply to G Stuart, at Mrs Bright's Boarding-house on C st.

FRI APR 12, 1850
Owner wanted: the subscriber has in his possession a watch which he has no doubt has been stolen. It was a present from Pres Andrew Jackson. Address Henry A London, Pittsboro, N C.

Died: on Apr 11, Kate Vernon, infant daughter of Daniel & Matilda B Smith, aged 8 months & 14 days.

Senate: 1-Memorial of Geo Ketcham & 84 other citizens of Indiana, who were ofcrs & soldiers in the last war with Great Britain, asking bounty land for their services. 2-Memorial from Brevet Col J F K Mansfield, of the U S engineers, for the settlement of his public accounts as disbursing agent of the Govn't, while superintending the construction of certain public works: referred to the Cmte on Military Affairs. 3-Memorial of Jos Byrd, which set forth that in acting as a private soldier in Florida against the Creek Indians, in the war of 1814, during the war with Great Britian, while out as a scout, belonging to a company of spies, he came upon a prize which was in possession of a British schnr, a quantity of merchandise. The crew of the schnr, supposing him to be attended by a larger company, weighed anchor & left a portion of the goods on the shore. They were chiefly goods designed for the Indian consumption, & were taken into camp & finally distributed among the troops stationed there at that time. The petitioner prays that he may be allowed a compensation: referred to the Cmte on Military Affairs. 4-Ptn of John P Skinner & the legal reps of Isaac Greene, asking to be released from a judgment against them as sureties for the late pension agent, Thos Emerson, of Vt: referred to the Cmte on the Judiciary. 5-Ordered, that the petition of Richd S Coxe, on the files of the Senate, be referred to the Cmte on the Post Ofc & Post Roads. 6-Cmte on Pensions: bill for the relief of Mgt E Carnes, widow of Peter H Carnes: ordered to be printed. 7-Cmte on Commerce: act for the relief of Williams, Staples, & Williams, & an act for the relief of Smith & Hersey, reported back the same without amendment, & recommended their passage. 8-Cmte on Pensions: bill for the relief of Camfield Averill: recommended its passage. 9-Cmte on pensions: bill for the continuance of a pension to Mary McRae: this is her sole dependence: bill was passed. 10-Cmte on Naval Affairs: memorial of Thos Marston Taylor, asking allowance for Treasury notes deposited in the Phoenix bank of Charlestown, Mass, & lost by the failure of the bank, submitted a report, which was ordered to be printed, accompanied by a bill for the relief of Thos M Taylor & Francis B Stockton: passed to a second reading. Same cmte: reported a bill for the relief of Purser T P McBlair: passed to a 3rd reading.

The barque **Sherwood** arrived at Boston on Wed, having on board Capt Hunt, of the brig **John Hill**, of & for Bristol, R I, from Cardenas, before reported lost, with all hands except the first mate, who was taken off & carried to Charleston. When rescued by the **Sherwood**, they proceeded to the wreck of the **John Hill**. The unfortunate crew must have met with a watery grave. There were 9 all told on board: Mr Alex'r Gifford, mate; Messrs Bowen & Vaughan, passengers; the cook, & 5 before the mast.

Mrd: on Tue last, by Rev Mr Pyne, Dr Jas H Causten, jr to Miss Annie Payne, both of Wash City.

Mrd: on Apr 11, by Rev L F Morgan, Mr Saml H Lamborn, of Ohio, to Miss Virginia E Kleiber, of Wash City.

Mrd: on Apr 10, by Rev G W Samson, Mr Chas Wilson to Miss Mary Thompson Bloxham, all of Wash.

Died: Apr 10, in Wash City, Juliet Virginia, infant daughter of Wm H & Sarah A Prentiss, aged 8 months.

SAT APR 13, 1850
Senate: 1-Ptn of Almanzor Houston, asking compensation for carrying the mail: referred to the Cmte on the Post Ofc & Post Roads. 2-Ordered, that the memorial of John P Walbach, on the files of the Senate, be referred to the Cmte on Military Affairs. 3-Cmte on Commerce: memorial of Enoch Baldwin, praying a return of duties wrongfully exacted, reported a bill for the relief of Enoch Baldwin & others: passed to a second reading.

House of Reps: 1-Cmte on Naval Affairs: bills for the relief of Wm Gove; of Benj Cressy; of Jas W Wilkins; & of Lot Davis; & also a bill granting a pension to Asel Wilkinson: committed. Same cmte: adverse report on the memorial of Saml T Anderson: laid on the table. Same cmte: discharged from the further consideration of the ptn of Ursula E Cobb, widow of Chas Cobb: referred to the Cmte on Invalid Pensions. 2-Cmte on Invalid Pensions: bills for the relief of Mary W Thompson & of Alanson Pool: committed. Same cmte: bills for the relief of Hamilton Carroll & of Fielding G Brown: committed. 3-Cmte of Claims: bill for the relief of Matthews, Hall & Wood: committed. Same cmte: bills for the relief of Geo Armstrong, of Maj E H Fitzgerald, of Monoah D Robison, & of Wm Kilgour: committed. Same cmte: adverse report on the ptn of Capt Francis Cicote: laid on the table. 4-Cmte of Claims: discharged from the further consideration of the ptns of Chas Waldron, & of the legal reps of the late Gen Robt Young: laid on the table. Same cmte: discharged from the further consideration of the ptns of Hendricks & Jones, next of kin of Robt Leckie, & of R S Coxe: laid on the table. Same cmte: adverse reports on the ptns of Geo Harvey, of Elliot Smith, & of Nathan Farnsworth: laid on the table. Same cmte: bill for the relief of Thos Crown: committed. Same cmte: adverse reports on the ptns of Howell & Coates & of Joshua Hillyard: laid on the table. 5-Cmte on Commerce: discharged from the further consideration of the memorial of Chas Massey, jr, & of the rector, warden, & vestry of the Chruch of the Advent, in Boston: laid on the table. Same cmte: discharged from the further consideration of the ptn of Capt Henry M Shreve: referred to the Cmte of Claims. 6-Cmte on Public Lands: bill for the benefit of John Ozias: committed. Same cmte: bill for the relief of Jasper A Malthy: committed. 7-Cmte on the Post Ofc & Post Roads: bill for the relief of Dunning R McNair: committed. Same cmte: joint resolution providing for the adjustment of the accounts of John D Colmarine, Pres of the Ohio & Mississippi Mail Line Co: committed. 8-Cmte on Revolutionary Pensions: adverse reports on the ptns of Catherine Adair, widow of Gen John Adair, of Ky; of Hannah Weston; of Mary B Francisco; of Anna L Scott; of Mott Wilkinson; of Nehemiah Holden; of citizens of Tenn for increase of pension to Jordan Milan; of Sianna Griffin; & of Jonathan Hutchins: laid on the table. Same cmte: reported a joint resolution for the relief of the children of Sarah Stokes, deceased: passed. Same cmte: bills for the relief of John Morrison, Adam Garlock, & Rebecca Freeman, widow of Pearson Freeman: committed. Same cmte: adverse report on the ptn of Jos Merchant: laid on the table. Same cmte: discharged from the further consideration of the ptn of the executor of Carter Page, praying the allowance of commutation pay for services during the Revolutionary war: laid on the table. Same cmte: adverse report on the ptn of Saml Gilman; of John Jones, of Ky; of Jeremiah Stilwell; & of Uriah Wilson: laid on the table. 9-Cmte on Invalid Pensions: bill for the relief of Thos Flanagan: committed. Same cmte: bill for the relief of Jonas D Platt; & of Peter Frost: both committed. Same cmte: discharged from the further consideration of the ptn of the legal reps of John Jackson, deceased: referred to the Cmte on Revolutionary Pensions. 10-Cmte on Military Affairs: ptn of Franz Schurmann, of Georgia, & the ptn of Jas H Rogers, of Texas: laid on the table. Same cmte: adverse report on the ptn of John Shaefer: laid on the table. Same cmte: bill for the relief of Josiah P Pilcher: committed. Same cmte: discharged from the further consideration of the memorial of the heirs of Jas Greer & of Richd Pool: laid on the table. Same cmte: discharged from the further consideration of the ptn of Jacob Saunders & other citizens of Pa: referred to the Cmte on Public Lands. Same cmte: discharged from the further consideration of the ptn of certain citizens of Pa, praying an amendment to the law relative to evidence in claims of disabled soldiers; also, the memorial of the General Assembly of the State of Alabama, in behalf of John Scott: referred to the cmte on Invalid Pensions. 11-Act for the relief of Mary McRae, for merely the renewal of a pension for 5 years: referred to the Cmte on Revolutionary Pensions. 12-Act for the relief of Mgt L Worth, widow of the late Gen Worth, of the army of the U S: read twice. 13-Bill for the relief of Solomon T Nicoll & Jas Clinch, of N Y C: bill laid aside to be reported to the House, with the recommendation that it do not pass. 14-Unanimous consent of the House to withdraw from the files the papers in the case of Saml T Winslow, for the purpose of referring the same to one of the Executive Depts. 15-Ptn of John Adams, of Pa, a Revolutionary soldier, praying Congress to grant him a pension. 16-Ptn of Mary Ann Williams, in behalf of the estate of her late father, John Ron, deceased, for relief. 17-Ptn of C B Culver & 33 others, of Mass, for the repeal of a patent reissued to Chas Goodyear.

Hon Jas Emott, a distinguished & remarkable member of the bar & bench of N Y, died at his residence in Poughkeepsie on Sun. Judge Emott was a member of Congress in 1812. He was 80 years old.

Mr Benj H Punchard, of Andover, Mass, who died recently, has left by his will the sum of $60,000 to be appropriated to the establishement & endowment of a High School for boys & girls, in Andover, South Parish.

Lost child: Thos McCue, aged 7 years, strayed from the residence of his mother on Thu; since when he has not been heard from. It is feared he may have fallen into the canal near 4½ st bridge. Any information in regard to him will be thankfully received by his mother, residing on 4½ st, near Md ave.

Zachary Taylor, Pres of the U S, recognizes C H H Papendick, who has been appointed Consul of Hanover, for the State of Wisconsin, to reside at the city of Milwaukee. Apr 12, 1850

Sudden & appalling death. A young man, Chas Wilson, employed in the Coast Survey Ofc, died very suddenly on Thu. He was married on Wed at Mrs Little's boarding house, & was found dead by his wife the next morning, when she attempted to awake him. Having taken a mixture on Wed, of opium & ether, it was believed by many that this draught was the cause of his death.

Mrd:on Apr 11, at St Patrick's Church, by Rev Wm Mathews, Mr John H D Richards to Miss Sarah C Brenner, both of Wash City.

Died: on Apr 12, Mr Richd Goldin, in his 47th year. His funeral will take place from his late residence, 7th st, between N Y ave & L st, at 3 o'clock, on Sunday.

Died: on Apr 12, Zachary Taylor, infant son of John E & Charlotte Moran. His funeral will be from their residence, on 6th st, 2nd door from I st, this evening, at 4 o'clock.

Died: on Apr 11, after a long & painful illness, Eliz D Smallwood. Her funeral will be from the residence of her sister, Mrs Marshall, Garrison st, Navy Yard, Sunday, 3 P M.

Silver & silver-plated ware, lamps, & girandoles, at auction, this evening, at the store formerly occupied by Mr Robt Keyworth. -Dyer & Brother, aucts

MON APR 15, 1850
Wash Corp: 1-Ptn from Timothy Buckley, for the remission of a fine: referred to the Cmte of Claims. 2-Bill for the relief of Wm B Wilson: passed. 3-Ptn of Fanny Buchanan, asking to be refunded certain taxes erroneously paid the Corp: referred to the Cmte of Claims. 4-Ptn of B L Jackson & Brother for the improvement of Canal st, between 6th & 7th sts: referred to the Cmte on Improvements. 5-Ptn of John H Clarvoe in relation to an error in the assessment of his property on square 436: referred to the Cmte of Claims. 6-Cmte of Claims: ptn of Edw Hammersly, asked to be discharged from the further consideration of the same: agreed to. 7-Cmte on Police: communication from Wm H Gunnell, proposing to rent certain grounds at the intersection of 6th st & the Canal for gas works, & the memorial of B I Semmes & Brother, & others, remonstrating against the same, asked to be discharged from its further consideration: laid on the table. 8-Ptn of Mr John F Rabbit for the remission of a fine: referred to the Cmte of Claims. 9-Ptn from Ignatius M Knott & 63 others, praying a modification of the present license laws in relation to the sale of intoxicating liquors: referred to the Cmte on Police. 10-Ptn of Allison Nailor, praying permission to erect a stable on square 227: referred to the Cmte on Improvements: passed. 11-Ptn of D A Gardner & others, for the improvement of N Y ave between 14th & 15th sts: referred to the Cmte on Improvements: passed. 12-Ptn of J T Clements & others, for the grading & gravelling of K st, from 4th to 7th sts: referred to the Cmte on Improvements.

For sale: an English Mocking Bird, warranted to be an excellent songster, together with the cage, will be sold a great bargain, on immediate application to John J Bogue, east side of Market, 4 doors from Bridge st, Gtwn, D C.

Supreme Court of the U S, Dec Term, 1849. Jos J Kennedy, trustee, & Henry Shultz, appellants, vs The Bank of the State of Georgia, the City Council of Augusta, John McKinne, & Gasaway B Lamar. Opinion of the Court: Henry Shultz & Lewis Cooper, in 1813, obtained from the State of S C a charter for a bridge over the Savannah river, opposite the town of Augusta, in Georgia, for the term of 21 years; & in 1814 the State of Georgia granted to them a charter for the term of 20 years. In 1816 Henry Shultz & John McKinne, being the joint owners of the bridge, formed a partnership in the business of banking, under the name of Bridge Company of Augusta; the bridge was valued at $75,000, & it, with other property named, constituted the partnership stock. In 1818 Shultz sold & transferred his interest in the partnership to Barna McKinne. In a short time the firm became embarrassed. They owed to the Bank of the State of Georgia the sum of $40,000; & they obtained from it a further loan of $50,000, with a view, as was stated, to relieve the Bridge Co. McKinnes mortgaged the bridge, 80 negroes, & some real estate, Jun 10, 1819. Shultz resumed his place in the firm, by procuring a transfer of Barna McKinnes interest. He advanced $15,000 of his own funds to pay deposites in the bank, & took other steps with his partner to sustain the credit of the Bridge bills in circulation. On May 4, 1838, the bank conveyed its interest in the bridge to G B Lamar for the sum of $70,000, by a quit claim deed. Jan 21, 1840, Lamar conveyed his interest in the bridge to the City Council of Augusta for the sum of $100,000. An abridgement of the case stands thus: I built the bridge, & got a charter from the States of S C & Georgia to collect toll. John McKinne became my partner; he mortgaged his share in this bridge for his private debts to the bank; the bank took that bridge from me by force to pay the debts of John McKinne & his partner, Jas Lambkin. I never owed to that bank one dollar. The bank got alarmed & sold to Lamar; he got alarmed & sold to the town council of Augusta. The bank is bound to me for all the money those parties received, & she may get it back from them as she can. The income of the bridge is $30,000 per annum. My claim on the bank stands now *$163,000, which is a little more than $2/3^{rds}$ of its capital. –Henry Shultz, Wash, D C, Apr 9, 1850 [Henry Shultz: foreigner by birth; arrived in this country in 1806; naturalized in 1814, & became an American citizen.] [Apr 17 newspaper: amount should read $1,063,000.]

Proposals will be received by the undersigned until Apr 20, for trimming & forming 7th st west, from south side of Mass ave to the centre of N Y ave, & gravelling the same.
–C P Wannall, Com'r 3rd Ward; Fra B Lord, Com'r 4th Ward; A Rothwell, L Storm, Assist Com'rs

Marshal's sale: by a writ of fieri facias: public sale, for cash, on May 18, on the premises, part of lot 2 in square 352. Seized & levied upon as the property of Jacob Bender, & will be sold to satisfy judicials 5 to Oct term, 1850, in favor of Thos H Gillis & Wm B Todd, executors of Seth J Todd. –Richd Wallach, Marshal

Faulkner's Shirt Manufactory: Pa ave, between 3rd & $4^{1/2}$ sts, open. Good hands wanted to make shirts. —Wm H Faulkner & Co

Among the persons killed by the explosion of the ill-fated steamer **Troy**, near Buffalo, was Dr Wright, of the firm of Avery & Wright, of Geddes, near Syracuse, N Y, where they conducted a large grain & provision business. On hearing of the death of Wright, Mr Avery started for Sandusky, for the interest of the firm, & the first intelligence his family had of him afterwards was the receipt of a telegraphic dispatch announcing his sudden death at Sandusky.

City Ordinances: 1-Act for the relief of John E Little: to be paid the sum of $19, amount due him for materials & repairing the lockup-house in the 6th Ward.

Quebec Village, Vt, Oct 11, 1850. Fatal accident at Taftsville, Vt, yesterday. Mr Jos Corbin was instantly killed by the breaking of the grindstone upon which he was grinding, in Messrs D Taft & Son's Axe & Scythe Factory. His head was crushed in a shocking manner. He was a respectable & industrious man. —Boston Journal

On Fri the son of Mr Alanson Bunce, of Centreport, Long Island, went into the grist mill belonging to the estate of Jos C Lewis. While playing in the corn & cob crusher, which was running at the time, his hand caught & he was drawn into the machine & killed instantly. The boy was about 12 years of age.

Fatal accident on Tue, by which Wm H Hoffman, son of Hezekiah Hoffman, of N Y, lost his life. While walking with others, he stumbled, & his gun discharged sending the contents through his head, producing instant death. He was about 20 years of age. —Goshen Democrat

The Hon Thos Jefferson Campbell, of Tenn, Clerk of the House of Reps of the U S, died at his lodgings in Wash City, on Sat, after an illness of about a week. His remains are to be conveyed forthwith to his residence in the State of Tenn for interment.

Appointments by the Pres: 1-Wills de Hass, of Va, to be Consul of the U S for Merida & Sisal, in Yucatan. 2-Curtius H Saunders, of Tenn, to be Consul of the U S for St Catherine's, Brazil. 3-J J Wickes, to be Assist Treasurer of the U S & Treasurer of the Mint at New Orleans, Louisiana.

Capt Sherman, of the barque **Agnes**, arrived at N Y from Rio Janeiro, reports that the U S ship **Ohio** sailed 2 days before for Boston. The 1st Lt died the night before the ship left Rio Janeiro. [No name given.]

Mr Stephen A Wright, who left South Kingstown several years ago for the West, & finally reached Calif, where he was settled when the discovery of gold was made, has just returned with a fortune of about half a million, with which, like a sensible man, he has come to live in the land of his birth. —Providence Journal of Fri

Mrd: on Apr 11, in Alexandria Co, Va, by Rev Wm Lockwood, Basil E Gantt, of Fairfax Co, Va, & Miss Maria W Paine, of Richmond, Va,

Mrd: on Mar 1, in Gtwn, by Rev Mr Everest, Mr Chas T Edmonston to Miss Mary Ann Trinnel, all of that place.

Orphans Court of Wash Co, D C. Apr 13, 1850. Letters of administration on the personal estate of Christopher C Berry, late of Cumberland, Md, deceased.
-Jos M Downing, adm

TUE APR 16, 1850
Mrd: on Apr 14, at Trinity Church, by Rev Wm Flannagan, Mr Chas F Edmonson to Miss Mary Ann Trunnel, all of Gtwn.

G C Grammer returns his sincere thanks to the members of the Fire Companies for the praiseworthy alacrity with which they arrested the fire that threatened the entire destruction of his property at 6th & E sts on Sunday last.

Zachary Taylor, Pres of the U S, recognizes Rudolph Petting, who has been appointed Consul of Nassau, for the State of Texas, to reside at Galveston. Apr 15, 1850

Senate. 1-Memorial of Geo Talcott, an ofcr in the army of the U S, asking to be allowed the pay & emoluments of a colonel of ordnance during the period for which he performed the duties of that ofc: referred to the Cmte on Military Affairs. 2-Ptn of John B Brooks, son & heirs of Jos Brooks, a Revolutionary soldier, asking compensation for his father's services: referred to the Cmte on Pensions. 3-Ptn of Wm Andrews, asking to be allowed bounty land for his services as a soldier in the battle of Tippecanoe & other Indian wars: referred to the Cmte on Military Affairs. 4-Memorial of Geo C Hutter, asking to be restored to his rank in the army: referred to the Cmte on Military Affairs. 5-Cmte on Naval Affairs: memorial of Elisha W B Moody, of Yarmouth, Nova Scotia, owner of the barque **Sarah**, asking renumeration for expenses incurred & losses sustained in consequence of the deviation of his vessel from her voyage, for the purpose of rescuing the crew & passengers of the American ship **Caleb Grimshaw**, burnt at sea in Nov, 1849: asked to be discharged from the further consideration of the same, & that it be referred to the Cmte on Commerce. 6-Same cmte: memorial of Thos Blanchard, asking Gov't to purchase his patent car machine for the use of the navy: asked to be discharged from the further consideration of the ptn of the same: agreed to. 7-Same cmte: memorial of John Thomas for compensation for the use of his patent, in floating dry docks, asked to be discharged from the further consideration of the ptn of the same: which was agreed to. 8-Cmte on Indian Affairs: memorial of Jas M Marsh, asking renumeration for property destroyed: ordered to be printed. 9-Cmte on Public Lands: ptn of Moses Pacquette & Theresa Brisbois, asking to be allowed to locate land set apart for said Pacquette by the Winnebago Indians, submitted an adverse report on the same: ordered to be printed.

Warfield Academy, Howard District, Anne Arundel Co, Md: Rev T J Shepherd, A M, Mr Wm T Crapster, Assoc Principals. The summer session commences on the first Wed of May next.

Com'rs sale of real estate in Alexandria: by virtue of the decree pronounced by the County Court of Alexandria Co, at its Jan term, 1850: public auction on Apr 29, of the following: 1-Brick dwlg with a large lot attached, containing about 6 acres, at the head of King st, Alexandria, Va, late the residence of Col Francis Peyton, deceased. 2-Oak Hill, situated on Quaker Hill, Fairfax Co, Va, contains between 18 & 20 acres of land: bldgs are substantial, but not in good order: has a 3 story brick house & frame kitchen. 3-Two story brick house & lot on King st, adjoining the dwlg of Mr Jos Gregg. 4-Two story brick house & lot on King st, adjoining the house on the corner of West & King sts, & the same owned by Mr Edw Burchell. 5-An undivided half of the 2 story brick house & lot at King & Commerce sts. 6-Two lots on the south side of Commerce st, near King st. 7-Two small frame Tenements & lots of ground on the east side of Peyton st, near the Virginia House. 8-Vacant lot on Peyton st. 9-Large lot at Prince & Commerce sts, subject to an unexpired lease of one or two years. 10-A ground rent of $15 per annum, secured on a frame dwlg on Commerce st, owned & occupied by Mrs Sarah Parks. –Robt G Violett, Christopher Neale, Com'rs of sale

Harrisburg, Apr 15. The House bill granting a divorce to Edwin Forrest without going to court, passed today by 42 yeas to 40 nays.

WED APR 17, 1850
Died: Galveston papers to Apr 5. Maj J P J O'Brien, an ofcr well known for this gallant exploits at Buena Vista, died on Mar 30, at Indianola, of cholera.

Senate: 1-Memorial from Jas Ralichison de Saint Vital & Anthony Villard, an architect, both French citizens, residents of Mexico for several years past, setting forth that on Dec 20, 1847, some American troops, coming from Vera Cruz to the city of Mexico, did, for the purpose of cooking their victuals & warming themselves, set on fire the old inn, [Venta Antique.] They are now verging on impending & utter ruin. As neutrals in politics between the 2 countries, the subscribers claim, in the name of their children, the just indemnification to which they are entitled: referred to the Cmte of Claims. 2-Memorial of Winifred N Kouns & W Neville Read, heirs of John Neville, an ofcr in the Revolutionary army, asking to be allowed commutation pay: referred to the Cmte on Revolutionary Claims. 3-Cmte of Claims: bill for the relief of Sarah Jane West: recommended its passage.

Trustee's sale of valuable lot #9 in square 317, on K st, between 11th & 12th sts: by deed of trust from E H Roper, recorded in Liber W B 83 folio 1. Sale on Apr 15.
–Dyer & Brother, aucts

Mrd: on Apr 16, at Trinity Church, by Rev Dr Butler, Jos Saxton, of Phil, to Mary H, daughter of late Jas Abercrombie, of Balt, Md.

Mrd: on Apr 9, at Greenville, by Rev B Grimsley, Mr John Pickett, of Fauquier Co, Va, to Miss Sallie A, eldest daughter of Geo L Kerfoot, of Clark Co, Va,

Mrd: on Apr 11, by Rev Mr McElfresh, Mr Daniel Robertson to Miss Mary Eliz Hurdle, all of Wash City.

The dwlg house of Mr Robt Brown, of Montg Co, Md, was totally destroyed by fire on Mon of last week, as was also the furniture contained therein. No insurance. A child of Mr Brown was badly burnt, & the balance of the family barely escaped.

THU APR 18, 1850
Senate: 1-Ordered, that the memorial of John A Bryan, on the files of the Senate, be referred to the Cmte on Military Affairs. 2-Memorial of Wm H Payne, in behalf of himself & a company of Florida volunteers commanded by him in the Seminole war, asking compensation for their services: referred to the Cmte on Military Affairs. 3-Cmte on Military Affairs: memorial of the widow of of Capt E G Elliot, of the U S army, asked to be discharged from the further consideration of the same, & that it be referred to the Cmte on Pensions: which was concurred in. Same cmte: memorial of Mary Morris Foot, widow of a late surgeon in the U S army, asked to be discharged from the further consideration of the same, & that it be referred to the Cmte on Pensions: which was concurred in. 4-Cmte on Commerce: memorial of Geo Dennett, for compensation for services performed while naval ofcr at Portsmouth, N H, reported a bill for his relief: ordered to a second reading. 5-Cmte on Military Affairs: ptn of Amelia Sophia Catharine Welmore, asked to be discharged from the further consideration of the same, & that it be referred to the Cmte on Pensions: which was concurred in. 6-Memorial of Chas Byrne & A H Cole, for themselves & other proprietors of a tract of land in the State of Florida, claimed under a Spanish grant, asking that they may be allowed to prove their title under the act of May 23, 1828: referred to the Cmte on the Judiciary. 7-Ptn of Benj F Rogers & Wm H Home, asking the adoption of a plan for the prospective abolition of slavery & slave trade in D C, & for the prohibition of slavery in the Territories of the U S: ordered to lie on the table. 8-Memorial from the heirs of Isaac Shelby, asking compensation for the services of their ancestor in the war of the Revolution: referred to the Cmte on Revolutionary Claims. 9-Ptn of Fernando A Underwood & H H Crane, heirs of John Underwood, deceased, asking the confirmation of his title to certain lands in the State of Florida: referred to the Cmte on Private Land Claims.

Extensive sale of lumber, lumber wagon, & cart, by order of the Orphans Court of Wash Co, D C. Sale on Apr 22, at the Lumber Yard formerly kept by Messrs Harvey & Lloyd, on 12th st: all that is in the yard. –Green & Tastet, aucts

Appointments by the Pres: 1-F A Beelen, of Pa, to be U S Consul for Angostrua, in the Republic of Venezuela. 2-Philip Clayton, of Ga, to be Second Auditor of the Treasury.

Mrd: on Apr 14, at the Catholic Chapel, at Harrisburg, Pa, Hon Linn Boyd, Rep in Congress from Kentucky, to Mrs Ann L Dickson, of Ebensburg, Pa.

Died: on Apr 16, in Wash City, Mary Eliz, only daughter of Francis H & Mary Darnall, aged 8 years, 10 months & 27 days.

Died: on Mar 20, at the residence of her sister, Mrs Dorothy Williams, in Montg Co, Md, Mrs Ann Harding, in her 74th year.

Died: on Apr 13, at *Palermo*, the residence of Mrs Brent, near Alexandria, Va, Francis Lightfoot Lee, in the 68th year of his life.

Rencontre took place at Far Rockaway, Long Island, N Y, on Tue last, between 2 neighbors, Mr Oliver Doxey & Mr Peter Pearsall, in which the latter was killed, by a blow with a club. Doxey has given bail for his appearance, & will be tried at the next Oyer & Terminer of the county.

Parker's refectory, furniture, & bar fixtures, at auction, on Apr 20, at the well known Refectory on D st, between 10th & 11th sts. -Dyer & Brother, aucts

On Sat week, along a street in Warrenton, Miss Lucinda Scott, of Warrenton, Fauquier Co, Va, jumped from a horse she was riding because the speed of the horse was greater than she was accustomed to. The shock which the accident gave her nervous system was so great as to prostrate it, & all efforts to produce a reaction proved fruitless. After lingering in considerable pain until Thu, she expired. -Alexandria Gaz

FRI APR 19, 1850
Potomac Herrings just received & for sale by John A Grimes, Commercial wharf, Gtwn.

Shocking affair occurred in the vicinity of this place last Monday. Thos D Forman, age 14 or 15 years, was out hunting, & having found some birds, he alighted from his horse to shoot them. Before firing, he fastened the rein to his wrist to hold his horse. At the report of the gun the horse took fright, & dragged young Forman after him until he kicked him loose. He was killed instantly. We sympathize with his afflicted relatives. –Holly Springs [Miss] Gaz

Senate: 1-Ptn of Mary A Berger, widow of John T Berger, who was an on board the U S propeller **Secretary Walker**, during the late war with Mexico, asking that she be allowed a pension: referred to the Cmte on Pensions. 5-Ptn of Saml Davis, a Revolutionary pensioner, asking an increase of pension: referred to the Cmte on Pensions. 3-Memorial of the heirs of Nathan King, an ofcr in the Revolutionary army, asking to be allowed commutation pay for the services of their ancestor: referred to the Cmte on Pensions.

Mr Edw Moore, of Newport, R I, left the Astor House on Apr 9, intending to go to Orange, N J, by the 4 o'clock train, but has not been heard of since. A reward is offered for any information that may lead to his discovery.

House of Reps: 1-Memorial of Thos Croxall & others, reps of late Capt Chas Croxall, of Md, praying relief for Revolutionary services. 2-Memorial of Thos Hope Palmer & other members of a military company of volunteers in the late Florida war, asking for compensation for losses of clothing & also for grants of land. 3-Petition of Mrs Frances Fenton, widow of Thos Fenton, soldier of Revolution, asking compensation for extra services performed by her brother. 3-Ptn of Priscilla Barns, sister & excx of the late Maj Geo Burd, asking compensation for services performed by her brother. 4-Resolved, that Robt E Hornor, acting Doorkeeper of the House of Reps, be & he is hereby dismissed. Mr Brown, member of the House from Mississippi, makes the following charges against Hornor: A-That Hornor made a false certificate, under & by virtue of which his brother drew pay as an ofcr of the House, at a time when his said brother was notoriously absent from Wash City, & held an ofc in the State of Wisconsin, the duties of which he was discharging, & for which he was receiving a salary from the U S. B-That he has dismissed from his place a page of this House without cause, &, in his attempted justification, made a false charge against the said page, calculated to disgrace him & subject him to criminal prosecution. C-That said Hornor has made false statements in regard to the manner of discharging his official duties. 5-Resolved, that a select cmte inquire whether Thos Ewing, Sec of the Interior, re-opened & paid to G W & W G Ewing a claim against the U S Treasury of $77,000, after the same had been adjudicated & rejected by the proper ofcr of the Gov't, before said Ewing was inducted into said ofc of the Interior. Whether Ewing re-opened & paid interest to the amount of $31,000, on the pension granted to Cmdor Jas _arron for services rendered in the Virginia navy during the Revolutionary war, after the principal had been fully paid & discharged. Whether said Ewing re-opened & paid a claim to a person or persons on behalf of the Chickasaw Indians of $108,000, after the same had been adjudicated & rejected by the proper ofcr of the Gov't, before said Ewing was inducted into the ofc of the Interior.

Appointment by the Pres: Chas W Cutter, to be Navy Agent for the naval station at Portsmouth, N H.

Serious accident at the Brooklyn Navy Yard on Sat. Mr John Megill, attached to the storekeeper's dept, was packing clothing which had been lying about for some time, & he came across a 6 ounce vial, & threw it into the stove, causing an instant explosion, blowing the stove through the floor. The vial is supposed to have contained fulminating powder. Mr Megill had his right arm badly injured which had to be amputated just below the elbow. -Advertiser

Zachary Taylor, Pres of the U S, recognizes A C Rhodes, who has been appointed Vice-Consul of his Majesty the King of the Two Sicilies, for the port of Balt. Apr 17, 1850

Household & kitchen furniture at auction: on Apr 23, at a house on G st, between 14th & 15th sts, the second door from Douglas' Green-house, the furniture of a gentleman declining housekeeping. -Dyer & Brother, aucts

St Louis Republican of Apr 9. Henry Co, Ill: outrages committed upon the Swedish colony located in that county. The 70 men engaged in these acts are from Cambridge & Rock River, Henry Co, & are headed by John Root. Root married Charlotte Louisa Johnson, but they did not live happily together, she left him & fled to her relatives for protection against his violence. On Mar 26, Root visited the colony, with a mob, to regain possession of his wife, but she had left. Root was irritated. Mar 27 Root & the mob returned & demolished some houses, & threatened the people. Mar 28 he burnt the hay stacks, & set fire to the bldgs at Little Hill. The colony suffered severely from the cholera last year, & 70 widows with their children are left dependant upon the colony for support. They resemble the Quakers & offered no violence to the mob. The colony deserves protection of the laws, & the offenders should not be suffered to go unpunished.

Wash Corp: 1-Ptn from Chas Monroe & others, for the improvement of 2nd st west, from D to C st north: referred to the Cmte on Improvements. 2-Ptn from Geo Mantz & others, for a change of the license laws in relation to the sale of spirituous liquors: referred to the Cmte on Police. 3-Ptn of Alex Mahon, for the remission of a fine: referred to the Cmte of Claims. 4-Ptn from W Jones, for the remission of a fine: referred to the Cmte of Claims. 5-Bill for the relief of John F Callan: decided in the negative. 6-Cmte of Claims: asked to be discharged from the further consideration of the ptn of Wm Furguson: & they were discharged accordingly. Same cmte: asked to be discharged from the further consideration of the ptn of Geo Stutz. 7-Cmte on Improvements: bill for the relief of Philip Ennis, reported the same with additional facts connected with the claim. 8-Ptn of Wm B Randolph & others, for improvement of 12th st west, south of the canal: referred to the Cmte on Improvements.

Foundation slates direct from the quaries for sale. Reasonable price.
-Matthew Waite, 6th st, between G & H sts

SAT APR 20, 1850
Senate: 1-Ptn of the heirs of Andrew D Crosby, deceased, late a purser in the navy, asking to be allowed a pension: referred to the Cmte on Pensions. 2-Ordered, that the memorial of Priscilla D Twiggs be taken from the files of the Senate, & referred to the Cmte on Naval Affairs. 3-Ordered, that the ptn of Wade Allen, on the files of the Senate, be referred to the Cmte on the Post Ofc & Post Roads.

Charge of kidnapping settled. Case of Jonathan Little: Huntingdon [Pa] Journal of Apr 16. The records of Md were here to prove Finley [the negro] a slave; the sons of his mistress were here, who knew him, & had authorized Little to take him; every thing requisite to prove the negro a slave, &, consequently, Little innocent upon the indictment. Upon these grounds the prosecution was abandoned. The settlement acquits Little

Mrd: on Apr 16, in Gtwn, by Rev Mr Lanahan, Mr A H Gatton to Miss Martha W Lewis, all of this place.

Mrd: On Apr 18, by Rev Mr Samson, Mr Jno House & Miss Mary C Speake, all of Wash City.

Died: on Apr 6, in Franklin, Tenn, Mrs Mary C B Lewis, formerly of Centreville, Fairfax Co, Va, in her 67th year.

Died: on Apr 19, in Wash City, Isaac Cooper, son of Wm H & Sarah A Prentiss, in Wash, aged 3 years & 6 months. His funeral will be from the residence of the parents on Vt av & H st, tomorrow, at 3 o'clock.

A private letter from Para River [Brazil] states that Lt Washington Reid, of the navy, died on board sloop of war **Albany**, on Feb 18 last, of bilious fever, in his 33rd year, son of Capt Sam'l C Reid, of N Y, & entered servce in 1832. The 1st Lt of the ship of the line **Ohio**, who died at Rio de Janeiro just before the ship sailed, was C M Armstrong, of N Y.

Reward-$50 for return of Frank Tillman, negro, age 19 years. -John P Bouic, Poolsville, Montgomery Co, Md.

The Northumberland House, the residence of John R Stith, of Northumberland Co, Va, accidentally caught fire & burnt down on Sat last, with almost all of the furniture.

Mrs Ireland & daughter, of Quincy, Ill, came to an awful death by freezing & starvation on the mountains during the past winter. They were on their way to Calif. They insisted upon the husband & father to leave them to their fate, & seek his own safety. We almost shuddered when our informant told us he did so.

Trustee's sale of valuable property: by deed of trust from the late Jas B Phillips: public auction on May 13, of lot 7 in square 449, corner of 7th & L sts, north. Also, for sale, on May 14, lots 11 & 13 in square 637, fronting on South Capitol st, between C & D sts, with a good 2 story brick house. –Henry May, trustee -Dyer & Brother, aucts

Methodist Protestant Church, on 9th st, has pews to rent. The Rev W T Eva, has been appointed Pastor of the Church. Rev S R Cox is to fill the pulpit tomorrow, at 11 o'clock.

The Board of Trustees of the Augusta Female Seminary will proceed on Mon, May 20, to elect a Principal to take charge of the institution. –Wm Frazier, Sec, Staunton, Va

The Albany Evening Journal announces the death in that city, on Wed, of the Hon Chas Humphrey, in his 59th year.

$100 reward for runaway negro man John Moore. He is supposed to have stolen a grey horse, the property of Mrs James; my saddle & bridle were stolen the same night. –C C Randolph

Notice: will be sold on Apr 23, at my Stables, on 8th st, 2 horses & one set of double harness, the property of J O'Mear, to satisfy livery due to me & unpaid. –Thos Baker

For rent: a brick house on G st, near the Treasury Dept, formerly occupied by Wm S Miller, member of Congress from N Y, but more recently by the Austrian Minister. Apply on N Y ave, near 15th st. -D A Gardner.

Household & kitchen furniture at auction: Apr 26, at the residence of Mr A Favier, on 19th st, between Pa ave & H st. –Dyer & Bro, aucts

MON APR 22, 1850
Died: in Jan last, in Calif, Dr John D Moore, eldest son of Alexander D Moore, lately of Wilmington, N C. He went out hunting in the hills near the mines about the middle of Jan last, & became separated from his friends in a snow storm, & was not found until a month afterwards, when his body was discovered in a ravine in an unmutilated state.

City Ordinances-Wash: 1-Act granting permission to Allison Nailor to erect a brick stable on lots 15 & 16 in square 227, in the Second Ward, provided said Allison will erect a brick bldg, & free from all combustible material, with the exception of floors, hay-racks, & frames for horses' stalls & doors. Approved: May 20, 1850.

Mr R Clark, fishing the Sycamore Landing on the Potomac, sent to the Mayor week before last a present of a rock fish [striped bass] the largest we have ever seen. It weighed 74 pounds.

Died: in Wash City, at the lodgings of his father, [the Hon Henry W Hilliard, of Montg, Ala,] on Sat, Henry W Hillard, jr, in his 17th year. The Pres had recently selected him as a Cadet in the Military Academy at West Point. His mind & character were both of the highest order.

Postmaster Gen established the following new Post ofcs for week ending Apr 13, 1850.

Ofc	County, State	Postmaster
South Maxfield	Penobscot, Maine	F Tomtillott
West Howland	Penobscot, Maine	Geo R Tomtillott
East Franklin	Franklin, Vt	Jacob Perkins
Southfield	Berkshire, Mass	Augustus Turner
Stanley Corners	Ontario, N Y	Lucius Stanley
Mortonville	Orange, N Y	John D Vail
Louisville Landing	St Lawrence, N Y	R D Marsh
Chanceville	Monmouth, N J	Henry Morford
Drakesville	Morris, N J	Richd Salmon
Olivet	Armstrong, Pa	John McGeary
Silver Creek	Schuylkill, Pa	Chas S Dobbins
West Manchester	Alleghany, Pa	Wm H Phelps
Dublin Mills	Bedford, Pa	A Weidman

Webster's Mill	Bedford, Pa	J S Zimmerman
First Fork	Clinton, Pa	S Norcross
Myersburgh	Bradford, Pa	E R Myer
Ransom	Luzerne, Pa	J D Gulick
Boston	Northampton, Pa	Saml Weller
Blue Mountain	Northampton, Pa	Enos Lehr
Five Points	Venango, Pa	Alex'r Grant
Clokey	Wash, Pa	E J Morgan
White Mills	Wayne, Pa	A M Atkinson
East Springhill	Wyoming, Pa	D L Crawford
Keyser's Bridge	Alleghany, Md	Wm H Myer
Tomkinsville	Chas, Md	Wm Rogers
Damascus	Montg, Md	N Worthington
Bruceville	Carroll, Md	Geo Mering
Naaman's Creek	Newcastle, Del	Geo Thompson
Reynolds	Licking, Ohio	Abel Pickering
Cairo	Stark, Ohio	A G Blair
Taylor	Richland, Ohio	John Jackson
Park	St Jos, Mich	Jacob Van Ness
Kenneys	Shichawassce, Mich	Augustus Turner
Choppeen	Wells, Ia	Saml C Caley
Cox's Mills	Wayne, Ia	Enos Thomas
Mount Moriah	Brown, Ia	Wm Milnes
Mooresburg	Pulaski, Ia	David Whitman
White River	Morgan, Ia	Jas D Newton
Pettys	Lawrence, Ill	Jos Petty
Ashby	Coles, Ill	David Porter
Selma	McLean, Ill	Geo Webster
Renault	Monroe, Ill	E W Maxon
Lowryville	Madison, Ill	Wm J Lowry
Brookfield	La Salle, Ill	Benj F Gage
Browning	Schuyler, Ill	A Dillworth
Willow Creek	Lee, Ill	Robt Blair
Cheney's Grove	McLean, Ill	Wm H Cheney
Fox Lake	Lake, Ill	Wm H Hall
Little Compton	Carroll, Mo	A Callaway
Olive Branch	Holt, Mo	G B Jeffries
Swan Ford	Taney, Mo	Joel Hall
Silver Spring	St Francis, Mo	Saml N Perry
Whitesville	Andrew, Mo	C Miller
Renick's Mills	Lafayette, Mo	Leonard H Renick
Garnder's Mills	Saint Clair, Mo	Jas Gardener
Tebo	Henry, Mo	F G Reaves
Irish Grove	Atchinson, Mo	Chas V Snow

Pasco	Dallas, Mo	H L Trantham
Blisk's Mills	Franklin, Mo	Isaac C Lund
Freel	Polk, Iowa	John Hull
Summerset	Polk, Iowa	John Lees
Sullivan	Jackson, Iowa	Michl O Sullivan
Herman	Dodge, Wis	E M B Drake
Schleisingerville	Wash, Wis	Jesse Wood
Muckwa	Winnebago, Wis	C E P Hobart
Wauonah	Columbia, Wis	Chas H Moore
Dellona	Sauk, Wis	Saml Northrup
Russell's Corner	Sauk, Wis	John B Russell
Springdale	Dane, Wis	Thos Miles
Rob Roy	Jefferson, Ark	Jordan N Embree
Dividing Ridge	Carter, Tenn	H W Johnson
Screamersville	Maury, Tenn	Wm Hickman
Jordan's Valley	Rutherford, Tenn	Blount Jordan
Rossland	Dickson, Tenn	Wm B Ross
Frozen Creek	Breathitt, Ky	Jos Sewell
Cavender's Creek	Lumpkin, Ga	R P Hogue
Junction	Calif Terr	John S Beener
Napa	Calif Ter	Chas Briggs
Santa Barbara	Calif Ter	Saml Barney
Placerville	Calif, Ter	Thos Nugent
Santa Cruz	Calif, Ter	Alex'r McLean
San Diego	Calif, Ter	R Rust
Los Angelos	Calif Ter	I Pugh
Mission San Jose	Calif, Ter	Jose Jesus Vallego
Weaverville	Calif, Ter	A Woodworth
Fremont	Calif Ter	Henry A Weeks
Forks of St Mary's River	Clackemas Co, Ore T	John Lloyd
Mollatta	Clackemas Co, Ore T	Harrison Wright
Champoeg	Marion, Ore T	Matthews
Santyam Forks	Linn, Ore T	Jacob Conser
Pleasant Hill	Benton, Ore T	Elijah Bristow

Names Changed:
Clintonville, Worcester Co, Mass, changed to Clinton.
Sherwood's Corners, Cayuga Co, N Y, changed to Sherwoods.
Mersereau's Ferry, Richmond Co, changed to Port Richmond. [No State given.]
Edgecomb's Corners, Saratoga Co, N Y, changed to South Galway.
Coursenville, Sussex Co, N J, changed to Wykertown.
West Branch, Clinton Co, Pa, changed to Chatham Run.
Seigfried's Ferry, Northampton Co, Pa, changed to Laubach.
Steam Mills, Oakland Co, Mich, changed to Mahopack.
Rock Lick, Marshall Co, Va, changed to Poplar Spring.

Cooper's Hill, *Wood Co, Va, changed to Fountain Springs.
Delphi, Marion Co, Va, changed to Sequatchie.
McMary's, Mecklenburg Co, N C, changed to Ellwood.
Porter's Landing, Ohio Co, Ky, changed to Pincheco.
Ogg's Mills, Madison Co, Ky, changed to Elliston.
La Fax, Kane Co, Ill, changed to Geneva.
Blue Island, Cook Co, Ill, changed to Worth.
Keepataw, Cook Co, Ill, changed to Palmyra.
Wiota, Camden Co, Missouri, changed to Lebanon.
Union Mills, Mahaska Co, Iowa, changed to Widow's Home.
Stoughton, Dane Co, Wisconsin, changed to Bass Lake.

Household & kitchen furniture at auction: on Apr 25, at the residence of G H Heap, Mass ave, between 11th & 12th sts, near the residence of N P Vansant. –Green & Tastet, aucts

Died: in Wash City, at the lodgings of his father, [the Hon Henry W Hilliard, of Montg, Ala,] on Sat, Henry W Hillard, jr, in his 17th year. The Pres had recently selected him as a Cadet in the Military Academy at West Point. His mind & character were both of the highest order.

In Chancery: Edw Hamilton et al, cmplnts, versus Matthew Hamilton, dfndnt. Richd R Crawford, the trustee in the above cause, reported he hath made the sale directed by the decree: at such sale W Keefe, for Mary C Ann Fullmore, was the highest bidder, & Fullmore became the purchaser of the same at the price of $555; & further, that the said Mary Ann Fullmore has paid the said sum of $555. –Jno A Smith, clk

The remains of the illustrious statesman, Mr Calhoun, designated for their interment in his native State of S C, will leave Wash City this morning. At Wilmington, they will embark on board a steamer for Charleston, & will go to Columbia, the capital of S C, the place of interment. Mr A P Calhoun & Maj P Calhoun, sons of Mr Calhoun, have arrived in the city.

Education. Rev D McCarter's Boarding School for Boys & Young Men, Strasburg, Lancaster Co, Pa: summer session will commence on the first Monday of May.
–Rev D McCarter, Principal & Proprietor

An elegant monument has been recently erected in the <u>New Haven Cemetery</u> to the memory of Mrs Ann, widow of the late Eldridge Gerry, one of the Signers of Declaration of Independence, & subsequently Vice Pres of the U S. Inscription on the front of the monument: "Ann, the widow of Eldridge Gerry, Vice President of the United States; his name is immortalized on the Declaration of his country's Independence-here, in the transcendant virtues of domestic life; both are embalmed in the veneration of their children." On the reverse side of the monument is the following inscription: "Born 12th August, 1763; died 17 March, 1849. This monument erected in memory of parental kindness, with the grateful devotion of filial love. -New Haven Journal & Courier.

The Columbia Telegraph announces the death of Col F W Davie, who died at his residence in Chester district on Apr 9, after a protracted illness. He was favorably known as a member of the Legislature of S C, having for years served with ability & efficiency as chairman of the Ways & Means Cmte.

TUE APR 23, 1850
For rent: 3 story brick house on Delaware ave, North Capitol Hill, adjoining the residence of Mrs Wm Brent, & lately occupied by Col G L Thompson. Apply to John C Brent, atty-at-law, Van Patten's Bldg, C st, or at Mrs Brent's, next door.

Senate: 1-Cmte on Private Lands Claims: house bill for the relief of Jos Richards, reported back the same without amendment, & recommended its passage. 2-Cmte of Claims: house bill for the relief of John Plunkett, submitted an adverse report on the same: ordered to be printed. 3-Cmte of Claims: House bill for the relief of Geo Collier & Wm G Peters: recommended its passage. 4-Documents submitted relating to the claim of Francis Mortimer, a Revolutionary soldier , to a pension: referred to the Cmte on Pensions. 5-Cmte on the Post Ofc & Post Roads: ptn of Saml W Chilson, asking pay for services under a contract with the Post Ofc Dept, was ordered to be printed, with a bill for the relief of Saml W Chilson: ordered to a second reading.

Died: on Apr 21, Capt Chas Ward, formerly of 4th Regt of artl, U S army, & late of the Pension Bureau. His funeral will be from his residence on 12th st, on Apr 23, at 4 o'clock.

Died: on Apr 15, at Cambridge, Ohio, Mrs Eliz J Evans, wife of Hon Nathan Evans, Member of Congress from 14th Congressional district of Ohio.

Masonic Meeting: this evening, 7½ o'clock. –G A Schwarzman, sec

Household & kitchen furniture at auction: on Apr 26, at the furniture Store of Mr T B Brown, on 7th st, near I. –Green & Tastet, aucts

Trustee's sale of real estate: by decree of the High Court of Chancery, passed Feb 28, 1850, the undersigned, as trustee, will offer at public sale, at *Marshall Hall*, on Jun 25, the real estate of Harriot R Marshall, a minor. It is in Chas Co, Md, & contains, by recent survey, 772 acres. It was formerly a part of the *Marshall Hall* estate. Mr W H Clagett will show the property. At the same time & place, & also under a decree of the High Court of Chancery, will be sold the real estate of Geo R H Marshall, minor, 758 acres. Mr Wm H Clagett will show the land. -Thos Marshall, Trustee [Port Tobacco Times]

The Mississippian, of Mar 29, records the death of Saml Stamps, Sec of State for the State of Mississippi. We learn also, from the N O Picayune, that Horace S Coley, Sec of the State of Illinois, recently died in that city, which he had visited for the purpose of his health.

From Mexico: on Mar 27, Don Juan de Dios Canedo, a Deputy of Congress, was assassinated in his own house in the city of Mexico. He had been stabbed more than 30 times, all on the left side of the body, & thus must have been killed while asleep. Private vengeance must have been the motive.

WED APR 24, 1850
Land for sale: I am authorized to sell the farm of the late Dr Worthington, containing nearly 360 acres. The Wash & Rockville Turnpike Road divides the farm, & the west side is bounded by Piney Branch Road. –Tho Carbery

Senate: 1-Documents relating to the claim of Saml Wilson, a Revolutionary soldier , to a pension: referred to the Cmte on Pensions. 2-Cmte on Commerce: memorial of J H Pulte, proposing a plan for extending the magnetic telegraph around the globe, made a report, which was concurred in. 3-Memorial of Susan Murphy, widow of Thos Murphy, asking that she may be allowed to institute legal proceedings for the purpose of proving the validity of her title to certain lands in the State of Florida: referred to the Cmte on Private Land Claims. 4-Memorial of Lydia Gibbs, asking indemnity for French spoliations prior to 1800: ordered to lie on the table. 5-Ptn of Silas Chatfield, a pensioner of the U S, asking to be allowed back pension: referred to the Cmte on Pensions. 6-Ordered, that the heirs of Nathl Ashby have leave to withdraw their petition & papers. 7-Mr Butler. I ask leave to withdraw the papers of Geo Harvey, agent of the British ship James Mitchell, from the files of the Senate. Adverse report was made by the Cmte of Claims; referred to the Cmte on Naval Affairs-accidentally discovered to be under a different name: Mr Yulee opposes the motion. [The first petition was of the heirs of Geo Harvey; the second application was for the relief of the owners of the ship **James Mitchell**. Harvey is understood to be a citizen of Charleston.] The motion to grant leave to withdraw the papers from the files was then put & lost. 8-Ptn of Robt Dixon & 75 other citizens of Louisa, Livingston Co, N Y, praying that slavery may be abolished in all the Territories of the U S.

Appointments by the Pres: 1-Wm B Kinney, of N J, to be Charge d'Affaires of the U S near the Gov't of Sardinia. 2-Chas Bunker, of Mass, to be U S Consul for the port of Lahaina, in the Island of Maui. 3-Jas Hendebert, of Mississippi, to be U S Consul for the port of Lyons, in France.

House of Reps: 1-Cmte on the Post Ofc & Post Roads: discharged from the further consideration of the ptn of Isaac Hill, of N H: laid on the table. Same cmte: discharged from the further consideration of the ptn of Armistead Neal: laid on the table.

For sale or rent: lot 32 in square A, containing about 5,000 sq feet, on Pa ave, near 3rd, with the house & improvements thereon. Formerly occupied by Mr Michl McDermott for the last 10 years under a lease for that time of $240 per annum. –Dyer & Brother, aucts & Commission Merchants

$50 reward for return of Va bank bills, rolled up in a piece of oilcloth: total of $700. –H L Turner, D st, between 13th & 14th sts.

There are 6 newspapers in the U S edited by ladies, namely:
Pittsburg Visiter, Mrs Swisshelm.
Windham Co Democrat, [Vt] Mrs C J H Nichols
The Lily, [Seneca Falls,] Mrs Bloomer
The Lancaster Gaz [Pa] Mrs Pierson
The Yazoo Whig, Mrs Horn
The Mountain Bough, Mrs Prewett

Died: yesterday, Mr Patrick McGarvey, of county Donegale, Ireland, in his 40th year, but for the last 10 years a resident of Wash City. His funeral will be at his residence on K & 27th sts, Thu, at 3 o'clock.

Died: on Apr 19, suddenly, in Wash City, Chas R Thompson, in his 46th year, of congestion of the brain. He leaves a wife & 6 children to lament their loss.

For sale: my farm, **Woodburn**, in Frederick Co: contains about 415 acres of land. The house is a stone dwlg, 2 stories high; with other out-bldgs. -J G Gray, Winchester, Va

THU APR 25, 1850
Wash Corp: 1-Nomination of Dr T B Frye, as a member of the Board of Health: unanimously confirmed. 2-Ptn of Jos W Nairin, in opening an alley: referred to the Cmte on Improvements. 3-Ptn of Wm Pettibone was taken from the files & referred to the Cmte of Claims. 4-Jas L Cathcart, associated with us as a member of this Board, resigns his seat, as he is greatly enhanced on his part to leave the city. 5-Bill for the relief of Patrick Wilson; referred to the Cmte of Claims. 6-Ptn of Jas M Wright & others, for a curbstone & footway on north side of square 515: referred to the Cmte on Improvements. 7-Ptn of John Scrivener, reporting the condition of the gutter on I st, between 8th & 9th sts: referred to the Cmte on Improvements. 8-Ptn of Vandora Mallion, praying a reduction of his taxes: referred to the Cmte of Claims. 9-Ptn of Sarah Myers, praying the remission of a fine: referred to the Cmte of Claims. 10-Ptn of John Sinon & others, for the improvement of Maine st, from 4½ to 3rd st: referred to the Cmte on Improvements. 11-Ptn of Wm Lord & others for flag footways at the crossings on north side of G st: passed.

House of Reps: 1-Cmte on Private Land Claims: discharged from the further consideration of the ptn of David Wier: referred to the Cmte on Manufacture. 2-Cmte on Revolutionary Claims: adverse report on the ptn of Peter Dygert: it was laid on the table. Same cmte: discharged from the further consideration of the same: & referred to the Cmte on Invalid Pensions. 3-Cmte on Private Land Claims: adverse report on the ptn of Jos Reynes: laid on the table.

Indianola, Texas, Apr 3, 1850. The remains of Maj John P O'Brien were followed to the grave by a large solemn procession. Col Reeve, Capts Wood & Coburn & Lt Garnett, of the army, acting as pall bearers. He leaves an afflicted widow & orphan children.

J B Bigelow has been elected Mayor of Brownsville, Texas. –N O Crescent

We understand from passengers by last night's train from Syracuse, that Mr Francis, conductor of the freight train on the Utica & Syracuse road, was killed in passing under the bridge east of the tunnel. He was on the top of the cars & knocked down when he came in contact with the bridge. He was much esteemed & we believe this was his first trip as conductor. –Oswego Com Times

Senate: 1-Ptn of Geo Horn, asking that a patent may be issued to him for a tract of land which he has occupied & improved, near Sacramento, Calif: referred to the Cmte on Public Lands. 2-Cmte on Pensions: to which was referred the resolution of the Senate of Feb 27 last, directing an inquiry into granting to the widow & heirs of David Linn, a soldier in the war of 1812, 5 years half-pay, asked to be discharged from the further consideration of the same: which was concurred in. 3-Cmte of Claims: claim of Danl D T Benedict, for certain pay & allowances, made an adverse report on the same: ordered to be printed. Household & kitchen furniture at auction: on May 2, at the residence of Mr O J Preston, on C st, between 12th & 13th sts. –Dyer & Brother, aucts

Detroit, Mich, Apr. The U S District Atty, Gen John H Norvell, returned here on Sun from Wash, when he was attacked with erysipelas, & lingered until today, when he died.

Mrd: on Apr 24, by Rev Mr Butler, Dr Ruel K Compton to Miss Rachel Dement, all of Wash City.

Mrd: on Arp 23, at St Matthew's Church, by Rev Jas B Donelan, Mr Jos Sessford to Miss Sarah Eliz Stewart, both of Wash City.

Household & kitchen furniture at auction: on Apr 30, at the residence of Mrs J S Brown, on 19th st, between G & H sts. -Green & Tastet, aucts

FRI APR 26, 1850
Appointments by the Pres-Postmaster: 1-Abraham Jones at Quincy, Ill
2-Oliver S Beers, at Mobile, Ala 3-Michl Musson, at New Orleans, La 4-Jas H Turner, at New London, Conn

House of Reps: 1-Cmte on the Military: adverse report on the ptn of Wm H Ker: laid on the table. 2-Cmte on Naval Affairs: bill for the relief of Wm Speiden: committed. Same cmte: joint resolution authorizing the Pres of the U S to accept & attach to the navy 2 vessels offered by Henry Grinnell, of N Y, to be sent to the Arctic seas in search of Sir John Franklin & his companions.

Senate: 1-Ptn from David C Ellsworth, asking the the Sec of State may be required to grant passports to all citizens of the U S who may demand them, without regard to color.

The Postmaster Genr'l has established the following new Post Ofcs for the week ending Apr 20, 1850.

Ofc	County, State	Postmaster
Leeds Station	Kennebeck, Maine	Geo Beals
No Pittston	Kennebeck, Maine	Jesse Gould
Dixmont Mills	Penobscot, Maine	Edmund Chase
Prospect Ferry	Waldo, Main	A Harriman
So Alabama	Genesee, N Y	B W Strickland
New Grafenburgh	Herkimer, N Y	Richd Holland
Amityville	Suffolk, N Y	Jas H Porter
Jefferson Valley	Westchester, N Y	Harvey Green
Marlboro	Chester, Pa	Bayard Neilds
New Milltown	Lancaster, Pa	Levi Hoover
Sweet Valley	Luzerne, Pa	Barton Moss
Port Providence	Montg, Pa	M Shoemaker
Branch Da'e	Schuylkill, Pa	D J Lewis
Pitman	Schuylkill, Pa	Saml Miller
Baley Creek	Tioga, Pa	Wm Lawrence
Mungo Park	Wash, Pa	Geo Atkins
Alpha	Green, Ohio	Jos Siddall
Kennon's Landing	Chas City, Va	J C Wilson
Bath Alum	Bath, Va	Wm H Allen
Chas Mills	Wash, Va	Jacob Morton
Lorenzoville Foundry	Shenandoah, Va	A Ludwick
Jerusalem	Davie, N C	Jos W Hodge
Trades Hill	Chatham, N C	E R Harton
Mills Gap	Rutherford, N C	Geo J Mills
Rose Hill	Mechlenburg, N C	John H Grier
Clark's Ford	York D, S C	John McGill
Haeyondale	Scriven, Ga	Jacob Freeman
Scienceville	Stewart, Ga	Jas M Granberry
Buncombe	Walton, Ga	Wm F Kennedy
Fox Grove	Burke, Ga	Elton Hodges
Newson	Bibb, Ga	Stephen Slocum
Whitewater	Fayette, Ga	John T Harper
Egypt	Effingham, Ga	Geo Foy
Gamble	Jefferson, Ga	E B Hook
Perry	Jefferson, Fla	Perry Barronton
Centre Star	Lauderdale, Ala	Wm J Fapp
Mount Hebron	Greene, Ala	Alex A Rogers
Spring Dale	Lafayette, Miss	M D Parks

Roma	Starr, Texas	H R Holland
Alfred	Henderson, Texas	E L Smith
Sand Spring	Anderson, Texas	Wm Stewart
Johnston	Poinsett, Ark	John Johnson
Reed's Creek	Lawrence, Ark	Jas C McGee
Caroline	Haywood, Tenn	Lorenzo T Heart
Flint Gap	Knox, Tenn	Wm Plumbe
Rich hill	Maury, Tenn	A W Blackman
Cherry Valley	Wilson, Tenn	Wilson T Cartwright
Loddy	Hamilton, Tenn	John Watson
Swan Creek	Warren, Ky	J P Smith
Bruin	Carter, Ky	Thos T Thompson
Hopewell	Livingston, Ky	Alex Davis
Devon	Henry, Ia	Andrew J Batson
Oak Woods	Grant, Ia	Turner W Fallis
Coffee Creek	Porter, Ia	Jesse Morgan
Dunlap's Prairie	Cook, Ill	M L Dunlap
Rayan	Fond du Lac, Wis	Robt C Wright
Sand Prairie	Richland, Wis	Johnson Young

Names Changed:
Water Valley, Erie Co, N Y, changed to Wait's Corners.
East Lexington, Green Co, N Y, changed to Jewett Centre.
Walling's Creek, Lee Co, Va, changed to Stickleysville.
Bolivia, Bolivar Co, Miss, changed to Content.
Knob Creek, Izard Co, Ark, changed to Cross Plains.
Camp Creek, Hancock Co, Ill, changed to Dallas, City.
Dodge Centre, Dodge Co, Wisc, changed to Juneau.

Rev Peter McEnally, of the Balt Annual Conference of the Methodist Episcopal Church, died very suddenly on Apr 19, near Phillipsburg, Pa, on the mountain. He has been for some time in feeble health.

To the unknown heirs of Paul Leathers, deceased. By an order of the Scott Circuit Court, the undersigned was directed to advertise for the unknown heirs of Paul Leathers, deceased, who was a native of Culpeper Co, Va, & who died intestate in Scott Co, Ky, in 1843, at the advanced age of 105 years, leaving his brothers & sisters & their descendants his only heirs at law & distributees of his estae, some of whom reside in N C, S C & Tenn, as is supposed. The estate is estimated at ten or fifteen thousand dollars.
-P Thompson, Mstr Com'r

Three story brick house for sale, in Gtwn, on the east side of High st, between Bridge & Gay st, it being lot 11 in square 19. At present occupied by Mr Sam'l McKnight, & belonging to the estate of Richard Ross, deceased. -Green & Tastet, aucts

Died: on Mon last, in Washington, after a brief illness, Bridget McGan, wife of Mr Saml Davey, aged 20 years. The deceased was a native of Dublin, Ire.

Cotton Factory at Public sale: under a deed of trust for the benefit of creditors, executed by the Avondale Mfgr Co, to the subscribers: the tract of land containing about 15 acres, with water-power, bldgs, & appurtenances known as the property. The factory is on the Patuxent river, near the village of Laurel, PG Co, Md. There are 11 bldgs on the property for the accommodation of the hands, 10 of which are double houses: all frame bldgs, in good order. -Thos S Alexander, Geo W Dobbin, trustees -Cannon, Bennet, & Co, aucts

Coal lands in Alleghany Co, Md, at Auction, by a decree of the Honorable Chancellor of Md, in his Court of Chancery, made in the cause of Dundas & al vs McCulloh, Abert, & Templeman, defending in said Court: auction on May 18, the following: tract called **Bank Property**, it being a resurvey of a part of **Western Connexion**, containing 1,622½ acres of land, according to the re-survey of Oct 10, 1836. Also, **Bank Territory**, being a re-survey of another part of **Western Connexion**, containing 6,322 acres, according to re-survey dated Sep 27, 1836. Also, another tract called **Bank Lot**, being a re-survey of another part of **Western Connexion**, contining 1,036½ acres, by re-survey dated Sep 22, 1838. All lands were conveyed to the Pres, Dirs, & Company of the Bank of the U S, by 3 deeds from Jas M Mason, dated May 19, 1830, recorded in the land records of Alleghany Co. Also, all that **Revolutionary Soldier's Lot**, being #2,487, containing 50 acres. Also, an undivided moiety of **Mount Pisgah**, said to contain 235 acres. Also, **Pleasant Ridge**, containing 281½ acres. -Rd Smith, trustee -Dyer & Bro, aucts

Lands in Hardy Co, V, for sale at Public auction: by deed of trust, executed on Jan 22, 1839, by Chas J Nourse & Rebecca M Nourse his wife, & Geo Templeman & Mary Templeman his wife, recorded in book 15, page 136, in the clerk's ofc in said county: sale on May 18: all those tracts of parcels of land in Hardy Co, Va, containing together 9,365¼ acres: tract of 4,480 acres, being part of Francis & Wm Deakin's tract of 25,500 acres, being the same land which was conveyed to Walter Smith, in trust, by John Templeman & wife, by deed dated Mar 31, 1809, recorded in book 6, page 396, in said county. Also, the lands in Hardy County aforesaid: executed in like manner by said Templeman & wife to said Walter Smith, in trust, dated Mar 31, 1809, recorded in said county in book 6, page 403, containing 5,609 acres: which tracts containing together 10,089 acres conveyed by Walter Smith to Jas M Mason, by deed dated Oct 13, 1825, excepting, from the above described 10, 089 acres, 345 acres sold to Jas Irons, Jan 29, 1836; 110¾ acres sold to M Hainline, Oct 8, 1836; 150 acres sold to R Davis, Dec 28, 1836; & 118 acres sold to Elisha Hays, Aug 21, 1837. -Rd Smith, trustee -Dyer & Bro, aucts

Mrd: on Mar 14, at the residence of Col J R Lewellyn, in Chicot Co, by Rt Rev Bishop Freeman, Hon Thos W Newton, of Little Rock, Ark, to Miss Amelia C Cordell, of Missouri.

Fine Horses for sale. They can be seen at the Nat'l stables, kept by Walker & Kimmell. –S Crim

Valuable farm at Public sale: by virtue of an order, passed in the matter of the application of Horace Capron, of PG Co, for the benefit of the insolvent laws, the subscribers, as trustees, will sell, on May 21, that farm called **Laurel Farm**, in PG Co, Md, containing 1,000 acres. There are 12 tenements in different parts of the farm, all in good order. -Tho S Alexander, Geo W Dobbin, trustees

SAT APR 27, 1850
House of Reps: 1-Ptn of Elisha Foster, of Chautauque Co, N Y, praying Congress to grant him a pension for injury received while in the service of his country, in the late war with Great Britain.

Cadets of the Military Academy. Gentlemen invited by the Sec of War to attend the examination of the Cadets of the Military Academy, to commence on Jun 1 next.
1-Chas B Haddock, N H
2-Geo W Benedict, Vt
3-Gen Jas B M Potter, R I
4-Gen Thos Cadwalader, N J
5-Capt Henry Dupont, Dela
6-Vincent Witcher, Va
7-Matthew J Williams, S C
8-Richd Hawes, Ky
9-Dr Geo R Grant, Tenn
10-Jas P Millikin, Ind
11-Col N B Buford, Ill
12-Geo H Hazleton, Mich
13-Jas S Rollins, Missouri
14-Capt Jas D Cobb, Ark
15-Saml A Roberts, Texas

For rent: 4 story brick house in **Pollard's row**, near the City Hall. Inquire of the subscriber at his House-furnishing Ware-rooms, Pa ave. -C W Boteler

Mathias M White, undertaker, N Capt st, advertises metallic burial cases. John L Wirt will fill orders during my absence, with the remains of Hon John C Calhoun.

MON APR 29, 1850
Terrible tornado at Nassau, N P, on Mar 29, which passed over the premises of Messrs Aaron Cambridge, Taylor, Duncome, Tynes, Maj Anderson, & others, utterly destroying everything in its course. The Bahama Gaz: 8 persons lost their lives, Mr Saml Dean, who had just married, was one of them. –Balt Amer

A few days ago Mr David Bell, of Fayetteville, N C, who had resided here with his family for just 12 months, was employed by the day as a draughtsman, in one of the bureaus of the War Dept. He worked up to Sat, the 20th, & was a corpse the Monday following. His worthy widow seeks an opening for a school whereby to maintain herself & 5 little ones. Address Mrs Gen Macomb, Mrs G J Abbott, or Miss Mary Moore, all near the corner of I & 17th sts, or to Mr Woodbury, teacher, H st, near the Lutheran Church.

Circuit Court-City Item: late Nicholas Travers, over 90 years of age, left his property to his sons, to exclusion of his daughters; not of sound disposing mind per testimony.

Appointments by the Pres:
Marshals:
Richard Wallach, for D C
Geo Little, for N C
Wm Paine, for Maine
Saml Garfield, for N H
Chas Devens, jr, for Mass
Allison A Pettengill, for Conn
Geo W Jackson, for R I
Saml Barr, for Dela
Thos H Kent, for Md
Goshorn A Jones, for Ohio
Solomon Meredith, for Indiana
John W Twichell, for Mo
Luther Chase, for Ark
Frederick G Smith, for La
Stephen B Shellady, for Iowa
Alex'r M Mitchell, for Minn
Wm M Brown, for Ga
Jas S Speed, for Ky

Land ofcrs: Ezra Rood, for Mich; & Marcus Boyd, for Missouri.

Died: of yellow fever, board U S ship-of-the-line **Ohio**, under command of Capt C K Stribling, that arrived in Boston on Apr 26 from Rio De Janeiro, after an absence of 3 years:
Lt Chas M Armstrong
Lt Henry Eld
Ass't Surgeon E J Bee
Midshipman Jos B Miller
Purser's clk Thos C Johnson

Annexed is a list of the surviving ofcrs:
Capt C K Stribling
Lts: Jos F Reed, Jno J Almy, Jno L Worden, Miles K Warrington
Actg Surgeon, N C Barrabino
Passed Assist Surgeon, S A McCreery
Assist Surg, Robt T McCoun
Actg Capt's Clerk, C Stribling
Marine Ofcrs, Capt J L C Hardy; 2nd Lt Jas Wiley
Midshipmen, Augustus N Lodge, Jas P Foster, Beverly Kennon, Wm H Ward, John T Wood, A B Cummings, Salmon A Buell
Boatswain, Moses Hall
Gunner, S M Beckwith
Purser, Saml Forrest
Chaplain, Peter G Clarke
Master, John Adams
Carpenter, Geo W Elliott
Sailmaker, Geo T Lozier

Household & kitchen furniture at auction: May 2, at the residence of Mrs Behler, on C st, between 4½ & 6th sts. –Green & Tastet, aucts

Orphans Court of Wash Co, D C. Letters of administration on the personal estate of John Mcleod, late of Wash Co, deceased. -Jas J Boyle, adm

Circuit Court of Wash Co, D C. In Chancery: Henry N Young vs Edw Hart et al. Ratification of sale of the premises to Chas Homiller for $2,300; endorsed by Henry Kengla. -Jno A Smith, clerk

Henry Clay, jr, son of gallant Lt Col Clay, of Ky volunteers, killed at Buena Vista, has been appointed a Cadet in U S Military Academy.

Died: Col B O Smith, age 42 years, Feb 21, at *Insinore*, his residence in Claiborne Co, Miss.

Died: on Apr 28, in Wash City, Capt Geo W Taylor. His funeral will be at his late residence, H & 18th sts, this afternoon, at 4 o'clock.

Miss M A Hughes will open on May 6, in the school room of Wesley Chapel, a School for Young Ladies, in which she will teach all the branches of the English education. Lessons also given in Music & Tapestry. Apply at the school or at her residence on D st, between 6th & 7th sts.

Died: on Apr 11, in Murray Co, Ga, Mr Richard L Glover, leaving a wife & 2 children, also, his mother, sisters, & relatives, in this his native city, Wash.

TUE APR 30, 1850
Dr W E Fulwood, Assist Surgeon of the U S army, died at Macon, on Apr 19. He was a native of Clark Co, Georgia.

Louis T Barney, a son of the distinguished Cmdor Barney, & in the earlier time of his life one of the most enterprising & useful citizens of Balt, is dead. He died at his residence in Balt on Wed, on the verge of 70 years. For a long number of years he was afflicted with disease, the effect of a paralysis which he suffered many years ago. He has since that time been living between life & death. -Patriot

David Humphrey, Sheriff of Jefferson Co, Va, died at the residence of his son, in that county, on Wed last. He emigrated to Jefferson Co [then Berkeley] near the close of the last century, & on the division of the latter county he was the first man commissioned by the Govn'r as a justice of the peace. During the late war with Great Britian he volunteered as a private, & at the battle of the White House he was so unfortunate as to lose his right arm.

Handsome residence for sale at public auction, in front of Sinclair's Hotel, in Leesburg, Loudoun Co, Va, on Jun 6, the beautiful residence known as *Rural Hill* or *The Hill*, near the town. The mansion is of brick & contains 9 rooms: the rear is attached to 8 acres. -G W Ball, Leesburg, Loudoun Co, Va

Mr Birge, clerk of the circuit court of Boone Co, Ill, was recently fatally wounded by the accidental discharge of his fowling piece.

Wash City Ordinance: 1-Act for the relief of Wm B Wilson: the sum of $7.75 to be paid Wilson for settlement of his laying a flag footway across Missouri ave, on the west side of 4½ st.

Died: on Apr 29, in Wash City, Mrs Lydia Brown, in her 63rd year. Her funeral will be from the residence of Geo W Thompson, 3rd & M sts, this afternoon, at 2 o'clock. Her friends & those of Mr Thompson & the Rev R T Nixon are invited to attend.

Senate: 1-Ptn from the heirs of Josiah Davenport, asking the confirmation of their land titles; also, a ptn from John B Eddins, to the like effect, both of which were referred to the Cmte on Private Land Claims. 2-Memorial of Isaac T Tinsley, in relation to certain bonds held by him of the late Republic of Texas, regarding his claim against the said Govt: referred to the Cmte on the Judiciary. 3-Memorial of J Eppes Cowan, legal rep of the heirs of Benito Vasquez, asking permission to locate a confirmed Spanish land claim: referred to the Cmte on Public Lands. 4-Ptn of Chas A Grignon, asking compensation for his services as an Indian interpreter: referred to the Cmte on Indian Affairs. 5-Ptn of Coombs Greenwell, asking compensation for an injury receive while in the performance of his duty as a machinist at the Navy Yard at Wash: referred to the Cmte of Claims. 6-Ordered, that Jos Walker have leave to withdraw his petition & papers. 7-Cmte on the Judiciary: memorial of Eliz L Blackburn, relict of the late Felix G Bosworth, a paymaster in the U S army, asking to be relieved from a certain judgment rendered against her as one of his sureties, submitted a report, which was to be printed, with a bill for her relief, which was passed to a second reading. 8-Cmte on Public Lands: ptn of Mark Bean & others, asking to be allowed indemnity for losses sustained by them in their removal under the treaty with the Cherokees of May 6, 1828, submitted a report for the relief of Mark Bean & Richd H Bean, of Ark: passed to a second reading. 9-Referred to the Cmte on the Post Ofc & Post Roads: act for the relief of Jas S Graham & Walter H Fennall. Also, an act for the relief of Brown & Tarbox.

Appointments by the Pres: 1-Edw Hamilton, of Ohio, to be Sec of the Territory of Oregon. 2-Wm V Brady, of N Y, to be Deputy Postmaster at N Y C, N Y.

Mrd: on Apr 18, by Rev Dr Balentine, Wm Boyd to Jane Wilson, both of Wash City.

Died: on Mar 12, on board the U S ship **Ohio**, on the passage from Rio Janeiro to Boston, Lt Henry Eld, jr, of New Haven, Conn. His disease was fever contracted at Rio Janeiro. He was on his return from a 3½ years cruise. He was one of the active young ofcrs of the U S Exploring Expedition during its arduous service; & in the Narrative of the Expedition by Capt Wilkes his name is frequently mentioned in terms of high commendation. [See Apr 29th newspaper.]

Andrew Coyle & Son having determined to close their present business with the least possible delay, offers their entire stock of Boots & Shoes, at greatly reduced prices.

Public sale, by a decree of the Circuit Court of Wash Co, D C, sitting in Chancery, in a cause wherein Eliz Ford is cmplnt, & Peter Brady, administrator of Wm Ford & John N Ford, dfndnts: public auction on Mar 2, of part of lot 1 in square 121, with a 2 story brick dwlg house; also, the east half of said lot 1 in said square, at the corner of 19th & F sts; also, lot 3 in square 8 & the south half of lot 18 in square 143, unimproved. Title is undisputable. –S S Williams, trustee -Green & Tastet, aucts

Ice Cream Saloon, on D st, between 11th & 12th sts, will open May 1. –J Aigler

Died: yesterday, in Wash City, at his residence near the Long Bridge, Brother Harris, of Equal Division Sons of Temperance #6. His funeral will take place this afternoon at 3 o'clock, from his late residence.

Farm for sale: by deed of trust from John G Gasy & wife to the subscriber, dated Apr 11, 1849, recorded in Liber 20, page 413, of the land records of Prince Wm Co, Va: sale of one undivided third part of a tract of land in Chappawamsick Creek, in said county, containing in all 262 acres. The farm is about 5 miles from Dumfries, with a dwlg-house on it. –Edw Swann, trustee -John Martin & Co, aucts

House of Reps: 1-Ptn of David Cowden, of Chautauque, N Y, praying Congress to grant him a pension for injury received while in the service of his country in the late war with Great Britain. 2-Memorial of John W Walker, praying for authority to construct a floating dock at the Delaware Breakwater. 3-Ptn of Stephen Howard, of Clarendon, Orleans Co, N Y, praying for a grant of land in consideration of services rendered by his father, Jonathan Howard, in the Revolutionary war.

Steamboat disaster: Cleveland, Ohio, Apr 29. The steamer **Anthony Wayne** blew up opposite Vermillion, on Sunday. Killed & missing were about 40. Passengers known to be killed are Matthew Falkner, of Sheffield, Mass, & Henry McDonough, of Choteau, Michigan. The schnr **Elmira** took the killed, wounded, & survivors to Sandusky.

WED MAY 1, 1850
Senate: 1-Mr Foote presented the credentials of the honorable Jefferson Davis, of Miss, elected a Senator from that State for the term of 6 years from Mar 4, 1852. 2-Ptn of Augustus H Evans, Danl D Page, & others, asking the confirmation of their title to a quarter section of land in the St Louis land district: referred to the Cmte on Public Lands. 3-Memorial from Wm A Nicholls, in behalf of himself & other ofcrs of the 2nd Regt of the U S Artl, asking that an appropriation be made for supplying the band attached to this regt with musical instruments: referred to the Cmte on Military Affairs.

Rooms for rent: inquire of Mr Kloman, one door above the Nat'l Intelligencer, 7th st.

At N Y on Mon, as a gang of laborers were working near the Darling, Albertson & Rose store, in Front st, destroyed by fire on Wed last, the peak of the gable of the adjoining bldg, owned by Stephen Whitney, fell with a tremendous crash. Dennison was killed outright, & Edw McCheyne had his legs broken. The remainder of the party still remained covered by a heavy mass of brick. They are: Hugh McCheyne, John Harvey, John Horgon, Wm Pratt, Michl Connor, John Driscoll, John Lavy, Tom Lehey, John Hays, & Patrick Barry. Similar accident occurred at the old Chemical Bank bldg, while a number of workmen were removing the old edifice, when a portion of the flooring gave way, burying them. Those badly hurt & conveyed to the hospital: Matthew Kearhan, John Golden, Michl Macleaven, John Trainor, Thos Karr, Patrick Brady, Saml Hunter, & Jas Hughes.

Phil: on Sun as 2 fire companies were proceeding to a fire, they were attacked by ruffians, & Peter Myers was stabbed in the heart & died. A few hours earlier, the house of Patrick Monaghan, Bedford st, was entered into & Monaghan was stabbed below the heart. He is in the hospital, but not expected to survive. –Phil Inquirer

Lots on the Island, in the east half of square 297, for sale by John Marron.

Persons having claims against Francis A Dunn will please present them to the subscriber, as the proceeds of the sale of Dunn's goods have been placed in his hands for settlement. –P W Browning

Notice: I want to purchase $10,000 worth of Family Servants. Call at King's Hotel. –Thos N Davis

Household & kitchen furniture at auction: on May 2, at the residence of the late Capt Jas Ward, 12th st, bet Md ave & B st, [Island.] -Dyer & Brother, aucts

THU MAY 2, 1850
Senate: 1-Memorial of Benedict J Heard, asking indemnity for losses sustained in consequence of the destruction of his property by the enemy in the last war with Great Britain: referred to the Cmte of Claims. 2-Memorial of the heirs of John Chalmers, asking indemnity for French spoliations prior to 1800: ordered to lie on the table. 3-Ordered, that the Sec of War be directed to communicate to the Senate the report of Capt Marcy, U S Army, of his expedition from **Fort Smith**, Ark, to Santa Fe, including his return trip, in command of a detachment of U S troops, during 1849. 4-Sec of State to inform the Senate what measures he has taken upon the memorial of Ladislas Wankowitz, great grand nephew of Gen Thaddeus Kosciusko, & Gaspard Tochman, atty of the heirs of Gen Kosciusko, complaining against Alex de Bodisco, Minister from Russia, accredited to the Gov't.

Died: on May 1, in Wash City, Roberta Ann, only daughter of Bushrod W & M L Reed, aged 3 years & 4 days. Her funeral will be from father's residence at 14 & F sts, today, at 3 o'clock.

I O O F Notice: Members to attend the funeral of Bro Philip Massa, of Schiller Lodge, #95, Phil, at the Odd Fellows' Hall. –Wm Cooper, sec

For sale: 3 story brick house on 6th st, near D, now occupied by Capt Tyler. Inquire of H F Condict, Pa ave, between 12th & 13th sts.

Dwlg & Seminary for rent: that desirable property now occupied by Rev Wm Love, on King st, Martinsburg, Va. Also, the large bldg occupied as the Berkeley Seminary, with a lot of ground. Possession given on Jun 10 next. Apply to John H Likens, Martinsburg, Va

Public sale: by decree of the Circuit Court of Wash Co, D C, sitting in Chancery, made in the cause of the U S vs David Ott's administrator & devisees: auction on May 27, on the premises, all that part of lot 2 in square 379 described, with improvements-a 3 story brick house. -Walter S Cox, trustee -Dyer & Bro, aucts

FRI MAY 3, 1850
Senate: 1-Memorial of Capt F Britton, of the U S army, asking compensation for extra services rendered in the Commissary & Quartermaster's depts. referred to the Cmte on Military Affairs. 2-Ptn of Victor Morass, asking the confirmation of his title to a tract of land in the Detroit land district, in Michigan: referred to the Cmte on Public Lands. 3-Report of Wm Carey Jones on the subject of land titles in Calif: referred to the Cmte on Public Lands. 4-Report of Thos Butler King, special agent to Calif, be referred to the Cmte on Public Lands. 5-Cmte on Pensions: ptn of Amelia Sophia Catharine Wetmore, asking a pension, reported a bill for the relief of Mrs Amelia Sophia Catharine Wetmore, widow of the late Capt Leonidas Wetmore, of the U S army: passed to a second reading. 6-Cmte on the Post Ofc & Post Roads: ptn of Wade Allen, of the firm of Allen & Kitchen, asking further allowances under their contract for carrying the mail, reported a bill for the relief of Wade Allen: passed to a second reading. 7-Senate considered the joint resolution for the settlement of accounts with the heirs & reps of Col Pierce M Butler, late agent of the Cherokee Indians: passed. 8-Bill for the relief of Gamaliel Taylor, late marshal of the district of Indiana, & his sureties: passed.

House of Reps: 1-Cmte on Naval Affairs: bill for the relief of the securities of Robt S Morse, deceased, late a purser in the U S Navy: committed. Same cmte: bill for the relief of Eli Darling: committed. Same cmte: discharged from the further consideration of the ptn of Wm B Bingly & wife: it was laid on the table. Same cmte: bill for the relief of Rebecca Winn: committed. 2-Cmte on Foreign Affairs: joint resolution of the Senate for the relief of John Hoagland, reported it back without amendment: committed. Same Cmte: adverse report on the memorial of Benj Rush, praying compensation for his services as Charge d'Affaires at London during the absence of Mr Stevenson: laid on the table. 3-Ptn of Hannah Phelps, widow of Saml Phelps, a Revolutionary soldier, late of Byron, Maine, praying for a pension.

A man missing: Danl Earner, about 23 years of age, left this city on Mar 29 last, for a short trip to Rockville, Md. He reached Rockville that night, & lodged at Kidwell's Hotel, which he left in the morning. He left all his clothes & other property here, & was to have returned in a day or two. Serious fears are entertained by his friends lest the money which he had in his possession should have made him the victim of some reckless villains. His many friends would be glad to hear of his whereabouts. Address Mr Wm Flaherty, D st, Wash.

Wm Rotch, one of the early founders of the whale fishery at New Bedford, Mass, died a few days ago.

There are twin-sisters residing near Keyport, N J, who have entered their 92nd year. [Names not given.]

Wash Corp: 1-Ptn from Nathl Plant & others: referred to the Cmte on Improvements. Same for the ptn from John Moore & others. 2-Ptn from C W Pairo: referred to the Cmte on Finance. 3-Ptn of W H Loudon: referred to the Cmte of Claims. 4-Cmte of Claims: act for the relief of Jas H Shreves & Harrison Taylor, an act for the relief of Jas A Wise, an act for the relief of W H Powell, & recommended that they do not pass: ordered to lie on the table. 5-Ptn of G Simmons, praying remission of a fine: referred to the Cmte of Claims. 6-Ptn of Wm H Phillip, praying that certain takes for removing a nuisance in square 229 may be remitted: referred to the Cmte on Improvements. 7-Ptn of Jas Mercer, praying remission of a fine: referred to the Cmte of Claims. Same for the ptn of Jas Burdear, for remission of a fine. 8-Cmte of Claims: asked to be discharged from the further consideration of the ptn of Sarah Myeres: so discharged. 9-Ptn of Geo E Kirk & others, for a flag footway across F st, at 7th: referred to the Cmte on Improvements.

Rev John A Jacobs, of the Catholic Church, died in Indianola, Texas, on Apr 7, one week after he performed the funeral rites of the late Major O'Brien.

Died: on Sat last, at Cherry Hill, N J, Rev David Bartine, of N J Conference of the Methodist Episcopal Church. He entered the ministry in 1791.

The Iron Business. Mrd, on Mar 20, near Toms river, N J, by Benj L Irons, Mr Jos Grant to Miss Amanda Irons; & on Mar 21, at Dover, N J, by Benj L Irons, Mr Hendrick B Irons to Miss Jedidah Ann Irons.

Three gentlemen, residents of Mountjoy, Lancaster Co, Pa, died suddenly last week of a disease similar to that of Asiatic cholera. Their names were Geo Schmaling, Moses Gardener, & Mr Light.

Alex'r Franklin, a young member of the Pittsburg bar, died on Thu last, of lock jaw, caused by a slight operation upon one of his fingers, which was crooked from an injury received in early life.

Mrd: on May 1, in Wash City, by Rev Jas Ryder, Pres of Gtwn College, Wm T Sherman, U S army, & Ellen Boyle Ewing, eldest daughter of the Hon Thos Ewing.

Mrd: on Mar 30, by Rev Dr Clement M Butler, John G Hedgeman, of the Treas Dept, to Cecelia Ashton, eldest daughter of the late Dr Noble Stuart, of Chas Co, Md.

Mrd: on Mar 15, at the residence of Franklin Steele, **Fort Snelling**, Minnesota Territory, by Rev Mr Gear, Brevet Major Saml Woods, U S Army, commanding the post, to Clavonie, daughter of the late Maj Wm B Barney, of Balt.

Mrd: on Mar 22, at Madison Barracks, Sackett's Harbor, N Y, S B Hayman, U S Army, to Mary Seymour, daughter of the late Maj Satterlee Clark.

Mrd: on Mar 25, at Boston, at the Stone Chapel, by Rev Dr Peabody, Louis Agassiz, Prof in the Lawrence Scientific School of Harvard College, to Eliz C Cary, daughter of the Hon T G Cary, of Boston.

The Montesquiou Trial: the trial of Raymond & Gonzalve de Montesquiou, upon a charge of killing T Kirby Barnum, which occupied the Criminal Court of St Louis for 4 weeks, was disposed of for the present, on Mar 29, by the jury being discharged, not being able to agree upon a verdict.

For sale in exchange for city property: the farm of Mrs H H Dyer, 72½ acres, on the Bladensburg Turnpike. Inquire of Mrs H H Dyer, on the premises, or Thos Carbery. -Dyer & Bro, aucts & commercial merchants.

Died: on Apr 17, at the Fremont House, in Galveston, Gen John Thompson Mason, a native of Va. He moved from Va to Ky in early life; he lived in Ky from 1811 to 1835. About 15 years ago he moved to Michigan, where his eldest son had previously been Govn'r, but died soon after. He also was afterwards Govn'r ex officio of the same State. He moved to N Y & 4 months ago came to Galveston.

SAT MAY 4, 1850
Appointment by the Pres: Nathan Hantch, to be Deputy Postmaster at Carlisle, Pa.

Mr Senator Berrien is detained at his home in this city by the serious illness of an interesting son. —Savannah Rep of Tues.

House & lot on Pa ave at auction: on Apr 9: lot 6 in square 380, with a 2 story frame house, adjoining Mr W Noell, Venetian blind manufacturer. —Noch Callan, atty -Dyer & Brother, aucts

Truste's sale of real estate at public auction: Apr 9, in front of the premises, near 4½ & N sts south, by deeds of trust duly recorded: in square 545, lots 35 & 36, corner of M & 3rd sts, with a 2 story frame house, nearly new. See Liber W B 114 folios 402 thru 404. Also, lots 49 & 50 on 3rd st. See Liber W B 110, folios 120 & 121. Also, lot 18 on 4½ st. See Liber W B 110, folios 157 & 158, of the land records of Wash Co, D C. The title to the above property is indisputable. -Saml Byington, trustee -Green & Tastet, aucts

Senate: Ptn of Martha Garrand, Allen Christian, Mgt Christian, John Christian, & Chas M Hestor, the heirs of Wm Christian, deceased, who was a capt in the Va Continental line, praying Congress to grant them the 5 years' full pay which was due to their ancestor under certain resolutions of Congress therein named.

$50 reward for runaway mulatto boy, aged 18 years. [No name given.] Deliver to me at Culpeper Court-house, Va: R J M Hall.

Zachary Taylor, Pres of the U S, recognizes Chas Hunt, who has been appointed Consul of Belgium, for St Louis, Missouri. May 3, 1850

Postmaster Gen est'd the following new Post ofcs for week ending Apr 27, 1850.

Ofc	County, State	Postmaster
Round Pond	Lincoln, Me	Parker Mears
Mapleville	Providence, R I	Danl S Whipple
Hope Falls	Hamilton, N Y	John Ressequire
Claryville	Sullivan, N Y	John Reynolds
Shongo	Alleghany, N Y	Jas R Wood
West Shongo	Allehany, N Y	G Hyde
Hughsonville	Dutchess, N Y	E Van Kloeck
East Sharon	Potter, Pa	Azel Lane
Mount Carmel	Northumberland, Pa	Feliz Lerch
Saint Chas	Butler, Ohio	Saml R Stewart
Boke's Creek	Union, Ohio	Amos S Davis
Grand Traverse	Michilimakcinac, Mich	Robt Campbell
Eldersburgh	Anne Arundel, Md	Francis M Shipley
Cooper's Gap	Rutherford, N C	Wm E Mills
Fort Prince	Spartanburg D, S C	A C Bomar
Meeting Street	Edgefield D, S C	J Smyly
Cedar Spring Asylum	Spartanburg D, S C	N P Walker
Greenfield	Poinsett, Ark	T F Arlege

Names Changed:
Boston, Northumberland Co, Pa, changed to Kautatinchunk.
Owing's Run, Carroll Co, Md, changed to North Branch.
Horse Creek, Polk Co, N C, changed to Pacolot.
Reed's Creek, Lawrence Co, Ark, changed to Barry.
West Dupage, Dupage Co, Ill, changed to Junction.
Springfield, Dodge Co, Wisc, changed to Lomira.

Foreign Items. 1-Rev Canon Bowles, the poet, whose controversy with Byron may be recollected by many, died at Salisbury, England, on Mar 7, at age 89. 2-Accounts from Russian announce that M Bodisco, Minister to the Czar to the U S, instead of being banished to Siberia, has been decorated by the Emperor with the grand cross of the order of Waldimar.

Mrd: on Thu last, by Rev Wm G Eliot, jr, of St Louis, Mo, John A Kasson, of St Louis, to Miss Caroline Eliot, daughter of Wm G Eliot, of Wash City.

Mrd: on May 2, at St John's Church, by Rev Smith Pyne, D D, Lt Geo Thom, of Corps of Topographical Engineers, to Miss Mary Lucia, daughter of Dr J F Griffin, of S C.

Died: on Apr 29, in Wash City, Mrs Mary Ringgold, wife of Maj Geo M Ringgold, Paymaster, U S Army. An affectionate mother, a devoted wife & warm friend, her loss is a sad affliction to her family & friends.

Died: on May 2, at the Four Mile Run, near Alexandria, Va, Miss Margaret Burns. Her funeral is tomorrow at 2 p m.

The brig **Lincoln**, Capt Averill, which left Boston on Jan 29 for San Francisco, was set on fire by lightning at sea on Mar 2, & continued to burn, notwithstanding the utmost exertions of the crew. On May 5 the crew of 11 & 2 passengers, being all on board, were taken off by the Danish ship **Maria Christina**, Capt Voss, from Rio Janeiro for Altona, & landed at Portland, England, Apr 5. Capt Averill speaks in the highest terms of the kindness shown to all, passengers & crew.

$50 reward for runaway negro man Edw Sprigg, about 24 years old.
-Mary Hall, Queen Ann, PG Co, Md

For sale, a superior finished Buggy, made to order, & of beautiful style. For sale low. Apply to John L Marceron, Grocer, Navy Yard.

Best quality school furniture for sale, at his school rooms, on F st, between 5th & 6th sts. –R H Patchin

Ohio land for sale: a small farm in Clermont Co, Ohio, upwards of 100 acres, within 2 miles of Batavia, the county seat of Clermont. Apply to Jas L Ranson, living in Charlestown, Jefferson Co, Va. Also, my house & lot in Charlestown, now being thoroughly repaired & improved; also, $1/4^{th}$ of the *Piedmont Farm*. Apply by letter, post paid, or in person, to Jas L Ranson, Charlestown, Jefferson Co, Va.

MON MAY 6, 1850
Brookeville Academy, E J Hall Principal; John C Williamson, Assist: located in Montg Co, Md, about 20 miles from Wash. Reference may be made to the following patrons: Chas E Sherman, Johnson Hellen, Mr A Green, Jas Adams, Cashier Bank of Wash; Dr J O Wharton, Balt; Mr R H Snowden, Anne Arundel Co, Md; & Mr J T Thomas, of St Mary's Co, Md.

The undersigned are authorized to employ a Teacher for Primary School #8, near Piscataway, PG Co, Md: John L Lambert, Randolph B Latimer, & Geo W Gardiner.

Appointments by the Pres: 1-Neil S Brown, of Tenn, to be Envoy Extra & Minister Pleni of the U S to the Court of His Majesty the Emperor of all the Russias. 2-Edw H Wright, of N J, to be Sec of the U S Legation at the Court of His Imperial Majesty the Emperor of all the Russias. 3-John D Diomatari, of Georgia, to be U S Consul for the port of Athens, in Greece.

Died: on May 2, Jos Samuel, son of Solomon & Eleanor Hubbard, in his 6th year.

Died: in Wash, A B Murray, aged 54, formerly of Balt. His funeral is on Tue, at 10 o'clock, from the corner of 3rd & Indiana av. [No death date given.]

Hon Franklin H Elmore, appointed Senator from the State of S C to fill the vacancy caused by the death of Hon J C Calhoun, arrived in Wash City last night, & has taken lodgings at Fuller's U S Hotel.

Orphans Court of Wash Co, D C. Letters of administration on the personal estate of Lydia Brown, late of Wash Co, deceased. -R T Nixon, adm

For rent: the dwlg of the 3 story brick house over Mr Brashear's store, on Pa ave. Apply to G C Grammer.

Interments in Wash for Apr 1850 - 58. –Thos Willer, M D, Pres of the Board of Health.

TUE MAY 7, 1850
Mr Archer Brackney, one of the passengers on the steamer **Wayne**, at the time of the explosion, was on his way from Lafayette, Ia, to Phil, with the remains of his wife & child, recently deceased. He succeeded in dragging his 2 living children from their rooms, & plunged into the water. He came in contact with the box containing his wife & child & for some time used it to keep them from drowning. The little 2 year old died in his arms, drowned by the waves that crashed over them. He and his little daughter were saved.

Zachary Taylor, Pres of the U S, recognizes Edwin Adelbert Oelricks, who has been appointed Consul of Bremen, for the port of N Y. May 6, 1850

Orphans Court of Wash Co, D C. Letters testamentary on the personal estate of Patrick McGarvey, late of Wash Co, deceased. -Jas W Sheahan, exc

Senate: 1-Memorial from Aaron Hayden & others, owners of the steamer **Admiral**, asking for equal & uniform law on the subject of alien passengers arriving in the U S, whereby they may be relieved from oppressive or unconstitutional State laws: referred to Cmte on the Judiciary. 2-Additional documents submitted relating to the claim of the legal reps or Rinaldo Johnson & Anne E Johnson: referred to Cmte of Claims. 3-Ordered that the legal reps of John Baptiste de Lomagne, on the files of the Senate, be referred to Cmte on Pensions. 4-Cmte on Indian Affairs: ptn of Chas A Grignon, asking compensation for services as an interpreter to the U S sub-agents for the Menomonee Indians, reported a bill for his relief: passed to a second reading. 5-Cmte on Public Lands: bill for the relief of Mariba Fairservice, reported back the same, with amendments. Same cmte: asking to be discharged from the further consideration of the ptn of Geo Horn. Same cmte: ptn of John Frazer & Wm Lindley, for the heirs of John G Glendenin, submitted an adverse report: ordered to be printed. Same cmte: ptn of Wm Wallis, asking to be allowed to locate certain land, submitted an adverse report: ordered to be printed. 6-The undersigned, ofcrs & soldiers of the war with England, commenced in 1812, & with the Indian tribes during that period, represent that they entered the said war, at different periods, & served out their engagements, & were honorably discharged. Your memorialists respectfully ask the passage of a law granting to all the ofcrs, musicians, & privates, regulars, volunteers, & militia, who served in the war of 1812 with England & with the Indian tribes, a part of public domain, to be appropriated to them according to their respective rank, as a just reward for their services.

R C S Brown	Elijah Parker	Philip Stevens
Wm Russell	Wm Oliver	Whitfield Bourn

David Matlock	A McLean	Wm Riley
Wm G Ramsey	Wm Steward	David Givins
Wm Howard	Jos Bryant	John V Gray
Jas Shinault	Joel Oliver	Thos Pruitt
John F Winfrey	Sam Rush	Russel Bates
John Pentz	Valentine Matlock	Jas Mitchell
John Phagan	Wm Ritchie	
David Burton	Hugh Foreman	

House of Reps: 1-Ptn of 1st Lt W T Sherman, U S army, for an increased pay while serving as assistant adjutant general in the Pacific military division in Calif. 2-Memorial of Jas S Green, A S Green, & others, children of Wm Green, an ofcr in the Revolutionary army, praying for land, or other compensation in lieu thereof, for the services of Wm Green.

St Louis, May 2. Dreadful accident at Laclede Saloon, last night, when J H Purkett's scholars & their parents assembled for amusement. The first floor gave way, carrying down some 200 persons into the cellar. The wife of Mr Chaster W Pomeroy, & the wife of Mr John Beakey, were killed instantly. Miss Mary Abbott is expected to die from her wounds. Mrs Emanuel Black had both legs fractured. Seriously injured: Mrs Johnston, teacher; Mrs Malay, Miss Sullivan, Mrs Reed, wife of the late Surveyor Gen; Miss Virginia Clark, & Miss Barlow. Slightly injured: Miss Gunn, Miss Mary Pomeroy, Mr P A Ladew, Mrs L T Carr, Miss Sarah Know, Dr Sykes, Miss Atwood, Miss Carter, Wm Waters, Mr Tucker, Miss Kate Clark, Miss Brewell, Mr Christopher, Mr Holmes, Mr Purkett, principal of the school.

WED MAY 8, 1850
Cadet appointments in 1850:
Maine: Levi B Browne: Wm O Otis, Chas G Sawtelle
N H: Thos J Treadwell, Ebenezer Gay
Mass: Henry L Abbott, Henry M Lazell, Chas O Higginbotham, Allen A Bursley
R I: Zenas R Bliss
Vt: Henry A Smalley, Breed N Hyde
N Y: Phillips Phenix, Stephen H Weed, Alex'r Annan, Peter Fonda, jr, Saml Ten Eyck, Wm De Mott, John A Black, Loomis L Langdon, Lemuel C Curtiss, Fazilo A Harrington
Pa: John T Greble, Wm A Leech, John V Jordan, Saml Kinsey, Jas W Phillips, Chas M Webb, D H Brotherton, Geo R Wilson, Waterman Palmer, jr, Geo McG Dick
Md: Richd Thomas, Wm P Scott
Va: Jas E B Stuart, Wm R Robertson, John Pegram, John T Scott, Chas G Rogers, Jas C Bennett, Milton T Carr
N C: A H Graham, Saml E Shepperd, Wm D Pender, Alex'r H Guion
S C: Stephen D Lee, Jno B Villipigue, Wm M Davant
Georgia: J T Mercer, Abner Smead, Wm J Daniel, Lewis H Kenan
Ky: W Yancey Eaker, Wm K Peyton, Ezekiel F Halloway; Henry Clay, jr, Peter Laskbroke, jr
Tenn: Robt C Crawford, Arthur J Nixon, Levi L Wade

Ohio: John McCleary
Louisiana: Michl R Morgan, Laurence B Haynes, Peyton R Splane
Indiana: Willis J Hargrove, Cyrus F Widup, Judson D Bingham
Illinois: Wm A Allen, Michl Kelley
Mississippi: Benj F Davis
Jno G Powell
Alabama: Jas Deshler
Wisconsin: Thos H Ruger
Oregon: Jos H Cornwall
Minnesota: Chas K Smith, jr
There were no vacancies from Conn, N J, Del, Mo, Ark, Mich, Fla, Texas, Iowa, or D C.
At Large:
Wm Croghan Jesup
Geo W C Lee
Jno R Smead
Robt C Wood
Geo A Gordon
Wm C Nicholson
Wm F Drum
Jno O Long
Jas G Montgomery
Thos J Wright
The last three are in the place of H W Hilliard, deceased, & Messrs White & McKee, declined.

P T Barnum, of Museum notoriety, has a country seat at Bridgeport, Conn, & has given some attention to farming & gardening of late, was elected Pres of the Fairfield Co, Agricultural Society.

Zachary Taylor, Pres of the U S, recognizes Monsieur Hachette, who has been appointed Vice-Consul of Belgium for the port of San Francisco, Calif. –May 7, 1850

Died: Apr 27, at *Roe Down*, Anne Arundel Co, Md, [the residence of his mother,] John J Dorsett, youngest son of the late Thos J Dorsett, in his 4th year.

Died: May 6, Jas French, of Fauquier Co, Va. His funeral will be from his residence on E st, today, at 4 o'clock.

Incendiaries abroad: the livery stable of Mr Dennis Pumphrey, 6th & C sts, was set on fire yesterday. The carpenter's shop of Messrs Allen & Thompson, at 12th & sts, was totally destroyed by fire. Jefferson Butler, a colored boy, age 12 years, was arrested yesterday on the charge of setting the carpenter's shop on fire.

Obit-died: on Apr 30 last, in Madison Co, Va, Presley N Smith, aged 58 years. His many virtues & excellencies of character will be long remembered by his numerous relatives & friends.

Saml D King: Land & General Agent, ofc of F st, near the Treas Dept.

The Universalist Church in Bridgeport, Ct, of which Mr Ballou is pastor, was entirely destroyed by fire on May 2. The bldg was erected about 3 years since at a cost of $4,500.

$25 reward for return of a light sorrel horse & blind bridle stolen from my stable on May 6. –F A Tschiffely, near *Franklin Row*, Wash

Senate: 1-Additional documents submitted relating to the claim of Maria Mason: referred to the Cmte on Military Affairs. 2-Ordered, that leave be granted to withdraw the papers on the files of the Senate relating to the claim of Wm Parkeson. 3-Cmte of Claims: House bill for the relief of the legal reps of Capt Geo R Shoemaker: adverse report on the same: ordered to be printed. Samt cmte: ptn & documents of Erskine & Eichelberger for a balance due them by John Gunter, a Cherokee Indian, prior to the Cherokee treaty of 1835, submitted an adverse report on the same: ordered to be printed. 4-Cmte on Military Affairs: memorial of Col J R Creecy, asking remuneration for services rendered & expenses incurred in raising & subsisting volunteers for the Mexican war, submitted a report, which was ordered to be printed, with a bill for the relief of Col Jas R Creecy, which was passed to a second reading. 5-Cmte on Military Affairs: memorial of Geo Poindexter, asking compensation for injury done his property near Louisville, Ky, by the troops encamped on it under command of Gen Wool, submitted a bill for his relief: passed to a second reading. 6-Cmte of Claims: ptn of Solomon Parsons, for himself & other heirs of Solomon Parsons, deceased, asking compensation for services of said Parsons during the Revolutionary war, asking to be discharged from the further consideration of the same, & that it be referred to the Cmte on Revolutionary Claims: which was agreed to. Same cmte: memorial of Wm Seely, asking remuneration for the losses & sacrifices of his father during the war of the Revolution, & for the services of his 2 sons during the war of 1812, asking to be discharged from the further consideration of the same: which was agreed to. 7-Mr Greene: I ask the indulgence of the Senate in behalf of a bill for the relief of Adj Gen Roger Jones, which I desire the Senate to take up & dispose of. The Senate then resumed the consideration of the bill to establish a Board of Accounts.

Trustee's sale: by deed of trust from Aaron M Gattrell, dated Jan 22 last, to the subscriber, & at the request of Chas W Pairo, the party beneficially interested, I will expose to sale at auction, on Jun 8, the following property: lot or parcel of ground in Wash City, being part of lot 1 in square 343; with improvements on the same. –W Redin, trust

Appointments by the Pres: 1-Geo C Bates, of Michigan, to be U S Atty for the District of Michigan. 2-Lester H Colton, of Wisconsin, to be U S Marshal for the District of Wisconsin.

Thos G Ford has purchased of Mr Thos Fitnam & Son all of their stock in trade in the Saddle, Harness, & Trunk business, at Wash Hall, corner of Pa ave & 6th st, & will re-open in a few days.

THU MAY 9, 1850
Died: on Apr 23, Hon Daniel Chipman, of Vt, aged 85 years, at his seat in Ripton.

In March last, Mrs Gerry House, of Wayne aged about 30, died from taking wild cherry tree bark & drinking it with gin. She died in 3 hours. It was the acid which is contained in this species of the cherry that caused her death. Dr N H Carey, of Wayne, in this county, was called to the patient, but too late to save her. –Augusta [Me] Farmer

Senate: 1-Additonal documents submitted relating to the memorial of A P Britingham: referred to the Cmte on Foreign Relations. 2-Mr Atchison, on leave, introduced a bill for the relief of the heirs of Nicholas Lachance: referred to the Cmte on Revolutionary Claims.

For rent or sale: Groc & Feed Store, 8th & L Sts, Wash. View of locating in the west. -J G Adams.

Mrd: on May 2, by Rev D Brainard, Lt S B Buckner, U S Army, to Miss Mary J Kingsbury, daughter of Maj J J B Kingsbury, U S Army.

Mrd: on May 7, at Balt, by Rev Mr Hoover, John B Lord, of Wash City, to Miss Sarah Jane Douglass.

Mrd: on May 8, by Rev E Ballantine, N H Johnson, of Centreville, Indiana, to Cath Coyle, daughter of John Underwood, of Wash City.

Died: on May 8, after a long illness, Mr Walter Mudd, in his 82nd year. He was a native of Chas Co, Md, but resided in Wash for the last 40 years. His funeral will be from the residence of his son-in-law, Saml H Taylor, 8th st near I st, this afternoon, at 3 o'clock.

Young Ladies' Academy, 7th st, between K & L sts: Mrs Bell proposes opening on May 13. She has permission to refer inquirers to the following friends:

Gen Totten, U S Army	Mrs Genl Macomb
Rev Mr McElfresh	Mrs G J Abbot
Rev Mr Allen	Miss Mary Moore
Mr Jno M Moore	Miss Ann Young, teacher
Dr Magruder	Mr G J Abbott, teacher
Dr Smoot	Mr H E Woodbury, teacher

Marshal's sale-in virtue of a writ of fieri facias: sale on May 22: of the following property, to wit: a life estate in one undivided fifth part of lot 23 in square B, in Wash City, together with all singular the right, title, interest, & estate of the dfndnt in the case, in & to the said premises, & the improvements thereon: seized & levied upon, & will be sold to satisfy Judcials 118, in favor of Esau & John F Pickrell. favor of Smith & Dyer. -R Wallach, mrshl of D C

Household & kitchen furniture at auction: on May 13, at the residence of Maj Ringgold, F between 19th & 20th sts. –Green & Tastet, aucts

Marshal's sale-in virtue of a writ of fieri facias, I shall expose to public sale for cash, on May 23: a life estate in one undivided interest in lot 21 in square B, in Wash City, with the improvements thereon. Seized & levied upon & will be sold to satisfy Judicials 119 to Mar term, 1850, in favor of Wm & Jas H McVeigh. -R Wallach, mrshl of D C

Marshal's sale-in virtue of a writ of fieri facias: sale on May 23, of a life estate in one undivided fifth part of lot 9 in square 403, with improvements; seized & levied upon, & will be sold to satisfy Judicials 74, to Mar, 1850, in favor of Smith & Dyer.
–R Wallach, mrshl, D C

FRI MAY 10, 1850
Notice: claims against estate of Barbara Vermillion, late of Wash Co, deceased, to be exhibited to me, on or before May 11, with vouchers. -R H Laskey, exc.

House of Reps: 1-Cmte on Revolutionary Pensions: bills for the relief of Isaac Cobb & Martha Dameron: committed. Same cmte: adverse reports on the ptns of Joshua Woodward, Stephen Allen, Eady Tuck, the heirs of Stephen Riggs, Eliz Wright, Wm Pierce, John Caldwell, Jacob Slingerland, the heirs of John Hill, Handley Donaldson, & Levi Foster. Also, upon the ptn of Uri Young & others, citizens of Warren Co, N Y: which were severally laid on the table. 2-Cmte on Invalid Pensions: bills for the relief of Wm Lynch; of Jas F Green; of Jas Mains; of Isaac Downs; & of Geo C Thomas: committed. Same cmte: discharged from the further consideration of the ptn of Saml Minifield: & it be referred to the Cmte on Revolutionary Pensions. 3-Cmte on Invalid Pensions: discharged from the further consideration of the ptn of Mrs Catherine Keller, widow of John Keller, deceased: referred to the Cmte on Revolutionary Pensions. Same cmte: bills for the relief of Gardner Henning; of Emily Stone; & of Sylvanus Blodget: committed. Same cmte: bills for the relief of Wm B Edwards, & of Maurice K Simons: committed. Same cmte: discharged from the further consideration of the ptn of Jesse W Hollister: laid on the table. Same cmte: adverse report on the ptn of John Lusk: laid on the table. 4-Cmte on Patents: bill for the extension of the privilege secured by letters patent therein mentioned to Zebulon Packer & Austin Parker: committed. 5-Cmte on Revolutionary Claims: discharged from the further consideration of the ptns of John Quinton & Peter Hilton: referred to the Cmte on Revolutionary Pensions. 6-Ptn of W G Howison, one of the auxiliary guards of Wash City, praying compensation withheld from him during the time of his sickness. 7-Ptn of David Steward, a soldier in the army of the U S in 1812, asking for a pension.

Mrd: on May 9, by Rev Mr Samson, Orlando H Donn & Miss Virginia Cook, all of Wash City.

Mrd: on May 7, at Cathedral in Balt, Md, by Rev Thos P Foley, Daniel J Foley & Miss Annie Maria Sanders, daughter of late Benedict J Sanders, all of Balt.

Mrd: on May 8, by Rev L F Moran, Mr Jno H Robinson & Miss Cath Mackaboy, all of Wash.

Mrd: on May 8, in Wash, by Rev Mr J E Weems, Mr Wm Upton to Miss Susan Redmun, both of Prince Wm Co, Va.

Geo Davis, son of Matthew L Davis, formerly a merchant of N Y C, but for 12 or 14 years a deputy collector of the port, died this morning. He was a competent & energetic ofcr, & thouroughly acquainted with the principles of commercial law. –Evening Post

Household & kitchen furniture at auction: on May 16, at the residence of Gen Eaton, on L st, between 20th & 21st st. –Dyer & Brother, aucts

By writ of fieri facias, at the suit of Bennona Jones, against the goods & chattels of Jas Spirling, to me directed: I have seized & taken in execution all the right, title, & interest of the said Spirling in & to one carryall; sale of same in front of the centre Markethouse, on May 16, at 9 o'clock. –H R Maryman, constable

SAT MAY 11, 1850
Wash Corp: 1-Ptn from Stephen Scott: referred to the Cmte on Improvements. 2-Ptn of Mrs Ellen Donohaugh: referred to the Cmte of Claims. 3-Ptn from French S Evans & others for a foot pavement: referred to the Cmte on Improvements. 4-Ptn from Wm Ashdown & 133 other citizens, praying Congress to grant power to the Corp to erect a bridge across the Wash canal at 6th st. 5-Cmte of Claims: ptn of R R Burr, a bill for his relief: passed. 6-Cmte of Claims: act for the relief of Edw Hammersly: passed. 7-Cmte on Police: bill for the relief of Wm W McCreery: praying to be indemnified for injuries sustained from falling into an exposed culvert, with additional evidence to support his claim: referred to the Cmte on Police. 8-Ptn from Philip Hawkins for the remission of a fine: referred to the Cmte of Claims. 9-Bill for the relief of John F Callan: referred to the Cmte of Claims. 10-Bill for the relief of Wm B Lewis: ordered to lie on the table. 11-Bills for the relief of B Mullany, & for the relief of Raub & Green: passed. 12-Ptn of David Miller, in relation to the bill recently passed for his relief: referred to the Cmte of Claims. 13-Ptn of Geo E Jellard & others, praying for the grading of K st from 12th to 13th sts: to be placed on file with the bill for the improvement of K st. 14-Ptn of Giles Dyer, praying the reimbursement of a certain amount erroneously paid for taxes: referred to the Cmte of Ways & Means. 15-Ptn of G & T Parker & others for the improvement of 6th st west: referred to the Cmte on Improvements. 16-Ptn of C L Coltman, praying payment of a balance due for constructing a reservoir at La ave & 7th st west: referred to the Cmte on Improvements. 17-Ptn from Wm Hodges in relation to a nuisance on square 877: referred to the Cmte on Health. 18-Cmte of Claims: ptn of Jas Mercer, discharged from the further consideration of the same; which was agreed to. Same cmte: ptn of G Simmons, asked to be discharged from the further consideration of the ptn of the same: which was agreed to. 19-Cmte of Claims: bill for the relief of Jas Burdine: read. 20-Bill for the relief of P Ennis was decided in the negative.

To let: a brick house with 6 rooms, with basement & large garden: on M st, between 19th & 20th sts, for the moderate rate of $150 per year, $12.50 per month, to a punctual tenant. –John T S McConchie

Boarding: Mrs MacPherson, on Pa ave, near 3rd st.

House of Reps: 1-Bill for the relief of Solomon T Nicoll & Jas Clinch, of N Y C: laid on the table. 2-Bill for the relief of Gamaliel Taylor, late marshal of the district of Indiana, & his sureties: referred. 3-Settlement of the accounts with the heirs & reps of Col Pierce M Butler, late agent for the Cherokee Indians: referred. 4-Bill for the relief of Wm Darby: referred. 5-Bill for the relief of Mgt L Worth, widow of the late Gen Worth, U S Army, was taken up.

Trustee sale of valuable real & personal property. Deed executed by John E Penman & wife, Daniel Penman & wife, Richard Thomson, & Marian Penman, dated Apr 19, 1849: sale on May 31 at the **Taylor Furnace**, 440 acres, Frederick Co, Md; & a tract of 600 acres; these 2 tracts conveyed to John E & Daniel Penman by Jas Bean & wife, Dec 1, 1848 & by deed of Mrs Magdalen Bean, widow of Jas Bean the elder, Jan 2, 1849, releasing to John & Daniel Penman a dower interest or estate which she had in a part of said lands. A brick dwlg house of good size is included in the improvements. There are also 2 smaller tracts of land adjoining these, one containing about 100 acres, & the other 3 acres, which were purchased of John W Piler. The two first named will be sold subject to a prior lien of $4,500 in favor of said Jas Bean. -Jos H Sherrard, trustee

Died: on May 7, in Phil, Capt Wm Lang, U S Marine Corps. He was a native of N Y.

MON MAY 13, 1850
1-A few weeks since a Mr G W Atwood, an American, came here from London with his lady, niece, & nephews, bound to San Francisco. This morning, the last of his family, he only remains to prosecute his voyage. 2-The sister of Rev Mr Pease, Seamen's Chaplain at this port, who arrived here in Jan last, died of this dreadful fever some 6 weeks ago. His wife was sick at the time, not expected to live, but has since recovered. Himself & children have also suffered of this fever.

A father & 4 children drowned: on Sun last: while Mr Leonard was crossing the Ohio in a skiff, it struck a flatboat moored on the shore, & in an instant all 5 were out of sight, a father, 2 sons, & 2 daughters. Mr Leonard worked in a foundry as a blacksmith. The wife & mother died some time since. The only remaining member of the family is one child. –Cincinnati Com of Mon last

Appointed members to compose the Levy Court of Wash Co, D C:
Henry Naylor	Lewis Carbery	Benj K Morsell
Chas H Wiltberger	Wm R Woodward	John F Cox
Chas R Belt	Robt White	Jas Crandell
Joshua Pierce	Saml Drury	

Killed: a few days ago, Master Bagley, age 10 or 12 years, son of Jas H Bagley, in Albemarle Co, Va, when powder exploded. -Richmond Whig

At the Lunatic Hospital, on Mon, Mrs Susan Gregg, aged 51 years, a native of Groton, Mass, died of general debility, supervening on tight lacing & insanity.

Mrd: on May 9, by Rev Mr Slattery, Mr Thos M Harvey to Miss Sarah E French, all of Wash City

Mrd: on May 9, by Rev Mr Fowler, Dr Jas Muschett, of Va to Miss Virginia M, daughter of N Tastet, of Wash City.

Died: Wm Wordsworth, the Poet, age 80 years, at his residence, **Rydal Mount**, near Ambleside. He was born in 1770 at Cockermouth, in Cumberland.

Died: on Fri, at Charleston, after a protracted & painful illness, in his 74th year, Hon Hon John S Richardson, an Associate Judge of the Courts of Gen Sessions & Common Pleas of the State of S C.

Household & kitchen furniture at auction: on May 17, at the Auction Room, Concert Hall, near Brown's Hotel, Pa ave, the personal effects of Capt G W Taylor, deceased. –W B Scott, adm -Green & Tastet, aucts

Postmaster General est'd the following new Post ofcs for the week ending May 4, 1850.

Ofc	County, State	Postmaster
Centre Rutland	Rutland, Vt	J P Proctor
South Franklin	Norfolk, Mass	Jos H Wadsworth
Batavia Kill	Delaware, N Y	Cyrus Mead
Carthage Langind	Dutchess, N Y	Gilbert Budd
New Russia	Essex, N Y	P S Whitcomb
Greenville	New London, Ct	Jas D Morey
Blanket Hill	Armstrong, Pa	J M Daily
Anderson's Mills	Butler, Pa	S M Anderson
Loveland	Clinton, Pa	Thos B Baily
New Athens	Clarion, Pa	Alex Armstrong
Clara	Potter, Pa	Sala Stevens
Turner Creek	Potter, Pa	Rufus H Howe
Cranesville	Preston, Va	Henry Harr
Higginsville	Hampshire, Va	Wm Parker
Winterpock	Chesterfield, Va	Egbert T Bass
Pulaski	Scott, Va	C R Curtis
Laurel Branch	Henrico, Va	C G Waldrop
Tomilson	Mason, Va	Wm Sayre
Mt Eminence	Orange, Va	Lewis Harvey
Shawsville	Montg, Va	Jas V Deaton
Alpine Depot	Morgan, Va	Chas A Swann
Fine Forks	Person, N C	Bedford Vaughan
Chalkville	Chester D, S C	Horndon Chalk
Cotosa	Walker, Geo	John N Murray

Greenwood	DeKalb, Ala	Jeptha Edwards
Mosely Hall	Madison, Fla	Louis M Mosely
Gay Hill	Wash, Texas	Francis Thompson
Woodruff	Pulaski, Ark	Conway Scott
Midway	Hot Springs, Ark	Edw P Kearly
Carey	Washita, Ark	Jas McFarlin
Chalk Bluff	Green, Ark	Nathan Harris
Kinnard's Store	Tennessee, Tenn	D C Kinnard
Mount Olivet	Bracken, Ky	Joshua Barlow
Underwood	Hopkins, Ky	Saml Rorer
Sulphur Lick	Monroe, Ky	Winford Daniel
Oak Spring	Ballard, Ky	Wm Porter
Farmersville	Caldwell, Ky	W W Throckmorton
Anselm	Gallia, Ohio	Abadiah Ralph
Laura	Miami, Ohio	Amos Hall
Henby	Montg, Ohio	Alex Dean
Six Corners	Richland, Ohio	Wm B Miller
Blissville	Marshall, Indiana	Wm M Dunham
Oak Grove	Montg, Indiana	John Aydelott
McCutchenville	Venderburg, Indiana	Saml McCutchen
Fillmore	Montg, Ill	Henry L Dickson
Lawn Ridge	Marshall, Ill	Chas Stone
Letcherville	Greene, Ill	Elihu Armitage
Truston	Bureau, Ill	A S Lathrop
Sentinel Prairie	Polk, Mo	Avington Simpson
Bridgeport	Jackson, Iowa	Robt S Dyas
Pleasant Ridge	Lee, Iowa	John Houtz
Fennimore	Grant, Wis	John M Reynolds
Poynett	Columbia, Wis	John Thomas
Black Earth	Dane, Wis	O B Haseltine
Wallace	Iowa, Wis	Chas Waldridge
New Calif	Grant, Wis	Wm Henry

Names Changed: Shirley, Piscataquis Co, Maine, changed to Shirley Mills.
Wilson, Piscataquis Co, Maine, changed to Shirley.
Harewood, Susquehanna Co, Pa, changed to Brackney.
Leon, Astabula Co, Ohio, changed to Richmond Centre.
Cutler's Corners, Hillsdale Co, Mich, changed to North Adams.
Wright's Mills, Jackson Co, Va, changed to Moore's Mills.
Fort Hamilton, Madison Co, Florida, changed to Stockton.
Cockrum's Cross Roads, Desoto Co, Miss, changed to Cockrun.
Tiptonsport, Carroll Co, Indiana, changed to Fountian.
Gross Point, Cook Co, Ill, changed to Ridgeville.
Yellow Spring, Desmoines Co, Iowa, changed to Kossuth.
Prairie House, Lee Co, Iowa, changed to Charleston.
Hawley's Corners, Winnebago Co, Wis, changed to Fisk's Corners.

Beautiful goods for sale: dress goods, shawls, mantillas, & embroideries. –Walter Harper, Pa ave, between 9th & 10th sts

Tea, sugar, & olive oil for sale: J T Radcliff, Odd Fellows' Hall, 7th st.

Trustee's sale of valuable lot: deed of trust executed by Gardiner Green to the subscriber, dated Dec 1, 1849, recorded in Liber I A S 9, folios 291 thru 294, of the land records of Wash Co, D C: sale on Jun 13, all that piece or parcel of ground known as *Devaughn's subdivision* of lot 1 in square 43, being the s e corner of said lot 1, marked A, containing 4,220 sq feet, more or less. Also, sale of 2 valuable horses & a stone wagon, by deed of trust from Gardiner Green to the subscriber dated Dec 1, 1849, recorded in Liber I A S, 9, folio 291 thru 294, of the land records of Wash Co, D C: one large Horse 6 years old & one large sorrel Horse 5 years old; also, one large Stone Wagon, nearly new. Sale on May 21. Terms cash. -David A Gardiner, trustee -C W Boteler, auct

U S Navy Yard, Wash, May 7, 1850. Com Chas S McCauley, the undersigned, master mechanics & others attached to the Wash Navy Yard, express the high respect they have for you as an ofcr & a gentleman, in the uniform courtesy & kindness extended to them during the 3 years' term of your command of this station. With our best wishes for your future health, prosperity, & happiness, we remain your obedient servants.

John Davis, of Abel	John H Peake	Wm Dixon
Wm M Ellis	Jonas B Ellis	John Clapham
Jas Tucker	A G Davis	Wm J Barry
Edw Foster	Thos Woodward	David McComb
Jos M Padgett	Wm H Bland	J Carberry
B B Curran	C H Gordon	Thos Altemus
Jas R McCathran	John F Tucker	Truxion Beale
Amos Woodward	Lewis Marceron	A G Herold
Richd Barry	Richd Barry	

News from the last steamer was of the death of Wm Wordsworth, the poet Laureate. He breathed his last on Apr 23, at **Rydal Mount**, his residence, near Ambleside, at the age of 80 years. The event was not unexpected, as he was attacked about a month previous with a serious illness, from which, at his advanced age, he could not easily recover. He was born in 1770, at Cockermouth, in Cumberland, of respectable parents of the middle class in society. Entered St John's College, Cambridge, in 1787, where he graduated, &, upon the death of Southey, received the title of Poet Laureate.

TUE MAY 14, 1850
Mrd: on Apr 9, at Cumberland, by Rev D H Bull, Chas P Manning & Mary Jeannette, only daughter of Col C M Thruston, of Cumberland.

Mrd: on May 12, at M P Parsonage, by Rev W T Eva, Mr John W Rudd to Miss Harriet M Davis, both of Alex, Va.

Senate: 1-Ptn of E P Hale, late Assist Surgeon to the 2nd Regt of Tenn volunteers, in the late war with Mexico, asking to be allowed extra pay & bounty land: referred to the Cmte on Military Affairs. 2-Ptn of Saml R Butterworth, asking compensation for his services in carrying the mail: referred to the Cmte on the Post Ofc & Post Ofc Roads. 3-Ptn of citizens of Indiana, in behalf of Wm A Mott, a soldier in the Black Hawk war, asking that he may be allowed bounty land: referred to the Cmte on Pensions. 4-Cmte on Indian Affairs: memorial of Thos Snodgrass, asking the reimbursement of expenses incurred in the removal of the Cherokee Indians, submitted a report, which was ordered to be printed, with a bill for his relief. 5-Cmte on Public Lands: memorial of Jas J Stark, of Florida, asking for a donation of land under the armed occupation act, made an adverse report on the same: ordered to be printed. 6-Cmte of Claims: memorial of Eugene Van Ness & John N Burch, executors of Nehemiah Brush, for property destroyed by the U S troops in Florida, made an adverse report on the same: ordered to be printed. 7-Cmte on Public Lands: ptn of Sydney S Alcott, submitted a report, which was ordered to be printed, accompanied with a bill for his relief: passed to a second reading. 8-Cmte on Pensions: memorial of Maj D LeLamogne, asked to be discharged from the further consideration of the ptn of the same: referred to the Cmte on Revolutionary Claims.

From the report of Brevet Maj E Steen, of the 1st Dragoons: Dona Anna, New Mexico, Sep 1,1849. I went in pursuit of a large body of Indians of the Apache tribe who had crossed the river & killed a number of citizens in the vicinity of El Paso, & within the territory of New Mexico. My command was of 30 men of my company, & about 20 citizens joined me with Lt F T Bryan, of the topographical engineers. We succeeded in driving them from any position they would take. I was wounded in the early part of the engagement, as also Sgt Snyder, of my company. After I was wounded, Lt Bryan led the charge. One man was killed, Cpl A E Norwood, of Co H, 1st Dragoons.

House of Reps: 1-Memorial of Thos Davis, praying for a pension.

Died: on May 12, in Wash, aged 62 years, Mrs Maria S Webster, relict of E W Webster, of Cuba. Her funeral will be at her late lodgings, at Mrs Allen's, Pa ave, between 10th & 11th sts, this morning, at 10 o'clock.

Southdown Rams for sale @ $25 each: the purest & highest breed stock in the country. Address Wm B Dobbin, Balt, Md.

Household & kitchen furniture at auction: on May 18, by order of the Orphans Court of Wash Co, D C: the personal estate of Patrick McGarvey, deceased, at his late residence, corner of K & 27th sts north. -Jas H Sheahan, exc -Green & Tastet, aucts

WED MAY 15, 1850
Senate: 1-Ptn of Jos H D Bowman, asking that a patent may be issued for certain lands entered by him at the land ofc at Ouschita, La: referred to the Cmte on Private Lands Claims. 2-Bill from the House of Reps for the relief of Solomon T Nicoll & Jas Clinch, of N Y C: referred to the Cmte of Claims.

Ladies with letters remaining in the Post Ofc, Wash, May 15, 1850:

Anderson, Mrs C
Abbott, Miss E
Anderson, Miss Ann
Boyd, Mrs Ann L
Ball, Mrs Ann C
Brown, Miss E
Byrne, Miss Judith
Brown, Miss R W
Boggess, Sarah
Bowen, Miss Ann R
Browne, Miss Cathy-2
Brown, Miss Ellen J
Brown, Mrs Mary E
Biscoe, Miss Sarah A
Brown, Mrs Mary
Crogan, Miss Alice
Carroll, Mrs Eliza
Chapman, Mrs M A
Clarke, Mrs M C
Cutts, Miss Mary E
Clarke, Ms Sarah A
Childs, Mrs Gen T
Cooly, Miss Marg N
Cook, Mrs Cecilia A
Campbell, Mrs Cath
Creighton, Mrs Cath
Canter, Mrs Revecca
Davis, Mrs Ann
Dunn, Bridgett
Dinsby, Emily
Durham, Mrs Flora
Diggs, Mrs Mary
Diggs, Mrs Susan
Dawson, Mrs Har O
Edelin, Mrs Sydney
Fowler, Mrs Eliza
Ferguson, Mrs F
Ford, Miss Francis
Forest, Miss Louisa
Fisher, Miss M A
Franks, Mrs M J
Fields, Mrs R A
Fletch, Miss Sarah
Glasgow, Mrs Mary
Gillard, Miss Mary
Glasgow, Mrs Mary
Gambel, Miss Saran
Gayle, Mrs Eliz
Glenn, Mrs Elix
Green, Mrs Mary A
Hartman, Miss C
Heap, Mrs Evelina
Harris, Miss H
Heany, Miss
Humphrel, Miss M A E
Hardin, Sarah Jane
Humphreys, Miss M
Harris, Sarrah J
Holladay, Miss Sarah
Hillery, Sarah M
Ingle, Mrs Mary
Juilan, Mrs Ann
Jackson, Mrs Ann
Jackson, Mrs Lucia
Jackson, Miss M
Johnson, Mrs R W
Jones, Mrs Susan
Jackson, Mrs Hester
Johnson, Ms Harriet
Jackson, Miss S
Johnson, Mrs Ann
Mulligan, Miss M
Myers, Miss C W
Marshall, Mrs Car
Macklin, Miss E H
Mudd, Mrs Frances
Melling, Mrs Jane
Morrison, Mrs L R
Miller, Mrs L
Miller, Mgt
Murray, Miss M A
Mitchell, Mrs Mary
Monday, Matilda
Moore, Mrs M E
Mayor, Miss Marg
Miller, Mrs M
McClelland, Mrs R A
McKinly, Miss E
McIntosh, Angeline
McMechan, Miss A B

Nelson, Miss Marg
Nally, Mrs Mary A
Orme, Miss Cor'a-2
O'Brien, Mrs E T
Oden, Miss Mary
O'Dwyer, Miss
O'Conner, Miss M
Pendleton, Mrs J S
Poole, Miss Rach'l
Parker, Miss Miss Pris'a
Penny, Miss M J
Reed, Mrs Caroline
Robinson, Mrs M J
Reader, Miss R A
Spencer, Mrs A O-3
Sheridan, Mrs Cath
Schenig, Mrs E J

Smith, Miss Jane E
Sullivan, Kate
Schank, Mrs R
Taylor, Miss B
True, Miss Frances
Thornton, Mrs L E
Thompson, Mrs M E
Vogel, Miss Emilie
Williams, Mrs Col
Willett, Mrs Car
Willett, Mrs E C
Williams, Miss Kate
Williams, Mrs P
Wilcox, Miss S A-2
Young, Mrs Marg't
Zelinger, Mrs Pris'a
-Wm A Bradley, P M

Mrd: on May 13, in Trinity Church, by Rev C M Butler, D D, Wm Gray, of Detroit, to Miss Mary Stewart, daughter of Chas H Stewart, of Wash.

Mrd: on May 14, in Gtwn, by Rev Edmund C Bittinger, the Rev B F Bittinger to Miss C Malvina Libbey, 2nd daughter of Jos Libbey.

Died: on May 14, Kate Mary, youngest daughter of Buckner & Catherine B Bayliss, aged 2 years, 1 month & 10 days. Her funeral will be at family residence, Missouri av, this afternoon, at 4 o'clock.

Died: on May 13, Mrs Grace Dinnies, mother of A J Dinnies, in her 67th year. Her funeral will be at her late residence at Mrs Thompson's, 9th & H sts, this afternoon, at 4 o'clock.

Died: on May 14, Louise Morris French, daughter of Rev J W French, aged 5 years. Her funeral will be from the Church of the Epiphany, today, at 5 o'clock.

Mr Jas M Power, late Canal Com'r of Pa, died at Alleghany city on Sunday. He had only arrived there in the morning from Cincinnati.

Dinah, an old negress, died in Norfolk a few days ago, at the age of 123 years. She was a servant in a family residing at the Great Bridge, when the memorable battle was fought there in 1775, between Col Woodford's Va troops & the British grenadiers under Capt Fordyce, & was at that time a grandmother, a fact which attests her age. She was blind for a number of years, but recovered her sight when past her 100th year; & having lost all her teeth, she cut an entire new set about the same time. She was remarkably sprightly & industrious to the last.

House of Reps: 1-Memorial of Lt J K Goldsborough, & other ofcrs of the U S Navy, praying Congress to authorize the Sec of Navy to frank through his Dept the private letters & papers addressed to ofcrs & men of the navy on foreign stations.

Trustee's sale of valuable property: by deed of trust to the subscriber, the following lots of ground in Wash City: [No date given for sale.]
Lot 9 in square 18
Lot 5 in square 61
Lot 7 in dquare 61
Lot 8 in square 81
Lot 7 in square 567
Lot 19 in square 863
Lot 9 in square 517
-John Marbury, trustee -Dyer & Brother, aucts
At the same time:
Lot 9 in square 268
Lot 18 in square 516
Lot 1 in square 636
Lot 9 in square 784
Lot 3 in square 759
Lot 1 in square 984
½ part of lot 15 in square 762
-Eliz Kervand -Dyer & Brother, aucts

Shannondale Springs, Jefferson Co, Va, leased by the undersigned for a term of years, is now undergoing thorough repairs. The analysis of the late Dr DeButts, in 1821, classed the principal fountain with the saline chalybeates, a combination of the most valuable description in the whole range of mineral water, & closely resembling those of the celebrated Bedford in compostion, operation, & efficacy. It is within 8 hours' travel from Wash & Balt. –Hall Osburn & Co

Notice: Distribution of estate of Simon Frasier, deceased, May 24. -Wm Bird, adm

THU MAY 16, 1850
The accounts of Cornelius W Lawrence, late Collector of the port of N Y, accounted for the enormous sum of $77,433,121, received during his term of ofc, & there was not a single error or discrepancy. –N Y Courier

Wash Corp: 1-Bill for the relief of Wm H Yates: indefinitely postponed. 2-Ptn of Jas Handley & others for the improvements of 7th st near G: referred to the Cmte on Improvements. 3-Ptn of Andrew J Joyce & others, for grading E st north, at 14th: referred to the Cmte on Improvements. 4-Cmte on improvements: bill for the relief of Philip Mohun: reported without amendment. 5-Bills for the relief of Peter Smith, & for the relief of Jas Burdine: passed. 6-Ptn from G W Emerson & others, butchers, in relation to the license on their carts: referred to the Cmte on Police. 7-Ptn from Wm Pegg, for the remission of a fine: referred to the Cmte of Claims. Same for ptn from A Addison, for remission of a fine. 8-Resolution authorizing Thos Lawson to enclose part of the alley in square 169: referred to the Cmte on Police. 9-Bill for the relief of R R Burr; & of John Dewdney: referred to the Cmte on Police. 10-Referred to the Cmte of Claims: relief of Edw Hammersly; of Bernard Mubriney; & of Raub & Green. 11-Bill for the relief of John F Callan: ordered to lie on the table.

Died: on May 7, in Fredericksburg, after a 2 days illness, Thos Lunsford Lomax. He had resided in King Geo Co, Va, for 20 years.

Died: John F Gross, aged 25 years, suddenly, from a fall into an ice-house. His funeral will be at his residence near Gtwn College, this afternoon, at 5 o'clock.

Senate: 1-Submitted: additional documents relating to the claim of Jas M Marsh to indemnity for losses sustained in consequence of a robbery committed on him by a band of Sioux Indians, while in the execution of his duty as a deputy surveyor of the public lands: referred to the Cmte of Claims.

Flour dealers & consumers will do well to call at the new Flour Store next door to Francis Dodge, Water st, Gtwn, of Isaac Paul.

FRI MAY 17, 1850
House of Reps: 1-Memorial of Dr D S Edwards, Surgeon of the U S Navy, asking to be allowed for servants, & forage for horses, while serving with the army in Mexico.
2-Ptn of Geo Hatch & others, citizens of Buchanan Co, Iowa, praying that slavery may be prohibited in all the Territories of the U S.

Statement exhibiting the names & political creed [Whigs-Democrats] of the heads of bureaus, their chief clerks, & the chief clerks of Depts who were in ofc on Mar 4, 1849; also, the names of the present incumbents, with their political faith, Mar, 1850:

Chief Clerks	Mar 4, 1849	Mar, 1850
State Dept	W S Derrick-	W S Derrick-w
Treas Dept	McC Young-d	J McGinnis-w
War Dept	R W Young-d	J Etheridge-w
Inte'r Dept	[blank]	D C Goddard-w
Post Ofc Dept		
Chief Clerk	W H Dundas-d	W H Dundas-d
Interior Dept		
Assist Sec Treas	[blank]	Allen A Hall-w
Chief Clerk	[blank]	G A Harrington-w
1st Comptroller	J W McCulloch-d	E Whittlesey-w
Chief Clerk	J Larned-d	E C Seaman-w
2nd Comptroller	A K Parris-d	A K Parris-d
Chief Clerk	J M Brodhead-d	J M Brodhead-d
1st Auditor	Wm Collins-d	T L Smith-w
Chief Clerk	Geo H Jones-d	M H Miller-w
2nd Auditor	J M McCalla-d	Philip Clayton-w
Chief Clerk	J F Polk-s	Wm Mechlin-w
3rd Auditor	Peter Hagner-w	J S Gallaher-w
Chief Clerk	Jas Thompson-w	Jas Thompson-w
4th Auditor	A O Dayton-d	A O Dayton-d
Chief Clerk	F H Gillis-w	F H Gillis-w
5th Auditor	S Pleasonton-w	S Pleasonton-w

Chief Clerk	Thos Mustin-w	Thos Mustin
6th Auditor	P G Washington-d	J W Farrelly-w
Chief Clerk	Thos E Brown-d	Thos E Brown-d
Treasurer	Wm Selden-d	Wm Selden-d
Chief Clerk	W B Randolph-w	W B Randolph-w
Reg'r Treasury	D Graham-d	T Haines-w
Chief Clerk	M Nourse-w	M Nourse-w
Solicitor Treas	R H Gillett-d	J C Clarke-w
Chief Clerk	B F Pleasants-w	B F Pleasants-w
Com'r Land Ofc	R M Young-d	J Butterfield-w
Rec'r Land Ofc	S H Laughlin-d	N Sargent-w
Chief Clerk Public Lands	John Robb-d	Davis-w
Chief Clerk Priv Land Claims	J S Wilson-d	J S Wilson-d
Chief Clerk Surveys	Jno Wilson-s	Jno Wilson-s
Com'r of Customs	[blank]	C W Rockwell-w
Chief Clerk	[blank]	J D Barclay-w
Com'r of Indian Affairs	W Medill-d	Orlando Brown-w
Chief Clerk	John Cochran-d	A S Loughery-w
Com'r of Pensions	J L Edwards-w	J L Edwards-w
Chief Clerk	J G Berret-s	Coombs-w
Com'r of Patents	Edmund Burke-d	Thos Ewbank-w
Chief Clerk	H H Sylvester-d	D W C Lawrence-w
Examiner	Chas Page-w	Chas Page-w
Examiner	W P N Fitzgerald-w	W P N Fitzgerald-w
Examiner	H B Renwick-w	H B Renwick-w
Examiner	L D Gale-w	L D Gale-w
Examiner	J H Lane-w	J H Lane-w
Examiner	T R Peale-w	T R Peale-w
Assist Examiner	Saml Cooper-d	Saml Cooper-d
Assist Examiner	[blank]	T J Everett-w
Com'r of Public Bldgs	C Douglas-d	I Mudd-w
U S Marshal	Wallace-d	Richd Wallach-w
City Postmaster	C K Gardiner-d	W A Bradley-w
Chief Clerk	J E Kendall-d	W H Gunnell-w
Navy Agent	W B Scott-d	J H Lathrop-w
Warden of Penitentiary	C P Sengstack-d	Thos Fitnam-w
Chief of Bureau of Provision & Clothing	Gideon Welles-d	Wm Sinclair-w
1st Assist Postmaster Gen	S R Hobbie-d	S R Hobbie-d
2nd Assist Postmaster Gen	W J Brown-d	Fitz H Warren-w
3rd Assist Postmaster Gen	John Marron-d	John Marron-d

The following remain in ofc:
War Dept
Chief Clk Q M Dept: W A Gardiner-d
Chief Clerk Engineers: F N Barbarin-w
Chief Clerk Topog Engineers: G Thompson-w
Chief Clerk Ordnance: Geo Bender-w
Chief Clerk Pay Dept: A Frye-[blank]
Chief Clerk Subsistance: R Gott-d
Chief Clerk Surgeon Gen: R Johnson-w
Chief Clerk Adjutant Gen: J M Hepburn-w
Navy Dept
Chief Clerk Bur of Yards & Docks: W G Ridgely-w
Chief Clerk Bur of Construction: P C Johnson-d
Chief Clerk Bur of Provisions & Cothing: W S Parrott-d
Chief Clerk Bur of Medicine & Surgery: M Poor-w

Public Act passed at the First Session 31st Congress: 1-For 15 days' services of Jos Bryan, as com'r to take testimony in pursuance of an inquiry by direction of the Sec of the Treasury, at $8 per day, $120.

Constable's sale: by writ of venditioni exponas, against Nathan Brown, at the suit of Jas Ball, I have levied on 1 frame house & lot on H st, between 9th & 10th sts. I shall proceed to sell the same on Jun 17, to satisfy said judgment. [Constable-blank.]

Senate: 1-Memorial of the heirs of Rafael Garcia, asking compensation for the occupation & use by the U S, as a military post during the Mexican war, of their property at Point Isabel in Texas: referred to the Cmte on Military Affairs. 2-Memorial of Foxall A Parker, an ofcr in the navy, asking the reimbursement of certain unavoidable & extraordinary expenses incurred by him while in command of the East India squadron in 1843, 1844, & 1845: referred to the Cmte on Naval Affairs. 3-Ordered, that the ptn of Parkinson Hocker, on the files of the Senate, be referred to the Cmte on Pensions. 4-Ordered, that the heirs of John Ireland have leave to withdraw their ptn & papers.

A letter from S Williams, missionary to China, dated Canton, Feb 25, says intelligence just receiver from Pekin of the death of the Emperor. His name was Taukwang, or the Glory of Reason, this being the title he assumed on his ascension. He was the 2nd son of Kiaking, & the 6th of the Tsing, or Mantchu dynaster, which has reigned since 1644. Taukwang ascended the dragon's throne in 1821, & has reigned 29 years. He was 69.

Edw McCarthy was killed on the Lowell railroad, at East Cambridge, last Mon. He was about 35 years of age, & leaves a family in East Cambridge. It appears he stepped from one track to the other to allow a train to pass.

Orphans Court of Wash Co, D C. Letters of administration on the personal estate of Mary Eleanor Ford, late of the city of Balt, Md, deceased. –H M Potter, admx

Loudoun Co farm for sale at auction: under authority of the last will & testament of Chas Gassaway, deceased: auction on Jun 27, the valuable farm called *Sugar Land Farm*: contains 678 3/4th acres. The bldgs are only ordinary for so large a farm.
–C B Gassaway, exc, F W Luckett, exc, of Chas Gassaway, deceased.

Household & kitchen furniture at auction: on May 21, at the late residence of A B Murray, deceased, corner of 3rd & D sts. -Green & Tastet, aucts

By decree of Circuit Court of Wash Co, D C, sitting in chancery, & passed in a cause wherein Wm Holmead & others are cmplnt, & Gregory Ennis & others dfndnts, I shall sell on Jun 7, lot 15 in square 534, with two 2 story frame houses thereon: fronts on 4½ st, near Md ave. –John F Ennis, trustee -Green & Tastet, aucts

Geo Janes, a deaf mute aged 19, was overtaken on last Sat by the cars on the Naugatuck railroad, & died in great agony in a few hours.

Mrd: on May 14, at the residence of her father, by Rev Edmund C Bittinger, Henry Barron, of Md, to Eliz A Davis, of Gtwn.

House of Reps: 1-Cmte of Claims: bill for the relief of the legal reps of Robt S Burroughs & Stephen Hopkins: committed. Same cmte: adverse report on the ptn of Jas Jones, of Indiana: laid on the table. Same cmte: bill for the relief of the legal reps of John H Pratt, deceased, of the administrators of Oliver Lee, deceased, & of Isaac Cook & others: committed. Same cmte: discharged from the further consideration of the ptn of Thos M O'Brien, of Harry Richardson, & of David Melville: laid on the table. Same cmte: bill for the relief of Melvina Cruyal: committed. Same cmte: discharged from the further consideration of the ptn of Isaac Hill: referred to the Cmte on the Post Ofc & Post Roads.
2-Cmte on Commerce: bill for the compensation of Jas W Low & others, for the capture of a British private armed schnr, during the late war with Great Britain: read twice. Same cmte: discharged from the further consideration of the ptn of Andrew A Jones: referred to the Cmte of Claims. Same cmte: discharged from the further consideration of the ptns of F Guilbeau & others, praying for the right of drawback to entend to Eagle Pass, in Texas; of Job Duncan, Thos M Newell, Wm S Payne, & Osmond Peters: laid on the table. Same cmte: discharged from the further consideration of the ptn of Thos H Abrahams & others, praying permission to build a bridge at Kittery, Maine: laid on the table. Same cmte: discharged from the further consideration of the ptn of Gorham Coffin & other citizens of Nantucket, praying that no change be made in the prime meridian for longitude: referred to the Cmte on Naval Affairs. Same cmte: discharged from the further consideration of the ptn of Joshiah Sturgis & other ofcrs in the revenue cutter service: referred to the Cmte on Invalid Pensions. Same cmte: bill for the relief of S Morris Waln & Ira T Horton: committed.

Died: on Apr 6, at Belmont, Mississippi, Joseph M Clark, formerly of Wash, aged 36 years.

Died: yesterday, after an illness of 14 days, Mgt Ann Virginia, eldest daughter of Solomon & Ann Maria Goddard, of Wash City, aged 2 years & 14 days. Her funeral will be at their residence 11th st, between L & M sts, at 4 o'clock, this day.

Died: on May 16, in Gtwn, at the residence of her father, Mr Jos Radcliffe, Fannie A, wife of Albert F Yerby, of Wash, aged 18 years. Her funeral is this evening, at 4½ o'clock.

Died: on May 12, at *Rouse's Point*, Clinton Co, N Y, Mrs Harriet G Mason, wife of Bvt Lt Col J L Mason, U S Corps of Engineers, aged 24 years.

SAT MAY 18, 1850

The Postmaster General has established the following new Post Ofcs for the week ending May 11, 1850.

Ofc	County, State	Postmaster
West Norfolk	Litchfield, Ct	N Humphrey
Ouleaut	Delaware, N J	Jas Humphrey
Low's Corner	Sullivan, N J	Abraham B Low
Denning	Ulster, N J	Gilbert Palen
Thornton's Mills	Rappahannock, Va	P Thornton
China Grove	Wmsburg D, S C	J J Dickson
Freetown	Jackson, Ind	Chas Rosenbaum
Cortland	Jackson, In	Jacob Brown
Indian Creek	Monroe, Ind	Jesse East
Homer	Jackson, Ind	Geo W Findley
Dorset	DeKalb, Ill	Wm Robertson
So Hollow	Jos Daviess, Ill	Henry Elson
Deerfield'	Lake, Ill	C Cadwell
Pilot Grove	Hancock, Ill	Nelson Andrews
Crooked Creek	Monroe, Md	Elijah Haden
Double Oak	Camden, Md	Ousley Cliborn
Monterey	Waukesha, Wis	A W Hackley
Rock River	Fond du Lac, Wis	W J C Robertson
Ashippun	Wash, Wis	E A Duncan
Wausau	Marathon, Wis	Chas Shuter
Warner's Landing	Crawford, Wis	John Warner

Name Change:
China Grove, Wmsburg district, S C, changed to Black Mings.

Purser Forrest, of the ship **Ohio**, a few days since employed a cab driver, Patrick Mahar, to carry him, with $300,000 in gold, from the Custom-house to the Navy Yard in Boston. On leaving the cab one of the bags, containing $1,000 was accidentally overlooked & the oversight would not have been detected until Jun 1. The driver found the bag under his seat the next day, & restored it at once to the Purser.

The U S steam frig **Saranac** sailed from Norfolk on Tue for Wash.
List of the ofcrs on board: Capt, Josiah Tattnall
Lts: T W Brent, Overton Carr, Wm May, Geo Wells
Chief Engineer: D E Martin
Master, J P Decatur
Surgeon, N Pinkney
Lt of Marines, J T Doughty
Purser, J J Jones
1st Assist Engineer, J W King
Assist Surgeon, M Duvall
Passed Midshipmen: M Quinn, A McLaughlin, S B Elliott, J P Hall, Thos Roney
2nd Assist Engineers: J Alexander, Wm F Lynch
3rd Assist Engineers: D P Mapes, R C Potts, C Fithian
Midshipmen: J D Rainey, B Gherardi, Jas Greer, J B McIntosh
Capt's Clerk, J J Tatnall, jr
Sailmaker, J Frazer
Boatswain, D Green
Purser's Clerk, J J Gwaltney
Carpenter, C Boardman

Mrd: on May 16, by Rev Mr Sampson, Mr E H Edmonston to Miss Virginia, youngest daughter of Capt J M Dellaway.

City Items: serious accidents. 1-Mr John Purdy of Wash City, coal & lumber merchant, standing on a pile of boards, the lumber gave way & to save himself from being crushed, Mr Purdy jumped on the pavement. He broke his left leg a little above the ankle. 2-John Wilson, a young man employed by Mr F Y Naylor, while at work yesterday on the roof of a bldg on Pa ave, fell into the yard below, & was seriously injured in the back & ankle.

MON MAY 20, 1850
City Ordinances-Wash: 1-Act for the relief of A Butler: fine imposed relative to keeping his tavern open on Sunday is remitted, provided he pay the costs of prosecution. 2-Act providing for the payment to Wm B Wilson a balance due for paving gutters: the sum of $59.39.

Appointments by the Pres: U S Marshals:
Thos S Hall, for the eastern district of Va.
Chas Bingham, for the southern district of Ala.
Wm McQuiston, for the northern district of Miss.
Henry F Tallmadge, for the southern district of N Y.
Anthony E Roberts, for the eastern district of Pa.
Chas H Knox, for the district of Michigan.
Atty: Wm H Caperton, for the district of Ky.
Geo Folsom, of N Y, to be Charge d'Affaires of the U S at the Court of his Majesty, the King of the Netherlands.

The English papers announce the death of the venerable Rev Richd Reece, Wesleyan minister, in his 85th year, on Apr 27. He was the oldest preacher in the Wesleyan Church, & was the first rep from the body to the Methodist Episcopal Church in the U S.

Thos Shriver [Whig] was on Monday last elected Mayor of Cumberland, & Messrs Fred'k Shipley & John Beal, [Whigs,] & John B Widener, Jesse Korns, Geo Hughes, & F B Tower [Democrats] were on the same day elected members of the Common Council.

Amos C Miller, aged about 11 years, hung himself in Newbury, Vt. He thought he would frighten his little brother by putting the rope slip-noose round his neck, but in doing so he accidentally hung himself. He was a son of Mr Richd Miller.

Chancery sale: by decree of the Circuit Court of Wash Co, D C: in a cause wherein Thos Kinnersley & others are cmplnts, & John L Hammond & others dfndnts: public auction, on Jun 18, of square 862, in Wash City. –Walter D Davidge, trustee -Dyer & Bro, aucts

Davis' Mill, Gtwn D C, at auction: by decree of the Circuit Court of Wash Co, D C, made on May 9, in the case of Wm S Herriman against administrators & heirs-at-law of Thos J Davis, deceased, & others: sale on Water St, in Gtwn, on Jul 15 next, that valuable Merchant Flour Mill, built by Thos J Davis, deceased. Bounded by the property of the late Gen John Mason on the east, with the old brick warehouse thereon, commonly called the Old Penitentiary. The property will be sold free of all incumbrance, except the widows' right to dower in 3/4ths of the mill lot & bldg & the whole of another lot, subject to which right it will be sold. -John Marbury, trustee -Edw S Wright, auct, Gtwn

Mrd: on May 14, at Shepherdstown, Jefferson Co, Va, by Rev C W Andrews, John G Lane, of Rose Hill, Rappahannock Co, Va, to Miss Helen Berry, daughter of Henry Berry.

Circuit Court of Wash Co, D C . J W Osborn & wife vs Chas S Matthews & others. In the matter of the real estate of the late Wm P Matthew. Commission under the act of direct descents. Com'rs having been made & filed on Apr 11 last, stating that the lot mentioned in the proceedings is not susceptible of division, & fixing the value thereof at $1,968, it is ordered by the Court, that the same is ratified. By order of the Court, Jno A Smith, clerk.

TUE May 21, 1850
Senate: 1-Memorial of Francis Pettit Smith, asking the renewal of his patent for an improvement in the method of propelling steam & other vessels: referred to the Cmte on Patents & the Patent Ofc. 2-Ptn of Richd Benson, Robt Waller, & other citizens of Iowa, asking that patents may be issued for certain lands entered by them at the Land Ofc at Dubuque, Iowa, under the military land warrants: referred to the Cmte on Public Lands. 3-Cmte on Pensions: ptn of Mary Farrar, asking a pension on account of the services of her husband as a capt in the service during the Revolutionary war, submitted a report asking to be dismissed therefore: ordered to be printed. Same cmte: ptn of Cyrus Wheelock, asking a pension on account of injuries received in the war of 1812: discharged from the further consideration of the ptn of the same: ordered to printed. Same cmte: ptn of Sarah Nichols, for a pension for services of her husband in the war of the Revolution, discharged from the further consideration of the ptn of the same. Same cmte: ptn of Jas Wright, an engineer in the revenue service, asking to be allowed a

pension: discharged from the further consideration of the ptn of the same. Same cmte: ptn of Peter Grover, asking a pension in consideration of injuries received while engaged in blasting rocks in the service of the U S: asking to be discharged from the further consideration of the ptn of the same. Same cmte: ptn of Frances P Gardiner, asking a renewal of her pension: ordered to a second reading. Same cmte: ptn of Nancy Bowen, asking to be allowed a pension, with a bill for her relief: passed to a second reading. Same cmte: ptn of David N Smith for arrears of pensions, with a bill for this relief: passed to a second reading. 3-Cmte on Indian Affairs: memorial of Geo Copway, an Indian chief, asking the organization of a new Indian Territory, east of the Mississippi, asked to be discharged from the further consideration of the ptn of the same: which was agreed to. 4-Cmte on Claims: ptn of Thos Maughan, Cullen Battle, & others, asking indemnity for Indian depredations during the Creek war in 1836-7, asked to be discharged from the further consideration of the ptn of the same, & that it be referred to the Cmte on Indian Affairs: which was agreed to. 5-Cmte on the Judiciary: memorial of Chas Byrne & others, proprietor of a tract of land granted by the Spanish Govn't to Don Pablo F Fontaine, in Florida, asked to be confirmed in their title: asking to be discharged from the further consideration of the ptn of the same, & that it be referred to the Cmte on Private Land Claims.

Circuit Court of Wash Co, DC, In Chancery. Michael Runner & wife, Jos Sherrick & wife, & others, heirs of Peter Ham, deceased, cmplnts, vs John Ham & David L Ham, & Enos Kessinger & Mgt Ann his wife, children of Jos Ham, deceased, et al, dfndnts-[Non residents]. Rg: John & Jos Ham overpaid $616.62 from previous distribution.
-Jno A Smith, clk.

Circuit Court of Wash Co, DC-In Chancery: Jas Moore, David Moore & Geo Moore, vs Robt P Dunlop & others, heirs-at-law of Eliz Dunlop. Jas Moore, sr, deceased, purchased in 1836, part of tract of land called *Mt Pleasant*, about 57 acres; purchase money has been paid; Jas Moore, sr, hath died, leaving cmplnts his heirs-at-law. Eliz Dunlop hath also died, leaving dfndts her heirs at law; that some of them are minors & others non-residents; & the object of the bill is to obtain a conveyance for the said land; & it appeared to the Court that the said Robt P Dunlop, Henry Dunlop, Mary Mines, Mgt Lulborough, Henrietta Dunlop, Geo Johnson, jr, Robt Peter & Roberta his wife, & Jas Laird, reside out of D C. Said cmplnts to appear on or before Oct 1 next.
-Jno A Smith, clerk

Appointments by the Pres: 1-Postmasters-Chas T Maddox, Balt, Md; Wm M Blackford, Lynchburg, Va; Frederick W Smith, Houston, Tex. 2-John Summers Smith, of N Y, to be Consul of the U S for the port of Malaga, in Spain.

Nashua, N H, May 14. Mr Allen committed suicide by hanging himself, but not before he strangled the youngest of his 11 children, a little girl just 2 years of age.
–Corres Boston Traveller

Household & kitchen furniture at auction: on May 27, at the residence of Mr Hamersly, on 12th st, near Pa ave. –Dyer & Brother, aucts

$150 reward for runaway negro man Alfred Clark, about 23 or 24 years of age. All reasonable expenses will be paid. –S P Franklin [Alfred was purchased by me from the estate of Col Crawford, of PG Co, in Mar 1842, & has absconded without the least cause of provocation.]

Circuit Court of Wash Co, D C, in Chancery. Michl Runner & wife, Jos Sherrick & wife & others, heirs of Peter Ham, deceased, cmplnts, vs John Han & David L Ham, & Enos Kessinger & Mgt Ann his wife, children of John Ham, deceased, et al, dfndnts. The bill states that part of lot 1, & lot 13, in square 118, in Wash City, & the dwlg house thereon, [late the estate of Peter Ham,] had been sold, & a distribution of the proceed made, in which the sum of $298.51 had been assigned to the dfndnt, John Ham, & a similar sum to the other dfndnts above named, as the children of Jos Ham, deceased; but that, on a previous distribution of the other estates, real & personal, of said Peter Ham, the said John & Jos Ham had been each overpaid the sum of $616.62 more than their proper share in the whole estate of said Peter Ham. The object of the bill is to have the said shares of the said John & Jos Ham in the property in Wash City divided among the cmplnts, the other children & descendants of said Peter Ham, so that there may be an approximation towards equality in the distribution of his estates according to his will. Because said dfndnts are non-residents of this District, the absent dfndnts are to appear on or before Oct 1 next, in this Court. –John A Smith, clerk

Died: on May 18, in Wash City, William Francis, youngest son of Cmder Wm H Gardner, U S Navy, aged 1 year & 11 months.

Constable's sale: by a writ of venditioni exponas, against the goods & chattels, lands & tenements of John & David Magers, I have levied one house & lot, east of 7th st, above the Cross Keys, as the property of John Magers, to satisfy an execution in favor of Anthony Holmead. Sale on Jun 18, in front of the premises. -Wm Coale, cnstbl.

Circuit Court of Wash Co, D C-in Chancery: Dillon vs Garretson & others. Ratify sale of lot 40 square 387, in Wash City, for $240, & lot 54 square 387 for $73.80, sold to Oliver Whittlesey. -Jno A Smith, clerk

Died: on May 19, after an illness of but 4 days, Jas N Fitzpatrick, son of John C Fitzpatrick, in his 21st year. His funeral will be from his father's residence on so B st, Capitol Hill, today, at 4 o'clock.

WED MAY 22, 1850
Mr Edwin Du Bose, an assistant employed on the Greenville [S C] & Columbia railroad, was drowned on Wed last, while attempting to cross Crimm's Creek, in Newberry district. His companion, Mr M Y Mills, a resident engineer of the same road, ventured in to save his friends, but his efforts failed.

Trustee's sale of part of lot 7 & 11 sq 74 in Wash; deed from late John Mullikin, dated May 31, 1849, for benefit of John Roberts; now occupied by Mrs Mullikin.
-G W Parker, trust

Trustee's public sale: by deed of trust from the late John Mullikin, dated May 31, 1849, recorded in Liber J A S #4, folio 450, made for the benefit of John Roberts, & at his request, I will expose to sale, at public auction, on Jun 7, part of lot 7 & lot 11 in square 74, in Wash City, wih bldgs & improvements thereon, & now occupied by Mrs Mullikin. –G W Parker, trustee

Senate: 1-Memorial of Seth M Leavenworth, asking compensation for damages sustained due to an alleged violation on the part of the Postmaster Gen of his contract for carrying the mail: referred to the Cmte on the Post Ofc & Post Roads. 2-Memorial of Edw Lynch, asking that an improvement invented by him, called a condenser & evaporator, may be attached to the boilers of the U S steamer **Jefferson**: referred to the Cmte on Naval Affairs. 3-Cmte of Claims: referred additional document in relation to the claims of Jas M Marsh, asked to be discharged from the further consideration of the ptn of the same: referred to the Cmte on Indian Affairs: agreed to.

Circuit Court of Wash Co, D C-in Chancery. Jas Carrico vs Geo C Bomford, Jas V Bomford, Geo W Irving Bomford, Richard C Derby & Louisa his wife, & John F Payne & Ruth his wife. Carrico contracted with the late Geo Bomford for the conveyance to him of certain portions of lot 4, 5, & 7, in square 214, & lot 2 in square 28, in Wash City: the price has been paid, but no conveyance executed; that said Geo Bomford has departed this life intestate; & that the said Geo C, Jas V, & Geo W J Bomford, Louisa Derby, & Ruth Payne are his children & heirs at law; & the object of the bill is to obtain a conveyance of the said parcels of ground. It appears that the dfndnts do not reside in this District. Same are to appear on or before Oct 1 next. -Jno A Smith, clk

Sale at residence of Miss McJilton, G St bet 14th & 15th sts, Wash City.

The cabinetmaker's shop occupied by Mr Valentine on 10th st, between D & E, was destroyed by an incendiary.

On May 19, Jesse Anderson, a young man, drowned in the Eastern Branch, when his skiff upset by a sudden gust of wind.

Land for sale: the farm of the late Dr Worthington, containing nearly 360 acres of land, about 3 miles from the Centre Market, & is one of the best farms in Wash Co. The west side is bounded by Piney Branch Road. –Tho Carbery

House of Reps: 1-Ptn of Chas R Pomeroy, V B Horton, & others, praying for the passage of a law to indemnity for French spoliations prior to 1800.

For rent: the second store west from 7th st & Pa ave, occupied for years as a dry-goods store. Also for rent a large boarding-house, over the above store & adjoining the store of W M Shuster & Co. Immediate possession. For terms apply to Anne R Dermott.

Household & kitchen furniture at auction: May 24, at the residence of Miss McJilton, G st, between 14th & 15th sts, next to Mr Douglas' greenhouse. –Green & Tastet, aucts

THU MAY 23, 1850
Wash Corp: 1-Jas Nokes nominated by the Mayor as Street Com'r for the eastern district of the city: considered & confirmed. 2-Act for the relief of Peter Smith: referred to the Cmte on Finance. 3-Act for the relief of Wm B Lewis; & of Jas Burdine: referred to the Cmte of Claims. 4-Ptn of Alex'r S Wadsworth & others, on gravelling K st: laid on the table. 5-Elected Com'rs:

C A Davis	V Harbaugh	Henry Ball
J W Sheahan	J C McGuire	Jas Crandell
S Duval	David Saunders	John R Queen
Willard Drake	F A Klopfer	Abel G Davis
D Hauptman	Thos H Havenner	G W Hinton
J F Ennis	Amon Woodward	J L Smith
Geo Crandell	Chas Monroe	R Wimsatt

A card of thanks to those firemen & citizens who so promptly hastened to rescue my property from the flames. –Richd Cruit

Postmaster Gen has est'd the following new Post Ofcs for week ending May 18, 1850.

Ofc	County, State	Postmaster
S Billingham	Norfolk, Mass	Paul Chilson
Asburnham depot	Worcester, Mass	John M Frost
Bald Hill	Norfolk, Mass	Elias Cook
East Boston	Suffolk, Mass	Geo H Plummer
Ore Hill	Litchfield, Ct	Philip Rockefeller
So Greenfield	Saratoga, N Y	Geo B Rowland
Cooksburgh	Albany, N Y	Geo Bellamy
Farmer's Hill	Dutchess, N Y	Willis H Haviland
Solsville	Madison, N Y	Nathl S Howard
Oswego Falls	Oswego, N Y	Jos E Willard
Laddsburgh	Bradford, Pa	Peter Stengere
Lamartine	Cairion, Pa	David Eshelman
Plain Grove	Lawrence, Pa	Hutchison Bovard
West Pike	Potter, Pa	Ira F Kilbourn
Forest Hill	Union, Pa	Ammon H Lutz
Principio Furnace	Cecil, Md	Oliver W Lund
Bay Hundred	Talbot, Md	Jas S Ridgway
Le Sourdsville	Butler, Ohio	John Hawkins
New Palestine	Clermont, Ohio	Wm R Lindsey
Olentaugy	Crawford, Ohio	Andrew Schreck
Poplar Ridge	Dark, Ohio	C C Alexander
Port Union	Hamilton, Ohio	Jas Patchell
Beech Land	Licking, Ohio	John C Alward
Skeel's Cross Roads	Mercer, Ohio	Sylvester Skeel
Pharr's Mill	Moore, N C	Jas J Pharr
Clear Spring	Greenville D, S C	Wm Goldsmith

Knob Lick	Daviess, Ky	Iona Downs
Camden	Schuyler, Ill	Alex McHatton
Fair Haven	Carroll, Ill	Danl P Holt
Phill's Creek	Jersey, Ill	E M Pease
Sardinia	Decatur, Ind	John T McCormick
Pay Down	Osage, Mo	Thos Kinsey
Michicott	Manetoowoc, Wis	Nahum Daniels
Saylorville	Polk, Iowa	John Saylor
Huron	Des Moines, Iowa	Jas Hemphill

Names changed: Cold Brook, Worcester Co, Mass, changed to Smithville.
Factory Village, Middlesex Co, Mass, changed to west Chelmsford.
Carrollton, Cattaraugus Co, N Y, changed to Limestone.
Baileyville, Centre Co, Pa, changed to Stove's Place.
Battow Island, Duval Co, Florida, changed to Mayport Mills.
Bee Creek, Wells Co, Ill, changed to Ossian.
Ogden, Cumberland Co, Ill, changed to Woodbury.

The Superior Court in session in Warrenton on the case of the Commonwealth against Fantleroy Carter, charged with the murder of Alex'r Welch. Case was given to the jury on May 9, who rendered a verdict of guilty of murder in the second degree, & fixed 15 years as the term of his confinement in the penitentiary. –Piedmont Whig

Died: on Mar 5, in Rio De Janeiro, of yellow fever, John McLeod Tilley, of Wash, in his 19th year.

House of Reps: 1-Cmte on the Judiciary: bill for the relief of Jas Lewis: committed. Same cmte: bill for the relief of the late Lt J E Bispham's executor: committed.
2-Cmte on Revolutionary Claims: adverse report on the ptns of the heirs of Jas Conway, of Dudley Hall, executor of John Brooks, deceased, & of the heirs of Nehemiah Stokely: which were laid on the table. Same cmte: adverse reports on the ptns of the heirs of Wm Cherry, of the executors of Dr Lackey Murray, & of Jas Geer: laid on the table.
3-Cmte on Revolutionary Claims: discharged from the further consideration of the ptn of Mary A Turner, widow of Jno L Turner, & it was referred to the Cmte on Revolutionary Pensions. 4-Cmte on Private Land Claims: bill for the relief of Jas T Shackelford: passed. 5-Ptn of Alex Hammett, American consul at Naples, to be recompensed for services rendered while acting charge d'affaires: presented.

Senate: 1-Ordered, that the memorial of David Vann & Wm P Ross, delegates to the Cherokee nation, on the files of the Senate, be referred to the Cmte on Indian Affairs. 2-Cmte of Claims: memorial of Adam D Stewart, a paymaster in the army, asking reimbursement of a sum of money paid by him for the recovery of certain stolen funds belonging to the U S, with a bill for his relief: passed to a second reading. 3-Cmte on Public Lands: ptn of Jacob W Cummings, a clerk in the Gen Land Ofc, asking additional compensation for services performed by him, submitted an adverse report on the same: ordered to be printed. 4-Cmte of Claims: House bill for the relief of Wm B Crews: recommended its passage.

Horses for sale. Apply at Robt Earl's Livery Stable, near West Market.

Obit-died: on May 19, Jas N Fitzpatrick, a native of Wash City. The amability of his manners endeared him to his family & friends.

FRI MAY 24, 1850
Wash City: on Wed, the blacksmith shop occupied by Mr Saml Bryan, B & 2nd sts, was set on fire & totally destroyed. Mr Wm Thompson's carpenter shop, near the blacksmith shop, was in great danger of being also burnt down, but the neighbors saved it. Mr Bryan is a poor man, &, in view of his loss, several well-disposed persons have offered to subscribe towards his relief. We hope it will be immediately set about.

A Telegraph dispatch from Madison announced the death of Ex-Govn'r Hendricks, who was the first Govn'r of the State of Indiana, & for some time a Senator in Congress from Indiana. He died suddenly on May 16.

Fatal accident at a Regatta: the boat **Doubloon**, on May 14, capsized in the race, & Meredith McLane, a sailmaker from Phil, drowned; a lad of about 17, name not given, also drowned. The remainder of the crew were exposed during the whole night, & were not discovered till the afternoon of the ensuing day.

The American Expedition in search of Sir John Franklin, the Arctic navigator, sailed from N Y on Wed: the vessel **Advance**, 144 tons, [2 years old,] & the vessel **Rescue**, 91 tons, [new,]: fitted out by the munificence of Henry Grinnell, of this city, at an expense to him of more than $30,000. The whole is under the command of Lt Edwin S De Haven, an enthusiastic & excellent ofcr of the U S navy. The men of the 2 vessels is 36. The ofcrs are: Lt Edwin S De Haven, Commanding; Passed Midshipman, S P Griffin, Acting Master; Wm H Murdaugh, T W Brodhead, R R Carter; Passed Assist Surgeon, E K Kane; Assist Surgeon, Benj Vreeland; Midshipman, W S Lovell; Boatswain, H Brooks.

Zachary Taylor, Pres of the U S, recognizes Godfrey Weber, who has been appointed Vice Consul of Denmark, for the State of Pa, to reside at Phil. May 22, 1850

Executors notice: claims against estate of Capt Wm Lang, late of U S Marine Corps, to be made known without delay, to Jas W Lisle, exc, 46½ Walnut st, Phil.

Senate: 1-Ordered, that the ptn of Ziba Baker, on the file of the Senate, be referred to the Cmte on Pensions. 2-Ordered, that the ptn of Robt Mitchell, on the files of the Senate, be referred to the Cmte on Indian Affairs.

Constable's sale: by virtue of a writ of fieri facias, I shall expose to public sale, for cash, in Wash City, on May 30, 1 barrel of new shad, seized & taken as the property of John W Hootman, to be sold to satisfy a judgment in favor of John T Armstrong.
-Wm Cox, constable

House of Reps: 1-Cmte on Private Land Claims: bill to provide the issuing of a land patent to Thos B Clarke: committed. Same cmte: discharged from the further consideration of the ptn of John P Smith, administrator of John Smith, & it was referred to the Cmte on the Revolutionary Claims. 2-Cmte on Private Land Claims: adverse report on the ptn of the heirs of Sarah Moore: laid on the table. Same Cmte: bill for the benefit of Jas P Roan: committed. Same cmte: adverse report on the ptn of the heirs of Jno Baptiste Valle, deceased: laid on the table. 3-Ptn of Chas Wm Carroll, asking compensation for injuries sustained by being unjustly arrested & imprisoned as a deserter from the army of the U S: presented. 4-Ptn of Stephen Simpson, sr, & one of the heirs of Geo Simpson, asking for compensation for services rendered to the Govn't by his father: presented. 5-Ptn of Dr Wm H Duncan, of Davies Co, Ky, praying Congress to remunerate him for liabilities incurred & moneys expended in the service of the U S with the late war with Mexico, & also for the professional services rendered to sick soldiers in said service.

House to let: on 9th st, between L & M sts. Inquire next door of W J Sibley.

In Chancery. A D Sheele vs John P Coulter et al. Ratify sale of 2 lots of ground, in Gtwn, called **Wilberforce**, on High & Gorman sts to Frederick Sheele for $300.
-Jno A Smith, clk.

Constable's sale: by virtue of 3 writs of fieri facias, against the goods & charrels, lands & tenements, of Nathan Brown, at the suits of Wm Cringley, C S O'Hare, & Miss C Hillyard: I have levied on 1 frame house & lot, on N st, between 9th & 10th sts, in Wash City: sale on Jun 17, in front of the premises. –A E L Keese, constable

SAT MAY 25, 1850
Philip Pearl, of Hampton, Conn, was accidentally killed on Fri last, when the frame of a bldg which was being torn down, fell upon him. He died 5 hours later. He was a Presidential elector in 1840, has several times been a State Senator, & has filled other public ofcs.

Died: on Fri last, at his residence in Batavia, N Y, Hon David E Evans. He was one of the earliest settlers of Batavia, having gone there in 1803.

Died: on May 24, Katherine, daughter of Wm H & Eliz Tenney, in her 5th year. Her funeral is tomorrow, at 5 o'clock.

$100 reward for runaway negro man Hanson Hawkins, about 25 years of age. He has a free wife in Wash City, D C. –Chas H Johnson, Dunkirk P O Calvert Co, Md.

Died: on Fri last, at his residence in Batavia, N Y, Hon David E Evans. He was one of the earliest settlers of Batavia, having gone there in 1803.

Died: on May 24, Katherine, daughter of Wm H & Eliz Tenney, in her 5th year. Her funeral is tomorrow, at 5 o'clock.

Senate: 1-Memorial from Alden Marsh, Professor of Surgery in the Albany Medical College, & several other medical professors, asking that Congress pass a law granting to medical ofcrs of the navy the same degree of rank relatively to ofcrs of the line in the navy as corresponding grades of medical ofcrs in the army possess, according to law relating to ofcrs of the line in the army, provided that the assimilated rank thereby conferred shall not entitle any medical ofcr in the navy to increased pay, & to take precedence of any ofcr who may be in legal command of any port, station, or vessel to which such medical ofcrs might be attached for duty: referred to the Cmte on Naval Affairs. [Three others, similar in all respects from: Troy, signed by Thos C Brintmoele, Pres of Rensselaer Co Medical College; one from Utica, signed by John McCall; & another from Lyons, Wayne Co, in the same State, N Y, signed by J B Pierce, Pres of the Wayne Co Medical Society.] 2-Memorial of J R Jefferson & other mail contractor, asking compensation for their services for carrying the mail: referred to the Cmte on the Post Ofc & Post Roads. 3-Memorial from the heirs of John Crosby, asking indemnity for French spoliations prior to 1800: ordered to lie on the table. 4-Ptn from Jas Stackpole, jr, praying that a limitation as to time may be fixed for the recovery of fugitive slaves, & that the citizens of one State in another State may be protected in the full enjoyment of all the privileges of citizenship as guaranteed by the constitution: ordered to lie on the table. 5-Memorial of the heirs of Jas Williams, asking indemnity for French spoliations prior to 1800: ordered to lie on the table. 6-Ordered, that the report of the Sec of the Interior of May 21, in relation to the claims of Alex'r Sanders, a Cherokee Indian to a pension, be referred to the Cmte on Pensions. 7-Cmte on Pensions: ptn of Mrs Lomax, widow of the late Maj Lomax, asking to be placed on the pension roll, with a bill for her relief: passed to a second reading. 8-Cmte on Commerce: memorial of Willis H Chase, of Florida, asking to be released from a certain judgment obtained against him by the U S for duties on railroad iron, asked to be discharged from the further consideration of the ptn of the same, & that it be referred to the Cmte on Finance: which was agreed to. 9-Bill was introduced for the relief of Capt Nathan Adams, of Tenn. Capt Adams, being called on service at a time when it was necessary to render his quarterly accounts, left his vouchers with a clerk to make up the account in his absence. He subsequently found that his clerk had died, & that his vouchers were pledged with a tavern keeper in New Orleans for a tavern bill. Part of the vouchers were recovered, but others were not found, to the amount of $350. Bill was read a third time & passed. 10-Cmte of the Whole: House bill for the relief of Jesse Sutton. Explanation: the com'rs were sent out shortly after the annexation of Texas, to negotiate a treaty with the Camanche & other Indians. Sutton was appointed a blacksmith. This individual discharged the duties, & now calls upon Congress to make him compensation. Bill was passed. 11-Bill for the relief of J H McClintock, Harrison Gill, & Mansfield Carter: passed. 12-Joint resolution for the relief of Saml Colt & B F Morse: referred to the Cmte on Finance.

The U S ship **Lexington**, John K Mitchell, Cmder, arrived at N Y on Thu from Rio Janeiro. The epidemic of yellow fever spread to all the neighboring towns. The following persons belonging to the **Lexington** have died since she left N Y on Dec 13 last. Deaths in order of their occurrence: Mar 2, Wm Jones, seaman, on Board at Rio Janeiro; May 16, Wm Ryan, do, do; 17th, passed midshipman Elias Vanderhorst, ashore; 21st, Moses Willisma, landsman, on board; 22nd, Richd Stillwell, do, do; 23rd, Nathl P

Prickett, midshipman, do; 24th, Jas Conner, quarter gunner, do; 25th, John Bruce, ordinary seamen; Apr 5, John S Whipple, passed assist surgeon, at sea; 6th, Michl Brooks, ofcr's steward; 7th, Jas Dawson, do; 26th, Danl D Chase, ship's stewart. This makes a total of 12, of whom 3 were ofcrs. Six were invalids from the ship **Brandywine** & the ship **Marion**. The deaths were by yellow fever, with the exception of Moses Williams & Jas Dawson.

$100 reward for runaway negro man Hanson Hawkins, about 25 years of age. He has a free wife in Wash City, D C. –Chas H Johnson, Dunkirk P O Calvert Co, Md.

House of Reps: 1-Bills objected to were: bill for the relief of the heirs of Joshua Eddy, deceased. Bill for the relief of the heirs of Larkin Smith; relief of the heirs of Lt Bartlett Hinds; relief of Chas Lee Jones; relief of Wm P Wallace & Jos R McFaden; & relief of Horatio N Crabb. 2-Ptn of David Heaston & 10 others, of Randolph Co, Indiana, praying Congress to grant bounty lands to the soldiers of the war of 1812. 3-Memorial of Wm Selden M D & 34 other physicians & surgeons in & out of the naval service, asking the passage of a law securing assimilated rank to the medical ofcrs of the navy.

Died: on May 20, at *Locust Grove*, Calvert Co, Md, suddenly, Capt John Beckett, in his 59th year. He was an ofcr of our army during the late war with Great Britain, & was actively engaged in service on the frontier through the whole contest. He was at the battle of York, & bore from the field Gen Pike, who was mortally wounded. He also participated in the capture of *Fort George*, & in the affair at Stoney Creek. At the invitation of Capt Woolsey, & permission of Gen Wilkinson, he went on board of our fleet, & was in the hardest fight that took place on Lake Ontario. He was in the battle of Chrystler's field, where Covington fell, & in the battle of Lyon's Creek he received a severe wound. At the close of the war, not wishing to continue in the army on the peace establishment, he advised the War Dept of his wish to retire from service. His name, however, was still continued on the register after the reduction of the army, & he then resigned his commission & retired to his patrimonial estate in Calvert Co, on which he was born & died. He served many years in both branches of the Legislature in his native State.

MON MAY 27, 1850
Died: yesterday, Mr Jno Bohlayer, sr, in his 57th year, a native of Wurtemburg, Germany, but for the last 30 years a resident of Wash City. His funeral will be at his residence, near the Navy Yard, tomorrow, at half-past 2 o'clock.

Notice: all persons are warned, at the peril of the law, not to trespass on the walks or grounds belonging to Gtwn College. –Jas Ryder, President

Died: on May 21, in Balt, in her 47th year, Mrs Ann Agnez Dowson, relict of late Robt H Dowson, & only daughter of late John Doloughrey. She was a native of & was raised in the city in which she died, beloved by all who knew her. She leaves an aged mother, a living brother, & an only daughter, & a large circle of admiring friends, who deplore her loss.

Unfortunate expedition to Trinidad Bay. From the San Francisco Journal of Commerce, Apr 16. Death of John H Peoples, Lts Bache & Browning, & 2 others. The brig **Arabian**, Capt Blunt, left here on Mar 10, on a trip of exploration to Trinidad bay. After pursuing her search, arrived here last evening, & from Capt Connor, a brave soldier who distinguished himself at Buena Vista, Mexico, & who was one of the party, we obtained the following melancholy termination of their expedition. On Mar 27, I left the brig **Arabian**, Capt Blunt, in a whale boat accompanied by Lts Bache & Browning, U S Navy, John H Peoples, Messrs Johnson, Cheshire, Baker, Robertson, & 2 seamen belong to the brig, for the purpose of examining the shore, being led to suppose, by seeing a schnr near the land, that there was a river or bay in the neighborhood, which afterwards proved to be a mistake. We determined to land at a point where the surf was not so bad as it unfortunately proved to be. We rode the first breaker out nobly, but the second one upset us, leaving us to struggle in the surf. John H Peoples was washed ashore; Lt Browning struck out for the shore, but did not make it; Lt Bache was unable to stand alone & swept under the water. W W Cheshire & one of the seamen also met a watery grave. The next morning we went to visit our boat for the purpose of securing our blankets, but the Indians has taken every thing & broken up the boat to get the nails out of her.

Public sale: by a decree of the High Court of Chancery. Sale: *Ellerslie*, late the residence of Henry Brawner, deceased. This farm is in Chas Co, Md, & contains 700 acres. –Henry May, trustee.

TUE May 28, 1850
Senate: 1-Ptn of Chas H Morrison, asking the confirmation of his title to a tract of land lying in the Bastrop grant, in Louisiana: referred to the Cmte on Private Land Claims. 2-Memorial of Thos H McManus, asking that he may be allowed the right of pre-emption to certain lands in the Greensburg land district, in Louisiana: referred to the Cmte on Private Land Claims. 3-Memorial of the heirs of Benj Page, deceased, asking indemnity for French spoliations prior to 1800: ordered to lie on the table. 4-Cmte of Claims: ptn of John Devlin, asking compensation for his services as a clerk in the 5th Auditor's ofc, with a bill for his relief: passed to a second reading. 5-Cmte on Private Land Claims: ptn of John H D Bowman, asking that a patent may issue for a certain tract of land entered at the land ofc at Ouachita, La: passed to a second reading. 6-Cmte on the Judiciary: ptn of Simon Greenleaf, asking a renewal of his copyright, reported a bill for his relief. Same cmte: memorial of John P Skinner & others, asking to be released from a judgment obtained against them as sureties of Thos Emerson, late pension agent for Vermont, submitted an adverse report on the same.

E B Grayson, agent for all claims against the Gov't arising from military services. Ofc on B st, between 3rd st & Railroad Depot.

Valuable improved poperty at auction: May 2: south part of lot 14, in square 348, 10th st, between D & E sts, improved by a good 2 story brick house, at present occupied by Mr John Skirving. [The purchaser, John Killiam, failed to comply with the terms of the sale, the property will be resold at his risk & expense, on Jun 4 next.] –Dyer & Bro, aucts

All persons indebted to O J Preston & Co, or D G Day, will please call on Mr Jno P Hilton, on 14th st, between H & I sts, who is legally authorized to collect & receipt for the same. —O J Preston & Co

Orphans Court of Wash Co, D C. Letters of administration, with the will annexed, on the personal estate of Dolley P Madison, late of Wash Co, deceased. -Jas C McGuire, adm with the will annexed

$100 reward fpr runaway negro woman Hagar, about 35 years of age. -W B Boggs, Gtwn

WED MAY 29, 1850
Senate: 1-Memorial of A J Frasier, & the report of the Sec of State thereon, on the files of the Senate, be referred to the Cmte of Claims. 2-Cmte of Claims: memorial of Peter N Paillett, asking indemnity for property destroyed during the late war with Mexico, passed to a second reading. 3-Cmte on Public Bldgs: memorial of Robt Mills, architect in Wash, in relation to the enlargement of the Capitol: ordered to be printed. 4-Mr Atchison asked leave to introduce a bill for the relief of the heirs of Col A G Morgan. 5-House bill for the relief of Jas T Shackleford: referred to the Cmte on Private Land Claims. 6-Bill for the relief of Jos P Williams: engrossed for a third reading.

Valuable farm at auction: on Jun 12, the farm recently occupied by Mr Lemuel J Middleton, containing 125 acres, situated on Rock Creek, about 2 miles from Gtwn, with a comfortable 2 story frame dwlg house. The farm utensils on the premises will also be offered. -C W Boteler, auct

Orphans Court of Wash Co, D C. Letters of administration on the personal estate of Saml H Laughlin, late of Wash Co, deceased. -Chas S Wallach, adm [Jun 6th newspaper: Col S H Laughlin's Library, Pa av at 6th, to be sold-administrator's sale of rare & valuable books]

One cent reward & no thanks: for runaway John Tho Nichols, a bound & indented apprentice to the Baking business, near 20 years of age. I forwarn all persons from harboring said apprentice, as the law will be enforced. —Geo W Hughes

Mrd: on May 28, in Gtwn, by Rev N Tillinghast, Wm Cole Bayly, 2nd son of J W Bayly, of the county Dublin, Ire, to Anna, youngest daughter of late A B Murray, formerly of Balt, Md.

Wash, May 28, 1850. Ofcrs of the navy met to express their condolences for the melancholy fate of their late brother ofcrs, Lts Robt L Browning & Richd Bache. Lt Wm W Hunter called to the chair, & Lt S Chase Barney, appointed sec. Lts Wm McBlair, John R Goldsborough, & Passed Midshipman Somerville Nicholson, were appointed a cmte to carry out the object of the meeting.

Zachary Taylor, Pres of the U S, recognizes Patrice Dillon, who has been appointed Consul of France for Francisco, Calif. May 28, 1850

Died: on May 28, Bridget Whalen Holohon, wife of John Holohon, in her 56th year, a native of Monaghan, Ireland, but for the last 33 years a resident of Wash City. Her funeral will be from her late residene, 7th, between G & H sts, today at 5 P M.

Beautiful residence & Market Garden at Public sale. By virtue of a deed of trust dated Apr 16, 1849, recorded in Liber J A S #4, folios 181, 182, & 183: sale on Jun 8 next, that beautiful residence called *Cazenova*, adjoining *Pearson's mill*, & formerly owned & occupied by John A Wilson, deceased, consisting of the whole of square 747, lots 8 through 14 in square 748, & the whole of square 750, with a large well built frame dwlg house & all necessary outhouses. The property lies between I st north, & between 2nd & 3rd sts east. –Chas S Wallach, trustee -C W Boteler, auct

THU MAY 30, 1850
Senate: 1-Memorial of Wm Archer, of Wash City, asking that Congress would pass an act to authorize the Pres of the U S to cause one or more ships to be stationed in the bay of San Francsco, to receive & safely keep all the gold collected: referred to the Cmte on Finance. 2-Ptn of Richd Mackall, asking compensation for property destroyed by the enemy during the last war with Great Britain: referred to the Cmte of Claims.
3-Memorial of the heirs of Eliz Frisby, asking indemnity for French spoliations prior to 1800: ordered to lie on the table. 4-Cmte on Military Affairs: memorial of Jas Edwards, asking payment for losses incurred by the destruction of his property during the Seminole war: asked to be discharged from the further consideration of the ptn of same, on the ground that an adverse report had already been made & concurred in by the Senate. Without regard to that fact, it had been referred to the Cmte on Military Affairs, without any additional evidence.

Valuable improved property at auction: on Jun 10, sale of part of lot 10 in square 429, fronting on 7th st, between G & H sts, with a 2 story dwlg-house upon it, with back bldgs & a store-house, occupied by Mr W S McPherson, as a grocery. Also, part of lot 9 in square 429, fronting on H st, between 7th & 8th sts, with 2 frame shops.
–Dyer & Brother, aucts

Hon Franklin H Elmore, a Senator of S C, expired at his lodgings in Wash City last evening, after a brief illness, & has thus early following to the tomb the eminent statesman whose vacant place he so recently arrived here to fill. [May 31st newspaper: Mr Elmore was a native of Laurens district, S C, & died in his 51st year. His father, Gen Elmore, was a native of Va, & an active soldier in the Revolution, serving under Gen Green, in his celebrated Southern campaign of 1781. His mother was a Miss Saxon, a name distinguished in the partisan war of the Revolution. He entered the S C College in Nov, 1817, & graduated 2 years afterwards with honor. As a husband & father, he loved & was loved with deep & tender affection. His funeral will take place tomorrow at 12 o'clock.]

Black & White-smithing: at his old stand, on C st, between 10th & 11th sts.
–C Buckingham

Died: yesterday, Geo Dunn, formerly of Annapolis, Md, at Marbury's Landing, Md, on May 29, suddenly after leaving the Mail Boat. He was at the time considerably inebriated. An inquest has been held.

Mr John G Smith, of Memphis, Tenn, who shot a waiter at the American Hotel, in N Y, while under an attack of lunacy on Sun last, has been removed to the lunatic asylum on Blackwell's island, & it has been found necessary to put the strait-jacket on him twice.

Died: on May 23, at New Brunswick, N J, aged near 83 years, Mrs Mgt Vanderhorst Ellis White, a native of Charleston, S C, relict of late Col Anthony Walton White, Brig Gen by Brevet & Patriot of the American Revolution.

Mr Solomon Shelter, of Allegheny city, has invented a machine to make horse shoes, which he thinks will turn out 1,800 shoes an hour.

Beautiful country residence for sale, containing 160 acres; a fine 2 story house, 44 by 20 feet; 8 miles from Wash. Inquire of Mr Jeremiah Orme, Gtwn, & Messrs Middleton & Beall, Wash. Possession immediately.

House for rent: 3 story brick bldg, ready furnished, in the six bldgs, First Ward, & now occupied by Mrs D D Porter. Apply to Mrs D D Porter.

FRI MAY 31, 1850
House of Reps: 1-Ptn of Jas Abercrombie, a director of the Girard Railroad Co, asking certain privileges in regard to the public lands. 2-Memorial of Dr Asbel Smith & other physicians for conferring on the surgeons of the navy assimiliated rank.

In Chancery: Wm G W White & brother, cmplnt, vs Edw N Roach, adm, & Ellen M Ellwood, widow, & Wm D Ellwood & others, heirs of Isaac T Ellwood, dfndnts. Claims against the estate of Isaac T Ellwood to be presented on Jun 10, City Hall, Wash. -W Redin, auditor

Died: on May 18, at his residence in Jefferson Co, Ohio, Capt Aaron Allen. He was one of the very first settlers of that county, & during the war of 1812 he commanded a company of volunteers & rendered important services to the army under Gen Harrison, in the N W Territory.

Real estate at public auction: on Jun 10, the real estate of which Thos Gittings, late of Montg Co, Md, died seized, situated in said county, on the road leading from Wash City to Colesville, & on the road leading from the Cross Roads to Bladensburg. This property will be offered in lots, from 84 to 137 acres. Mr Jedediah Gittings, or Mr Martin L Gittings, living on the premises will show the property. -Wm Viers Bouic, trustee

Governess wanted: a lady who is well qualified to teach all the branches of a good English education: salary $500 per annum. –John W Phillips, Warrenton, Va

SAT JUN 1, 1850
Ladies with letters remaining in the Post Ofc, Wash, Jun 1, 1850.
Adams, Mrs Pris L
Ashe, Mrs Eliz H
Bell, Mrs Eliza A
Baker, Mrs Ch W
Browne, Miss Cath
Brooks, Miss Eliza
Brannon, Miss Ellen
Bates, Miss Eliz-2
Bell, Miss Eliza B
Barton, Mrs Lizzie
Boston, Miss Han
Blanche, Miss Jane
Brent, Mrs Judge
Baker, Mrs Lucy
Barney, Mrs Mary
Bowser, Miss Mar
Bridgman, Mrs M
Belt, Miss M A-2
Blackston, Miss M
Beall, Miss Inda M
Bird, Mrs Rebecca
Brooke, Miss S F
Blount, Miss Mary
Calvert, Miss Ann
Clemmons, Mrs A M
Creighton, Miss C S
Chum, Miss M J
Callaghan, Miss M-2
Campbell, Miss M A
Clarke, Miss S A
Dupee, Mrs Amelia
Dorr, Mrs Car
Deakins, Mrs Jane
Donoho, Mary
Dunlop, Miss S
Evans, Mrs A C U N
Eckardt, Mrs M
Espy, Mrs Lydia
Ears, Miss Sarah
Fennelly, Mrs M A
Foley, Mrs Cath
Fitzgerald, Mrs F A
Fitzhugh, Miss M L
Ginity, Mrs Alice
Grace, Miss Eliz
Green, Mrs
Gorman, Mrs
Gamwel, Sarah
Hock, Miss Anna
Hall, Miss Ann M
Howard, Mrs Eliz
Humphreys, mres E
Hastings, Mrs F H
Harris, Miss Hen-2
Hinson, Mrs Julia
Herbert, Mrs John, or otherwise Dixon
Harden, Mrs S E
Henderson, Mrs
Henry, Mrs
Holliday, Miss M A
Hesler, Mrs
Hillsman, Miss M L
Harmanson, Mrs R-2
Harley, Mrs Susan
Hurley, Miss V A
Ireland, Miss M E-2
Johnson, Miss Cath
Jackson, Miss Han
Jennings, Mrs J
Johnson, Mrs Mary
Jones, Miss Marg
Johnston, Miss T A
Jones, Agnes
Kern, Mary A
King, Miss Marg
Kuhn, Mrs R D
King, Miss Sallie
Lee, Miss Ann
Litton, Miss Jenny
Lyon, Mrs F
Lawrence, Mrs M A
Lallum, Mrs Ellen

Lovocat, Miss R
Locke, Miss Sarah J
Landre, Mrs Sarh
Mills, Miss A V C
Mason, Anna W-2
Martin, Fanny
Moore, Mrs Lucinda
Moore, Mrs M E
Murray, Miss M J
Maher, Miss Mary
Mullin, Mrs Mary
Murray, Mgt
Marshall, Mrs M
Magyer, Mrs M E
Mariott, Mrs M
Macrae, Miss J-5
McCoy, Martha
McAbee, Miss C
McCallion, Bridget
McPherson, Ellen
Nichols, Mrs Ann C
Nelson, Miss Eliz
O'Donnell, Miss M G
Porter, Mrs Ev-2
Porter, Mrs Eliza C
Price, Mrs Eliz
Petticord, Miss Vic
Pinkney, Mrs Louisa
Rosher, Mrs Abigail
Reed, Mrs Caroline
Rosier, Mrs Cath
Ratcliffe, Miss E
Ross, Miss Eliza
Ross, Mrs Eliz
Rising, Miss Jane
Robinson, Miss M
Reeder, Miss M A
Robinson, Miss M J
Russell, Miss Susan
Richards, Mrs S C
Smith, Miss America
Sibley, Mrs H H
Spalding, Mrs Mary
Sheekels, Miss C
Saltonstall, Miss C
Saeville, Miss D E
Saunders, Emily
Sawyer, Mrs E
Saunders, Mrs Delia
Smith, Miss Jane O
Somerville, Mrs R C
Stokes, Mrs Sarah
Tyler, Miss Ann F
Trunnell, Ann M
Thompson, Mrs C
Triplett, Miss Ann E
Thompson, Miss J
Tredwell, Miss J M
Thrift, Mrs Dinah S
Taylor, Miss Lititia
Thornton, Miss S J
Underwood, Miss Cassre
Wilson, Miss Ann-3
Wayman, Mrs
Wells, Miss C E-2
Wilkinson, Miss U-2
Wells, Mrs V S
Winslow, Mrs C H
Weister, Eliz
Wren, Miss Melvina
Wilkins, Mrs S
Zekind, Mrs D
-Wm A Bradley, P M

Zachary Taylor, Pres of the U S, recognized Felix Lacoste, who has been appointed Consul Gen of the French Republic, to reside in N Y. Senor Don Buenaventura Alcalda, who has been appointed Vice consul of the Mexican Republic for Brownsville & Fronton de Santa Isabella. Don Jose Antonio Pizarro, who has been appointed Vice Consul of the Mexican Republic for Balt. Senor Don Felix Merino, who has been appointed Vice Consul of the Mexican Republic for Phil. Senor Don Juan Herbst, who has been appointed Vice Consul of the Mexican Republic for Pittsburg. -May 31, 1850

Jos C G Kennedy, of Pa, has been appointed Superintendent of the Census, under the act of May 23, 1850.

In Chancery: Circuit Court of Wash Co, D C. U S, vs D Ott's administrator et al. The trustee has reported that he has sold the western part of lot 2, in square 379, fronting on Pa ave, to Jos Bryan, for $5,275. –Jno A Smith, clerk

Appointments by the Pres: 1-Robt P Letcher, of Ky, to be Envoy Extra & Minister Pleni of the U S to the Mexican Republic. 2-Orlando Brown to be Com'r of Indian Affairs. 3-Jas McDowell, of Ohio, to be Consul of the U S for the port of Dundee, in Scotland.

Died: on Wed, Jas H Lynch, an esteemed citizen of Richmond, Va, after a brief illness of only a few hours. He was one of the oldest citizens of Richmond, & was in his 78th year. –Richmond Enquirer

City Ordinances-Wash. 1-Act for the relief of R R Burr: the sum of $265.62 be paid to him as the balance found due to him on the settlement of his accounts as police ofcr for the 4th Ward. 2-Act for the relief of John Dewdney, the sum of $20 to be paid him for reimbursement to him for conveying unmanageable persons from the first Ward to the city workhouse from 1844 to 1849, inclusive.

The funeral of the Hon F H Elmore was performed this mornng. The corpse was removed from Mrs Wells', on Capitol Hill, to the Senate Chamber. Services were by Rev Mr Gurley, Chaplain of the House of Reps. The funeral cortege proceeded to the <u>Congressional Burial Ground</u>, where the body for the present is deposited.

Arctic Expedition: ofcrs & men of the expedition on the brig **Advance** & brig **Rescue**: the **Advance**-E J De Haven, cmder; Wm H Murdaugh, 1st ofcr; Wm S Lovell, 2nd ofcr; Elisha H Kane, surgeon. Men: Wm Morton, Jas Smith, Edw Boyd, John Bunnon, Lewis Coster, Edw Wilson, Thos Dunning, Henry Derode, Wm Holmes, Gibson Caruther, Danl Vaughan, Wm Weast, Chas Berry, & Edw C Delano. The **Resuce**-S P Griffin, cmder; R R Carter, 1st ofcr; Henry Brooks, 2nd ofcr; Benj Vreeland, surgeon. Men-Rufus C Boggs, Jno Williams, Robt Bruce, H G White, Wm Benson, Wm Lincon, J A Knaup, Smith Benjamin, David Davis, Jas Johnson, Jas Stewart, Alex'r Daly, & W J Kurner.

$25 reward for runaway negro woman Daphna, about 24 years of age. She has relations in Wash, & at Col C R Belt's, D C, where she is probably lurking.
–Wm I Belt, Forest of PG Co, Md

The funeral of the Hon F H Elmore was performed this mornng. The corpse was removed from Mrs Wells', on Capitol Hill, to the Senate Chamber. Services were by Rev Mr Gurley, Chaplain of the House of Reps. The funeral cortege proceeded to the <u>Congressional Burial Ground</u>, where the body for the present is deposited.

Mrd: on May 30, at St Matthew's Church, by Rev Jas Donelan, Mr Jno A Brenner to Miss Catharine E Brannan, both of Wash City.

Postmaster Gen has est'd the following new Post Ofcs for week ending May 25, 1850.

Ofc	County, State	Postmaster
Melrose	Middlesex, Mass	Geo W Barrett
West Sterling	Worcester, Mass	Jacob N Tolman
Summitville	Allegany, N Y	Jos Cole
Clymer Centre	Chautauque, N Y	A Maxwell
North Hamden	Delaware, N Y	Allen Stoodley
No Bridgewater	Oneida, N Y	Elisha Baker
Academy	Ontario, N Y	N W Randall
Amboy	Oswego, N Y	Robt G Carter
Pucketas	Westmoreland, Pa	John S McKean
Franklinville	Carroll, Md	Jas Steele
Taylor's Island	Dorchester, Md	Thos H Keene
Whetstone	Morrow, Ohio	Jacob Merret
Austin's Lake	Kalamazoo, Mich	Moses Austin
Big Spring	Ottowa, Mich	John S McClain
Gravel Run	Washtenaw, Mich	Roswell Curtis
Hilliardsville	Henry, Ala	Wash'n H Peacock
Oglethorpe	Macon, Geo	P J Pemerton
Sparta	Chickasaw, Miss	Geo T Baber
Looxahoma	De Soto, Miss	John Thompson
Monterey Landing	Concordia P, La	Saml C Scott
College Mound	Kaufman, Texas	John J Beck
Pilot Grove	Grayson, Texas	B Clements
Powellton	Harrison, Texas	Thos D Powell
Otte's Landing	Marion, Tenn	W Pryor
Rover	Bedford, Tenn	Wm Taylor
Dadsville	Marion, Tenn	Nicholas Smith
Gulistan	Davidson, Tenn	John L Hadley, jr
New Milford	Winnebago, Ill	Anson Barnum
Buck Branch	De Kalb, Ill	Conway B Rhodes
Myers' Mills	Vermillion, Ill	Elijah Briggs
Eliza	Mercer, Ill	Jas M Mannon
Fair Point	Cooper, Mo	Geo L Bell
Mount Airy	Randolph, Mo	Lewis Meadows
Pigeon Grove	Columbia, Wis	Saml Herreman
Nelson's Landing	Chippewa, Wis	Jas J Gilbert
Centre	Rock, Wis	Jeremiah Root
Mosalem	Du Buque, Wis	Thos Brasher
Pembina	Pembina, Min T	Norman W Kittson
Log Prairie	Wahuatah, Min T	David Olmstead
Sauk Rapids	Benton, Min T	Jeremiah Russell

Names Changed: Little Falls, Herkimer Co, N Y, changed to Rockton.
Simmonsville, Providence Co, R I, changed to Olneyville.
Vancluse, Wood Co, Va, changed to St Mary's.

Dark Corner, Carroll Co, Miss, changed to Ceralvo.
Baker's Creek, Bladen Co, N C, changed to Lyon's Landing.
Short's Point, McLean Co, Ill, changed to Independence.

MON JUN 3, 1850
Farmers & Mechanics' Bank, Gtwn, stockholders meeting on Jul 1, at 12 o'clock.
–Wm T Lang, Cashier

For rent: large 3 story brick house adjoining the Six Bldgs. Will be rented either with or without furniture. Inquire of Mrs Worthington, on the premises.

Appointments by the Pres: 1-Robt Birchett, to be Deputy Postmaster at Lynchburg, Va. 2-Isaac Hendershott, to be Deputy Postmaster at Springfield, Ohio.

Bvt Col AEneas Mackay, Deputy Quartermaster Gen U S Army, died at St Louis on May 22.

Cmdor Cooper, of the U S Navy, died on Sat, at his residence in Brooklyn, at the age of about 57 years.

Died: at his residence near Williamsport, Pa, a few days ago, the Hon John Cummings, aged 84 years. He had been elected Sheriff 4 times, first in 1798, & filled the ofc of Associate Judge of Lycoming Co, for a period of 17 years.

Sold: Col Horace Capron's property was sold at public auction on Tue of last week. It was divided: 600 acres to Thos S Wilson, of Balt-$46 per acre, sum $27,600; 125 acres to Saml Cecil, of Anne Arundel Co, Md-$11.24 per acre, sum $1,106.25. 325 acres withdrawn by the trustees. It is understood that Mr Wilson intends to build a beautiful mansion upon the property he purchased. The Avondale factory was sold some days after in Balt.

Died: on May 31, Anne Moss, the infant daughter of Wm H & Gertrude West.

Orphans Court of Wash Co, D C. Ordered that Wm D Nutt, exc of Alex'r Hunter, deceased, late of D C, give notice in regard to distribution of said estate. -Wm F Purcell. -Ed N Roach, Reg/o wills

TUE JUN 4, 1850
Wm P Hudson, a printer, formerly of Boston, is stated to have died on board of the barque **John W Cater**, bound from the Columbia river to San Francisco. The date of his death is not given, though it must have occurred sometime after Mar 20, 1850. The deceased was formerly publisher of the Oregon Spectator, & it is said has left a large amount of property in Oregon & Calif.

Died: yesterday, in her 53rd year, Mrs Mary J Lauck, consort of Isaac S Lauck, formerly of Martinsburg, Va. Her funeral is this afternoon at 5 o'clock.

The Alleganian states that on Tue last, as Mr A McDonald, a resident of Morgan Co, Va, was passing along the track of the Balt & Ohio railroad, about 24 miles east of Cumberland, he was run over & dreadfully mangled. He died on Wed.

Arrest of Foreign Defaulters. Thos Ormsby & Thos Conolly, 2 passengers by the packet ship **Yorkshire**, which arrived at N Y on Sat week, were arrested & charged with having embezzled L25,000, from the bank of Cork, Ireland.

The frig **Congress** will not proceed from Norfolk to Cuba until Thu next. The following is a list of her ofcrs: Cmdor, Isaac McKeever; capt, Jas M McIntosh; lts-1st, Thos Turner; 2nd, Geo R Gray; 3rd, A A Holcomb; 4th, C R P Rodgers; 5th, Gough W Grant; purser, A J Watson; acting master, D M Fairfax; fleet surgeon, Thos Williamson; capt of marines, A S Taylor; passed assist surgeon, Wm A Nelson; assist surgeon, Geo H Howell; cmdor's sec, Robt Glover; passed midshipmen, Edw Simpson, R J D Price; midshipmen, D H Lynch, John Warters, Thos H Looker, John E Johnston, Edwin F Gray, P C Johnson, jr, Washington Totten; purser's clerk, J W Jones; capt's clerk, John T Stoneall; boatswain, Geo Smith; gunner, J M Ballad; carpenter, J G Thomas; sailmaker, R C Rodman.

House of Reps: 1-Ptn of Moses Barrett, for encouragement in the invention of a fog-bell. 2-Ptns of Dr John C Warren & others, & of Dr O W Holmes & others, of Boston, in behalf of the medical ofcrs of the navy. 3-Ptn of Thos Grisham, of Cherokee Co, Texas, praying for a pension, on account of injuries received in the last war with Great Britain. 4-Memorial of Phoebe Wood & Silvia Ann Wood, asking a grant for the invention of a plough. 5-Ptn of Chas H Buxenstein, of Montg Co, Pa, for an increase of pension. 6-Memorial of Dr John R Rhinelander, in favor of the medical ofcrs of the navy of the U S.

Mrd: on Jun 3, at the Fourth Presbyterian Church, by Rev John C Smith, Wm A Page, of Genr'l Land ofc, to Miss Eliza Jane Dunbar, of Carlisle, Pa.

Mrd: on Jun 3, at Church of Ascension, by Rev Mr Gillis, Mr S Augustus H Poe, of N Y, to Miss Harriet N, eldest daughter of E N Stratton, of Wash City.

Died: yesterday, Robert G Barry, son of late Jas D Barry, in his 36th year. His funeral will be from his mother's residence, N J ave south, tomorrow, at 4 o'clock.

Died: on May 31, at Harrisburg, Mgt Espy, wife of Prof Jas P Espy, in her 55th year. She was a devoted wife & most affectionate sister, &, next to her husband, her sisters will feel her loss most severely.

Died: on May 30, after a severe illness of 3 days, of scarlet fever, at his father's residence, near Beltsville, PG Co, Md, John C Herbert Hunter, age 3 years,1 month & 7 days, son of Lt Thos T Hunter, U S Navy. His body was interred in <u>Green Mount Cemetery</u>, near Balt, Md.

Died: on Apr 11, in Rio Janeiro, where he had gone for his health, Rev Thos Meredith Jenkins, of Gtwn College, age 31 years & 5 months. He went there last summer, & was almost restored, when, seeing some American families heavily afflicted with the yellow fever, he went about day & night to assist the sick, but fell a victim himself to the raging malady, having contracted the disease on the 5th.

Senate: 1-Memorial of Alfred G Benson, asking that he may be authorized by law to enter into contract with the U S for transporting the mails & mail agents of the Gov't between San Francisco, Calif, & China: referred to the Cmte on the Post Ofc & Post Roads. 2-Additional documents relating to the ptn of the widow of Jas Wright: referred to the Cmte on Pensions. 3-Ptn of Chas H Buxenstein, a pensioner of the U S, asking an increase of pension: referred to the Cmte on Pensions.

The death of Rev John N Maffit, at Mobile, which is announced by telegraph, has caused some regrets among his friends here. There is, however, some doubt as to the truth of the dispatch. [Jun 5th newspaper: Rev John Newland Maffitt, of the Methodist Episcopal Church, died suddenly at Mobile on May 28, from an affection of the heart.]

WE JUN 5, 1850
On Mon, while 2 Irish laborers, Michl Cronin & Timothy Sullivan, were employed with others, under the superintendence of Mr Essex, in cutting away a bank on Second st, the earth suddenly gave way, & covered Cronin & Sullivan. Cronin is in very dangerous condition at his lodgings, being attended by Dr Eliot. Sullivan is at the Wash Infirmary. Cronin is a single man; Sullivan has a family living at Gtwn.

Senate: 1-Ptn of the reps of Wm Armstrong, deceased, asking compensation for extra services by said Wm Armstrong, while Agent for the Choctaw Indians west of the Mississippi: referred to the Cmte on Indian Affairs. 2-Cmte on Military Affairs: memorial of Capt F Britton, asking compensation for extra services in the Commissary's & Quartermaster's Depts: asked to be discharged from the further consideration of the ptn of the same: which was agreed to. 3-Cmte on Finance: resolution for the relief of Saml Colt & B F Morse, reported the same without amendment, & asked its immediate consideration: which was agreed to: & was considered as in the Cmte of the Whole.

Died: on May 16, at **Keswick**, his late residence, in Albemarle Co, Dr Mann Page, in about the 58th year of his age.

Died: on Jun 2, in Gtwn, D C, Henrietta Steptoe, aged 71 years. Near 50 years of her life were devoted exclusively to nursing the sick. Her funeral will be from residence of her daughterr, Mrs Barker, 4th st in Gtwn, today, at 10 o'clock.

Official: Information received at the Dept of State from John Parrott, late U S Consul at Mazatlan, Mexico, of the murder, on Mar 12 last, of Dr Richd Thompson, supposed to be from the State of N Y, while on the road from the city of Durango to that port.

For sale: my farm, upon which I live, in Montgomery Co, Md: improvememts are a log dwlg-house & kitchen, stable, tobacco house, & other out-bldgs. Contains about 144 acres. I wish to remove to the State of Missouri. -John Hardy.

House of Reps: 1-Leave granted to withdraw from the files of the House the ptn & papers in the case of Palmer Branch.

THU JUN 6, 1850
Mr Enos Routzahn, sr, aged about 50 years, a most worthy & influential farmer, residing about 4 miles north of Middletown, Fred'k Co, Md, died suddenly on Mon. He was assisting the workmen engaged in completing a new Lutheran Parsonage, & by some means, lost his balance, & was precipitated to the ground amidst a mass of rock & lumber, dreadfully lacerating his head & limbs. He was carried home, & died on Tue.

Circuit Court of Wash Co, D C-in Chancery. Sarah Kuhns, John Eschbach, & Fred'k Reglin & Catherine his wife, cmplnts, & Paul Kuhns, Baumgardner & Eliz his wife, Baumgardner & Barbara his wife, Baumgardner & Hillina his wife, Jacob Kuhns, Enos Kuhns, Abraham Kuhns, John Kuhns & Malinda Kuhns, & all other unknown heirs of Paul, John, Peter, Sally & Polly Kuhns, & others, dfndnts. Wm Kuhn, sr, by will dated in 1821, gave Wm Kuhns, jr, a legacy of $1000, & to Sarah Kuhns & Catherine Reglin, a legacy of $100 each, to be paid on death of his wife, & all residue of his real & personal property he gave to the heirs of Paul, John, Peter, Sally, & Polly Kuhns, on the death of his wife, who was to enjoy the whole of his estates during her life & after her death the same were to be disposed of as above stated; that said Wm Kuhns soon afterwards died, that his widow Catherine Kuhns hath also departed this life; that his personal estate was inconsiderable, & was mostly worn out & consumed during the life of his said widow; that he died seized of part of lot 261 in Beatty & Hawkins' addition to Gtwn, D C, & a part of #252 in the same addition, & of lot #13 in *Wilberforce* near the said town; that said Wm Kuhns, legatee, hath also died, intestate, & that the cmplnt John Eshbach is his administrator; that the heirs of said Paul, John, Peter, Sally, & Polly Kuhns, so far as known, are Paul Kuhns, Eliz, Barbara & Hillina Baumgardner, & their respective husbands, & Jacob, Enos, Abraham, John & Malinda Kuhns, & Sylvester, Jos, & Michael Kuhns. All except the last 3, reside out of D C, as do all other heirs, if any, of said Paul, John, Peter, Sally & Paul Kuhns. All to appear in this Court on or before the first day of the next Oct term.   -Jno A Smith, clk

Household & kitchen furniture at auction: on Jun 8, by order of the Orphans Court of Wash Co, D C. Sale at Centre Market, of the household stuff & kitchen furniture of the late Col Sam *McLaughlin. –Chas S Wallach, adm -C W Boteler, auct
+
Administration sale of rare books: order of the Orphans Court of Wash Co, D C. Sale on Jun 8, at the store lately occupied by Thos Fitman, corner of Pa ave & 6th st, the Library of the late Col Saml H *Laughlin. –Chas S Wallach, adm -C W Boteler, auct [*Note McLaughlin/Laughlin.]

Died: on May 28, at Port Gibson, Mississippi, aged 38 years, Fred'k J Poor, son of Moses Poor, of Wash City.

For sale or rent: a 3 story brick house on L, between 9th & 10th sts. Also, 3 small tracts of land near the city. Apply to Z Jones, on 9th st, between L & M sts.

FRI JUN 7, 1850
Senate: 1-Cmte on Pensions: joint resolution from the House for the relief of the children of Sarah Stokes. The widow Stokes died leaving the sum of $300 due to her. The resolution is merely to authorize the Dept to pay that sum to her administrator for the benefit of her children. The Com'r on Pensions says he had no objection to its passage. The resolution was laid over. 2-Memorial of Dr Thos M Morton, asking that he may be recognized as Surgeon for Col Doniphan's regt, instead of Assist Surgeon: referred to the Cmte on Military Affairs. 3-Memorial of G Thos Howard, asking that a bill may be passed granting him compensation as bearer of despatches from Texas to the U S, with documents in relation to the annexation of Texas: referred to the Cmte on Foreign Affairs. 4-Ptn of J R Jefferson, asking compensation for carrying the mail: referred to the cmte on the Post Ofc & Post Roads. 5-Memorial of Wm F Wallace & Jos R McFaddin, asking the reimbursement of the duties paid on merchandise imported by them while acting as sutlers to the army in the Mexican war: referred to the Cmte of Claims. 6-Memorial of Ernest Eude, Clement Duhamel, & Jos Derbis, asking compensation for a vessel & cargo plundered by guerrillas during the late war with Mexico: referred to the Cmte of Claims.

Death in the pulpit. Rev Wm D Allen, of the M E Church, died suddenly on Sun, at Wood's Church, in Chesterfield Co, Va. It is said he had ruptured a blood vessel. Mr Allen was an unmarried man.

Died: on Sat last, at the Naval Hospital, Norfolk, Va, Lt John Harding Marshall, of the U S Navy. He was a native of Louisiana, & appointed to the Navy 30 years ago. He was nearly at the head of the list of Lieutenants at the time of his death.

Mrd: on Jun 4, in Balt, by Rev Mr Randou, Dr Wm F McLenahan, U S N, to Kate Ridgely, daughter of late Mark Desabaye, of Ga.

Mrd: on Jun 3, by Rev Mr Finkle, Mr Enoch Ridgeway to Miss Henrietta F Ecklof, all of Wash City.

Died: on Jun 6, Henry V Hill, an old & respectable citizen of Wash, in his 60th year. His funeral will be from their residence on Capitol square, this afternoon, at 4 o'clock.

In Chancery. Wm H Herriman & others against the administrators & heirs at law of Thos J Davis, deceased. The creditors of the late Thos J Davis, of Gtwn, & others interested in his estate are notified to attend the statement & audit of the individual claim of Wm Winn, one of the administrators, against the estate, at my ofc, in City Hall, Wash, on Jun 12, at 10 o'clock. —W Redin, auditor

Postmaster Gen established the following new Post ofcs for the week ending Jun 1, 1850.

Ofc	County, State	Postmaster
Steep Falls	Cumberland, Me	Andrew Hobson
West Peru	Oxford, Me	Lyman Bolster
E Wakefield	Carroll, N H	Oliver Nutter
Bondville	Bennington, Vt	Josiah G Sumner
Buck Hollow	Franklin, Vt	Parker Farnsworth
So Canaan	Essex, Vt	Hiram S Cooper
Carolina Mills	Wash, R I	Bashford Kenyon
Leeds	Hampshire, Mass	Thos Musgrave
So Amboy	Middlesex, N J	Lucius D Morse
New Sharon	Monmouth, N J	M S Earle
Auburn	Schuylkill, Pa	Isaac Hoffmeister
Jones Mills	Westmoreland, Pa	Clement Hubbs
Tyrell	Venango, Pa	J N Tyrell
Seneca Mills	Montg, Md	John Drill
Lakesville	Dorchester, Md	John D Staplefoot
Conoccheague	Wash, Md	Robt M Small
Middle River	Allen, Ohio	C Hotchkiss
Bascom	Seneca, Ohio	Thos C Wilson
Laceyville	Harrison, Ohio	Jesse H Lacey
Haskellville	Lawrence, Ohio	Jas Haskell
Pleasant Valley	Morgan, Ohio	Stephen Dunbar
Chichasaw	Mercer, Ohio	Saml Patty
Town House		Wm R Winneford
Edge Hill		Jas E Jones
Clover Green	Spottsylvania, Va	Wm R Powell
Colvin's Tavern	Culpeper, Va	John R Colvin
Concord	Appomattox, Va	John R Davidson
Post Oak	Iredell, N C	A A Sharpe
Lowell	Johnston, N C	N T Perkins
Roseborough	Laurens D, S C	John Duncan
Long Cane	Abbeville D, S C	H S McCaslin
North Saluda	Greenville D, S C	Juliet Good
Colonel's Ford	Pickens D, S C	Geo W Phillips
Cold Well	White, Ark	Elijah Little
Shoal Creek	Johnson, Ark	John Cravens
Mayfield	Jackson, Tenn	M A Bassham
Redwood	Grainger, Tenn	P Godwin
Elliott's X Roads	Clinton, Ky	Wm Bramlette
Van Buren	Anderson, Ky	Jacob W Lindle
Cofer	Hardin, Ky	Robt Hunk
Carpentersville	Putnam, Ia	Ezra Whitney
Royton	Delaware, Ia	Wm Mitchell
Big Rock	Kane, Ill	Robt Summers

Scottsville	Macoupin, Ill	Sargeant Goble
Clay	La Salle, Ill	E S Beardsley
Recruit	Allen, Ill	Asa Dillon
Chesapeake	Lawrence, Mo	John S Richmond
Hester	Marion, Mo	Eliz Coons
Half Way	Polk, Mo	John Vanderford
Black Oak Point	Hickory, Mo	J T Powers
Welaunee	Winnebago, Wis	D H Nash
Buffalo Lake	Marquette, Wis	Datus N Root
Oakfield	Fond du Lac, Wis	Wm J Ripley
Indianapolis	Nahaska, Iowa	Jas Bridges
Douglass	Fayette, Iowa	Danl McDuffie

Names Changed:
Oakland, Hartford Co, Conn, changed to Manchester Station.
Greene, Harrison Co, Ohio, changed to Hopedale.
Middlebury, Livingston Co, Mich, changed to Middletown.
East Ford, Green Co, Ky, changed to Cannonsburg.
Marion, Jefferson Co, Fla, changed to Wamkeenah.
Lofun's Store, Butts Co, Georgia, changed to Worthville.
Coopersville, Fentress Co, Tenn, changed to Wright's X Roads.
Dutchman's Point, Cook Co, Ill, changed to Niles.
Thorn Grove, Cook Co, Ill, changed to Bloom.
Amazon, Boone Co, Ill, changed to Park's Corners

Wash Ordinances: 1-Act for the relief of John Fletcher: the sum of $34.54 be paid to him for gravelling Third st east from Va ave to N st south. 2-Act for the relief of Wm B Lewis: fine for an alleged violation of the law in relation to auction, be the remitted: provided Lewis pay the costs of prosecution. 3-Act for the relief of Raub & Green: fine imposed for the alleged violation in relation to using the water from fire plugs on Pa ave, is hereby remitted: provided they pay the costs of prosecution. 4-Act for the relief of David Miller: to be paid the sum of $2.45, the cost paid by Miller on a fine imposed on him by Justice Grubb. 5-Act for the relief of Peter Smith: the sum of $55.89 to be reimbursed to Smith, being the amount erroneously paid by him in person & by his trustee for taxes on part of lot 15 in square 377. 6-Act for the relief of P Ennis: to pay him the sum to be in addition to the compensation allowed under his contract, & in full claim for that service, provided it does not exceed $50. 7-Joint Resolution authorizing Thos Lawson to enclose part of the alley in square 169: immediately in the rear, & bounded north & south by lots 6 thru 10, owned & held by said Lawson.

Suitable reward for the return of a pair of fine Gold Spectacles, with smoked glasses, which were lost on Jun 3, by Mrs J L Daniel, in or about the Patent Ofc. Return to Mrs Daniel at Mrs Gordon's, Capitol Hill.

U S Patent Ofc, Jun 6, 1850. Beriah Swift, of Wash, N Y, praying for the extension of a patent: improvement in cutting & shaving dyewoods, for 7 years from expiration of said patent, which takes place on Aug 10, 1850. –Thos Ewbank, Com'r of Patents

SAT JUN 8, 1850
House of Reps: 1-Ptn & papers of John O'Donald, a soldier of the war of 1812, praying for a pension. 2-Ptn of Henry Dennis, of Md, for compensation for Revolutionary services.

Dept of State, Wash, Jun 7, 1850. Information received from R M Harrison, U S Consul at Kingston, Jamaica, of the deaths of J B Pratt & Abner Moulton, who were passengers in the steamer **Crescent City**, bound from Chagres to N Y, on or about May 20 last. The above were drowned while the steamer was lying at Kingston, on May 18 & 19, 1850.

U S Patent ofc: petition of Edw M Chaffee, of New Brunswick, N J, praying the extension of his patent that expires Aug 31, 1850: improvement of manufacture of India rubber. –Thos Ewbank, Com'r of Patents

Mrd: on Jun 4, by Rev Mr Morgan, Mr John F Day to Miss Catherine Virginia Fridley, both of Wash City.

Died: on Jun 6, at Annapolis, Md, Mrs Catherine Mitchell, formerly of Wash City, in her 24th year. May her soul rest in peace. –W

North Branch of Potomac land for sale, in Hardy Co, Va: 2,309 acres, more or less, in Alleghany Co, Md. Apply by letter to the subscriber in Gtwn, D C. –Wm D C Murdock

Constable sale: of sundry property of Ann Powers, under a writ of fieri facias issued by J W Beck, Justice of the Peace, to satisfy a debt due to Ann Eliza Lindenberger.
–Wm A Mulloy, Constable

MON JUN 10, 1850
Appointment by the Pres: Luther Severance, of Maine, to be Com'r of the U S to the Sandwich Islands.

Furnished rooms for rent: one parlor & 4 chambers, [lately occupied by the Judges of the Supreme Court.] Enquire of P Brenner, Pa ave, near 4½ st.

The St Louis Times, of May 28, states that Mr Josiah Gregg, the author of the Commerce of the Prairies, died at Clear Lake, in Calif, on Jan 25 last.

Died: on Jun 8, at the residence of her son, Professor Gale, Mrs Eliz Gale, aged 89 years. From early life she has been a disciple of Christ & a useful member of the Baptist Church.

Died: on Jun 8, in Wash City, of scarlet fever, Isabella Clyne, 2nd child of Wm A & Jane F Mulloy, aged 5 years & 11 days. Her funeral will be from the residence of her father, 3rd & E Capitol st, this afternoon, at 3 o'clock.

The last steamer from Calif brings intelligence of a sad accident which resulted in the death of Mr John H Beeckman, lately a merchant of N Y C, & son of Henry Beeckman, one of its oldest & most respectable citizens. Mr B had been on a visit to the new town of Butterville, & was returning to Sacramento city in a whale boat, when changing his position in the boat, his gun accidentally discharged, causing his immediate death. He had anticipated an early return to his family, from whom he had been separated more than a year. –N Y Com Advertiser

Valuable mills & lands for sale. Being in feeble health, & wishing to curtail my business, I have determined to sell the whole or some part of the property where I reside, on Cedar Creek, Fred'k Co, Va, containing 500 acres. Apply to me or Isaac F Hite, in the neighborhood, & to Dr Robt T Baldwin & Messrs Barton & Williams, of Winchester. -Philip Swann.

$500 reward for 3 negro slaves named Sanford Lee, [about 40,] John Lee, & Jane Lee, [25,] who left this city Sat. They are probably with their brother Henry Lee, a free man, who has his free papers with him, obtained a few days ago from the clerk of the court. [No name given.] [Jun 12th newspaper: Apply to Capt J H Goddard, Auxiliary Guard.]

TUE JUN 11, 1850
Died: on May 16, at his residence, in Albemarle Co, of pneumonia, Dr Mann Page, in his 59th year. As a father, husband, friend & citizen, he possessed all the best attributes of the Christian, patriot, & neighbor. For 30 years he was a consistent member of the Episcopal Church. –Richmond Whig

Senate: 1-Additional document relating to the memorial of the legal reps of Rinaldo Johnson, deceased: referred to the Cmte of Claims. 2-Cmte on Private Land Claims: bill for the relief of Jas T Shackleford: asked its immediate consideration: passed. 3-Mr Borland. Bill for the relief of Cincinnatus Trousdale & John G Conolly, of Arkansas. The facts are: during the Mexican war the battalion commended by myself was ordred to do duty at points distant from the main army which was commanded by Gen Wool. Under an order by him, I appointed 2 persons to perform the services of adjutant & quartermaster. Those persons were the parties for whose relief I have brought in this bill; & they were appointed by me, with the approval of Gen Wool. They were not commissioned ofcrs, for there were not commissioned ofcrs to spare for the performance of those duties. One was a non-commissioned ofcr, & the other was a private; & they performed those duties from Sep 26 to Nov 18, acting under the orders of the commanding general. Upon the presentation of their accounts at the accounting ofcs here at Wash, the equity of the claim was admitted; but, under the regulations of the dept, they could not be paid. I introduced a bill, therefore, to allow them that amount-to allow to one of them his pay as adjutant, & the other his pay as quartermaster, for the time specified. Bill was subsequently passed.

The remains of Com Geo W Rodgers, who died at Buenos Ayres some 18 months ago, [& whose remains have lately been brought to his native country,] were re-interred at New London, Conn, Wed last.

The unfortunate Michael Cronin, who was so seriously injured on Jun 3, by the caving in of a bank of earth on 2nd st, died last Sat at the Washington Hospital. His remains were decently interred on Sun at St Patrick's burial yard. Mr Essex & a number of the fellow laborers of the deceased attended his funeral.

Died: on Jun 6, Henry B, infant son of Saml & Sarah J Lewis, aged 5 months.

Died: on Jun 10, Emily, daughter of Albert Greenleaf, in her 3rd year.

WED JUN 12, 1850
Appointments by the Pres: 1-J Hosford Smith, to be U S Consul at Beirout. 2-Wm Stowe, to be Deputy Postmaster at Springfield, Mass. 3-Darius Perrin, to be Deputy Postmaster at Rochester, N Y.

Died: on Jun 1, Mrs Eliz Waller, wife of Wm Waller, of Wmsburg, & daughter of ex-President Tyler.

Died: yesterday, Mr Chas Whitman, aged 58 years, a native of Mass, but for many years a resident of Wash City. His funeral will be from his residence, Capitol Hill, this afternoon, at 4 ½ o'clock.

Circuit Court of Wash Co, D C-in Chancery. Geo Peter & others, cmplnts, vs Geo Hamilton Peter, Sarah J Peter, John P C C Peter, John Leonard & Susan H his wife, Jas B Beverly & Jane his wife, Wm Ramsay, W Wadsworth Ramsay, A Douglass Ramsay, David P Ramsay, Marion Ramsay, & Allen Ramsay, heirs of David Peter, dfndnts. The ptn of Jas Dundass & others, assignees of the late Bank of the U S, & of Geo Peter, filed in the above cause, states that they are creditors of the late David Peter, & that a balance of debt is still due to the said Dundass & others of $16.195.88, & to said Geo Peter of $9,178.67; that the sum of $3,738.39, or thereabouts, is in hands of G W Peter, trustee for sale of **Mill Seat**, as the portion of the proceeds due to said David Peter. Object of the bill is to have the same applied towards the balance of debts so due as aforesaid, & it appearing that the said dfndnts above named, heirs of said David Peter, do not reside in this District. Ordered they appear in this Court, on or before the first day of the next Oct term. -Jno A Smith, clk

Senate: 1-Joint resolution for the relief of Sam B Colt & J F Morse: read a third time & passed.

THU JUN 13, 1850
Appointments by the Pres: 1-Benj Riddells, to be U S Consul for Chihuahua, in Mexico. 2-Danl Ringo, to be Judge of the District Court of the U S for the District of Arkansas.

Cmder Stribling is to take command of the U S Naval School at Annapolis, in place of Cmder Upshur, & Lt Tilton is ordered as 1st Lt in place of Lt S S Lee, whose terms of service have expired.

Among the passengers from Europe in the ship **Atlantic** are G W Kendall, of the N O Picayune, & Mr A Dudley Mann, who went out as a special agent of the Gov't during the late revolutionary struggle in Hungary.

House of Reps: 1-Ptn of Henry & Robt Blow, of Southampton, Va, praying for arrears of pension due Henry Blow, deceased, for his services in the late war with Great Britain. 2-Ptn of Sarah Smith for a pension.

The English brig **Emblem**, Capt Finch, which was supposed to have been lost on the ocean, has arrived at Portsmouth, Va, after a passage of 87 days from Newport, Wales, with over 200 tons of T iron for the Seaboard Railroad. The Portsmouth Pilot states the 4 of the crew of this brig were in a state of mutiny when the pilot boat **Fashion**, Capt Wherrett, of Balt, boarded her 60 miles at sea, on Jun 5, to whom Capt Finch surrendered the command of the brig. On reaching Portsmouth the British Consul boarded her, heard the case of the mutineers, &, with the presence of a file of marines from the ship **Pennsylvania**, put the 4 men in irons. Their names are Wm Daisy, Wm Low, Chas Johnson, & Patrick Chill-3 Irishmen & 1 Dane.

Window glass for sale: all sizes on hand. –Robt Nally, Alexandria, Va

Zachary Taylor, Pres of the U S: 1-Recognizes Arthur T Lynn, who has been appointed Consul of Her Britannic Majesty at Galveston. 2-Geo Benvenuto Mathew, who has been appointed Consul of Her Britannic Majesty, for the States of North & South Carolina.

Senate: 1-Additional documents in relation to the claim of Silas L Loomis: referred to the Cmte of Claims. 2-Ptn of Asahel Brainard, a pensioner, asking an increase of his pension: referred to the Cmte on Pensions. 3-Memorial from citizens of Licking Co, Ohio, asking Congress to authorize Asa Whitney to construct a railroad from the Mississippi valley to the Pacific ocean, on the plan proposed in his memorial to Congress: referred to the Cmte on Roads & Canals. 4-Memorial of Col Ward B Burnett, asking for the allowance of expenditures made by the Common Council of N Y C, in raising the First Regt of N Y Volunteers: referred to the Cmte on Military Affairs. 5-Memorial from John S Gilbert & Zeno Secor, asking additional compensation for contructing the dry dock at Kittery, in Maine: referred to the Cmte on Naval Affairs. 6-Memorial from the legal reps of Chas Porterfield, deceased, asking bounty land commutation pay, & the reimbursement of advances made for the public service: referred to the Cmte of Claims. 7-Ptn from Francis Ayler & Chasteen Scott, citizens of Boone Co, Ky, asking indemnity for slaves that escaped into Ohio, & which they are unable to recover for want of the passage of necessary laws by the U S: referred to the Cmte on the Judiciary.

Moore's Union House, Wash: on C st, between 4½ & 6th sts, recently known as the Exchange Hotel, has been refitted, improved, & furnished anew, & will be opened on Mon next, by the subscriber, lately of the Croton Hotel, N Y C. –John L Moore

In the Balt Clipper: "further from Cuba: execution of Capt Duperu. Among the prisoners executed at Cardenas was Capt Duperu, well known in New Orleans as a brave & gallant spirit. He was a Virginian by birth, of French extraction, & spoke the French language like his mother tongue." I take great pleasure in assuring you, that I am alive & in excellent health. I was not one of the unfortunate expedition who sailed for Cuba under the command of Gen Lopez. –Alphonso M Duperu, late Capt 3rd Dragoons.

Mrd: on Jun 4, in Richmond, by Rev Dr Jones, Mr Robt W Hughes, of Richmond, & Miss Eliza M Johnston, adopted daughter of Gov Floyd & daughter of late Hon Chas C Johnston, of Wash Co, Va.

Mrd: on Jun 11, by Rev Peter B O'Flannagan, Mr Saml J Noland to Miss Eliz A Frank, both of Wash City.

Mrd: on May 28, in Gtwn, by Rev Mr Murray, Mr Simeon Garratt to Miss Ann Virginia Ball, both of Wash.

Mrd: on Jun 10, at St John's Church, by Rev Mr Pyne, J I Washington, of Westmoreland, Va, to Mary D, daughter of the late Geo D Ashton, of King Geo, Va.

Circuit Court of Montg Co, Md-in Equity. March Court, 1850. Barnet T Norris vs Thos S Read, adm of Henry A Collier, deceased, Ann Collier, widow of Jos P Collier, Henry A Collier, John W Collier, Jos E Collier, Mary N Collier, Wm T Collier, & Berkhart L Collier, children of Jos P Collier, deceased, Thos S Reid & Rachel his wife, Ann Eliza Clarke, Jas H Clarke, heirs-at-law of Henry A Collier, deceased, & Geo W Peter. The original & amended bills in this case state that Henry A Collier, late of said county, died intestate; & that the personal estate of Henry Collier was granted to said Thos S Reid, & that the personal estate of said Henry A Collier is wholly insufficient for the payment of the debts of the said Henry A Collier; that said Henry A was, at the time of his death, seized in fee of a lot of land in Poolesville, in said county, & also had an equitable interest in other lands in said county, & which have descended to the widow & children of the said Jos P Collier & to Rachel Reid, & to Ann E Clarke & Jas H Clarke, children of Henry Clarke, deceased; that said widow & children of said Jos P Collier do not reside in this state; & that said children of said Jos P Collier are infants under the aged of 21 years; that the said Barnet T Norris is a creditor of said Henry A Collier, & sues as well for himself as for the other creditors of the said Henry A Collier, who may come & distribute to the expense of this suit, & prays that said Thos S Reid may account for the personal estate of said Henry A Collier; & that the real estate of Henry A Collier may be sold for the payment of his debts, & for general relief. Notice is given to the said Ann Collier, Henry A Collier, John W Collier, Jos E Collier, Mary M Collier, Wm T Collier, & Berkhart L Collier, widow & children of said Jos P Collier, deceased, to appear on or before the 2nd Mon of Nov next in this court. -T H Wilkinson, Nich'l Brewer.
-S T Stonestreet, clk, Montgomery Co Crt [Md].

Died: on Jun 7, at **Bellevue**, her late residence, in her 85th year, Mrs Eliz Lowe, relict of the late Lloyn M Lowe, formerly of PG Co, Md.

Died: on Jun 7, at Woodsfield, Ohio, of consumption, Miss Eleanor Morris, in her 19th year, daughter of Hon Jos Morris.

Died: yesterday, in Wash City, Mrs Grace Auld, aged 51 years. Her funeral will take place this morning at 10 o'clock.

Died: on Jun 4, at Louisville, Ky, Mrs Henretta M Addison, aged 73 years, daughter of the late Hon Wm Pace, one of the signers of the Declaration of Independence from Md, & relict of Thos G Addison, of Md. She went to Louisville in 1831, & died at the residence of her son-in-law, Henry E Thomas.

Died: on Jun 9, at the residence of his father, **Prospect Hill**, Essex Co, Va, Geo M B Garnett, in his 18th year.

Died: on May 30, at the residence of his father, near Beltsville post ofc, PG Co, Md, of scarlet fever, after an illness of 3 days, John C Herbert Hunter, son of Lt Thos T Hunter, U S N, aged 3 years, 1 month & 7 days. His remains were interred in Green Mount Cemetery, near Balt, Md.

FRI JUN 14, 1850
Fatal affray at Memphis, Jun 11. On Sat the case of Farmers' & Merchants' Bank came up before the court, on the part of Dr J Fowkes & others, that the assets of the Bank should be placed under their control. The motion was resisted by Gen Coe, as atty for a portion of the creditors. Messrs Coe & Connell left the court room, & were met by Trigg & his friends, when a personal assault occurred. Coe shot & killed Trigg. Coe was shot in the back & fell mortally wounded. Gaines & Connell were seriously injured.
-Telegraphic

Died: on Jun 10, of scarlet fever, Emily, in her 3rd year; on Jun 13, Albert Wm, in his 12th year, children of Albert & Emily Ann Greenleaf.

A Visit to **Mount Vernon**. A letter of introduction from an honorable Secretary procured us an entrance to the house, where we were most hospitably received by Mr & Mrs Washington. I was quite charmed with the easy grace of the lady, & the frank politeness of the gentleman, & left them grateful for their politeness, & sincerely regretting the embarrassment of their position. While we were there, 2½ hours, I witnessed the arrival & departure of 6 parties, all of whom were admitted to the house. Where is the generosity, the magnimity, the justice of the American people, that they can permit the Heirs of Washington, the guardians of his remains, to be taxed & harassed in this manner? Let Congress purchase the Residence & Tomb of Washington, & appoint suitable persons to preserve & protect the property, & act as guides to visiters; & keep the grounds as they were in the lifetime of Washington. All modern improvements, I think, would be in bad taste. Congress, & Congress alone, can remedy this evil. Being a Lady, I do not presume to discuss the constitutionality of these suggestions; I leave that to wiser heads. —Mrs C -Wash, Jun 8, 1850

Mrd: on Jun 13, in Wash City, by Rev Mr Pyne, Alexander F Warley, U S Navy, to Miss Emilie C W, only daughter of Capt Francis Forrest, U S Navy.

Navy Dept-Jun 13, 1850: information received of the decease of the 2 daughters of the Hon John P Gaines, Govn'r of Oregon, at St Catharine's, Brazil, in Mar last. The youngest, Miss Harriet, died on board the U S ship **Supply**, on the 18th; & the elder, Miss Florella, died on shore on May 20. [See notice in Jun 15th newspaper.]

Stock of Confectionary & Fancy Store at auction: on Jun 15, the entire stock of Mrs E Palmer, near the market. –Edw S Wright, auct

In Chancery, Mar Term, 1850. Jacob Snider, jr, vs John Vaughan's heirs. The trustee in this cause have reported the sale of lots 14, 16, & 17 in square 583, for $300; in square 585, lots 6, 11, & 16 for $216; in square 587, lots 11 & 16 for $32.08; in square 589, lots 14 thru 18 for $48.84; in square 643, lots 3, 7 thru 11, & 16 for $35.23; to Jacob Snider, jr, the cmplnt, & the terms of the sale have been complied with. –Jno A Smith, clerk

On Wed, before the Supreme Judicial Court of Mass, the application for a writ of error in the case of John W Webster, now under sentence of death, was presented by his counsel, & ably argued for the application by the Hon C B Goodrich. But few persons were present, except members of the bar, which was numerously represented.

The brig **Porpoise** destined for the coast of Africa left on Sun last, preparatory to departing. List of her ofcrs: Lt Commanding, Jas L Lardner; Acting Lt, J Hogan Brown; Purser Jos C Eldridge; Passed Assist Surgeon, J J Brownlee; Acting Master, Reginald Fairfax; Passed Midshipmen, John M Brooke, Chas W Woolley; Midshipman, Julius G Heilsman; Capt's Clerk, John L Forney.

House of Reps: 1-Ptn of Hyacinth Ropelle for the passage of an act granting him a patent of a certain tract of land. 2-Ptn of Adam Weir, jr, & 91 other citizens of Wash Co, Pa, for an Agricultural Bureau.

Butter & Egg Depot: fronting the Nat'l Hotel, Pa ave. –Richd Cruit

Obit-died: on Apr 28 last, in Wash, Capt Geo W Taylor, aged 43 years, the well known submarine armor & diving bell man. At the commencement of the present Administration, Mr Sec Preston contracted with Capt Taylor to go to Gibraltar & examine the war steamer **Missouri**, sunk at that point some 5 or 6 years ago. He made the examination, & reported his observations to the Dept. While on this duty he lost his health, & repaired to Madeira. But this failing to restore his health, he proceeded to Havanna, for a few months. Still being feeble, he concluded to seek a colder climate, & left Havana for N Y. This change he thought braced him up, & improved his health. Soon afterwards he came to the seat of Gov't. But here his lungs were more oppressed, & he kept on declining until Apr 28, when he died, leaving a wife & daughter, & a circle of friends. .

Valuable real estate at public sale: by decree of Fred'k Co Court, as Court of Equity, the subscribers will offer, on Jun 28, at Ijamsille, on the Balt & Ohio Railroad, all the real estate of which Plumer Ijams, late of Fred'k Co, deceased, died possessed. 1-The *Homestead*, containing 190 acres; with a 2 story brickdwlg & all necessary out bldgs: about 8 miles from Fred'k. 2-*Davis' Farm*, about 80 acres, adjoining the *Homestead* on the west. 3-The *Mill*, Saw-mill, Miller's House, with a lot of 16½ acres attached. 4-The *Ijamsville Property*, about 18½ acres, with a storehouse & warehouse, depot, & blacksmith shop.

SAT JUN 15, 1850
Public sale of real estate: Circuit Court of Wash Co, D C, sitting in Chancery, in the cause wherein Wm G W White & Jas L White, trading as White & Bro & others, are cmplnts & Edw N Roach, administrator of Isaac T Ellwood & others, are dfndnts, proceed to sell lots 26 & 27 in square 262, fronting the mall, near 7th st west. Lot 27 has on it 2 handsome frame houses. Lot 26 adjoins lot 27, with no improvement.
–S S Williams, trustee -Green & Tastet, aucts

Mrd: on Jun 13, by Rev L J Gilliss, Mr John H McChesney to Miss Mary E King.

Died: on Mar 6, at sea, Fred'k Robinson, eldest son of Wm Strong, associate Judge of U S Crt for Oregon Territory; aged 6 years.

Valuable property for sale: by authority of the powers invested in me by the last will of Patrick McGarvey, late of Wash Co, deceased: sale on Jun 19, of lot 1 & lot 11 in square west of square 4, in Wash City, [being the same property sold by the undersigned as trustee to the said McGarvey on Nov 27, 1848,] with the improvements: located at 27th & K sts, opposite the Wash brewery. The interest which McGarvey had in & to the premises, which is to be sold, will be stated at the sale. Terms cash.
–Jas W Sheahan, exc -Green & Tastet, aucts

Died: of yellow fever, in the harbor of St Catharine's, Brazil, on board the U S storeship **Supply**, on Mar 19 last, in her 17th year, Miss Harriet P; & on Mar 22, Miss Florilla, age 19 years, daughters of Hon John P Gaines, of Ky, Govn'r of Oregon Territory. [See Jun 14th notice on the above.] On Mar 6, at sea, of yellow fever, Fred'k Robinson, eldest son of Hon Wm Strong, Assoc Justice of the U S Court for Oregon Territory, in his 6th year. On May 19, of yellow fever, Danl Williams, seaman on board the **Supply**. The **Supply**, with the several families of members of the Territorial Gov't of Oregon, arrived at Rio Janeiro, on her voyage to the N W coast, on Feb 22. Yellow fever prevailed there with terrible devastation to life, in the harbor among the shipping, & on shore near the commercial anchorage. The **Supply** sailed on Mar 4, & ran into St Catherine's to complete the arrangements on board incident to so long a cruise. The second day out a death in one of the families, witnessed his burial in the deep. The two sisters, so beloved in life, now sleep side by side in a beautiful spot on the mountain above the residence of Mr R Cathcart, Acting American Consul. Perennial flowers give a sad impressive beauty to the scene.

To let: finished brick houses on Mass ave, between 6th & 7th sts west. Inquire of Jas B Phillips, corner of 6th & H sts, or to E Owens, near Willard's Hotel.

For rent: the house on N J ave, now in the occupancy of Mrs Whitman, with or without furniture. Apply at the premises, or to Jas Adams, at the Bank of Wash.

100,000 sawed laths: 27,000 feet dressed Carolina flooring, for sale by Jos Fugitt, La ave, between 9th & 10th sts.

Household & kitchen furniture at auction: by deed of trust, executed by Thos L Potter, recorded in Liber J H S 9, folios 80-82, of the land records of Wash Co, D C: sale at the furnishing store of said Potter, E & 10th sts, Wash City, on Jun 19. –Jas W Barker, trustee -C W Boteler, auct

Zachary Taylor, Pres of the U S, recognizes Jas F Melinx, who has been appointed Consular Agent of France for Cincinnati, Ohio. -Jun 14, 1850

$3 reward for return of a black Cow, that strayed from the subscriber, living at 6th & P sts, in the rear of the old Poor-house. –Franset Diller

MON JUN 17, 1850
Senate: 1-Submitted: documents relating to the claim of Gustavus Heimberger, an ofcr in the late war with Mexico: referred to the Cmte on Pensions. 2-Memorial of Jas J Strang, Geo J Adams, & Wm Marks, Presidents of the Church of the Saints, Apostles of the Lord Jesus Christ, asking that Congress will pass a law giving the consent of the nation that the saints may settle upon & forever occupy all the uninhabited lands of the islands in lake Michigan, & to cease to sell the same to other persons, & asking of the people of the U S, as they have not allowed their brethren to remain in peace with them, they will at least suffer them to remain there, separate from them. The memorial sets forth that 10,000 men, women, & children were illegally expelled from the State of Missouri, plundered of their possessions, exiled from their homes, & driven in destitution & hunger, & in continual danger. Ptn was referred to the Cmte on Public Lands. 3-Mr Underwood. I rise to present a resolution of inquiry. I claim to be the descendant collaterally of John Rogers; & as the heirs of his, some 15 or 20 years ago, my family drew from the Treasury some three or four thousand dollars; & recently another family claiming to be the heirs of this gentleman have drawn twelve or fourteen thousand dollars for the same services. John Rogers was a captian in the Va State line. I claim to be the nephew of his man, &, according to tradition in our family, he died a few years after the Revolution, without having been married, or having children, & for that time we have been paid a claim. The other family say that the true John Rogers lived a great many years longer, & as the amount of the half-pay would be in proportion to the time he lived, the second family got about 3 or 4 times as much as my family was paid. A man by the name of Williams, some 14 or 15 years ago, wrote to an old uncle of mine, now in his 85th year, who received this money as the administrator of his deceased brother, & asked by what authority he received the money which was paid to him. My under stated he received it because he was the administrator of the estate of Capt Rogers; because he had the

diploma of Capt Rogers as a member of the Cincinnati Society, identifying him as the true Capt Rogers; because he held 2 commissions of Capt Rogers, establishing his indentity, & that he & his family had inherited the property of Capt Rogers. We have heard no more from Mr Williams, until I came on here, when I found out that money had been paid out to them. The Sec of the Interior informed me that a bundle of papers had been filed as proofs, which he had examined before the claim was paid, whereas that of my living uncle rested on a single affidavit, made by an old soldier . The object of this resolution is to get the Judiciary Cmte to take up this matter, & that they ought to provide some means by law for the reclamation of money thus paid through fraud or through mistake. The resolution was adopted.

100 acres of Montg Co land at auction: on Jun 27, [belonging to Mr Tucker, who intends leaving the county,] situated on the old Rockville Rd, adjoining the farm of Wm Huddleston. –Dyer & Bro, aucts

House of Reps: 1-Cmte on Revolutionary Pensions: discharged from the further consideration of the ptn of Mary A Turner & John L Turner: referred to the Cmte of Claims. Same cmte: discharged from the further consideration of the ptn of Wm Randall, heir of Richd R Randall, deceased: referred to the Cmte on Revolutionary Claims. Same cmte: bill for the relief of the heirs of John Jackson, deceased, & a bill for the relief of Mary Martin: committed. Same cmte: adverse reports on the ptn of Philip Taber, of Eunice Page, of Hannah Phelps, of Eliz Huntsman, of Adam P Campbell, son of Patrick Campbell, of John Bain, of Francis Wallace, of Saml Merrifield, of Wm Quail, of Peter Hilton, of Buckley Hutchins, & Danl Risdon, of the surviving ofcrs & soldiers who assisted in the defence of New Orleans, of Jas Pitman, of Mgt Field, of Jane Sexton, & of the heirs of Rachel Rowell: laid on the table. Same cmte: reported a bill for the relief of John Adams, of Blair Co, Pa: committed. 2-Adverse reports on the ptns of Stephen Howard, of Valentine Sevier, & of the ofcrs of volunteers in the late Mexican war: laid on the table. 3-Cmte on Revolutionary Pensions: discharged from the further consideration of the ptn of the widow of Lt Noah Wise: laid on the table. 4-Cmte on Invalid Pensions: bill for the relief of Chas Hinkle: committed. Same cmte: adverse report on the ptn of Saml Spalding: laid on the table. Same cmte: discharged from the further consideration of the ptn of David Troxil: referred to the Cmte on Revolutionary Pensions. Same cmte: adverse report on the ptn of Jefferson Cook: laid on the table. Same cmte: bill for the relief of John Hazen: committed. Same cmte: bill for the relief of John W Robinson, of Thos Howard, an invalid seaman, & of Ichabod Weymouth: committed. Same cmte: adverse reports on the ptns of Mich White, of Washington Denham, of Wm Ferguson, & of Isaac Always: laid on the table. Same cmte: bill for the relief of Jas Butler: committed. Same cmte: adverse reports on the ptns of Robt Trevit, of Edw Taylor, of John English, & of Stephen A Corey: laid on the table. 5-Cmte on Invalid Pensions: discharged from the further consideration of the ptns of Jos Morrison, of Danl Palmer, of Richd G Caswell, of Apollos Hitchcock, of Isaac Graham, of Saml C Mabson, of Elnathan Phelps: laid on the table. Same cmte: adverse report on the ptn of Mary B Rice: laid on the table. Same cmte: bill authorizing the Com'r of Patents to grant an extension of a patent of Andrew Moore, jr, for an improvement in capstans: committed. Same cmte: discharged from the further consideration of the ptn of John

Pettibone: referred to the Cmte of Claims. 6-Cmte on Military Affairs: bill for the relief of Joel Henry Dyer: committed. Same cmte: adverse report on the ptn of Jas Armstrong: laid on the table. 7-Ptn of Sarah Kirby, widow of Robt B Kirby, to be placed on the pension list. 8-Ptn of Stephen Spalding, of Gasconade Co, Missouri, a Revolutionary soldier, for relief. 9-Ptn of Ben Heatherby, a soldier in the Revolutionary war, for relief. 10-Ptn of Saml Chase Barney & Mary E his wife, for a change of circuit court in the District of Columbia, or a change of venue to Balt.

Postmaster Gen has established the following new Post ofcs for week ending Jun 8, 1850.

Ofc	County, State	Postmaster
Groswoldville	Franklin, Mass	R White
Assabes	Middlesex, Mass	Amory Maynard
Mount Rose	Mercer, N J	Alfred S Cook
Freeland	Northumb'd, Pa	John B Lowe
E Lewiston	Mohoning, Ohio	Philip Fetzer
Baltimore	Barry, Mich	John Baker
Cottrellville	St Clair, Mich	S B Grummond
Kimberlin	Giles, Va	H Neel
Henry	Spartanburg D, S C	Saml N Drummond
Freesoil	Cherokee, Ga	N J Garrison
Jernigan	Orange, Fla	W Patrick
Ridgley	Macon, Ala	E J Hays
Barbour	Choctaw, Ala	Noah Barbour
Farmersville	Posey, Ia	Jos Phillips
Milo	Bureau, Ill	Isaac Southerland
Naausay	Kendall, Ill	M Smith
Pine Creek	Ogle, Ill	Benj Brubaker
Bruckville	Morgan, Ill	Louis Reinback
Lamburg	Iroquois, Ill	Jas Lamb
Elm Grove	Lewis, Mo	N H Slaughter
Capse's Creek	Newton, Mo	David Ferguson
Valley Prairie	Barry, Mo	W F H Frazier
New Holsein	Calumet, Wis	Rudolph Puckner
Linn	Lucas, Iowa	W H H Linn
Concord	Louisa, Iowa	Jas Latta
Glen Dale	Muscatine, Iowa	Saml D Viele

Names Changed:
Bucksnort, Scott Co, Miss, changed to Homwood.
Lott's Creek, Bradley Co, Ark, changed to Eagle Creek.
Fountain, Racine Co, Wisc, changed to Mount Pleasant.
Mount Pleasant, Racine Co, Wisc, changed to Caledonia.
Monpelier, Madison Co, Iowa, changed to Winterset.
Nebraska, Potawatamie Co, Iowa, changed to Council Bluff.
Eatontown Landing, Monmouth Co, N J, changed to Ocean Port.

Ferdinand E Hassler writes that in 1819 his father presented the American Philosophical Society his papers upon the coast survey, which, for some reason or other, were not published until 1825.

Mrd: on Jun 6, in Richmond, Va, by Rev Dr Jones, Judge Wm Daniel, jr, of Lynchburg, & Miss Eliz H Cabell, daughter of Judge Wm H Cabell, of Richmond.

House of Reps: 1-Cmte on Military Affairs: discharged from the further consideration of the memorial of Jas Hardy, Peter Woods, & others, asking an extension of the benefits of the various acts of Congress granting bounty land & extra pay to soldiers & marines who sereved in the late war with Mexico, to the seamen in the U S Navy: laid on the table, for the reason that a bill had been reported from the Cmte on Naval Affairs. 2-Same cmte: discharged from the further consideration of the ptn of John Read & others, ofcrs & soldiers of the war of 1812, & other citizens of Lawrence Co, Pa, praying donations of land to the ofcrs & soldiers engaged in said war: referred to the Cmte on Public Lands. Same cmte: bill for the relief of John H B Rolls: committed. 3-Cmte on naval Affairs: bill for the relief of John W Simonton: committed.

Piscataway Academy commenced on Jun 1. The subscriber has now in his possession the most flattering certificates as to his qualifications, from the following literary gentlemen, under whom he was a student for several years: Miles Carey, Principal of the Lynchburg Academy; H J Christian, Prof of A L in Richmond College, Richmond City, Va. Thos B Robertson, Prof of Math in Richmond College, & N Webster, Prof of N Science in Richmond College. Cmte: T D Jones, M D; & B L Gwynn.
–Richd Herndon Rawlings, Piscataway, Md

Grand Division Sons of Temperance, D C: meeting this evening, at 7½ p m.
–R G Campbell, G S

TUE JUN 18, 1850
$200 reward for negro man Dennis, about 36 years old. Rachel Piles, near Tenallytown, Montgomery Co, Md.

Appointments by the Pres:
John R Bartlett, to be Com'r for running the boundary line between the U S & the Republic of Mexico.
Ebza C Coffey, to be Receiver of Public Moneys at Kaskaskia, Ill.
John W Ashmead, to the U S Atty for the Eastern District of Pa.
Jas M Clark, to be U S Atty for the District of Rhode Island.
J Prescott Hall, to the U S Atty for the Southern District of N Y.
Wm Halsted, to be U S Atty for the district of N J.
Chas H Merritt, as Agent to take the Census of New Mexico.
Brigham Young, as Agent to take the Census of Deseret.
J N Johnson, as Agent to take the census of Calif.

John Pickrell & John Dickson, Gtwn, D C, have formed a Co-partnership, under the firm of Pickrell & Dickson, to carry on the Lumber, Wood & Coal business, at the old Lumber Yard on Water st, Gtwn, lately & for many years occupied by King & Pickrell.

New daily paper in Wash City: The Southern Press, edited by Ellwood Fisher & Edwin De Leon, & to be published daily by G A Sage & Herr M Heath, made it's first appearance yesterday in this city.

Painful event at Triadelphia, Md, on Jun 9. A little daughter of Jas Dwyer, about 6 or 7 years of age, walked out with a dog & after a 2 or 3 hours absence, her parasolete was found on the bridge over the Patuxent river, & the little dog intently looking into the river from the bridge. Upon searching, her body was found in the river, life extinct. She supposedly accidentally fell in, on crossing the bridge.

The U S ship **St Mary's**, bearing the broad pennant of Cmdor Geisinger, arrived in Hampton Roads on Fri, after a passage of 80 days from Batavia. She sailed from Macao on Feb 22 for Manila. The object of the visit to Manila was to bring to the U S for trial, 5 American seamen, who were in prison there, charged with having set fire to the American ship **Massachusetts**, of New Bedford, at the Marian Island. There are also on board 3 prisoners from the Pacific squadron, sent home under commutation of sentence of death by court-martial. List of Ofcrs: Cmdor D Geisinger; Lts, J B Marchand, C Ap R Jones, W E Boudinot; Acting Lts, A C Rhind, D Ochiltree, [master;] Purser, C Anderson, Surgeon, S R Addison, Lt of Marines, F B McNeil; Com Sec, Fred Schley; Midshipmen, J L Breese, D L Braine, C L Haralson, J H Rowan, jr.

For sale: 2 three story brick houses, in the 1st Ward. Apply at Jos Boulanger's, G st, near War Dept.

Senate: 1-Cmte on Pensions: ptn of Fred'k Dixon, of Jackson Co, Iowa, asking remuneration for wounds received in the late war with Great Britain: passed to a second reading. Same cmte: ptn of John W Mount, asking an increase of his pension for the loss of his right eye in the late war with Mexico: asking to be discharged from the further consideration of the same: which was agreed to. Same cmte: ptn of citizens of Clay Co, Indiana, asking that a pension be granted to the widow of Thos West, late a soldier in the war with Mexico: asking to be discharged from the further consideration of the same: which was agreed to. Same cmte: claim of Famous Mortimer, for an increase of pension: asking to be discharged from the further consideration of the ptn of the same: which was agreed to. Same cmte: ptn of Silas Chatfield, asking arrears of pension: asking to be discharged from the further consideration of the ptn of the same: which was agreed to. Same cmte: House bill for the relief of Wm Whicker: recommended its passage. Same Cmte: House bill for the relief of Anna Griffin: recommended its passage. Same cmte: House bill for the relief of Jacob Zimmerman: reported back the same with an amendment. 2-Ordered, that the memorial of Seneca G Simmons, on the files of the Senate, in relation to his liability for money stolen from his possession during the Mexican war, be referred to the Cmte on Military Affairs, & that the papers of the same memorialist on file, asking compensation for services as secretary of the Creek & Osage com'rs, be referred to the Cmte on Indian Affairs. 3-Ordered, that B F Mullen have leave to withdraw his ptn & papers from the files of the Senate. 4-Mr Clay. I have received a ptn from John M McGuire, a citizen of Indiana, a person with whom I was acquainted many years ago, who was a volunteer in the late war with Great Britain. He has never yet received anything from the Gov't for his services except the pay he received. The ptn is accompanied by a certificate of the very honorable discharge he received from his commanding ofcr, with whose signature I am well acquainted. He asks of Congress some remuneration for his services in consideration of their value & of his present destitute condition: referred to the Cmte on Military Affairs. 5-Cmte of the Whole: regarding the ptn of Geo Poindexter: for injury sustained in consequence of the occupancy of his land by the Ky regt: land is known as Oakland race course. Mr King: what is the amount? Mr Davis: about $1,500. The bill was ordered back to the Senate, read a third time, & passed. 5-Bill for the relief of Mrs Margaret Hetzel, widow & administratrix of A R Hetzel, late Assist Quartermaster in the U S Army. It appears that her husband died on Jul 20, 1847, at Louisville, Ky, in attempting to reach home after a most laborious service at the city of Vera Cruz, during the siege by the U S troops, leaving the memorialist, his widow, & 3 children. The deceased served in the quartermaster's dept more than 12 years previous to his death; his accounts have all been settled at the Treasury. Consideration of the bill was postponed.

Commission on Claims against Mexico: 1-Memorial of Francis Meyer, filed Apr 12, 1850, & claiming for advances & services in the expedition of Gen Mina, in 1816, was submitted, examined, & suspended. 2-That of Elisha H Saubnier, filed May 15, 1850, & claiming for expulsion from Vera Cruz in 1846, was submitted, examined, & ordered to be received. 3-That of Geo W Van Stavoren, claiming for tobacco seized at Vera cruz in 1839, was submitted, examined, & ordered to be received. 4-That of Benj T Reed, for himself & others, claiming for un-repaid deposites of cash in the custom-house of Monterey, Calif, made in 1845 & 1846, was submitted, examined, & suspended. 5-That of Jos Bolles, seaman, claiming for confiscation of property & imprisonment of person at Monterey, Calif, in 1810, was submitted, & leave given to withdraw, with a view to amend. 6-That of Jas Kelly, mariner, claiming for imprisonment & consequent loss of property, at Monterey, Calif, in 1840, was submitted, examined, & suspended.

Constable's sale: by writ of fieri facias: sale on Jun 25, on the public space, near the Centre Market House: sale of sundry articles, to satisfy 2 judgments recovered against the said Timothy Buckly in favor of the Corp of Wash. –J W Busher, Police 5th Ward

Criminal Court: following gentlemen were summoned to serve on the Grand Inquest.

Peter Force- Foreman	John W Martin	W D C Murdock
Geo Lowrey	Saml McKenney	John Dickson
Michl Shanks	Robt White	Peter M Pearson
Robt Farnham	Evan Lyon	Wm Sothoron
Isaac Clarke	Henry Haw	Stanislaus Murray
Geo Parker	Thos Blagden	Peter G Washington
Wm Easby	Thos Bates	Wm Collins
Craven Ashford	Geo W Young	

1-Nicholas Watkins, found guilty of a common assault: sentence postponed. 2-Wm Webster, convicted at the last Dec term of breaking into a house & beating a women, was sentenced to pay $5 & costs. [Jun 24th newspaper: Watkins found guilty of a common assault: to suffer 4 months imprisonment in the county jail, & fined $1.]

Died: on Jun 17, Mary Augusta France, youngest child of Jos Henry & Mary Eliz France, aged 1 year, 4 months & 23 days. Her funeral is this afternoon, a half past 4 o'clock.

Died: on Mon, of teething, Frances Marion, youngest child of John J & Mary G Mulloy, aged 10 months & 2 days. Her funeral is this morning, at 10 o'clock, from the residence of her parents, on South B st, Capitol Hill.

Died: on Jun 17, in Wash City, of disease of the heart, Mary, daughter of Jas Mead, in her 27th year. Her funeral will be this afternoon, at 4 o'clock, from the residence of her father, on F st, between 5th & 6th sts, near the Navy Yard.

$150 reward for runaway from the farm of E Ray, near Rock Creek Church, Wash Co, D C, negro man Henry Smith, about 26 or 27 years of age. –Enos Ray

WED JUN 19, 1850
A suit has been brought by Nathl Childs, late Teller of the Bank of the State of Missouri, against that institution, for defamation, false imprisonment, & malicious prosecution. He has laid the damages at $50,000.

The steamship **Constitution**, recently built in Phil, has been purchased by Capt Bissell, late of the U S navy, who intends taking her to the Pacific.

Skowhegan Free Press: Mr Goodrich, now in Calif, wrote his father, in Bingham, Maine, that out of a company of 30 in number, who left *Fort Independence* about a year ago for Calif, he was the only person who survived the journey, the remaining 29 having either died of the cholera, exposure, or were killed by the Indians. –Boston Journal

Senate: 1-Ordered, that the ptn of John Bronson, on the file of the Senate, be referred to the Cmte of Claims. 2-Cmte on the Judiciary: memorial of Louisiana Eliz Lee Alice Ripley, [now Mrs Lawson,] the only surviving child of the late Eleazer W Ripley, asking payment for the amount due her father by the U S courts, submitted a report in writing; which concludes that it is inexpedient to grant the claim. The report was ordered to be printed.

Commission on Claims against Mexico: 1-Memorial of Robt M Forbes & of John A Parker, claiming for losses by Mexican invasion of Texas in 1836, was submitted, examined, & held under further consideration. 2-That of Henry Cheatham, claiming for seizure on board of schnr **Champion** in 1837, imprisonment & loss of property, was submitted, examined, & ordered to be received.

Died: on Jun 14, at his residence in Fred'k Co, Md, Thos C Shipley, in his 69th year.

Six cents reward: for runaway indented apprentice to Coach Painting, John Everett. –Michl McDermott, living on Pa ave, & 3rd. [Jun 20th newspaper: in answer to the above notice, offering a reward for me, I deem it proper to state that I was 21 years old on Jun 15, & that I never consented to be bound for a longer period than I should be 21 years old. I shall resist any effort on the part of Mr McDermott to hold me to further service. –John S Everett.]

For sale, at public auction, on Jul 23 next: lot 273, 15, 218, part of 41, 42, 51 thru 54, 57, part of 17, 18, 26, part of 29, 30, 58, 59, 70, 71, 27, 35 thru 37, 24, 25, 48 thru 52, 83, 103, & part of lot 1, in Gtwn, by the will of John Hoye, late of Cumberland, Md, deceased. For information apply to John Marbury, Gtwn. -Geo Smith, of Alexandria, exc of the will of John Hoye, deceased.

Looking for Catherine Devine, between 12 & 13 years of age: she left her mother's residence on I st bet 11th & 12th sts on Jun 11. Anyone knowing her whereabouts will confer a great favor on a distressed mother by giving her such information as will lead to her recovery. -Catherine Devine

For sale: the beautiful residence of the late Saml Burche, on N J ave, north of the Capitol: with about 2 acres of ground attached. Apply to Mrs Burche on the premises.

THU JUN 20, 1850
Senate: 1-Memorial of Anna De Neufville Evans, heir & legal rep of John de Neufville & Son, asking the repayment of advances made by her ancestors in the Revolutionary war: referred to the Cmte on Revolutionary Claims. 2-Ptn of Robt Butler, containing additional evidence in relation to his claim to compensation for property taken for public use. 3-Additional documents presented relating to the memorial of the legatees of Thos D Anderson, deceased: referred to the Cmte on Foreign Relations. 4-Ordered, that the ptn of John H Kimball, administrator of Eliz Bingham, deceased, on the files of the Senate, be referred to the Cmte on Pensions.

Commission on Claims against Mexico: 1-Memorial of Dr Geo East, claiming for expulsion from Chihuahua, in 1846, for imprisonment, & consequent losses on goods, was ordered to be received. 2-That of Archibald Stevenson, claiming for expulsion from the same place, at the same date, for confinement, & losses in his business as hotel-keeper: ordered to be received. 3-That of Pierre Seuzeneau, administrator of Emile Seuzeneau, claiming for expulsion from Matamoras, in 1846, was also ordered to be received. 4-That of Eli H Hammond, claiming for robbery of horse & mules, within Mexican limits, by Apache Indians, in 1844, was examined. The memorial does not set forth a valid claim against Mexico, under the treaty of Feb 2, 1848, & therefore rejected. 5-Memorial of Danl Davis, withdrawn by leave on Jan 24 last, in order to establish the identity of the memorialist, was re-submitted & filed anew, as authenticated in the particular where it was formerly defective.

Circuit Court of District of Columbia: Wm B Kibby et al vs Hill, ux et al. Trustee's sale of real estate at public auction on Jul 13 next, of lot 6 in square 461, in Wash City, fronting on 7th st, with improvements, consisting of a warehouse. –J M Carlisle, trustee –Dyer & Bro, in Wash City, aucts

Mrd: on May 7, in New Albany, Indiana, by Rev J M Bishop, Francis C Goode, of Cincinnati, [formerly of Wash City,] to Miss Sarah W Crane, of the former place.

Mrd: Jun 11, at **Snow Hill**, Md, by Rev Mr Olmstead, Rev Isaac W K Handy to Miss Sallie S, daughter of late Dr John S Martin.

Mrd: on Jun 18, by Rev S A H Marks, Mr Ezekiel Green Simpson to Miss Mary Ann Sweeny, both of Wash Co.

FRI JUN 21, 1850
Commission on Claims against Mexico: 1-Memorial of Thos B Cotterell, claiming for seizure, of schnr **Essex**, at Matamoras, in 1837, being taken up for consideration, the Board came to an opinion that the claim is a valid one against the Republic of Mexico, & the same was allowed; the amount to be awarded subject to the future action of the Board. 2-That of Danl Davis, claiming for imprisonment as one of the crew of the schnr **Julius Caesar**, the Board came to an opinion that the claim is a valid one against the Republic of Mexico, & the same was allowed; the amount to be awarded subject to the future action of the Board. 3-That of Henry Cheatham, claiming for seizure of his person, on board of schnr **Champion**, in 1837, the Board came to an opinion that the claim is a valid one against the Republic of Mexico, & the same was allowed; the amount to be awarded subject to the future action of the Board.

Appointments by the Pres: 1-Chas R Webster, to be U S Consul for Tehuantepec & Huatalco, in Mexico. 2-Wm Tudor Tucker, to the U S Consul for Bermuda. 3-Edmund Flagg, to be U S Consul for the port of Venice, in Austria. 4-Anson Dart, to be Superintendent of Indian Affairs in the Territory of Oregon.

Mrd: on Jun 19, by Rev C M Butler, John H Semmes, of Wash City, to Eliza Wadsworth, daughter of late Saml Robertson, Purser, U S Navy, formerly of Norfolk, Va.

Died: on Jun 20, Col John Carter, late of S Carolina. His funeral will be from his late residence in Gtwn, on Jun 21, at 4 o'clock.

Died: on Jun 20, in his 42nd year, of apoplexy, Mr Henry T Harvey. His funeral will be this evening, at 5 o'clock, from his late residence, G st, between 12th & 13th.

Died: on Jun 20, Jos Henry, infant son of Eliz & the late John H Smoot, aged 20 months & 6 days. His funeral will be from his mother's residence. on 7th st, this afternoon at 4 o'clock.

Died: on Jun 20, after a short illness of 4 days, John Algoma, infant son of Wm G & Anne Wheatley. His funeral will be from their residence on Capitol Hill, today at 5 P M.

Died: on Jun 19, at *Fort Washington*, Md, Mrs Eliz M, consort of Lt T S Everett, U S A.

Died: on May 5, at *Fort Winnebago*, Capt Gideon Low, formerly of the U S Army, in his 62nd year. Capt Low served as an ofcr of the army during the war of 1812, & was stationed at Green Bay as early as 1828, from whence he removed to *Fort Winnebago* in 1831, where he has since resided.

Mr E Fuller, of Ludlow, Mass, lately died there at the great age of 98 years, while sitting in his chair. The Springfield Daily Post says that shortly before his decease he was gratified in beholding his great-great-great grandchild, for he was the venerable living rep of a 5th generation. He preserved his faculties unimpaired, & died full of years peacefully & still.

Senate: 1-Cmte on Foreign Relations: referred the several memorials relating to the conduct of Capt David Cook in saving the crew of the American ship **Caleb Grimshaw**, reported a joint resolution authorizing the presentation of a gold medal to David Cook, master of the English barque **Sarah**: passed.

We the undersigned certify that on Jun 8, 1846, John Everett appeared before us, with a person whom he represented as his aunt & dearest friend, for the purpose of being bound to Michl McDermott to learn the trade of Coach Painting. He then represented his age, on the 16th day of the then coming Aug, as 16 years. His representing himself to be an orphan boy, & being desirous of being indented as above set forth, we, as Justices of the Peace for Wash, D C, bound him, from his own representations, until the 16th day of Aug, 1851, to M McDermott. –Thos C Donn, J P; B K Morsell, J P

SAT JUN 22, 1850
Stray cows on my premises: one red & white, the other white & black. Owner can get them by coming forward & proving property & pay expenses. –Jas Little, near Bayne's Burial Ground

Cleveland Herald: The steamer **Griffith**, when 14 miles below Cleveland, this Mon, was discovered to be on fire around her smoke pipe, on the main deck, about 3 miles from shore. Capt Roby gave orders for the woodpiles to be thrown over, which was done. The cabin & deck passengers were then jumping over in crowds. The Capt remained on board until the last, with his family, until the flames drove them off. He then threw over his wife, children, mother-in-law, & the barber's wife, & jumped in himself, & remained on the surface a moment with his wife in his arms, when they sank together. The only females saved were the barber's wife & 3 of the steerage passengers, 2 of whom were Germans. On board in all were 330 persons.

Mrd: on Jun 20, by Rev Mr McElfresh, Mr Saml V Hurdle to Miss Grace Calvert, both of Wash City.

Mrd: on Jun 20, by Rev Mr Lanaham, Michl Nash & Miss Ann Maria, 3rd daughter of late Robt Clarke, all of Wash.

Postmaster Gen est'd the following new Post ofcs for week ending Jun 5, 1850.

Ofc	County, State	Postmaster
Oramel	Allegany, N Y	Wm H Hampton
Edenton	St Lawrence, N Y	Benj F Partridge
Chappaqua	Westchester, N Y	David F Brett
Frenchtown	Hunterdon, N J	A G M Prevost
Milford	Hunterdon, N J	N Runkle
Foundryville	Columbia, Pa	J B Dodson
Stony Creek	Somerset, Pa	Jacob Phillippi
Cherry Mills	Sullivan, Pa	Wm M Covanhovan
Windsor	York, Pa	Peter Herman
Ney	Defiance, Ohio	D Cummins
Miltonsburgh	Monroe, Ohio	Vance Johnson
York	Union, Ohio	Henry Tobey
Henries' Ford	Gilmer, Va	Asa Andrews
Barclaysville	Cumberland, N C	Nathan King, jr
Evans' Mills	Chatham, N C	R A Stuart
Packsville	Sumter D, S C	Henry Kelly
Indian Hill	Abbeville D, S C	Thos J Lyons
Holly Grove	Stewart, Geo	Jos Wood
St Illa	Ware, Geo	Burrell Sweat
Mount Hickory	Chattooga, Geo	G B T Maddox
Home Spring	Holmes, Fla	Dempsey Fennell
Big Oak	Kemper, Miss	Eli G Gibson
Fremont	Pontotoc, Miss	H W Young
Bethlehem	Marshall, Miss	H Journegin
Sonet	Natchitoches P, La	Joshua Dyess
Buckhorn	Bienville P, La	Jas D Mines
Spring Creek	Collins, Texas	Jas G Vance
Earpville	Upshur, Texas	S J Taylor
Chappell	Dallas, Ark	C C Terrell
Ashland	Wayne, Tenn	Saml C Mitchell
Lamar	Marion, Tenn	J A Lamb
Rocky House	Sumner, Tenn	O Staley
Milford	Bracken, Ky	Wm Best
White Oak	Bartholomew, Ia	Wm Horobert
Moselle	Jos Daviess, Ill	Jas Beaty
Ulso	Washington, Wis	John Howe
Mapleton	Waukesha, Wis	J M Breek
Timber Creek	Marshall, Iowa	Wm C Smith
Richmond	Washington, Iowa	Jehiel Tyler

Post Ofc Names Changed:
South Greenfield, Saratoga Co, N Y, changed to Middle Grove.
Waterville Corners, Erie Co, N Y, changed to Glenwood.
Cameron, Steuben Co, N Y, changed to North Cameron.
South Cameron, Steuben Co, N Y, changed to Cameron.
Rowland, Hillsdale Co, Mich, changed to Bird.
The Grove, Cook Co, Ill, changed to Northfield.
Northfield, White Co, Ill, changed to Enfield.
Pea Ridge, Marion Co, Geo, changed to Buena Vista.
Forestville, Stevenson Co, Ill, changed to New Erin.
Monroe, Cook Co, Ill, changed to Maine.
Wickliffe, Cook Co, Ill, changed to Palatine.
Palmyra, Cook Co, Ill, changed to Lemont.
Bremen, Dupage Co, Ill, changed to Pierce.
Bachelor's Grove, Cook Co, Ill, changed to Bremen.
Cazenovia, Cook Co, Ill, changed to Leyden.
Flag Creek, Cook Co, Ill, changed to Lyonsville.
Trenton, Cook Co, Ill, changed to Palos.
Cooper's Grove, Cook Co, Ill, changed to New Bremen.

Died: on Jun 21, in Wash City, Geo Royal, son of Rev R R & E M Gurley, aged 7 months & 23 days. His funeral will be from his father's residence on 12th st, this day, at 9 o'clock.

Died: on Jun 20, in Wash City, Wm Robertson, son of G W & Susan D Humphreys, aged 3 months & 2 days.

Died: on Jun 21, after a short but painful illness, in her 5th year, Adelia A C, 2nd daughter of J B & Sarah Jane Morgan. Her funeral will be from the residence of her parents, 12th st, between G & H, Sat, at 10 o'clock.

Commission on Claims against Mexico: 1-Memorial of John Bensley, claiming, as proprietor of a traveling circus company, for the detention, in 1844, at San Louis Potosi, by the Govn'r of that State, of John A Farrington, an apprenticed rider in that company, being taken up for consideration, together with the proofs & documents connected therewith, the Board came to an opinion that the claim as aforesaid is not a valid one against the republic of Mexico, & the same was accordingly not allowed. 2-That of Henry May, administrator of Mrs Ann P Bouldin, deceased, claiming for pension to her son, Capt David H Porter, under the special act of the Mexican Congress, on May 27, 1828, being taken up for consideration, the Board came to an opinion that the claim is a valid one against the republic of Mexico, & was allowed accordingly; the amount to be awarded subject to the future action of the Board.

Freehold Institute-a Boarding School for Boys: located in Freehold, Monmouth Co, N J. –O R Willis, A M Parents & guardians in Washington are referred to Dr Blake, Hon Wm A Newell, & Hon Jas G King, of the House of Reps, of N J.

Excursion to *Piney Point*, on Jul 3, the superb steamer **Baltimore** will leave the wharf at Wash at 8 o'clock A M & Alexandria at 9 A M, & will take in wood at Aquia Creek & arrive at *Piney Point* about 5 P M, & at Balt in the course of the night. Returning, the **Baltimore** will leave Commerce st wharf, Balt, at 4 P M on Tue & Fri, arriving at Alexandria at 10 A M & at Wash at 11 A M on Wed & Sat. Passage from Wash to Marbury's-$1,00; to Piney Point $2.00; to Balt $2.50; excursion tickets to Balt with privilege of returning next afternoon $3.00. Meals & state-rooms extra.
-Geo Mattingly, Agent

The advertisement by J W Busher, Police 5th Ward, inserted in the paper, being calculated to injure my credit, I am obliged to notify the public that the seizure of my goods was a trespass, for which I sued the parties concerned, & which several days later, the goods were ordered to be surrendered to me. I assure my creditors that I am able to keep my engagements. –Timothy Buckley

House of Reps: 1-Ptn of Mrs Mary Deany, widow of Lt Jas A Deany, of the U S infty, who died in the service of the U S, asking for a pension. 2-Ptn of Geo S Kline, of Columbia Co, Pa, asking for a pension on account of disabilities incurred while in the service of the U S in the Mexican War. 3-Two memorials, signed by more than 300 citizens of Pa, protesting against the renewal of the patent granted to Austin & Zebulon Parker for pretended improvement in the reaction waterwheel. 4-Ptn in behalf of the heirs of Maj Wm Jackson, for compensation for services of said Maj Jackson, for compensation for his services as a Deputy Commissary of Forage in the Revolutionary war: referred to the Cmte on Revolutionary Claims. 5-Memorial of F Forrest, a captain in the U S Navy, asking repayment of the amount unjustly & illegally deducted from his pay.

Trustee's sale of square 750, by virtue of a deed of trust dated Apr 16, 1849, recorded in Liber J A S 4, folios 181 thru 183, the subscriber will sell at public sale, on Jun 29, square 750 located between I & K sts north, & 2nd & 3rd sts east. –Chas S Wallach, trustee -C W Boteler, auct

MON JUN 24, 1850
Deaths by drowning: 1-Cyrus Barker, age 20 years, a clerk in a store in Providence, R I, went beyond his depth & drowned. He was an only son. 2-Three boys drowned at Great Falls, N H, on Jun 18. They were the sons of Messrs Joshua Edwards, Saml C Lord, & Andrew Wentworth. 3-Mr Wm H Cocken, a native of Halifax, N S, & a student of law at Phil, was drowned while bathing in the Delaware on Thu, when seized with cramp. 4-Mr D H Klein, of Cumberland, Md, drowned on Sat week whilst bathing in the canal near that town. He was in the prime of manhood & a gentleman of great promise.

The Portsmouth, N H Journal of a recent date records the death in that place, on Jun 9, of John Melcher, the oldest practical printer in N H, & probably in the U S. He was about 90 years of age.

Mathew L Davis, long known from his connexion with politics, died on Fri at the residence of his son, at Manhattanville, near N Y. He had never fully recovered from the stroke of paralysis which he sustained some years since at Wash, though his recent illness was rather the result of his great age than any specific disease. —Cour & Enq

Jacob Hays, the oldest ofcr of the N Y city gov't, & oldest police ofcr in the country, died on Fri. He had no defined disease, but expired from the effects of age & a complete prostration of the powers of nature. He was in his 79th year. Mr Hays was born in Westchester Co, in 1772, he was appointed to ofc in 1801 by Edw Livingston, then Mayor of the city, & has been High Constable of N Y for nearly half a century. —N Y Tribune

Among the passengers on board the steamer **Griffith**, destroyed by fire near Cleveland, was a party of 31 English emigrants, principally from Cambridgeshire. Most were intending to settle in Medina Co, Ohio, where they have relatives & friends. Robt Hall, himself saved, lost his mother, wife, 2 sons, 2 daughters, 2 brothers, & 2 sisters. Wm Waters, himself saved, lost his wife & son. Jos Money, a lad, was saved; his father & 2 sisters lost. The following entire families were lost: Thos Rhodes, wife, 2 sons & 3 daughters; Wm Walker, wife & son; Wm Taylor, wife, 2 sons, & 2 daughters. 150 dead bodies have been found. Arrangements were set on foot at Cleveland, to have all these bodies disinterred, that they might be transported to that city, & be consigned to separate graves.

On Tue, while the steamer **Bay State** was on her route from N Y to Fall River, Mrs Fay, who, with her husband, Rev C H Fay, were among the passengers, was found to be missing. The boat was searched, but she was not to be found. It was ascertained, that while in a partially deranged state of mind, she had jumped overboard & was drowned.

Sea Bathing, Cape Island, N J: Congress Hall, formerly kept by J Miller, is open for the reception of visiters. —W B Miller, proprietor

Mrd: on Jun 4, at Quincy, Ill, by Rev Geo P Giddings, J Chas P De Krafft, U S Navy, to Eliz S, daughter of Albert J Pearson, of Quincy, Ill.

Mrd: on Sat, by Rev John C Smith, Mr Geo C Walker to Miss Mary E Wallingsford, both of PG Co, Md.

Died: on Jun 21, at N Y C, of congestion of the brain, after a sickness of 4 hours, aged 34 years, Mary Eliz, wife of Henry G Wheeler, & daughter of late John Clough, U S Navy.

Died: on Jun 23, Eliza M Cheshire, daughter of late Archibald Cheshire, of Wash City. Her funeral will be from the residence of her mother, 12th st, this day, at 4 o'clock.

Died: on Jun 20, at Oak Hill, Loudoun Co, Va, her late residence, Maria Hester, wife of Saml L Governeur, & daughter of the late Jas Monroe, 5th Pres of the U S.

Died: on Jun 18, at Elkton, Md, Mary Clinton, eldest daughter of Henry C Mackall, aged 8 years, 4 months & 16 days. [Gtwn & Alexandria papers please copy.]

Died: on Sat, at *Sidney*, near this city, [the residence of her brother-in-law, Erasmus J Middleton,] Miss Mgt Eliz Ross, in her 20th year.

O'Ferrall's Boarding House, Bath, Berkeley Springs, Va, will be ready for company by Jul 1. Assisting in the management is his father, Mr John O'Ferrall, who is well known to the public as a boarding-house keeper. The public's respectful servant, P F K O'Ferrall.

Balt-Jun 20: the trial of Capt Wm K Gardiner, of the brig **Frances Jane**, & his mate, Wm Humphreys, indicted for the manslaughter of the cook of the vessel, a colored man, Wm Thomas, alias Thompson, was closed in the U S District Court today by the conviction of both the accused of manslaughter. The evidence exhibited a most cruel treatment towards the deceased. He was forced, under threats, to eat slop & refuse until he actually died from the deleterious & poisonous effects of the abominable filth. [Jun 28th newspaper: sentence of the Capt & his mate: on Tue, at Balt: each to pay a fine of $1,000 & costs, & to be confined in jail for 3 years, & to remain in prison until the fine & costs are paid. This is the full penalty of the law.]

Farm for sale: deed of trust from Robt W Burrows & wife, dated Oct 6, 1849, recorded in Liber J A S, folio 320, land record of Wash Co, D C: public auction on Jul 5, of a part of *Haddock's Hills*, containing 46½ acres. -Edw Swann, trustee -J Martin & Co, aucts

St Mary's Co Court-Court of Equity. Thos J Griffin & Wm J Heard, vs Henry N Kirk & others. Cmplnts having filed their bill for partition or sale of real estate, & it being alleged that Benj Simms & Mary his wife, & Philip Chandler & Virginia his wife, & Jas Nelson & Jane his wife, are non-residents of Md. Same to to appear by the first Monday of Dec next. -Peter W Crain. -Wm T Maddox, clk St Mary's Co Crt

The brig **Excellent**, of New Orleans, arrived at Norfolk on Jun 19, in charge of Lts Bruce & Gansevort. The brig was captured off the coast of Africa, by the U S ship **John Adams**, on suspicion of being engaged in the slave trade. Left the African squadron all healthy.

Notice is given that Johann Baron Von Racknitz, is the owner of 336 square leagues of land, between the Rio Grande & the Nucces, in the former State of Tamaulipas, Mexico, but now within the U S: granted to him by Mexico, & his title is confirmed by the guaranties & assurances contained in article 10 of the treaty of Guadalupe Hidalgo, concluded between the U S & Mexico Feb 2, 1848. –Johann Baron Von Racknitz

Household & kitchen furniture at auction: on Jun 25, at the residence of Mr Tucker, on 1st st. –Edw S Wright, auct

We have this day seen a pamphlet entitled "A Short History of the Washington Gaslight Company," to which is appended the signature of Brown, Giddings & Co. We have never granted to the author the use of the signature of said firm.
–W Giddings -Jas Crutchett

TUE JUN 25, 1850
Killed: Col Dupree was killed recently by his son-in-law, J S Graves, in Hinds Co, Mississippi. The parties had a difference for some time previously. Dupre had pulled Graves from his horse, & cut him several times with a knife, when Graves drew his pistol & shot the colonel. Mr Graves gave himself up to the authorities & was acquitted.

Died: on Jun 24, of consumption, Mrs Susan Henry, of Coshocton, Ohio, wife of Jas Henry, of the same place. Her funeral will take place from the residence of her husband, on 1st st, near the Capitol, this morning, at 10 o'clock.

Trustee's sale of valuable house & lot: in Chancery: Circuit Court of Wash Co, D C. C H Wiltberger et al vs Cain et al. Public auction on Jul 17 of: lot 8, in square 728, in Wash City, & part of lot 7 in square 728, adjoining said lot 8, fronting 24 feet on East Capitol st, with a 3 story brick house & back bldg. –Chas H Wilterger, trustee

Senate: 1-Cmte on Indian Affairs: memorial of Susan Coody & others, asking indemnity for losses sustained by depredations committed by U S troops, submitted a favorable report: ordered to be printed. 2-Cmte on Private Land Claims: ptn & papers of Priscilla *Prewett, submitted a report, which was ordered to be printed, with a bill for the relief of the heirs & reps of Uriah *Prewitt, deceased. [*2 splgs.]

WED JUN 26, 1850
Wash Corp: 1-Cmte on Unfinished Business: ptn of J W Nairn: referred to the Cmte of Claims. 2-Ptn of B Jose & others, for paving an alley in square 168: referred to the cmte on Improvements. 3-Ptn of A Lehmann, praying remission of a fine: referred to the Cmte of Claims. 4-Act for the relief of Wm Dowling: referred to the Cmte on Improvements. 5-Ptn of Chas J Wise, praying indemnity for the loss of a horse which fell into the canal from one of the bridges: referred to the Cmte of Claims. 6-Act for the relief of W W McCreery: referred to the Cmte on Police. 7-Ptn of S A Peugh, for the improvement of a part of 7th st east: referred to the Cmte on Improvements.
8-<u>Nominations from the Mayor</u>:
*Jos Radcliff, 1st Clerk
*W E Howard, 2nd Clerk
*Jas H Carlisle, Atty
*Jacob Kleiber, Messenger
*Geo Bean, Inspector of Tobacco
*Jacob Kleiber, Inspector of Flour & Salted Provisions.
*Jas A Tait, Com'r of the western section of the Canal
Jos Cross, Com'r of the eastern section
*Caleb Buckingham, Inspector of Fire Apparatus

*Chas A Davis, *Geo H Fulmer, & Theodore *Wheeler, Com'rs of the Asylum *Dr Geo M Dove, Physician to the Asylum

Police Constables:
*O E Hazard
*W H Barnaclo
*J F Wollard
*E G Handy
*R R Burr
*Wm Martin

*W H Mulloy
*Jas M Busher
*Josiah Adams
Ignatius Howe
John Magar
Jas Ennis

Com'rs of the Markets:
Ignatius Mudd
Wm Orme
John H Goddard
Leonard Storm

Edw Queen
Lemuel Barnes
Geo H Fulmer

Clerks of the Markets:
*Fielder B Poston
*John Waters
*Hy B Robertson

*Peter Little
*Wm B Wilson

Inspectors & Measurers of Lumber:
*Wm G Deale
*Benj Bean
*Wm Burroughs

*John W Ferguson
*John G Robinson
*Jesse Plowman

Wood Corders & Coal Measurers:
*Saml Kilman
*Richd Wimsatt
Henry Haliday

*John B Ferguson
Washington Brunner

Gaugers & Inspectors: *Elexius Simms & *Florian Hits
Measurer of Grain, Bran, Shorts, & Shipstuff: *John B Ferguson.
Com'rs of the West Burial Ground: *Wm Wilson, *John Wilson, & *John C Harkness. *Guy Graham, Sexton.
Com'rs of the East Burial Ground: *John P Ingle & *F Y Naylor. *Thos J Barrett, Sexton.

Chimney Sweeps:
*John Lewis
*Jas Burgess
*Roger Moffett

*W A Robinson
N B Wilkerson
John Davis

Scavengers:
*Jas Hollidge
*W Johnson
*Jas Hollidge
*Saml Curson
*Thos Greaves

*Hanson Brown
*G T McGlue
*John Cox
*John Downs

[*Jul 8th newspaper: those confirmed.]

House of Reps: 1-Papers relating to the claim of Wm Y Hansell, Wm H Underwood, & the legal reps of Saml Rockwell, were withdrawn from the files of the House for the purpose of reference to the Executive Dept.

Senate: 1-Cmte of Claims: ptn of Alex'r Y P Garnet, assist surgeon U S navy, asking compensation for extra services: passed to a second reading. 2-Memorial of D L Dix, asking a grant of public land for the establishment of an asylum for the indigent curable & incurable insane in the U S.

Appointments by the Pres: 1-Asa R Carter, to be Receiver of Public Moneys at Augusta, Miss. 2-Willis H Gibson to be U S Marshal for the Northern District of Ala. 3-Anson G Henry, of Ill, & Henry H Spaulding, of Oregon, to be Indian Agents for the Territory of Oregon. 4-John P Gaines, Beverly S Allen, & Alonzo H Skinner, to be Com'rs to negotiate treaties with the Indian tribes in Oregon.

Oregon: Maj J S Hathaway, U S A, in a fit of mental derangement, had attempted to commit suicide by cutting his throat. Hopes were entertained that the wound inflicted would not prove mortal.

House of Reps: 1-Memorial of Mrs Rachel Maule: asking indemnity for French spoliations prior to 1800. 2-Ptn of Timothy Cavan for an increase of pension.

Real Green Turtle just received from Nassau, N P, via Balt: a lot of the finest real Green Turtle which has been in this city this season, will be served up in soup & steaks, in best style. —Wm F Benter, Wash Hall, corner of 6th & Pa ave

Household & kitchen furniture at auction: on Jun 28, at the residence of Mrs Whitman, on N J ave, 2nd hours south of the Capitol. -Dyer & Brother, aucts

$3 reward to whoever will return to me a good sized black & white milch cow, that left my place Jun 22. —Julius A Peters, Wine Store, Pa ave, near 10th st

U S Patent ofc-Petition of W Schley, adm of John Schley, deceased, of Augusta, Ga, extension of patent which expires Oct 27, 1850: improvement in picking & breaking wool.

THU JUN 27, 1850
Indiana State Journal: the suit of John Norris, of Boone Co, Ky, vs Leander B Newton, E B Crocker, & 7 others, for the recovery of damages for aiding & abetting the escape of slaves, after more than a week's investigation before the Circuit Court of the U S, was determined on Wed last in favor of the plntf. A verdict of $2,856 was given by the jury against the dfndnts, as the value of the slaves & other damages.

For sale: a negro woman who has 4 years & 6 months to serve as a slave. She is perfectly honest, a good cook, chambermaid, or nurse. Apply to Mrs Inch, Navy Yard, or to Murray & Semmes, Pa ave.

Appointments by the Pres:
Abbott Lawrence, to be Envoy Extra & Minister Pleni of the U S at the Court of the United Kingdom of Great Britain & Ireland.
Bailie Peyton, to be Envoy Extra & Minister Pleni of the U S to the Republic of Chili.
Geo P Marsh, to the Minister Resident of the U S at Constantinople.
Isaac Nevitt Steele, to be Charge d'Affaires of the U S to the Republic of Venezuela.
Julius C Kretschmar, to be U S Consul for the port of Nassau, in the island of New Providence.
Henry L Norris, to be U S Consul for the port of Para, in Brazil.
Nicholas A McClure, to be U S Consul for the port of Acapulco, in Mexico.
John C B Davis, to the Sec of the Legation of the U S near her Britannic Majesty.
Jesse B Holman, to be Sec of the Legation U S at Santiago de Chili.
Willis H Gibson, to be U S Marshal for the northern district of Alabama.
Edw Wm Johnston to be Sec to the Board of Com'rs on Mexican Claims.
John D Barclay & Wm McNeir to be Justices of the Peace, Wash Co.

Christian Meadows & Wm Warburton, alias Bristol Bill, were sentenced to 10 years each in the State prison at Danville, Vt, on Fri, for conspiring to rob the bank. The moment the sentence was announced Bristol Bill rose from his seat behind the bar, reached over, & stabbed Wm N Davis, in the neck, inflicting a severe but not mortal wound. Mr Davis had been engaged as one of the counsel for the prosecution, & Bill declared that it was his intention to kill him.

Died: on Jun 16, at Key West, of consumption, Lt J Harkins, U S Army, one of the members of the Cuba expedition. [Jul 29th newspaper: correction: we are requested, by proper authority, to correct the statement that Mr Harkins belonged to the U S Army. There is no ofcr of that name borne on the Army rolls.]

There still remains in Florida 22 companies of Artl. 5 companies of the 2nd Artl are at Indian river, commanded by Maj Lowd; one company of 2nd Artl at Miamie river, commanded by Maj Woodbridge; 4 companies of 3rd Artl, under Col Steptoe, are ordered to *Fort Meade*, where there are now 3 companies of the 1st Artl, under command of Capt Vodges; 2 companies of the 4th at Chokonickla, commanded by Capt Roberts; 2 companies of the 4th Artl at *Fort Hamer*, commanded by Maj Morris; one company of the 4th Artl at Charlotte Harbor, commanded by Brevet Capt Rains; one company [mounted] of the 4th Artl at *Fort Meade*, commanded by Capt Getty; & 3 companies of Artl at Calockahatche, commanded by Maj Ridgely. The Indians were coming in slowly, & in the course of a few months, it is hoped that they will be induced to emigrate. Gen Twiggs left Tampa on Jun 13, & is now on a brief visit to this city.

Hazelfield for sale: valuable farm in Jefferson Co, Va, on the public road from Charlestown to Martinsburg: 600 acres of land: large dwlg house, out-houses, & stabling. Mr Montg Slemons, living on the farm, will show it. Address J R Tucker, Winchester, Va, or the subscriber at Kerneysville, Jefferson Co, Va. –H Tudor Tucker, Agent for Mrs A E Tucker.

Commission on Claims against Mexico: 1-Memorial & supplementary memorial of Geo W Van Stavoren, claiming for expulsion from Tampico in 1846, were submitted, examined, ordered to be received.

FRI JUN 28, 1850

An elderly gentleman named McEntire was instantly killed at Hagerstown on Tue by the premature explosion of a blast of powder used in quarrying stones.

Mr Geo Burall, a brakesman on one of the burden trains on the Balt & Ohio Railroad, was killed on Fri last at Paterson's Creek. He was getting on the cars while they were in motion, missed his aim & fell, when the cars passed over his body, killing him instantly.

In Harsimus, N Y, on Sun, Thos Doyle was killed by lightning. He was lying on a bed, in the same room with 2 other persons.

Died: in Troy N Y, Jun 24, Sarah French Bradley, widow of Wm Bradley, age 78 years.

Died: Gen Zacharias Huntington, of Norwich, Conn, age 86, on Jun 23. He was one of the oldest & most respected citizens of Norwich. He died without any apparent disease, simply from exhaustion of the vital powers-the breaking up of the worn-out machinery, of life. He was the worthy sire of that worthy son whom, a little more than 2 years since, we were called to mourn, snatched by death, from his place in the Nat'l Senate, & the wide sphere of influence which he filled in his native State.

On Mon last, Joab C Bartlett, postmaster at Grout's Corner, in Montague, Franklin Co, was brought before Chas L Woodbury, U S Com'r, to answer to allegedly stealing 2 letters, said letters containing small sums of money. The dfndnt waived an examination, &, in default of bail in $10,000, was committed to answer at the term of the District Court, which will commence today. –Boston Post [Jul 27th newspaper: Bartlett sentenced to 10 years' confinement in jail.]

Senate: 1-Memorial of the heirs of Benj Marvin, asking compensation for his services in the Revolutionary war: referred to the Cmte on Revolutionary Claims. 2-Additional document submitted in relation to the claim of the legal reps of Rinaldo Johnson: referred to the Cmte of Claims.

Mr Fiorentino & M Amader Achard, men of celebrity in the literary circle of Paris, fought a duel not long since, in which the latter received a bullet in his chest. A fatal result was apprehended.

Appointments by the Pres: 1-Wm M King, Surveyor & Inspector of the Revenue at Portland, Oregon. 2-Wm Porter, Surveyor & Inspector of the Revenue at Nesqually, Oregon.

Died: on Jun 23, at Stirling, Cayuga Co, N Y, Thos Phoenix, formerly Dist Atty of N Y, in his 71st year.

Postmaster Gen has est'd the following new Post Ofcs for the week ending Jun 22, 1850.

Ofc	County, State	Postmaster
Rumford Point	Oxford, Me	Otis C Bolster
Clifton	Penobscot, Me	Thos Parks
Goshen	Addison, Vt	John Caper
North Wilson	Fairfield, Ct	Lewis Olmstead
Scarsdale	Westchester, N Y	Wm S Popham
Gypsum	Ontario, N Y	Marcus Persons
Estelville	Atlantic, N J	M Hogan
Port Perry	Alleghany, Pa	Wm J Morrison
Rapho	Lancaster, Pa	F Arford
Wellsville	York, Pa	Abraham Wells, jr
Hickory Hill	Chester, Pa	Jas B McDowell
Bridgeville	Dorchester, Md	I W C Nicols
Mahala	Adams, Ohio	David Naylor
Woodington	Darke, Ohio	Sam T Mendenhall
Big Plain	Madison, Ohio	Wm H Holmes
Bear Creek	Montg, Ohio	Michl Neff
Dunlevy	Warren, Ohio	Benj A Stokes
Redding's Mills	Berrien, Mich	Benj Redding

Names Changed: Wilsonville, Adams Co, Pa, changed to Bendersville.
St Clair, Bedford Co, Pa, changed to Saint Clairsville.
Norwegian, Schuylkill Co, Pa, changed to Saint Clair.

Commission on Claims against Mexico: 1-Memorial of Thos O Larkin, late U S Consul at Monterey of Calif, claiming for supplies furnished to the Mexican Gov't of that territory in 1845 & 1846, the amount of which, war meantime intervening, he could not recover from the Mexican Gov't, was submitted & ordered to be received. 2-Memorial of Jas Kelley, vessel's mate, claiming for imprisonment & consequent loss of property at Monterey of Calif in 1840, together with the proofs & documents connected therewith, came to an opinion that the claim is a valid one against the Republic of Mexico; the same was allowed accordingly, the amount to be awarded subject to the future action of the Board.

Died: on Jun 24, in Troy, N Y, Mrs Sarah French Bradley, widow of Wm Bradley, in her 78th year.

The Carlist refugee, Cabrera, has married in London a daughter of R Vaughan Richards, a lady of immense fortune.

$100 reward for runaway negro boy Frank Roshier, 19 or 20; has relations at Mr Thos Osborn's & Mr Horatio C Scott's, near Marlborough. –Z B Beall, living near Upper Marlborough, PG Co, Md

SAT JUN 29, 1850
Mr E J Thomas, merchant of N Y, died at Saratoga Springs, Fri last. While arranging for his return home, he fell & instantly expired. He was married on Jun 5, to a daughter of Bishop Brownell, & was on the bridal tour with his wife, when suddenly snatched from life.

Senate: 1-Joint resolution for the relief of Chas F Sibbald: this is a decision in regard to a land title. This individual goes upon land which the Gov't claims. He erects mills, in order to cut off the timber & send it to market. The Gov't drove away this individual. Ultimately he succeeded in getting a decision of the court in favor of the claim he set up, to a portion of the lands, at least. Congress passed an act authorizing the settlement & payment of his claim. It was adjudicated by the comptroller under the act of Congress. And he comes forward now, not presenting additional evidence, & asking adjudication on that evidence, but he asks that a kind of board shall be created in order to settle this claim. Mr Sibbald was a prosperous merchant at Phil. He let this business, & invested all his capital in these lands, erecting saw mills, & getting vessels to carry on an extensive business in Florida. All the acts passed for his relief, have been for the purpose of giving him indemnity for the loss of his sawmill, & the actual loss sustained by the wrongful interference of the Gov't. Resolution laid on the table.

Dr Jas Gunnell, jr, offers his professional services to the citizens of Wash. Ofc on 7th st, below D st south.

Marshal's sale: by writ of fieri facias: public sale on Jul 9, on the premises, Pa ave, between 17th & 18th sts, of household & kitchen furniture seized & levied upon as the property of Lemuel Williams, & will be sold to satisfy judicials 77 to Oct Term, 1849, ___ Williams & Kennedy vs Lemuel Williams. –R Wallach, Marshal District of Columbia

Died: on Jun 28, Jane, infant daughter of Southey S & Mary Ann Parker, aged 11 months & 3 days. Her funeral will be at their residence, H st between 21st & 22nd sts, this afternoon, at 4 o'clock.

By a Board of Army Surgeons convened on May 15, in N Y C, for examination of Assist Surgeons for promotion & of applicants for appointment to the Medical Staff of the Army, Assist Surgeons Chas H Laub, Richd H Coolidge, & Alex'r S Wotherspoon were examined & found qualified for the promotion. The following applicants for the appointment of Assist Surgeons in the Army were also examined & approved:
Saml W Crawford, Pa   Chas Page, Va
Wm H Tingley, Pa   Archibald Taylor, Va
John J Milhau, N Y   Chas Sutherland, Pa
Aquila T Ridgely, La

House of Reps: 1-Memorial of Geo Rogers, of N Y, offering to the Congress of the U S, for purchase, the painting, by Jas Burns, of the apotheosis of Geo Washington.

Commission on Claims against Mexico: 1-The Board resumed the consideration of several cases partially considered: & came to an opinion that the claims of John P Schatzell, French Strother, Joachim Fox, Henry Gisner, Henry Breeze, Adolphe Seuzeneau, Geo S Miller, Pierre Seuzeneau, administrator of Emile Seuzeneau, Sidney Udall, Elihu D Smith, Geo East, & Archibald Stevinson are valid claims against the Republic of Mexico, & allowed the same accordingly; the amounts to be awarded to the said claimants subject to the future action of the Board.

MON JUL 1, 1850
The Grand Jury in the U S District Court returned true bills of indictment yesterday, for violation of the Act of Congress of 1818, by setting on foot an expedition against the Island of Cuba, against John A Quitman, [Govn'r of Mississippi,] Judge Cotesworth Pinckney Smith, [of the Supreme Court of Mississippi,] John Henderson, [late Senator from that State,] J L O'Sullivan, [late editor of the Democratic Review, & son of a former Minister to Spain,] John F Pickett, [late Consul at Turks' Island,] Theodore O'Hara, [late Major in the U S Army,] C R Wheate, Peter Smith, A Gonzalez, Thos Theodore Hawkins, W H Bell, N J Bunch, L J Sigur, [State Senator] Donatien Augustin, Brig Gen, & cmder of the Legion, & Gen Narciso Lopez. Writs were issued for the arrest of the parties, most of whom are absent from the city. Strong efforts will be made to bring these cases to trial before the adjournment of the court.

Another massacre on the plains: supposed by the Apache Indians. Mr Ardinger, just in from Santa Fe, brought the mail. At Wagon Mound, this side of Moro, the first American settlement, the bodies of 10 Americans were found, pierced with bullets & arrows. From papers in their pockets it was ascertained that the party consisted of Messrs T W Flourney, Benj Shaw, John Duty, Moses Golstein, Clay, Williams, Hendrickson, Freeman, & others not recognized.

$400 reward for runaway negro men John Ellis, 23, & Dick Generee, 26. –Sarah Ann Talburtt, admx of Jesse Talburtt, deceased

Capt Josiah Sturgis, long known as an efficient ofcr of the revenue service, & for many years past engaged on the Boston station, died suddenly on board the cutter **Hamilton**, in that harbor, on Fri last. He had no indication of previous illness, & is supposed to have died from disease of the heart.

Criminal Court-Wash: last Fri, Mary McPherson, alias Mary Ennis, an old offender, was found guilty of larceny, & sentenced to 1 year in the penitentiary.

Mr Thorn's son, who was shot by a negro last Thu, continues in critical condition. The slug lodged in the boy's groin has not been extracted.

Died: on Jun 27, in Montg, Ala, Mrs Mary Hilliard, mother of Hon Henry W Hilliard, in her 70th year.

For sale: farm in Augusta Co, near Staunton, Va, 1,010 acres, called **Bearwallow**, the estate of the late Chapman Johnson. Contains 2 dwlg houses, & all necessary out-bldgs. It is at present occupied by Mr Simpson F Taylor as tenant. Wm B Johnson, brother of Geo Nicolson Johnson, is at Staunton. -Geo Nicolson Johnson, for himself & other devises of C Johnson, deceased.

Orphans Court of Wash Co, D C. Letters of administration on the personal estate of Henry T Harvey, late of Wash Co, deceased. -Mary Ann Harvey, Michael R Combs, adms

TUE JUL 2, 1850
Appointment by the Pres: Jonas B Ellis, to be Warden of the Penitentiary for the District of Columbia.

Charlotteville Advocate: Maj Edmund Broadus died at his residence, at the Univ of Va, on the 27th ult, aged 60 years. He was a resident of Culpeper until the fall of 1846, & had represented that county in the House of Delegates for 10 or 12 years.

Senate: 1-Memorial of G Huntington, asking the enactment of an international copy right law: referred to the Cmte on Patents & the Patent Ofc. 2-Documents submitted in relation to the claim of John R Pritchard to an increase of pension: referred to the Cmte on Pensions. 3-Adverse reports lying over, taken up & concurred in: from the Cmte on Public Lands: memorial of Jas J Stark; the ptn of settlers on townships 43 & 44, in Missouri; & the ptn of Jacob W Cummins. From the Cmte on Pensions: ptn of Peter Grover; the documents relating to the claim of Chas Larrabee; & the ptn of Mary Farrar. From the Cmte of Claims: ptn of Asa Andrews; & ptn of Eugene Vanness & Jno M Brush, executors of Nehemiah Brush. From the Cmte on the Judiciary: ptn of Jno P Skinner & the legal reps of Isaac Greene, asking to be relieved from a judgment obtained against them as sureties for Thos Emerson, late pension agent for Vermont.

Mrd: on Jun 11, by Rev W D Dutton, Rev Hugh A Brown, of Charlotte Co, Va to Miss Matilda C Little, of Winchester, Va, daughter of late Jas Little.

Mrd: on Jun 27, by Rev Jas B Donelan, Mr John T Holohan to Miss Eliza Jane Smith, all of Wash City.

Died: on Jul 1, John D Lee, artist. His funeral will be at house of Mr Jas O'Bryon, on D st, between 12th & 13th sts, this afternoon, at 4½ o'clock. [I O O F notice of same.]

Died: on Jun 29, in Wash City, Wm Johns, in his 49th year.

Salubria for sale: fine country seat on the Leesburg Turnpike, adjoining the first toll gate, 5 miles from Gtwn: contains 53 acres; improvements are all new, commodious, & tasteful. The dwlg is a Grecian Doric Cottage, 53 feet front & 48 feet deep. Apply to J F Callan, E & 7th sts.

WED JUL 3, 1850

Appointments by the Pres: 1-Luke Lea, of Mississippi, to be Com'r of Indian Affairs, vice Orlando Brown, resigned. 2-Geo P Fisher, of D C, to be Com'r under the act of Congress approved Mar 29, 1850, entitled "An act to carry into effect the Convention between the U S & the Emperor of Brazil, of Jan 27, 1849." 2-Philip A Searle, of N Y, to be Clerk to act under the Commission in the performance of the duties prescribed by the same act as above.

Cmdor Wm B Shubrick, recently returned from the command of the Pacific Squadron, has been appointed to command the Navy Yard at Phil, & leaves the city this day to assume that command.

On Sat last a locomotive engine exploded a short distance above Clapville, Mass, & John Managin, the engineer, was instantly killed.

For rent: commodious & well furnished dwlg on N Y ave, between 9th & 10th sts. The house is new & contains 9 chambers, exclusive of dining room, parlor, & kitchen, with good cellar. Inquire of Jos Bryan.

Senate: 1-Ptn of Henrietta Elsey, widow of a deceased surgeon in the army, asking to be allowed a pension: referred to the Cmte on Pensions. 2-Cmte on Military Affairs: memorial of Ward B Burnet, asking the repayment of the expenses incurred by the Common Council of N Y C in raising volunteers: passed to a second reading. 3-Resolution for the relief of Chas F Sibbald: laid on the table.

Mr Wm H Downey, formerly editor of the Chambersburg Whig, died very suddenly at his residence, near Charlestown, Jefferson Co, Va, on Tue last, of an attack of apoplexy.

Household & kitchen furniture at auction: Jul 11, at the residence of E W Johnson, on F st, opposite the Patent Ofc. –Dyer & Brother, aucts

Criminal Court-Wash-Monday. 1-Wm Noland found guilty of stealing a parcel of leather, the property of J Payne, of Gtwn: sentenced to 2 years' imprisonment in the penitentiary. 2-Jos Goddard, guilty of receiving stolen goods: sentenced to 3 months in jail. 3-Nelson Simms & Lewis Hanks were acquitted of receiving stolen goods. 4-Yesterday, Archibald Sterrett, a youth, was found guilty of stealing $260, the property of Wm Benter, but recommended to the mercy of the Court. 5-Patrick Rady found guilty of setting fire to the blacksmith's shop of Saml Bryan. 6-Jos S Brown, negro boy, found guilty of arson, in setting fire to a stable in the First Ward.

Mrd: on Jul 1, in Wash, by Rev Mr Butler, Thos Pattison, U S Navy, to Miss Serafina Catalina Webster, of Matanzas, Cuba.

Died: on Jun 28, at Bladensburg, Md, Mary Anna, only child of Thos & Milicent Catharine Granger, aged 19 months & 1 day.

In Chancery: Jun 7, 1850: Ratify sale of the property in the cause of Jas Dundas & others, against Jas W McCulloh & Geo Templeman & others, made & reported by the trustee, Richd Smith, be ratified & confirmed. The amount of sales: $7,053.59½.
–Louis Gassaway, Reg Cur Can

THU JUL 4, 1850

Mount Vernon-from the Custis recollections & private memoirs of the life & character of Washington. Our tableau opens in 1753, when Washington crosses the threshold of *Mount Vernon*; in 1754 he was entrusted with the defence of the frontier of his native colony. Having attracted the notice of Gen Braddock, the provincial soldier in 1755 was requested by the British veteran to accompany the latter in the ill-fated expedition to **Fort Du Quesne**. At the close of the Seven Year's War, the provincial colonel becomes a private citizen, & returns to *Mount Vernon*. In 1759, our tableau exhibits a gay & joyous scene, while the old halls ring against with the reception of a bridal party, & Washington enters *Mount Vernon* a prosperous & happy bridegroom. Many happy years glide happily along until 1774, when Patrick Henry & Edmund Pendleton arrive at *Mount Vernon*. They are there to accompany Washington to the first Congress where the soldier had been called by the voice of the country, to change the duties of the field for those of the Senate house. In 1775, while a member of the first Congress, Washington is appointed to command in chief the armies of the Colonies, then assembling to do battle for the rights & liberties of unborn generations. For 6 years his home is in the field. In 1781 the long deserted halls of *Mount Vernon* are animated by the presence of the Cmder in Chief of the combined armies of America & France, accompanied by the Count de Rochambeau & a brilliant suite, who halt but for a single day, being en route for Yorktown. In 1783 the war had ended. In 1784 Lafayette bids adieu to Washington at *Mount Vernon*. Four years passed in the employments of agriculture, & in social & domestic intercourse. In 1787, his country calls upon her chosen son to leave the tranquil shade of *Mount Vernon*. In 1789 Mr Secretary Thomson declares he is charged, by the Congress then assembled in N Y, with the duty of announcing to Geo Washington, a private citizen, his election to the Presidency of the U S of America.

Yesterday, Mr Chas Wright, carpenter, at work on the roof of the new Trinity Church, at C & 3rd sts, fell about 50 feet. He is a worthy citizen, & owes his life to his presence of mind in seizing hold of a rope, which in some measure broke the force of the fall. He is very seriously injured, though we believe none of his bones are broken.

Senate: 1-Memorial of Jas F Babcock, administrator of the estate of Maj Fred'k D Mills, setting forth that Mills was a major in the 15th regt of infty, & that he was killed at the battle of Cherubuco, before the gates of Mexico, & that his horse, equipments, apparel, & other property fell into the hands of the enemy at the time of his death, for which the administrator seeks compensation: referred to the Cmte of Claims. 2-Ptn of Jonathan D Roberts, administrator of Olive Folsom, widow of a Revolutionary soldier, asking to be allowed arrears of pension: referred to the Cmte on Pensions.

A mail robber, Chas M Gearhart, was convicted last week at Wmsport, Pa, & sentenced to 10 years in the penitentiary. Another mail robber, Geo Baldwin, of Susquehanna Co, Pa, formerly postmaster at Great Bend, was convicted on the charge of embezzlement of letters containing money from the U S mail, & on Fri last sentenced to 10 years in the penitentiary.

Richd L Mackall promoted to the situation of Chief Clerk in the ofc of the 4th Auditor of the Treasury, which was made vacant on Jul 1 by the resignation of Thos H Gilliss. Mr Gilliss was appointed Principal Chief in the ofc of the Accountant of the Navy upon its establishment in 1798. In 1817, that ofc was abolished, & the accounts of the Navy were directed to be settled in the Treasury Dept, by an ofcr constituted for that purpose, to be called the 4th Auditor of the Treasury, Mr Gilliss was made the Chief Clerk in the new ofc, & continued to hold the same place until his recent withdrawal from the public service in consequence of his great age. Less that 2 months more would have completed the 52nd year of his appointment. –Republic

Died: on Jul 3, in Gtwn, D C, after a protracted indisposition of nervous debility, in her 64th year, Mrs Christiana Sothoron, consort of Dr Wm Sothoron. Her funeral will be from her late residence on Bridge st, this afternoon, at 5 o'clock.

Drowned: on Jul 4, while bathing in the Potomac River, Wm F Tehan, S J, Prof at Gtwn College.

Suicide: a young man, Geo S White, from Loudoun Co, Va, committed suicide on Sunday last, by throwing himself into Cahokia Creek, near Morris' Mills, on the opposite side of the river. He had arrived in this city on Jun 29. –St Louis Int, 21st

House of Reps: 1-Memorial from Miss T L Dix for a grant of land. Mr Carter objected to presenting the memorial. 2-By unanimous consent, the ptn & papers in the case of Eleanor Washburn were withdrawn from the files of the House, for the purpose of reference to the Pension Ofc.

Household & kitchen furniture at auction: on Jul 8, at the residence of N H Starbuck, on F st, between 13th & 14th sts. –C W Boteler, auct

Criminal Court-Wash-yesterday. 1-Luther Johnson found not guilty of stealing jewelry & handkerchiefs. 2-Geo W Wright, charged with the same offence, found not guilty.

Household & kitchen furniture at auction: on Jul 9, at the residence of Orlando Brown, late Com'r of Indian Affairs, on Pa ave, between 14th & 15th sts. –Dyer & Brother, aucts

Boarding: Miss Briscoe, corner of Pa ave & 7th sts, over Shuster's dry goods store. Single gentlemen or families accommodated.

SAT JUL 6, 1850
Two young students of Oglethrope Univ, near Milledgeville, one named Luce, the other McCutchen, were instantly killed on Jun 26, by lightning.

Postmaster Gen has established the following Post Ofcs for week ending Jun 29, 1850.

Ofc	County, State	Postmaster
Flume	Grafton, N H	Richd Taft
Green Bank	Burlington, N J	Saml Sappington
Greenwood Furnace	Huntingdon, Pa	Wm H Benner
Nelsonport	Potter, Pa	Mason Nelson
Clayton	Berks, Pa	A B Bechtel
Steuben	Crawford, Pa	Isaac M Stedman
Woodvale	Fayette, Pa	Wm Walker
Porter	Jefferson, Pa	Henry Snyder
Simpsonville	Anne Arundel, Md	Chas Simpson
Benevola	Washington, Md	Jon Newcomer, jr
Berlin X Roads	Jackson, Ohio	L W Salmens
North Star	Darke, Ohio	John M Houston
Breck	Darke, Ohio	Josiah Johnson
Meadow Branch	Jackson, Ohio	Saml S Vandevort
Oetia	Mercer, Ohio	Jonas P Wood
Ridgeway	Muskingum, Ohio	Noah M Grandstaff
F_at	Pike, Ohio	David Sampson
Sampson	Darke, Ohio	Jas Battem
Culver Creek	Delaware, Ohio	Fred'k Gemmill
Summit	Summit, Ohio	Geo W Marsh
So Assyria	Barry, Mich	Saml H Young
Gun Lake	Barry, Mich	Nathan Barlow
Ecorce	Wayne, Mich	David Le Blanc
Cedar Springs	Wythe, Va	J G Keesling
Cox's Mills	Gilmer, Va	John S Cox
Summerville	Cumberland, N C	Jas W Cotton
Stony Fork	Wataga, N C	Alfred Miller
Auman's Hill	Montg, N C	John J Leach
Little Mills	Richmond, N C	J T Andrews
Campobella	Spartanburg D, S C	David Patton
Songtown	Fairfield D, S C	John E Peay
Bee Tree	Kenshaw D, S C	Wm L Pickett
Merritt's Bridge	Lexington, S C	Chas Plunkett
Thickety Ford	Spartanburg, S C	Wm Lipscomb
Euharley	Case, Geo	A G Burge
Seven Island	Butts, Geo	Leroy M Wilson
Fancy Hill	Murray, Geo	M J Murphy
Straight Neck	Cherekee, Ala	Saml M Barkley
Slossburg	Lauderdale, Ala	Wm Sloss

Green Hill	Lauderdale, Ala	Chas Mckluskey
Post Oak	Valla Busha, Miss	Jordan Williams
Collamer	Copiah, Miss	Clarke Spears
Yellowbush	Chichasaw, Miss	Edw W Lane
New River	Columbia, Florida	Wm Z Herndon
Bossier Point	Bossier P, La	Richd Combs
Connell's X Rds	Bossier P, La	T A Snider
Rochester	Jackson, La	Wm B McDonald
Cut Off	Drew, Ark	Peter Farquhar
Anvil	Clark, Ark	L J Evans
Bartson	Humphreys, Tenn	J B Adams
Sylco	Polk, Tenn	A McKissic
Temp'ance Hall	De Kalb, Tenn	A M Robertson
Chesterfield	Grundy, Tenn	Stephen Marlow
Obian	Hickman, Ky	A Wetherford
Dallasburg	Owen, Ky	R Vallandingham
Beechey Mire	Union, Ia	Robt G Kercheval
Fairfax	Monroe, Ia	Isaac Woolery
Clermont	Richmond, Ill	O A Battson
Steady Run	Keokuk, Iowa	Geo Fell
Salt Creek	Davis, Iowa	F C Humble
Francis Creek	Manitoowoc, Wis	Jos Lamerre
Pheasant Bran'h	Dane, Wis	Wm Darling
Arena	Iowa, Wis	C W Matthews
Waldwick	Iowa, Wis	Ezra A Hall

Names Changed:
Councills Store, Ashe Co, N C, changed to Boone.
Lawrenceville, Montg Co, N C, changed to Swift Island.
Bridgeville, Coffee Co, Ala, changed to Bentonville.
Gim Wolf, Marshall Co, Miss, changed to Tiro.
Cash, St Francis Co, Ark, changed to Gage's Point.
Gum Creek, Cherokee Co, Texas, changed to Jacksonville.
Bayard, Shelby Co, Ky, changed to Eminence.
Pottsville, Wash Co, Ky, changed to Bakers.
Quarles, Racine Co, Wis, changed to Union House.

Dr John W Webster confesses to the murder of Dr Geo Parkman. On Nov 23rd he came into the laboratory & immediately said: Are you ready for me, sir? Have you got the money? I replied, no, Dr Parkman, & stated my condition. He would not listen to me. I could not stop him and soon my temper was up. I seized a stick of wood that was at hand & gave him a blow on the side of his head. He fell instantly upon the pavement and did not move. I got some ammonia & applied it to his nose, but without effect. I tried to recuscitate him, but found he was absolutely dead. *The confession goes on to state the manner in which the body was dismembered, but these details are so horrible that we must be excused from copying them. *Copied as written in the newspaper.

Senate: 1-Additional documents relating to the ptn of the heirs & reps of Wm Somerville: referred to the Cmte of Claims. 2-Cmte on Printing: referred the motion to print the Report of the Sec of War calling for Lt W H C Whitney's reconnoissances of the western front of Texas, reported in favor of printing same: agreed to. 3-Cmte of Claims: memorial & documents of Wm P Wallace & Co, reported a bill for the relief of Wm P Wallace & Jos R McFadden: passed to a second reading. Same cmte: memorial of Wm B Hill, adm of Gilbert Stalker, deceased, submitted an unfavorable report: ordered to be printed.

Capt Isaac Hedge, well known in New Bedford & Salem as a shipmaster from those ports, & formerly of Barnstable, committed suicide on the passage from San Francisco to Panama by first cutting his throat & then jumping overboard.

There was one death by drowning on Jul 4, of a highly esteemed scholastic named Tehan, belonging to Gtwn College. He was seized with a cramp while swimming, & sank. The corpse has not been recovered. In another accident on Jul 4, Chas D Simonton fell from a tree and suffered the loss of one of his arms. He was a promising youth who was attached to the Union's corps of Reporters. He was endeavoring to suspend a swing from a tall tree, when the limb on which he stood broke & precipitated him to the earth. He was conveyed to the residence of his brother, in Wash City, where amputation was found to be indispensable.

Mrd: on Jul 2, in Fred'k City, by Rev Mr Chas Stonestreet, Wm R Collins, of Wash, to Virginia Stipes, of Harper's Ferry, Va.

Mrd: on Jul 2, by Rev Mr Lanahan, Mr Saml L Bryen to Miss Mgt A How, all of Wash City.

Mrd: on Jul 2, by Rev Mr Butler, Mr Chas V Gordon, of Wash City, to Mrs Julia C Holmes, daughter of Henry Bry, of Lousiana.

Died: on Jul 3, in his 5th year, Douglas F, youngest son of Wm H Dundas, of the Post Ofc Dept.

Died: on Jul 4, Jas Goddard. His funeral will be from his mother's residence, **Steamboat Wharf**, this morning, at 9 o'clock.

Died: on Jul 5, after a severe & painful illness, Susan Roberta, daughter of Robt W & Catharine C Latham, aged 6 years, 8 months & 20 days. Her funeral will be from her father's residence on F st, in Union Row, this afternoon, at 5 o'clock.

Died; on Jul 2, at Morristown, N J, Geo Franklin Turner, youngest son of Surgeon Geo F Turner, U S Army, aged 1 year & 7 months. He leaves his mother in Morristown, his father is absent in Calif.

Died: on Jul 5, Wm Buist, native of Scotland; long known as a successful florist of Wash City.

MON JUL 8, 1850
On Thu last a little boy, Hugh McWilliams, one of the Sabbath school children attached to Ryland Chapel, who went out to spend the day at Roach's farm, was saved from drowning in the Potomac by the promptness of Mr Peter Hepburn, of Balt, a son of Mr Peter Hepburn, who resides on the Island. Mr Hepburn plunged into the river & resuced the little fellow from a watery grave.

Wash Corp: 1-Nominations from the Mayor: Henry C Bowen, as Superintendent of Chimney sweeps in the 7th Ward, in place of John Davis. *Benj S Gittings, as Intendant of the Asylum. *John Dewdney, as Police Constable of the 1st Ward. *Luke Richardson, as Scavenger of the 2nd Ward. *Wm M McCauley, as Sealer of Weights & Measures. [*Confirmed.] 2-Ptn of Isaac Newton, praying remission of a fine: referred to the Cmte of Claims. 3-Ptn of J H Clarvoe & M Radcliff, praying a change in the alley in square 436: referred to the Cmte on Improvements. 4-Ptn of Geo Page, asking permission to make certain improvements at the southern termination of 7th st west: referred to the Cmte of Wharves. Ptn of Geo Page, praying remission of a fine: referred to the Cmte of Claims. 5-Ptn of D A Hall, praying that the gutter on the north side of C st, between 4½ & 6th sts, may be relaid: referred to the Cmte on Improvements.

Senate: 1-Cmte of the Whole: act for the relief of Richd H Barrett: it appears that permit 73 was granted to Barrett, under the act of Aug 4, 1842, for the armed occupation & settlement of a part of the Territory of Florida, on Apr 15, 1843, who made settlement, built a house, & cultivated more than 5 acres. On Jul 28, 1844, a letter was addressed from the Land Ofc in Wash to the register & receiver at St Augustine, informing them that permit 73 had been annulled, which embraced lands within 2 miles of the military post established at Pilatka; consequently the claimant did not make final proof of continued residence & cultivation. Letter of Brig Gen W J Worth, reports that the post was virtually abandoned on Mar 19, 1843, nearly one month previous to the issuing of the permit 73 to Richd H Barrett. Bill was read a third time & passed. 2-Cmte of the Whole: bill for the relief of E A McNeil, widow of Gen John McNeil: portion of the report proposed to the widow of Gen McNeil a pension for 5 years: McNeil was not in the service at the time he died: he was a civil ofcr under the Gov't: bill laid on the table.

Some days since, at Dixon, Ill, Mrs Eaton was thrown against a wall, breaking her neck, when the horse attached to her buggy, became frightened and reared furiously. She died immediately. Her 2 sons, who were with her, were injured severely.

Died: on Jul 7, Mrs Agnes Elliott, relict of late Richd Elliott, in her 70th year. Her funeral will be from her late residence on N Y ave, between 12th & 13th sts, this morning, at 10:30 A M.

Died: on Jul 7, in Gtwn, Lewis Warfield, infant son of Rev Stephen G & Isabella V Gassaway, aged 7 weeks & 4 days. His funeral will take place this afternoon at 6 o'clock.

Died: on Jul 6, Wm Ross, son of late Richd Ross, of Montg Co, Md, in his 22nd year.

Criminal Court, Wash: 1-John S Brown, a colored boy, not more than 14 years of age, was found guilty of setting a stable on fire: sentenced to one year in the penitentiary. 2-Patrick Rady, about 18 years old, was convicted of arson: not sentenced: motion for a new trial. 3-Eliz Beckett, a free negress, an old offender, guilty of stealing a pair of shoes, sentenced to 18 months' imprisonment in the penitentiary.

Fred'k Netcke, a German, stole a watch from Mr Wm Voss, on Pa ave, in his silversmith's shop. He was arrested near the Railroad Depot by ofcr Busher & committed for trial. The watch has not been recovered.

Meeting held on Jul 5, 1850: Tribute of respect to the memory of Wm F Tehan, S J, by the Students of Gtwn College: Wm J Rice, of Md, John C Hamilton, of D C, Wm H Wills, Md, Lafayette J Caniell, La, Mathews Lancaster, Md, Orlando Brown, Tenn, Wilfred B Fetterman, Pa. –Dominick A O Byrne, Chairman. John McManus, Sec

House of Reps: 1-Ptn of Benj Thomas, postmaster at St Clairsville, Ohio, for an alteration of the law regulating the compensation of postmasters, & for an increase of his compensation. 2-Ptn of B Thomas, asking for additional compensation to certain postmasters.

Classical, Mathematical, & Commercial School, on F st, between 5th & 6th sts, will henceforth be conducted by Mr Richd Ford, A M, Trinity College, Cambridge, England. He has been for 10 years successfully engaged as a teacher, & for a considerable time held a mastership in one of the largest public schools in the north of England.

Marshal Hall for sale: lies in Chas Co, Md, contains 377½ acres: dwlg is of brick, 2 stories high, with necessary out-bldgs. It has about 1 mile of beach attached. To see the farm call upon Mr Wm H Clagett, on the farm. The steamboats will land persons at the door. For terms address Thos Marshall, Gtwn.

Orphans Court of Wash Co, D C. Letters testamentary on the personal estate of John Carter, late of said county, deceased. –John Marbury, exc

TUE JUL 9, 1850
Situation wanted: a German wants a situation as Gardener. Apply at Shadd's Tavern, near the Railroad depot.

Household & kitchen furniture at auction: on Jul 12, at the residence of C Bestor, 7th & D sts. –Green & Tastet, aucts

Senate: 1-Ptn of Jas Giddings & others, citizens of D C, setting forth their belief that they are in possession of such advantages in the manufacture of gas as will make their enterprise one of great public utility, & of great economy, & ask that an act may be passed to incorporate the Union Gas Ligth Co of D C: referred to the Cmte on D C. 2-Memorial of J N Sewall, asking that provision may be made for certain debts of the Chippewa Indians, agreeable to the 4th article of the Treaty of 1837, concluded between the U S & those Indians: referred to the Cmte on Finance. 3-Ptn of G K Lewis, of Cameron Co, Texas, setting forth that the portion of the country lying between the Nueces & Rio Grande rivers was overrun by hordes of savages, compelling him to abandon his home, & making a complete wreck of his property: referred to the cmte on Indian Affairs. 4-Memorial of Jonathan Elliot, U S Commercian Agent of San Domingo, asking to be reimbursed for expenses incurred in maintaining refugees in his house, during the civil war in the Dominican republic: referred to the Cmte on Foreign Relations.

Mail robbers at the present term of the U S District Court for Illinois found guilty: Francis M Shaw, about 14 or 15 years of age, sentenced to 3 months in jail; Lander M Cutchen, to 4 years in the penitentiary; Thos Boyd, to 10 years in the penitentiary. Jos K Bates & David Wallace, charged with mail robbery, have their trials at Chicago. Thos M Cutchen was not found guilty of the charge of robbing the mail. The indictment against him for perjury was quashed. –Springfield Jrnl

Lt Brown, of the navy, & Dr Henry A Ford, were upset in the Chesapeake bay, in a sailboat, on Thu week, off Buzzard Point. They crawled up on the bottom of the boat, & were taken off by a yawl.

Accidents on Jul 4: 1-Duncan McLane, a sailor, was killed, in Boston, by the bursting of a swivel. 2-Saml Domkee, of West Haven, Conn, had his hand & arm badly broken & lacerated, by the premature discharge of a swivel. 3-Geo Palmer, of East Haven, aged 20 years, received a wound from the bursting of a swivel, from which he died on Jul 5. 4-At New Haven, a little girl named Nora Welch ran before a cannon, at the very moment the match was applied for its discharge. As the smoke cleared away, she was seen lying upon the ground dead, the top of her head having been blown away. 5-A son of Mr Banning, in New Haven, was very seriously injured by the burning of a pack of crackers in his pantaloons pocket. 6-At Saratoga, N Y, Ferdinand Haight, a printer, & J Hodgman, a blacksmith, 2 respectable young men, each lost an arm, & were otherwise dreadfully injured, while firing a salute, by the premature discharge of a cannon. 7-At Lansingburg, N Y, by a similar accident, Mr Cassidy had both hands blown off, & was fatally injured. Messrs Butler & Davenport each lost an arm. 8-At Reading, Pa, Mr B Umstead had his right arm shattered & his eyes much injured, by the premature discharge of a cannon. 9-At N Y, Addison Bilby, aged 21, a machinist, was struck by a steel ramrod which passed through into the right lung, producing a wound which soon proved fatal. It was carelessly fired from a cannon. 10-At Phil, Jane Barret, a young lady, aged 13 years, was drowned by the upsetting of a boat in the Schuylkill; one of her male companions, in attempting to save her, was also drowned. Geo F Fenders, aged 50, was drowned while bathing. A lad named Jones was also drowned while bathing.

Killed: on Thu, Jul 5, Mrs Susanna Bowles, a widow lady, who resided at the head of St Clement's Bay, was struck by lightning. She lived until the following day, but exhibited no signs of consciousness. -Leonardtown Beacon, Md

Mrs Fanny Kemble has left this country for England, on account of the sudden illness of her father, Chas Kemble, of whose low state of health we have been apprized by almost every last arrival for a year.

Zachary Taylor, Pres of the U S, recognizes Auvied Von Witzleben, who has been appointed Consul of Nassau for San Francisco, in Calif. -Jul 8, 1850

Died: on Jul 6, at Gtwn, Presly S, in his 4th year, eldest child of Ignatius & Eliz E Lancaster, late of Chas Co, Md.

Died: on Jul 6, Geo Wm, infant son of Jos F & Esther M Moffett, aged 8 months & 7 days.

Died: on Jul 8, John Henry Peak, infant son of Wm & Eleanor Peak, aged 5 months & 10 days.

Died: on Jul 4, of cholera infantum, Mary Anna, youngest child of Geo W & Mary Ann Robinson, aged 11 months & 10 days.

$10 reward for return of a pocket-book that was lost between the Waverley House & Capitol Hill, on Sat, Jul 7. Please leave at P A De Saules, Waverley House, Pa, & receive the above reward.

WED JUL 10, 1850
Senate: 1-Cmte of Claims: ptn of Jas A Goff, of Fla, praying compensation for horses impressed in the service of the U S during the Seminole war by order of an ofcr in the service of the U S, submitted a reverse report to the same: ordered to be printed. 2-Bill for the relief of Jas Wormley: introduced. 3-Bill granting a pension to Sarah Crandall: referred to the Cmte on Pensions.

A young man named Chas Sutherland, residing near Covington, Ky, killed his aged father on Tue last. He was shot as he lay asleep by the side of his wife, the stepmother of the young man. The murderer was arrested the same day.

Albany, Jul 8. Rufus Pemberton, formerly a clerk in the city post ofc, was arrested yesterday on the charge of robbing the post-ofc. He confessed & implicated 2 persons named Bramkall & Gaylor, both of whom have been arrested.

The Manchester, N H, murder. The long examination in this case ended in the discharge of Horace Wentworth & Wm C Clarke, & in the committal of Asa & Henry T Wentworth for trial for the murder of Jonas Parker some 6 years ago.

A fatal tragedy at Wilmot, Ga, on Jun 9. Mrs Miller, wife of a respectable farmer, who had exhibited signs of derangement, dressed her 4 children & went out for a walk. Nothing further was heard of them for a number of days, when the body of the eldest boy was found drowned on the beach. Is is supposed the mother proceeded to a cliff overhanging the shore, &, having fastened the children to her side with a cord, or a part of her dress, plunged with them into the water.

Died: on Sat, Jul 6, at Balt, Geo H Hughes, a native of Balt, & only brother of the late Christopher Hughes. He was a most useful citizen.

Died: on Jul 9, Mrs Louisa J Newman, wife of T A Newman, & daughter of late J Van Riswick. Her funeral will be from her late residence on Prospect st, Gtwn, at 3 o'clock, this afternoon.

Died: on Jun 27, of cholera, in her 29th year, in Cincinnati, Ohio, Freedom Eliz Durfee, wife of Jas H Durfee, & only sister of Geo R Herrick, of Wash.

Died: on Jul 9, in Wash City, in her 20th year, Sophia A Baker, daughter of Thos D & Susanna J Perrie, formerly of Chas Co, Md. Her funeral will be at the residence of her mother, Mrs Perrie's, on H st between 9th & 10th sts, tomorrow, at 4 o'clock

Died: on Jul 9, Mr P N Tracy. His funeral will be at his late residence on the Heights of Gtwn, this morning at 9 o'clock.

Died: last week, Rev Coombs, a Priest at Leonardtown, Md.

Died: on Jul 6, Miss Mary O'Neill, aged 74 years.

House of Reps: 1-Ptn of John Fraziers & John Read, citizens of Lawrence Co, Pa, praying Congress to grant them relief as the sureties of Jos S Boyd, the late & defaulting postmaster at Newcastle, in said county. 2-Ptn of F C Cox, a soldier of the Mexican war, asking for relief.

Zachary Taylor, Pres of the U S, recognizes Otto Frank, who has been appointed by His Majesty the King of Hanover, Consul of Hanover for San Francisco, Calif. Jul 9, 1850

THU JUL 11, 1850
$30 reward for the return of 2 diamond rings, stolen from the house of Prof Page, Jul 9.

Died: on Jul 9, in Wash City, Nicholas Burke Boyle, late U S Consul at Mahon, & youngest son of late John Boyle. His funeral will be from the residence of his mother, 4½ st, bet Pa & C sts, this morning, at 10 o'clock.

Died: on Jul 9, in Gtwn, after a brief illness, Mr Conrad Hogmire, in his 57th year. His funeral will be from the Union Hotel, this afternoon, at 5 o'clock.

Millard Fillmore, Pres of the U S. Dept of State, Wash, Jul 9, 1850. The melancholy & most painful duty devolves on us to announce to you that Zachary Taylor, late Pres of the U S, is no more. He died at the Pres' Mansion this evening, at half-past 10 o'clock. Your obedient servants:
John M Clayton, Sec of State
W M Meredith, Sec of the Treas
T Ewing, Sec of the Interior
Geo W Crawford, Sec of War
Wm Ballard Preston, Sec of the Navy
J Collamer, Postmaster Gen
Reverdy Johnson, Atty Gen
Mr Fillmore's reply: Wash, Jul 9, 1850. I have just received your note conveying the melancholy & painful intelligence of the decease of Zachary Taylor, late Pres of the U S. I have no language to express the emotions of my heart. The shock is so sudden & unexpected that I am overwhelmed with grief. I shall avail myself of the earliest moment to communicate the sad intelligence to Congress; & shall appoint a time & place for taking the oath of ofc prescribed to the President of the U S. You are requested to be present & witness the ceremony. Respectfully, yours, Millard Fillmore
Message received by the hands of Geo P Fisher, from the late Vice Pres of the U S: Zachary Taylor, late Pres of the U S died in the midst of his family, in full possession of all his faculties. Among his last words were these, which he uttered with emphatic distinctness: "I have always done my duty; I am ready to die; my only regret is for the friends I leave behind me." Zachary Taylor was born in 1784, in Orange Co, Va; in 1808 he was appointed, during the Presidency of Mr Jefferson, lt in the U S army; he rose in 1812 to the rank of capt; & after the declaration of war with Great Britain in that year, he was breveted major by Pres Madison for his memorable & gallant defence of **Fort Harrison**, with a handful of men, against a large body of savages. In 1832, he then advanced to the rank of colonel, he distinghished himself in the Black Hawk war; was ordered into Florida in 1836, & for his signal services against the savage Seminoles was created a brevet brig gen & cmder-in-chief in Florida. He was transferred to the command of the division of the army in the Southwestern portion of the Union; was ordered to Texas in 1845; advanced to the banks of the Rio Grande; & afterwards, beginning with the battles of May 8 & 9, 1846, at Palo Alto & Resaca de la Palma, & ending with Bueno Vista, her overthrew, with fearful odds against him, & signally defeated the most skilful of the Mexican generals, Ampudia, Arista, Paredes, & even the Pres of Mexico himself. His history is a part of the history of this country. Only once before in our history has the ofc of Pres of the U S been made vacant by death-the case of the lamented Harrison.

Phil papers announce the death of a venerable member of the Fraternity of Printers, Adam Ramage, at the age of 80 years.

FRI JUL 12, 1850
The Remains of the Pres will be removed to the East Room of the Executive Mansion this morning, & at 2 o'clock the doors will be opened to the public.

Wash Corp: 1-The Mayor nominates Wm Wheat as police ofcr, & withdraws Ignatius Howe, previously made: confirmed. 2-Ptn from Chas Dyson, for the remission of a fine: referred to the Cmte of Claims. 3-Ptn of Alex Mahon: referred to the Cmte of Claims. 4-Act for the relief of Jas H Shreeves & Harrison Taylor: referred to the Cmte of Claims. 4-Ptn of Wm Pegg, of Jas Burdine, of A Addison, & of Mrs Ellen Donohaugh: referred to the Cmte of Claims. 5-Act for the relief of Saml Gregg: passed. 6-Bill for the relief of Geo Sinclair: passed. 6-Ptn of Jas B Greenwell, respecting his contract for erecting & keeping pumps in repair: referred to the Cmte of Claims. 7-Ptn of Thos Baker & others, for improvement of D st north, from 7th to 8th st west: referred to the Cmte on Improvements. 8-Ptn of Geo Parker & others, respecting the drainage of the alley on square 533: referred to the Cmte on Improvements. 9-Cmte of Claims: asking to be discharged from the further consideration of the ptn of Geo Page: agreed to. 10-Cmte on Improvements: bill for the relief of Wm Dowling: passed. 1-Cmte on Police: bill for the relief of Wm McCreery, recommitted to the same cmte.

Copartnership: R T McLain has associated with him in the Dry Goods business Mr J M Harry, to be conducted under the firm of McLain & Harry.

The Funeral of the late President, Zachary Taylor, will be solemnized on Sat, Jul 13, at 12 o'clock; religious services to be performed by Rev Dr Pyne, at the Executive Mansion, according to the usage of the Episcopal Church, in which church the deceased most usually worshipped. The body to be afterwards taken from the Pres' House to the Congress Burying Ground, accompanied by a Military escort & Civic Procession, & deposited in the receiving tomb.

The U S Marshall for D C, having been charged with the civic portion of the Funeral Procession of the late Pres, has selected the following Aids & Assistants for that occasion, who will report to him as soon as possible.

Jos H Bradley
W B Randolph
Dr Thos Miller
John C Harkness
W H Edes
R King Stone
J L Henshaw
W H Winter
John A Linton
W B B Cross
A S H White
J H McBlair
Washington Nailor
Thos Tench
Edw H Fuller
Isaac Hall
Jonah D Hoover
John A Hunnicutt

A H Kirkwood
John E Reeside
W C Reddall
D C Goddard
J E Etheridge
C P Wallach
W F Anderson
W E Kennaugh
P H Brooks
C W Boteler, jr
Jas Bernard
Beverly Tucker
B L Jackson
John B Sullivan
W B Magruder
S R Hobbie
Francis Dodge, jr
O M Linthicum

Maj Lewis
W F Bayly
J T Towers
Geo H Harrington
Geo M Phillips
Walter D Davidge
Geo Jillard
Wm T Dove
Marian Burche
Marshall Brown
John T England
Thos H Fisher
Chas Thomas

T B J Frye
J T Bangs
J F Coyle
L J Middleton
S J Anderson
E H Metcalfe
W A Kennedy
W B Sasscer
Chas McNamee
John B Clagett
H B Sweeney
–Richd Wallach, D C

New Saddle, Harness, & Trunk Manufactory, on Pa ave, 2 doors east of the Nat'l Hotel. –Francis A Lutz

Died: on Jun 26, of consumption, at Wirtland, near Monticello, Fla, Dr Henry Grattan Wirt; youngest son of late Wm Wirt, of Md. For a year past, increasing infirmity compelled him to withdraw from an extensive medical practice, in which it was his happiness to have exhibited for a few years that of intelligence & skill. He leaves his widow and 2 infant children. -Tallahassee

My companions were all massacred on Apr 23, 1850, by the Umah Indians at the Calhoun Ferry. Killed were the Doctor, [no name given;] Capt John J Glanton, San Antonio, Texas, Thos Harlin, of Texas, Henderson Smith, of Texas, Wm Perrit, of Texas, Dr A L Lincoln, of St Louis, Missouri, Thos Wilson, of Phil, Pa, John Gunn, of Missouri, Jas M Miller, N J, John Dorrey, Missouri, & a negro man, John Jackson, of N Y C. Those now living of those concerened in the ferry are Wm Carr, of Canada, Marcus L Webster, of Texas, & myself. I may be killed, but we will try to exterminate the whole race of Umah Indians. –Jos A Anderson

Orphans Court of Wash Co, D C. In the case of Wm Ward, exc of Jas Day, deceased: Jul 30th appointed for the settlement & distribution of the estate of the deceased, with the assets in the hand of the executor. -Ed N Roach, Reg/o Wills

Died: on Jun 28, in Tallahassee, Fla, W H Brockenbrough, age 37.

SAT JUL 13, 1850
For sale: Trinity Church edifice, on 5th st, near City Hall. Apply to Dr Wm P Johnson, A H Lawrence, of Jos Ingle.

Arrangments for the Funeral of the late Pres Zachary Taylor. The doors of the Pres' House will be opened at 9 o'clock this morning, for the admission of Heads of Depts, Foreign Ministers, & others, who, by order of the Cmte of the two Houses of Congress, are entitled to admission.

Appointments by the Pres: 1-Gen Balis M Edney, of N C, to be U S Consul for the port of Palermo, in Sicily. 2-Bennett Riddell to be U S Consul for Chihuahua, in Mexico. 3-Geo McNeir to the Justice of the Peace in & for the District of Columbia.

Mr John Walter, of Smithsburg, Wash Co, Md, on a wager of $10, cut on Sat 6 acres & 18 perches of wheat, making 203 dozen sheaves.

For sale: *Hazlefield*, Jefferson Co, Va, 600 acres. -H Tudor Tucker, agent for Mrs A E Tucker.

Died: on Jul 11, Mr Mason E Clark, of Wash City. His funeral will be from his late residence on 10th st, at 8½ a m today..

Died: on Jul 11, after a brief illness, Frederick William, son of A E L & Catharine Keese, of Wash City, aged 5 months & 15 days. His funeral will be from their residence on 13th st, between C & D sts, on Jul 14, at 3 o'clock..

Died: on Jul 12, Mrs Rebecca Tree, a native of Pa, but for the last 25 years a resident of Wash, aged 83 years. Her funeral will be at the residence of her son, L Tree, 12th st & N Y ave, on Sun, at 3 o'clock.

MON JUL 15, 1850
Died: on Fri, Henry Burr, infant son of Jas W & Matilda Simonton.

Died: Jul 14, William, infant son of Jas & Eliz Parsons, aged 11 months. His funeral will be this Mon at 4 o'clock from his father's residence, F & 7th sts.

Died: on Jul 3, in Morristown, N J, Geo Franklin, son of Dr G F Turner, U S Army. The death of this lovely boy is rendered more deeply distressing to his bereaved mother by his father being absent in Calif. Tue Jul 16, 1850

The Funeral of the late Pres Zachary Taylor, deceased: immediate relatives of the deceased in attendance: Col Taylor, his brother, Dr Wood, Col Bliss, the Hon Jefferson Davis, & others who are nearly allied. The procession extended nearly 2 miles. Gen Taylor's horse, <u>Old Whitey</u>, full caparisoned, was attended by a groom. The family of the late Pres rode in 3 carriages. The magnificent Funeral Car was prepared by Messrs Haslup & Weeden, at their Coach Factory, in Wash City. The running gear was obtained from Mr Chas Goddard, of Balt. The body was 11 feet long & 6½ feet wide. On Sat evening, the family of Gen Taylor removed from the Pres' Mansion to the residence of Mr Meredith, whose hospitality is accepted for a few days. The afflicted relict of the late Pres will for the present take up her abode with her friends in Balt.

$10 reward for the return of a pocket book stolen from the subscriber, on Pa ave, on Sat, while the funeral of the Pres was passing. Return to me at the Patriotic Bank, Jas Mankin.

TUE JUL 16, 1850
Senate: 1-Cmte on Foreign Relations: to inquire into allowing Jno P Brown the pay of charge d'affaires for the time he discharged the duties of that station at Constantinople. 2-Documents were submitted in relation to the claim of A H Evans & others: referred to the Cmte on Public Lands. 3-Memorial of H B Babcock, asking that the Sec of Navy may be authorized to purchase the right to manufacture, for naval purposes, an anti-friction metallic compound: referred to the Cmte on Naval Affairs. 4-Documents relating to the claim of Jim Capers for a pension: referred to the Cmte on Pensions. 5-Memorial of Jordan L Mott, in behalf of the inventors of the U S, asking the enactment of a law to provide greater security & protection of the rights of patentees.

Died: on Jul 1, at Longwood, near Natchez, Sargeant S Prentiss, of New Orleans, aged about 42 years. He was a native of Maine; emigrated to Mississippi about 1826. He passed a year or two as tutor in a private family in the neighborhood of Natchez, & pursued his legal studies under the instruction of Gen Felix Huston. He soon moved to Vicksburg. He leaves a wife & children to mourn his death.

We have a letter written by Geo R Bradley, dated Liberty, Jun 21, which gives the sad account of the fate of one of the Calif emigrating companies. The writer says that his wagon, to which were attached his brother & himself, from Union Co, Ill, H J Osteller, from Chester, Ill, & two of the McDills, from Union Co, Ill, left Independence in a company of 27 persons on Jun 11; they lost 10 men due to cholera & small-pox breaking out among them. On the return route there were 7 more deaths. –St Louis Repub

Mrd: on Jul 11, at Chillicothe, Ohio, by Rev L Freeman, Seneca W Ely, Editor of the Scioto Gaz, to Miss Agatha Eustace Bell, daughter of the late Chas Bell, of Pickaway Co, Ohio.

Died: on Sun, at the residence of Rev R R Gurley, near the Irving House, on 12th st, Rev Thos Bailey, of Little Compton, R I. His funeral will take place today at 9 o'clock A M.

Died: on Sunday, at *Sidney*, near Wash City, the residence of her brother-in-law, E J Middleton, Sarah Ann Ross, in her 28th year. Her funeral is this afternoon, at 4 o'clock. Carriages will be in readiness at the residence of her brother-in-law, A E Perry, in Wash City, at quarter past 3 o'clock.

Died: on Sat, at *Sidney*, near Wash City, the residence of her father, Ellen, infant daughter of E J & Ellen Middleton, aged 9 months.

Died: on Jul 8, at the residence of her husband, Maj Jas H Griffin, in the village of Piscataway, PG Co, Md, Mrs Juliana E Griffin, aged 33 years, leaving behind a husband & 3 children.

Died: on Jul 15, Eleanor Hubbard, aged 4 years & 4 days, 2nd daughter of Jos Henry & Mary Eliz French. Her funeral is this evening at 4½ o'clock.

Died: on Jul 15, in Gtwn, suddenly, of organic disease of the heart, John Kurtz, aged 64 years.

The wife of J W Moore & her youngest sister, aged 14, of Chatham Four Corners, attempted at night recently, to fill a spirit gas lamp, while the lamp was lit. The flames immediately communicated to the liquid, & the lamp exploded, setting fire to both. The latter died in a few hours. –Albany Jour

Grand Military & Civic Excursion: the Walker Sharpshooters will have their second annual excursion on Jul 16. Cmte:

Lt W J McCollam	Serg E C Eckloff	W D Servin
Lt Jas Ward	Serg R Downing	Jas Lewis
Ensign W Gallant	John Goddard	
Serg Curtis	B Hurst	

Complete Book & Job Printing Ofc for sale: formerly owned by Theodore Barnard. Apply to John T Towers.

$5 reward for return of strayed gray mare. Return to Owen Carroll, living near Beltsville, PG Co, Md.

WED JUL 17, 1850
Senate: 1-Cmte on Finance: memorial of J S Toley & Co & Lewis Kinney & Co, asking the return of certain duties: discharged from the further consideration of the memorial: laid upon the table. 2-Cmte of Claims: bill for the relief of Gideon Walker: ordered to be printed, adverse to the passage of the bill.

Criminal Court-Wash: Tue: 1-Jacob Rowles, convicted of petit larceny, in stealing chickens of the value of $3.75, the property of Jos H Knott, was sentenced to 6 months in jail, & fined $10 & costs. 2-Thos Huysey, charged with arson, was found guilty.

$10 reward for recovery of a bay horse that escaped from me on the Navy Yard Hill on Jul 3. –John E Dement

Mrd: on Jul 16, at St John's Church, by Rev Mr Tillinghast, Mr Jas C Sprigg, of Cumberland, to Miss Lucy E, daughter of Thos B Addison, of Gtwn, D C.

Died: on Jul 16, Mrs Susan Green, after a protracted illness of 7 weeks. Her funeral will be from her late residence in the First Ward, this day, at 4 o'clock.

Died: on Jul 16, Henry Clay, son of Francis & Annie Conway Carman, aged 9 weeks.

Died: on Jul 15, Eleanor Hubbard, 2nd daughter of Jos Henry & Mary Eliz France, aged 4 years & 4 days.

Died: on Jul 16, at his residence, in Wash City, Peter Hagner, late 3rd Auditor of the Treasury, in his 78th year. [Jul 18th newspaper: the friends of the late Peter Hagner, & of his family are requested to attend his funeral this morning at 8 o'clock. The body will be conveyed to Annapolis, Md.] [Jul 25th newspaper: Peter Hagner was born in Phil, Oct 1, 1772, was the son of Valentine Hagner, a worthy citizen of that city, who served with credit in the war of the Revolution.]

Pres Millard Fillmore: Great Grandfather-John Fillmore, common ancestor of all of that name in U S; born about 1700, in one of the New England States; his son, Nathaniel Fillmore, father of Millard was born at Bennington in '71; removed to Summer Hill, Cayuga Co, where Millard was born Jan 7, 1800. About 1802 he removed to Sempronius, now Niles, same County, resided there until 1819; removed to Erie County, where he still lives. In 1826 Millard married Abigail Powers, youngest child of Rev Lemuel Powers, deceased, by whom he has a son & a daughter.

THU JUL 18, 1850
Mrd: on Jul 15, in Wash City, by Rev J B Donelan, Mr Alphonsos L R Hilton & Sarah Ellen Anderson, all of Wash City.

Mrd: on Jul 9, by Rev Mr Hodges, Adelbert Pomnietezritzky to Miss Sarah Ann McAlwee, all of Wash City.

Died: on Jul 15, Robt King, son of Eli & Mgt Davis, aged 9 months & 22 days.

Senate: 1-Ptn of David L Palmer, asking indemnity for loss sustained in consequence of illegal seizure of a cargo of live oak by the Gov't: referred to the Cmte on the Judiciary. 2-Cmte on Private Land Claims: bill for the relief of the legal reps of Martin Fenwick: ordered to be printed. Same cmte: memorial of Thos H McManus, asking confirmation of his land title: passed to a second reading. 3-Cmte of Claims: memorial of D A Watterston, asking payment for services performed as a clerk to the Surveyor General of Louisiana: passed.

Died: on Wed, in Wash City, , Henry St Geo Tucker, eldest son of Beverly & Jane S Tucker, aged 7 years & 2 months.

FRI JUL 19, 1850
Drowned: Mr J W Nuthall, keeper of the Lighthouse at Piney Point, Md, on Fri last. He was in a boat with his wife & servant boy, when the boat capsized. Mr Nuthall sank & could not be recovered. Mrs Nuthall & the boy were saved. –Alexandria Gazette

Dedication of the new Methodist E Church, on Dunbarton st, Gtwn, on Sabbath next, Jul 21. Rev Henry Slicer will preach at 11 a m. the Rev J T Peck, D D, Pres of Dickinson College will preach at 3½ p m; & Rev B H Nadal, A M, will preach at 8 p m.

Died: yesterday, in Wash City, Katharine Broadus, youngest daughter of Hon R W Thompson, of Indiana, aged 5 years, 5 months & 12 days. Her funeral will be from the house of Mrs Lenox, E between 10th & 11th sts, today, at 12 o'clock.

The subscriber, wishing to engage in other business, offers for sale the Sullivan County Whig printing establishment at a very low price. The Whig has been published for 6 years & has a circulation of nearly 800 subscribers. Address John W Hasbrouck, Bloomingburgh, N Y

SAT JUL 20, 1850
Pres Fillmore yesterday removed his residence to the Presidential Mansion.

Mrs Gen Taylor, Col & Mrs Bliss, & Dr Wood & family left this city on Thu & arrived safely at the Eutaw House, in Balt, where they intend remainng for some time.

The Rev Theodore Parker gave so much offence to some of his congregation by his sermon against the late Pres Taylor, on Sun last, that they rose & quit the church.
--Boston Transcript

We learn that 250 U S troops left N Y on Jul 15, under command of Lt Saml D Sturgis, for **Fort Leavenworth**, by the Lakes.

Mrd: on Jul 11, at **Sherwood Forest**, seat of Ex-Pres Tyler, in Chas City Co, Va, by Rev W T Levell, pastor of the Episcopal Church in Chas City, Rev H M Dennison, late Pastor of Episcopal Church in Williamsburg, [now of Brooklyn, N Y,] to Miss Alice Tyler, daughter of ex-Pres. Tyler.

Mrd: on Thu, by Rev John C Smith, Mr Jas W Shiles to Miss Ann B Forsyth, both of Alexandria.

Yesterday Thos, alias Tom Cook, convicted of grand larceny, was sentenced by Judge Crawford to 2 years in the penitentiary.

Notice: by virtue of 7 writs of fieri facias, at the suit of Amos Green, against the goods & chattels of Jas M McRea, I have seized a large assortment of furniture & accessories of said McRea, to be sold on Jul 27, in front of Centre Market house.
--H R Maryman, constable

Wash Corp: 1-Ptn frm Hugh Tenny & others, in relation to the assessment of their property: referred to the Cmte on Finance. 2-Resolution for the relief of Thos J Barrett: referred to the Cmte of Claims. 3-Nomination of Henry Haliday, as wood corder, was confirmed. 4-Act for the relief of Jas McGuire: referred to the Cmte of Claims. 5-Ptn of Robt F Magee, praying remission of a fine: referred to the Cmte of Claims.

MON JUL 22, 1850
Dissolution of co-partnership between Hyatt & Frasier, by mutual consent. Jas Frasier will continue the business. –R G Hyatt, Jas Frasier, 3rd door west of 8th st, opposite Centre Market

Postmaster Gen has est'd the following new Post Ofcs for the week ending Jul 13, 1850.

Office	County, State	Postmaster
Wilson's Mills	Osford, Me	Jas M Wilson
Wentworth's location	Coos, N H	C J Drake
St Stoddard	Cheshire, N	M W McClure
West Canaan	Grafton, N H	Gordon B Pattee
Barton's Landing	Orleans, Vt	John Drew
Pine Meadows	Litchfield, Ct	F Lawrence
Jamestown	Newport, R I	Benj Congdon
East Galway	Saratoga, N Y	Noah Vibbard
Bennettsburg	Tompkins, N Y	Caleb Keep
Stanwix	Oneida, N Y	S Wade
Bruin	Butler, Pa	Wm Porter
Hayesville	Chester, Pa	Jas Haynes
Fayette Springs	Fayette, Pa	Wm Sprowl
Salunga	Lancaster, Pa	John G Freeland
Sweet Air	Baltimore, Md	Robt Agnew
Gustine	Adams, Ohio	Jas F McAdow
Coddingville	Medina, Ohio	Geo McCodding
Ayersville	Defiance, Ohio	Jos P Ayers
Vandalia	Cass, Mich	T T Wilcox
Whigville	Lapier, Mich	Stephen Grinnell
Uffington	Monongalia, Va	Wm D Smith
Clingman	Cleveland, N C	John W Williams
War Hill	Hall, Geo	Allen Langford
Marblehead	Gilmer, Geo	Jas Simmons
Coxville	De Kalb, Ala	Thos G A Cox
Duck Spring	De Kalb, Ala	Wm Mullin
Hendricksville	De Kalb, Ala	Joab Hendricks
Good Water	Coosa, Ala	Wm Adkins
Trion	Tuscaloosa, Ala	Geo Collins
Kiomatia	Red River, Texas	T G Wright
Rapp's Barrens	Fulton, Ark	Isaac Howard
Canadian	Mississippi, Ark	Wm L Ward
Cerro Gordo	Grundy, Tenn	Wm Dugan
Cherry Flat	Rutherford, Tenn	Wm H Cayce
Arrington	Williamson, Tenn	Wm Osborne
Menelos	Madison, Ky	John Dozier
Houston	Jackson, Ia	David Bowman
Cross Roads	Vanderburg, Ia	S Ruark

New Hope	Spencer, Ia	Wm Harris
Anthony	Delaware, Ia	Otho Upp
Turnback	Dade, Mo	Nathan Rutledge
Waupaca	Marquette, Wis	E C Session
Pine River	Marquette, Wis	Henry Long
Almond	Portage, Wis	Jas F Moore
Leyden	Rock, Wis	John McMillon
Allen's Grove	Scott, Iowa	Geo Hederick
Mormon Hill	Marshall, Iowa	Thos Gordon
Brookfield	Jackson, Iowa	Amosa Nims
Oak Spring	Davis, Iowa	C M Hurless
Davis Creek	Washington, Iowa	Chas G Maynard

Names Changed: East Bristol, Hartford Co, Conn, changed to Forestville.
Hall's Mills, Albany Co, N Y, changed to Medusa.
Shandaken Centre, Ulster Co, N Y, changed to Shandaken.
Pacolet, Rutherford Co, N C, changed to Horse Creek.
Gallatin, Stark Co, Ill, changed to Dorrance.

Died: on Jul 16, at New Haven, Conn, Mrs Eliz Baldwin, aged 85 years, wife of Hon Simeon Baldwin, & daughter of Hon Roger Sherman. She retained to the last a vivid remembrance of the scenes of her youth. But a few days since, we had the pleasure of listening to her minute description of Gov Trumbull, Col Humphreys, Gen Washington, & others. Mrs Baldwin leaves her husband of four score & ten years, after a union of 60 years. –New Haven Journal

Deacon Loring, one of the oldest booksellers & printers in New England, a warm hearted patriot, educated in Ben Russell's ofc, first editor of the Christian Watchman, & every way a worthy time honored old gentleman, died at his residence in Boston, on Jul 9.

Chas W Sutherland, a youth of some 17 or 18 years, shot & killed his father a few days since about 5 miles back of Covington, Ky. He endeavored to make his escape, but was arrested & lodged in the Covington jail. –Louisville Courier

Died: on Jul 21, of consumption, Jas Mitchell, in his 35th year. His funeral will be from his late residence on 6th st, today at 3 o'clock.

Died: on Jul 20, in Gtwn, Eliza, daughter of Richd S & the late Eliza Cox, aged 6 months & 17 days.

Died: on Jul 1, at Bladensburg, Mrs Catharine E S Stephen, wife of Edmund B Stephen, of PG Co, Md, & eldest daughter of L P W Balch, of Jefferson Co, Va, in her 35th year.

Ladies & Gentlemen forming the Vocal Dept of the Wash Philharmonic Society are to meet at my residence on Jul 24, at 8 o'clock. –A T Kieckhoefer, Pres: 13th st, between E & F sts

On Sat last, the Pres nominated to the Senate, the following gentlemen, & all nominations were confirmed by that body.
Sec of State: Danl Webster, of Mass
Sec of Treas: Thos Corwin, of Ohio
Sec of War: Edw Bates, of Missouri
Sec of Navy: Wm A Graham, of N C
Sec of Interior: Jas A Pearce, of Md
Postmaster Gen: Nathan K Hall, of N Y
Atty Gen: John J Crittenden, of Ky

Commencement of Columbian College took place on Wed last in the large Baptist Church on E st: prayer by Rev Dr Bacon, Pres of the College. Orations by members of the graduating class:
Wm J Arrington, Louisville, Geo
Elbert C Catchings, Clinton, Geo
Andrew F Davidson, Charlotte Co, Va
Julius E Grammer, Wash
B Johnson Hellen, Wash
Wm J Houston, Kenansville, N C
Asa B Richardson, Jefferson, Maine
Clement C Speiden, Wash
Wm P Solomon, Franklin Co, N C
Wm A Tyree, Amherst Co, Va
Thos Pollard, King & Queen Co, Va

First Degree in the Arts [A B] was conferred on the following graduates:

Wm J Arrington, Ga	Wm J Houston, N C
Jas W Asbury, Ga	Robt G Lewis, N C
E T Blake, Wash	David H McCoy, Pa
Elbert G Catchings, Ga	John T Mercer, Ga
A F Davidson, Va	A B Richardson, Maine
Caleb Davison, Oleny, Eng	W P Solomon, N C
Edw L Force, Wash	C C Speiden, Wash
Julius E Grammer, Wash	Thos R Thornton, Ga
Thos B Greer, Va	Wm A Tyree, Va
Robt Hall, Va	Jas J Wallace, Ga
B J Hellen, Wash	Joshua C Wood, Miss
J Byron Hilliard, N C	

Candidates for the Second degree, [A M:] Robt French, D C; Wm T Headren, Va; & Thos Pollard, Va
Honorary Degree of Master of Arts was conferred on: Stephen M Allen, of Mass; & Danl Witt, jr, of Texas
The Honorary Degree of D D was conferred on: Rev J T Jones, of Siam, & Rev C D Mallory, of Georgia.

The undersigned, engaged in other business, is desirous of renting out the Republican House, now kept by him. Apply to John Foy.

Senate: 1-Additional documents presented in the case of the legal reps of Gen Nathl Greene: referred to the Cmte on Revolutionary Claims. 2-Ptn of Chas Hibbs, principal messenger in the ofc of the Com'rs of Pensions: referred to the Cmte on Military Affairs. 3-Amos Holton has leave to withdraw his petition & papers.

TUE JUL 23, 1850
Farmers' Hotel, Fredericksburg, Va: leased by the subscriber for a term of years. His table at all times shall be supplied with the best the market affords. –C A Tackett

Senate: 1-Bills referred-act for the relief of Geo Poindexter; relief of Judith Worthen, deceased; relief of Mrs Mgt Hetzel, widow & admx of R R Hetzel, late Assist Quartermaster in the army of the U S. 2-Memorial of B B French, asking the House to cause him to be employed to compile & prepare for its use a Parliamentary Manuel. 3-Ptn of Bethiah Black, daughter & heir of Geo Black, a Revolutionary ofcr, asking to be allowed a pension: referred to the Cmte on Pensions. 4-Memorial of Robt Mills, architect, of Washington, proposing to furnish a plan for a nat'l mausoleum in Wash City, for the reception of the remains of all the Presidents: referred to the Cmte on Public Bldgs.

Rappahannock Academy, Caroline Co, Va, will commence on Oct 2 next, & continue until the last day of Jul, 1851. Geo G Butler, A M, Rev Alex Shiras, Assoc Principals.

Another Mail Robber Deteched. Morgan Ashcroft, mail carrier, was arrested at York district, S C, on Jul 11, by Thos P Shallcross, special agent of the Post Ofc Dept, for robbing the mail, & has been committed for trial.

Household & kitchen furniture at auction: on Jul 26, at the house lately occupied by Y N Ashton, at Pa ave & 22nd st. –Green & Tastet, aucts

Dr S W Everett informs the citizens of Wash, that he will give his attention to the practice of Medicine & Surgery, & that he has removed his ofc to Lane & Tucker's bldg, Pa ave, above 4½ st, where he may be found at all hours.

In Chancery: sale of the real estate of Geo R H Marshall, made & reported by the trustee, Thos Marshall, be ratified & confirmed: the amount of sales to be $5,495.
–Louis Gassaway, Reg Cur Can

House of Reps: 1-Bill for the relief of Capt Nathan Adams, of Tenn: referred to the Cmte of Claims. 2-Bill for the relief of Simon Greenleaf: referred to the Cmte on the Judiciary.

Died: yesterday, William P, infant son of Jas M & Anna E McKnight, aged 8 months. His funeral will be from the residence of Mrs Preston, on 12th st, this afternoon, at 4 o'clock.

Mrd: on Jul 16, in Annapolis, by Rev Mr Brooke, Dr Abram Claude, Mayor of Annapolis, to Rachel Ann, daughter of Washington G Tuck.

Mrd: on Jul 2, in Balt, by Rev Henry Slicer, at Eutaw St Methodist Episcopal Church, Benjamin E Gittings, of Wash, & Rachel Marriott Thompson, 4th daughter of late John Thompson, of Balt.

WED JUL 24, 1850
We understand that Maj Gen Winfield Scott has been appointed Sec of War, & Cmdor Lewis Washington Sec of the Navy, until the arrival of the new Secs of those respective Depts.

House of Reps: 1-Cmte of Claims: adverse report on the ptn of John A Rodgers: laid on the table. Same cmte: bill for the relief of John H Baker: committed. Same cmte: bill for the relief of Capt Geo Simpton, of Galveston: committed. Same cmte: adverse reports on the ptns of Zachariah Lawrence, Edw Devitt et al, G De Lirac, Elisha Button, & Jos C Doxey: laid on the table. 2-Cmte of Claims: bill for the relief of the legal reps of J J Bulow, jr, deceased: committed. 3-Cmte of Commerce: bill to grant a register to the barque **James Patton, jr**, now the Grenadian barque **Bogota**, owned by John Benson an American citizen residing in N Y C: which was read twice.

Mrd: on Jul 23, in Wash, by Rev Mr Hodges, in Christ Church, Mr Evert M Topping, of Balt, to Miss Sallie B Hebb, of Wash.

We learn by the wreck of the ship **Elizabeth**, from Leghorn, on the shore of Long Island, on Fri last, several lives were lost, among them the Marquis & Marchioness D'Orsoli, with their child, & a lady named Celesta Paulina, formerly a resident of this city. The Marchioness D'Orsoli was better known to our citizens as Margaret Fuller, having acquired her new name recently by marriage in Italy. Eight lives in all were lost.
–N Y Courier [The ship had on board Power's statue of the late Hon John C Calhoun. It is hoped the statue will be saved.]

Mrd: on Jul 23, in Christ Church, Wash, by Rev Mr Hodges, Evert M Topping, of Balt, to Miss Sallie B Hebb, of Wash.

Died: on Jul 23, Wm H Turner, formerly of Port Tobacco, Md, aged 24 years.

$50 reward for the apprehension & conviction of the person or persons who cut the cushions of the omnibus of J Q Adams, the door panels of the omnibuses John Tyler & Geo Washington, & the side panel of the Thos Jefferson during the past week.
–Reeside & Vanderwerken

Criminal Crt-D C: 1-Christiana Brown, guilty of larceny, sentenced to 1 year in the penitentiary. 2-Thos Huysey, guilty of arson: 2 years in penitentiary. 3-Nelly Butler, guilty of larceny: 4 months in jail & $1 fine. 4-Cordelia Digges, guilty of forgery: 2 years in the penitentiary. 5-Archibald Sterrett, guilty of larceny: 1 year & 6 months in the penitentiary.

Orphans Court of Wash Co, D C. Jul 24, 1850. Letters of administration on the personal estate of Zachary Taylor, late Pres of U S, deceased. -W W S Bliss, adm

THU JUL 25, 1850
Senate: 1-Ptn of Wm H Harrison, asking to be allowed a pension in consideration of an injury received in the revenue service: referred to the Cmte on Pensions. 2-Introduced: bill for the relief of L E A Lawson, sole surviving heir of Gen Eleaser W Ripley, deceased: ordered to be printed.

Two young gentlemen from Utica, Chas B Foster & Theodore C Bradish, were ascending the Catshill Mountail on Fri, the former lost his footing & fell over a precipice of 80 feet upon the rocks below. He was picked up, with his thigh broken, & his teeth knocked in, alive, but insensible. The injury it is thought must prove fatal.

Mrd: on Jul 23, by Rev Mr Marks, Mr Sam'l August to Miss Lydia Ann Lowman.

Died: on Wed, of bilious dysentery, Josiah Melvin Baird, adopted son of Josiah & Elleanor M Melvin, aged 15 years & 24 days. The friends of the family & those of his father, David A Baird, are invited to attend his funeral will be from the residence of Josiah Melvin, on 10th between G & H sts, today at 4 o'clock.

Died: on Jul 16, Amos Baker, of Lincoln, Mass. He was age 94 years of age on Apr 9th last. He was the last survivor of the Concord Fight, & the only man living who bore arms on Apr 19, 1775. He was present at the late celebration at Concord.

Died: on May 23 last, at Steubenville, Ohio, Dr Wm F Lowrie, of Hannibal, Mo, & formerly of Wash, D C. He leaves an affectionate wife & 4 little children to mourn his loss.

Died: on Tue, Joseph T, 4th son of Rich'd R Burr, in his 15th year. His funeral is this afternoon at 2 o'clock, at the residence of his father, F & 3rd sts.

For rent: house on F st, between 6th & 7th sts, recently occupied by the Sec of War. Refer to Dr Robt Arthur, Pa ave, near 13th st, or to John F Webb, Odd-Fellows' Hall.

Bldg lots for sale, in square 279. Inquire of Mrs Callan, F st.

For sale: valuable & highly improved Jas River Estate: well known as the ***Rowe***, on the north side of the Jas River, in Chas City Co, Va: containing 700 acres. Bldgs consist of a 2 story wooden dwlg house & necessary out-bldgs. -Robt B Bolling

FRI JUL 26, 1850
Mrd: on Jul 25, by Rev J C Smith, the Rev Thos Jones, of Sussex Co, Va, to Anne S Mustin, of Wash.

Died: on Jul 24, in Wash City, of dropsy, John Hogan, of Utica, N Y, in his 48th year.

Died: on Jul 25, Mr Thos Tonge, in his 34th year. His funeral from his late residence, 6th st, between H & I sts, on Jul 27, at 10 o'clock.

The subscribers, having purchased the Flouring Mill formerly owned by the late Thos J Davis, have entered into a copartnership, to carry on the Milling business, under the firm of Boyce, Taylor & Co, & are prepared to receive grain. –W M Boyce, Vincent J Taylor, W D Beall

Household & kitchen furniture at auction: on Aug 6, at the residence of the Hon J Collamer, late Postmaster Gen, on N Y ave, near 14th st. -Dyer & Brother, aucts

For rent the whole or part of Mrs Humphries Cottage, on 9th st, between G & H sts. Apply on the premises.

Two story brick house at Auction: on Jul 31, on half lot 10 in square 881, fronting on south K st, near 7th, next door to Mr S Scott's. The property is sold to satisfy ground rent due Jacob Smull. Terms cash. -Green & Tastet

St Louis, Jul 17: sudden death: the heat during the past 2 days has proved fatal to 5 persons, among them Hugh McCartney, one of the superintendents. -Republican

Charlotte Hall School: the Principalship of this institution has become vacant by the resignation of Rev Saml G Callahan, the trustees will meet on Sep 24, when appointment of principal will be made. Applications addressed to the Register [post paid] will be laid before the board on that day. –H Fowler, Reg C H School

SAT JUL 27, 1850
Miss Mary Ann Lynes, a native of N Y, aged 34 years, was accidentally drowned late on Wed night, at the Fulton Ferry, while returning home from Brooklyn, in company with her brother, who, at the time she fell, had hold of her hand. In getting off the boat she got near the edge of the boat, which struck the piles, & shook the boat so violently that she was precipitated into the water. In the fall her neck was broken.

Wash Corp: 1-Cmte of Claims: asked to be discharged from the further consideration of the ptn of Jas Burdine: discharged accordingly. 2-Act for the relief of Chas Stewart: passed. 3-Cmte on Unfinished Business: ptn of Wm Pettibone, for the remission of a fine: referred to the Cmte of Claims. 4-Cmte of Claims: asked to be discharged from the further consideration of the ptn of Mrs Ellen Donohugh: discharged accordingly. 5-Act for the relief of A F Tottchinder: referred to the Cmte of Claims. 6-John Magar confirmed as police constable for the 7th Ward.

City Ordinance-Wash: 1-Act for the relief of Saml Gregg: the sum of $86.77 be paid him for the balance due him for trimming, forming & gravelling Missousi ave from 3rd to 6th st. Approved: Jul 20, 1850

House of Reps: 1-Cmte of Claims: report made through mistake, on the application of John A Rogers: resubmitted. 2-Cmte on Revolutionary Claims: bill for the relief of Judith Worthen, deceased: committed. Same cmte: adverse reports on the ptns of the heirs of Capt Wm Christian, John Arlee, Abraham Van Ingen, the heirs of Derville Hart, heirs of Capt John McAdams, Jonathan Shafer, one of the heirs of Christian Orendorf, & of the heirs of Col Wm Nelson: severally laid on the table. Same cmte: bill for the relief of the heirs of Phillip R Rice: committed. Adverse reports on the ptn of the heirs of Lt Saml Waples, & of Eliz W Beachey: laid on the table. Same cmte: bill for the relief of the legal reps of Capt John De Treville: committed. Same cmte: bill for the relief of Abigail Stafford: committed. Same cmte: bill for the relief of Chas J Davis, administrator of Capt John Davis, an ofcr in the war of the Revolution: committed. Same cmte: adverse report on the ptn of Stephen Hoyt, & other heirs of Stephen Hoyt, deceased: laid on the table. Same cmte: adverse reports on the ptns of the heir of Wm Grymes, of Mary M Talfair, heir of Israel Pearce, & of the heirs of Casper Rouse: laid on the table. 3-Cmte on Revolutionary Claims: discharged from the further consideration of the ptn of Mrs Mary Barrey, of Boston: referred to the Cmte on Revolutionary Pensions. 4-Cmte on Private Land Claims: bill allowing Wm H Wells the bounty land which would have been due his brother Lemuel Wells, had he lived, as a private soldier in the late war with Great Britain: committed. Same cmte: adverse report on the ptn of Peter Bellinger: laid on the table.

Died: on Sunday last, at Middleton, Conn, Passed Midshipman Edw F Tattnal, eldest son of Capt Josiah Tattnal, U S Navy, aged 26 years.

Accident at Boonton, Morris Co, N J, on Sat last: Harriet Glover, 13, & Phebe Moore, 14, drowned when they fell from a narrow footbridge over Rockaway river, on their way to gather berries.

The owners of the house on square 728, commonly called the Brick Capitol, now occupied by Mrs H V Hill, are to meet at the Dirs' rooms of the Bank of Wash on Tue next. –John P Ingle, trustee

Mrd: on Jul 25, by Rev C M Butler, Edmund Barry to Julianna H, daughter of Col David Butler, all of Wash City.

Sharp's Patent Rifle: newly invented rifle is constructed as to admit of its being loaded at the breech & to supply itself with caps. It can be loaded & fired 12 times per minutes: highly recommended by Gen T Rusk, the honorable U S Senator from Texas. This patent rifle is manufactured by A S Nippes & Co, Manayunk, Phil Co, Pa, who have the exclusive right to apply Dr E Maynard's patent primer to Sharp's rifle. Messrs Baden & Brother, Pa ave, Wash City, are agents of the subscribers. –Benj Butterfield, Albert S Nippes

For sale: small 3 story brick house, H st north, east of 18th st; has a good woodhouse & water at the door. Inquire of H W Balmain, Second Auditor's Ofc.

Academy of the Visitation, Gtwn, D C: Annual Distribution of Premiums took place on Jul 24: premiums presented by the most Rev Archbishop. Gold Medal in the Senior Class was awarded to Miss Gertrude Fetterman, of Pittsburg, Pa. Premiums were awarded to:
Isabel Cole, of Detroit, Mich
Ann Herty, of Milledgeville, Ga
Josephine Briscoe, of Wash City, D C
Imogen Penn, of Lynchburg, Va
Virginia Foote, of Jackson, Miss
Lucy Shackelford, of Culpeper Co, Va
Ellen Roach, of Wash, D C
Catharine Tilghman, of Eastern Shore, Md
Amanda Clare, of Wash, D C
Mary Ann Borremans, of Wash, D C
Rosa Ford, of Wash, D C
Marion Ramsay, of Wash, D C
Mary Ward, of Warrenton, Va
Harriet Thayer, of Petersburg, Va
Maria Yerby, of Richmond, Va
Jane Neale, of Chas Co, Md
Georgiana Hill, of Wash, D C
Hannah Manly, of Newbern, N C
Julia Young, of Wash, D C
Alice Berry, of Gtwn, D C
Anna O'Donnoghue, of Gtwn, D C
Victoria Branch, of Petersburg, Va
Mary Jane Jones, of Wash, D C
Eliz Poe, of Gtwn, D C
Mary White, of Charleston, S C
Virginia Magruder, of PG Co, Md
Amelia Stoops, of Gtwn, D C
Geraldine Bellinger, of Charleston, S C
Mary Watkins, of Newbern, N C
Carolina Roland, of Montg Co, Md
Arabella Foote, of Jackson, Miss
Sarah Robinson, of Montg, Ala
Adele Branch, of Petersburg, Va
Mary Spalding, of Wash, D C
Mary Peabody, of Wash, D C
Mary Cammack, of Gtwn, D C
Carolien Godfrey, of Detroit, Mich
Mary Brawner, of Wash, D C
Mary H Osborn, of Gtwn, D C
Rosa Gibson, of Richmond, Va
A C Stoops, of Gtwn, D C
Mary De Ford, of Newburyport, Mass

Caroline Brent, of Montg Co, Md
Alice Semmes, of PG Co, Md
Maria Smoot, of Gtwn, D C
Anna Waring, of Montg Co, Md
Mary Payne, of Gtwn, D C
Eliza O'Donnoghue, of Gtwn, D C
Eliz Schenck, of Dayton, Ohio
Lucy Gwin, of Calif
Emma Magruder, of PG Co, Md
Alice Murray, of Gtwn, D C
Josephine Laub, of Wash, D C
Sarah Middleton, of PG Co, Md
Rose Walsh, of Wash, D C
Eliz White, of Charleston, S C
Lavinia Clements, of Gtwn, D C
Gertrude Greenhow, of Wash D C
Charlotte Turner, of King Geo Co, Va
S Hurdle, of Gtwn, D C
P Atchison, of Gtwn, D C
S Palfrey, of Franklin, La
Frances Digges, of Chas Co, Md
Henrietta Taylor, of Cumberland, Md
Nora Bonner, of Wash, D C
F Turner, of King Geo Co, Va
Cecilia Lyon, of Balt, Md
L Bonner, of Wash, D C
Virginia Laub, of Wash, D C
M T Osborne, of Gtwn, D C
Josephine Clements, of Gtwn, D C
Rosa Queen, of Wash, D C
A Bateman, of Gtwn, D C
Cora Semmes, of Gtwn, D C
Virginia Gross, of Gtwn, D C
Ada Semmes, of Gtwn, D C
Josephine Freeman, of Chas Co, Md
E May, of Gtwn, D C
Margaret Jewett, of Wash, D C
Eliz White, of Wash, D C
Mary Harris, of Bienville Parish, La
Caroline Canfield, of Auburn, N Y
Josephine Hinton, of Delaware, Ohio
Florence Greenhow, of Wash, D C
Susan Sasscer, of PG Co, Md
Christina Williams, of St Augustine, Fla
Caroline Poe, of Gtwn, D C
Julia Swann, of Alexandria, Va

Catharine Edelin, of Calvert Co, Md
Pauline Blache, of New Orleans
Delia Walker, of Wash, D C
Nina Fremont, of Wash, D C
Ellen Waring, of Montg Co, Md
Lucy Rainy, of Gtwn, D C
Miss Mary Brooks, of Gtwn
E McAtee, of Gtwn
Adelaide Goszler, of Gtwn, D C
Victoria Brent, of Chas Co, Md
E Wilson, of Bladensburg
Margaret Duer, of Cincinnati
Rosa Porche, of New Orleans
Amanda Lepretre, of New Orleans
E de Vaudricourt, of Wash, D C
Dora Murray, of Gtwn, D C

Mrd: on Jul 9, in the parish of Lafayette, La, at the residence of Govn'r Mouton, by Rev Calvin A Frazer, Bvt Capt Franklin Gardner, Adjut of 7th U S Inf, to Miss Mathilde Mouton, daughter of Alexander Mouton.

Died: on Fri, Jos Lawrence, son of Dr Flodoardo & Lydia M Howard, in his 6th year. His funeral will be from the residence of his father, F st north & 10th west, this afternoon, at 5 o'clock.

In virtue of a distress for house rent, I shall expose to public sale, on Aug 3, 1850, 2 milch cows, seized & taken under a distrain as the property of Edmund Hagan, to satisfy rent due in arrears to Benj F Greene. –Wm A Mulloy, bailiff

Boarding: at Miss Briscoe's, 7th & Pa ave, over Shutter's Dry Goods Store. Families, single gentlemen, & transient visiters, on moderate terms, can be accommodated with board or with rooms only.

Hon R I Bowie is, for the present, detained from his seat in the House of Reps: in consequence of the death of a very near relative.

Postmaster Gen established the following new Post Ofcs for week ending Jul 20, 1850.

Ofc	County, State	Postmaster
Marion Mills	Wash, Me	E Whitney
Sutton's Mills	Essex, Mass	Laban Sawyer
Manville	Providence, R I	Alex W Fenner
Collamer	Windham, Ct	Danl Gordon
W Perrysburgh	Cattaraugus, N Y	John Tousey
Springfield Centre	Otsego, N Y	Mark Waly
Wmsville	Kent, Del	John H Johnson
Alert	Butler, Ohio	John Iseminger

Timber Ridge	Rockbridge, Va	Jos Taylor
Long Branch	Franklin, Va	S P Aldridge
Winchester	Union, N C	Jas D Smith
Moultrie	Spartanbrug D, S C	J R Wilkins
Marengo	Laurens D, S C	Wm G Coleman
Harkinsville	Anderson D, S C	Jas W Lewis
Esom Hill	Paulding, Geo	Jas Wheeler
Cotoma	Montg, Ala	Amos Jones
New York	Sumter, Ala	John A McConnell
Holly Spring	Dallas, Ark	Richd C Key
Baptist Mission	Cherokee N, Ark	Evan Jones
Cox's Creek	Bullitt, Ky	H McCullough
Bear Wallow	Barren, Ky	Christopher Carden
Worthington	Greene, Ia	M P Eddy
Parma	Shelby, Ia	Alfred Phelps
Waterford	Laporte, Ia	Arad Davis
Leedsville	Vanderburgh, Ia	Saml Hutchinson
Bloomville	Will, Ill	Geo W Allen
Dimmick	La Salle, Ill	A Long
Amazon	Madison, Iowa	Emanuel J Henkle
Indian Prairie	Van Buren, Iowa	A T Brooks
Green Bush	Polk, Iowa	Closbery Jones
Eureka	Winnebago, Wis	Lester Round
Roxo	Marquetto, Wis	Geo L Leatherbury
Freedom	Sauk, Wis	Jas Christie
Eolia	Dane, Wis	Chas H Bradley

Names Changed:
Woodville, Abbeville, district, S C, changed to Greenwood.
Greenwood, Laurens district, S C, changed to Woodville.
Leesville, Boone Co, Ill, changed to South Prairie.
Tyro, Jefferson Co, Mo, changed to Glenfinlas.
Wanonah, Columbia Co, Wis, changed to Portage city.

MON JUL 29, 1850
Appointments by the Pres: 1-John C Clark, of the State of N Y, to be Solicitor of the U S Treasury. 2-Thos L Smith, of the State of N Y, to be First Auditor of the U S Treasury. 3-Ignatius Mudd, of D C, to be Com'r of the Public Bldgs.

Word received yesterday by Gen Jesup, announcing the death of that distinguished ofcr & excellent man, Brig Gen [by brevet] Richd B Mason, of the U S Army, who had retruned from Calif. He breathed his last in St Louis on Jul 25, a victim to the cholera. –Union

The American mail steamer **Atlantic** sailed from N Y on Sat for Liverpool, taking out 130 passenges, among whom are A C Bullitt & Geo W Kendall.

Danl H Pearson was executed for the murder of his wife & children, [in Wilmington, Mass, on Apr 11, 1849,] on Fri last within the yard of the jail at East Cambridge. Pearson confessed having perpetrated the dreadful crime.

Died: on Jul 25, in Wash City, at the residence of John S Gallagher, Catharine, daughter of R H & Harriet E P Gallagher, of Richmond, Va, aged 1 year.

Died: on Jul 15, at Montgomery Hall, near Staunton, Augusta Co, Va, Mrs Ann Montgomery Peyton, widow of late John Howe Peyton, & daughter of John Lewis & Mary Preston. She was born at Sweet Springs, Mar 3, 1803, & was married Sep 13, 1821 & from that time resided in & near Staunton, She was the mother of 10 children, all of whom were assembled around her dying bed. In all the relations of neighbor, friend, mistress, wife, & mother, she exhibited the virtues which constitute & adorn the character of a Christian lady.

Miss Mgt Ann Thornton was found dead in her bed, in one of the rooms of the Delavan house, at Albany, on Fri last. An examination showed she had not committed suicide, but rendered it probable that she had taken some medicine, which had operated very powerfully & caused great pain, to allay which, she had taken an overdose of chloroform, which had caused her death. Her family reside near Thornton's Ferry, N H. For the past 2 years she had been in Mississippi, & had been the principal in charge of the Jackson Female Academy, at Jackson, the capital of that State. A strong letter of recommendation was found in her papers signed by Chas G Atherton & Franklin Pierce, both of whom have been U S Senators from N H. Her grandfather was Matthew Thornton, one of the signers of the Declaration of Independence, & her father's brother was formerly an ofcr in the U S Treasury Dept, & then Charge d'Affaires to Lima. She evidently was on her way to visit her family & relatives in N H.

Chapman Coleman, son-in-law of Govn'r Crittenden, died at his residence in Louisville, Ky, on Sun last. His death leaves a deep void in our community.

Mrd: on Jul 26, by Rev Dr Duchachet, Capt D J Sutherland to Annie D, daughter of Maj A A Nicholson, U S Marine Corps.

For sale: my place, 20 acres, east side of Rock Creek, between Maj John P Heiss & Joshua Pierce. Twenty minutes ride from Pa ave, by 14th st. Improvements are a handsome cottage, with a separate bldg for kitchen & servants' room & stabling Terms easy. -Julius A Peters, on premises, or at his store, Pa av near 10th st.

For sale: 2 story brick dwlg on west side of Green near Bridge st, the lot fronting 25 feet with Bridge st. Apply to Judson Mitchell, or A F Offutt & Co.

TUE JUL 30, 1850
Col Manlius V Thompson, formerly Lt Govn'r of Ky, & cmder of a regt of volunteers from Ky during the Mexican war, died at his residence in Gtwn, Scott Co, on Mon of last week.

Mrd: on the Sabbath, by Rev John C Smith, Mr Sydney Danforth Bassett to Miss Mary Fergusson, all of Wash City.

Died: on Jul 26, near the Navy Yard, in Wash City, of cholera infantum, after 7 days' illness, Mary Handley, daughter of Dennis & Mary Callaghan, aged 9 months & 1 day.

Died: on Jul 29, after a few days' illness, Mr Jas Johnston, in his 83rd year. His funeral will be tomorrow, at 5 P M, from his late residence on the corner of First & E Capt sts.

Died: on Jul 29, after a few days' illness, Mr Dennis Tuomey, native of the county of Cork, Ireland, in his 60th year, & for the last 24 years a resident of Wash City. His funeral will be this afternoon at 4 o'clock, from the residence of Nicholas Ferritor, D st, between 12th & 13th.

For rent: a new frame house, just finished, containing 8 rooms, well finished, located on 4th st, between F & G sts. Rent $9 per month. -L Saur, 7th st, between D & E sts.

A card-Dr T P Hereford, late of Va, has settled in Washington, on the Island, & offers his professional services to the citizens of Wash. His ofc is at Mrs Fraser's, on 7th st, near Md ave.

WED JUL 31, 1850
Mr Jas D Hall, of Boston, came to an untimely death in that city on Thu last, from having been accidentally poisoned. Being unwell, his family physician was called, who left a prescription for 10 grains of calomel. A neighboring apothecary prepared the dose, but carelessly sent corrosive sublimate instead of calomel. [Aug 3rd newspaper: Mr Wakefield, the apothecary in Boston, who, by mistake, put up a poison which caused the death of Mr Hall, assist assessor, was on Mon arrested on the charge of manslaughter, & gave bail of $5,000 to appear for trial.]

Judge Lynch. At Indianapolis, Ind, lately a man named Moorehouse was tried & acquitted on a charge of assault with intent to kill his son. A public meeting was held, & he was warned to leave the place, which he did immediately.

On Mon night, while Mr Catoir was giving an exhibition of fire works, one of them struck Miss Cecelia Leonard, a very accomplished young lady of our own town, killing her in a most horrible manner. -Shreveport [La] Gaz, Jul 17

Gen Jose Antonio Paez, formerly Pres of Venezuela, & one of the founders of that Republic, whence he had been recently exiled, arrived in Phil from St Thomas last Fri. He comes to this country, it is stated, with a view to making it his future residence.

Pretty farm for sale: the farm on which I reside: near Good Hope: about 60 acres, with a dwlg with 5 rooms, a servant's house, stable, carriage-house, smoke & hen-house. Apply on the premises, or 3rd story of Winder's new bldg. –Edw M Clark

Died: on Jul 29, in Gtwn, Albert Eccleston, 3rd son of Dr J A & Mary S Ritchie, in his 6th year.

Died: on Jul 4, in his father's residence in Cincinnati, Ohio, Jas F Janney, aged 20 years.

Died: yesterday, in Gtwn, Mrs Mary E C Rodier, wife of C H Rodier, in her 27th year. Her funeral is from the residence of her husband, in Gtwn, on Bridge st, this Wed, at 5 o'clock.

Household & kitchen furniture at auction: Jul 31, at the residence of Mrs Marsolette, Va ave, near the Navy Yard. —Green & Tastet, aucts

THU AUG 1, 1850
Envoys Extra & Ministers Pleni of Foreign Gov'ts presented to the Pres yesterday at the Executive Mansion.
Russia: M Alex'r De Bodisco, Envoy, & M Edw Stoeckl, 1st Sec of Legation.
Great Britain: Rt Hon Sir H L Bulwer, Envoy
France: M Sain de Bois le Comte, Envoy; M A de Bouboulon, Sec of Leg; M J Marie, M Poussieloue, & M Philibert, Attaches
Spain: Don A Calderon de la Barca, Envoy
Portugal: Cmder J C de Figaniere E Morao, Minister Resident
Prussia: M Magnus Charge d'Affaires ad interim
Belgium: M Henri Bosch Spencer, Minister Resident
Denmark: M Steen de Bille, Charge d'Affaires
Brazil: Chevalier Sergio Terceiro de Macedo, Envoy
Chile: Don Manuel Carvallo, Envoy; Don Francisco s Astaburuaga, Sec of Legation
Peru: Don J M Tirado, Envoy
Mexico: Don Angel Huici, Attache

Senate: 1-Memorial of Adam Hays, a hospital surgeon during the late war with Great Britain: referred to the Cmte on Pensions. 2-Petition of Martha Jarnigan, asking compensation for certain property stolen by the Indians during recent hostilities in Fla: referred to Cmte on Indian affairs.

FRI AUG 2, 1850
Land for sale: being desirous of locating my servants in Texas the ensuing fall, I will sell privately the farm on which I reside, lying mostly in Madison Co, on the Rapid Ann river, midway between Orange Courthouse & Barboursville, containing 750 acres. Refer to the Hon Jeremiah Morton, Washington, Mr Robt B Somerville, Richdmond, Va, & the subscriber on the premises, whose address is Liberty Mills, Orange Co, Va.
—Geo A Smith

It appears that there is little hope, at least for the present, of recovering the statue of Mr Calhoun, on board the wreck of the ship **Elizabeth**, the sea having made a complete breach over the place where she sunk. A buoy has been placed over the wreck, with a view to further efforts to recover the statue.

Senate: Bill for the relief of John Mitchell: passed.

Mrd: on Jul 30, by Rev Mr Donelan, Mr Jos F Crown to Miss Priscilla Ann Walters, all of Wash City.

Mrd: Jul 30, by Rev W T Eva, Mr John P Lair to Delilah Thompson, both of PG Co, Md.

Mrd: on Thu last, by Rev Mr Edwards, Mr Chas McDonald to Miss Ann Maria Wallace, all of Wash City.

Mrd: on Jul 18, at Edenton, N C, by Rev Saml J Johnston, J T Pickett, of Fauquier Co, to Eliz J, eldest daughter of the late Malachi Haughton.

Mrd: on Thu, in the 4th Presbyterian Church, by Rev John C Smith, Mr John W Thompson to Miss Janet McGill, all of Wash City

Died: on Jul 30, Thos Tomlinson, aged about 37 years.

Handsome farm of 420 acres for sale: near Poolesville, Montg Co, Md: with a good stone dwlg house & kitchen, brick dairy, & pump in the yard. –Martin H Batston, Trustee, Triadelphia Factory, Md

Household & kitchen furniture at auction: on Aug 4, at the residence of the Hon Geo W Crawford, late Sec of War, situated on F st, between 6th & 7th sts.
–Dyer & Brother, aucts

SAT AUG 3, 1850
Accident on the Erie Railroad, on Wed, near Lackawaxen, caused the death of 2 drovers, Henry C Clapp, 19 years old, in charge of sheep & swine, from Menton, Ohio, nephew of Alex'r Campbell, of Bethany College, Va, & Mr Bondall, in charge of cattle, from Corning, N Y.

Balt, Aug 2. Bloody murder perpetrated in Harford Co, Md: the victim was Mr Henry Hammond, a well know citizen of that place. He was shot through the heart yesterday while engaged in his garden at his farm, near Perrymansville. The murder was deliberate & the perpetrator has not yet been discovered. Mr Hammond was a native of Balt, & among our best families, & resided in the city until within a few years back, when he removed to Harford.

On Jul 4, the 18 year old son of Dr Walker, of Wash, Texas, was in a small tree when he was struck by lightning & killed.

Carlo Bassigallope, a skilful Italian musician, died in Providence, on Sat, from the effects of poison. Only in this country but 3 months & spoke English very imperfectly, feeling unwell, went to purchase some cream of tartar, but pointed to a bottle marked tart emetic, which he insisted was what he wanted. It caused his death soon after.

House of Reps: 1-Cmte on Agriculture: discharged from the further consideration of the ptn of Wm H Paddock, of N Y, praying the establishment of an Agricultural Bureau at Wash: laid on the table. 2-Cmte on Indian Affairs: resolution for the settlement of the accounts with the heirs & reps of Col Pierce M Butler, late agent of the Cherokee Indians: reported the same back without amendment. 3-Cmte on Indian Affairs: discharged from the further consideration of the ptns of S L Fremont, Jas McNutt, Capt J G Barnard, Wm Hutchinson, Hamilton P Bee et al, Benj Moore, & Chas G Layton: laid on the table. 4-Bill for the relief of Wm Maxwell, late Marshal for the district of Georgia: passed. 5-Cmte on Military Affairs: bill for the relief of Jacob P Montgomery: passed. Same cmte: adverse report on the claim of Joel M Acker; which was committed. Same cmte: discharged from the further consideration of the ptn of H G Fant: laid on the table. Same cmte: bill for the relief of Wm H Owen, a private in Capt W B Gray's company of Texas rangers: committed. 6-Cmte on Naval Affairs: bill for the relief of Wm Guinard: committed. Same cmte: bill for the relief of Jos Radcliff: committed. Same cmte: act for the relief of Thos M Taylor & Francis B Stockton: committed. 7-Cmte on Revolutionary Pensions: act for the relief of Mary Mac Rea: reported the same back without amendment. Same cmte: adverse reports on the ptns of Wm K Blair, John W Campbell, Jno C Van Duzen & others, Eliza Kirby, Henrietta M Stewart, & Rebecca L Weaver: laid on the table. Same cmte: adverse reports on the ptns of Saml T Harrison et al, heirs of Wm Harrison, deceased, Mary Deany, Eliza Vethake, Levi Nichols, Wm E Parkman et al, Ann Temple Green, Maria Nicholson & Eliz R Nicholson, Abigail Davis, & W B Goodwin: laid on the table. Same cmte: bill for the relief of Susannah Tarn, widow of Jno Tarn, deceased, & a bill for the relief of Christina Weber, widow of John Weber, deceased: committed. Same cmte: act for the relief of Margaret L Worth, widow of the late Gen Worth, of the army of the U S, reported the same back with the recommendation that it do no pass. Same cmte: adverse reports on the ptns of Jos Herndon, Jos Carter, Jos Plumb, & Fred'k Fishback et al, heirs of Col Yates: severally laid on the table. Same Cmte: bill for the relief of Capt Robt Wilson: committed. Same cmte: adverse report on the ptn of Sarah Foster: laid on the table. Same cmte: adverse reports on the ptns of the children of Josiah Knight, John Ferris, & Francis Nutinack: laid on the table. 8-Cmte on Invalid Pensions: bills for the relief of Amos Knapp & Hugh W Wormley, of Ala: committed. Same cmte: bills for the relief of Collin Andrews & Mrs Catharine Clarke: committed. Same cmte: adverse reports on the ptns of Asa Derrington, Jos Cross, David Cowder, Michl Bailey, & Jacob Carder: laid on the table. Same cmte: bills for the relief of Cornelius Hughes, of John Campbell, & of Isaac Seymour: committed. 9-Cmte on Invalid Pensions: adverse reports on the ptns of Robt Ramsey, Richd Robinson, Enoch Dobyns, Danl Matzanbaugh, Saml Smith, David Boomer, Moses W Hunt, Gen Willis Foulke, Isaac Plummer, John Oothoudt, Danl Palmer, & Bela Sprague: laid on the table.

Powder Mill Explosion, on Mill Creek, near St Clair, Schuylkill Co, Pa, on Mon last, instantly killed Theobald Sherrer, one of the workmen. John Scharr, another workman, although not killed outright, died 6 hours later. Two lads, 17 & 10 years of age, sons of Mr Solomon McKinney, of Barry township, were instantly killed. Mr Danl Dengler, of Barry, also fell a victim to the explosion. -Pottsville Emporium

Senate: 1-Cmte on Pensions: ptn of Wm Ferguson, asking arrears of pension, submitted a report in wirting, which was ordered to be printed, adverse to the prayer of the petitioner. Same cmte: adverse report on the ptn of Isaac F Miller, for an increase of pension. Same cmte: ptn of John B Brooks, asking compensation for services of his father during the Revolutionary war: adverse report thereon. Same cmte: bill for the relief of Benj P Smith: recommended its passage. 2-Cmte on Indian Affairs: memorial of J K Rogers, legal rep of the widow & children of David Cordery, deceased, a Cherokee Indian, asking compensation for the value of a reservation under the treaties of 1835-36: passed to a second reading. 3-Cmte on the Judiciary: bill for the relief of Wm Maxwell, late U S marshal for Ga: recommended its passage. 4-Bill for the relief of Isaac Seymour: a soldier who was wounded in the Florida war, but on account of the failure of the official report of his case, he failed to get a certificate which would have secured a pension, & he has been without a pension from that time. Having lost a limb, & being really in extreme poverty, not being able to obtain a livelihood for himself, the House passed an act for his relief: passed by the Senate. 5-Bill for the relief of John P Montgomery: referred to the Cmte on Military Affairs. 6-Engrossed bill for the relief of John Miller was read a third time & passed.

Irregularities in the receipt of letters at the post ofc at Geneva, N Y, directed an investigation by Mr Holbrook, the special agent, which resulted in the arrest of John E Bean, a clerk in the Geneva ofc.

Mrd: on Wed last, by Rev Mr Ballantine, Thos G Rice, of Boston, to Miss Ellen, daughter of J Collamer.

Mrd: on Aug 2, in Wash City, by Rev G W Samson, Peter Slingerland to Miss Martha McEwing, both of Laurel Factory, Md.

Died: on Jul 22, at Moorefield, Va, Mary V L Cassin, consort of John H Cassin, & eldest daughter of Dr Mortimer D Williams, in her 22nd year.

Died: yesterday, in Wash City, Catharine, youngest child of Geo & Julia Phelps. Her funeral will take place this day at 2 o'clock.

MON AUG 5, 1850
The stage from Harrisburg, Pa, broke through the Cumberland Canal bridge on Aug 1, & Benj D Jones was killed, & 10 other passengers were very badly injured.

Died: on Aug 2, in Wash City, in her 41st year, Mrs Ursula Gardner, consort of David A Gardner, formerly of Brooklyn, N Y, but for several years past a resident of Wash City.

Longevity-John Vanhooser, living in Jefferson Co, Tenn, is 122 years of age. He voted for Gen Washington for the Presidency. The Knoxville Reporter states that until lately he could walk to & from town, a distance of 6 miles, without fatigue. His daughter aged 80 lately paid him a visit. He is a German by birth, & emigrated to the U S a century ago.

A duel was fought near New Orleans on Jul 22, between Col Bunch & Capt Lewis, two of the Cuban invaders. The quarrel was some alleged misconduct of Col Bunch while the Creole was at Cardenas. Capt Lewis was shot through both thighs, but not so severely wounded that he could not have continued the fight, had a second shot been demanded.

Correction: the name of Miss Edith O Henshaw, as receiving the silver medal for best scholarship in the female dept of the First District School, was omitted in the list furnished to us. We add the following names: Sarah Ellen Burgess & Julia Prosperi.

Mr J L Clapp, of Painesville, Ohio, was one of the victims of the late terrible disaster on the Erie railroad, caused by the breaking of a bridge near Lackawaxen. He was discovered buried among the fragments of the car, directly beneath an ox, which was still alive, & at times greatly distressed Mr Clapp by kicking him in his breast. It was impossible to extricate him until the ox was removed. He thought he could endure the weight of the ox until it could be killed & removed piecemeal. It was shot, but in its dying struggles kicked Mr Clapp so violently in the breast as to deprive him of life. He spoke much of his family in Ohio, during the ordeal, stating that he had a wife & 4 children.

Appointments by the Pres: 1-Thos L Crittenden, of Ky, to be U S Consul for the port of Liverpool, England. 2-Henry Boyce, of Louisiana, to be Judge of the District Court of the U S for the western District of Louisiana. 3-Edmund M Evans, to be Sec to sign in the name of the Pres all patents for lands sold or granted under the authority of the U S.

Died: on Jul 21, at Blanhiem, near Bladensburg, PG Co, Md, Miss Fanny C Nicholson, daughter of Cmdor John Nicholson, of Kent Co, on the eastern shore of Md.

Died: on Aug 4, Howard Lee, infant son of Dr Chas G Page, aged 5 months. His funeral is this evening at 5 o'clock.

Chas Emory has been arrested near Springfield, Ill, while in the act of stealing sundry packages from the mail bags on the stage route to the East.

House of Reps: 1-Cmte on Invalid Pensions: adverse reports on the ptns of Jas McCauley, John Pearl, & Saml Campbell: laid on the table. Same cmte: discharged from the further consideration of the ptns of Jno B Cunningham & Jeremiah Hess: laid on the table. 2-Cmte on Patents: bill to extend a patent to the heirs of Jethro Wood, deceased: read twice. 1-Bill introduced for the relief of Jos Arnow & Peter Arnow, heirs of Jos Arnow, late of Florida, deceased: referred to the Cmte of Claims.

$100 reward for runaway negro Margaret, who was induced by a quasi free negro Ben Lanham; & for her to take $30 in gold. She is about 18 years old, a good seamstress, & supposed to be pregnant. –S L Lewis

Liberal reward for return of a black boy, John Pinkney, who ran away on Aug 2. —Geo Beale, Bloomingdale, near Wash, D C

TUE AUG 6, 1850
Millard Fillmore, Pres of the U S, recognizes Giulio Cesare Vertu who has been appointed Vice Consul of the Two Sicilies for port of N Y. Apr 5, 1850

Postmaster Gen est'd the following new Post Ofcs for the week ending Jul 27, 1850.

Ofc	County, State	Postmaster
Snow Falls	Oxford, Me	L White
Pike	Washington, Me	John Balch
West Salisbury	Addison, Vt	Jas S Messer
W Cornwall	Addison, Vt	Benj F Haskell
East Thetford	Orange, Vt	Wm Slade
Derby Centre	Orleans, Vt	John M Culver
Campbell's Mills	Windham, Ct	C Campbell
Ireland Corners	Albany, N Y	E H Ireland
Checkered House	Oswego, N Y	Saml Crosby
Portsmouth	Dauphin, Pa	John Ringland
Juniata Crossings	Bedford, Pa	Jas W Dickinson
Mt Chesnut	Butler, Pa	Jas Anderson
Bridgeport	Huntingdon, Pa	David Irons
Cherry Valley	Washington, Pa	E Smith
Blemen	Carroll, Md	John Yuob
Tampico	Darke, Ohio	Wm Thompson
St Henry's	Mercer, Ohio	Fred Seewald
Cable	Guernsey, Ohio	Chas Swan
Hamburgh	Preble, Ohio	A Sterling
Grand Ledge	Eaton, Mich	H A French
Augerons	Jackson, Va	Danl Woodruff
Dovesville	Rockingham, Va	U Wittick
Reems Creek	Buncombe, N C	J R Weaver
South Fork	Ashe, N C	B C Galloway
King's Creek	Caldwell, N C	A Kaxton
Warriors' Creek	Caldwell, N C	Jas Watt
Nathan's Creek	Ashe, N C	A McMillan
Palona	Greenville D, S C	David Clary
Camp Ground	Appling, Geo	J Hall
Liberty	Jackson, Ala	E W Williams
Bethlehem	Chambers, Ala	A B Camp
Mountain Stand	Marshall, Ala	C W Bryan
Gold Mines	Marion, Ala	Peter Gilpin
Ponta	Lauderdale, Miss	Wm V Raney
Monroe	Perry, Miss	O C Rhodes
Sentrell's Store	Caddo P, La	W Sentrell

Elm Spring	Crawford, Ark	Wm Barrington
Cove	Polk, Ark	J McDaniel
Hoodsville	Jefferson, Ark	Jona R Hood
Palmer's Store	Weakley, Tenn	John W Palmer
Manlyville	Henry, Tenn	Wm C Manly
Crooked Ford	Morgan, Tenn	A Agee
Red Spring	Polk, Tenn	Wm Mills
Plum Grove	Blount, Tenn	Alex Cook
Pleasant Hill	Henderson, Ky	A J Vorment
Shiloh	Callaway, Ky	E P Chandler
New Frier	Cook, Ia	A H Taylor
Rogers Farm	McLean, Ia	E Rogers
Crooked Creek	Clinton, Ia	J L Johnson
Woodsboro'	Montgomery, Ia	Wm Wood
Beaver Creek	Pulaski, Ia	M Kelley
Massillon	Allen, Ia	John Shaffer
East Liberty	Allen, Ia	D Stendabecker
Deeds Creek	Kosciusko, Ia	Geo W Ryerson
Greenwood	Marquette, Wis	S C Dow
Weyauwega	Winnebago, Wis	Ben Birdsall
Hubbleton	Jefferson, Wis	L M Grigg
Sharon	Appanoose, Iowa	Thos Swearinger
Smith's Ferry	Jackson, Iowa	Wm Smith
Lindville	Monroe, Iowa	David J Prather

Names Changed:
Kedron, Washtenaw Co, Mich, changed to Chelsea.
Druham's Ford, Marion Co, Iowa, changed to English Settlement.
Metcalf Furnace, Carter Co, Ky, changed to Star Furnace.
Cherry Grove, Lauderdale Co, Ala, changed to Lauderdale Factory.
Steam Mills, Choctaw Co, Miss, changed to Bankston.
Short Bend, Cook Co, Ill, changed to Wanksaik.
New Erin, Stephenson Co, Ill, changed to Elleroy.

Orphans Court of Wash Co, D C. Letters of administration on the personal estate of Wm Cockrell, late of Wash Co, deceased. –J T Clark, adm

Appointments by the Pres: 1-John J Walker, Collector of the Customs, Mobile, Ala. 2-Manuel J Garcia, Naval Ofcr, New Orleans, La.

Mrd: on Aug 4, at St Peter's Church, Capitol Hill, by Rev Mr Lennahan, Mr Wm E Chafee to Miss Lidia A Wood, both of Wash City.

Senate: 1-Cmte on Public Lands: ptn of Robt Butler, closing with a resolution that the prayer of the petitioner ought to be granted: which was agreed to.

Letter dated Aug 3 from Harper's Ferry: death by cholera of Erasmus Bell, Lewis E Gore, Jos Baylis, & Michl Gomph. –Balt American
+
Died: at Harper's Ferry, of cholera: Erasmus Bell, Lewis E Gore, Jos Baylis & Michael Gomph. -Balt Americ.

Died: on Aug 2, at the residence of his grandfather, Geo F De La Roche, at Gtwn, D C, of bilious dysentery, Geo Clinton, in his 6th year, only son of G Clinton & Eliza M M Frailey, of Balt, where his remains were deposited in Green Mount Cemetery. Of such is the Kingdom of Heaven.

Died: on Aug 3, at his residence in Phil, Cmdor Jacob Jones, U S Navy, in his 83rd year. He was a native of Delaware, in the war of 1812, & contributed to establish the naval renown of our country. While in command of the brig **Wasp**, he captured the British brig **Frolic**, of superior force, & was voted a sword by each of the States of Delaware, Mass, & N Y. He was, until recently, the Govn'r of the Naval Asylum, near Phil.

Land Warrant Lost: #44162, in favor of Robt A Richardson, late a Cpl in Capt Walker's Co D, Regt U S Voltigeurs, dated Feb 7, 1849, lost in the mail between Wash & Appomatox, Va. A caveat against said warrant has been entered at the Gen Land Ofc. -R W Latham Co.

WED AUG 7, 1850
Senate: 1-Cmte on Military Affairs: bill for the relief of Jacob P Montgomery: recommended its passage.

U S vs Lewis F Carley: Carley was convicted at the Criminal Court, before Judge Crawford, of manslaughter, in stabbing Brown, the U S marine, on board the U S ship **Alleghany**, on the high seas, in 1848: question was whether he could be put upon his trial for the second time for the same offence. Further hearing of the case will be had.

Lightning on Sat at Village Green, near Chester, Delaware Co, Pa, struck & killed Mr Dunton & his wife.

House of Reps: 1-Ptn of Susan Tool, of Pa, a widow & relict of Jacob Tool, deceased, who was a soldier of the late war, praying that Congress may grant her 160 acres of bounty land. 2-Ptn of Hon C H Atherton, praying to be allowed interest on his money during the time the Gov't had the use thereof, & to be remunerated for his expenses incurred in entering into a contract with the Gov't, which contract the Gov't failed to perform on their part. 3-Ptn of Leonard Scott & Co & others, publishers of periodicals, on the subject of postage.

Mrd: on Aug 6, by Rev Jas B Donelan, Mr Ethan Allen Edmonston, of PG Co, Md, to Miss Mary Virginia, 2nd daughter of Saml Sherwood, of Wash City.

Died: on Aug 3, at his residence, **Greenleaf's Point**, in his 70th year, of consumption, Jas Gill. He was a good citizen, a kind parent, & an honest man.

Died: on Aug 6, in Wash City, Mr Henry W Howard, formerly of Montg Co, Md, after a short but painful illness. His funeral will be this Wed at 4 o'clock, from the residence of Mr Theo Sheckles, on 7th st, between L & K sts.

Died: on Jul 20, in N Y C, Mgt Major, widow of the late Danl Major, Parish of Lisburn, county Antrim, Ireland, in her 70th year.

Died: Jul 25, at **Fort Moultrie**, S C, Anita, wife of John B Porter, M D, Surgeon, U S Army, & daughter of late Josiah Smith, of St Augustine, Fla.

Notice. Per order of the Orphans Court of Wash Co, D C. Thos J Johnston, administrator of the estate of Thos J Johnston, deceased, will be at the court room on Aug 24, for the purpose of paying all past claims against said estate.

Circuit Court of Wash Co, D C-in Chancery. Wm Holmead & al, vs Gregory Ennis, executor heirs of Moran. Order of ratification nisi. Trustee reports the sale of lot 15 in square 534, in Wash City, to Alice Moran for $287, & the purchaser has complied with the terms of the sale. Ratify same. –Jno A Smith, clerk

Navy Dept: Aug 5, 1850. As a mark of respect to the memory of Cmdor Jacob Jones, a distinguished ofcr of the U S Navy, who died in Phil on Aug 3, the flags of the Navy Yards, Stations, & vessels of the U S Navy, will be hoisted at halfmast, & 13 minute guns fired at noon on the day after the receipt of this order. Ofcrs of the Navy & Marine Corps will wear crape on the left arm for 30 days. –Wm A Graham, Sec of the Navy

Interments in Wash, D C for Jul, 1850: 134. Ofc of the Board of Health: Thos Miller, M D, Pres.

THU AUG 8, 1850
Robt Read, was on Mon last unanimously elected Pres of the Farmers & Mechanics' Bank of Gtwn in the place of John Kurtz, deceased.

Senate: 1-Memorial of McKean Buchanan, a purser in the navy, asking indemnity for losses sustained by him in consequence of an illegal order of his commanding ofcr: referred to the Cmte on Pensions. 2-Ptn of Orris Crosby, asking the correction of an error in the act approved Aug 8, 1846, allowing him a pension as a private, instead of surgeon's mate: referred to the Cmte on Pensions. 3-Bill for the relief of the heirs & reps of Col Alex'r G Morgan: referred to the Cmte on Military Affairs.

Mrd: on Jul 23, at New London, Conn, by Rev J W Dennis, S S Bassett, U S Navy, to Louisa Ellen Albertson, of New London.

Mrd: on Aug 6, by Rev Mr Hanson, Mr Josiah Hitchcock to Miss Catherine A Turner, all of Wash City.

For sale: farm called **Summerville**: in Loudoun Co, Va, containing 825 acres, near **Ball's Mill**, about 6 miles from Leesburg, the county seat. There is a frame dwlg, 2 stories high, & other ordinary out-houses. Address the subscriber, Leesburg, Loudoun Co, Va: Chas W Blincoe.

$50 reward for runaway servant Isabella, or Issy, who took with her her child Malvina, about 6 years old; both mulattoes. Issy is about 45 or 50 years of age. She may be harboring about the farm of Mr Thos Crawford, near the **Old Fields**, as she has numerous acquaintances in that part of the State. –Philip Ennis

FRI AUG 9, 1850
Died: on Aug 2, of congestion of the brain, in her 6th year, Ann E Bell, daughter of the late David B Bell, of N C.

Died: on Aug 7, in Newport, Ky, Mrs Harriet E Jones, consort of Michl Jones, in her 40th year.

Died: on Aug 9, in Springfield, Miss Bancroft, age 17, only daughter of Mr Bancroft, of Springfield, Mass.

Died: on Tue, at Bedford Springs, John Swan, Superintendent, on the part of the State of Md, of the Nat'l Road, of inflammation of the stomach.

SAT AUG 10, 1850
At the house of Mr Pyper, in Thetford, Mich, on Tue week, Mr Pyper's mother, who was nearly blind, & 2 of his children were alone in the house, when the elder of the children, in playing round the stove, set her clothes on fire. The grandmother, child, & youngest child who was in her arms, were all set on fire. The old lady did not have the power to take any effectual means to extinguish the flames.

From the Salem Register: died, in this city, on Aug 14, Hon Nathl Silsbee, aged 77 years & 6 months, one of our oldest & most respected citizens.

The police of Wash City on Thu arrested a white man, Wm L Chaplin, & a runaway slave, Allen, the former being in the act of conveying the slave who was captured, & another named Garland, who made his escape, out of the District & the ownership of their masters, towards a free state. The police watched Chaplin's movements & traced him to a point on the Montgomery road near the residence of Francis P Blair. Allen & Chaplin were both committed to jail yesterday.

Died: on Aug 8, in Wash City, after an illness of 10 days, Mrs Eleanor Dewees, relict of late Col Wm Dewees, of Wash City, in her 70th year. Her funeral is this afternoon, at 4 o'clock, from her late residence, corner of 13th & G sts.

Postmaster Gen est'd the following new Post Ofcs for the week ending Aug 3, 1850.

Ofc	County, State	Postmaster
Carver's Harbor	Waldo, Me	David Vinal
Glanville	Fairfield, Ct	Henry S Banks
Pine Valley	Chemung, N Y	C L Ten Brook
North Greece	Monroe, N Y	Alfred Phelps
Reed Island	Pulaski, Va	Gordon Dobbins
Hall's Cross Roads	Franklin, N C	Thos R Simpson
Marysville	Paulding, Geo	W C Walker
Williamstown	Madison, Miss	John L Smith
Huntsville	Choctaw, Miss	Jos J Thomas
Waco Village	Milan, Texas	S P Ross
Cozby	Hamilton, Tenn	Wm Cozby
Friendship	Blount, Tenn	David Morgan
Thompsonville	Washington, Ky	Jos M Kirkland
Saint Peters	St Charles, Mo	Jos G Spalding
Claysville	Boone, Mo	Edwin Bass
Hardinsburg	Montgomery, Ill	Jas Cummings
Kent	Stephenson, Ill	Abram Reber
Packwaukee	Marquette, Wis	Wm Euen, jr
Cross Plains	Dane, Wis	Sylvester Morgan
Warwick	Marquette, Wis	Ransom Wright

Name Changed: Moniteau, Moniteau Co, Missouri, changed to Jamestown

The Boston Courier announces the decease of Col Wm P Winchester, one of the most esteemed citizens of Massachusetts. [No death date given-current item.]

Cholera at Harper's Ferry, Va: on Aug 7th there were 7 deaths, amongst them the Rev Jos G Haye, M. D. & Mr Carroll, proprietor of the United States Hotel.

Died: on Thu, after a brief illness, in his 27th year, Alphonse Labbe, son of late F C Labbe, & a clerk in the ofc of the clerk of the Supreme Court. His funeral will take place on Sun at 4 o'clock, from the residence of his sister, on Pa av near Williard's.

Died: on Aug 8, in Wash City, after a long & painful illness, Mary Emily, 4th daughter of Thos & Mary Smith, in her 13th year. Her funeral is Sat at 4 o'clock.

Died: on Aug 9, in Wash City, Geo Salvage, sr, aged 20, 2nd son of Geo Savage. The deceased had been long & painfully afflicted with a pulmonary disease. His funeral will take place at his father's residence on Sun, at 4 o'clock.

Died: on Jul 26, at his residence in Montg Co, Md, in his 50th year of his age, Thos John Bowie, eldest son of late Washington & Mgt C Bowie, leaving a widow & 2 children, with a large number of relatives & friends, to lament their irreparable loss.

Positive sale: I offer that beautiful & healthy residence & farm *Volucia*, on the Little River turnpike, 3 miles from Alexandria, containing about 166 acres of good land: the house is a good substantial 3 story brick. Terms liberal. –Ann D Macrae

The Hon Mr Chase has been absent from the Senate by the illness of a member of his family, & the death of his infant daughter.

Senate: 1-Resolved, that John B Wallack have leave to withdraw his petition & papers. 2-Ptn of Catharine G Finney, a descendant & one of the heirs at law of an ofcr of the Rhode Island brigade, in behalf of herself & others, asking Congress to provide for the just payment of the commutation pay due to that brigade. 3-Cmte on Revolutionary Claims: memorial of Haym M Solomon, asking indemnification for advance made by his father during the Revolutionary war: ordered to a second reading. 4-Cmte on the Post & Post Ofc Roads: memorial of John T Sullivan, asking compensation for executing the binding of the laws & instructions to Postmasters, for the use of the Post Ofc Dept: ordered to a second reading. 5-Cmte of Claims: ptn of John McAvoy, a soldier in the war with Mexico, submitted a report in writing, which was ordered to be printed, adverse to the prayer of the petitioner. 6-Cmte on Pensions: bill for the relief of Eliphas C Brown: recommended its passage.

Lost or Stolen: A warrant or bounty land Certificate (unassigned) #66045, for 160 acres, dated Nov 13, 1849, issued of Frederica Muller or Miller & others; widow & minor children of Frederic Muller or Miller, deceased, late a Private in the 4th Regt of Artl of the U S. -Alfred Schucking

Thos Cornock, a native of London, & a resident of Washington for 10 years, is returning to London the end of Sept.

MON AUG 12, 1850
Senate: 1-Memorial of Eliza C Bache, widow of Geo M Bache, late a lt in the U S Navy, asking that a gratuity may be extended to her in consideration of the death of her husband, who was drowned at sea in the execution of his duty: referred to the Cmte on Naval Affairs. 2-Cmte on pensions: bill passed the House granting a pension to Eliphas C Brown: @ $18 per month: passed.

There is good reason to hope the statue of Mr Calhoun will be recovered from the wreck of the ship **Elizabeth**. Lt Maxwell Woodhull knew the position of the box enclosing it, which was unknown a day or two since.

Mrd: on Aug 8, at *Allison's Park*, near Rockville, Md, by Rev Alfred Griffith, Chas Slemmer, of Gtwn, D C, to Mary H Willson, daughter of the late Sam'l Willson of Rockville Md, of the former place..

Mrd: on Aug 1, by Rev Thos Myers, Mr Wm Finch, of N Y, to Miss Mgt A Gibson, of Wash, D C.

Mrd: on Aug 6, by Rev Thos Myers, Mr Richd Perkins to Miss Mary Morgan, both of Wash Co, D C.

Mrd: on Aug 8, by Rev Thos Myers, Mr John W Lusby to Miss Jane Vermillion, both of Wash D C.

Died: on Aug 10, at Harper's Ferry, Va, Wm Collins, of Wash City, in his 51st year. His funeral will be from his late residence, in the First Ward, this afternoon, at 5 o'clock.

Died: on Jul 24, at Noblesville, Indiana, of cholera, Lucius H Emmons, late a clerk in the Gen Post Ofc Dept.

Died: on Aug 6, in Wash, at the Navy Yard, John Thomas, age 1 year & 12 days, son of Richd N & Rebecca Peake.

Died: on Aug 11, in Wash City, Jas Albert, youngest son of Wm & Mgt Morgan, aged 17 months & 10 days.

Died: yesterday, in Wash City, after an illness of 3 days, Jos Franklin, aged 1 year & 4 months, son of Nicholas & Sarah Snyder. His funeral is this afternoon at 3 o'clock, from the residence of his parents, 11th st, between L & M sts.

Died: on Aug 7, Sallie Read, infant daughter of John A Lockwood, Surgeon U S Navy.

The Jasper Co correspondent of the Lafayette [Ia] Courier, writes that a daughter of Mr Geo Grissell, about 12 years old, committed suicide near Rensselaer, on Jul 23, by hanging herself to the joist of the house with a bridle. He little brother could not obtain assistance before she died. -Ex paper

TUE AUG 13, 1850
On Sat, in Phil, a large new 5 story brick double store house, on Granite st, belonging to Jesse Godley, fell with a crash: Alex'r Brady was severely hurt; Saml Mickey & Michl Murphy were killed; Thos Mickey & John Hagerty, were seriously injured, & Patrick Anderson was slightly injured.

Millard Fillmore, Pres of the U S, recognizes Henri Vermot, who has been appointed Vice Consul of the French Republic, for Balt.

Mrd: on Aug 11, on the Island, in Wash City, by Rev J E Weems, Wm T Tucker to Miss Mary E Maharney.

Died: on Jul 28, at St Paul, Minn, Alex'r, son of Gov'r Ramsey, aged 4 years.

Tragedy in Texas. Mr Wiley, living upon the Sabine, near Van Zandt, had separated from his wife. He visited her to propose a division of the property, & shot her dead with a pistol. He was overtaken & killed in Rusk Co by a number of citizens.

Martin Ragan, an Irish laborer, age about 22 years, was stabbed to death yesterday, in Wash.

Information wanted of Edmond Fahey, who came to this country with his sister in Apr, 1849, from Woodford Co, Galway, Ireland; when last heard of he was employed somewhere near Phil. Any information respecting him would be thankfully received by his sister Bridget Fahey, of Wash, or his cousin, Hugh Touhy, at the Navy Yard, Wash. Phil & Balt papers will please copy.

WED AUG 14, 1850
Wash Corp: 1-Ptn from R J Roach & others asking to have water conveyed in iron pipes from the public spring on 13th st along the line of 9th & 12th st: referred to the Cmte on Improvements. 2-Ptn of W W Edwards, asking for a refund of money he paid for a license: referred to the Cmte on Claims. 3-Cmte on Claims: resolution for the relief of T J Barrett: laid on the table. 4-Cmte on Claims: act for the relief of John Maguire: passed. Same cmte: act for the relief of Chas Dyson: passed. 5-Nomination of W Brenner for wood corder was taken up, considered, & rejected. 6-Nomination of J Ennis as police constable for the 7th Ward: rejected. 7-Cmte on Claims: act for the relief of Alex'r Mahon: passed. Same cmte: act for the relief of A F Totchinder: laid on the table. Same cmte: ptn of A Lehman: asked to be discharged from the further consideration of the ptn of the same: laid on the table. 8-Ptn from Wm McPeak & others, praying for the paving of an alley in square D: referred to the Cmte on Improvements. 9-Ptn from Benedict Jost, asking for the remission of a fine: referred to the Cmte on Claims. 10-Ptn from P Clapdon & others, for pavement on south side of K st: referred to the Cmte of Claims. 11-Cmte of Claims: act for the relief of Chas Stewart: passed. 12-Cmte of Claims: asked to be discharged from the further consideration of the ptn of W W Edwards: discharged accordingly. 13-Nomination of Isaac Stoddard, as Police ofcr for the 7th Ward: rejected. 14-Nomination of Geo B Bowen, as superintendent of chimney sweeps for the Second Ward, in place of N B Wilkinson whose nomination was withdrawn at his own request. The nomination was confirmed. 15-Act for the relief of the heirs of Jas Nairn: ordered to lie on the table. Same for the act for the relief of Isaac Newton. 16-Cmte on Claims: asked to be discharged from the further consideration of the ptn of John D Boyd: which was agreed to. 1

Mr Bancroft's only daughter & eldest child died at Springfield, Mass on Aug 9, aged 17 years, & had been visiting in the family of her uncle, Mr Bliss, in that town, for some weeks. She was in good health until within a few days of her death.

On Fri Jul 19, Dr S C Geren was poisoned by taking strychnine through mistake for morphine, from which he died in a few hours. -Mississippi Democrat

Orphans Court of Wash Co, D C. Sale of carriage horses, carriage, built to order last year by Ogle, in Phil, superior double harness; & other particulars of Maj D Hunter, U S A, at Keller's Pres Square.

Senate: 1-Ptn of Mrs Lewright Browning, widow of Robt L Browning, asking to be allowed a pension: referred to the Cmte on Pensions. 2-Cmte of Claims: memorial of Jas F Babcock, administrator of the estate of Maj Fred'k D Mills, asking compensation for a horse, equipment, & other property which fell into the hands of the enemy at the gates of Mexico: passed to a second reading.

City Ordinances-Wash. 1-Act for the relief of Henry S Wood: to be paid the sum of $16.75, a balance due him for work done on 3rd st east & A st south. 2-Act for the relief of Chas Stewart: sum of $35.57 be paid him, for a balance due him for laying stone gutters across 16th st.

THU AUG 15, 1850
Senate: 1-Additional documents relating to the claim of A P Brittingham: referred to the Cmte on Foreign Relations. 2-Ptn of Barbara Riley, widow of a Revolutionary ofcr, asking to be allowed a back pension: referred to the Cmte on Pensions. 3-Ptn of Charlotte Lynch, daughter & heir of Col Grey, of the Revolutionary army, asking to be allowed a pension: referred to the Cmte on Pensions. 4-Ptn of Francis G Beatty & Saml Walker, asking compensation for injuries received by the falling of the scaffold on which they were at work: referred to the Cmte of Claims. 5-Cmte on Military Affairs: memorial of Brevet Col Jos K F Mansfield, of the U S Corps of Engineers: passed to a second reading.

Mrd: on Aug 13, by Rev N T Eva, Jas B Williamson to A N Eberle, all of Wash City.

Mrd: on Aug 6, by Rev W T Eva, John F A Howell to Ann Matilda Anderson, all of Wash City.

Mrd: yesterday, in Wash City, by Rev C A Davis, Peter C Bogardus, U S Navy, to Miss Susan A Newman, eldest daughter of late Lewis A Newman, of Phil.

Mrd: on Aug 13, by Rev Mr Smith, Mr Wm Nichols, of Pa, to Miss Mary Hellriggle, of Wash City.

Died: last evening, in her 60th year, Mrs Eliz Hoburg, relict of the late John Hoburg, of Wash City. Her funeral will be at her son-in-laws, Mr Peter Gallant, on Mass ave, between 5th & 6th sts, this afternoon, at 5 o'clock.

Died: on Aug 12, at Old Point, of consumption, Jas H Thompson, in his 30th year.

Died: on Aug 12, in Wash City, after a severe illness, Pickett, aged 4 years & 7months, youngest son of the late Thos R Hampton, formerly of Fauquier Co, Va.

Died: on Aug 9, in Balt, Md, Joseph, son of John D & Eliza Geo Early, aged 4 years, 2 months & 14 days.

Died: on Sat last, in Harper's Ferry, Va, of the prevailing epidemic, Mr Wm Collins, of Wash City, aged 51 years. The sudden & unexpected decease of this truly faithful & worthy man has left a widow & 9 children to mourn a loss to them irreparable.

The subscriber will sell at private sale lot 18 in square 457, on E st, having thereon the large commodious 2 story brick house now occupied by Richd S Coxe. Also, lot 27 in square 950, & other lots in the Eastern part of Wash City. Call on the subscriber at Mr Wimsatt's, on Pa ave, or upon D A Hall, at his ofc, C & 3rd sts. -A D Benning

$300 reward for runaway black negro Margaret Sarah Tate, 19 years old.
–S L Lewis, 4½ st

Mr Cornelius Tims, of Wash City, drowned on Tue, on an excursion on Potomac River with Nat'l Greys, in the steamer **Columbia**. Mr Tims imprudently got into the small boat that was suspended at the stern of the steamer. Unfortunately it overturned & Mr Tims fell into the river. Every attempt was made to save him.

Mrs Ness, the wife of Dr *Ness, one of the Reps in Congress from Pa, died at his residence in York, Pa, on Aug 10. [Aug 16 correction: This is a mistake, a distant relative died in Balt last week, & the N Y papers copied the notice; hence the mistake. Dr *Nes lost his wife about 5 years ago. He has been quite ill, but is better.] *2-splgs.

FRI AUG 16, 1850
Appointments by the Pres: 1-Alfred Ray, Thos Donoho, Jos W Beck, John McCutchen, Aquilla K Arnold, Paul Stevens, Robt Clarke, John Page, Bladen Forrest, Benedict Milburn, & Anthony Hyde to be Justices of the Peace for Wash Co, D C. 2-Absalom Fowler, to be U S Atty for the District of Arkansas. 3-John Turnbull Van Alen, of N Y, to be Charge' d'Affaires to the Republic of Ecuador. 4-Dwight Webb, of Michigan, to be U S Consul for the port of Fouchou, in China. 5-Horation J Harris, to be U S Atty for the southern district of Mississippi. 6-Elisha H Allen, of Mass, to be U S Consul at the port of Honolulu, in the Sandwich Islands. 7-Wm M Martin, to be U S Assist Treasurer, at Charleston, S C.

Naval Affairs: 1-We learn from the Norfolk Courier that Cmder Edw C Rutledge, of S C, has resigned his commission in the navy, which places Lt T D Shaw, of Phil, at the head of the list for promotion. 2-Cmder Hugh N Page has received his commission as Capt in the Navy. 3-Cmder Geo A Magruder is to be ordered to the ship **St Mary's**. 4-Lt A D Harrell has been detached from the Coast Survey, & ordered to the frig **Raritan**, to sail in a few days for the Pacific. 5-Cmder John L Saunders is ordered to be detached from the U S rendezvous at Norfolk, his term of service having expired when his successor reports for duty. 6-The U S surveying steamer **Jefferson**, Lt commanding T A Jenkins, from Cape Hatteras, & the U S surveying brig **Washington**, Lt commanding Sands, from the Capes of Delaware, arrived at Norfolk on Sunday.

House of Reps: 1-Memorial of Edw Stabler & others, of Montgomery Co, Md, praying an appropriation of $25,000 for the erection of a plank road through the District of Columbia to the Montgomery line.

Henry A Schoolcraft, of Sacramento, Calif, is now on a visit to his relatives in Albany: age about 25 years: went out to Calif as a private soldier in Col Stevenson's regt. After his discharge from the U S service he was employed as book-keeper for Capt Sutter, & has since accumulated an estate valued at $350,000. He states that during his stay with Capt Sutter $15,000,000 of that gentleman's money passed through his hands.

Wash City News: Francis Camper was arrested & charged for the murder of Martin Ragan. Trial to be held at the next Dec term of the Criminal Court.

A requisition from Govn'r Thomas, directing the delivery of Chaplin, charged with an assault with intent to kill Mr Richd Butt & Mr Wm Smithia, in Montg Co, Md, was placed on Wed in the hands of ofcr Handy. Chaplin will first be tried in our Criminal Court for abducting Allen & Garland, the 2 runaway slaves found in Chaplin's carriage on Aug 8. [Dec 23rd newspaper: Mr Chaplin was on Thu liberated from the jail of Montg Co, $19,000 bail having been entered for his appearance at Howard Dist court. Bail to the amount of $6,000 had been given in this District. He passed through Balt on Thu on his return home. –Republic]

Mrd: on Aug 14, at Rock Creek Church, by Rev H W Woods, Mr Titian R Peale, of Wash, to Miss Lucinda McMullen, of N Y.

Died: yesterday, Joel Curtis Perry, in his 19th year. His funeral is on Fri, at 4 o'clock, from residence of his brother, Wm M Perry, La av beweent 6th & 7th sts.

Died: on Aug 15, Miss Margaret Catharome Johnston, in her 15th year, daughter of Mr John Johnston. Her funeral is today from his residence, 2nd st east, Capitol Hill, this evening, at 4 o'clock.

Died: on Aug 14, of cholera, at Chicago, Ill, Dr Geo W Wentworth, one of the Aldermen of that city, aged 29 years, son of Hon Paul Wentworth, of Concord, N H, & brother of Hon John Wentworth, M C, of Chicago, Ill District.

Died: on Aug 13, in Wash City, Mr C E Tims, in his 29th year. His funeral will be from the residence of his mother, Capitol Hill, Fri, at 10 o'clock.

Died: on Aug 1, after a lingering illness, at the Estill Springs, Ky, Wm Taylor, late of Point Coupee, La. He was born in Va, but soon removed to Ky with his father, Edmund Taylor. Orphaned at an early age. He was a relation of the late Pres. He was a devoted husband.

Died: on Aug 9, after a severe & protracted illness, at Auburn, his family residence near Piscataway, Md; Mr Wm H Lyles, in his 74th year. He leaves the wife of his bosom & his bereaved children.

Died: on Aug 8, in Wash City, Jane Eliz, in her 14th year, daughter of John & Hannah Dewdney.

SAT AUG 17, 1850
Book & Job Printing: having purchased the printing materials lately owned by Mr Theo Barnard. Business at the old stand, Pa ave & 11th sts, over Mr Robt Farnham's Bookstore. –Henry Polkinhorn

Jas Campbell has been convicted at Westchester, Pa, of the murder in the second degree, in causing the death of his wife, has been sentenced to 12 years confinement in the Eastern penitentiary. It was one of the most brutal homicides ever perpetrated. Campbell & his wife were each aged about 60 years, & had been married about 30 years.

Official: War Dept: Aug 7, 1850. Genr'l Orders #23. Promotions & Appointments in the U S Army, made by the Pres, by & with the advice & consent of the Senate, since the publication of the Army Register, Jan, 1850.
I-Promotions
Quartermaster's Dept
Maj Chas Thomas, Quartermaster, to be Deputy Quartermaster Gen, with the rank of Lt Col, May 23, 1850, vice Mackay, deceased.
1st Regt of Dragoons
Lt Col Thos T Fauntleroy, of the 2nd Dragoons, to be Col, Jul 25, 1850, vice Mason, deceased.
Capt Geo A H Blake, of the 2nd Dragoons, to be Major, Jul 25, 1850, vice Boone, promoted.
1st Lt Richd S Ewell, to be Capt, Aug 4, 1849, vice Eustis, resigned.
2nd Lt Clarendon J L Wilson, to be 1st Lt, Aug 4, 1849, vice Ewell, promoted.
Brevet 2nd Lt Chas H Ogle, to be 2nd Lt, Aug 4, 1849, vice Wilson, promoted.
2nd Regt of Dragoons
Maj Nathan Boone, of the 1st Dragoons, to be Lt Col, Jul 15, 1850, vice Fauntleroy, promoted.
1st Lt Fowler Hamilton, to be Capt, Jul 25, 1850, vice Blake, promoted.
2nd Lt Jas M Hawes, to be 1st Lt, Jul 25, 1850, vice Hamilton, promoted.
Brevet 2nd Lt N G Evans, of the 1st Dragoons, to be 2nd Lt, Sep 30, 1849, vice Pleasanton, promoted.
Brevet 2nd Lt Geo H Stuart, to be 2nd Lt, Nov 1, 1849, vice Bicknell, deceased.
Brevet 2nd Lt Horace F De Lano, of the 1st Dragoons, to be 2nd Lt, Jan 13, 1850, vice Hawes, promoted.
Brevet 2nd Lt Beverley H Robertson, to be 2nd Lt, Jul 25, 1850, vice Givens, promoted.
1st Regt of Artl:
Maj Levi Whiting, to be Lt Col, Apr 1, 1850, vice Pierce, deceased.
Capt Justin Dimick, to be Major, Apr 1, 1850, vice Whiting, promoted.

1st Lt Isaac S K Reeves, to be Capt, Apr 1, 1850, vice Dimick, promoted.
2nd Lt John H Dickerson, to be 1st Lt, Apr 1, 1850, vice Reeves, promoted.
Brevet 2nd Lt Absalom Baird, of the 2nd Artl, to be 2nd Lt, Jul 8, 1850, vice Dickerson, promoted.
2nd Regt of Artl:
Brevet 2nd Lt Edw R Platt, of the 3rd Artl, to be 2nd Lt, Jul 8, 1850, vice De Russy, deceased.
3rd Regt of Artl:
1st Lt Henry B Judd, to be Capt, Feb 13, 1850, vice Wade, deceased.
2nd Lt John Hamilton, to be 1st Lt, Feb 13, 1850, vice Judd, promoted.
Brevet 2nd Lt Johnson K Duncan, of the 2nd Artl, to be 2nd Lt, Oct 31, 1849, vice McDonald, resigned.
Brevet 2nd Lt Chauncey McKeever, of the 1st Artl, to be 2nd Lt, Jul 27, 1850, vice Heck, resigned.
4th Regt of Artl:
1st Lt John W Phelps, to be Capt, Mar 31, 1850, vice O'Brien, deceased.
2nd Lt Geo W Hazzard, to be 1st Lt, Mar 31, 1850, vice Phelps, promoted.
2nd Lt Orlando B Wilcox, to be 1st Lt, Apr 30, 1850, vice Fahnestock, resigned.
Brevet 2nd Lt Delavan D Perkins, of the 2nd Artl, to be 2nd Lt, Mar 31, 1850, vice Hazzard, promoted.
Brevet 2nd Lt Wm A Nimmo, to be 2nd Lt, Apr 30, 1850, vice Wilcox, promoted.
1st Regt of Infty:
Lt Col Bennet Riley, of the 2nd Infty, to be Col, Jan 31, 1850, vice Davenport, resigned.
1st Lt Geo W F Wood, to be Capt, Jun 26, 1850, vice Gardenier, deceased.
2nd Lt Eugene E McLean, to be 1st Lt, Jun 26, 1850, vice Wood, promoted.
Brevet 2nd Lt Edw D Stockton, of the 7th Infty, to be 2nd Lt, Aug 31, 1849, vice Denman, promoted.
Brevet 2nd Lt Seth M Barton, of the 3rd Infty, to be 2nd Lt, Apr 19, 1850, vice Hudson, deceased.
Brevet 2nd Lt Richd W Johns, of the 6th Infty, to be 2nd Lt, Jun 26, 1850, vice McLean, promoted.
2nd Regt of Infty"
Maj Wm R Jouett, of the 3rd Infty, to be Lt Col, Jan 31, 1850, vice Riley, promoted.
1st Lt Julius Hayden, to be Capt, Jun 30, 1850, vice Patrick, resigned.
2nd Lt Henry B Hendershott, to be 1st Lt, Jun 30, 1850, vice Hayden, promoted.
Brevet 2nd Lt Saml B Holabird, of the 1st Infty, to be 2nd Lt, Jun 30, 1850, vice Hendershott, promoted.
3rd Regt of Infty:
Capt Gouverneur Morris, of the 4th Infty, to be Major, Jan 31, 1850, vice Jouett, promoted.
Brevet 2nd Lt Duff C Green, of the 5th Infty, to be 2nd Lt, May 22, 1850, vice Mason, deceased.
4th Regt of Infty:
1st Lt Henry D Wallen, to be Capt, Jan 31, 1850, vice Morris, promoted.
2nd Lt Edmund Russell, to be 1st Lt, Jan 31, 1850, vice Wallen, promoted.

5th Regt of Infty:
2nd Lt Thos H Neill, to be 1st Lt, Jul 31, 1850, vice Read, resigned.
Brevet 2nd Lt Thornton A Washington, of the 6th Infty, to be 2nd Lt, Jul 31, 1850, vice Neill, promoted.

6th Regt of Infty:
Brevet 2nd Lt John S Tidball, of 4th Infty, to be 2nd Lt, Mar 31, 1850, vice Howe, deceased.

7th Regt of Infty:
1st Lt Chas H Humber, to be Capt, Jul 16, 1850, vice Britton, resigned.
2nd Lt Wm K Van Bokkelen, to be 1st Lt, Jul 16, 1850, vice Humber, promoted.
Brevet 2nd Lt Thos G Williams, of the 2nd Infty, to be 2nd Lt, Jul 16, 1850, vice Van Bokkelen, promoted.

II-Appointments.

Inspector General's Dept.
Brevet Lt Col Geo A McCall, Major of the 3rd Infty, to be Inspector Genr'l, with the rank of Colonel, Jun 10, 1850, vice Duncan, deceased.

Medical Dept:
David L Magruder, of Va, to be Assist Surgeon, Feb 1, 1850, vice Barbour, resigned.
Wm J H White, of D C, to be Assist Surgeon, Mar 12, 1850, vice Ryer, resigned.
Rodney Glisan, of Md, to be Assist Surgeon, May 2, 1850, vice Fullwood, deceased.
Elisha P Langworthy, of N Y, to be Assist Surgeon, May 16, 1850, vice Ballard, resigned.

Pay Dept:
John R Hagner, of D C, to be Paymaster, Jan 9, 1850, vice C Andrews, resigned.

Ordnance Dept:
Thos Thorp, of La, to be Military Storekeeper, Aug 2, 1850, vice Butler, removed.
Jas W Simmons, of Texas, to be Military Storekeeper, Aug 2, 1850, vice Maulsby, resigned.

III-The following named cadets, graduates of the Military Academy, are attached to the Army with the Brevet of 2nd Lt, to take rank from Jul 1, 1850:

Brevet 2nd Lt attached to the Corps of Engineers.
Rank
1-Cadet Fred'k E Prine

Brevet 2nd Lt attached to the Corps of Topographical Engineers
2-Cadet Gouverneur K Warren

Brevet 2nd Lts attached to the Dragoon Arm.
11-Cadet Wm T Magruder: Co B, 1 Drgs
15-Cadet Lucius M Walker: Co B, 2 Drgs
18-Cadet Robt Ransom, jr: Co K, 1 Drgs
24-Cadet Jonas P Holiday: Co K, 2 Drgs
27-Cadet Wm R Calhoun: Co H, 1 Drgs
28-Cadet Robt Johnston: Co G, 1 Drgs
29-Cadet Thos Bingham: Co H, 2 Drgs

Brevet 2nd Lt attached to the Regt of Mounted Riflemen.
19-Cadet Eugene A Carr: Co H

Brevet 2nd Lt attached to the Artl Arm:
4-Cadet Cuvier Grover: Co G, 1 Art
5-Cadet Powell T Wyman: Co H, 3 Art
6-Cadet Jos H Wheelock: Co L, 3 Art
7-Cadet Jacob Culbertson: Co E, 4 Art
8-Cadet Oscar A Mack: Co K, 3 Art
9-Cadet Hugh E Dungan: Co K, 4 Art
10-Cadet Achilles Bowen: Co L, 2 Art
12-Cadet Adam J Slemmer: Co B, 1 Art
13-Cadet Richd Arnold: Co A, 1 Art
14-Cadet jas P Flewellen: Co K, 2 Art
16-Cadet John A Mebane: Co F, 2 Art
17-Cadet Armistead L Long: Co E, 2 Art
21-Cadet Amos Beckwith: Co D, 1 Art
22-Cadet Chas S Winder: Co M, 4 Art
Brevet 2nd Lts attached to the Infty Arm:
20-Cadet Wm P Carlin: Co K, 6 Inf
23-Cadet Francis H Bates: Co B, 4 Inf
25-Cadet Elisha G Marshall: Co E, 4 Inf
26-Cadet Nicholas B Pearce: Co E, 7 Inf
30-Cadet Austin N Colcord: Co F, 4 Inf
31-Cadet Robt Macfeely: Co G, 4 Inf
32-Cadet John W Alley: Co G, 3 Inf
33-Cadet Wm L Cabell: Co B, 7 Inf
34-Cadet Jas H Wilson: Co G, 1 Inf
35-Cadet Henry C Bankhead: Co E, 5 Inf
36-Cadet Alden Sargent: Co B, 6 Inf
37-Cadet Robt G Cole: Co A, 5 Inf
38-Cadet John J A A Mouton: Co D, 7 Inf
39-Cadet Jos T Haile: Co D, 1 Inf
40-Cadet Jas L Corley: Co I, 6 Inf
41-Cadet Retus S Searle: Co H, 8 Inf
42-Cadet J E Maxwell: Co K, 3 Inf
43-Cadet Fred'k M Follett: Co A, 3 Inf
44-Cadet Donald C Stith: Co I, 5 Inf
IV-Casualties Resignations, 10
Col Wm Davenport, 1st Infty, Jan 31, 1850.
Brevet Maj Marsena R Patrick, Capt 2nd Infty, Jun 30, 1850.
Capt Forbes Britton, 7th Infty, Jul 16, 1850.
1st Lt Simon S Fahnestock, 4th Artl, Apr 30, 1850.
1st Lt Wm Read, 5th Infty, Jul 31, 1850.
2nd Lt John H Heck, 3rd Artl, Jun 27, 1850.
Brevet 2nd Lt Henry L Brown, 3rd Infty, Mar 31, 1850.
Brevet 2nd Lt Washington C Tevis, Mounted riflemen, May 12, 1850.
Assist Surgeon Saml L Barbour, Jan 31, 1850.
Assist Surgeon Wm H Ballard, Apr 30, 1850.

Deaths, 12
Brevet Brig Gen R B Mason, Col 1st Dragoons, Jul 25, 1850, at Jefferson Barracks, Mo.
Bvt Col Aeneas Mackay, Dept Quartermaster Genr'l, May 23,1850, St Louis, Mo.
Lt Col Benj K Pierce, 1st Artl, Apr 1,1850, N Y, N Y
Bvt Lt Col Richd D A Wade, Capt 3rd Artl, 13 Feb 1850, *Fort Constitution*, N H
Bvt Maj John P S O'Brien, Capt 4th Artl, Mar 31, 1850, Indianola, Texas
Capt John R B Gardenier, 1st Infty, Jun 26, 1850, Dardanell Springs, Ark
1st Lt Lewis Neill, 2nd Dragoons, Jan 13, 1850, *Fort Croghan*, Texas
Bvt 1st Lt Edwin Howe, 2nd Lt, 6th Infty, Mar 31, 1850, *Fort Leavenworth*, Mo.
2nd Lt John De Russy, 2nd Artl, 8 Jul 1850, *Fort Monroe*, Va
2nd Lt Thos J Mason, 3rd Inf, 22 May 1850, Socorro, N Mex
Assist Surgeon Wm E Fullwood, Apr 17, 1850, Macon, Ga.
2nd Lt Walter W Hudson, 1st Infty, Apr, 19, 1850, *Fort McIntosh*, Texas/Died of wounds received in skirmish with the Indians.
V-The ofcrs promoted & appointed will join their proper Regts, Companies, & Stations without delay; those on detached service, or acting under special instructions, will report by letter to the commanding ofcrs of their respective regts & corps.
VI-The usual leave of absence allowed by the regulations is hereby granted to the several graduates; at the expiration of which [Sep 30th] they will join their proper Stations & Regts. The Brevet 2nd Lt assigned to mounted Regts, [except those under special instructions,] will repair to Carlisle Barracks & report for temporary duty on the expiration of their leaves.
VII-Acceptances on non-acceptances of appointments will be promptly reported to the Adj Gen of the Army; & in the case of acceptance, the ofcr will immediately subscribe to the Rule & Regulations enjoined by the 1st article of war. He will also report his birth-place, & the State from which appointed. By Order: R Jones, Adj Gen
Memoranda: Change of date, made by & with the advice & consent of the Senate.
The date of Col J B Walbach's Brevet of Brigadier Gen, changed from May 30, 1848, to Nov 11, 1823.
Transfers & correction of dates of commission, by & with the advice & consent of the Senate.
2nd Lt Wm Silvey, of the 3rd Artl, in the 1st Artl, [Co B,] to date Nov 6, 1849, vice Chalfin, promoted.
2nd Lt Beekman Du Barry, of the 1st Artl, to the 3rd Artl, [Co F,] to date Feb 13, 1850, vice Hamilton, promoted.
2nd Lt Wm H Lewis, of the 1st Infty, to the 5th Infty, [Co B,] to date Oct 7, 1849, vice Harrison, deceased.
2nd Lt Thos Wright, of the 5th Infty, to the 2nd Infty, [Co G,] to date Oct 16, 1849, vice Gardner, promoted.
2nd Lt John Withers, of the 2nd Infty, to the 4th Infty, [Co G,] to date Jan 31, 1850, vice Russell, promoted.
The above Lts will join their Companies without unnecessary delay.
The appointments of Cadets J K Duncan, E D Stockton, J W Frazer, & A Cumming to be Brevet 2nd Lt, to date from Jul 1, 1849, instead of Jul 2, 1849, as announced in General Orders #38, of 1849. And they are restored to their relative rank in the Army according to the order of precedence determined by the Academic Board.

Postmaster Gen est'd the following new Post Ofcs for week ending Aug 10, 1850.

Ofc	County, State	Postmaster
East Eden	Hancock, Me	Richd Higgins
West Danby	Tompkins, N Y	John Patchin
West Macedon	Wayne, N Y	J B Van Vleit
Eden Valley	Erie, N Y	Jos Webster
Bernhard's Bay	Oswego, N Y	John Bernhard
New Gretna	Burlington, N Y	Jos B Cramer
Monroe	Bedford, Pa	H Markle
Cascade	Lycoming, Pa	Henry Stevens
Dry Ridge	Somerset, Pa	Valentine Hoon
Well's Corners	Erie, Pa	Wm Wells
Fitz Henry	Westmoreland, Pa	Henry B Miller
Kellersville	Monroe, Pa	M Kiser
Ridge Hall	Balt, Md	John Whiteford
Taylorsville	Anne Arundel, Md	Alex Richardson
Gap Mills	Balt, Md	C Kennell
Maria Stein	Mercer, Ohio	Mathias Gast
Medway	Clark, Ohio	D J Stiles
Stovertown	Muskingum, Ohio	Uriah Parker
Ball	Knox, Ohio	Jas Walker
Pleasanton	Athens, Ohio	F Burnham
Bengal	Clinton, Mich	Cortland Hill
Dug Spur	Carroll, Va	A J Durnell
Richd Valley	Wythe, Va	Elias Repass
Hampden Sidney College	Prince Edward, Va	J A Shelton
Bethlehem	Gilmer, Va	Jos Bennett
Greenwood	Doddridge, Va	W W Chapman
Independence	Grayson, Va	A Cornus
Alston	Fairfield D, S C	Nathan Feaster
White Oak	Fairfield D, S C	John Cockrell
Mountvideo	Elbert, Geo	Richd S Hill
Steam Factory	Muscogee, Geo	P V Guerry
Towaligga	Butts, Geo	Thos McKibben
Bug Hall	Macon, Ala	E W Touey
Wolf Creek	Wilson, Ala	Saml Young
Highland	Shelby, Ala	R S Griffin
Spencerville	Marengo, Ala	Lysander Adams
Banner	Lafayette, Miss	Wm C Redwin
Pea Ridge	Benton, Ark	Robt Wallace
Alder Cock	Independence, Ark	Henry Niell
Clifton	Hardin, Tenn	S S Rickets
Snow Hill	Hamilton, Tenn	A E Jones
Slack	Mason, Ky	Thos Griffith

Proviso	Cook, Ill	Augustin Porter
Oakley	Macon, Ill	J Ricketts
Prairie Creek	Logan, Ill	Henry B Stevens
Harvey's Point	Polk, Iowa	Stephen Harvey
Hamilton	Marion, Iowa	Henry Edwards
Hillsborough	Washington, O T	Abraham Sulger
Wahcoota	Wabashaw, M T	B F Aiton
Fort Bridger	N T	Louis Vasques

Names Changed:
Blemen, Carroll Co, Md, changed to Kroh's Mills.
Pearson's Mills, Cumberland Co, N C, changed to River Side.
Littletonville, Knox Co, Ill, changed to Truro.
Cedar Creek, Warren Co, Ill, changed to Denny.
Duck Creek, Brown Co, Wisc, changed to Oneida.
Mitchell's Landing, Obion Co, Tenn, changed to Line.

Mrd: on Aug 16, by Rev Mr Marks, Mr Edw Hazle to Miss Mary Jane Hays of Wash Co.

Mrd: on Aug 18, in Gtwn, by Rev Mr Lanahan, David W Bevans, of Piney Point, Md, to Ellen B Hunter of Wash City.

Died: on Aug 16, in Wash City, Theodore J, son of Theodore & Susan A Sniffin, aged 14 months & 10 days.

MON AUG 19, 1850
Died: on Aug 16, in Wash City, Miss Martha Lippett, age about 80 years.

Died: on Aug 18, in Gtwn, Mrs Eliz Ann Tilley, consort of H W Tilley, in her 39th year. Her funeral is today at 5 o'clock.

Died: Aug 15th, Chas R, son of Overton & Jane Castell, aged 14 months.

Eliz, the only daughter of Rev Gorham D Abbott, was so severely injured a few days since at Long Branch, N J, by a kick from a horse, that she died on Tue.

House of Reps: 1-Memorial of Capt Lavalette, of the U S Navy, asking to have refunded to him a sum of money paid to an interpreter.

Lynnfield, Mass, Aug 15, 1850. Drowned in a paddle boat excursion on the Suntang Lake this afternoon: Robt Shirtleff & his wife Eliz Shirtleff. They had been married but a short time. Catharine L Adams; Mrs Mary Howard; Mary Augusta Howard; 2 children of Mr Ephraim Brown; Mrs Mehitable Alley, wife of Mr Jacob Alley; Miss M A Johnson; Miss Young; daughter of Mr Washington Alley; Maria Cheever; 2 children of Mr Joshua Garland.

TUE AUG 20, 1850
Wash Corp: 1-Ptn from Margaret Ferris, in relation to the taxes on her property: referred to the Cmte on Finance. 2-Cmte of Claims: act for the relief of B Jost: rejected. 3-Cmte of Claims: act for the relief of Louis Simon: read twice.

City Ordinances-Wash. 1-Act for the relief of Jacob A Bender: sum of $80.40 to be paid him for pumping out the reservoir at E & 9th sts west, & lining the same with bricks & cement, & furnishing materials. 2-Act for the relief of John Fletcher: the sum of $234.11 be paid to him, a balance found to be due for grading & gravelling north H st, between 16th & Rock Creek.

Senate: 1-Memorial of Emily C B Thompson, widow of Capt Thompson, late of the U S Navy, asking an increase of pension: referred to the Cmte on Naval Affairs. 2-Ptn of M Jean Deplaigne, a French subject, residing in Mexico, asking indemnity for the loss of certain property seized by the naval force of the U S, after the surrender of Frontera de Tabasco, in Mexico: referred to the Cmte of Claims. 3-Ordered, that the ptn of Rebecca Bright, widow of Jacob Bright, on the files of the Senate, be referred to the Cmte on Naval Affairs. 4-Cmte on Indian Affairs: memorial of Theodore E Elliot, asking payment for a boat sold to R M Butler, the Indian agent, reported a bill for his relief, & asking the unanimous consent of the Senate to consider it at once.

Teacher wanted to instruct in the Primary School #1, Bladensburg district. Good Luck Post Ofc, PG Co, Md: Clement Baden, Richd G Cross, Henry Phillips.

Died: on Aug 13, in Boston, Capt Louis C F Fatio, late of the U S Revenue Marine, in his 47th year.

Mrd: on the Sabbath, by Rev J C Smith, Mr Columbus Furtner to Miss Georgiana Williams, all of Wash City.

Pianos for sale or rent: F C Reichenbach, 12th st, above F st.

For sale: until Aug 24, a fine likely negro gril, 8 years old, for a term of 22 years. She is healthy & of a very industrious family. Apply to Mrs Inch, near the Navy Yard, where every information will be given.

Rugby Academy: Boarding & Day School: will resume the first Mon in Sep next: corner of K & 14th sts. –G F Morrison

Christopher McKiernan, insolvent debtor, has applied to be discharged from imprisonment: hearing on Aug 24. –Jno A Smith, clerk

WED AUG 21, 1850
Senate: 1-Ptn of John G Mount: referred to the Cmte on Pensions. 2-Cmte on Military Affairs: referred the documents relative to the claim of Ebenezer Dumont, for a horse killed in Mexico: reported without amendment.

Died: on Aug 19, near the Navy yard, John Thos, son of Francis & Jane E Keithly, aged 1 year & 7 months.

J Evans Young, late U S Commercial Agent at the port of Curacoa, & formerly of Rockland, Delaware, died of typhus fever on Jul 11, at Curacoa, in his 41st year.
—Phil North American

Phil explosion killed Wm L Bachman, David Mulford, Marcus Marcus, Caroline Marcus, Abigail Catharine Drake, & others, by the explosion at the store of Mr John Brock, occupied by Messieurs John Brock, Sons & Co, Belger & Buiz, & others, in Water st, on Jul 9, 1850, at the fire which occurred on that day.

For sale: my residence on Md ave, near the east park of the Capitol, with about an acre of ground attached to the house. Inquire on the premises, or address me personally.
—S J Anderson

Orphans Court of Wash Co, D C. Letters testamentary on the personal estate of Eleanor Dewees, late of Wash Co, deceased. -A B Smith, exc

Orphans Court of Wash Co, D C. Letters of administration on the personal estate of Wm Collins, late of Wash Co, deceased. -Wm R Collins, adm

Drowned off Gloucester, Mass, by upsetting of a boat: Capt Fuller & son, of Gloucester, Mr Griggs; & a boy named Inglis, of N Y, Francis Edwin Dubois, of Boston, age 16.

St Mary's Female Institution, near Bryantown, Chas Co, Md, Aug 7, 1850. Distribution of premiums to:

Eliza F Dyer, of Wash, D C
Annie Downey, of Chas Co
Mary C Thompson, Chas Co
Eleanor R Boarman, Chas Co
Mary Sophia Du Bernard, of Balt, Md
Martina Dyer, of Wash, D C
Ellen Jameson, of Chas Co
Susan Kenny, of Balt, Md
Beatrice Gardiner, of Chas Co
Mary Jane Hamersley, Chas Co
Emily Boarman, of Chas Co
Eliz Bowling, of Chas Co
Maria Conlan, of Wash, D C
Mgt Marshall, of Chas Co
Edwardina Pye, of Chas Co
Mgt Conlan, of Wash, D C
Marian Burch, of Chas Co
Mary Stewart, of Chas Co
Martha A Gibbons, PG Co,
Sarah Gibbons, of PG Co, Md
Eliz A Sasscer, of PG Co, Md
Susanna Sasscer, PG Co, Md
Sarah M Stone, of Chas Co
P A Scott, St Mary's Co, Md
Maria McDaniel, of Chas Co
Sarah Burtles, of Chas Co
Rebecca Bryan, of PG Co, Md
Mary Hamilton, of Chas Co
Sarah Blundell, of Balt, Md
Mgt T Martin, of Balt
Helen Dyer, of Chas Co
Mary M Dyer, of Wash, D C
Kate Hamilton, of Chas Co
Mary L McLean, of Balt, Md
Mgt Fusting, of Catonsville, Balt Co, Md

THU AUG 22, 1850
Senate: 1-Memorial of Edwin James, senior, & Edwin James, junior, deputy surveyors of the public lands in Iowa, praying to be indemnified against loss in consequence of the unlawful annulment of their contract by the surveyor general of St Louis, Mo, for surveying public lands: referred to the Cmte of Claims. 2-Memorial of John B Walbach, asking compenson for services rendered in 1801, & for expenses & losses incident to said services: referred to the Cmte on Military Affairs. 3-Cmte on Private Land Claims: bill for the relief of Mrs Maria Taylor, to allow the bill to have its 2nd reading, in order that it might be considered & disposed of at once. 4-Cmte on Pensions: memorial of Mrs Lewright Browning, widow of the late Robt L Browning, a lt in the navy of the U S: ordered to a 2nd reading. Same cmte: memorial of John W Mount, for an increase of pension: ordered to a 2nd reading. 5-Cmte on Commerce: bill for the relief of Chas A Kellet, reported back the same without amendment.

Orphans Court of Wash Co, D C. Letters testamentary on the personal estate of Patrick Magee, late of Wash Co, deceased. -W B Magruder, exc

For sale: desirable property: 2 story brick dwlg-house & lot on N Y ave, between 13th & 14th sts. Inquire of the subscriber, at Mrs Clark's, on 10th st, near Pa ave. –John Heart

For sale: 2 commodious 2 story frame houses on B st, opposite the Smithsonian Bldgs, belonging to the estate of the late Evan Evans. Apply to Mrs Evans, at R Cruit's, F st, or W B Magruder, Exc of E Evans.

Country Board: the subscriber having completed his large & commodious bldg at Meadow Bank, Spa Springs, on the Bladensburg road, is prepared to accommodate a large number of boarders. Inquire on the premises of Robt W Burrows.

The Misses Grimshaw's Boarding & Day School, Wilmington, Delaware, will begin Sep 1. English Dept: Misses C & I Grimshaw; Music: Miss Agnes Young, Mr Chas Grobe, & Mr W J Lemon. French: M D'Ouville & Miss C Grimshaw.

Died: on Aug 18, at *The Refuge*, Chas Co, Md, Mrs Catherine Merrick, in her 51st year, wife of Hon Wm D Merrick. For years she suffered the agonies of a most acute disease.

Died: on Tue, Alice, youngest child of Chas H & Mary Ellen James. Her funeral is this evening, at 5 o'clock, from the residence of Mrs E James, F st near 10th st.

Mrd: on Aug 20, by Rev Mr Morgan, Mr Christian Hourch, of Balt, to Miss Eleanor T Patton, daughter of J V Patton, of Wash City.

Phil Pa: Mr Chas Burd was robbed and murdered on Monday.

FRI AUG 23, 1850
The Hon Jesse Miller died at Harrisburg, Pa, of congestion of the liver, on Tue. At the time of his death he was the editor of the Harrisburg Keystone.

Rev Mason Chesney, of the Methodist Episcopal Church, drowned at Fincastle, Va. He was well known in Baltimore, Md. Last winter he attached himself to the Balt Annual Conference, when he was appointed to the Fincastle circuit, which he was traveling with great promise. [No death date given-current news item.]

Mobile Advertiser: the elegant & magnificent edifice, **Mansion House**, at Mobile, kept by Chas Cullum, is in ruins. It was entirely consumed by fire on Aug 13. The house was insured for $37,000, & the furniture for $20,000.

House of Reps: 1-Cmte of Ways & Means: refunding to Jos Jos Chance, Bishop of Natchez, the duty paid on a Cathedral bell presented to said Bishop by Prince Alex'r Torlonia, of Rome, $250. Agreed to.

Mrd: on Aug 11, in Green Bay, Wisc, by Rev Jas Porter, Jos B Collins, U S Army, to Miss Agnes B Jones, of the former place.

Died: on Aug 11, in St Mary's Co, Md, in her 19th year, Charlotte, wife of Dr Alex'r McWilliams, & daughter of late Henry N Kirk.

Senate: 1-Memorial of Duff Green, agent of the Georgia Exporting Co, asking that the Sec of the Navy be authorized by law to contract with that company for the construction & employment in the mail service of the Gov't of 5 steamships: referred to the Cmte on Printing. 2-Cmte on Pensions: memorial of Robt Armstrong, asking to be allowed a pension: ordered to a 2nd reading. 3-Cmte on Pensions: ptn of Charlotte Lynch, only surviving child of Lt Col Ebenezer Gray, a Revolutionary ofcr: ordered to a 2nd reading.

SAT AUG 24, 1850
Senate: 1-Memorial of Salvadorah McLaughlin, admx of John F McLaughlin, asking compensation for a steam vessel lost in the public service, in the Gulf of Mexico, during the late war with Mexico: referred to the Cmte on Naval Affairs. 2-Cmte on Naval Affairs: memorial of Susan Decatur, asking that the prize money due for the capture & destruction of the frig **Philadelphia**, in the harbor of Tripoli, may be distributed among the captors, & protesting against any portion of the same being paid to Priscilla D Twiggs, or her sisters; & the memorial of Jos K Boyd, asking remuneration for aiding in the capture of the said frig: ordered to a 2nd reading. 3-Cmte of Claims: memorial of John Tucker, asking compensation for military services in Florida, in 1838: passed to a 2nd reading. 4-Bill for the relief of Al loh-la: passed.

Died: yesterday, in Wash City, of dropsy on the chest, Mr Daniel Homans, aged 64 years-an honest, upright man, a good neighbor, & a good citizen. His funeral will take place from his residence on A st south, on Capitol Hill, on Sun next, at 3:30 p m.

Died: on Aug 22 of paralysis, of which he had been afflicted for more then 2 years, Geo Ellsworth, aged 67, a native of Hempstead, Long Island, N Y, but for nearly the last 50 years a resident of Wash City. His funeral will take place this Sat, at 2:30 o'clock, from the dwlg of his son-in-law, Ferdinand Jefferson, on 11th st, between E & F sts.

Postmaster Gen est'd the following new Post Ofcs for week ending Aug 17, 1850.

Ofc	County, State	Postmaster
Water Valley	Erie, N Y	John Barton
E Houndsfield	Jefferson, N Y	N Jones
Engellville	Schoharie, N Y	Philip Becker
French Mountain	Warren, N Y	Geo Brown
S W Oswega	Oswega, N Y	S G Place
Warner	Warren, Pa	Wm H Talcott
Prosperity	Washington, Pa	T D Minton
Pittsburgh	Darke, Ohio	Chas Wellbaum
Grape Grove	Greene, Ohio	Wm Lewis
Durbin's Corner	Williams, Ohio	Geo W Durbin
Wadesville	Clark, Va	John H P Stone
Timber Grove	Washington, Va	J S Reeve
Cramberry Pl'ns	Carroll, Va	Andrew Cock
White Road	Forsyth, N C	Geo V Fulph
Ellisville	Bladen, N C	David Jones
Sweetwater Factory	Campbell, Geo	Jas Rogers
Delray	Upsom, Geo	Wm O Smith
Mills Bridge	Pike, Geo	Thos J Allen
Southerland	Jefferson, Fla	W G Moseley
Mosley's Grove	Dallas, Ala	Lewis P Moseley
Rock Creek	Franklin, Ala	Chas Womble
Court House	Franklin, Ala	John Miller
Detroit	Marion, Ala	Wm D Davidson
Highland	Tishemingo, Miss	Robt W Paden
Waxahackie	Ellis, Texas	Jos Whittemberg
Prospect	Burleson, Texas	J W Thomas
Trier	Bexar, Texas	Jas Head
San Gabriel	Williamson, Texas	Thos J Allen
Hermitage	Decatur, Tenn	Thos B Garrard
Scott's Hill	Henderson, Tenn	Wm Brigance
Racoon	Laurel, Ky	M D Hardin
Wooldridge's Store	Christian, Ky	G H Dobyns
Jones' Nursery	Clark, Ky	F Jones
Highland	Bath, Ky	L Yeates
Barr's Store	Macoupin, Ill	Benj D Barr
Winthrop	Kane, Ill	S S Ingham
Texas	Randolph, Ill	John Ralls, jr
Pike Creek	Ripley, Mo	Jas Snider

Names Changed:
Salt Lake, Calif Territory, changed to Salt Lake City, Utah Territory.
Hill's Bridge, Halifax Co, N C, changed to Ringwood.

For sale: small neat 3 story brick house on H st, near 18th st. Apply to H W Balmain, 2nd Auditor's Ofc.

Late from Mexico: the wife of Capt Eustis, U S Army, died at Santa Fe, on Jul 20.

Notice: committed to the jail of Chas Co, Md, as a runaway, on Aug 19, negro man Wm Gozmere, about 60 years of age. He has a pass to travel through any of the States, signed by David Butts, David Kinsloe, & Harvey Olstine, of Panola Co, Miss. The owner is to come forward, prove property, pay charges, & take him away; otherwise he will be discharged according to law. –J R Robertson, Sheriff

MON AUG 26, 1850
Senate: 1-Bill for payment of compensation to Dr Thos O Edwards for his services as examiner into the practical operation of the law for the prevention of the importation of spurious & adulterated drugs & medicines, under appointment from the Sec of the Treas of Oct 10, 1848, $250. 2-Cmte of Ways & Means: pay a balance found by the accounting ofcrs to be due to Jose Yznardy, former Consul at Cadiz, in Spain, the sum of $1,228.80; & to ascertain how much of said sum is due by descent or devise, or in any other manner, to the late Jos M Yznardy, or his heirs.

Mrd: on Aug 20, by Rev Dr Baynham, Jas C Welling, of N YC, to Genevieve Hamilton, daughter of Col Henry T Garnett, of Ingleside, Westmoreland Co, Va.

Died: on Aug 24, Ann Jennet, only child of Sayles J & Mary Bowen, of Wash City, aged 7 years, 1 month & 28 days.

Died: on Jul 17, at her residence, in PG Co, Md, after a protracted illness, borne with calm submission, Rachel, wife of Dennis Duvall, in her 55th year.

Female teacher wanted: salary of $250, with board, & washing included.
–Thos Goode, Hot Springs

The <u>Misses Rooker's Academy</u> for Young Ladies, 6th & F sts, will be re-opened Sep 2.

TUE AUG 27, 1850
Senate: Additional documents submitted in relation to the claim of C M Hitchcock, exc of R S Hunter, deceased: referred to the Cmte on Indian Affairs. 2-Documents submitted relating to the claim of Rhoda Frisbee, widow of a Revolutionary soldier, asking a pension: referred to the Cmte on Pensions. 3-Resolved, that the Cmte on Pensions report on allowing a pension to Emilee Hooe, of Prairie du Chien, widow of Brevet Maj Alex'r Seymour Hooe, in consideration of the entire loss of his right arm by a cannon shot in the battle of Ressca de la Palma, at the commencement of the late war with Mexico, & of his consequent death in Dec, 1847, while he was in command at Baton Rouge, in Louisiana, & as is generally believed, a result occasioned by the effect of that wound. Documents were referred accordingly.

Jas Wade, a tailor by trade, was arrested yesterday by Ofcr Wollard, charge with robbing a magistrate named Dobney, at Gettysburg, Pa, of $300. He was found at a tavern near the Centre Market.

Mrd: on Sat evening, by Rev John C Smith, French Strother, of Alabama, to Miss Susan Petty, of Culpeper Co, Va.

Mrd: on Aug 20, at New Haven, Conn, by Rev G W Perkins, Dwight Foster, of Worcester, Mass, to Miss Henrietta P Baldwin, daughter of Roger S Baldwin, of New Haven.

Died: on Jul 30, at **Fort Kearny**, on the Oregon route, after an illness of 10 days, from injuries caused by his horse falling on him, Lt Rufus A Roys, U S Corps of Engineers.

To Teachers. The subscriber, wishing to change his business, offers for sale the good will & fixtures of the school, well known as Columbian Academy, on 9th st, between G & H sts. –L F Churchill

Household furniture at auction: on Aug 29, by deed of trust from J F Tucker to the subscriber, recorded in Liber J A S #12, folios 482 thru 484, one of the land records of Wash Co, D C, at the store formerly occupied by said Tucker, on Pa ave, between 9th & 10th sts: an extensive assortment of new & second-hand furniture.
–John Mills, trustee -Green & Tastet, aucts

WED AUG 28, 1850
Orphans Court of Wash Co, D C. Letters of administration on the personal estate of Wm C Ross, late of Wash Co, deceased. -Augustus E Perry, adm

Orphans Court of Wash Co, D C. Letters of administration on the personal estate of Sarah A Ross, late of Wash Co, deceased. -Augustus E Perry, adm

Orphans Court of Wash Co, D C. Letters of administration on the personal estate of Mgt E Ross, late of Wash Co, deceased. -Richard L Ross, adm

St John's College, Annapolis, Md, will resume Sep 21. –Hector Humphries, Pres

Left her home on Tue last, Mary Eliz Hudson, about 13 years of age. I hereby forwarn any person from harboring or trusting her on my account. Any person finding the said girl will confer a favor on me by delivering her to Mr A Clements, 9th & Pa ave.
–Mary Anna Hudson

Senate: 1-Memorial of Eliz Armistead, widow of Gen W K Armistead, late of the U S Army, asking relief in relation to certain disbursements made by her late husband, & disallowed by accounting ofcrs of the treasury: referred to Cmte on Military Affiars.
2-Memorial of Jos J Graham, of Wythe Co, Va, setting forth that, in southwestern part of Va & East Tenn, there are a great many hardy & patriotic young men anxious to remove

west, & asking authority of Congress to organize a regt of dragoons, of not less than 1,000 men, to constitute a part of the army of the U S for a term not less than 3 nor more than 5 years, & that after their term expires a grant of a half section of land be made to each, upon condition of the actual settlement of the same: referred to the Cmte on Military Affairs. 3-Memorial of Mrs Myra Clark Gaines, widow of Maj Gen Edmund P Gaines, setting forth the long & arduous military services of her late husband, the battles in which he was engaged, with foreign Powers as well as various Indian tribes, & the wounds received: asking to be allowed a pension: referred to the Cmte on Pensions. 4-Memorial of the heirs of Herman & Mayard Blannerhassett, formerly residing on an island in the Ohio river, setting forth that the property was taken possession of by an armed body of militia, called out under a proclamation of the Pres in Dec 1806; that the cellars were broken open, & the provisions & liquors taken, & the property destroyed: referred to the Cmte of Claims. 5-Additional documents submitted in relation of the claim of Peter U Morgan, administrator of John Arnold, deceased, & Geo G Bishop: referred to the Cmte on Patents & the Patent Ofc. 6-Cmte on Military Affairs: bill for the relief of Edw Everett, late a sgt in the U S army: recommended its passage. 7-Cmte of the Whole: bill for the relief of John Devlin: engrossed for a 3rd reading.

THU AUG 29, 1850
Senate: 1-Cmte on Indian Affairs: memorial of Mary Jernigan, asking indemnity for property taken by the Indians in Florida, asked to be discharged from the further consideration of the same: which was agreed to. 2-Bill for the relief of John Devlin: passed.

Mrd: on Aug 20, Cambridge, Mass, by Rev Mr Frothingham, Lt Henry A Wise, U S Navy, to Charlotte Brooks, daughter of the Hon Edw Everett.

Mrd: on Aug 22, by Rev J G Butler, Mr Thos Wm Anderson to Miss Sarah Clarinda Burton, 3rd daughter of Mr Chas Burton, artist.

Died: on Tue, in Gtwn, John M Hepburn, in his 61st year. His funeral will be from his late residence, West st of Gtwn, Thu at 5 o'clock. Mr Hepburn has been, for the last 37 years, one of the most faithful public servants, having served all this time in the ofc of the Adj Gen of the army.

Mr Isaac N Cardoza, a venerable & worthy citizen of Powhatan, Va, drowned on Mon, in the Jas River, having made a mis-step from the cabin of the packet boat on way to Richmond with his daughter & niece, to attend the nuptials of latter.

Mrs Ellen Jones' School, for Juvenile Pupils, will re-open on the first Mon in Sep, at the same place, H & 21st sts.

House of Reps: 1-Ptn of Washington Bonifant, Dr Washington Duvall, & 92 other citizens of Montg Co, Md, praying an appropriation for the construction of a plank road from Washington to the Montg Co line.

Public Schools-Wash: Teachers for the ensuing year:
1st Dist School: Saml Kelly, Principal; Mrs Henshaw, Assist
Primary School 1-Mr A Lindsly
Primary School 2-Mrs Rodier, Principal; Miss King, Assist
Primary School 3-Miss Waggaman, Principal; Miss Anderson, Assist
Primary School 4-Miss Washington
2nd Dist School: Dr Watkins, Principal; Mr W W Demain & Mrs Randolph, Assists
Primary School 1-Miss Standiford
Primary School 2-Miss Randolph
Primary School 3-Mr Fill
Primary School 4-Mrs Ogden, Principal; Miss Billing, Assist
Third Dist School: Mr McCormick, Principal; Mr Goldsmith, Assist
Primary School 1-Miss Sherman, Principal; Miss Bulger, Assist
Primary School 2-Miss Bradley; Mrs Clark, Assist
Primary School 3: Mrs Martin
Primary School 4: Miss Moss
Fourth Dist School: J E Thompson, Principal; Mrs Hinton, Assist
Primary School 1-Miss Wells
Primary School 2-Miss English
Primary School 3-Miss Milburn

FRI AUG 30, 1850
Appointments by the Pres, with the advice & consent of the Senate:
Henry D Turner, Assistant Treasurer of the U S at St Louis, Missouri.
Attorneys of the U S:
Thos E Deblois, for Maine
Wm W Stickney, for N H
J Bowman Sweitzer, for Pa
Benj H Smith, for Va
Hiram W Husted, for N C
Henry Williams, for Ga
Jefferson F Jackson, for Ala
Peter Hamilton, for Ala
Geo W Lahin, for Wisc
Stephen Whicher, for Iowa
Geo W Call, jr, for Fla
Wm R Harkley, for Fla
Woodson L Ligon, for Miss
Logan Hunton, for La
Laurence P Crain, for La
W F Kercheval, for Tenn
Chas N Gibbs, for Tenn
Samson Mason, for Ohio
John D Cook, for Mo
Ofcrs of the Customs:
Levi Jones, Saluria, Texas
Thos L Shaw, Gtwn, S C
Jas E Gibble, Beaufort, N C
Saml Cooper, Middletown, Conn
Wm Henry Peete, Fairfield, Conn
Hiram Lenox, Burlington, N J
Fred'k S Thoms, Newark, N J
Chas M K Smith, Perth Amboy, N J
Wm M Gallagher, Presque Isle, Pa
Thos Ireland, Annapolis, Md
John D Whitford, Newbern, N C
John H Dilworth, St Mary's, Ga
Wm J Grayson, Charleston, S C
Robt W Alston, St Mark's, Fla
Danl Remick, Kennebunk, Maine
Lory Odell, Portsmouth, N H
Albert L Catlin, Vt
Saml L Thaxter, Fall River, Mass
Hooper C Hicks, Vienna, Md
Wm S Mallicote, Yorktown, Va

Geo W Charles, Camden, N C
Hiram Roberts, Savannah, Ga
Jas Gwinn, Vicksburg, Miss
Cornelius L Russell, Cuyahoga, Ohio
Jacob Russell, Chicago, Ill

Danl Dwight, Teche, La
Oliver York, Stonington, Conn
John Youngs, Sandusky, Ohio
Jonathan R Bullock, Bristol & Warren, R I

Surveyors:
David Fitz Randolph, for the port of New Brunswick, N J
Wm Face, for Hampton, Va
Edwin Morrison, for Smithfield, Va
Robt Edmonds, for Carter's Creek, Va
Henry Love, for Dumfries, Va
Geo W McGlaughon, for Windsor, N C
Wm J Phillips, for Matagorda, Texas
Robt S Cushman, for Albany, N Y

Appraiser: Artemon Hill, for the port of New Orleans, La.

Naval Ofcrs:
John McClintock, for Portsmouth, N H
Thos J Clark, for Newburyport, Mass
Moses Richardson, for Providence, R I
Thos K Carroll, for Balt, Md
Thos Gatewood, for Norfolk & Portsmouth, Va

Postmasters:
Wm Brewster, at Taunton, Mass
Fred'k G Edwards, at Louisville, Ky
John McGrew, at Alleghany City, Pa
Nathan Fiske, at Cambridge, Mass
L A Moody, at Chicopee, Mass
Whitney Jones, at Lansing, Mich
Chas Lyman, at Montpelier, Vt
John King, at Peoria, Ill
Thos Lefavour, at Pawtucket, R I
Richd G Savery, at Rome, N Y
W G Wollcott, at Whitehall, N Y
David Smith, at Jersey City, N J
Jas M Todd, at Frankfort, Ky
Fred'k J Coffin, at Newburyport, Mass
Caleb Clark, at Ann Arbor, Mich
Edw Lemist, at Roxbury, Mass
Chas E Ford, at Batavia, N Y
Alonzo M Griffin, at Natchez, Miss
B S Williams, at Detroit, Mich
Edw W Lincoln, at Worcester, Mass
Henry H Matthews, at Elmira, N Y
Ezra S Hamilton, at Hartford, Conn
Wm Oliver, at Cincinnati, Ohio
Benj F Arndt, at Easton, Pa
Andrew Mortimer, at Pottsville, Pa
Wm P Millard, at Galena, Ill
Philo S Johnson, at Watertown, N Y
David Powers, at Sandusky, Ohio
John S McCully, at Trenton, N J
Isaac Dillon, at Zanesville, Ohio
Francis A Wells, at Steubenville, Ohio
Rodney Wilbur, at Newark, N J
Robt A Barnard, at Hudson, N Y
Henry Rhoads, at Reading, Pa
Alex'r W Russell, at Indianapolis, Ind
Saml Ware, at Kensington, Pa
Thos H Sill, at Erie, Pa
Aner Austin, at Lynn, Mass
Thos L Fullock, at Portsmouth, N H
Jas C McGraw, at Cumberland, Md
Gold S Silliman, at Brooklyn, N Y
Nathan Merrill, at Charlestown, Mass
Geo L Whitney, at Canandaigua, N Y
Barzilai Slosson, at Geneva, N Y
Hoses H Fetts, at Lewiston, N Y
John F Bodley, at Vicksburg, Miss
Henry L Bowen, at Providence, R I
Abner Y Ellis, at Springfield, Ill

Cherry Ames, at Oswego, N Y
Lewis L Watson, at Vincennes, Ind
Eli D Anderson, at Maysville, Ky
Wm Woodward, at Middletown, Conn
Luther P Blodget, at Burlington, Vt
Danl Brawley, at Lafayette, Ind
Geo Robinson, at Ogdensburgh, N Y
C P J Arion, at Madison, Ind
Richd B Alexander, at Tuscumbia, Ala
Jos Burton, at Augusta, Maine
Joshua W Carr, at Bangor, Maine
Martin Pond, at Montgomery, Ala
Jas Hersey, at Manchester, N H
John B Robertson, at New Haven, Conn

Peter Banker, at Schenectady, N Y
Geo F Wentworth, at Dover, N H
John Dunham, at Norwich, Conn
Saml W Eager, at Newburgh, N Y
Geo R Barr, at Abingdon, Va
Andrew H Jordan, at Columbus, Miss
Zephainiah T Conner, at Macon, Ga
Geo Wade, at Bridgeport, Conn
Archibald Gamble, at St Louis, Mo
Alfred Gilman, at Lowell, Mass
Jas Ford, at Fall River, Mass
Jas G Burr, at Wilmington, N C
Augustus Clarke, at Northampton, Mass

Senate: 1-Cmte on Indian Affairs: memorial of Lewis Ralston, asking indemnity for loss of improvements of which he was dispossessed contrary to the treaty with the Cherokees of 1835 & 1836: asked to be discharged from the further consideration of the same: agreed to.

This is the day assigned for the execution of Prof John W Webster, at Boston. The appointed time is 8 o'clock. His family visited with him for the last time yesterday afternoon. He was calm & penitent. [Aug 31st newspaper: thousands have congregated, the housetops all around are covered with persons anxious to see, hundreds may be seen at the doors & windows, the throng is immense. Prof Webster was brought out & ascended the platform about 9 o'clock. He remained there until a quarter to ten, when the drop fell, & his spirit passed from time to eternity. He died almost without a struggle. His body has been taken back to the cell, where it remains until night. It will then be taken to Cambridge & given to his family for interment.]

SAT AUG 31, 1850
Senate: 1-Cmte on Foreign Relations: memorial of G T Howard, asking compensation as bearer of dispatches from Texas to the U S with documents in relation to the annexation of Texas, reported a bill for his relief: passed to a 2nd reading. 2-Cmte on Revolutionary Claims: memorial of Anne de Neufville Evans, with a joint resolution in relation to the accounts of John de Neufville & Son: ordered to a 2nd reading.

Naval Appointments: by the Pres, with the advice & consent of the Senate. 1-Stephen Champlin to be a capt in the Navy. 2-Richd B Tunstall to be Assist Surgeon in the Navy. 3-Richd T Allison, Nixon White, John J Jones, & John Johnson, to be Pursers in the Navy. 4-Jedediah H Lathrop to be Navy Agent, Washington. 5-Edwin O Perrin to be Navy Agent, Memphis.

Mrd: on Thu, in Gtwn, by Rev John C Smith, Capt Albert Dayton, of N Y, to Miss Emily Baker, of Gtwn..

Died: on Aug 22, after a brief illness, at the residence of his father, in Montg Co, Md, after a brief illness, Rev Luther J Etchison, of Balt Annual Conference, in his 24th year, & the 3rd of his ministry.

Died: on Aug 28, in Wash City, Francis Middleton Schreiner, eldest son of Mr Henry J Schreiner, of the Navy Dept, late of Gettysburg, Pa, in his 18th year. His funeral will be today at 3:30 o'clock, from the residence of his father, on Capitol Hill.

Died: on Aug 24, after a protracted illness, at the residence of Geo Kneller, Norfolk, Va; Louis Beeler, aged 76 years, a native of Germany, but for the last 30 years a resident of Alexandria, & for 17 years of Washington.

Died: on Aug 28, in Wash City, after a long & painful illness, Jacob, son of John A & Rebecca Young, late of Balt.

House of Reps: 1-Bill for the relief of Winthrop S Harding: passed.

The ancestors of Paul Revere emigrated from France to the Island of Guernsey on the revocation of the edict of Nantes; & his father was sent to Boston at age 13, to learn the trade of a goldsmith. Paul Revere was born in Boston, Jun 1, 1725, died May 1818, aged 84. He was brought up in his father's business, as a goldsmith. In the war of 1756 he served with reputation on the frontiers, against the French & Indians, as lt in the Mass troops. During the Revolutionary war Paul Revere was major & afterwards lt colonel, in a regt of artl, raised for the defence of the State. Paul Revere was first Pres of the Massachusetts Charitable Mechanic Assoc.

For rent or sale: large commodious brick dwlg on Pa ave, between 1st & 2nd sts, adjoining the residence of the subscriber. Inquire of John Purdy.

MON SEP 2, 1850
Appointments by the Pres, with advice & consent of the Senate.
Land Ofcrs--<u>Receivers of Public Moneys;</u>
John W Norton, at Shawneetown, Ill
Blenford Johnson, at Edwardsville, Ill
Jas T B Stapp, at Vandalia, Ill
Walter Davis, at Springfield, Ill
John H Murphy, at Danville, Ill
Henry V Sullivan, at Quincy, Ill
John H Kinzie, at Chicago, Ill
Bernard F Hempstead, at Wash, Ark
Wm H Ringo, at Helena, Ark
Wm Goodrich, at Clarksville, Ark
Chas P Bertrand, at Little Rock, Ark
Seneca W Ely, at Chillicothe, Ohio
Wm Sheffield, at Defiance, Ohio
Saml Merriwether, at Jeffersonville, Ind
Robt N Carman, at Vincennes, Ind
Thos Allen, at Clinton, Mo
John T Hughes, at Plattsburg, Mo
Gideon Fitz, at Jackson, Miss
Geo R Clayton, at Columbus, Miss
Jas W Drake, at Pontotoc, Miss
Rosemond de Armas, New Orleans, La
John H Dinkgrave, at Monroe, La
John Corkern, at Greensburg, La
John Laplace, at Natchitoches, La
Chas L Stevenson, Mineral Point, Wisc
Chas H Williams, at Milwaukee, Wisc
Moses S Gibson, at Willow River, Wisc
Nathl G Wilcox, at Stillwater, Minn Terr

Registers:
Ferdinand Maxwell, at Kaskaskia, Ill
Jas M Davis, at Vandalia, Ill
Jas M McLean, at Palastine, Ill
Turner R King, at Springfield, Ill
Danl Clapp, at Danville, Ill
Henry Asbury, at Quincy, Ill
Silas Noble, at Dixon, Ill
Henry F Mooney, at Helena, Ark
John E Manley, at Clarksville, Ark
Wm E Powell, at Champagnole, Ark
Jas H Patterson, at Batesville, Ark
Wm W Adams, at Little Rock, Ark
Wm H Etter, at Washington, Ark
Jas H Sterman, at Fayetteville, Ark
Anthony Walke, at Chillicothe, Ohio
Abner Root, at Defiance, Ohio

Wm H L Noble, at Indianapolis, Ind
Jas Scott, at Jeffersonville, Ind
John C Clark, at Vincennes, Ind
Saml B Todd, at Fayette, Mo
Greer W Davis, at Jackson, Mo
John Dade, at Springfield, Mo
Thos E Birch, at Plattsburg, Miss
Austin Morgan, at Jackson, Miss
Chas Fitz, at New Orleans, La
Evariste de Bouillon, Opelousas, La
Henry O McEnery, at Monroe, La
Hugh Y Waddell, Natchitoches, La
Paraclete Porter, at Milwaukee, Wisc
Francis P Catlin, at Willow River, Wisc
Abraham Van Vorbes, at Stillwater, Minn Terr

Mrd: on Aug 29, by Rev Dr Butler, Lt John S Garland, U S A, to Mary Truxtun, daughter of John H Houston, of Wash City.

Died: on Aug 29, in Phil, Pa, Wm Sager, age 23 years. Married but 1 month, he suffocated to death by inhaling gas from spirits of nitre, in labortory of Smith & Hodgson, where he was engaged in the manufacture of the article. His death took place almost immediately after encountering the fumes from the vessel that had the nitre.

Mrd: on Aug 27, at Circleville, Ohio, Jas McQueen to Miss Eliz D Lawrence, daughter of Gen H Lawrence, all of that place.

Mrd: on Aug 26, in Richmond, by Rev R B C Howell, Mr John Graeme, jr, to Miss Virginia, daughter of Mr Wm Booth, all of Richmond City.

Died: on Aug 31, at her residence, on 4½ th st, Mrs Catherine Boyle, consort of the late John Boyle, in her 63rd year.

Died: on Aug 21, at his residence, Newstead, Loudoun Co, Va, Geo M Grayson, in his 56th year. He faithfully fulfilled every duty of a husband, father, & master.

Died: on Jul 29, at the residence of Geo T Beale, PG Co, Md, Solomon Weeks, school teacher, formerly a resident of N Y.

House of Reps: 1-Ptn of Mary Haskins, of North Dansville, Livingston Co, N Y, praying for a pension. 2-Memorial of John T Parker, of Shelby Co, Ky, praying Congress to authorize & require the Navy Dept to purchase hemp from him, as prepared for the Gov't, equal to the standard heretofore required by the Dept.

M A Tyson & Sister's Seminary, F st, between 12th & 13th sts, will be resumed on Sep 16th. [Ad]

For rent: house & lot on 16th st west, near I st, opposite Cmdor Morris. It is now occupied by Mr Marie, Sec of the French Legation. Possession in a few days. Inquire of Jas Carrico.

Wash City: erection of 2 handsome brick bldgs by Messrs Lane & Tucker: the window shutters are made to slide into the brick wall above, thus the handling & removal of window shutters is entirely avoided. This was introduced into the stores lately erected in Balt. The outside doors fold back into a recess made in the wall, The inner doors are of handsome glass sash: the glass sheets cost upward of $500. They are of the best English plate, which we understand has never before used in this city; it is said not to be liable to be dimmed by vapor as the French glass. Employed upon the bldg: Messrs Dufief & Entwisle, architects & carpenters; John Davis, painter; N Rider, castings; M G Emery, stone work; Jas Skirving, Tinner; & J W Thompson, Plumber.

I certify that A W Manning, of Wash Co, D C, brought before me a stray roan mare, & one sorrel horse. –John L Smith, J P [Owner is to come forward, prove property, pay charges, & take them away. –W A Manning, Eastern Hill, D C, near Anacostia Bridge.

City Ordinance-Wash. Act for the relief of Josias Adams: sum of $50 be allowed to him for his services as a police ofcr for 6th Ward, from 13 Jun 1849 to Jun 1850

TUE SEP 3, 1850
Millard Fillmore, Pres of the U S, recognizes John Searle, who has been appointed Consul of Portugal for Calif, to reside at San Francisco. Sep 2, 1850

Mr O Hinton, agent for the Ohio Stage Co, was arrested at Cleveland on Aug 25, on a charge of robbing the U S mail, on Aug 15, of a large amount of money. A guard of 3 ofcrs was put over him during the night, but at 1 o'clock he managed to escape. A reward of $500 is offers for his arrest & confinement in any jail in the U S. [Sep 9 newspaper: Hinton has been retaken at Wellsville, Ohio, & safely lodged in jail.] [Sep 19th newspaper: Cleveland, Ohio, Sep 16. Preliminary examination of Hinton closed on Sat. He was adjudged guilty, & bail was fixed at 15,000. The prisoner was not able to procure bail, & left by stage for Columbus, with Gen Jones, U S Marshal, where he will await his trial in the Franklin Co jail.]

Geo Corser, son of S S Corser, Superintendent of the Atlantic & St Lawrence railroad, was killed on Fri, while returning with a train of cars, of which he was conductor. He was on top of a car when it came in contact with a bridge, knocking him off.

Last week, a 12 year old son of Mr John Gilpin, of Centre township in this county, died when a yellow jacket flew into his mouth & stunk him at the top of his throat. In 20 minutes he was dead. Swelling had set in which closed the windpipe.
–Cambridge, Ohio, Times

Albert Francis, brakeman on the Syracuse & Utica railroad, while walking on the top of the cars near Syracuse, fell between them & the wheels passed over him, cutting off his legs & lower part of the body. He lived about 20 minutes after the accident.

For rent: 3 story brick house on F st, between 13th & 14th sts, long established as a hotel & boarding house. –Abraham Butler

Mrd: on Aug 28, at Middleton, Conn, by Rev Mr Jarvis, John M Storey, of Havana, to Caroline Augusta, youngest daughter of late E W W Webster, of the Island of Cuba.

Died: on Sep 2, Yelverton Peyton Bowen, in his 27th year. His funeral will be today, at residence of his brother-in-law, Wm T Duvall, on Missouri ave, near 4½ st, at 3:30 p m.

Died: on Jul 23, at Santa Fe, New Mexico, Mrs Eliz Lloyd Easton, wife of Capt Langdon C Easton, & daughter of Col Benj L Beall, U S A. She leaves a devoted husband & 3 children.

Died: on Sep 1, after a short illness, Georgianna Sessford, aged 8 months, youngest daughter of John H & Susan S Sessford.

For sale or rent: two 3 story brick houses in the First Ward. -J Boulanger

Two story brick house at auction on Sep 4, on part of lot 10 in square 881, fronting on South K st, near the Navy Yard. Sold to satisfy gound rent due Jacob Small, & by his order. –Green & Tastet, aucts

Senate: 1-Memorial of Saml Perrine, setting forth that he has charge of the surf-boat with appurtenances, station #7, on Jersey coast, between Sandy Hook & Little Egg Harbor; & that it is attended with considerable trouble, & consumes much time, & asking that compensation may be allowed him: referred to the Cmte on Naval Affairs. 2-Document submitted in relation to the claim of Rufus Hoyt to an increase of pension: referred to the Cmte on Pensions.

Appointment by the Pres. A J Jones: Postmaster at Harrisburgh, Pa.

The N Y Commercial Advertiser of Sat announces the death of John Inman, one of the editors of that journal. Mr Inman was in his 47th year, & for the last 20 years has been connected with the press of N Y.

WED SEP 4, 1850
Cincinnati Gazette chronicles the death of 2 esteemed citizens of that city: John A D Burrows, age 39, merchant; & James M Douglass, age 43, teller in the Franklin Bank. Mr Burrows has been a prominent merchant for past 16 years. Mr Douglass was a resident of the city since boyhood.

Mexican Items: 1-Gen Romulo Diaz de la Vega has been appointed Commandant-Gen of the State of Mexico. 2-Gen Pena y Banagan, Commandnat-Gen of the State of Vera Cruz, died of cholera at Jalapa on the 2nd inst.

Postmaster Gen established the following new Post Ofcs for week ending Aug 24, 1850.

Ofc	County, State	Postmaster
White Hall	Balt, Md	John Wise
Ewing	Hocking, Ohio	Warren Chapman
Davidson Centre	Genesee, Mich	G Townsend
Peninsula	Ontonagon, Mich	S O Knapp
Cuba	Rutherford, N C	Jas P Webb
Lowery	Barnwell D, S C	H Easterlin
Curcton's Bridge	Henry, Ala	Jas W Curcton
Spring Port	Panola, Miss	A J Holcombe
Bloomfield	Kemper, Miss	W H Stephenson
Lafayette Springs	Lafayette, Miss	H D McIntosh
McCutchans'	St Charles P, La	Saml McCutchan
Turkey Creek	Hunt, Texas	C Shepherd
Providence Hill	Tyler, Texas	A Savell
Cotton Plant	Rusk, Texas	Chas Kuykendall
Linn Flats	Nacogdoches, Texas	R E Wynnes
Rough & Ready	Monroe, Ark	M M Green
Bethel	Giles, Tenn	J C Roberts
Trion	Jefferson, Tenn	John Cowan
Shady Hill	Henderson, Pa	J L McCollum
Arlington	Bureau, Ill	Jas Waugh
Keeneville	Wayne, Ill	John Keen
Bull Mills	Yancy, Mo	R Jones
Alto	Fond du Lac, Wis	Wm S Gillet
Johnstown Centre	Rock, Wis	Edwin G Matthews

Names Changed:
Worcester, Marquetto Co, Mich, changed to Marquette.
Mouth of Prater, Tazewell Co, Va, changed to Slate Creek.
Schoofield's Store, Bledsoe Co, Tenn, changed to Nine Mile.
Brookfield, Lasalle Co, Ill, changed to Scott.
Polkville, Macon Co, Maine, changed to Newburg.
O'Neil's Mills, Polk Co, Oregon Territory, changed to Nesmith's.
Forks of Mary's River, Benton Co, Oregon Territory, changed to Marysville.

$100 reward for the person who mutilated a State block of stone forwarded to the Wash Nat'l Monument, to be placed in that edifice. The watchman was not absent more than 10 minutes. By order of the Board of Mgrs: Thos Carbery, Chrmn of Bldg Cmte.

Died: on Aug 24, in North Carolina, Rev Jas Osbourn, formerly of Balt, & Pastor of Navy Yard Baptist Church in Wash City in 1818, aged 70. He was extensively known, & greatly esteemed.

Senate: 1-Cmte on Pensions: House bill for the relief of Skelton Felton, reported back the same without amendment & recommended its passage. 2-Ptn of Isaac Seymour, a pensioner of the U S, asking to be allowed a back pension: referred to the Cmte on Pensions. 3-Cmte on Military Affairs: memorial of Jos J Graham, asking authority to raise a regt of volunteers to serve on the frontier, asked to be discharged from the further consideration of the ptn of the same: which was agreed to. Same cmte: to inquire into granting a pension of 5 years to the widow of Lt Col Zenon Mackay, late of the U S army. 4-Resolution for settlement of the accounts with the heirs & reps of Col Pierce M Butler, late agent for the Cherokee Indians: passed.

THU SEP 5, 1850
House of Reps: 1-Resolved, that the payment by the Sec of the Interior of $32,382.50 to the administrator of Cmdor Jas Barron as commutation pay for the naval services of the said Barron, during the Revolutionary war, was made in violation of law. Resolved, that ofcrs of the navy, during the war of the Revolution, are not entitled to commutation pay. Resolved, that the payment of compound interest in the case of Cmdor Jas Barron was made in violation of law. 2-Resolved, that the sum of $56,021.49 paid to Messrs Corcoran & Riggs, as assignees of Wm M Gwinn, was justly due the Chickasaw Indians, & was improperly paid to Corcoran & Riggs.

For sale or exchange for city property: a farm, containing 60 acres 2 miles east of the Navy Yard, near Good Hope, having a 2 story frame house, stable, carriage-house, & other necessary out-bldgs. For terms apply to Geo M Phillips, F & 15th sts.

$5 reward for recovery of a large light-red cow that strayed.
-G B McKnight, Third st

Improved property at auction: on Sep 12, parts of lot 17 & 18 in square 496, fronting F st near 4½ st, with a good 2 story frame house, kitchen & garret. It is opposite the residence of Geo Mattingly, & next adjoining Mr Page's windmill. –Dyer & Bro, aucts

FRI SEP 6, 1850
Robt Wickliffe, jr, late Charge d'Affaires to Sardinia, died at his residence in Ky, on Aug 29.

On Fri, a man named Potter, a Mason by trade, & his 8 year old son, belonging to Topsfiled, Mass, while on a gunning excursion, in the Ipswich Marshes, sunk into the mud & were drowned when the tide began to rise.

Mr Alex'r Hale, son of Hon Nathan Hale, of Boston, met with a sudden death on Aug 24. Being engaged in surveying a route for a railroad at Pensacola, Fla, a schnr was observed driving on shore during a severe storm. Passed Midshipman Dyer, Mr Hale, & 4 seamen jumped into a boat & went to the rescue, & had made one trip in safety, when on returning to render further aid, their boat was capsized & Mr Hale drowned. He was in his 23rd year, & a graduate of Harvard College.

Wash Corp: 1-Ptn of T P Brown & Marshall Brown, asking authority to construct an area of certain dimensions on their premises: referred to the Cmte on Improvements. 2-Cmte on Finance: statement of a balance due A C Kidwell for relaying & widening the gutter on D st: referred to the Cmte on Improvements. 3-Cmte of Claims: asked to be discharged from the further consideration of the ptn of Ignatius W Atchenson. 4-Bill for the relief of B Jost: referred to the Cmte of Claims. 5-Bill for the relief of John Dewdney: passed.

On Mon last, during a storm, Mr & Mrs Edmund P Gatchell, on their return from a visit, missed their way while driving over the inundated roads, & were precipitated into a gully, where they drowned.

City Ordinances-Wash. 1-Act for the relief of John Maguire: fine imposed for an alleged violation of the law in relation to manufacturing & dealing in hats, is remitted: provided he pay the costs of prosecution. 2-Act for the relief of A Addison: fine imposed for a violation in relation to wagons & carts, is remitted: provided he pay the costs of prosecution.

Senate: 1-Cmte on Naval Affairs: ptn of the widow of Jacob Bright, whose husband was killed in the public service, asking for a pension; & the ptn of Wm Brown, asking to be allowed a pension; & the ptn fo Emily C B Thompson, widow of Capt Chas Thompson, asking that her pension be increased & continued during her life: asked to be discharged from the further consideration of the ptns & they be referred to the Cmte on Pensions. Same cmte: asked to be discharged from the further consideration of the ptn of Cmdor Danl Turner, & that it be referred to the Cmte of Claims. Same cmte: memorial from Jos P Pierson, asking the adoption of his patent condenser to the engines of the steam naval marine; from Edw Lynch, asking an appropriation for the purpose of altering the boilers of the U S steamer **Jefferson** so as to apply his improvement for supplying them with a freer supply of fresh water; from Moses J Hill, claiming to have made a valuable discovery applicable to the naval service, & asking that its value & practicability may be tested; from H B Babcock, asking Congress to purchase his patent-right for a new anti-friction metallic compound for the use of the Gov't; & from Ralph Bulkley, asking an appropriation to test his method of extinguishing fire: asked to be discharged from the further consideration of the above memorials: agreed to. 2-Resolved, that the Cmte on Military Affairs inquire into granting a pension of 5 years to the widow of Lt Col Zenon Mackay, late of the U S Army. 3-Bill to make compensation to Walter Colton came up & was passed. 4-Bill for the relief of Lewright Browning, widow of the late Lt Robt L Browning: to be placed on the list of naval pensions for the period of 5 years, & to allow to her the pension now provided by law for the widows of lts of the navy who died in service.

The Boston papers record the death of Danl P Parker, long known as an eminent & successful merchant of that place, who died on Sat, in his 69th year.

The wife of Hon Josiah Quincy, senior, died at their country residence in Quincy, Mass, on Sun at the advanced age of 80 years.

Miss Charlotte Ann Mooers, a young lady at Green Bay, Wisc, was sitting in her father's house, on Jul 30, singing with her sister, Mrs Lathrop, when she was struck by lightning. Miss Mooers was enveloped in flames, lay upon the floor, & appeared quite dead. Her mother breathed into her mouth, followed by her father, until she began to be restored to consciousness. She regained her sight & could speak, & hopes were raised of her recovery. She lingered for 20 hours, & then sunk away in death.

Mrd: on Sep 4, by Rev Jas Laurie, D D, of Wash City, Mr Isaac Hulse, of Balt, to Miss Mgt Jackson of Accomac Co, Va.

Died: in Wash City, after a short illness, Eugene Columbus, youngest son of John H & Mgt A Plant, age 1 year, 2 months & 16 days. [No death date given-current item.]

Died: on Aug 21, at Pittsburg, Pa, Mary Ann Lowry, in her 70th year. She was for many years a resident of Wash.

SAT SEP 7, 1850
Senate: 1-Mr Underwood: I rise to ask a favor for a woman who lives in my neighborhood, of the name of Sarah Jane West, widow of Gardner West, who was musician in Capt Patrick H Gardner's company of volunteers, [Co K of Col Williams' regt of Ky volunteers.] The bill from the House was passed: she is to be paid 3 months' extra pay, & 2½ months' pay, to which her deceased husband was entitled at the time of his death; & the Com'r of Pensions is directed to issue to her a certificate for 160 acres of land, & to place her name on the pension roll, & allow the 5 years' pension payable to the widow of deceased soldiers who served in the war with Mexico. It is said that he deserted in Mexico, but that is a mistake. I believe he was assassinated in the city of Mexico. Bill passed. 2-Bill #207, which is a bill reported from the Judiciary Cmte for the relief of Eliz L Blackburn, the widow of a soldier who was killed at Vera Cruz: he was a paymaster, & killed with a large sum of money in his hands. On examining his trunk there was found to be a small deficiency, for which the Gov't obtained judgement against the widow. The cmte were unanimously of opinion that she ought to be released from it, & the bill is for that purpose. The bill provides that Eliz L Blackburn, [late Bosworth,] be, & she is hereby, released & discharged from the judgment rendered against her as one of the securities of her late husband, Felix G Bosworth, a paymaster in the U S army, first rendered for $2,362.49, but afterwards reduced by the accounting ofcrs of the Treasury to $1,672.49. Bill passed. 3-Cmte of the Whole: bill for the relief of Isaac Watts Griffiths, to increase his pension. Engrossed for a 3rd reading. 4-Bills passed: relief of Wm Hardin; relief of Chas F Sibbald; relief of John M McIntosh; & relief of Lewright Browning. 5-Bill for the relief of Charlotte Lynch: provides there shall be allowed & paid to her, only surviving child of Lt Col Ebenezer Gray, of the 6th regt of the Connecticut line, who served in the army of the Revolution from the beginning of the war to its close: engrossed for a 3rd reading. Ebenezer Gray retired from the army, with a constitution broken down by disease contracted in the service; that the only compensation on which he or any member of his family ever received was his pay in depreciated currency, & the 5 years' commutation allowed in 1783, which depreciated to a few cents on the dollar; & that the ofcrs did not receive the benefits of that. 6-Bill for

the relief of Maj Fred'k D Mills: engrossed for a 3rd reading. 7-Cmte of the Whole: bill for the relief of Chas Reeder, Walter R Johnson, & the legal reps of Thos P Jones: Sec of Navy to cause their accounts to be audited & adjusted, for their services as a board of examiners in relation to steam boiler explosions: not to exceed $100 per month. It was the impression of Mr Dickinson that these men were fully paid already. Bill laid over. 8-Bill for relief of John M McIntosh: to pay him $164, that being the joint amount of 2 accounts against the Gov't, duly certified to be correct, in favor of John Clutes & Jacob Hart, for $82 each; the amounts being on duplicate certificates, the originals having been lost & considered as cancelled. [Clutes was a teamster at *Fort Macomb*, Fla; Jacob Hart, similar services; accounts stolen on Apr 7, 1840.] Engrossed for a 3rd reading. 9-Cmte of the Whole: bill to provide for the final settlement of the accounts of Jonathan Kearsley, late receiver of public moneys at Detroit; & of John Biddle, late register of the land ofc at that place. The petitioners were register & receiver at the land ofc at Detroit, in 1831, 1835, & 1836. The amount of compensation for land ofcrs is $500, & he is entitled to 1 per cent on the business until it amounts to $3,000. Bill was laid on the table.

Mrd: on Sep 4, in St John's Church, Gtwn, D C, by Rev C M Butler, D D, Robt F Lilburne, of Md, to Miss Emeline V Hopkins, of Gtwn.

Mrd: on Aug 26, in Cincinnati, by Bishop McIlvaine, Wm J Flagg, of N Y C, to Miss Eliza Longworth, daughter of Nicholas Longworth, of the former place.

Died: on Sep 6, in her 88th year, Mrs Susannah Scaggs, wife of Richd Scaggs, & daughter of Fred'k Holtzman, of Fred'k Co, Md. Mrs Scaggs was a resident of this District for 55 years. Her funeral will be Sat, at 10 o'clock, on 18th st, between K & L sts.

Died: on Sep 6, in Wash City, after a lingering illness, in her 64th year, Mrs Dorcas Galvin, a native of Balt Co, Md, & for the last 40 years a resident of Wash City. Her funeral will take place from her residence, on C, between 3rd & 4½ sts, on Sun, at 3 o'clock.

Died: on Aug 23, at the hospital of Detroit, after a few hours illness, of cholera, Sr Mary Loyola [Ritchie,] a native & former resident of Gtwn, in this District. Many years have passed since she left this community. For 20 years she served in the holy cause of Charity.

Farm for sale: the subscriber will sell his farm on the road to Port Tobacco, adjoining the lands of Messrs Bladen & Berry, containing about 180 acres, with a nearly new dwlg-house & out-houses. Terms will be made known by Messrs G & T Parker, Pa ave, or by the undersigned, Zadock Williams, Coombs' Wharf, Eastern Branch.

Executor's sale of land: by provisions of the last will & testament of Robt Threft, deceased: sale on Oct 2, of the tract of land owned by Threft, in Fairfax Co, adjoining the lands of Col Geo Minor & others, containing 250 acres. –Geo N Threft, exc of Robt Threft, deceased -Madison Courthouse [See Sep 10th newspaper.]

Postmaster Gen established the following new Post Ofcs for week ending Aug 31, 1850.

Ofc	County, State	Postmaster
So Raymond	Rockingham, N H	Jacob Elliott
Fessenden Mills	Rockingham, N H	R B Jackson
East Woburn	Middlesex, Mass	Henry Ramsdell
Mills' Mill	Allegany, N Y	A S Ladd
Fordham	Westchester, N Y	John Berrian
Brown's Mills	Burlington, N J	B Woodward
Groveville	Mercer, N J	Jos Walter
Shelltown	Monmouth, N J	Thos C Rogers
Walnut Mills	Monmouth, N J	Miss Sarah Waln
No Chatham	Lycoming, Pa	Saml Mapes
Hickorytown	Montgomery, Pa	Jas Wood
Nauvoo	Tioga, Pa	Danl W Canfield
Bald Eagle	York, Pa	Jos H Thompson
New Plymouth	Vinton, Ohio	H S Brinkley
Woodyard	Athens, Ohio	Robt Figley
Renrock	Morgan, Ohio	Firman Dye
Morris' Church	Campbell, Va	A J Jennings
Fillmore	Cleveland, N C	A L Elliott
Hornsborough	Chesterfield D, S C	John C Mangum
Chaseville	Murray, Geo	D W Chase
Hecla	Carroll, Tenn	Wm Akers
Merry Oaks	Hamilton, Tenn	Sam Hunter
Marble Hall	Hawkins, Tenn	J D McFarland
Snider's	Washington, Ky	Jacob Snider
Staffordsburg	Kenton, Ky	John Carroll
Prestonville	Carrol, Ky	Ira M Collyer
Koro	Winnebago, Wis	Jas H Foster
New Glarus	Green, Wis	G C Panchard
Booneville	Boone, Iowa	Saml H Bower
Paris	Linn, Iowa	R C Powell

Names Changed:
Pierce, Dupae Co, Ill, changed to Sagone.
Drake's Creek, Shelby Co, Ill, changed to Big Spring.
Nisqually, Lewis Co, Oregon Territory, changed to Olympia.

MON SEP 9, 1850
Mrd: on Sep 4, by Rev Jas Laurie, D D, Isaac Hulse of Fla to Mgt L, daughter of Thos Jackson, of Gtwn, D C.

Mrd. On Aug 22, in the Presbyterian Church, Portsmouth, Va, by Rev V Eskridge, Mr G B Davids of N Y to Miss Mary F Hughes, of Wash.

Died: Sep 7, after a severe illness of only a few hours, Mrs Cath McAlwee, relict of late Mr Aaron McAlwee.

Died: on Sep 5, in Phil, Walter Hellen, aged 35 years. His friends, & those of his brother-in-law, T L Moody, are invited to attend the funeral, from his residence on G st, this afternoon, at 3 o'clock.

$15 reward: strayed from the commons on Capitol Hill, 3 cows. Reward if brought home. –J Hepburn, Capitol Hill, near Hay Scales

Farmers' Hotel, Rockville, Montg Co, Md. The subscriber can accommodate 10 or 15 boarders on reasonable terms. This village is perfectly healthy, with fine water & pure air. –Francis Kidwell

Paris, Aug 22, 1850. Tremendus loss that French literature has just sustained, in the death of the distinguished writer Honore de Balzac who died on Sun last; of dropsy of the heart. It would seem that the cold to which he was subjected during his late sojourn in Russia, whither he went to marry the Russian countess, whom he had loved so long, contributed powerfully to the development of the disease. He went in search of happiness & fortune. He found both, but brought back death.

Rev Dr Adoniram Judson, aged 62 years, Missionary to Burmah, died at sea on board the French barque **Aristide Marie**, of Bordeaux, on Apr 12th, & was buried at sea. Mrs Judson & children survive. [Sep 12th newspaper: Dr Judson embarked for the East in 1812, & has been more than 38 years in the missionary service.]

TUE SEP 10, 1850
Executor's sale of land: by provisions of the last will & testament of Robt Thrift, deceased: sale on Oct 2, of the land owned by Thirft, in Fairfax Co, adjoining the lands of Col Geo Minor & others, containing 250 acs. –Geo N Thrift, exc of Robt Thrift, deceased [See Sep 8th newspaper.]

House for rent: occupied by Mrs Macdaniel, on the east side of 4½ st, near Pa ave, will be for rent after the adjournment of Congress.

House of Reps: 1-Ptn by Mr Kaufman, of Texas, praying for compensation for the seizure of the schnr **Marcia M Briggs**.

The U S surveying steamer **Walker**, arrived at Portsmouth on Fri from the sea-coast of Md & Va, S P Lee, Lt Commanding; B Westcott, Master; J A Pettit, Surgeon. On Jul 14, Henry Cavener & John Patrick were drowned in the surf. She is to be relieved by the vessel **Legare**. -Pilot

Dissolution of the copartnership, in the trade of Booksellers & Stationers, under the firm of Gooch & Waters, by mutual consent. -John Gooch, N Ramsey Waters

Senate: 1-Ptn of Isaac Ackerman, asking an increase of pension: referred to the Cmte on Pensions. 2-Memorial of Wm Y Hansell, Wm H Underwood, & the reps of Saml Rockwell, deceased, former counselor & atty for the Cherokee Indians within the limits of Geogeia, asking Congress to make provision by law for the payment of their respective claims: referred to the Cmte on the Judiciary. 3-Ordered that Saml Hook, a Revolutionary soldier, have leave to withdraw his papers. 4-Cmte on Indian Affairs: memorial of P E Thomas & others, in behalf of the Seneca Indians, asking payment of money due them, & withheld by a sub-agent of the U S. 5-Cmte on Indian Affairs: memorial of certain Seminole Indians, who were in the service of the U S under the command of Wm G Sanders, submitted a report, which was referred to the Cmte on Fiannce, recommending that an amendment be made to the bill making appropriation for the military serice, setting apart $1,018,92 for the payment of said warriors. 6-Cmte on Indian Affairs: Memorial of David Vann & Wm P Ross, delegates of the Cherokee nation, in relation to a balance due under the treaty of 1835, & land reserved under the treaty of 1819; asked to be discharged from the further consideration of the same, which was agreed to. 7-Cmte on the Judiciary: bill for the relief of Winthrop S Harding: requested that it might be immediately considered. 8-Cmte of Claims: bill for the relief of Chas Reeder, Walter R Johnson, & the legal reps of Thos P Jones: accounts to be audited and the sums found to be due them be paid. 9-Bills passed: relief of Charlotte Lynch; relief of Chas A Kellett; relief of Eliz L Blackburn; increase pension of Isaac Watts Griffith; & relief of the administrator of Maj Fred'k D Mills, deceased. 10-Cmte of the Whole: bill for the relief of Hiram Moore & John Haskell.

Appointments by the Pres, with the advice & consent of the Senate.
1-*Danl D Barnard, of N Y, to be Envoy Extra & Minister Pleni to Prussia.
[*Oct 19th newspaper: Hon D D Barnard, his wife & daughter, sailed from N Y on Wed, in the ship Zurich, for Havre.]
Wm Strong, of Ohio, to be an Assoc Justice of the Supreme Court of the U S for the Territory of Oregon.
John S Gallaher, of Va, to be 3rd Auditor of the Treasury.
Wm Irvin, of Pa, Marshal of the U S for the Western District of Pa, vice Alex'r Irvin, removed.
Thos Ewbank, Com'r of Patents.
Consuls:
Wm Carroll Sanders, of Ala, for the city of Rome, in place of Nicholas Brown, recalled.
Lorenzo Draper, of N Y, for the port of Havre de Grace, in France, vice Wm J Staples, recalled.
Edw Kent, of Maine, for the port of Rio de Janeiro, in Brazil, vice Gorham Peaks, recalled.
Wm R Glover, of Monterey, for the city of Monterey, in Mexico.
Wm R Hayes, of Conn, for the island of Barbadoes, vice Noble Turner, recalled.
Ralph King, of La, for the port of Bremen, vice Wm H Robinson, recalled.
John L Hodge, of Pa, for the port of Marseilles, in France, vice Danl C Croxall, recalled.
Fayette M Ringgold, of D C, for the port of Arica, in Peru.
Benj H Norton, of Mass, for the port of Pictou, in Nova Scotia, vice Luther Brackett, recalled.

Albert Lange, of Indiana, for the port of Amsterdam, in the Netherlands, vice Chas Nicholls, recalled.
Jos Mosier, of N Y, for Ancona, in Italy, vice Jas E Freeman, recalled.
Alex'r H Clements, of D C, for the port of Messina, in Sicily, vice T W Behn, recalled.
Nathan Burchard, of N Y, for Basle, in Switzerland, vice Geo H Goundie, recalled.
Zabdial W Potter, of Md, for the port of Valparaiso, in Chili, vice Wm G Moorhead, recalled.
Jas F Waddell, of N C, for the port of Matamoras, in Mexico, vice Thos W Slemons, recalled.
J B Wilbor, senior, of N Y, for the port of Nice, in Sardinia, vice Victor A Sasserne, removed.
Lewis Baker, of N Y, for the port of Laguyra, in Venezuela, vice John P Adams, recalled.
Thos M Rodney, of Delaware, for the port of Matanzas, in the Island of Cuba, vice Simeon M Johnson, resigned.
Reynold Frenckall, for Helsingfors, in Russia.
Henri Stuckle, for Algiers.
John M Fessenden, at Dresden, in Saxony.
Pablo Auguera, for the port of Barcelona, in Spain.

Died: on Sep 8, in Wash City, Mr David Fitzgerald, a native of Ireland, in his 32nd year. His funeral is today at 3 o'clock, from the residence of his father, on H near 5th st.

Notice: by order for distress, I shall expose to public sale, for cash, on Sep 14, goods & chattels of Jas Stoops for house rent due & in arrears to Cornelius Boyle, & will be sold to satisfy the same. —R R Burr, bailiff

Household & kitchen furniture at auction: on Sep 13, at the residence of Mr Bowen, 12th & F sts. —Green & Tastet, aucts

2 valuable tracts of land for sale: one in Montg Co, Md, containing 70 acres; one of 40 acres of land on the heights of Gtwn. For terms apply to Nich Callan, Notary Public, F st.

Wm D Brook, insolvent debtor, has applied to be discharged from imprisonment: hearing on Sep 16. —Jno A Smith, clerk

To let: new brick house, with back bldg, on D st, between 6th & 7th sts. Inquire of J Galligan & Son.

WED SEP 11, 1850
Trustee's sale of improved property: on Sep 17, by deed of trust from Dickerson Nailor & wife, recorded in Liber W B 136, folios 384 thru 386, of the land records for Wash Co, lot 20 in square 367, with improvements, fronting on 9th st, between L & M sts.
—J F Callan, trustee; Dyer & Brother, aucts

Senate: 1-Memorial of Geo Mackay, asking compensation for services rendered a deputy surveyor of public lands in Florida: referred to the Cmte on Public Lands. 2-Ptn of Isaac Houston, asking compensation for services in carrying the mail: referred to the Cmte on the Post Ofc & Post Roads. 3-Cmte on Indian Affairs: memorial of Jonathan Lewis, asking indemnity for depredations committed by the Indians while residing among the Cherokees as a blacksmith, asked to be discharged from the further consideration of the same: which was agreed to. 4-Cmte of Claims: ptn of Saml Boots, asked to be discharged from the further consideration of the same, & that it be referred to the War Dept, which was agreed to. 5-Bill for the relief of Chas Reeder, Walter R Johnson, & the legal reps of Thos P Jones: passed. 6-Bill for the relief of John Le Roy, an express rider in the late war with Mexico, to allow him a pension of $20 per month, to commence on Feb 22, 1847, & continue during life: engrossed for a 3rd reading.

Died: on Aug 29, at Niagara, Canada West, John Virginius, only child of Lt John Newton, Corps of Engineers, U S Army, aged 11 months & 19 days.

Orphans Court of Wash Co, D C. Letters of administration, with the will annexed, on the personal estate of Daniel Homans, late of Wash Co, deceased. -Rhoda L Homans, admx, W A

Balt Sun: dispatch received by Rev John Hurst, of this city, announcing the death, at Louisville, Ky, on Sun last, of Rev Henry B Bascomb, one of the Bishops of the Methodist Episcopal Church, South. Bishop Bascomb had been ill for some time.

Cecil Co Democrat says the census taker in that county noted these aged persons: Mary Wilmer, near Cecilton 108 years old; Mark Simpers, near Elkton, 106 years old; Jos S Lusby, Back Creek, 102 years old. The first named is a white woman, & the rest colored.

THU SEP 12, 1850
Appointments by the Pres: 1-Lemuel Wilson, to be Register of the Land Ofc at Newnansville, Fla. 2-John P Gaines, of Ky, to be Govn'r of the Territory of Oregon. 3-Buckingham Smith, of Fla, to be Sec of Legation to the Mexican Republic. 4-P Sheward Johnson to be Atty of the U S for the District of Delaware.

Dr Jas W Roach, of St Mary's Co, Md, met with a serious accident at Piney Point on Aug 31. He broke 3 ribs when jumping from a steamboat to the wharf, his foot slipped, & he fell upon the wharf.

Louis Philippe, late King of France, died Aug 26, at his residence in Claremount. He is survived by the Queen and his children and grandchildren.

Capt Dawson, cmder of the steamer **Virginia**, a western boat, was found not guilty on the charge of manslaughter, for the explosion on board said boat.

The subscriber offers for sale the Farm upon which he resides, about 3 miles from Wash, lying in Va, containing 61 acs. Inquire of Selby Parkers, Fancy Store, Pa ave, or L Aborn, F & 18th sts, or to Jas Fraser, on the premise.

For sale or rent: 2 story brick house near the Navy Yard gate.
-Wm M Ellis, Navy Yard

Senate: 1-Memorial of Jas C Booth & Campbell Morfitt, chemists of Phil, proprietors of an invention for refining gold upon a new & economical plan, asking that it be adopted for the use of the mints of the U S: referred to the Cmte on Finance. 2-Cmte of Claims: House bill for the relief of Chas Stuart: recommended its passage. 3-Cmte on Indian Affairs: memorial of Richd Fields, asking payment of a balance due him for services as special agent to the Seminole Indians, asked to be discharged from the further consideration of the ptn of: which was agreed to.

Mrd: on Sep 10, by Rev Mr Gossage, Mr Jacob D Hutton, of Balt, to Miss Kate S Suter, of Havre de Grace, Md.

Mrd: on Jul 28, by Rev Mr Slatery, Mr Patrick Hagerty to Miss Mary Ann Cryer, all of Wash City.

Died: on Sat last, after a long & painful illness, Mrs Sarah Little, youngest daughter of late Jos Dougherty; in her 46th year.

Died: on Sep 10, in Fairfax Co, Va, after a long & painful illness, Mrs Mary Burch, wife of Mr Wm S Burch of Wash City.

Died: on Aug 29, in Tuscumbia, Ala, Dr Alex'r Spotwood Moore, in his 61st year. He was born in King Wm Co, Va, Oct 10, 1789; graduate of the Medical School in Phil, & a successful practioner.

Died: on Sep 10, Julia Martina, daughter of Patrick A & Mary J Byrne; aged 11 months & 20 days. Her funeral is today at 4 o'clock.

Mr & Mrs Oldham, of Ky, who were crossing the Ohio River on their way home from Cincinnati, in a skiff, upset & both drowned.

Died: on Aug 27, in Saline Co, Mo, Col Benj Chambers, in his 87th year. Col C was born in Pa near Chambersburg, entered the army at 16, & served in the Regt of Pa volunteers commanded by his father. After the Revolution he settled in Indiana, and the last 30 years has resided in Missouri.

Daniel Eaton, of Wash, D C, fell from the steamer **Empire State**, on Friday & drowned. He was on his way to New Bedford to ship for a whaling voyage.

FRI SEP 13, 1850

Died: on Tue, at his residence in York, Hon Henry Nes, Rep in Congress from Pa. He has been ill for a long time. He was born in York, York Co, Pa, was age 52 years.

New York Mirror: at Newport on Tue, Gracie Lawrence, son of W Beach Lawrence of N Y C, age 17 years, accidentally shot & killed himself. He had gone with his little brother, about 7 years of age, on a gunning expedition. When he was shot, his brother ran to the nearest farm house for assistance, & on returning, found him dead.

Mrd: Sep 11, at Trinity Church, by Rev Dr Butler, Herman C Adams, jr, of N Y, to Miss Frances M Burr, of Wash City.

Mrd: on Sep 10, at St Rose's Church, Montg Co, Md, by Rev Mr Lynch, Mr M T Fitzgerald, of Balt Co, to Miss Cecelia Ashton, daughter of the late John Scott.

Died: on Sep 10, Violella Dent, infant daughter of Jas & Deborah Mankin.

Died: at the residence of his father, at **Oak Springs**, Fairfax Co, Va, of typhoid fever, Albert Gallitin Bates, in his 25th year. [No death date given-current item.]

Died: on Sep 11, after an illness of nearly 4 months, Jno Laskey, a native of Cornwall, Eng, but for the last 30 years a resident of Wash City. His funeral is on Fri, at 2 o'clock, from his late residence, 13th st, near Md ave.

Postmaster Gen established the following new Post Ofcs for week ending Sep 7, 1850.

Ofc	County, State	Postmaster
Millbridge	Washington, Maine	Warren Leighton
Greenland Depot	Rockingham, N H	Jas B Rand
Seneca River	Cayuga, N Y	Wm H Mills
Graysville	Herkimer, N Y	Chas Johnson
Suffern	Rockland, N Y	H Springsteen
Forks of Buffalo	Marion, Va	A Prichard
Smith's Grove	Davie, N C	Enoch G Clouse
New Prospect	Winston, Miss	R D Brown
Barney's	Phillips, Ark	Zeniri Barney
Old Town	Phillips, Ark	Jas W Muncy
Mooney	Phillips, Ark	Miles Knowlton
Griffins	Johnson, Ark	Sidney B Cozart
North Bend	Stark, Ind	Chas Tibbett
Hickory Point	Lake, Ind	Henry A Nichols
Cottonville	Jackson, Iowa	Saml Cotton
Onion River	Sheboygan, Wis	W G Mallory

Names Changed:
Tye River Mills, Nelson Co, Va, changed to Piedmont.
Stony Battery, Newberg district, S C, changed to Frog Level.

House of Reps: 1-Ptn of Jos Nock, asking for a settlement of his account at the Post Ofc Dept.

Springfield, Mass. Accident on the Boston & Albany Rail Road today, Sep 10, 1850, took the lives of Col Saml Jones Mumford, Lawyer-N Y C; Miss Roessle, of Albany, daughter of the proprietor of Delavin House in Albany; & Mr Whitmore of Leicester, Mass. Jas Hagerman was badly injured-one leg broken; & Amasa Richardson, of North Adams, was much hurt.

Register's Ofc, Aug 31, 1850. The following is a list of the persons who have taken out licenses under the laws of the Corp during the months from Feb thru Jun, 1850.
Auction: Dyer, E C & G F

Boots & shoes
Brashears, T W
Crandell, Jas
Drury, J H agent
Drury, T
French, Michl
Hoye, Thos W
Janney, H
Redstreak, W J
Short, E
Yeatman, H

Burn'g of Moscow: Young, W H

Cart:
Adams, Caleb
Ayler, Thyson
Adams, Saml-2
Allen, Benj
Adams, Robt-2
Acton, O-2
Addison, A
Anderson, W
Brent, Elton
Beall, Thos J
Brereton, Wm H-2
Brown, Robt
Bean, C
Barnes, Wm-2
Batemen, A
Buckley, J S
Brown, Hanson
Boone, John B-2
Bean, Geo-2
Butler, M-2
Brown, Arthur
Brereton, John
Besschlin, John
Bird, Wm
Bryant, Ellen
Burke, Henry
Brooks, Hanson
Bayliss, Thos
Barr, Wm
Burgess, John
Burgess, Jas
Buckner, Thos
Brown, jr, J
Barrett, Geo
Bates & Brother-2
Brooks, E
Barrett, Thos J-2
Barnes, Jas-2
Bridget, Arthur
Brown, John
Chew, Philip
Chew, John
Cruttenden, Harvey-2
Casanave, Peter-2
Chapin, H L
Cross, Lloyd-4

Conlan, P
Cook, Saml-2
Connell, Dennis
Clarke, Wm-2
Crowley, Wm
Crowley, Wm
Clarvoe, J H
Cameron, G-2
Caho, Jos M
Chapin, H L
Cartwright, jr, W
Daniel, J T
Duvall, W L-6
Duvall, W L-3
Dowling, Wm-2
Dove, Wm T
Duvall, W L-3
Dowell, John
Dent, Bruce-2
Deevers, L
Delany, L
Deeven, Wm
Daniel, J T
Dove, Jas
Davis, Richd-2
Dyson, Chas
Davis, Henry
Edes, Philip
Emery, M G
Ennis, Philip-2
Elzey, S
Ford, Wm
Fisher, A
Fletcher, John-2
Fugitt, Jos
Fowler, Jas
Ferrity, N
Fletcher, John
Fletcher, Wm-2
Green, M
Geldermeister, H-2
Greer, T J
Green, Patrick
Gill, John-2
Gibson, Caleb
Greer, A A

Grimes, C W
Hill, Isaac
Hoover, Andrew-2
Horsthamp, H
Hill, Isaac
Hyde, R A
Heitmiller, A
Hagerty, Wm-3
Harshman, J
Haislip, H-2
Harvey & Co, J S-4
Hicks, Chas
Hanson, Chas
Haymes, John
Hanson, Geo
Hopkins, J & G-2
Jackson, Pompey
Isaac, Hester
Jones, Andrew
Jones, Alfred
Johnson, Tounly
Jolly, John
Jones, Noah
Jarboe, B
Kibball, Alex
Knight, H
Lee, Michl
Little, Peter-2
Linkins, Jos
Linkins, Walter-2
Lyons, Chas-2
Loveless, John
Lewis, Thos
Lewis, Octavus
Loomis, W
Linkins, Danl-2
Lamble, K H-2
Lindsley, M S
Mason, Jos-2
Magruder, Fielder
Madison, C
Mohun, Philip
Mitchell, Rebecca
Middleton, Eliza
McKelden, John C
Mothershead, John-2

Miller, Chas
Mester, Isaac
Morum, Elijah
McGlue, Geo T-2
Miller, John
McInerney, Thos
Moran, W M
Mackey, M
Madison, C
Noerr, A-2
Nalley, J T
Noble, Martha-2
Newton, Benj
Neale, Levi
Nepp, Danl
O'Donohue, P & T
O'Hare, C S
Owens, Jas
Otterback, Philip
Pulizzi, V
Purdy, John
Paine, Saml
Powers, John
Pettibone, John
Peterson, Henry
Pumphrey, J
Prather, H-3
Prather, O J
Riley, T
Raub & Green
Reed, Isaac
Riley, Thos W-4
Richards, Wm
Rooker, J B
Redfern, Saml
Reed, A
Rhodes, Jas
Richardson, Luke
Ragan, Danl-2
Railey, Thos
Richards, Alfred-3
Rawlings, Wash'n
Rady, J
Risin, Chas
Reed, Isaac
Stevenson, Jos

Sharrell, J F
Sewall, Richd
Stewart, L W
Somerville, A
Simms, A
Sampson, H
Smoot, A E-3
Salsbury, J
Smoot, Saml
Selby, Thos
Stone
Smallwood, R T
Stewart, Geo-2
Simmons, Augustus-2
Saffler, Thos
Sibley & Co, W J-2
Stewart, Chas-2
Shipley, S L
Scott, Ann
Sibley, C
Saunders, A
Scott, G B
Stone, W
Stott, Saml
Simmes & Son
Stewart, Wm
Smith, Warren
Smallwood, J
True, Susannah
Thomas, Saml
Tyler, Robt
Travers, M W-2
True, S J
Thompson, Geo
Thomas, Henry
Tuxton, Stewart
Taylor, Jno H-2
Usher, John
Webster, Rezin
Waters, E-2
Warder, Wm-2
Williams, Z-2
Ward, Helen
Waters, G
Wilson, Wm A
Walker & Peck-2

Wilson, John
Wise, Wm-2
Worden, Wm
Wood, H F
Wise, Wm-2
Williams, Jesse-3
Wood, Edw

Wilson, Patrick
Whitmore, Ann
Woods, Jos
Wright, Jas
Woodland
Warner, Saml
Young, J M

Circus
Robinson & Eldred
Rice, Danl-2
Stone & McCollum

Commission: Dyer & Brother

Concert
Dumbolton, J A-2
Swiss Bellringers

Dog:
Anderson, S J-2
Arth, P
Andrews, Mil
Anderson, Garret-2
Adolph, M
Abert, J J
Ball, Wm
Brashears, W
Brent, Eliz-2
Benner, H
Brown, Jas
Bean, Wm
Barber, Jos & C
Boyle, C
Broadbeck, Jacob
Bache, A C
Beasley, Jos
Burns, G
Briel, Michl-2
Brown, J F
Boscoe, Arthur
Barber, Geo
Boston, Robt
Brown, Michl
Barron, H L
Burnett, Alex'r

Brown, M J
Beckett, W
Brooks, H
Burrell, John
Butler, Walter
Bell, Henry
Blagden, Thos
Bayly, W L
Barnes, John
Buete, H
Brown, Wm-2
Barnhill, J L
Curson, Saml
Combs, R M
Cross, T B
Castell, John-2
Clark, J T C
Casparis, J
Crutchett, J-2
Chubb, J M
Clarke, Wm
Colt, C A
Clarke, Robt
Coke, Wm
Clarke, H A
Clark, J W

Caden, Jas
Clephane, L
Caldwell, J P
Clements, J N
Contee, Eliz
Clements, J T
Costen, John
Connor, John
Cruit, Richd
Cox, Clement
Collard, Geo
Corcoran, W W
Chew, John
Cassell, John T
Chauncey, J S
Cardwell, D C
Dyer, Giles
Downer, Joel
Davis, A G
Dunnington, C W C
Davis, G M
Drury, S P
Dodson, J P
Donohoo, W J
Downs, J W
Dankworth, F
Diggle, Jas
Dulany, C
Dent, Bruce
Dozier, Kitty
Dodson, Jas
Davis, J Y-2
Downs, John
Diggs, M
Donoho, Ellen
Detter, Thos
Dillow, W
Evans, J D
Elliot, Wm P
Eddy, S
Espy, John
Ergood, Jesse
Everett, Thos J
Eberley, A
Fitzgerald, M A
Fitzgerald, J

Frailes, Chas
Fugitt, F J-2
Feeney, Wm
Fleet, M
French, Jas
Fleming, John
Fisher, M P
Fletcher, Henry
Fisher, D
Farrall, J M
Francis, Hannah
Goodrich, J
Greer, Henry
Grey, Emma
Gray, W J
Graham, Susan
Gordon, J A
Greer, A A
Galt, M W
Guyer, B-2
German, Franklin
Graham, H
Gibbs, John F
Green, J W
Greenwell, C
Granger, J H
Gladman, Asa
Green, E T
Greenwell, E
Gassaway, Richd
Gantt, Jas T
Greason, Wm
Goodall, Thos
Gibson, Jno
Giveny, Bernard
Hoffman, Henry
Hall, E
Harris, A
Harbaugh, V
Hancock, A
Holroyd, Jno
Hart, Albert
Hazel, Z-2
Haite, E
Hoover, A
Hager, C

Handy, S W	Knight, R T
Hamilton, S	King, Z M P
Hutton, H	Knott, Geo A
Herold, A G	Kummer, Chas
Hall, Eliz	Linkins, Wm
Howard, Jno	Lowe, Jos
Hickman, J L	Little, J F
Handy, Saml	Lauxman, W
Hickman, Jos	Lehman, A
Harris, Morgan	Lewis, Saml
Handy, E G	Lepreux, L
Hume, F	Latham, W
Holland, Isaac	Loudon, W H
Howard, Jas	Laub, J Y
Hayne, L	Lightfoot, G
Indermaner, J	Linkins, Danl
Imbrecht, J D	Linkins, L
Iddins, Jas	Lee, Richd
Johnson, Isaiah	Leisintzer, E
Johnson, John	Leddy, O
Jones, Raph'l	Lawson, Wm
Jeffers, Mary A	Lindsley, L C
Jordan, Harriet	Lee, Mary
Johnson, L	Lee, Josias
Jenkins, Eliz	Lee, Jos
Jones, Levi	Masi & Co, F
Johnson, Jas	Masi, S
Jones, Peter	McKin, J F
Jones, Noah	Middleton & Beall
Johnson, T	Miller, John
Jenifer, Robt	Martin, J W
Jefferson, F	Mann, Jas
Jost, B	McKean, S M
Kibbey, J B	Murray, S
Kleindeinst, J P	McDermott, M-2
Kelly, Saml	Marshall, W
Kidwell, A	Magar, John
Keefe, W N	Mechlin, A H
Kloman, Chas	McGregor, P
Klopfer, C	McPeak, Wm
Kibbal, A	Merullat, Chs
King, Robt	Mansfield, Jno
Kauffman, C	Miller, R A
Kersey, I F	McCoy, B M
Kelly, John	Maxwell, Dr
Kendrick, G H-2	Michum, Wm B

McCarthy, C F
Milburn, Timothy
Martin, Wm
Mitchell, Jno
Maguirek Jas
Marden, Phil
Mills, R T
Marshall, Thos
Massey, G T
Naylor, F Y
Nottingham, Wm
Nepp, Danl
Neale, Levi
Ofenstein, C
O'Donoghue, P & T
Owner, J
Ourand, John
Orem, J B
Parker, G & T
Parris, S P
Pettit, Chas
Plant, G H
Prout, Jonathan
Ponderock, F
Pumphrey, J
Perkins, Saml
Pumphrey, L-2
Prentiss, W H
Peake, Jno
Poletti, Jos
Parson, Jas
Pettibone, John
Poston, J F
Ross, A
Rawlings, D
Rone, A L
Randall, H K
Raub & Green
Ross, J W
Rappetti, Jos
Richardson, L
Reed, B W
Riley, P C-2
Raymond, J
Railey, B J L
Richards, W H

Ross, Danl
Randon, B
Ricketts, Jas
Ruff, J A
Reider, Eliz
Robinson, A J
Reid, A
Rous, A-4
Roach, E N
Shad, B-2
Stepper, A
Springman, J
Schwartze, A J
Seman, Chas
Smith, Thos-2
Scott, S E
Smoot, John
Smallwood, D-2
Smith, Jos
Smith, G B
Sweeting, Ellen
Stock, J G
Smith, Wm
Sinon, John
Simpson, Jno T
Somby, D
Smith, Edw
Spicer, Fred'k
Simmes, Wm
Stewart, J C
Stutz, F
Speaks, Letitia
Simms, R E
Scott, L
Seymour, Richd
Travers, E-2
Tucker, J
Talbot, Wm
Turner, Henry
Tophman, Geo
Thompson, G W
Talley, W D
Turpin, J S
Tilghman, H H
Turner, Thos
Thomas, Chs

Tschiffely, F H
Tench, T P
Tilghman, Rose
Thomas, J H
Thompson, J R
Talbot, Geo
Topham, Geo
Thomas, Wm
Tuston, J B
Trummer, Henry
Vonderlick, J
Vaudricourt, J
Werner, J H T
Wilson, J D
Whitwell, J C
Willet, V
Wirt, J L
Watson, Jas

Wallach, R
Wilkerson, E
Winter, Wm H
White, W G W
Wilcox, J A
Wilson, Jas
Winchester, Robt
West, John-2
Wood, E
Webb, W B
Warner, Nicholas
White, Jas L
Warner, Chas
Westerfield, D
Wallace, Wm
Wilkerson, Wm
Wiggeman, B
Young, McC

Dray
Bacon & Co, Saml
Davidson, John-2
Hall, Edw
Jackson & Bro, B L
Kibbey & Co, J B
Middleton & Beall
O'Brien, Jas

Ober, S J
Pullin, Jas
Parker, Geo & Thos
Ryon, R J
Stevenson, Jos
Semmes & Br, V J
Wise, C J

Giant & Dwarf: Turner, G W

Hack
Cowling, E
Gibson, John
Harrington, R H

Jasper, Wm
Smallwood, Dennis

Hats & Caps
Ruff, Jno A

Huckster
Atkins, D
Banks, J
Bicksler, John
Bardona, P
Biggs, H D
Cruit, Richd
Campbell, W W

Crowley, W
Dowling, Wm
Garret, M-2
Glascock, Geo
Hawkins, E
Harris, M
Howell, W P

Howell, H
Johnson, W C
Kale & Springman
Lane, John
Leddy, O
Langdon, Jas
Laskey & Co, Jno
Mullikin, J W
Newmeyer, L
Oyster, D W
Paxton, Jno
Rabbit, Jno

Ins Agency
De Selding, C-2
Latham, R W
McKean, S M

Merchandise
Adamson, Richd H
Alexander, Jno
Burroughs, Thos
Barker, Jacob
Boyle, Christopher
Clarke, L F
Cruit, Richd
Clements, W A
Cropley, E S
Clements & Daley
Clark, John D
Follansbee, J V
Foster, E agent
Faulkner, W H
Fenwick, Jno H
Galt & Co, Sarah
Gross, Jas
Green, Edwin
Gooch, John
Hager, C
Heger, J F
Iardella & Bro, N M
Jackson & Smith
Kumner, Chas
Lewis, Sinah E
Liesberger, H

Roth, A
Sennot, Geo
Sherwood, S
Sherwood, Perry
Shreve, C K
Thorn, J S E
Wilson, Wm
Wagner, Mary
Wallace, A
Worthington, L W
Weed, Isaac C

Pairo, C W
Webb, Pollard

Morgan, Ann
Morgan, A C
Munch, C H
Mitchell, Wm
Marshall, Wm
Malone, Lawrence
Morgan, Thos P
Magruder & Calvert
McCafferty, Wm
Mankin, Wm
Nourse, Jas
O'Meara, W C
Pilling, Alice
Perkins, W H
Page & Co, Geo
Radcliff, J T
Reeve, Saml
Seitz, Geo
Sibley & Co, W J
Stoddard, Isaac
Sanderson, Thos J
Turpin, Susan
Thomson & Davis
Thomas, Geo
Yerby, G W

Omnibus: Vanderwerken, N C & Co-9

Peddling
Edwards, Wm W
Fribourg, Victor

Retail
Byrne, C R
Brown, Jas A
Birth, Wm W
Emmerman, E
Fisher, C
Greenwell, J B
Hungerford, H
Keefe, Wm
Liphard, J H
Lynch, Jas
Marceron, P T

Martin, John W
Magnus, Fred'k
Murray, Jno F
Quigley, Francis
Riggles, Thos
Thompson, Jas
Trunnel, W D
Waters, Theo
Wise, Wm
William, M

Shop
Berry, Jas A
Holtzman, Jas H-2
[fish wharf]
Hooper, G K
Miller, Francis

Rollins, Joshua
Schadd, F
Smith, Jno
Thoma, Lorenzo
Wren, Geo W

Slut
Benter, W T
Barnhill, J L
Emendrout, Jos
Gunton, Thos
Harrison, Jos
Hunt, H W

Jackson, Pompey
Pumphrey, L
Porter, W T
Peters, Mary
Westerfield, D

Stage
Goffers, W J
Reeside & Vanderwerken-7

Tavern
Adams, Notley
Crutchett, John P
Jordon, M

Moore, Jno L
Shadd, C

Theatrical
Adelphia Theatre-9

Wagon

Ayler & Thyson
Burnett, Enoch
Butler, M
Besschlin, John
Brown, Thos
Ballenger, Francis
Briscoe, Henry
Blagden, Thos
Brown, Robt
Barber, Geo
Brown, Jas A
Ballinger, Francis
Bates & Brother
Bohlayer, J
Bond, Jos
Craig, Wm
Cross, A V
Cocknell, Geo H
Clarke, Wm
Cameron, G
Douglass, L
Dunlop, Henry
Donovan, Wm
Davidson, John
Desmond, Dennis
Emery, M G
Emerson, Geo W
Fugitt, Jos
Fosbee, Moses
Fuller, E H
Fister, John
Favier, A
Fitzgerald, D
Fisher, M
Geldermeister, H
Ginnetty, Thos
Green Edwin
Grupe, Wm
Guyer, V
Glick, J H
Gillispie, Alex
Green, J R
Hager, C
Havenner & Bro
Howard, Jno
Heitmiller, A
Horning, G T
Hamersley, Edw
Hughes, G W
Hager, F
Jackson & Smith
Jones, Alfred-3
Jones, Saml W
Johnson, Jas
Jones, Noah
Krafft, Jno M-2
Key, Saml
Kibball, Alex
Lenman & Bro
Lederer, C
Lee, Josias
Mason, Jos-2
McKelden, John C-3
Miller, Michl
McGarvey, Jno
Moore, Wm
Mills, Robt T
McGarvey, P
Magee, Saml
McGregor, N M
Miller, Chas
Miller, Jos
Murphy, John
Miller, Jacob
McDevitt, Jno
Martin, A W
McKinsley, W
Noerr, A
Newton, Isaac
Newell, Moses
O'Donohue, P & T
Pywell, R R
Purdy, John-2
Paine, Saml
Parker, Albert
Pettibone, John-3
Prather, Jos
Pearson & Co, P M
Page & Co, Geo-2
Page, L S

Prather, H D
Reeve, Saml
Riley, John
Roux, A
Reilly, Terence
Stevenson, Jos-2
Slade, Wm
Swigart, Jos
Stepper, Andrew
Sibley & Co, W J
Sibley, Jas
Shedd, Jas J
Santer, W
Straub, Jos

Simmons, A
Todschinder, F
Tompkins, R
Thoms, Chas
Tinney, Chas
Thomas, Geo
Visser, J
Van Renwick, J
Webb, A J
Wonderlich, John-2
Wilson, Wm
Waggoner, Jno
Wood, Edw
Young, John

Persons fined during the months of Feb thru Jun, 1850.

Cart
Burgess, Jno
Carey, John-2
Cross, Jos
Cameron, G-2
Fletcher, Jno-2
Fields, Geo

Jackson, P
Lyndsley, M-2
Prather, Hugh D
Scott, Geo B
Thorn, Henry
White, Patrick-3

Circus
Rice & Rosston-2
Robinson & Eldred

Stone & McCallem-2

Dealing in exchanges: Pairo, C W

Dray: Semmes & Bro, V I

Exhibition: Harman, Benj; Walleinstein & Co

Huckstering
Bode, Geo
Dunnington, Jno
Pardonnes, P

Rabbit, John

Keeping bar open on Sunday: Howard, G T

Keeping a dog:
Avery, Geo
Abert, Col
Aylmer, R R
Anderson, Garrett
Alexander, C
Butler, Richd

Brent, Elton
Brereton, John
Brown, Hanson
Brown, Jas
Burdine, Jas
Barnhouse, R

Black, Moses
Brooks, Hanson
Carter, Luke
Coltson, Josiah
Clark, Stephen
Church, Alfred
Cross, Edw
Cammett, David
Douglass, Wm
Denham, A
De Haven, Lt
Douglass, Catherine
Dant, W
Evans, H
Evans, J D
Foskey
Frisby, Wm
Francis, Richd
Fleming, John
Goings, Patrick
Garrett, Milton
Geore, Wm
Gordon, Jas A
Gildermeister, Henry
Hughes, Enoch
Handy, Wm
Hazel, Z-2
Howard, G T
Jarvis, Layora
Ingle, John
Johnson, John
Jones, Henry
Johnson, J
Kaufman, Geo
Loudon, W H
Lightfoot, Geo

Lewis
Little, Jas
Little, Jno E
Milne, Andrew
Moenster, C O
Mattingly, G
Miller, Jas
Marshall, Mgt
Nalley, John
Owner, Jas
Pegg, Wm
Peters, Mary
Poletti
Robinson, Jno
Ritter, Ephraim
Robb & Green
Reily, Mary
Robey, L
Scott, W B
Speiden, Wm
Swartz, A
Smoot, S C
Semmes, Sampson
Seitz, Geo
Stewart, Geo
Thomas, Jno
Tucker, Jas
Terrill, Edw
Thomas, Jos
Thompson, Miss
Waller, J D
White, Patrick
Wise, Wm
Washington, B
Watts, W

Keeping a slut
Dunnington, Ann
Dodson, Jas
Harrison, Jos
Jackson, Pompey

Peters, Mary
Smith, Mrs
Watts, W

Merchandise: Sutherland, Isabella

Non-residential merchant: Taylor, Jane A

Peddling
Bartlett, W O
Morse, O P

Wolf, Aaron

Selling books: Derby, C L

Selling Goods:
Alexander, Jno
Fairchild, L W

Pillings, Mrs

Selling liquor
Collins, Dennis
Cavanaugh, Thos
Desmond, Dennis
Flint, C W
Gross, Jas
Lee, Moses

Murphy, Mary
Miller, Francis
Nalley, Jas T
Renny, Jas
Rigdon, E
Smith, Mgt

Selling liquor on Sunday
Butler, Ab'm
Benter, B T
Benter, Wm
Bresnehan, Cornelius
Lehman, A

Maher, Jas
Stutz, F
Schadd, Chris
Shadd, Francis
Walker & Shadd-2

Selling Lumber: Blagden, Thos

Selling matches: Hawkins, Philip

Selling merchandise: Hodgskins, G

Wagon
Atkins, David
Addison & Cochrill
Bruce, Chas
Bond, J
Berkley, Enos
Cameron, G
Donovan, J
Freeman, John
Hammersley, E
Haward, Thos

Lokey, J B
McGregor, N
McKinstree, W
Rawlings, David
Riley, T B-2
Seitz, Geo
Sims, J M
Umphrey, Mary
Wolf, Aaron
Wheatley, Geo-2

SAT SEP 14, 1850
Household & kitchen furniture at auction: on Sep 18, at the residence of Mr Saml T Drury, I & 10th sts. –Dyer & Bro, aucts

Valuable Farm, furniture, stock, & farming utensils for sale, at auction, on Sep 25, at the residence of H H Dent, near Tenallytown, on the road leading from Gtwn to Rockville. The farm contains 77 acres, more or less: improvements are a good new 2 story brick dwlg-house, containing 16 rooms; & necessary out-bldgs. –Green & Tastet, aucts

Edwin Forrest, the tragedian, was arrested at the Astor House, N Y, on Wed, on the complaint of his wife, Catherine Forrest, & held to bail in the sum of $10,000 to keep the peace so far as Mrs Forrest is concerned, she being fearful of an assault from him. Mrs Forrest has commenced a suit for divorce against Mr Forrest.

Senate: 1-Cmte of Claims: asked to be discharged from the further consideration of the ptn of John Hollohan, who asked compensation as a day watchman: discharge was agreed to.

Millard Fillmore, Pres of the U S: To all whom it may concern. Wm Montgomery Stewart, of the State of Md, has been appointed Vice Consul of his Majesty the Emperor of all the Russias, for the ports of Calif. Sep 13, 1850

Mrd: on Sep 12, by Rev Jas B Donelan, Mr John Douglas West & Miss Catharine Dulany, all of Wash.

Mrd: on Sep 5, by Rev Geo W Samson, William B Magill, of Va, to Miss Mary Jane; & at the same time, Geo H Carter, of Va, to Miss E Louisa, daughters of Wm J Bronaugh, of Wash City.

Mrd: on Sep 7, by Rev Thos Myers, in the Ebenezer M E Parsonage, Mr James H Fisher to Miss Margaret E Cryer, both of Wash.

Mrd: on Sep 12, by Rev Mr Hodges, Danl T Johnson to Jane C Anderson, both of the District of Columbia.

Mrd: on Sep 7, in Frederick Cty, Md, by Rev Dr Trapnell, N B Meade, of Clarke Co, & Miss Eugenia Turner, of King Geo Co, Va.

Died: on Sep 7, at West Point, N Y, Brevet Maj Wm H Shover, Capt of 3rd Regt of Artl, & instructor of Artl & Cavalry at the Military Academy. He has fallen a victim to disease contracted while on arduous service in the Mexican War, having served with distinction as a subaltern of Ringgold's [afterwards Bragg's] Battery throughout the campaign, under Gen Taylor, &, after his promotion, in the Valley of Mexico. His bereaved widow & child mourn the irreparable loss of an affectionate husband & father.

Died: on Sep 11, in Alexandria Co, Lucius Cary Selden, son of late Dr Wilson C Selden of Loudoun Co, Va. His funeral will be from the residence of Rev E R Lippitt, in the neighborhood of Alexandria, today, at 11 o'clock.

Appointment by the Pres: Alex'r H H Stuart, of Va, to be Sec of the Interior, vice Thos M T McKennan, resigned.

Household & kitchen furniture at auction: by order of the Orphans Court of Wash Co, D C: on Sep 18, at the residence of Mrs Galvin, deceased, on C st, between 3rd & 4½ sts. –J P Pepper, J W Hicks, excs -Green & Tastet, aucts

Jenny Lind's first concert in America, was on Wed, at the Castle Garden. Last night a crowd of row-boats collected on the river in the rear of the garden. Throngs of people on the Battery were eager to catch a glimpse of the great songstress.

Orphans Court of Wash Co, D C. Letters testamentary on the personal estate of Dorcas Galvin, late of Wash Co, deceased. –John P Pepper, Josiah W Hicks, excs

MON SEP 16, 1850
Mexican Boundary Commission: letters received from Com'r Bartlett, dated Indianola, Texas, Aug 31: one death has occurred, that of Richd Sullivan, the servant of Capt Southerland. Mr M W T Chandler, of Phil, had been detained at New Orleans by sickness, but, being convalescent when the party left, was expected to rejoin it before its arrival at San Antonio. N E Worthington, of Washington, because of feeble health, was compelled to return.

Orphans Court of Wash Co, D C. Letters of administration on the personal estate of Nicholas B Boyle, late of Wash Co, deceased. -Chas S Wallach, adv

TUE SEP 17, 1850
Senate: 1-Communication from Jas Robertson, complaining of injuries alleged to have been received & grievous wrongs inforced on him by false imprisonment at the instance of certain persons in the employment of the Senate, asking that he may be indemnified for the same: referred to the Cmte on the Judiciary. 2-Ptn of Marcus Spalding, asking the Senate to pass the bounty land bill: asked to be discharged from the further consideration of the ptn of same: which was agreed to. 3-Cmte of the District of Columbia to which was referred the memorial of Thos Wilson & others, asking the passage of a law to incorporate a joint stock company, reported a bill to incorporate the Pioneer Cotton Mfgr company of Gtwn, D C: ordered to a second reading. 4-Cmte on Patents & the Patent Ofc: bill for the relief of Hiram Moore & John Hascall: objection was made, & bill was not considered. 5-Cmte on Military Affairs: referred the following memorials, to wit: memorial of the Legislature of Missouri, in favor of a grant of land to teamsters who served in the war with Mexico, & the memorial from Gen Hugh W Dobbin, asking remuneration for services in the war of 1812: asked to be discharged from the further consideration of the same: which was agreed to. Same cmte: memorial of C J Cook & A A Lockwood, asking compensation for their property, destroyed by a party of U S soldiers in the town of Fredericksburg, Texas: asked to be discharged from the further consideration of the same: which was agreed to. 6-Cmte on Public Bldgs: memorial of Gilbert Cameron, asking that a contract be made with him to complete the wings of the Patent Ofc, he having been the lowest bidder: asked to be discharged from

the further consideration of the same: which was agreed to. Same cmte: ptn of Jas J Fowler: to be paid $42.81, being a balance due for carpenter's work done on the public stable in the service of the Senate: passed. 7-Cmte on the Post Ofc & Post Roads: referred documents in relation to the claim of Wyche & Latham, asking compensation for extra services: ordered to be printed, accompanied with a joint resolution for the benefit of Wyche & Latham. Same cmte: ptn of Richd S Coxe, asking compensation for legal services as counsel to the Post Ofc Dept: passed to a second reading.

House of Reps: 1-Bills referred: relief of John M McIntosh; relief of Wm Hardin; relief of Isaac Watts Griffith; relief of Eliz L Blackburn; relief of the administrator of Maj Fred'k D Mills, deceased; relief of Chas A Kellett; relief of Charlotte Lynch; & relief of Chas Reeder, Walter R Johnson, & the legal reps of Thos P Jones. Also, granting a pension to John Le Roy. 2-Act for the relief of Leuright Browning, was read twice. 3-Cmte on Printing: memorial of Wm M Belt, asking to be discharged from his contract as public printer. The two Houses are satisfied that the contract is one of great loss to the contractor. –Wm McWillie, Chairman of the Cmte on Printing. [Belt is released from his contract. Thos Ritchie & Messrs Gales & Seaton appointed to execute the printing contracted for & by Belt.] 4-Cmte of Claims: adverse report on the ptn of Iris W Bates: laid on the table. Same cmte: act for the relief of Capt Nathan Adams, of Tenn: passed. Same cmte: bill for the relief of Dr W P A Hail: committed. Same cmte: adverse reports on the ptns of A H Patterson, Joel Byington, & Gilbert Stalker: laid on the table. Same cmte: act for the relief of Theodore Offutt: committed. Same cmte: adverse report on the ptn of Nathan Wintinger: laid on the table. Same cmte: joint resolution for the relief of C W Morgan, Wm R Rodman, & Edw Merrill: committed. 5-Resolution sent to the Clerk's table: Clarke Mills, the artist who had been employed to cast the bronze statue of Gen Andrew Jackson, has been much delayed for want of proper metal for the work. A quantitiy of brass cannon was found to contain an undue proportion of tin for the purpose of casting in bronze. There is in possession of the Gov't a quantity of old copper, which would be available to Mr Mills, & the brass is precisely suitable for the purpose of casting cannon. Cmdor Warrington recommended the exchange of metal, & being a joint resolution relating to the equestrian statue of Gen Jackson, was passed.

For rent: the house on F, between 13th & 14th sts, now occupied by the Hon Meredith P Gentry. Possession given on Oct 1. Inquire of Raymond W Burche.

Appointments by the Pres: 1-Capt Wm H Smiley, of Rhode Island, commercial agent for the Falkland Islands. 2-John Black, commercial agent at point de Galle, in the Island of Ceylon.

Stockholders of the Citizens' Omnibus Co meeting on Sep 18, at 7:30 p m.
-Jas Keleher, Treasurer

Mr Jas R Ware, one of the boarders at the Eutaw House, Balt, fell from his chamber window, in the 5th story, on Sat, & was instantly killed.

Mrd: Sep 12th, by Rev D W Bates, John W Hauptman, of Wash City, to Miss Rachel M Wantland, youngest daughter of Thos Wantland, of York Co, Pa.

Mrd: on Sep 11, in the 2nd Presbyterian Church, Alexandria, by Rev Joshua N Danforth, Mr Geo W Bush, of Wilmington, Del, to Miss Emma Noble, eldest daughter of Rev J N Danforth.

Mrd: on Sep 9, in Batavia, N Y, by Rev Jas A Bolles, D D, Mr Thos Underwood, formerly of Wash, to Miss Ann E Wilson, 2nd daughter of John Wilson, of former place.

Died: on Sunday, Dr John McCreary, late of Somerset, Pa.

Died: on Sep 14, in Wash City, Constance Virginia, daughter of Wm & Martha Bell, aged 4 years, 10 months & 25 days.

Died: on Sep 15, in her 29th year, Mrs Angelina Coolidge, wife of Dr Richard H Coolidge, U S Army. Her funeral is this afternoon, at 4 o'clock, from St John's Church.

Died: Sep 11, of congested fever, at **Cherry Hill**, Chas Co, Md, [the residence of Mr Wm Rennoe,] T M McIlhany, in his 42nd year. The deceased, with his family, was called to see his daughter, [Mrs Rennoe,] who was very ill, & whilst there was attacked with the same disease, which terminated fatally in the course of 8 or 9 days.

WED SEP 18, 1850
The U S sloop of war **Saratoga**, bound to the East Indies, sailed from Norfolk on Sat. The following is a list of her ofcrs: Cmder, Wm S Walker; Lts, J R Goldsborough, Wm L Maury, John C Howell, Wm A Wayne; Purser, J Geo Harris; Surgeon, Thos L Smith; Acting Master, Saml Edwards; Assist Surgeon, Thos B Steele; Lt Marines, M R Kintzing; Passed Midshipmen, Albert Allmand, John Madigan, R W Scott; Midshipmen, Chas W Flusser, Jos D Blake, Oscar F Johnson; Capt's Clerk, John S Sewall; Boatswain, Chas Smith; Gunner, W H Hamilton; Carpenter, Leonard Moses; Sailmaker, H T Stocker.

Mrd: in Wash City, by Rev O B Brown, Mr Robt McClelland to Miss Rosanna Moore, late of Fred'k, Md. [No date-current item.]

On Sat Joshua Pusey ascended with a balloon from Reading, Pa. He says that at about an altitude of 2 miles, he was overtaken in a snow storm, &, what was strange to him, was that the snow flakes ascended.

Pittsburg, Sep 17, 1850. Wm & Melchoir Beltzhoover, hotel keepers, 4 miles from this city, were murdered last night by an Irishman, who stopped at the hotel. Both were stabbed-one died instantly, the other died today. The murderer has been arrested.

$50 reward for runaway negro Hannibal Butler, age about 20 years.
-Levi Osbourn, living in PG Co, near Marlboro, Md.

Senate: 1-Memorial of Edw Dexter, of Massachusetts, setting forth that in Jun, 1809, he entered at the custom-house, in Providence, 40 chests of tea; that in Jul he took our 26 chests for exportation, & gave bond for the payment of duties, & consigned them to John G Ladd, of Alexandria, D C, to be exported at the earliest opportunity, all of which appears by documentary evidence; before exportation were wholly consumed by fire, to the total loss of said teas, & all incidental expense added to the obligation of the memorialist; he paid the bonds at maturity to the Gov't at the rate of .32 per pound; & prays Congress to reimburse him the full amount of duty paid, with interest thereon. Referred to the Cmte on Finance. 2-Memorial of Ambrose W Thompson, proposing to establish a line of steamships to carry the U S mail between Phil & Antwerp, in Belgium, touching at Portsmouth, England, & Havre, France. Provided, that the U S subscribes $2/3^{rd}$ of the cost, in U S stock bearing an interest of five per cent payable in twenty-five years. Referred to the Cmte on Naval Affairs. 3-Memorial of Wm Archer, proposing a plan for preventing the exportation of the gold collected in Calif in an uncoined state, & for creating a fund for the construction of a railroad from Wash City to San Francisco, Calif: referred to the Cmte on Finance. 4-Ptn of Wm Hurst; also the ptn of Marianus Lang; also the ptn of John W B Schrieber; each asking to be allowed an increase of pension: referred to the Cmte on Pensions. 5-Ptn of Mary B Renner, asking compensation for property destroyed by the enemy during the last war with Great Britain: referred to the Cmte of Claims. 6-Ordered, that Solomon Walls have leave to withdraw the documents relating to his claim. 6-Memorial of Miss D L Dix, of Boston, asking that grants of public lands may be made for the relief & support of the indigent insane in the U S: [Mr Dickinson says that Miss Dix, a lady of fortune, & of accomplished education, has devoted herself to relieve the sufferings of those unfortunate beings:] referred to a second reading. 7-Cmte on Patents & the Patent Ofc: documents in relation to the application of Thos J Godman for an extension of his patent for scalding hogs by steam: passed to a 2nd reading. 8-Cmte on Public Bldgs: memorial of Robt Grant, asking an appropriation for the purpose of lighting the public bldgs & grounds: asked to be discharged from the further consideration of the same: which was agreed to. 9-Cmte on the Military Affairs: ptn of Jos Byrd, asking that he may be paid the value of a quantity of merchandise captured by him while in the service as a private soldier in 1814, when being landed from a British schnr on the coast of Florida, & which was distributed among the troops then stationed in Florida: asked to be discharged from the further consideration of the same: which was agreed to. 10-Cmte on the Post Ofc & Post Roads: bill for the relief of Isaac Houston: ordered to a second reading. Same cmte: ptn of Saml F Butterworth, asking compensation for carrying the mail: ordered to a second reading. Same cmte: act for the relief of Jas S Graham & Walter H Finnall: reported back the same without amendment. 11-Cmte on Revolutionary Claims: memorial of the heirs of Wm Beatty, asking remuneration for services of Beatty during the Revolutionary war: asked to be discharged from the further consideration of the same: which was agreed to.

THU SEP 19, 1850
By two writs of distrain, I shall expose to sale, for cash, on Sep 28, sundry goods & chattels, seized & taken as the property of P H Grimes, to be sold, to satisfy rent in arrears due to Richd G Briscoe. -J L Henshaw, M D

Senate: 1-Ordered, that the ptn of Saml Crassin, on the files of the Senate, be referred to the Cmte on Pensions. 2-Little chance of of action on the papers of Capt A P Brittingham, & he desires to withdraw them. Motion cannot be made at this time. 3-Cmte on the Judiciary: asked to be discharged from the further consideration of the ptn of Jas Robertson, asking indemnity for injuries received & imprisonment suffered by him: which was agreed to.

Mrd: on Sep 17, in the Ebenezer Parsonage by Rev T Myers, Mr Wm Davis to Mrs Mary Ann Davis, both of Wash City.

Died: on Sep 18, Mrs Teresa Byrne, aged 67 years. Her funeral is Fri, at her late residence, on 12th st, near N Y ave, at 9 o'clock. A solemn Mass of Requiem will be offered at St Patrick's Church for her repose.

Died: on Sep 18 of consumption, Frances Olivia Clarke, in her 25th year. Her funeral is today at 4 o'clock, from her late residence on I st, between 9th & 10th sts.

Music: Jos Trug, Prof of Music & member of the Wash Philharminic Society, offers his services to the public as an instructor on the Violin & Violoncello. Refer to the Pres of the Society, or the Conductor, Prof Berlyn, & orders left for him shall have immediate attention.

FRI SEP 20, 1850
Senate: 1-Cmte on Military Affairs: bill for the relief of Robt L Blair: asked its immediate consideration. 2-Cmte on Pensions, to which were referred the following petitions: of Freeman Blakely, asking an increase of pension; of Susannah Rose, widow of a Revolutionary soldier, asking a pension; of Wm C Sterret, asking a pension; of Martin Dubois, a Revolutionary soldier, asking an increase of pension; of the heirs of Gen Wm C Keene, asking a continuance of the pension granted him; of Garret Burns, asking a pension; of the citizens of Wash Co, Pa, asking that a pension be granted to Eliz Porter, widow of a soldier of the war of 1812, made a written report in each case, asking to be discharged from their further consideration. 3-Bill for the relief of Peter M Pallet was taken up; but the motion was lost. 4-Cmte on Naval Affairs: ptn of Eliza Bache, widow of Geo M Bache, late Lt in the navy, asking the same allowance that was granted in the case of the U S brig **Somers**, reported a general bill for the relief of the widows & orphans of the ofcrs & seamen lost from the U S brig **Washington**, on Sep 8, 1846: did not receive its second reading.

City Ordinances-Wash. 1-Act for the relief of John Woods: to pay him $154.17, for grading & gravelling on D st, authorized by act of Nov 12, 1849. 2-Act to pay a balance due Chas Stewart for certain flag footways: sum of $97.34 to be paid Chas Stewart, jr, a balance due him. 3-Act for the relief of John Woods: to be paid $23.50, the sum being due him for finishing that part of Vt ave within the First Ward. Approved: Sep 15, 1850

Orphans Court of Wash Co, D C. Letters of administration on the personal estate of Nicholas B Boyle, late of Wash Co, deceased. -Chas S Wallach, adm

Wash Corp: 1-Ptn of Nicholas Snyder, for remission of a fine: referred to the Cmte of Claims. 2-Ptn of Jas H Blake, praying the payment of a prize ticket in a lottery: authorized by act of the Corp of Jul 24, 1815: referred to the Cmte of Claims. 3-Ptn of Jas Casparis, praying a reduction of the amount of tax on his bowling & ten-pin alleys: referred to the Cmte on Police. 4-Ptn of Elias Barnes, praying permission to enclose a portion of an avenue: referred to the Cmte on Improvements. 5-Ptn of John McDuell & others, respecting the conveyance of water to I & 14th sts: referred to the Cmte on Improvements. 6-Act for the relief of John H Mullen: referred to the Cmte of Claims. 7-Act for the relief of A C Kidwell. 8-Cmte of Claims: bill for the relief of Thos Dant: read twice.

Postmaster Gen established the following new Post Ofcs for week ending Sep 14, 1850.

Ofc	County, State	Postmaster
Green Creek	Cape May, N J	Seth Miller
Deas Creek	Cape May, N J	Chas K Hulme
Slate Hill	York, Pa	V G Stubb
White Ash	Alleghany, Pa	H Morrow
Cottage	Huntingdon, Pa	Wm Walker
Bower Hill	Washington, Pa	John Bower, jr
Hygeia	Hamilton, Ohio	D S Burnet
A d	Lawrence, Ohio	R Davidson
Russell's Place	Lawrence, Ohio	F Russell
Simmons'	Lawrence, Ohio	Chas W Simmons
Thivener	Gallia, Ohio	Henry Halley
Number One	Wayne, Ohio	John Kunkle
Mead's Mills	Wayne, Mich	J M Mead
Green Oak Centre	Livingston, Mich	A S Warner
Oak Plans	Livingston, Mich	Josiah Holden
Proctor	Allegan, Mich	Wm S Miner
Mount Clifton	Shenandoah, Va	A Hammon
Harper's Home	Brunswick, Va	Thos E Ballard
Nottoway C H	Nottoway, Va	W H Hallowell
Carolina Female College	Anson, N C	Saml W Neal
Pugh's Hill	Franklin, N C	Wm Powell
Brushy Flat	Watauga, N C	Silas Murphy
Rivers' Bridge	Barwell D, S C	John A Varn
Cowpen Branch	Barwell D, S C	Wm M Chitty
Yauhanna	Gtwn D, S C	L A Grier
Walker's	Colleton D, S C	M Hiers
Hollingsworth	Habersham, Geo	F G Moss
Spring	Henry, Geo	C W Oslia
Centre Hill	Stewart, Geo	E B Swinners
Bear Range	Bibb, Ala	T R Honeycut
Fremont	Itawamba, Miss	Geo W Williams

St Cloud	E Feliciana P, La	J S Peacocke
Isle Breville	Natchitoches P, La	P Oscar Chaler
Camp Creek	Jefferson, Ark	Jos McClung
Laputa	Franklin, Ky	John Childers
Pashawn	La Grange, Ia	Amos Davis
Grassy Valley	Harrison, Ia	Geo W Wold
Pilot Knot	Crawford, Ia	Saml Mansfield
Laketon	Wabash, Ia	B C Whitacre
Starfield	Peioria, Ill	Thos J Moore
Walker's	McDonough, Ill	John M Walker
Globe	Johnson, Mo	Jacob Tyler
Greenport	Cedar, Mo	Wm R Powell
Prospect Grove	Scotland, Mo	A Brite
St Leger	Ozark, Mo	Adam Sriver
Hickory Grove	Jackson, Iowa	Wm Keister
Grove Creek	Jones, Iowa	Geo Rutherford
Dundas	Calumet, Wis	Elias Beach
Grand Marsh	Columbia, Wis	S C Fletcher
Delaware	Indian County, Neb T	Jas Findlay

Names Changed:
Mount Linneus, Marion Co, Va, changed to Farmington.
Tullyton, Greenville district, S C, changed to Cedar Falls.
Prattsville, Monroe Co, Georgia, changed to Colaparchee.
Warrior Bridge, Choctaw Co, Ala, changed to Bladen Springs.
Matacha, Itawamba Co, Miss, changed to West Fulton.
Wright's X Roads, Fentress Co, Tenn, changed to Coopersville.
Rock Spring, Jackson Co, Tenn, changed to North Springs.
Shannonville, Decatur Co, Tenn, changed to Bath Springs.
Drury's, Rock Island Co, Ill, changed to Walnut Valley.
Widows' Home, Mahaska Co, Iowa, changed to Union Mills.
Marysville, Benton Co, Oregon Territory, changed to Forks of Mary's river.
Avery's, Benton Co, Oregon Territory, changed to Marysville.
Champoig, Marion Co, Oregon Territory, changed to Buteville.

Wash Corp: 1-Ptn of S Hocking & G Robb: referred to the Cmte on Police. 2-Cmte on Improvements: permission granted to T P & M Brown to widen an area at the corner of 6th & C sts: passed. 3-Act for the relief of Philip Mohun: passed. 4-Bill for the relief of Jesse Williams: passed. 5-Cmte on Police: act for the relief of E G Handy: passed. 6-Act to pay Saml Cursen for removing a nuisance in the 3rd Ward: passed. 7-Ptn from Cornelius Brosnahan for the remission of a fine: referred to the Cmte of Claims.

Died: on Sep 16, at West Point, N Y, Brevet Maj W P Bainbridge, Capt 4th Regt of Artl, of chronic dysentery, contracted in Mexico.

Land Warrant # 5295, issued Sep 1849, in favor of Hugh McQueen & land warrant # 5358, issued 2 Oct 1849, in favor of Daniel Devies, lost in mail between this place & Galveston, Texas. A caveat against said warrant has been entered at the Gen Land Ofc. –R W Latham & Co

SAT SEP 21, 1850
Senate: 1-Memorial of Thos Ginnaty, an alien, resident of Wash, asking that he may be allowed to hold certain property purchased by him in said city: referred to the Cmte on the Judiciary. 2-Cmte of Claims: ptn of Thos B Winston, asking that the amount of a judgment obtained against him might be refunded, submitted an adverse report thereon: ordered to be printed. 3-Cmte on the Judiciary: memorial of Wm Y Hansell, Wm H Underwood, & the reps of Saml Rockwell: recommending the adoption of the following amendment to the Indian appropriation bill: for payment to be distributed in the following manner: to W Y Hansell-$11,146; to W Underwood-$9,045; & to the legal reps of Saml Rockwell-$10,144. 4-Cmte on Foreign Relations: memorial of A P Brittingham, asked to be discharged from the further consideration of the same: which was agreed to. 5-Engrossed bill authorizing the settlement & payment of the account of Robt L Blair, for the subsisting & transportation of companies K & D of the 5th Regt of Tenn Volunteers from Jonesborough to Knoxville, in 1849: passed.

The Hon Rufus Choate, Hon Jos Bell, Col Isaac O Barnes, & Chas L Woodbury, all of Boston, returned home by the ship **Canada** from their visit to Europe.

Dr Walter Smith, Surgeon of the U S Naval Hospital, died at his residence in Brooklyn on Thu. He entered the service on Jun 5, 1820, & has been surgeon at the navy yard at Charlestown, at Washington, we believe, & for 2 or 3 years past at the naval hospital at the Brooklyn yard.

Intelligence has reached Boston of the death of the Rev Addison Searle, Chaplain of the U S frig **Cumberland**. He died on the passage to Alexandria, & was buried at sea.

Death of Ky fat boy: Andrew Brand died at Albany, Sep 18, after an illness of about 4 weeks. He was a native of Calhoun, Davis Co, Ky & was in his 16th year & weighed no less than 537 lbs. He came to Albany to attend the State Fair, but was attacked with illness.

Household & kitchen furniture at auction: on Sep 25, at the residence of Rev G W Samson, on E st, between 9th & 10th sts. –Dyer & Brother, aucts

Household furniture & blacksmith's tools at auction: on Sep 23, the personal estate of Bennet Lucas, deceased, at his late residence, near Easby's ship yard. –Dyer & Bro aucts

Jos Mansfield, son of Mr Edw Mansfield, of Portland, Me, was accidentally shot & killed last week in a hunting accident. One of the other lads, Isaac Scott, leveled his gun at some birds & fired just as Mansfield sprang up before the gun.

Mrd: on Sep 16, at Montrose, Pa, by Rev H A Riley, R W Barnard, of Gtwn D C, to Katherine Theodocia, daughter of Geo Fuller, of Montrose.

Died: on Sep 11, in Chas Co, Md, after an illness of one week, T M McIlhany, aged 42 years. He was a native of Loudoun Co, Va, but for the last few years a resident of Wash. He was summoned to attend the sick bed of a dying daughter in Md, where he fell victim to the disease which carried him off. Died: at the same place & in the same County, on Sep 14, Wm W Rennoe, son-in-law of the above, aged 26 years. Cut off in the bloom of life & usefulness, an affectionate husband, son & brother, a warm hearted generous friend & companion.

Died: on Sep 19, in Wash City, Charles Edward, youngest son of Wm C & Nancy Ann Goddard, of Wash City, aged 5 months. His funeral will be this evening at 4 o'clock, from the residence of his parents, on 10th, between N Y ave & K st west.

Two story brick house at auction: on Sep 26: part of lot 10, in square 881, fronting on south K st. The property is sold to satisfy ground rent due Jacob Smull, & by his order. –Green & Tastet, aucts

Appointments by the Pres: 1-Geo Lunt, of Mass, to be U S Atty in & for the District of Mass. 2-C Goethe Baylor, of Texas, to be Consul of the U S of America for the port of Amsterdam, in the kingdom of the Netherlands, in place of Albert Lange, resigned. 3-Wm D Lewis, Collector of Customs for the District of Phil, Pa.

Dreadful riot recently, growing out of the land troubles, at Sacramento city, in the course of which Mayor Bigelow was badly wounded & the City Assessor & many others killed. The Lt Govn'r declared martial law, & steamers had been dispatched to San Francisco for troops & other assistance. [Sep 23rd newspaper: Mr Woodland was lying dead; Mayor Bigelow was badly wounded. -Jno McDougal-Aug 14, on board steamer **Senator**.]

MON SEP 23, 1850
Senate: 1-Memorial of Robt Grignon, a half-breed of the tribe of Menominee Indians, asking that the treaty of 1836 may be carried out as originally intended, & that the sum of $1,000 may be paid him for each year for 20 years, as contained in the original treaty; but which had been stricken out by the Senate when the treaty was ratified Feb 15, 1837: laid on the table, due to the brief period allowed before the close of the session. 2-Memorial from Jos K Boyd, one of the captors of the frig **Philadelphia**, asking the Senate to relieve his anxiety by passing the bill for the relief of the captors, or laying it on the table, & in the event of its failure to be permitted to withdraw all the papers from the archives: which was laid on the table. 3-Mr Dodge, of Iowa, submitted documents in the case of Polly Thomas, widow of a Revolutionary soldier, asking a pension: referred to the Cmte on Pension. Also, documents in relation to the claims of Sarah Shatts, heirs John Walker & Mary Greer, heirs of Jas McKinney, to bounty lands for services in the war of 1812: referred to the Cmte on Private Land Claims. 4-Cmte on Military Affairs: bill for the relief of the heirs & reps of Col Alex'r G Morgan, reported back the same with

amendments. 5-Cmte on Public Lands: memorial of Jas J Stang, J Adams, & Wm Marks, presidents of the Church of the Saints, [styling themselves servants of the living God, the fellow servants of the martyred saints,] asking Congress to pass a law giving the consent of the nation to allow the saints to settle open & forever occupy all the uninhabited lands of the island in Lake Michigan, & to cease to sell the same to other persons: asked to be discharged from the further consideration of the ptn of the same: which was agreed to.

Mrd: on Sep 19, by Rev Mr Slattery; Mr Jos F Hodgson to Miss Mary Isabella Handly, all of Wash City.

Died: on Sep 20, Greenwood, Montgomery Co, Sep 20; Allen Bowie, aged 10 months, infant son of Allen Bowie & Hester Ann Davis.

Millard Fillmore, Pres of the U S: recognizes Chas Defly, who has been appointed Consul for the Republic of France, at Richmond, Va. -Sep 20, 1850

Brevet Maj John H Miller, of U S Army, died at the residence of Dr Porter, near Pitts, Pa, Sep 12. Maj Miller was son-in-law of the late Hon John Norvell, and husband of Mrs Miller, who so mysteriously disappeared from Niagara Falls a few months ago. She has lately returned to her mother in Michigan. The family of Mr Novell has been sorely afflicted during the last few months, in the death of its head, a son, & a son-in-law.

The Will of Louis Phillipe-Count of Neuilly, just presented for probate in Paris. It is said the per centage coming to the State upon the division of this estate will be $2,000,000.

WED SEP 25, 1850
Senate: 1-Memorial of Robt Piatt, asking compensation for services as a Deputy Commissary of Purchases during the war of 1812: referred to the Cmte of Claims. 2-Cmte of Claims: ptn of Edw Tracey & others, praying an extension of the act for the relief of J P B Gratiot & the legal reps of H Gratiot to all persons who paid mineral rent, submitted an adverse report on the same. 3-Resolved, that there be paid to Jacob Dodson the same extra compensation that was paid to the laborers at the last session of Congress: the sum of $50. 4-Resolved, that the Sec of the Navy is directed to purchase the right to use the patent suction & force pump & fire engine of Simon P Keese, & the sum of $25,000 is hereby appropriated. 5-The pay of the engineer, Ward B Burnett, at the navy yard, Phil, be $2,347, commencing at the time of his appointment on Feb 1, 1849: agreed to. 6-Cmte of Naval Affairs: the Sec of the Navy is authorized & directed to enter into contract with Saml D Dakin, John S Gilbert, Zenor Secor, & Rutherford Moody, for the construction, with all reasonable dispatch, of a sectional or balance floating dry deck, basin, & railway, at such harbor on the coast of the Pacific ocean as he may select. 7-Cmte on Indian affairs: memorial of C M Hitchcock, exc of R J Hunter, deceased, asking compensation for corn furnished to the Cherokee Indians in 1836, under the authority of Big Gen Wool & J R Schermerhorn, commissioner for negotiating the treaty with the Cherokees, from May 26 to Jul 16, 1836, $1,236.25: amendment ordered to be printed. 8-Cmte of Claims: bill for the relief of Chas Ahrenfeldt & John F H Vogt: recommended its passage.

I hereby certify that Chas Wilson, of Wash Co, D C, brought before me as an estray trespassing upon his enclosures, a small dark bay horse. –Jas Crandell, J P [Owners to call, pay charges, & take him away. –C Wilson, near the Navy Yard]

Millard Fillmore, Pres of the U S, recognizes Ferdinand Ludwig Brauns, who has been appointed Consul Gen of Saxony, to reside in Balt. Sep 17, 1850.

Mr Marcial A Carbajah, a native of old Spain, will give lessons in the Spanish language at his lodgings, in 8th st, near Pa ave, at Mr Tromma's, or at the rooms of such as may desire.

Furniture & store fixtures at auction: on Sep 27, at the residence of Mr Lindsley, 14th & Md ave, next to the Long Bridge.

Appointments by the Pres: 1-Jos A Shearman to be Deputy Postmaster at Utica, N Y. 2-Aaron P Hughes to be Deputy Postmaster at Nashua, N H.

House of Reps: 1-Ptn of J Bigelow, Saml H Tuner, J F Callan, & David A Hall, asking the enactment of a law incorporating the "Wash Dock & Transportation Co," for the reception & transportation of merchandise: referred to the Cmte on the Dist of Columbia. 2-Cmte on the Judiciary: ptn of Thos Ginnatty, a foreigner, asking to be allowed to hold certain property: to be engrossed for a 3rd reading. [Ginnatty is an Irishman who has been in the country about 9 years, & within the last 2 years has given notice of his intention to become a citizen of the U S.]

Mr Fred'k Rotham, a ship carpenter of Phil, & his son, aged 10 years, were drowned in the Delaware river on Sat, when their small boat, in tow of the steamer **Henlopen**, was suddenly swamped. They were returning from a gunning excursion.

Law of the U S passed at the First Session 31st Congress. Act to suppress the slave trade in the Dist of Columbia. From & after Jan 1, 1851, it shall not be lawful to bring into the Dist of Col any slave whatever for the purpose of being sold, or for the purpose of being placed in depot, to be transferred to any other State or place, to be sold as merchandise. If any slave shall be brought into the said District, such slave shall thereupon become liberated & free.

Sudden death: Mr Edmund Varden, chairmaker, died suddenly yesterday while seated in a chair at a refectory, supposed to be from disease of the heart. Aged 35 years. His funeral is from the residence of his aunt, Mrs Shields, on 5th st, today at 4 P M.

Mrd: on Sep 19, at Fleetwood, in Culpeper Co, Va, by Rev John Cole; Geo G Thompson to Eliza, daughter of the Hon John S Barbour.

Mrd: on Sep 17, in Lenoir Co, N Carolina, by Rev W W Hawks; H W Blount, M D, to Miss Winnie B, eldest daughter of late Gen Jas B Whitfield.

Died: on Sep 22, in Gtwn, at residence of Mr Jos Libbey, Mr John S De Merritt, in his 39th year. He was a native of Durham, N H, but for the last 13 years a resident of New Orleans, La, of the firm of Stevenson, De Merritt & Co, of that place..

Died: on Sep 23, Mgt Jane, aged 1 year & 11 months, youngest daughter of John & Sarah O'Donnell. Her funeral will be from the residence of Mr F H Elwell, near the Navy Yard, this evening, at 3 o'clock.

Died: on Sep 22, in Phil, Mason H Stansbury, draughtsman in the Topographical bureau, 3rd son of A J Stansbury, of Wash City.

City Ordinances-Wash: 1-Act fot the relief of John Dewdney, police ofcr of the First Ward: the sum of $9 to be paid to him for conveying unmanageable persons from said Ward to the city work-house, that amount being a balance due him for the years 1848 & 1849. 2-Act for the relief of O J Prather: to be paid $118.80, being the amount due him agreeably to the Surveyor's bill filed in the Register's ofc. 3-Act granting permission to Messrs T P & M Brown to widen an area at the corner of 6th st west & C st north.

Land at private sale: in pursuance of the will of the Rev John Brackenridge, & of a decree of the Warwick Co Probate Court, in Indiana, against the heirs of said Brackenridge & the Board of Education of the Presbyterian Church, & by deed of trust, with the will annexed, I will sell **Mill Seat**, adjoining the land of Mr Abner Pierce, in Wash Co, D C, supposed to contain 53 acres, & possesses superior water power, which has been in use for many years to propel a paper mill under Geo Broadrup. There is a stone mill house & dwlg house. Inquire of J B Mitchell, Phil; Walter S Cox, & Wm Noyes, Gtwn. –John A Brackenridge, Administrator W A

Died: on Sep 6, at Norfolk, Va, Alice, daughter of Lt Chas H & Mattie Poor, aged 4 years & 6 months.

Valuable real estate in Wash & Gtwn for sale: by deed of trust from the heirs at law of Nicholas Burke Boyle, deceased, dated Sep 20, 1850, executed for the purpose of the settlement of the estate of said Boyle: sale of lot 19 in square 635, adjoining the property of Wm P Elliot, immediately north of the Capitol, lot 5 & part of lot 4 in square 32, with the bldgs & improvements thereon, being the slaughter-house on north F st, formerly occupied by Godfrey Hager, & part of lot 9 in square 347, with the frame house thereon, on the south side of F st north, near 10th st; & also lot 299 in Beatty & Hawkins' addition to Gtwn, with bldgs & improvements thereon. –Chas S Wallach, trustee

For sale: residence of the undersigned, 12th st, between G & H sts. Brick house-2 stories, with basement & attic. –Presley Simpson

Corn at auction on Sep 28, on the premises, on the farm at present occupied by Mr Hutchinson, formerly the residence of Parson Brackenridge, lying between the farms of Messrs Riggs & Middleton. The field is near the Rock Creek Church road.
–Green & Tastet, aucts

THU SEP 26, 1850
Senate: 1-Compensation to Henry La Reintrie, late Sec to Cmdor Shubrick for his services as secretary to the legation of the U S near the Gov't of Chili, from Jan 6, to Apr 28, 1849: $590.40: amendment was rejected. 2-Cmte of the Whole: bill for the relief of Mrs A M Dade, widow of the late Maj F L Dade, of the U S army. Maj Dade fell at Dade's massacre during the war in Florida. She is now in extreme indigence, what little property she once had having been swept away from her, & is dependant for support upon the sweat of the brow of an aged father, now 70 years old. She is a resident of Florida: passed. 3-Bill for the relief of Frances P Gardiner, widow of Capt Geo P Gardiner, who was the second in command, & who also fell in Dade's massacre: passed.

Distressing affair yesterday on Pa ave: Claudius Mathieu, a silversmith in the employment of Messrs Galt & Brother, fired 5 discharges from a revolver at Joshua L Skidmore, a carpenter by trade, also living in Wash City, & dangerously wounded him. The act was in a fit of jealousy. Mathieu has not yet been arrested.

Army order, War Dept, Wash, Sep 21, 1850. Ofcrs of the army appointed members of the Board of Ofcrs of the Army.
Maj Gen Winfield Scott, Pres of the Board
Brevet Maj Gen Thos S Jesup
Brevet Maj Gen John E Wool
Col I B Crane, 1st Artl
Brevet Col C A Waite, 8th Infty
Surgeon Thos G Mower
Paymaster David Hunter
Brevet Lt Col Henry L Scott, 4th Infty, Recorder

Signor Sarti, the proprietor & manufacturer of the extraordinary anatomical figures in wax recently exhibited in this city, died at the Massachussetts Gen Hospital yesterday. He was a native of Florence, & a most accomplished man. He leaves a young widow, an English lady of rare excellence. -Boston Trans, Monday

Massacre of Calif emigrants: the Stark Co, Ohio, Democrat has the news that 5 citizens of Canton, & a man from Wisc, were murdered by Indians on Pitt river, on Jun 28 last. They were Wm McCurdy, Saml D Kaufman, Edward Meffert, Levi Barrell & Henry Kaufman. The Wisc gentleman was Daniel E Washburn from Janesville, in Wisc. He leaves a wife & family. Saml D Kaufman also leaves a wife & family.

Died: on Sep 25, in his 67th year, John McArann, native of the county of Antrim, Ire, for 43 years a successful Botanist in Phil, & for the last 10 years, a resident of Wash. His funeral will be Fri, from his late residence on G st near 17th, at 10 o'clock.

Died: on Sep 24, after a lingering illness, Ignatius A King, aged 77 years. His funeral is today from the residence of his daughter, Mrs Barbara Parker, G st, between 22nd & 23rd sts, at 4 o'clock.

Died: on Sep 21, in Gtwn, Wm Ellershaw Guy, aged 23 years.

Dissolution of the copartnership existing under the name of Dyer & Brother, by mutual consent. Mr Geo F Dyer will settle the accounts of the late firm. Also of the unsettled business of the late Robt W Dyer, deceased. –Edw C Dyer, Geo F Dyer [The undersigned have formed a copartnership under the firm of Dyer & McGuire, & will continue at the old stand. –Edw C Dyer, J C McGuire.]

$50 reward for runaway colored girl Charlotte Bell, about 21 years of age, & somewhat advanced in pregnancy. –Edw Mattingly, Wash

By 2 writs of fieri facias, at the suits of Richd G Briscoe & Jos S Clarke, trading under the firm of Briscoe & Clarke, against the goods & chattels of John E Dement: sale of the interest of said Dement in one lot of hay, containing about 10 stacks, to be sold on Oct 3, in Wash Co, D C. –H R Maryman, constable

FRI SEP 27, 1850
Died: on Aug 28, in Tuscaloosa, Ala, after a painful & lingering illness, at the advanced age of 75 years, Mrs Agnes Payne Williams, wife of the Hon M D Williams. This venerable lady was born in Pittsylvania Co, Va, on Jun 2, A D, 1775, where, more than half a century ago, she was married to Judge Williams, the afflicted husband who still survives her. After a residence of some years in N C, she removed with her husband, in 1810, to Madison Co, Ala. In 1818, she became a resident of Tuscaloosa, where she has ever since resided, an object of love & affection to her numerous descendants.

Mrd: on Sep 25, at Trinity Church, by Rev Wm Pinkney, Edw Bostick, of Beaufort, S C, to Maria, youngest daughter of the late Judge Wm D Martin, of S C.

Died: yesterday, in Wash City, Mrs Catherine Devina, in her 38th year. Her funeral is this afternoon at 4 o'clock, from her late residence at 11th & F sts.

From Havana: Sentenced to death or long imprisonments, charged with emigrating contemporaneously to the U S & establishing a club in N Y C entitled a Cmte of promoting the political interest of Cuba, for the purpose of disseminating in the island & in Porto Rico their insidious designs against the Gov't of her Majesty, & conspiring to overthrow it. Those sentenced to death by strangulation: Ambrosio Jose Gonzalez, Juan Manuel Macias, Jose Maria Sanchez, Iznago Cirilia Villaverde, & Pedro Aguero. Those sentenced to 10 years' imprisonment beyond the sea: Victoriana de Arrieta, Gaspar de Batancourt y Cisneros, Christval Madan.

Wm Wilcox, an American seaman, who was captured on an island called Key Chalupas, near Cardenas, on the day after the invasion of that town by the Lopez expedition, having been convicted of taking an active part, was on Aug 12, condemned to 12 years imprisonment at Ceuta, in Africa. The sentence was confirmed by the Auditor on the 17th, & approved by Count Alcoy on the 19th.

Fatal railroad accident on Tue on the Erie Railroad, about 2 miles of Owego, by coming in contact with a cow. Mrs Kendrick, wife of Saml Kendrick, of Rochester, was instantly killed, & Mr Thos Johnson, of Elmira, a clerk of the company, & Mr F Ingraham, of Buffalo, were badly injured.

Rev Gilbert Cumming Weld, well known correspondent of the N Y Journal of Commerce, died at Sacramento City on Aug 9, of typhoid fever. He died at age 32 years, leaving & widow & 3 children. His signature was: W.

Senate: 1-Cmte on Naval Affairs: memorial of Julius Meiere, asking an allowance for house rent, furniture, & fuel, while a professor of mathematics in the navy: recommendation that it ought not to be granted. 2-Same Cmte: memorial of John J Glasson, U S Navy, on behalf of the crew of the U S schnr **Falcon**, asking prize money for captures made during the late war with Mexico: recommending that the prayer of the petitioner ought not to be granted. 3-Cmte on Military Affairs: memorial of Mrs Eliz Armstead, widow of the late Gen Walter K Armstead, reported a bill for the relief of the legal reps of the late Gen: passed.

Household & kitchen furniture at auction: on Oct 2, at the house well known as Butler's Hotel, on F st, between 13th & 14th sts. -Dyer & Maguire, aucts

SAT SEP 28, 1850
Mrd: Sep 26, by Rev F S Evans, Andrew Dove to Eliza Jane Devers, of Fairfax Co, Va.

Senate: 1-Memorial of Wm C McMaster: referred to the Joint Cmte on the Library. He asked Congress to authorize him to paint full-length portraits of all the Presidents, to be placed in the Pres' House. Cmte was discharged from the further consideration of the subject.

Wash Corp: 1-Ptn of Peter K Kane, praying the restoration of his hogs found going at large: referred to the Cmte of Claims. 2-Ptn of Isabella Webster, praying remission of a fine: referred to the Cmte of Claims. 3-Ptn of Robt Beale & others, for the improvement of A st, between 2nd & 3rd sts: referred to the Cmte on Improvements. 4-Ptn of J W McElfresh, praying remission of a fine: referred to the Cmte of Claims.

Mrd: on Sep 19, at the residence of Mrs Mary Booton, by Rev S H Mirick, Mr Jno H McClung to Miss Martha F, daughter of the late Sinclair Booton, all of Madison Co, Va.

Mrd: on Sep 26, by Rev Mr Ballintine, David W Mahon to Jane O Smith.

Died: on Sep 26, after a short illness, in Wash City, Anna Maria, youngest child of Wm Duane & Eliz E Wilson, aged 27 months. –Wash, Pa & Steubenville, & Ohio papers copy.

Appointments by the Pres:
John Wilson, to be Principal Clerk of Public Lands in the Gen Land Ofc, under the act of Jul 4, 1836.
John M Moore, to be Principal Clerk of Surveys in said ofc, vice Joh Wilson appointed as above.
Bradley B Meeker, of Ky, to be an Assoc Justice of the Supreme Court of the U S for the Territory of Minnesota.
Elias Wampole, of N J, to be Indian agent in Oregon.
U S Attys:
Amory Holbrook, for the District of Oregon.
Saml R Rogers, for the Eastern District of Tenn.
Jas R Lawrence, for the Northern District of N Y.
Wm T Joynes, for the Easter District of Va, vice Robt C Nicholas, whose commission had expired.
Philip R Fendall, District of Columbia.
Ofcs or the Customs:
Collectors:
Chas Peters, for the Dist of Frenchman's Bay, [Ellworth,] Maine
Jeremiah Baily, Wiscasset, Maine
Nathl G Marshall, York, Maine
Danl Kibly, Passamaquoddy, [Eastport,] Maine
Wm C Hammet, Bangor, Maine
Luther Jewett, Portland & Falmouth, Maine
Bela B Haskell, Waldoborough, Maine
David Bronson, Bath, Maine
Maurice C Blake, Belfast, Maine
Wm R Easton, Natucket, Mass
Jas Gregory, Marblehead, Mass
Henry W Kinsman, Newburyport, Mass
Leavitt Thaxter, Edgartown, Mass
Ebenezer Bacon, Barnstable, Mass
Philip Greely, jr, Boston, Mass
Edw W Lawton, Newport, R I
Wm R Watson, Providence, R I
Nicoll Fosdick, New London, Conn
Gideon S Sacket, Cape Vincent, N Y
Danl McCulloch, Sackett's Harbor, N Y
Wm Ketchum, Buffalo, N Y
Ephraim Buck, Bridgetown, N J
Geo P Kane, Balt, Md
John H Allen, Oxford, Md
Jos Eaches, Alexandria, Va
Jefferson Minor, Tappahannock, Va
Wm Garnett, Norfolk, Va
Silburn H Trigg, Richmond, Va
Wm F Bowden, Petersburgh, Va

R H J Blount, Washington, N C
Robt G Rankin, Wilmington, N C
Jos Ramsey, Plymouth, N C
Chas R Railey, Natchez, Miss
Isaiah D Hart, St John's [Jacksonville,] Fla
Robt Mitchell, Pensacola, Fla
Saml J Douglass, Key West, Fla
Benj S Hawley, Apalachicola, Fla
Wm R Smith, Texas, [Galveston]
Chas W Hill, Miami, [Maumee,] Ohio
Chas E Avery, Michilimackinac, Mich
Naval Ofcrs:
Adam S Coe, for the Dist of Newport, R I
Philip Hone, N Y, N Y
Wm Brown, Salem & Beverly, Mass
Jas G Green, Wilmington, N C
Bryan Maxell, Savannah, Ga
Surveyors:
Jos Gunnison, for the port of Eastport, Maine
Bazaleel Cushman, Portland, Maine
Wm T Averill, Ipswich, Mass
Allen Putnam, Salem, Mass
Lonson Nash, Gloucester, Mass
Thos Foss, Marblehead, Mass
Asa B Waite, North Kingston, R I
Jos Paddock, Newport, R I
John G Needhan, Pawtuxet, R I
John M Spencer, East Greenwich, R I
W H S Bayley, Bristol, R I
Chas Randall, Warren & Barrington, R I
Jos Taylor, Middletown, Conn
Penfield B Goodsell, Hartford, Conn
Ezra Hotchkiss, New Haven, Conn
Giles Blague, Saybrook, Conn
Francis W Fitch, New London, Conn
John D Kellogg, Troy, N Y
Philip J Grey, Camden, N Y
Henry Woods, Pittsburgh, Pa
John B Abell, Town Creek, Md
Wm Coad, St Mary's River, Md
Elias T Griffin, Balt, Md
John Blackstone, Lewellensburgh, Md
John T Stamp, Nottingham, Md
Geo W P Smith, Snow Hill, Md
John A Chew, Havre de Gace, Md
Chas T Stuart, Alexandria, Va

Thos P Bagwell, Accomack C H, Va
Isaac H Parker, Norfolk, Va
Wm Gray, Port Royal, Va
John Cowan, Wilmington, N C
Wm Y Leitch, Charleston, S C
Thos Bourke, Savannah, Ga
Robt B Stille, New Orleans, La
John C O'Grady, Madisonville, La
Henry Dart, Pontchartrain, La
Robt C Thompson, Louisville, Ky
Wm K Hunter, Nashville, tenn
Wm W Greene, St Louis, Mo

Appraisers:
Corn's Savage, for the Port of N Y, N Y
John C Martin, for Phil, Pa
John H Withers, for Phil, Pa
Hugh W Evans, for Balt, Md
Wm P White, for Savannah, Ga
Robt F Canfield, for New Orleans, La

Eliphalet Barker, a large wholesale dry goods dealer in Boston, has failed. Not by operations in trade, but by speculations in real estate, which he holds to the amount of nearly half a million.

Postmaster Gen established the following new Post Ofcs for week ending Sep 21, 1850.

Ofc	County, State	Postmaster
North Thetford	Orange, Vt	David W Closson
Boylston Centre	Worcester, Mass	John B Heywood
East Pepperell	Middlesex, Mass	Jos A Tucker
Onoville	Cattaraugus, N Y	E D Fenton
Hibernia	Dutchess, N Y	A B Merrit
Searsville	Orange, N Y	Geo Hunter
White's Corners	Potter, Pa	John H White
Mount Freedom	Pendleton, Va	Wm S Arbogast
Maple Hill	Davidson, N C	Wm D Wood
Peter's Creek	Stokes, N C	David Hall
Smeltzer's Creek	Pickens D, S C	Nathan Lusk
Big Creek	Edgefield D, S C	Chas Nickerson
Bradford	Coosa, Ala	Wm K Simpson
Sibley's Mills	Wilkinson, Miss	Benj F Sibley
Peach Creek	Panola, Miss	Wm C Maxwell
Snow Creek	Marshall, Miss	L P Dishony
La Salle	Calhoun, Texas	Chas Mason
Watensaw	Monroe, Ark	Geo W Taylor
Philipsville	Weakley, Tenn	Thos H Philips
Dublin	Graves, Ky	S S Brown

Lacona	Jefferson, Ky	Jesse Hester
Saltillo	Morgan, Ky	Saml McGuire
Nairn	Scioto, Ohio	Laughlin Noble
Danby	Ionia, Mich	John Compton
Bowne	Kent, Mich	Justus G Beach
Mountain Spring	Martin, Ia	Josiah Pierce
Ash Grove	Irequois, Ill	John Nunamaker
Warsaw	Portage, Wis	Jasper Stowell
Rome	Jefferson, Wis	Aaron J Ball
Well's Landing	Dubuque, Iowa	Hiram Weld

Names Changed:
Lockport, Erie Co, Pa, changed to Plates.
Warner, Warren Co, Pa, changed to Steam Mills.
Dunnington's Depot, Berkeley Co, Va, changed to Van Clevesville.
Paradise, Macon Co, Tenn, changed to Alton Hill.
Drennon's Ridge, Henry Co, Ky, changed to Franklinton.

I offer my house on 11th st, near Pa ave, for rent for 5 years. I also offer my house fronting on Pa ave, now occupied by the Messrs Tate as a Lace store. This tenement has a handsome 3 story back bldg, for a family, as well as a front house, over the lace store; both of these have 10 chambers, parlor, kitchen, & basement. The whole of the poperty now rents for $1,350 per annum, insured in Phil. Apply to Jos K Boyd, through the Post Ofc, which will be attended to.

MON SEP 30, 1850
Senate: 1-Memorial from Ward Morton, a Capt of marines, asking to be allowed certain arrearages of pay; but he took occasion to observe that it was too late for the present session, & asked that the memorial be laid on the table: which was agreed to. 2-Moved that Robt Mayo have leave to withdraw his papers; but objection having been made, the leave was not granted. 3-Cmte on Commerce: ptn of John McColgan, asking to be discharged from the further consideration of the ptn of the same. 4-Cmte of the Whole House: bill for the relief of Lt Henry F Evans, to increase the pension from $14 to $40 per month. A more desperate case of daring was never exhibited by mortal man; he literally stood in a shower of lead, the flag he carried was pierced with 19 balls, & the flag-staff shot out of his hand. He himself received 5 wounds. Bill was amended by striking out $40 & inserting $20. This bill is for an old man, who cannot live very long. He was disabled in the service of his country; he has become blind, & it is unpleasant to have an incumbrance of that sort. Case was submitted to the Cmte on Pensions. 5-Cmte of the Whole: bill for the relief of Ebenezer Dumont: passed. 6-Bill authorizes the accounts of Col Jos K F Mansfield, of the Engineer Corps: to be engrossed for a third reading.

A large number of distinguished gentlemen have been invited by the Canal Board to be present at the opening of the <u>Chesapeake & Ohio Canal</u>. The celebration will probably take place about Oct 9. -Balt Patriot

Appointments by the Pres:
Chas J McCurdy, of Conn, to be Charge d'Affaires of the U S at the Court of his Majesty the Emperor of Austria.
Consuls:
Saml Bromberg, of Wisc, for the port of Hamburg, vice Philo S White, recalled.
Robt B Davidson, of Tenn, for the port of Rio Grande, in Brazil.
Day O Kellogg, of N Y, for the port of Glasgow, in Scotland.
Jas Foy, of Pa, at Dublin, in Ireland.
Chas Andony, of Mobile, Ala, at Napoleon Vendee, the capital of the dept of Vendee, in France.
Fred'k Karl, of Pa, for port of Bordeaux, in France, vice John Warren Grisby, recalled.
Jos Rodney Croskey, of Pa, for the ports of Southampton & Cowes, in the United Kingdom of Great Britain & Ireland, vice Chas W Fenton, resigned.
Chas Benjamin, of Conn, for port of Demarara, in Guiana, vice Saml J Marsters, recalled.
Alex'r M Ross, of N Y, for Puerto Cabello, in the Republic of Venezuela, vice Southy Grinalds, recalled.
Jean Baptiste Chas Antoine, at Sedan, in France.
Wm H Ropes, of Mass, at the port of St Petersburgh, in Russia.
John U Petit, of Indiana, for the Island of Maranham, Brazil.
Wm N Adams, for the port of Santiago de Cuba.

Postmasters:

Jos Mitchell	at Nantucket, Mass
Abraham Stryker	at Princeton, N J
Geo Updegraff	at Hagerstown, Md
Calvin Gold	at Shawneetown, Ill
Julius M Ackley	at Ithaca, N Y
Solomon Parmele	at Lockport, N Y
Geo W Dole	at Chicago, Ill
Nathl Wilson	at Lawrence, Mass
Richd Milton	at Winchester, Va
John C McCallister	at Jackson, Miss
Ofcrs of the Customs:	
Collectors:	
Chas J Abbott	District of Penobscot, [Castine,] Maine
Fred'k G Low	Gloucester, Mass
Wm T Russell	New Bedford, Mass
Hugh Maxwell	N Y, N Y
Elias Pond	Genesee, [Rochester,] N Y
John D Thompson	Little Egg Harbor, [Tuckerton,] N J
Henry Addison	Gtwn, D C
Oliver M Hyde	Detroit, Mich
Jacob Richardson	Oswego, N Y

Surveyor: Wm K Bond, Port of Cincinnati, Ohio
Naval Ofcr: Peter C Ellmaker, Dist of Phil, Pa
Appraiser: Matthias B Edgar, Port of N Y, N Y

Land Ofcrs: Receivers:

Richd M Thruston	at Fayetteville, Ark
Henry Acker	Saut Ste Marie, Mich
Blanton P Box	Champagnole, Ark
Thos T Russell	St Augustine, Fla
Solomon F Halliday	Neuwansville, Fla
Mordecai Mobley	Dubuque, Iowa
Wm H Wallace	Fairfield, Iowa
Easton Morris	Iowa City, Iowa
John H Thompson	Indianapolis, Ind
John Beard	Crawfordsville, Ind
Smallwood Noel	Fort Wayne, Ind
Robt H Griffith	Palmyra, Mo
Stephen F Page	Ionia, Mich
Horace Mower	Kalmazoo, Mich
Edgar Conklin	Green Bay, Wis

Registers:

Andrew Backus	at Saut Ste Marie, Mich
Geo H Slaughter	Mineral Point, Wis
Danl Sigler	Winamac, Ia
Thos McKnight	Dubuque, Iowa
Geo Wilson	Fairfield, Iowa
Saml Brenton	*Fort Wayne*, Ia
Andrew McCallen	Shawneetown, Ill
Hercules R W Andrews	Tallahassee, Fla
Alex'r Spaulding	Green Bay, Wis
Louis S Lovell	Ionia, Mich
Lansing B Mizner	Detroit, Mich
David B Webster	Kalamazoo, Mich
Cornelius Rosevelt	Genessee, Mich

Surveyors General:

Benj A Putnam	for Florida
Lorenzo Gibson	Arkansas
Robt W Boyd	Louisiana
Meriwether L Clark	Illinois & Missouri

Indian Agents:

David D Mitchell, Superintendent of Indian Affairs at St Louis, Mo.
John R Chenault, to be Indian agent at Osage River.
Jas S Calhoun, at Santa Fe
Luke Lea, *Fort Leavenworth*
Gabriel W Long, Chickasaw agency
Philip H Raiford, Creed agency
Wm Butler, Cherokee agency
John Drenner, Choctaw agency
Chas P Babcock, Mackinac agency

Mrd: on Sep 26, by Rev Mr Morgan, Mr Wm Warfield, of Balt, to Mrs Martha Lowe, of Wash.

Died: on Sep 20, at Greenwood, Montg Co, Md, Allen Bowie, aged 10 months, son of Allen Bowie & Hester Ann Davis.

Died: on Sep 25, at **Mount Hebron**, Elk Ridge, Md, in her 68th year, Milcah, consort of Chief Justice Thos B Dorsey.

For rent: large 2 sotry brick dwlg on 11th st, between G & H sts. For particulars inquire of Geo W Barry.

For rent: large 4 story brick house on C st, between 3rd & 4½ sts, next door to the Hon R C Winthrop's, formerly the residence of the late Dorcas Galvin. Inquire of J P Pepper, at A Lee's.

In Chancery: Wm Holmead & others, against Gregory Ennis, Alice Moran, widow, & Mary Ann, Michl, John Thos, & Rosa Moran, adm, & heirs of Patrick Moran. The creditors are to file their claims on or before Oct 10 next. –W Redin, auditor

The first coal by canal: the canal boat **Southampton**, belonging to the transportation line of Messrs McKaig & Agnew, is now loading with coal from the mines of Frostburg Coal Co, at the wharf of the Md Mining Co at Cumberland, Md, & will depart for Alexandria in a few days.

TUE OCT 1, 1850
Appointments by the Pres:
Chas Howard Edwards, of N J, to be Clerk to the Com'r under the Convention with Brazil, in place of Philip N Searle, resigned.
Postmasters:

J A L Lee	at Columbus, Ga
Wm Dickey	Paterson, N J
Saml Pitkins	Saratoga Springs, N Y
John H Tweedy	Milwaukee, Wisc
Eathan A Warden	Auburn, N Y
John J Cochrane	York, Pa
Simeon Bailey	New Bedford, Mass
Joshua Dunn	Portland, Maine
Geo P Conrad	Newark, Ohio
Chas R Barstow	Owego, N Y
Fred'k H Fessenden	Brattleboro', Vt
Asa Chapman	Middlebury, Vt
Steuben Butler	Wilkesbarre, Pa
Archibald F Stewart	Meadville, Pa
Nicholas Pearse	Chambersburg, Pa
Jas McDermot	Washington, Pa

Jos M Knox	Circleville, Ohio
John W Ogden	Keokuk, Iowa
Oliver Cocke	Burlington, Iowa
Jacob Hammer	Mansfield, Ohio
Willis Kinsman	Hanover, N H
Milton N Scott	Apalachicola, Fla
Jacob Fauble	Fred'k, Md
Jos C Cole	Monroe, Mich
Caleb R Williams	Richmond, Ind
Saml Stophlet	**Fort Wayne**, Ind
Jesse B Moffat	Terre Haute, Ind

Died: on Sep 18, at his residence in Somerville, N J, Col Isaac Southard, [brother of the late Hon Saml L Southard,] in his 67th year. Col S was for several years a member of Congress from N J, as was also his father & brother. For several years he filled the post of State Treasurer, & other ofcs.

List of Acts passed at the First Session of the 31st Congress: Privilege of franking letters & packages extended to Sarah Polk; & to Mrs Mgt S Taylor. Refund fine imposed on the late Dr Thos Cooper, under the sedition law, to his heirs. Relief of:

Jesse Sutton
Brown & Tarbex
Richd H Barrett
Benj P Smith
Camfield Averill
Eliphas C Brown
Skelton Felton
Winthrop S Harding
Smith & Hersey
Jacob Zimmerman
Sarah Jane West

Thos Dennis
Isaac Seymour
Chas Stuart
Wm Whicher
Jos P Williams
John Mitchell
Jas T Shackleford
D A Watterson
Leuright Browning
Children of Sarah Stokes, deceased
Capt Nathan Adams, of Tenn

Wm Maxwell, late Marshal for the dist of Ga
Al-lo-lah & his legal reps & their grantees
Thos Ginnalty to hold & transmit certain real estate
Conrad W Faber, Leopold Bierwith, & Theodore Victor
Settlement of accounts with the heirs & reps of Col Pierce M Butler, late agent for the Cherokee Indians.

Orphans Court of Wash Co, D C. In the case of Richd L Page, adm of Wm B Page, deceased: the administrator & Court have appointed Oct 22nd next for distribution of the said estate, of the assets in the hands of the adm. –Ed N Roach, Reg/o wills

Private sale of a 3 story brick dwlg, ofc, & lots, on 8th st, between E & F sts. Apply to W T Steiger, at the Gen Land Ofc.

WED OCT 2, 1850
Appointments by the Pres:
Danl M Barringer, of N C, to be Envoy Extra & Minister Pleni of the U S at the Court of Her Catholic Majesty, vice Romulus L Saunders, recalled at his own request.
Horation J Perry, of N H, to be Sec of Legation at the same Court.
Judah Benjamin, of Louisiana, to be Dirst Judge of the U S for Northern District of Calif.
John P Healey, of Mass, to be Dist Judge of the U S for the Southern Dist of Calif.
Calhoun Benham, of Calif, to be Atty of the U S for the Southern Dist of Calif.
J M Jones, of San Jose, Calif, to be U S Atty for the Southern Dist of Calif.
David F Douglass, of Calif, to be U S Marshal for the Northern Dist of Calif.
Augustus Humbert, to be Assayer in Calif.
Chas Kemle, of Missouri, to be Indian agent at the Upper Platte Agency, vice Thos Fitzpatrick.
Courtland Cusing, of Indiana, to be Charge d'Affaires of the U S at Quito, in the Republic of Equador.
Jos Buffington, of Pa, to be Chief Justice of the Supreme Court of the U S for the Territory of Utah.
Perry E Brocchus, of Ala, to be an Assoc Justice of the Supreme Court of the U S for the Territory of Utah.
Zerubbabel Snow, of Ohio, to be an Assoc Justice of the Supreme Court of the U S for the Territory of Utah.
Brigham Young, of Utah, to be Govn'r of the Territory of Utah.
Broughton Davis Harris, of Vt, to be Sec of the Territory of Utah.
Jos L Haywood, of Utah, to be U S Marshal for the Territory of Utah.
Seth Blair, of Utah, to be U S Atty in & for the Territory of Utah.
Redick McKee, of Va, Geo W Barbour, of Ky, & O M Wozencraft, of Calif, to be Indian Agents for Calif.
Pablo Noriego to be Marshal for the Southern Dist of Calif.
Elisha Whittlesey, of Ohio, to be First Comptroller of the Territory.

Consuls:
Wm H Smiley, of Rhode Island, for the port of Rio Negro, in the Argentine Republic.
Isaac C Bates, of Mass, for Aix la Chapelle, in Prussia.

Deputy Postmasters:

Jas Kidd	Albany, N Y
Isaac R Harrington	Buffalo, N Y
Geo H Harrison	New Albany, Indiana
Geo W Gordon	Boston, Mass
Chauncey Abbot	Madison, Wis
Hezekiah D Mason	Toledo, Ohio
Aaron F Perry	Columbus, Ohio
Danl M Haskell	Cleveland, Ohio
Eldad Smith	Racine, Wis
Thos Clowes	Troy, N Y
John McKeen	Brunswick, Maine
Isaac Platt	Poughkeepsie, N Y
Wm Jackson	Syracuse, N Y

Littleberry H Wilcox	Columbia, Tenn
F S Latham	Memphis, Tenn
Edw R Hunter	Portsmouth, Va
Henry H J Naff	Wilmington, Dela
Simeon King	Kenosha, Wis

Wash City Item. Jos Skidmore, the unfortunate man who was shot down one day last week by Claudius Mathieu, is considered to be in a dying state. [Oct 7 newspaper: coroner's verdict: Skidmore was killed by one to five successive pistol bullets, maliciously shot at him by Mathieu.]

For sale: the house in which I live, near the Navy Yard, the former residence of Dr M Williams. It is a double house, containing room for a large family. Inquire of N Young, near Navy Yard.

Household & kitchen furniture at auction: on Oct 8, at the residence formerly occupied by Mrs Vancoble, deceased, on 4½ st. –Green & Tastet, aucts

Death of a Aeronaut. The Bordeaux journals, which arrived this morning, announce the death of Lt Gale, the aeronaut, who made an ascent with the Royal Cremorne balloon, on the back of a pony, from the Hippodrome of Vincennes, at Bordeaux. It was the first time he had every made such an ascension. The descent, which took place near Bordeaux, proved fatal to him. The horse had been released from his slings, & the peasants who held the ropes of the balloon, misunderstanding the directions, let go, & the balloon rose suddenly. Mr Gale clinged to the ropes. It was thought he had climbed up into the car, but this was not the case. His dead body was found in a woods, with the limbs all broken. He has left a wife & 8 children.

Mrd: on Sep 30, by Rev F S Evans, Mr Wm A Webster to Miss Catharine Ferguson, daughter of Mr John Ferguson, of the Treasury Dept.

THU OCT 3, 1850
Appointments by the Pres:
Jas C Booth, of Pa, to be Melter & Refiner of the U S Mint at Phil.
Jas W Osborne, of N C, to be Superintendent of the Branch Mint at Charlotte, N C.
Andrew W Redding, of Ga, to be Superintendent of the Branch Mint at Dahlonega, Ga.
Robt H Moore, of Ga, to be Coiner of the Branch Mint at Dahlonega, Ga.
Matthew F Stephenson, to be Assayer at the Branch Mint of the U S at Dahlonega, Ga.
Ofcrs of the Customs
Collectors:
Wm B Smith, District of Machias, Me.
Lathrop, Cook, Niagara [Lewiston,] N Y
Ezra Smith, Champlain [Plattsburgh,] N Y
Jas C Barter, Oswegatchie [Ogensburg,] N Y
John M Hannon, St Augustine, Fla
Wm Freret, New Orleans, La

John H Williams, Pearl River [Shieldsboro',] Mi
Wm M Gallaer, Sonomo [Benicia,] Calif
Madison Walthall, San Joaquin [Stockton,] Calif
H E Robinson, Sacramento [Sacram City,] Calif
Wm C Ferrell, San Diego, Calif
Chas Cavileer, Minnesota [Pembina,] Min
Chas W Hill, Miami [Toledo,] Ohio
Levi Jones, Saluria [La Salle,] Texas
Allen W Hatch, Milwaukee, Wis
Naval Ofcr: Jacob Alex'r Cost, San Francisco, Calif
Appraisers:
Geo G Campbell, Port of N Y, N Y
Abm Kintzing, jr, San Francisco, Calif
J Vincent Brown, San Francisco, Calif
Assist Appraisers:
E E D Skinner, Port of Greenport, N Y
Benj Reddick, Suffolk, Va
David W Sanders, Jacksonville, N C
Thos Wolf, Memphis, Tenn
Chas B Applegate, New Albany, Ia
Wm Brown Butler, Evansville, Ia
Hart Fellows, San Francisco, Calif
Jas B Stevens, San Pedro, Calif
John McKelway, of N J, Commercial Agent for the Island of Curacao, vice Evans H Young, deceased.
Alex'r M Ross, of N Y, to be Consula at St Catharine's, in Brazil.

Mrd: on Oct 2, in the Church of the Epiphany, by Rev J W French, Dr Lewis A Edwards, U S A, to Miss Eulalia Emma, daughter of the Hon T Hartley Crawford, all of Wash City.

Mrd: on Oct 2, by Rev Mr Lynch, Dr R E Smith, of Opelousas, La, to Catherine, daughter of Lewis Carbery, of Gtwn, D C.

Official-War Dept. Gen Orders 29. Adj Gen Ofc, Wash, Oct 1, 1850.
Promotions & appointments in the U S Army, since publication of general orders #23 of Aug 7, 1850:
I-Promotions:
2nd Regt of Artl:
2nd Lt Jefferson H Nones, to be 1st Lt, Sep 10, vice Weld, deceased.
Brevet 2nd Lt John C Moore, of the 4th Regt of Artl, to be 2nd Lt, Sep 10, 1850, vice Nones, promoted.
3rd Regt of Artl:
1st Lt Edw O C Ord, to be Capt, Sep 7, 1850, vice Shover, deceased.
2nd Lt John S Mason, to be 1st Lt, Sep 7, 1850, vice Ord, promoted.
Brevet 2nd Lt John Kellogg, of the 4th Regt of Artl, to be 2nd Lt, Spe 7, 1850, vice Mason, promoted.

4th Regt of Artl:
1st Lt Thos L Brent, to be Capt, Sep 12, 1850, vice Miller, deceased.
1st Lt Thos Williams, to be Capt, Sep 16, 1850, vice Bainbridge, deceased.
1st Lt John C Pemberton, to be Capt, Sep 27, 1850, vice Shiras, appointed Commisary of Subsistence, who vacates his regimental commission.
2nd Lt John Gibbon, to be 1st Lt, Sep 12, 1850, vice Brent, promoted.
2nd Lt Clermont L Best, to be 1st Lt, Sep 16, 1850, vice Williams, promoted.
2nd Lt Richd C Drum, to be 1st Lt, Sep 27, 1850, vice Pemberton, promoted.
Brevet 2nd Lt Rufus Saxton, jr, of the 3rd Regt of Artl, to be 2nd Lt, Sep 12, 1850, vice Gibbon, promoted.
Brevet 2nd Lt Edw McK Hudson, of the 3rd Regt of Artl, to be 2nd Lt, Sep 16, 1850, vice Best, promoted.
Brevet 2nd Lt Cuvier Grover, of the 1st Regt of Artl, to be 2nd Lt, Sep 27, 1850, vice Drum, promoted.
2nd Regt of Infty:
Brevet 2nd Lt Alfred Cumming, of the 8th Regt of Infty, to be 2nd Lt, Aug 31, 1850, vice Russell, resigned
5th Regt of Infty:
1st Lt John C Robinson, to be Capt, Aug 12, 1850, vice Norvell, deceased.
2nd Lt Wm W Burns, to be 1st Lt, Aug 12, 1850, vice Robinson, promoted.
Brevet 2nd Lt John W Frazer, of the 2nd Regt of Infty, to be 2nd Lt, Aug 12, 1850, vice Burns, promoted.
II-Appointments.
Subsistence Dept
Capt Alex'r E Shiras, [4th Artl,] to be Commissary of Subsistence with the rank of Capt, to date from Mar 3, 1847, the date of his former commission.
1st Lt Wm B Blair, of the 2nd Artl, to be Commissary of Subsistence, with the rank of Capt, Sep 27, 1850.
1st Lt Wm T Sherman, of the 3rd Artl, to be Commissary of Subsistance, with the rank of Capt, Sep 27, 1850.
1st Lt Isaac Bowen, of the 1st Artl, to be Commissary of Subsistence, with the rank of Capt, Sep 27, 1850.
III-Casualties
Resignation:
2nd Lt Robt M Russell, 2nd Infty, Aug 31, 1850.
Brevet 2nd Lt John J A A Mouton, 7th Infty, Sep 16, 1850.
Deaths:
Brevet Maj Wm P Bainbridge, Capt 4th Artl, Sep 16, 1850, at West Point, N Y.
Brevet Maj John H Miller, Capt 4th Artl, Sep 12, 1850, near Pittsburg, Pa.
Brevet Maj Wm H Shover, Capt 3rd Artl, Sep 7, 1850, West Point, N Y.
Capt Spencer Norvell, 5th Infty, Aug 12, 1850, Saratoga, N Y.
Brevet 2nd Lt Rufus A Roys, Engineers, Jul 30, 1850, **Fort Kearny**, Oregon Route. Commission vacated under the provisions of the 7th section of the act of Jun 18, 1846.
Capt Alex'r E Shiras, 4th Art.,* appointed Commissary of Subsistence. *Regimental commission [only] vacated.
By order,: R Jones, Adj Gen

Jacksonville Hotel: the subscriber, having become the purchaser & sole proprietor of this well known Hotel, can accommodate over 150 persons. –Saml Buffington, Jacksonville, East Florida.

Dissolution of the copartnership between Stevens & Peaco, by mutual consent. –R C Stevens, Wm H Peaco. Wm H Peaco will continue the business at the old stand, 8th Pa ave, Wash. "Ladies Fancy & Trimming Business."

Laws of the U S passed at the 1st Session 31st Congress. 1-Payment to Lewis A Thomas & Thos Rodgers, $500, for services rendered in defence of 2 Sioux Indians, indicted in the district court of the U S for Iowa Terr, holden in Dubuque Co, Aug 11, 1845, for the murder of 2 white men. 2-To pay the Central Bank of Ga, assignee of H W Jarnegan & Co & others, $21,040. 3-For the redemption of the daughter of Mr & Mrs Jas M White, who was captured by the Indians on the borders of New Mexico, $1,500, to be expended under the direction of the Sec of the Interior. 4-Payment of the awards of Gen Wm B Mitchell, com'r under the treaty of Chicago of Sep 26, 1833, with the Pottawatamies: the sum of $88,589.32. 5-The sum of $39,901.67, to be paid by the Creek agent to the surviving chiefs of the McIntosh party of the Creek Indians, to be divided among the chiefs & warriors, the friends & followers of the late Gen Wm McIntosh, who have not received their proportion of the sum of $100,000, stipulated by the treaty between the U S & the Creek nation. 6-Settle the accounts of the companies of Texas Mounted Rangers, commanded by Capts B F Hill, J W Smith, J Roberts, J S Sutton, S P Ross, H E McCulloch, J W Johnson, & C Blackwell: shall not exceed $72,000. 6-Payment to David Taylor, rep of Cul-sut-tee-hee, or Hog, for proceeds of property sold by the U S agents, & erroneously paid by Govn'r P M Butler to another than the rightful claimant. 7-Payment to S B Lowry, for services rendered as interpreter & assistant conductor to a delegation of Winnebago Indians, Oct 13, 1846: $305. 8-Payment to Henry M Rice, for expenses as one fo the delegates from the Winnebago nation to Wash City, in 1846: $670. 9-Payment to So-le Emathla, a Seminole Indian, this amount stolen from him by U S soldiers at New Orleans: $125. 10-To the Choctaws: Life annuity to chief, [Bob Cole,] $150.

Weverton Manufacturing Co, Md: meeting on Oct 11. –John G Chapman, Pres

FRI OCT 4, 1850
The Portsmouth [Va] Pilot states that on Sat the immense boiler of the U S steamer **Saranac** was put into its place, & this ship will soon be ready for sea service. The ofcrs of the **Saranac** are: Josiah Tatnall, Capt; T L Brent, Wm O Carr, W May, Geo Wells, Lts; N Pinckney, Surgeon; J J Jones, Purser; J T Dougherty, Lt Com Marines; A N Smith, Acting Master; M Duvall, Passed Assist Surgeon; S B Elliott, J P Hall, Passed Midshipmen; B Gheradi, J D Rainey, DeG Livingston, Midshipmen; W W W Wood, Chief Engineer; J W King, W F Lynch, T A Jackson, Assist Engineers.

Foote & McCaffray, the former convicted of the murder of a young girl, his adopted sister, & the latter of the murder of 2 elderly people named Mr & Mrs Smith, were executed on Wed, at New Haven, Ct.

Appointments by the Pres: 1-Abel Underwood, to be U S Atty for the District of Vt. 2-Walter C Maloney, to be U S Marshal for the Southern District of Florida.

Postmaster Gen established the following new Post Ofcs for week ending Sep 28, 1850.

Ofc	County, State	Postmaster
New Castle	Rockingham, N H	N W Tarlton
High Ridge	Fairfield, Conn	Isaac Jones
Fillmore	Allegany, N Y	A S Dudley
Mapleton	Niagara, N Y	A B Rankin
Osceola	Lewis, N Y	R A Hubbard
Toddsville	Otsego, N Y	A H Todd
New Brighton	Richmond, N Y	Robt Morris
Knox Corners	Oneida, N Y	Jas C Knox
Kettle Creek	Monmouth, N J	Ivins Irons
Westport	Clinton, Pa	N Butler
W Brownsville	Washington, Pa	John F Dawson
Lamira	Belmont, Ohio	O G Metcalf
Dyson's	Guernsey, Ohio	S B Allison
Pipestone	Berrien, Mich	Wm Boughton
Palo Alto	Onslow, N C	D W Sanders
Kennimore	Jackson, Ala	Jacob Kennimore
Prairie Hill	Montgomery, Ala	K Jones
Oak Hill	Franklin, Ala	Israel Burns
Filton	Marion, Miss	Jordan Johnson
Sulphur Springs	Madison, Miss	Saml D Graham
Friar's Point	Coahoma, Miss	R C Fair
Palestine	Washington P, La	John McGaha
Jameson	Owen, Ky	Geo D Jameson
Tobacco Port	Stewart Tenn	Nathan Brandon
Rockbridge	Green, Ill	Geo D Rundle
Summer Hill	Stoddard, Mo	John W Pigg
Montello	Marquette, Wis	Justus N Dart

Names Changed:
Waln's Mills, Monmouth Co, N J, changed to Walnford.
Stearn's Mills, Newaygo Co, Mich, changed to Croton.
Cross Plains, Izard Co, Ark, changed to Benbrook's Mills.
Harford, Des Moines Co, Iowa, changed to Danville.

Teacher wanted: salary will be 250 or $300; school-house is situated about a mile east of the Anacostia bridge, lately owned by Mr Beale. Apply to Selby B Scaggs, Long Old Fields post ofc, PG Co, Md.

Teacher wanted: Trustees of the Rockville Academy, Montg Co, Md, wish to employ a gentleman qualified in all the branches of English education. The compensation amounts to about $500 per annum. By order of the Board: Richd I Bowie, sec.

Teacher wanted: a gentleman, raised & educated at the South, would be preferred. Address John Ravenscroft Jones, at Lawrenceville, Brunswick Co, Va.

For rent: brick house on L st, between 15th & 16th sts. Apply on the premises to Alex'r Borland, or to Jas B Clark, at Winder's bldg, 17th st west.

SAT OCT 5, 1850
Trustee's sale of valuable land in PG Co, Md. By decree of the Court of Chancery of Md, passed Aug 19, 1850, wherein Thos C Worthington & others are cmplnts, & Sarah F Contee & others are dfndnts: sale in Nov 12, all that valuable plantation called **Park Hall**, of which the late Mrs Sarah Slater died seized & possessed, consisting of about 270 acres, more or less. The estate adjoins the estate of Jos K Roberts, [the dwlg plantation of the late Govn'r Kent,] & is about 8 miles from Upper Marlboro. Improvements consist of a large brick dwlg & necessary out bldgs. –Alex'r Randall, Thos G Pratt, trustees

Horrible murder at West Chester, Pa, on Sat last. The teacher at Rocky Hill school, Phebe Sharpless, was found dead in the school, weltering in her blood. In the course of the day, Geo Pharoah was arrested on suspicion of the murder. The young lady, aged about 28, was the daughter of Aaron Sharpless.

Mrd: on Oct 3, in PG Co, Md, by Rev F S Evans, Mr Robt Downing, of Wash City, to Miss George-Anna Markward, daughter of Mr Wm Markward.

Mrd: on Thu, by Rev John C Smith, Mr Jno T Rye, of Gtwn, to Miss Martha Munroe, of Wash City.

Mrd: on Oct 3, by Rev Jas Donelan, Chas G Eckloff to Eliz Twomey, of Wash City.

Mrd: on Oct 3, by Rev Mr Alig, Mr Jas McEleyett, of Wash, to Miss Mgt Wright, of Va.

Died: on Sep 16, at Pensacola Navy Yard, Chas H Winder, youngest son of Cmder Geo N Hollins, U S Navy.

Died: on Oct 1, at Seneca Quarries, Montg Co, Md, in his 43rd year, Mr Wm Clark, a native of Murrayshire, Scotland.

Died: on Sep 28, at Jersey City, of consumption, Robt O Ellis, formerly of Wash City, in his 24th year.

Teacher wanted: at the village of Piscataway, PG Co, Md: salary is $350, payable semi-annually; good accommodation can be had for $100. Address John W Ward, Horatio Edelen, Trustees, Piscataway.

MON OCT 7, 1850
Naval appointments by the Pres. by & with the consent of the Senate.
Lts:

Van Rensselaer Morgan	Israel C Wait
Madison Rush	John H Parker
Danl Ammen	Wm B Muse
Henry Rolando	Geo W Rodgers
Andrew Weir	Archibald McRae
John S Taylor	Robt H Wynan
John H Brown	Edw A Barnett
Edw F Beale	Nathl C Bryant
Edw T Nichols	Geo B Balch
John P Decatur	Jonathan M Wainwright
Edw L Winder	Foxhall A Parker
John K Duer	Isaac G Strain

Surgeon: Edw J Rutter
Assist Surgeon: Jas F Heustis
Chaplain: Edw C Bittinger

The U S mail steamship **Southerner**, Capt Berry, when about 160 miles from the port of N Y, a sail was discovered on the larboard bow, close at hand, & coming right down upon her. It was instantly seen that a collision must take place. The Southerner's engine was reversed, but it was too late. Life-boats were manned, but the lost vessel, the barque **Israel Meade**, Capt T R Brown, which had left N Y on Wed, bound for Savannah, Ga, collided. Persons lost, as far as reported: passengers: Mrs Catherine Bradley, of Conn; Miss Harriet Grannis; Mrs Amerit Barnes, of Macon, Ga; Mrs Barnard, of Wilmington Island, Ga; Miss C Barnard, of Wilmington Island, Ga; Master John Barstown, of Wilmington Island, Ga; Dr Maginnis, lady, & child, of Macon, Ga; H Grannin, Conn; Mr Cornis, Conn; 2 Messrs Adams, of London; J H Brown, capt's son. Crew: John Smith, Mass; Francis Butler, Sanannah, Ga; Jas Draper, Dungarian Island; Robt Moore, England; Richd ___, England; cook, name unknown; Jas McGlover, N Y, 2nd cook; Mrs Crady, stewardess.

Mrd: on Oct 6, by Rev Mr Donelan, Christopher Krofft to Miss Mary Boyle, both of Wash.

Mrd: on Oct 2, at Chantilly, Fairfax Co, Va, by Rev Mr Lockwood, Louis A Cazenove, of Alexandria, Va, to Harriotte, eldest daughter of the late C Calvert Stuart, of Chantilly.

Mrd: on Sep 30, by Rev J B Condit, D D, Josiah H Davis, of Alexandria, to Mrs Sarah Wells Martin, of Newark, N J.

Died: on Sunday, Julia, wife of Mr John E Bates. Her funeral is on Mon, at 3 o'clock, from the Ebenezer Methodist Episcopal Church, near the Navy Yard.

Died: on Oct 6, in his 55th year, Robt Moore, a native of Bristol, England, but for the last 30 years a resident of Wash City. His funeral will take place today at 1 o'clock, from his late residence on 18th st, between H & I sts.

Died: on Sep 30, at **Walnut Grange**, [the residence of her mother, near Beltsville, PG Co, Md,] after an illness of 3 days, of inflammation of the bowels, Mrs Sarah Carlyle Fairfax, wife of Lt A B Fairfax, U S Navy, & daughter of the late Hon John C Herbert, of Md.

Died: on Oct 3, after a night's illness, in her 3rd year, Eliza, daughter of Wm E & Eliza M Crossfield.

Ichabod Sprague, of Riga, N Y, died on Sun last, at age 74 years. He settled upon the farm which he owned & occupied at the time of his decease, about 40 years ago. He was in a painful accident on Sep 21, riding in a buggy with his wife, when the horse kicking violently, fractured Mr Sprague's leg. Amputation was necessary on Tue, but his advanced age could not bear up against the shock. He has left numerous descendants & a large property.

Died: on Oct 4, aged 6 months & 10 days, Robt Rose, infant son of Robt R & Anne E Fitzhugh.

The Phil papers have announced the death of Mr Judah Dobson, of that city. He was for many years a prominent bookseller, having succeeded his father, Mr Thos Dobson, who was one of the earliest publishers in America. The son, Mr Judah Dobson, married the daughter of the late Zachariah Poulson, the proprietor for many years of the American Daily Advertiser. As a linquist, he had no superior in America.

The Hon Chester Butler, a worthy member of Congress, representing the 11th district of Pa, died on Sat last, in Phil, where he had arrived on his way home from Washington.

The Criminal Court of St Louis, on Sep 25, sentenced Benj Savage, convicted of aiding slaves to abscond from their owners, to 10 years confinement in the penitentiary.

Sudden death. Dr Thos Hammond, of Shepherdstown, Va, died suddenly at the Wheatfield Inn, at Balt, on Fri, from disease of the heart.

Tom Thumb's house, now bldg in Bridgeport, is said to be a remarkable edifice.

Nat'l Greys meeting this evening at the Armory, 7:30 p m. By order: Jas H Shekell, Sec.

We have this day associated ourselves together, under the name of Waters & Brown, for the purpose of transacting a general Grocery & Commission business, in the house recently occupied by John H Waters & Co. –John H Waters, Chas H Brown, Gtwn

The copartnership existing between John H Waters & Co, is this day dissolved by mutual consent. –John H Waters, J F Wheatley

Orphans Court of Wash Co, D C. Letters testamentary on the personal estate of Theresa Byrne, late of Wash Co, deceased. –Cornelius Boyle, Catharine O'Bryen, excs

Orphans Court of Wash Co, D C. Letters of administration on the personal estate of John Murphy, late of Wash Co, deceased. –John F Ennis, adm

Marshal's sale: by writ of fieri facias: sale of part of lot 18 in square 407, seized & levied upon as the property of Owen Connolly, & will be sold to satisfy judicials #114, to Oct Term 1850, in favor of Bartholomew McGowan. –Richd Wallach, Marshal D C

TUE OCT 8, 1850
Millard Fillmore, Pres of the U S, recognizes F E Dixon, who has been appointed Vice Consul of the King of the Kingdom of the Two Sicilies to reside at Phil, Pa. Oct 5, 1850.

Died: on Oct 7, in Wash City, Mary Beeler, consort of the late Lewis Beeler, aged 60 years. Her funeral will take place from the residence of her son-in-law, G W Phillips, in **Pollard Row**, at half past three o'clock this evening.

Two little boys, [6 & 8 years old,] David L Lester & Geo Lester, were murdered in Albany Co, N Y, by injuries inflicted by Reuben Dunbar & other persons unknown. Dunbar has been arrested & confined in jail. He is a step-son of David Lester, the uncle of the children. Dunbar is the son of Mrs Lester by a former husband. The elder boy was strangled; the younger boy was struck with a fatal blow. [Dec 13th newspaper: the trial of Reuben Dunbar, indicted for the murder of Stephen & David Lester, at Waterloo, on Sep 28 last, concluded on Tue with a verdict of guilty. Among the painful attendants of the case was that the prisoner had only been married 2 weeks, & that the most important witness against him was his own mother.]

Mrd: on Oct 3, by Rev Mr Donelan, Wm L Ross, of Wash, to Miss Mgt A Whelan, of Gtwn, D C.

Mrd: on Oct 1, at Brookland, Fauquier Co, Val, by Rev A D Pollock, Dr B W Allen, of Ringwood, Va, to Helen Mary, eldest daughter of Wm McCoy.

Died: on Aug 14, in Monterey, Calif, Dr Wm L Booth, Assist Surgeon of the U S Army.

The late Maj Jas Galloway, of Greene Co, Ohio, died some weeks ago, by a gangrene which attacked the extremity of the right foot. He died in his 68th year. Maj Galloway was born at the Low Dutch Station near Louisville, Ky, in 1782, son of Jas Galloway, sen, who emigrated to the Station as early as 1780, from Pa; & in 1798 emigrated to Ohio & settled in what is now Greene Co, bringing with him his family. He was a Major of militia in the war of 1812.

Situation wanted as a Wet Nurse, by a mother with a young child, who can come well recommended. Apply at Mrs Cratty's, north Capitol st, Capitol Hill.

A lost dog: strayed away from a lady at Mr Perrine Washington's, an uncommonly small dog. Liberal reward at Mr W's, F & 6th sts.

House & lot for sale: 2 story brick house on Indiana ave, near 2nd st. Apply to Chas H Lane, or to Wm Tucker, Pa ave.

WED OCT 9, 1850
Supreme Court of the U S: Dec Term, 1849, #106. John Hagan, surviving partner of the late firm of John Hagan & Co, appellant, vs Wm H Pope & Saml Brick, administrators of Leroy Pope, deceased. Mr Atty Gen Johnson, of counsel for the appellant, having suggested the death of Wm H Pope, one of the appellees in this cause, moved the court for an order, under the 28th rule of court, to make the proper reps parties. It is now ordered that unless the proper reps of said Wm H Pope, deceased, shall voluntarily become parties within the first 10 days of the ensuing term, the appellant shall be entitled to open the record, &, on hearing, have the same reversed, if it be erroneous.
–Wm Thos Carroll, clerk Sup Crt

Senate: 1-Bill for the relief of Wm Paddy: passed. 2-Relief of the children of Sarah Stokes, deceased: passed.

The Rt Rev Archbishop of Canada died at Quebec on Oct 4.

Wm Croghan: the death of this gentleman, noticed a few days ago, is likely to produce a great change in a portion of the O'Hara estate. He was the oldest son of Maj Wm Croghan, who lived in Va on the breaking out of the Revolutionary war, & served under Washington. Maj Croghan was an early settler of Ky. The subject of this notice was born there at Louisville. His sister, wife of Gen Jesup, Dr John Croghan, & Col Geo Croghan, have all died within the last 18 months. Wm Croghan took up his residence in this city some 20 years ago, & purchased a beautiful spot near whe city, where he passed a quiet life. After the fire of Apr 10, 1845, hundreds of dollars were given away by him to sufferers. The grave has seldom closed over one more constant in his acts of charity.
–Pittsburg Chron

Capt Dunham & others were dangerously wounded when the steamer **Kate Fleming**, from Louisville for Cairo, burst both her boilers on Sunday, & burnt to the water's edge. Ten others are reported killed & missing.

A fatal affray occurred at Alexandria, La, on Oct 14, between S L Wells & J W Gordon, young lawyers & cousins. Wells attacked Gordon with a cane, when Gordon shot him in the side. He died in less than 24 hours. Gordon was bailed at $1,000, a nominal sum.

The Magnetic Telegraph Co, [Morse Line,] the first ever established by any company in the U S, is now prepared to transmit any number of messages which may be required of it. The ofcs are in Washington, Balt, Phil, & N Y. –Wm M Swain, Pres

$400 reward for arrest and delivery to the D C Marshal of Claudius Matthieu, who stands charged with the unlawful killing of J L Skidmore, in Wash City, Sep 18. Matthieu is a white man, born in Phil, aged about 34 years. Address Capt Goddard, Wash.
–Walter Lenox, Mayor of the city of Washington.

Mrs Grafton, the mother of the mate of the barque **Georgiana**, now under sentence of death in Havana for participation in the Lopez expedition, has made a pilgrimage to Cuba to solicit mercy for her son. She took letters from Mr Webster & the Spanish Minister at Wash to the Count Alcoy. He promised to represent the case.-N Y Sunday Times

Died: on Sat last, in Wash City, of consumption, Mrs Mary M Remington, in her 33rd year, leaving a large circle of friends to mourn her loss.

For sale: the place in Montg Co, Md, near Poolsville, part of *Hermitage*, late the property of Dr John Bowie, containing between 200 & 300 acres. Address Geo W Bowie, Upper Marlboro, Md.

Deed of trust from Saml C Forbes, dated Oct 1, 1845, recorded in Liber W B 123, folios 385 thru 389, of the land records of Wash Co, D C, I shall offer at public sale on Oct 8, lot 4 in the subdivision of lots 1 & 2, in square 556, in Wash City. –D A Hall, trustee -Dyer & McGuire

In Chancery. J & J Williams & Co, vs Jas Williams, Jno V Emick, P L Cox, trustee, S Stettinius, & others. The cmplnts, at Oct term, 1847, of the Circuit Court of D C, recovered judgment against Jas Williams for $500, with interest from Jul 1, 1846, & costs; that an execution was levied on goods & chattels in possession of said Williams, which were replevied by Lemuel Williams, & are not sufficient to satisfy said judgment; that the only other property of Jas Williams consists of an equitable interest in lots 26 & 27, in reservation 10, lot 9 in square 457, & lot 2, in square 160; that said Jas Williams conveyed lot 9, in square 457, to P L Cox, to secure certain notes executed in his favor amounting to $2,416, by indenture recorded Liver W B 129, folios 361, & conveyed all the aforesaid property to Lemuel Williams to secure notes endorsed by Saml Stettinius & others, by indenture recorded in Liber W B 134, folios 234, & executed certain other deeds of trust of lot 27, reservation 10 aforesaid. It further states that sundry judgments were obtained against said Williams prior to that of cmplnts, one a judgment in favor of Jno V Emick for $385, with interest from Dec 19, 1840, with costs. It prays that the property aforesaid may be sold to pay off the incumbrances & judgments according to their priority; &, forasmuch as P L Cox, S Stittinius, & Jno V Emick are non-residents, asks an order of publication against them. Same to appear in court on or before the 4th Monday of Mar. –Jas S Morsel, Assoc Judge Circuit Court of D C

THU OCT 10, 1850
We regret to learn of the total destruction by fire of the First Presbyterian Church & Session House, under the pastoral care of Rev W H Hornblower, in Paterson, N J, on Sat last. Some persons had been repairing the work of the spire, in doing which fire had been used in soldering, & from this it is supposed the accident took place.

On Sat last, during the thunder storm, lightning struck Mr Michl Kahoe, while at work on the steeple of the First Presbyterian Church, now in progress of erection in this village. He survived the injury only a few hours. –Watertown [N Y] Reformer

The New Orleans Bulletin notices the item going the rounds of the press, that Mrs Connor, of Washington, [who claims to be the widow of Gen Van Ness,] had come into possession of a property in New Orleans of $500,000, & says the article is based on the fact that Mrs Connor is one of the nieces of Mr Jos Fowler, of New Orleans, recently deceased. Mr Fowler had 6 brothers & sister, who either survive or have left children, & Mrs Connor will therefore come in for one-sixth part of the estate, as one of the heirs at law, as Mr Fowler died without a will. Her share will fall very far indeed below $500,000, as the entire estate will not exceed $1,200,000.

Died: on Sep 30, at his residence, near Marlborough, PG Co, Md, Philemon Chew, in his 62nd year, after a long & distressing illness.

$5 reward for return of a lost horned cow. –Juliet V Howison, 9th st, between E & F sts.

House for rent or lease: I have just finished & have ready, one of the best houses in our city. It is near G & 10th sts, & has good water, & a pump of the very best being in the kitchen. -Jas Caden

A lovely young lady, Miss Anna R Neil, the daughter of Jesse Neil, died very suddenly on Thur, through a mistake in preparing a prescription at the apothecary store of Dr Chamberlain. Dr Scoffin prescribed 30 grains of quinine to be divided into 6 doses, one every 3 hours. Dr Chamberlain, being out of town, his store was in charge of a young man, a student of medicine, who sent 30 grains of morphine, instead of the quinine. –Phil Ledger

FRI OCT 11, 1850
Mrd: on Oct 8, in the First Baptist Church, 10th st, by Rev O B Brown, Mr Henry H McPherson, jr, to Miss Mary A Clarke, daughter of Isaac Clarke. Also, Mr Wm J H Dorsey to Miss Josephine A France, daughter of John France.

Died: yesterday, in Gtwn, after a long & painful illness, Mr Wm Grindage. His funeral is this afternoon at 4 o'clock from Mrs Lang's Hotel.

I certify that Francis Morrow, of Wash Co, D C, brought before me a stray Mare.
-John D Clarke, J P [Owner is to prove property, pay charges, & take her away.
-Francis Morrow, 17th & R sts, Wash.]

Millard Fillmore, Pres of the U S, recognizes Philippe Jacques Franz, du Canton de Berne, who has been appointed Consul of the Swiss Confederation for Michigan, Wisconsin, Iowa, & Minnesota, to reside at Detroit. Also, recognizes J B Fah, du Canton de St Gall, who has been appointed Consul of the Swiss Confederation for Louisiana, Mississippi, Alabama, Tennessee, & Arkansas, to reside at New Orleans. –Oct 9, 1850

U S ship **John Adams**, Madeira, Aug 28, 1850. Passed Midshipman Thos B Wainwright, late acting master of this ship, died on Aug 14. He was reported ill 2 days after leaving Portendick, on the coast of Africa, supposed to arise from inflammation of the stomach, & daily became worse, after 15 days' illness. The body of the deceased was given to the deep on Aug 15. –L M Powell, Cmder

Mount Zephyr for sale: on Dec 19, the above named farm, containing about 600 acres, lying in Fairfax Co, Va: a portion of the original **Mount Vernon** estate, & was devised by Judge Bushrod Washington to the subscriber, in trust for the children of Bushrod Washington, jr, deceased. The improvements are a 2 story frame dwlg & out bldgs. Mr St Shuster, residing on the farm, will show it. Any further information will be given by the subscriber at Gtwn, D C. –G C Washington, trustee

Orphans Court of Wash Co, D C. Letters of administration on the personal estate of Chas R Edelen, late of said county, deceased. –Richd J Wood, adm

Notice: I do hereby forwarn all persons from harboring or employing my black boy Benj Reid, known to be in this city. He is about 14 years of age. –John D Harrison, Alexandria, Va

Senate: 1-Cmte on Revolutionary Claims: asked to be discharged from the further consideration of the ptn of Fred'k Vincent, administrator of Le Caze & Mallet, & from the further consideration of the ptn of the heirs of Edw Buncombe. 2-Cmte on Finance: discharged from the further consideration of the ptn of Wm A Seely.

For rent: a small farm on North Capitol st, adjoining the land of Mr David Moore & Capt Boyle, about a mile & a half from the city. It has a very neat 2 story frame dwlg with necessary out-bldgs. Inquire of Mr Geo E Moore, on the premises.

SAT OCT 12, 1850
Appointment by the Pres: Robt G Campbell to be Secretary to sign, in the name & for the Pres, all patents for lands sold or granted under the authority of the U S, in place of Edmund M Evans, resigned.

Rev O B Brown, having resigned the Pastorship of the First Baptist Church of Wash, 10th st, was succeeded by Rev Stephen P Hill, of Balt, on Oct 1.

The following is a list of persons who have taken out licenses under the laws of the Wash Corp during the months of Jul, Aug, & Sep, 1850.
<u>Bunker Hill</u>: Bartholomew & Co [1 week]

<u>Cart license:</u>
Ashton, C H B
Bryan, John
Beckett, W
Deevers, L

Jasper & Fink
Jackson, Pomfrey
Kendall, G W
Mudd, J T

Pumphrey, R-2
Pearle, Rezen
Peterson, Eliz
Prather, O J-2
Stone, Thos

Simms, J M-2
Talburt, Wm
Winchester, Robt
White, Geo
White, Patrick-2

Dog license:
Brenner, P
Bruner, W
Boses, Martin
Beale, Robt
Coltman, C
Croggin, Isaac
Conner, John
Davis, W-2
Dawes, Rufus
Ehrmantrout, Jos
Eliot, Johnson
Edelin, Sarah
Freeland, Susan
Ferral, Dennis-2
Hess, J P
Hedgman, J G
Haliday, A
Jones, J B
Jameson, E
Keese, A E L
Kidwell, A C
Kloman, Chas
Kirby, Saml
Kelcher, J
Lord, Wm

Laub, J Y
Lusby, J W
Lee, Chas
Magruder, Fielder
Norman, J
Nicholls, J N
Narden, Jos
Naser, Ellen
O'Mara, W C
Peters, Thos
Pendleton, A G
Peterson, Eliz
Riley
Raub, J P
Ricard, J G A
Rutter, Emilia
Riggs, jr, E
Sauter, John
Shaine, John
Simmons, John
Stonestreet, Wm
Thomas, Chas E
Tibbitts, E
Tasker, Thos

Concert: Nightingale Serenaders-4

Hack: Masi, Vincent; Poston, J F

Hats, caps, etc
Bastianelli & Co, T
Brawner & Co, W H
[transfer]

Combs, R M
Hyatt, R
Magruder, T J

Huckster:
Brereton & Bro
Bayliss, C
Cruit, Jas

Davis, A
Donaldson, E G
Fernstein, Peter

Gross & Co, J
Hughes, Rebecca
Mackey, Wm
McNier, Wm
Morrison, Robt
Mankins & Gates
Och, Geo
Preston, W

Scott, John
Stewart & Co, J C
Simms, J M
Tucker, Jas
Webb, A J
Wilson & Co, J L
Wollard, H-2

Merchandise:
Brown, J D
Hyatt, R G
Hodgkins & Meredith
King, Thos S
Lutz, F A
Lehman, Chas
Lusby, J M
Midherst & Heard

Munch, C H
Newton, Aug A
Rose, Susan V
Sinon, Louis
Tucker & Co, S M
Webb, A J
Worthington, T H
Wakeling, Igs

Retail:
Brawner & Co, W H
Fenwick, J H
Kleindienst, Jno P
Lloyd, J M
Noland, S S

Olive, Henry
Quigley, Francis
Reeves, John C
Sullivan, Timothy
Tuomey, Jeremiah

Shop:
Christopher Boyle
Bridewell, Moses T
Collins, Dennis
Gensler, Henry
Kuhl, H

Kutzenberger, John
Rainey, S A
Schad, B
Schwartz & Ruper
Usher, John W

Slut: C Wilcox

Stage: Reeside & Vanderwerken-2

Stages: Trustees Joint Stock Co-2

Tavern: Columbus & Burch; Ehrmantrout, Jos

Theatrical: Adelphi Theatre

Wagon:
Beale, Robt-3
Buckley, T K

Carroll, D
Donovan, W

Green, A
Henke & Maack
King, Thos S
Mason, E
Queen, Henry E

Simms, J M
Stewart, Geo
Skirving, Jas
Visser, J & J

Persons fined during the months of Jul, Aug, & Sep, 1850.
Allen, J H: theatrical
Bouer, John: selling liquor
Eberback, Jno H: concert
Entwisle, Wm B: slut
Farnham, Robt: dog
Farrel, Dennis: dog
Hughes, Wm: selling liquor
Hughes, Wm: selling liquor on Sunday
Knoblock, John: slut
Lewis, Wm B: selling liquor
Santmeyer & Piper: theatrical-2
McElfresh, Wm: dog
McQuigley, Mary: selling goods
Rupple, G: selling liquor on Sunday
Schwearing, F: selling liquor on Sunday
Simmons, Louis: selling goods
Wall, Columbus O: wagon
Young, Wm: slut

Wash City Ordinances: 1-Act for the relief of Isaac Newton: that the fine imposed on him for running a wagon without its being numbered, is remitted, the said Newton paying the costs. 2-Act for the relief of Isaac Newton: to refund to him $5, the sum having been paid by him for an fine imposed on him by Wm Thompson.

Dissolution of copartnership under the firm of Shanks & Wall, by mutual consent. -M Shanks, Wm Wall. [Mr Wall will continue the business.]

For rent: on Nov 7, the 3 story house on Pa ave, near Gadsby's Hotel, now occupied by Dr Towle. –Edw Sims

Hong Kong, Jul 22, 1850. The U S flag ship **Plymouth**, from a 5 months' cruise, arrived at Macao on the 9th inst, & is now at Hong Kong. All well. The ship **Marion** is at Macao, with several mild cases of sickness on board. The ship **Dolphin** sailed today for Manilla & San Francisco, on her way to Boston. Her ofcrs were almost entirely changed previous to her departure, & are now as follows: Thos J Page, Lt commanding; Gustavus V Fox, Exec Ofcr; Geo P Welsh, Acting Lt; Clark H Wells, Acting Lt & Master; Owen Jones Wister, Assist Surgeon; John J Cornwell, Midshipman; Chas L O Hammond, Midshipman; Jas Y Hudson, Capt's Clerk; Richd P Robinson, Master's Mate.

The Portsmouth [Va] Pilot states that Capt Hugh N Page has received orders to repair to the Pacific squadron, & take command of the U S frig **Savannah**. He will depart in the steamer of the 20th for Calif.

Dept of State, Wash, Oct 11, 1850. The Charge d'Affaires of the U S at Rome has informed of the decease of John L Pell, of New Orleans, who died at Aguapendente, in the Papal States, on Aug 28. His effects were to be transferred to the Legation of the U S at Rome.

Mrd: on Oct 3, at Knightly, Talbot Co, Md, by Rev Dr Spencer, Lt Col R C Buchanan, U S Army, to Sallie Murray Winder, daughter of the late Capt Edw S Winder, U S Army.

Died: on Oct 11, Mrs Caroline Sophia DeVaughan, wife of Thos S DeVaughan, in her 30th year. Her funeral is Sunday, at 4½ p m, from her late residence on 4th st.

Died: on Oct 11, Percy Lee, aged one year & 2 weeks, son of Wesley T & Matilda King. His funeral is from the residence of G W Venable, at 3 o'clock, this evening.

MON OCT 14, 1850
For rent: 4 story house on Md ave [Island,] between 6 & 7th sts. –John P West

I certify that Chas W Fowler, of Wash Co, brought before me as an estray, a red cow. –J L Smith [Owner is to prove property, pay charges, & take her away. –Chas W Fowler, about 2½ miles from old Bladensburg rd.]

Wash City Items: improvement on Louisiana ave: Within the last few years the handsome dwlg of Mr B F Middleton has been erected on the south side of La ave, & the dwlg, now occupied by Mr Stettinius, was enlarged & elevated so as to present a noble front. Very recently Mr W A Bradley has enlarged & raised his handsome dwlg, on the same side of the avenue. On the opposite side Mr Hellen has erected a handsome 4 story brick bldg, which reflects much credit upon the contractor, Mr Morsell. The removal of a rickety frame bldg next to the residence of the Hon D Webster, adds to the improvements.

Mrd: on Oct 10, by Rev Mr Hodges, Mr Geo T Allen to Miss Mary Brown, all of Wash City.

Mrd: on Oct 8, in Martinsburg, Berkeley Co, Va, by Rev D F Sprigg, Dr Edw Jaquelin Harrison, of Cumberland Co, Va, to Miss Betty Carr, eldest daughter of David Holmes Conrad.

For sale: the farm now occupied by the subscriber on Columbia Turnpike, in Alexandria Co: with comfortable improvements. –Saml D King

Wanted immediately, for the Md Military Academy, an experienced Classical Teacher, an unmarried gentleman. Address John H Allen, Oxford, Talbot Co, Md.

Trustee's sale of real estate in Washington: by deed of trust from Bazil Simms, in favor of the undersigned, dated May 20, 1846: sale of lot 5 in square 790 on Pa ave, with a 2 story frame dwlg & rope walk. Also, after the sale of the above: lot 5 in square 791, & lots 18 & 19 in square 795. –W M Addison, trustee

Household & kitchen furniture at auction: on Oct 17, at the residence of Mrs Braden, Pa ave, between 14th & 15th sts. –Dyer & McGuire, aucts

Household & kitchen furniture at auction: on Oct 17, at the residence of Madam Clavadatcher, on Pa ave, between 9th & 10th sts. –Dyer & McGuire, aucts

Household & kitchen furniture at auction: on Oct 18, at the 2 houses occupied by Mr Hackney, on 11th & D sts. –Dyer & McGuire, aucts

TUE OCT 15, 1850
Household & kitchen furniture at auction: on Oct 17, at the residence of Capt E B Boutwell, at 14th & N Y ave. –Green & Tastet, aucts

Trustee's sale: by decree of Montg Co Court, as Court of Equity, passed in the case of Wm Holmes, administrator of Richd Holmes & others, vs John Braddock, the subscriber, as trustee, will offer on Nov 5, parts of lots 40 & 41 in the town of Rockville, Montg Co, which was mortgaged by John & Iver Campbell to Wm Holmes, & afterwards sold by Richd Holmes to John Braddock, on which there is a large brick bldg, situated for a boarding-house or tavern, & formerly known as Dawson's tavern. –R J Bowie, trustee

Orphans Court of Wash Co, D C: sale of furniture on Oct 16, at the late residence of E J Sylvester, on Bealle st. –Ed S Wright, auct

The opening of the Chesapeake & Ohio Canal, so far completed as to be in a navigable condition from Cumberland to tide water, was celebrated on Thu last, in Balt.

Trustee's sale of valuable property at auction: by deed of trust from Richd W Cook & wife, dated Dec 8, 1848, recorded in Liber J A S #1, of the land records of Wash Co: sale on Nov 15, of lot 16 in square 950, on G st, between 9th & 10th sts, with a substantial frame house. –Walter Lenox, Henry Naylor, trustees -C W Boteler, auct

Household & kitchen furniture at auction: on Oct 21, at the residence of Lt Shields, on Capitol Hill, near the north Capitol gate. –Green & Tastet, aucts

Trustee's sale of very valuable property at auction: by deed of trust from Chas H Van Patton & wife, dated Feb 21, 1848, recorded in Liber W B 142, of the land records of Wash Co, D C: sale on Nov 16, of lot 1, in subdivision of lots 1 & 2, in square 490, on C st. Also, part of lot 25 in square 490. Improvements are valuable, being the premises formerly occupied by the late Dr Thos Sewell. –Walter Lenox, Henry Naylor, trustees -C W Boteler, auct

By 2 writs of venditioni exponas, I will expose to public auction, on Nov 16, all the right, title, & interest in & to lot 6 in square 75, together with the improvements thereon, in Wash City, D C, as the property of Thos Llewellin, seized & taken in execution at the suit of Michl Thompson. –H R Maryman, constable

WED OCT 16, 1850
Wash Corp: 1-Bill for the relief of J H Eberbach: passed. 2-Bill for the relief of Patrick Flynn: referred to be Cmte of Claims. 3-Ptn from J C Fitzpatrick & others, asking for a change in the grade of B st south: passed. 4-Bill for the relief of Chas Stewart: decided in the affirmative. 5-Ptn of Jas Kinslay for remission of a fine: referred to the Cmte of Claims. 6-Bill for the relief of Wm A Mulloy; act to pay Saml Curson for removing a nuisance in the 3rd Ward; & the act for the relief of E G Handy: reported without amendment. 7-Cmte of Claims: asked to be discharged from the further consideration of the ptn of Jas H Blake, praying the payment of a prize ticket in a certain lottery: report was agreed to.

Mr Wm Burdick, of Newport, R I, while eating supper on Wed, choked himself with a piece of beefsteak & died. –Courier & Enquirer

Ladies with letter remaining in the Wash Post Of, Oct 15, 1850.

Alvey, Mrs Mary	Cooke, Mrs C A
Bennett, Miss Clara	Cuthbert, Miss A B
Barnard, Mrs E A	Crannin, Miss F
Beall, Miss Eliza	Clemens, Mrs M A
Bell, Miss Eliz	Carroll, Maria
Burman, Mrs E	Christian, Miss M
Bell, Miss Eliza B	Casey, Mrs Sarah
Brooks, Mrs Julia	Crooks, Mrs S E
Barber, Mrs J L	Carlon, Miss Sallie
Blake, Miss F J	Davis, Mrs Arena
Blake, Mrs J M	Devaughn, Miss C
Bleart, Laura	Dayton, Mrs H C
Blair, Mrs	Dalton, Mrs Susan
Brown, Mrs M B	Devaul, Mrs
Beard, Mrs Matilda	Dunlop, Mrs Mary
Beall, Mrs Mary G	Donelan, Miss Susan
Butler, Miss M J	Edmonson, Miss E
Ball, Mgt A	Eyre, Miss Sarah
Bosworth, Mrs	Forbes, Miss Eliz
Baggett, Miss O	Fenwick, Miss M V
Becket, Miss Ruth	Green, Mrs A E
Brown, Mrs Rebecca	Gales, Miss A M
Bowles, Miss Sylvian	Grimes, Mrs Cath
Barry, Mrs Sarah	Gibbons, Miss E
Brown, Miss C J	Geoghan, Miss E
Bell, Mrs John	Galloway, Mrs F A

Greene, Mrs Henry
Gardiner, Mrs M
Hailstock, Mrs Ann
Hayes, Mrs Mgt
Howard, Mrs Eliza
Howard, Miss E
Hays, Miss Honor'h
Haust, Miss Kun'de
Hume, Mrs Priscilla
Hunt, Mrs Maria
Jones, Mrs Eliza D
Johnson, Mrs Mary
Jordan, Mrs Pauline-2
King, Mrs C C
Kidwell, Miss Ellen
Kissick, Mrs Jane-2
Longdon, Mrs Eliz
Lowrie, Mrs Eliz
Lewis, Mrs Lucy
Lucas, Mary
Leech, Miss Mary A
Larner, Mrs Mary
Lucas, Miss Mary J
Miller, Mrs Anna
Martin, Emily
Morton, Mrs Ellen
Miles, Kitty
Middleton, Mrs
Maurice, Mrs Maria
Morris, Mrs Matilda
Madella, Mrs Rebec
McCarthy, Miss H
Neil, Miss Eliz
Naylor, Miss Mary
Nelson, Miss Marg
Noble, Patsy T
O'Bryan, Mrs John
Osborn, Miss M
Oldom, Virginia
Page, Mrs Dora
Pope, Mrs Eliza
Porter, Mrs Eliza
Potter, Miss A M
Posey, Mrs Mary K
Peters, Mrs Mary
Paterson, Sarah
Raub, Mrs Ann E
Ratcliff, Catherine A
Rosier, Miss C
Roby, Miss Eliz
Raggan, Miss Mary
Rice, Mrs Maria
Robinson, Mrs M J
Raggio, Nicolla
Rice, Miss Sallie
Royston, Miss Sarah
Shoemaker, Mrs A
Sullivan, Miss Ann
Sullivan, Catherine
Smith, Miss E
Smith, Miss Eliza B
Starbuck, Miss Annie
Smith, Miss Rachel F
Smith, Miss Virginia-2
Stewart, Miss Frances
Tyler, Miss Ann T
Thompson, Miss B
Thornton, Mrs Jane
Throckmorton, Mrs Mary
Triplet, Mrs Sarah
Vance, Miss Mary J
Williams, Miss B
Wilson, Mrs C S
Williams, Hillery S
Ward, Mrs Mary L
Williamson, Mrs Maria A
Wallace, Mrs N F
Whitney, Miss S A
Young, Miss Fanny
Young, Miss Marg
Young, Miss Addie
Young, Mrs Sarah A
-Wm A Bradley, P M

Obit-died: on Oct 6, Mrs Julia H Bates, consort of John E Bates, who departed after a brief illness of a few hours; a young lady of fervent piety, & a consistent member of the Methodist Episcopal Church. Her bereaved mother & devoted husband mourn her loss.

Mrd: yesterday, by Rev Littleton F Morgan, Mr Jos Hedrick, formerly of Va, to Miss Susan Jane, eldest daughter of Mr Saml McElwee, of Wash City,

Mrd: on Oct 15, by Rev John C Smith, J M Tastet to Harriet Mason, daughter of Thos Mustin, of Wash City.

Mrd: on Oct 15, by Rev J C Smith, David Walker to Kate E, daughter of Thos Mustin, both of Wash.

Mrd: on Thu last, by Rev Mr French, Mr John Henry Berckmann, formerly of Frankfort on-the-Maine, to Mrs Mary Ann Wilson, of Wash.

Died: on Oct 12, Mrs Henrietta Collins, aged 32 years, consort of Jas H Collins.

For rent: brick dwlg, 2 stories, garrets, & basement, on First st, in the most pleasant part of Gtwn. Apply to W H Tenney

Valuable farm for sale: on Oct 30, the Farm on which Saml M Beall formerly resided, & now under rent to Saml K Beall, lying on the road leading from Seneca to Gtwn. farm is divided into 2 tracts, one containing 165 acres, & the other 60, with a frame dwlg & out-bldgs. –Josephus Beall, at Rockville, Montg Co, Md

Orphans Court of Wash Co, D C. Letters of administration on the personal estate of John W Butler, late of Wash Co, deceased. –Edw Owens, adm

THU OCT 17, 1850
Waterloo for sale: this Farm, on which the late Josiah Tidball resided, near the village of Upperville, in Fauquier Co, Va, contains about 800 acres. The dwlg house is handsome & comfortable, with all out-bldgs suitable to a gentleman's residence. Communicate with either of the undersigned, residing in Winchester, Va: Thos A Tidball, or Jas Marshall, excs of Josiah Tidball, deceased.

City Item: a white woman of very dissipated habits, named Mgt Loman, was found dead yesterday in a stable behind *Hazell's row*, on Capitol Hill.

Mrd: on Oct 15, at the Relay House, by Rev A D Jones, Wallace Eliot, of Wash, to Miss Eugenia E Lowe, of Balt Co.

Mrd: on Oct 15, by Rev Mr Dana, Lt W W Russell, U S Marines, to Virginia, daughter of Capt Geo Fletcher, of Alexandria, Va.

Mrd: on Oct 9, at Trinity Church, N Y, by Rev John Blake, Chaplain U S Navy, Capt W A T Maddox, U S Marine Corps, to Miss Sarah E W Moughon, daughter of the late Wm Moughon, of Columbus, Georgia.

Mrd: on Oct 15, at **Mount Pleasant**, by Rev Jas B Donelan, Mr Terence Drury to Mrs Louisa O'Neal, eldest daughter of Louis Vivans.

Died: on Oct 15, after a short illness, Jane Willet, aged 24 years. Her funeral is today at 2 o'clock, from the residence of Mrs Eliz Smoot, on 7th st east.

Died: on Oct 8, of consumption, Mary Jane Stone, aged 10 years, daughter of the late Wm B & Sally Stone, formerly of Stafford Co, Va.

Battles of the Revolution:

Were fought	When fought	American Com	Loss	British Com	Loss
Lexington	Apr '75		84		245
Bunker Hill	Jun '75	Warren	453	Howe	1,054
Flatbush	Aug '76	Putnam	2,000	Howe	400
W Plains	Oct '76	Washington	300	Howe	300
Trenton	Dec '76	Washington	9	Rahl	1,000
Princeton	Jan '77	Washington	100	Maw'd	400
Bennington	Aug '77	Stark	100	Baum	600
Brandywine	Sep '77	Washington	1,200	Howe	500
Saratoga*	Oct '77	Gates	350	Burg'e	600
Monmouth	Jun '78	Washington	230	Clinton	400
Rhode Island	Aug '78	Sullivan	211	Pigott	260
Briar Creek	Mar '79	Ashe	300	Prevost	16
Stoney Point	Jul '79	Wayne	100	Johns'n	600
Camden	Aug '81	Gates	720	Cornwallis	523
Cowpens	Jan '81	Morgan	72	Tarle'n	800
Guilford	Mar '81	Greene	400	Cornwallis	523
Eutaw Springs	Sep '81	Greene	555	Stewart	1,000

*5,752 British taken prisoners.
The surrender of Cornwallis at Yorktown, Oct, 1781, closed the war: prisoners 7,073.

Trustee's sale of improved property at auction on Oct 28, by deed of trust from Arnold Bowie, recorded in Liber J A S 12, folios 241 thru 244, of the land records of Wash: sale of lot 12 in square 55, with a neat frame tenement. –C W Boteler, auct

Appointments by the Pres: 1-Chas S Todd, of Minn, Oliver P Temple, of Tenn, to be Com'rs to procure information, collect statistics, make presents to & treaties with the Indian tribes on the borders of Mexico, as authorized by the act of Congress approved Sep 30, 1850. 2-Geo W Barbour, Redick McKee, & O M Wozencraft, to be Com'rs to make treaties with Indians in Calif, as authorized by the act of Congress approved Sep 30, 1850. 3-Simeon Francis, of Ill, to be Indian Agent in Oregon, vice Anson G Henry, resigned.

Public auction: by decree of the Circuit Court of Wash Co, D C, sitting in Chancery, in a cause wherein Richd Owen is cmplnt & John Ennis & others are dfndnts: sale on Nov 8, of lots 5 & 6 in subdivision of part of lot 5, in square 518, with a 2 story frame house, fronting on north H st, near 5th st. –John F Ennis, trustee -Green & Tastet, aucts

Notice: the heirs at law [non-resident] of Fanny Lindsay, deceased, being Opie Lindsay, Thos Lindsay, Robt Lindsay, & Wm Lindsay, sons of Opie Lindsay, late of this county, or their reps, are notified that I am prepared to pay over to them, or their proper atty, their respective dividends of the said decedent's estate. –Thos Moore, adm of Fanny Lindsay, deceased: Fairfax Court-house, Va.

Orphans Court of Wash Co, D C. Letters of administration, with the will annexed, on the personal estate of Geo W Taylor, late of said county, deceased. –Rebecca Taylor, admx de bonis non W A.

FRI OCT 18, 1850
We learn by a Brief of his holiness Pope Pius IX, dated Jul 19, the See of N Y has been erected into an Archiepiscopal See, with the Sees of Boston, Hartford, Albany, & Buffalo as Suffragan Sees. By this the Rt Rev Bishop Hughes is elevated to Archbishop.

Mrd: on Oct 15, by Rev E Ballantine, John C Whitwell, of Wash, to Augusta, daughter of the late Augustine Newton, of Alexandria, Va.

Died: on Thu last, in Germantown, Pa, Chas Provest, aged 46 years. He was Burgess of the borough at the time of his death, & a most valuable citizen. He was suddenly called by a short but severe illness, in the vigor of his years.

Marshal's sale: by writ of fieri facias under the lien law, I shall expose to public sale, for cash, on Nov 11, all the right & title of John Rynex in: bldgs erected on lots 2 & 3, in Peter's, Beatty's, Threlkeld's, & Deaken's addition to Gtwn, on south side of Water st: purchased by Rynex from Miller & Duvall, consisting of a large brick moulding house: to be sold to satisfy judicials 68, in favor of Wm C & Simon J Temple.
–Robt Wallace, late Marshall of D C

Household & kitchen furniture at auction: on Oct 22, next door to the residence of Judge Cranch, at the residence of a gentleman declining housekeeping. –Green & Tastet, aucts

Rare chance for a good business: being desirous of emigrating to Calif, I offer my stock of Groceries & unexpired term of lease. Inquire personally or by letter to Wm C Harper, High st, Gtwn.

Fulford Boarding School for Boys, near Sandy Spring Post Ofc, Montg Co, Md, will commence on Nov 12. –Isaac Bond, Principal Teacher. Anna Stabler, Principal of the Boarding Dept.

SAT OCT 19, 1850
Westchester Village Recorder: Mr Jos Hunt, one of the oldest residents of the county, was seized with symptoms of hydrophobia on Tue, & after suffering much pain & anxiety, died on Fri following. He was a man of robust constitution, about 70 years of age. To relieve his sufferings, chloroform was administered by inhalation.

Five men have been arrested who are believed to be the perpetrators of the daring robbery of the U S mail on Sat in Phil. The prisoners are Thos Veich, Jas Bell, Thos Brannin, John McCarty, & Robt McDowell.

Millard Fillmore, Pres of the U S, recognizes Gustavus Street, who has been appointed Vice Consul of Brazil, at Charleston, S C. Oct 17, 1850

Mrd: on Oct 17, at the Second Presbyterian Church, Alexandria, by Rev J N Danforth, Mr Alfred Campbell Belt, of Loudoun, to Miss Mary Rebecca Mills, of Alexandria. Also, John D Beach to Rosetta Whaling.

Mrd: Oct 17, by Rev Mr Hodges, Mr Alfred Burdine to Miss Lucy Ann Beyer, all of D C.

From Calif: 1-The following passengers, on board the ship **Crescent City**, died on the passage between Chagres & N Y: John W Haskill, of Boston; Edw Cuthbert, of Newbern, N C; Saml Strickland Rodman, of N Y; & John Houghton, of Windsor, Vt. 2-Mayor Bigelow, of Sacramento city, since the amputation of his arm, is fast recovering. 3-Henry M Nagle, an extensive banker, has failed for a very large amount. This caused a run on all the banking houses, but they have held out, with the exception of the one mentioned.

Household & kitchen furniture at auction: on Oct 23, at the residence of Mrs Tims, on Capitol Hill, [the flag will designate the house.] -Green & Tastet, aucts

MON OCT 21, 1850
The Postmaster Gen has est'd the following new Post Ofcs for week ending Oct 12, 1850.

Ofc	County, State	Postmaster
Morristown	Lamoille, Vt	J C Noyes
S Royalton	Windsor, Vt	Lyman Benson
W Hawley	Franklin, Mass	T S Allen
Rock Valley	Hampden, Mass	R W Ludington
West Haven	New Haven, Conn	Jas Reynolds
Moore's Forks	Clinton, N Y	P P Douglass
Bull's Head	Dutchess, N Y	F B Schultz
Clinton Furnace	Dutchess, N Y	Paul C Upton
Perry's Corner	Dutchess, N Y	A Levings
Caughderoy	Oswego, N Y	Wm H Rice
Hayfield	Crawford, Pa	Wm V Morse
Rundell's	Crawford, Pa	M Rogers
Highville	Lancaster, Pa	Jacob Miller
Limetown	Washington, Pa	M Sanders

Fallen Timber	Cambria, Pa	J Hartzell
Whittlesey	Medina, Ohio	Earl Moulton
Oakfield	Kent, Mich	W Horton
Holly Neck	Nansemond, Va	J S Haslitt
Gilmer's Store	Guilford, N C	J W Gilmer
Mellburg	Grenville D, S C	John Weaver
Chinquepin Gr	Gwinnett, S C	S H Freeman
Melendez	Benton, Fla	Wm Hope
Kowaliga	Tallapoosa, Ala	J G Yarbrough
Atwood	De Kalb, Ala	Thos Logan
Valley Grove	Lafayette, Miss	F Holmes
Hancock	De Soto, Miss	R C Hancock
Longtown	Panola, Miss	J S Fowler
Albemarle	Assumption P, La	M Albagnac
Wadeboro	Livingston, La	Chas Myers
Lake Charles	Calcasieu, La	John Hager
Blue's Point	Crittenden, Ark	Spencer Hall
Nolansville	Bell, Texas	W D Eastland
Providence	Wilson, Tenn	P C Baird
Palmyra	Simpson, Ky	Wm B Jones
Brown's Valley	Montgomery, Ia	John D Stilwell
N Stewart	Orange, Ia	John W Rice
Pearl Prairie	Pike, Ill	David Hess
Raneysburg	Washington, Ill	Wm Raney
Ash Ridge	Pulaski, Ill	J B Mabry
Birch Pond	Crawford, Mo	E Inman
Goggin's Mills	Macon, Mo	Sterling Coulter
Pennys	Macon, Mo	John H Penny
Hall	Lawrence, Mo	L J Estes
Spring Mills	Crawford, Mo	B Eldridge
Yellow Springs	Des Moines, Iowa	Elijah Wood
Hopkin's Grove	Polk, Iowa	Josiah Hopkins
Willow Creek	Marquette, Wis	A P Noyes
Oregon	Dane, Wis	Egbert Bennett
Sacramento	Marquette, Wis	B F Longworthy
Syracuse	Marion, Or T	Jacob Couser

Names Changed:
Morristown, Lamoille Co, Vt, changed to Morrisville.
Ironville, Blair Co, Pa, changed to Tyrone.
Aukenytown, Knox Co, Ohio, changed to Shaler's Mills.
Poinsett, Hamilton Co, Indiana, changed to Nicklesonville.
Wahcootah, Wabashaw, Minnesota Terr, changed to Red Wing.
Adamsville, Panola Co, Miss, changed to Moon.
Scott's Ferry, Albemarle Co, Va, changed to Scottsville.

On Sep 22 thirty-five persons dined at the camp of Saml Saffell, at Middle Settlement camp-ground, in Blunt Co, Tenn. They were all taken violently sick, & soon discovered that arsenic had been mixed with the food. Mr Saffell & his niece, Mrs Longbottom, died shortly after. No clue as to the fiend who perpetrated the awful deed.

Wash Corp Ordinances: 1-Act to pay Saml Curson for removing a nuisance in the Third Ward: sum of $22 paid to Curson. 2-Act for the relief of Philip Mohun: sum of $22.56 paid to him, the balance of his bill for laying a flag footway. 3-Act for the relief of Chas Stewart: to be paid $437.90 for work done on lowering the pavement on Pa ave & E sts.

Mscl: 1-Wm S Carman, formerly of N Y, died at San Francisco. He was riding in the city & took hold of the twig of a tree which penetrated his skin, & later was discovered to be poison. –Pacific News of Sep 15. 2-Mr Harper, from Wash, was shot at Mariposa mines on Sep 2 by the accidental discharge of his pistol. [Oct 28th newspaper: Regarding the death of Mr Harper, from Wash. May Heaven sustain an aged & widowed mother, overwhelmed with grief by this untimely event.]

By deed of trust from C Eckloff & wife, recorded in the land records of Wash Co, D C, in Book W B 147, folios 90 to 95, we shall sell, on Nov 23, parts of lots 1 & 2 in square 292, in Wash City, which front on Pa ave, upon which is a 2 story brick dwlg & back bldgs. -Green & Tastet, aucts

Orphans Court of Wash Co, D C. Letters of administration on the personal estate of Talliaferro M McIlhany, late of said county, deceased. –Ann McIlhany, admx

Mrd: on Oct 10, at St Louis, Mo, by Rev E C Hutchinson, R S Holmes, M D, [late of the army,] to Annie M, daughter of Maj Benj Walker, U S Army.

Died: in Calif, by accidentally falling from the steamer **Yuba** on her passage from Marysvlle to Sacramento, Mr Henry C Duralde. He was the son of the late Martin Duralde, of New Orleans, & a grandson of the Hon Henry Clay, by whom he was reared, as his mother died when he was quite a child. [No death date given-current item.]

Died: on Sep 24, in the Cherokee nation, Dr Wm Butler, Agent for the Cherokees. In the war of 1812 he was a Surgeon in the Navy, but retired to private life; was then after several years elected to Congress from the Pendleton & Edgefield districts, S C. He was a brother of the present Senator from S C.

Fatal accident at West Point, on Sep 15, which resulted in the death of a daughter of the late Prof Kinsley. Mrs K was taking a drive with her son & 2 daughters, in a carriage drawn by one of Capt Duncan's artl horses, which became alarmed & ran off, when one of the ladies caught one rein & drew the horse to the side of the road, where there was a stone wall. The animal leaped the wall, dashing the carriage to pieces, killing the youngest child, & seriously injuring Mrs Kinsley, her son, & other daughter.

Died: on Oct 2, at *Oak Hill*, the residence of his mother, in Fairfax Co, Va, Capt Andrew Fitzhugh, U S Navy, in his 56th year.

TUE OCT 22, 1850
$10 reward for return of a dark sorrel Horse, which was missed from the commons on Oct 6. Supposed to be stolen. –Lloyd Cross, Md av, between 9th & 10th sts, Wash.

Phil papers announce the death of Cmder Edmund Byrne, of the U S Navy, which occurred at his residence in Bristol township on Thu last. He entered the Navy in Feb, 1814.

On Tue last, Catherine Leonard, residing in Reade st, NY, was cruelly beaten by her husband, Peter Leonard, while intoxicated, & died from its effects. Leonard was arrested & committed to prison.

Appointments by the Pres: 1-Thos Butler King, Collector of the Customs, San Francisco, Calif. 2-Saml Barney, Collector of the Customs, Monterey, Calif. 3-A Randall, Surveyor of the Customs, Santa Barbara, Calif.

Mr Wm E Gilbert, in the employ of the Ordnance Dept, was killed at San Antonio, Texas, on Sep 21. He was shot by Mr Yarrington, who it is stated, acted in self defence. Mr Gilbert having broke a cane over his shoulder & inflicted a shot wound in his back with a revolver. He was admitted to bail in the sum of $1,000.

Died: on Oct 19, Thos L Thruston, eldest son of the late Judge Thruston, of Wash City. He was well known & highly esteemed in this community. His death will be long lamented by his family, as well as by a very numerous circle of friends.

Died: on Oct 21, of consumption, Mrs Sally Stone, formerly of Stafford Co, Va, leaving an amiable family to mourn her loss.

Mr Edw E Haviland & his Albert H Clarke, left West & Co, on Mon last, on a gunning excursion. A sudden gust of win capsized the boat & Mr Haviland died on Mon. Mr Clarke got on shore. They both came in the steamship **Republic** some 3 weeks since. He is from N Y C; Clarke is from Pa. –San Francisco Herald

WED OCT 23, 1850
E H C Griffith, arrested in Rochester in Sep of last year on a charge of robbing the post ofc in that city, had his trial before the U S Circuit Court last week, & was acquitted.

One day last week a dispute occurred between David Masters & Henry Johnson, near Millville, about some buckwheat growing on a piece of land in dispute between them. A scuffle ensued, & the wife of Johnson threw a stone at Masters, which accidentally hit her husband on the head & killed him. –Columbia [Pa] Democrat

Died: on Oct 17, at the residence of his father, at Binghampton, N Y, Manco C Dickinson, only son of the Hon Danl S Dickinson, aged 22 years, a young man of high promise & attainments.

Died: on Oct 22, in Wash City, Jas B B Wilson, in his 32nd year. His funeral is this evening at 4 o'clock, from **Smith's Row**, Gtwn.

Died: on Oct 8, Mrs Susannah Spalding, a native of St Inigoes, St Mary's Co, Md, but for the last 40 years a resident of this District, in her 61st year.

Died: on Oct 21, Cecelia Rose, youngest daughter of Richd L & Martha E Spalding, aged 2 years. Her funeral is this day at 3 o'clock, on 5th st, 3 doors from K st.

Died: on Oct 8, at Holland, Mass, Lucius F, son of Rev Amos Babcock, aged 22 years. For nearly 5 years the deceased lay without being moved an inch, or a change of clothes being made. This could not be done without putting him in great agony,&, in the opinion of about 20 physicians who were consulted, without causing death. The original cause of his condition was a shock occasioned by his making a misstep or slide on the brink of a precipice, where nothing but a small twig or bush saved him from instant death.

Died: on Oct 22, suddenly, of convulsion, Mary, eldest daughter of Wm & Laurantine Ryan, aged 3 years, 3 months & 18 days; a child of unusual loveliness, but unhappily as delicate as beautiful. Her funeral is today at 3 P M, from their residence, F st near 15th st.

Notice: we have this day associated with us Mr Chas St J Chubb as a member of our firm, which will hereafter Chubb, Schenck & Co. –Chubb & Schenck

Dissolution of the law partnership of Davidge & Semmes, on Nov 20 next. Walter D Davidge will continue the practice. Thos J Semmes will remove to New Orleans & practice his profession in that city.

THU OCT 24, 1850
The remains of the lamented Pres Taylor will be removed from Wash tomorrow, in the 6 o'clock train to Balt, in charge of Col Jos P Taylor & Col Bliss. They will proceed from Baltimore by an express train to N Y, thence by the Pa railroad to Pittsburg, & from there by an Ohio steamer to Louisville, Ky, the appointed final resting place of the old Patriot. [Nov 1st newspaper: the remains of the late Pres Taylor arrived at Pittsburg on Sun, & on Mon were escorted to the steamboat landing by a procession, civil & military, in which the citizens generally united.] [Nov 2nd newspaper: the remains of Gen Taylor reached Louisville, Ky, yesterday, & were buried in the family cemetery, 8 miles from the city. There was a solemn procession & a general suspension of business on the occasion.]

Mrd: Oct 22, by Rev V Palen, Mr Ferdinand Perpignon to Miss Eliz Mills, both of Wash.

$100 reward for the apprehension & conviction of the person or persons who set fire to my premises on Oct 22. –S M Burche

By Geo White, of Alexandria. Com'rs sale of real estate, by decree of the Circuit Court of Alexandria Co at its Jun term, 1850: public auction on Nov 2, of that beautiful tract of land, of which John Biddle Chapman died seized, in said county, containing 465½ acres. The estate will be divided into 4 parts. –Jos H Bradley, Christopher Neale, Com'rs Mr Jas Birch, who lives adjoining, will show the land.

The U S sloop-of-war **St Mary's**, Cmder Magruder, bound to the Pacific, dropped down to Hampton Roads on Mon. The following is a list of her ofcrs: Cmder, Geo Magruder; Lts, Wm S Young, Jas S Biddle, Robt H Wyman, John J Walbach; Lt Marines, G R Graham; Passed Assist Surgeon, John S Abernethy; Assist Surgeon, Richd H Tunstall; Master, Thos G Corbin; Passed Midshipmen, Jonathan Young, D A Forrest, T A Forrest; Midshipmen, Wm H Ward, Robt M Caldwell, Augustus Lodge, Benj Loyall; Boatswain, Geo Williams; Carpenter, Jas Meade; Cmder's Clerk, John Curry, jr; Purser's Steward, A W Hancock; Gunner, ___ Hutchinson; Sailmaker, W B Fugett.

Furnished house for rent. Inquire of W H Upperman, Pa ave, Wash.

FRI OCT 25, 1850
Wash Corp: 1-Bill for the relief of Geo Garrett: passed. 2-Bill for the relief of J E Dunawin: passed.

The remains of the late Com Jacob Jones are to be removed from Phil to Wilmington, Del, for final interment, on Sat next. He was the gallant son of Delaware.

Trustee's sale of Fancy Dry Goods, on Nov 1, in the store of Saml T Drury.
-Fred'k Fickey, trustee -Dyer & McGuire, aucts

Died: on Oct 23, Jesse E Dow, a native of Conn, but for many years a resident of Wash City, & recently a member of the City Council. He was much esteemed for his literary talents & amiable dispostition. His funeral is tomorrow, at 12 o'clock, from his late residence on G st, between 14th & 15th sts.

SAT OCT 26, 1850
N Y Evangelist: Congressional Burying Ground: for years the question has been asked, What shall be done with **Mount Vernon**? While it remains in the family of Washington, the public are at ease. My mind glows that the mighty dead of our nation be gathered as they fall at Washington in the public service, & be gathered around the Father of the country. Let the janitor occupy the house, while it shall stands, & improve the farm. What a place of interest it would be. Never would the remains of John Quincy Adams or John C Calhoun have been transported to their distant homes could they have found a resting-place beside the Father of his country. Let **Mount Vernon** become the **Mount Auburn**, the **Greenwood**, the **Mount Hope** of the country. –M J

The Zanesville Gaz records the death of Mr & Mrs John Grieve, who were in the habit of rowing & sailing up the Muskingum in the afternoons, & taking their evening meal along.

Tue their boat was found bottom side up, & the shawl & basket of Mrs Grieve. Their bodies had not been found.

In the U S District Court, at Balt, on Thu last, Henry Rehren & August Kesting, 2 of the Germans convicted of transmitting forged papers to the Pension Ofc in this city, to obtain land warrants, were sentenced to the Penitentiary for 10 years each. Wm Ogden Niles, of Wash, through whose unwearied energy in the public service these frauds were ferreted out, received a written commendation, signed by the jurors & ofcrs of the Court.

MON OCT 28, 1850
P M Deshong, the professed mathematician, died on board the steamer **City of Toronto**, between Kingston & Toronto, on Oct 19. His death was caused by apoplexy.

Judge Gantt died on Oct 18 at his residence in Greenville, S C, in his 86th year. He was raised to the Bench in 1815, & held that position until 1842, when he resigned.
–Charleston Mercury

A counterfeit note manufactory was broken up at St Louis on Oct 17, & Henry Lovejoy, an engraver, Alvin Bowen, & Mr McAfee were taken into custody.

City Ordinances-Wash. 1-Act for the relief of A C Kidwell: pay him $10.63, the balance due for relaying & widening the gutter on square 457. 2-Act for the relief of Jas A Wise: the fine imposed on him for a violation in relation to riding across pavements, is remitted, provided he pay the cost of prosecution. 3-Act for the relief of Chas Dyson: fine imposed for violation of the law in relation to huckstering is repealed, provided he pay the cost of prosecution. 4-Act for the relief of B Jose: $10 be paid to him, to reimburse him for fine imposed by Saml Drury. 5-Act for the relief of Jesse Williams: the fine imposed for violation in relation to burying dead animals, is remitted: provided he pay the cost of prosecution. 6-Act for the relief of John H Mullen: $10 to be paid him, being the amount erroneously paid by him to constable John S Hutchins. 7-Act for the relief of E G Handy, a police constable, to be paid $126.43, in full settlement of his accounts to Jul 1, 1850. 8-Act for the relief of John A F Tottchinder: to be refunded $10, the sum paid for a fine imposed on him. 8-Act for the relief of Geo W Garrett: fine imposed on him for $40, for hiring 2 slaves who had not been registered, is remitted: provided he pay the costs of prosecution.

Among the passengers in the steamer **Europe**, which left N Y on Wed for Liverpool, were the brothers Montesquieu, who had been confined at St Louis for some time on the charge of murder. One was proved innocent & the other declared a maniac.

TUE OCT 29, 1850
The undersigned, having resolved to abandon his present business, offers for rent his large & well known public house, the Columbian, corner of E & 8th sts. Possession given immediately. –J H Eberbach

At a Circuit Court of Louisa Co, on Sep 13, 1850: Wm R Hackett & Edw Poindexter, excs of Jas Michie, deceased, plntfs, against Sarah Bramham, Mary McArthur, Ann Johnson, Geo Michie, John Tatum & Eliz his wife, ___ Michie & Ann his wife, Robt Michie, Janetta Michie, John Michie, Matthew Michie, Jos Michie, Robt G Willis & Eliza his wife, Sally Chiles, Geo Bramham, Bushrod Bramham, Jas Bramham, John Bramham, Caroline F Bramham, Ellen Bramham, Harriet Bramham, Jas M Bramham, Caroline Winston, Ann Winston, Ada A Winston, Bickerton T Winston, Fred'k Fleming, Wm Fleming, & John Fleming, Matthew Anderson, Mary E Anderson, Saml M Anderson, Sarah A Anderson, & Ella Carr Anderson, dfndnts. John Hunter is appointed guardian ad litem for the infant dfndnts, Mary E Anderson, Saml M Anderson, Ella Carr Anderson, Fred'k Fleming, Wm Fleming, John Fleming, Caroline Winston, Ann Winston, & Ada Ambler Winston, whereupon the said infants, by their said guardian ad litem, filed their answer, & the subpoenas in this cause appearing to have been duly executed upon all the dfndnts, Sarah Bramham, John S Bramham, Carolien F Bramham, Ellen Bramham, Harriet Bramham, Janetta Michie, Bushrod W Bramham, Caroline Winston, Ann Winston, Ada Ambler Winston, Bickerton T Winston, Robt Michie, Matthew Anderson, Mary E Anderson, Saml M Anderson, Sarah A Anderson, & Ella Carr Anderson, & more than 2 months having elapsed as well since the return day of the said subpoenas as since the filing of the plntfs' bill, & the said dfndnts still failing to appear & answer, the said bill is taken for confessed as to them; & the plntfs having proceeded in the mode prescribed by law against all the non-resident dfndnts, to wit: Jas M Bramham, Geo H Bramham, Mary McArthur, Geo Michie, Ann Johnson, John Michie, Matthew Michie, Jos Michie, Robt G Willis & Eliza his wife, Sally Chiles, John Tatum & Eliz his wife, ___ Michie & Ann his wife, & the said non-resident dfndnts still failing to appear & answer the bill is taken for confessed as to them also. Whereupon this cause came on to be heard upon the bill taken for confessed as aforesaid, & the exhibits filed therewith, & the answer of the infant dfndnts, & was argued by counsel on consideration whereof the court is of opinion, & doth decide, that the widow, Henrietta Michie, not having renounced the provisions of her husband's will, her executors are not entitled to any portion of the personal estate as to which he died intestate, but that the same must be divided among his next of kin, according to their respective rights & interests. The court is further of opinion, & doth decide, that the legacy in favor of the slaves created a trust in the widow & executrix for their benefit, which they could not enforce, but which she was authorized to carry into effect as far as she chose, & that the amounts paid out for or distributed among them are to be credited against the estate, whether paid out by her or the succeeding executors prior to this date, but that the whole of the said legacy, now remaining unpaid, lapses & falls into the undisposed of portion of the estate, & is distributable in like manner. The court is further in the opinion, & doth decide, that the legacies referred to in the bill carry interest in favor of the legatees, respectively, from the end of the year, in which the widow, who was the life tenant, died. And the court doth adjudge, order, & decree that one of the commissioners of this court shall state & settle the accounts of Henrietta Michie, as executrix of Jas Michie, deceased, & also the accounts of the plntfs as executors of the said Jas Michie, deceased; in making which settlement he shall take as a basis the exparte settlements already made, but subject to be surcharged & falsified by any of the parties. The said commissioner shall also state & settle legatee accounts with the respective legatees, under the will of Jas Michie, deceased, the said commissioner shall, as to the undisposed of portion of the estate of Jas Michie, deceased, state a distribute account, showing among whom & in what proportions the same must be distributed; in order to enable him to do which he is directed to advertise, in one or more newspapers printed in Richmond, Wash City, for all persons claiming to be next of kin & distributes of said Jas Michie, deceased, to appear before him & prove their relationship; & the said commissioner shall report to the court the names & residence of all persons who are next of kin & distributes of said Jas Michie, deceased, & the shares of his estate to which they are entitled. –John Hunter, clerk [Parties interested in the foregoing decree are to proceed to take the accounts therein directed at my ofc, in Louisa court-house, Va, on Feb 12 next. –F W Jones, Com L C C]

Wash City: elected School Trustees last night:

R Farnham	T Donoho	J W McKim
J F Haliday	V Harbaugh	S Byington
G J Abbot	Jas Adams	W B Randolph
P F Bacon	F S Walsh	P M Pearson

Final examination of Wm Greason, charged with assaulting & robbing Wm Richards of his pocket-book, containing $1,190, on Oct 21, took place yesterday. He was dismissed the assault charge, but held to bail in the sum of $1,200 on the charge of robbery. On the charge of assault & battery, made by Greason against Richards & his brother, the justice decided to hold them to bail in the usual sum to answer at the next Criminal Court.

Telegraphic dispatch from New Orleans says: Hon John M Harmanson, Rep in Congress from La, died here on Fri last, after a lingering illness. John McDonough died here of cholera on Sat. He was a native of Baltimore, a noted miser, estimated to be worth over 10 millions of dollars. [Oct 30th newspaper: Mr John McDonogh, of New Orleans, whose death we mentioned yesterday, has bequeathed one eighth of the net revenues of his estate during 40 years, not to exceed $25,000, to the Colonization Society. He settled in New Orleans while Louisiana was a colony of Spain. He employed a clergyman for regular religious services for his numerous slaves, to all of whom he gave some education. He amassed an immense fortune, estimated at several millions of dollars.] [Nov 6th newspaper: Mr McDonogh was buried on Sep 27 in the cemetery erected by himself, near his residence at **McDonoghville**, for his negroes. In his will he left $6,000 & some landed property in Balt to his sister & her children.]

Virginia: in the Circuit Court for Clarke Co, Oct 14, 1850. In Chancery. Nathl Burwell, exc of Nathl Burwell, deceased, plntf, against John Bannister, Wm Barrow, Francis Bright, Wm Lewis, Matthew Moody, Matthew Friss, Susannah Riddle, & others, creditors of Gen Thos Nelson, deceased, dfndnts. The plntf in this cause, Nathl Burwell, exc of Col Nathl Burwell, the elder, having departed this life, the suit abates as to him; & the adms de bonis non, with the will annexed of the said Nathl Burwell, the elder, having been granted to Robt T Baldwin, high sheriff of Fred'k Co, who has filed his bill of reviver & supplemental bill, & the dfndnts therein named having filed their answers, on motion of the plntf it is ordered, that the suit be dismissed as to the other dfndnts mentioned in the original bill, & by consent of parties, it is ordered that this suit stand

revived in the named of the plntf, Robt T Baldwin, sheriff, adm de bonis non, with the will annexed of Thos Nelson, deceased, Wm F Wickham, adm de bonis non, with the will annexed of Jas Maclurg, deceased, & John Thos Briggs, exc of Thos Hunt, who was surviving partner of Thos & Rowland Hunt, merchants, of London; whereupon, by like consent, this cause came on this day, to be heard on the original bill, the bill of revivor & supplememtal bill, & the answers & exhibits, & was argued by counsel. On consideration whereof the Court doth refer it to Hugh H Lee, master com'r of the Court, to take an account of all claims against the estate of Gen Thos Nelson, deceased, provided for in the deed of Jan 30, 1788, & of the trust fund referred to in the proceedings in this cause; &, after making a deduction for all reasonable charges & the costs of this suit, that he apportion the same among the creditors, & in doing so he is to take for correct the statement made by Robt Andrews, Robt Saunders, & David Jamison, in the proceedings referred to, unless good cause to the contrary be shown before him by some of the parties concerned, & report to the Court with such matters as he may deem pertinent, or any of the parties may require. It is ordered, that Hugh H Lee, the receiver in this cause, do forthwith call in all moneys lent out from the said trust fund, that the same may be ready for distribution at the next term of this Court. All creditors of Gen Thos Nelson, deceased, are required to appear within 4 months, to do what is necessary to protect their interest, the object of this suit being to distribute the fund arising from the sale of Gen Nelson's property among his creditors.
–Hugh H Lee, C C [Feb 24, 1851, is the day fixed for taking the account directed by the foregoing decree, at the courthouse of Clarke Co, Va[&.

The Postmaster Gen has est'd the following Post Ofcs for the week ending Oct 19, 1850.

Ofc	County, State	Postmaster
Dugway	Oswego, N Y	John B Kellogg
West Berlin	St Clair, Mich	John Whitcomb
Mamskating	Sullivan, N Y	Wm Jordan
Patchin	Erie, N Y	Geo Brindley
Martinsville	Niagara, N Y	Abner D Hunt
Gentsville	Walton, Fla	John Gent
Portland	Whitesides, Ill	Solomon M Seely
Seneca	Whitesides, Ill	Wm Maynard

Re-established: Hickory Tavern, Harford, Md: John Waun.

Mrd: on Oct 24, at Pittsburg, by Rev T B Lyman, Geo S Lovett, of Wash City, to Caroline, daughter of Anthony Beelan, of Pittsburg.

Died: on Oct 27, Mr Wm A Clements, in his 41st year. His funeral is today at 11 o'clock, at his late residence, on 5th st, near Mass ave.

Died: on Oct 27, in full assurance of a blessed immortality & eternal life, Mrs Cecelia Hallaran, in her 78th year, consort of the late Wm Hallaran, a native of England, & for the last 35 years a resident of Wash City. Her funeral is this afternoon at 3 o'clock, from her late residence, on 8th st, near H st.

Died: on Oct 22, at Middleburg, Va, Miss Caroline Virginia Turner, daughter of the late Maj Thos Turner, of Kinloch.

WED OCT 30, 1850
Orphans Court of Wash Co, D C. Letters of administration on the personal estate of Malichi Lowe, late of said county, deceased. –Eliz Lowe, admx

Orphans Court of Wash Co, D C. Letters of administration on the personal estate of Eliz Gale, late of said county, deceased. –L D Gale, exc

Died: yesterday, at the residence of his brother-in-law, J F Wollard, on 9th st, John M Porter, after an illness of 3 weeks, in his 36th year. His funeral is today at 3 o'clock.

Died: yesterday, suddenly, at the City Hotel in Wash City, Mr L Jacobs, of Arkansas.

Estray cow came to my premises. Owner is to prove property, pay charges, & take her away. –Wm Holmead, near the old Race Course.

Household & kitchen furniture at auction: on Oct 30, at the residence of Mrs Totten, on 14th st, between F & G sts. –Dyer & McGuire, aucts

THU OCT 31, 1850
Valuable real estate at private sale: having been appointed trustees by the last will & testament of Isaac Riley, late of Montg Co, deceased, to sell the parcel of land of which said Riley died seized & possessed, lying on old Gtwn road, adjoining the land of Richd Magruder & others: contains 85 acres, with a frame dwlg house & log kitchen. Property shown by Saml W Magruder, who lives in the immediate neighborhood. If not sold by Nov 25, it will be disposed of at public auction. –Saml W Magruder, Edw M Veirs

Farm & abundance of ship & bldg timber & wood land for sale: in PG Co, near Scaggs' Crossing, on the Balt & Wash Railroad: with a good 2 story dwlg house: contains 363 acres. Refer to Mr Boteler, my present tenant, or to Thos Baldwin, of Bladensburg. Apply to the subscriber, Leonardtown, Md, for terms. –H G S Key

Judge Jas Wilson died at his residence in Steubenville, Ohio, on Thu last, of cholera morbus, aged 64 years. He died after about 12 hours' severe suffering. He was temporarily editor of the Aurora, in Phil, while Col Duane was absent in the army in 1812-1813. Mr Wilson removed to Steubenville & became the proprietor & editor of the Western Herald, which he continued to publish for more than 25 years. The papers prior to that time was published by Col John Miller, 19th Regt of Infty, the same who distinguished himself at *Fort Meigs*, & during the war with Great Britain, & was afterwards Govn'r of Missouri. –Cincinnati Gaz

Mayor Barker arrested again. The Mayor of Pittsburg was arrested on Sat, charged, on oath of John Barton, with an assault & battery with intent to kill. Col John Ross became security in the sum of $3,000, conditioned for his keeping the peace.

The Grand Jury of Manchester, N H, have found no bill against the Wentworths, who were charged with the murder of Jas Parker at Manchester 6 years ago, & they have been finally discharged.

Household & kitchen furniture at auction: on Nov 4, at the residence of Dr Towle, Pa ave & 3rd st. –Green & Tastet, aucts

Balt, Oct 30. The grandson of Gen Lafayette arrived last evening, & is stopping at the Eutaw House.

Persons having claims against a balance due from the U S to Geo Darling, seaman, deceased, to present them at the ofc of the 4th Auditor of the Treasury within 2 months from Oct 30. Treasury Dept.

I forewarn all persons from buying or trading for 2 notes drawn by the subscriber & made payable to Danl Rowland, one for $19.61 & the other for $75, as I have sufficient offsets against the same. –O E P Hazard

Milton James was hung at Mount Carmel, Ill, on Oct 11 for the murder of Jos K Miller. At least 5,000 persons witnessed the execution, of whom 1/3rd were females.

Mrd: on Oct 29, by Rev Wm Matthews, Geo D Livingston, of N Y C, to Miss Anne C Sweeny, daughter of the late Geo Sweeny, of Wash City.

Mrd: on Oct 29, by Rev Jas P Donelan, Mr Edw Dawson to Miss Virginia Hurley, all of Wash City.

Mrd: on Oct 27, by Rev G G Goss, Mr Jos F Norwood to Miss Virginia Leach, both of Wash City.

Mrd: on Oct 29, in St Ann's Church, at Annapolis, by Rev Mr Nelson, Passed Midshipman Robt F R Lewis, U S N, to Henrietta, only daughter of the late Dr Thos Cowman.

FRI NOV 1, 1850
Wash Corp: 1-Ptn from Jas A Williams in relation to license to keepers of livery stables: referred to the Cmte on Finance. 2-Ptn from John A Sauer, asking to be indemnified for damages sustained by him by an error in locating his lot by the Surveyor, upon which he had made an improvement: referred to the Cmte on Improvements. 3-Cmte of Claims: bill for the relief of Patrick Flynn: rejected. 4-Cmte of Claims: asked to be discharged from the further consideration of the ptn of Philip Ennis: discharged accordingly. 5-Ptn from Nicholas Snyder for remission of a fine: referred to the Cmte of Claims. 6-Act for the relif of W W McCreery: passed. 7-Ptn of John F Coyle & others, for conveyance of water to Missouri ave: referred to the Cmte on Improvements. 8-Cmte of Claims: discharged from the further consideration of the ptn of J W McElfresh, asking the remission of a fine. 9-Act for the relief of John Cox: read twice.

The N Y papers announce the death of Benj De Forrest, one of the oldest & most respectable merchants of that city. He died on Sunday, at the advanced age of 80 years.

Mrd: on Oct 23, in Stanton, Va, by Rev T T Castleman, Peirce Crosby, U S N, to Matilda S, daughter of J C Bowyer.

Died: on Sep 23 last, at Louisville, Ky, of consumption, after a long & painful illness, Miss Catharine Connelly, late of Wash City.

Died: on Oct 25, in Petersburg, Va, Bessie Stanly, youngest child of J Travis & Mary Armisted Rosser, aged 3 years, 4 months & 11 days. Blessed are the dead, she has gone to God.

Millard Fillmore, Pres of the U S, recognizes Fred'k A Stokes, who has been appointed Vice Counsul of the Oriental Republic of Uruguay for the port of Galveston, in Texas. Oct 30, 1850

I hereby forewarn all persons against buying or trading for 3 promissory notes drawn by the undersigned, dated Sept 16, 1850, to Francis Selden: for $50; for $75; & another for $75. For good reasons I will not pay them. –B Milburn

The subscriber offers for sale part of lot 8 in square 461, being the premises known as the Steamboat Hotel, on 7th st, between Pa ave & the canal; part of lot 3 in square 292 on Pa ave, between 12th & 13th sts, with a warehouse now occupied by Mr O'Bryon & others, with 2 small brick tenements on D st; lot 4 in square 371, with improvements, corner of 10th & K sts; lot 11 in square 299, on Md ave; lots 1, 2, & 11 & 22, in square 368, 9th & M sts; lots 1 & 10, at 9th & Mass ave; lot 2 in square 865; & lot 12 in square 559. Terms & other information made known upon application to the subscriber. –Walter Lenox

SAT NOV 2, 1850
The Postmaster Gen has est'd the following Post Ofcs for the week ending Oct 26, 1850.

Ofc	County, State	Postmaster
Okanchee	Waukesha, Wis	Albert McConnell
Brewer's Station	Putnam, N Y	J F Frost

Names Changed:
Mud Creek, Steuben Co, N Y changed to Savona.
Oramel, Allegany, N Y, changed to Rounsville.

Capt Johnson, of the yacht **Twilight**, has succeeded in recovering the statue of the Hon John C Calhoun, which was lost some months ago from a vessel that was wrecked off Fire Island. The statue has been but slightly injured. Part of the right arm, mostly covered by drapery, has been broken.

Mrd: on Thu, by Rev John C Smith, Mr Henry W Darnall, of PG Co, to Miss Ann E Moore, of Wash City.

Circuit Court of Wash Co, D C-in Chancery. Wm H Irwin against Alex'r H Lawrence, adm, & Priscilla Dines, heir-at-law of Hanson Dines, deceased. By decree of said court, I will offer at public auction, on Nov 13, part of square 797, in Wash City, on south I st; & also lot 12 in square 798. –Richd H Laskey, trustee -John Martin & Co, aucts

Died: on Nov 1, in Wash City, Mrs Bridget McGowan, in her 50th year. Her funeral is this afternoon, at 2 o'clock, from her late residence, on G st, near N J ave.

First Canal Boat from Cumberland: the first boat laden with coal has reached this city, direct from Cumberland. Those present can never forget the scene on Jul 4, 1828, when the then Chief Magistrate of the Republic broke ground on the Chesapeake & Ohio Canal, amid all the pomp & circumstance of a splendid civic festival..

MON NOV 4, 1850
Fatal occurrence on Sat evening, as the cars were on their way to Balt, a man named Dalton jumped off the platform of the car in which he was a passenger and the cars passed over his legs. He survived only about 2 hours.

Circuit Court of Culpeper Co, Va, on Mon last, the Grand Jury were sworn and a number of witnesses summoned in the matter of Wm Grayson, [a free negro charged with the murder of David H Miller, who had been found guilty, but to whom the General Court granted a new trial, & who had been forcibly taken from the jail & hung by a crowd of people] were sent before them. The Grand Jury, after deliberation, refused to make any presentment. –Alex Gaz

Boarding: Mrs Jane Taylor, on Pa ave, between 4½ & 6th sts; transient boarders by the day, week, or month. [Ad]

Accident at Orono, Maine, last Tue, when workmen were removing edgings, near Babcock mills, four were drowned: Jos Clark, of Orono, owner of the property, aged about 55; Jos W Wilson, of Palmyra, who leaves a family of 2 children in Bangor; John W Whiton, of Saco, unmarried; & Saml A Curtis, of Exeter, aged 24, unmarried. Mr Clark leaves a widow & several children, some of whom are grown up.

Murder in Motamensing, Phil: on Mon night, Mr Slaven, a watchman, was shot. He died on Fri from his wounds. This is the 6th murder within a few months in that district. -Phil Inquirer

Mr Edw Winden was killed in Parsonfield, Me, on Oct 14th. He was shot at while obtaining fruit from a neighbor's garden. A man with him was severely wounded.

TUE NOV 5, 1850
Forrest Hall Restaurant, in Gtwn, fitted up to serve friends & the public. Located in the basement of Forrest Hall & will be opened on Nov 6. –Jas H Holtzman, Proprietor, has 10 years in the business.

Mr John D Johnson complains that too much credit has been awarded to him for having recovered the statue of Mr Calhoun. He says the Hon Hugh Maxwell, collector of this port, has been constant in valuable counsel, & rendering effective aid through the services of the U S cutter **Morris**, Capt Waldron, who, with ofcrs & crew have been for months waiting for its rescue. Mr Whipple, of Boston, in his marine armor, has also for a long time rendered aid, without which all other efforts would have been fruitless.

For sale, a likely negro woman, about 30 years of age, & is a plain cook, ironer, & washer, & farm hand. Apply to Dr Melvin, F st, & 9th & 10th sts, on the Island.

To the heirs of Jesse Jopling, deceased: under decree of the Circuit Superior Court of Albemarle Co, Va, pronounced in the case of Jas Jopling & others against R B Patteson, adm with the will annexed of Jesse Jopling, deceased, & others, I will disburse a sum of money to each of the cousins [or their descendants] of the said Jesse, viz, the children of Jas Jopling, Joshiah Jopling, Thos Jopling, Martha Griffin, Ann Childress, Jane Davis, Rebecca Martin, Lucy Powell, & Hannah Allen. –D J Hartsook, Receiver, Howardsville, Va

Died: yesterday, Mary, infant daughter of Francis & Josephine King, aged 2 months & 21 days.

Public sale of the most valuable property in Wash City: by decree of the Circuit Court of Wash Co, D C-in Chancery, wherein John Withers is cmplnt & the heirs & reps of Jas Long are dfndnts: public auction on Nov 30, on the premises, the houses & premises at the corner of Pa ave & 6th st, in Wash City. –Jos H Bradley, Richd Wallach, trustees

WED NOV 6, 1850
Hon Saml Young died at his residence in Ballston, N Y, on Sunday, it is supposed of aopolexy. He was about 72 years old. He filled many stations under the State Gov't.

It appears on the Danvers Bank case, that there is some doubt whether John C Page, the son of the cashier, who was shot by Mr Bateman, the watchman, under the impression that he intended to rob the bank, had any such intention at all. He had been out on a drunken frolic and was left near the door of the bank, in which his father lived, drunker than he had ever been seen before, returning in a carriage from Salem, about 2 a m.

A Life of Maj Lemuel Purnell Montgomery, a gallant ofcr of the U S army, who was killed at the battle of the Horseshoe on Mar 27, 1814, is in preparation by Rev J T Headley, & is to be published by Baker & Scribner, 145 Nassau st, N Y C. Maj C P Montgomery, a brother of the deceased, will act as an agent to collect materials for the work. –N Y Evening Post

Mrs Ann H Clark will open Winter Millinery on Nov 7 at her fashionable saloon, Gtwn.

New Shoe Store just opened on E & 7th sts. –B F Duvall

Appointments by the Pres: 1-Alex'r Ramsay & Richd W Thompson, to be Com'rs to negotiate a treaty with the Mississippi & St Peter Sioux Indians for the extinguishment of their title to lands in Minnesota Territory, & with Indians & half-breeds for the extinguishment of their titles to the lands on the Red River of the North, in said Territory, under the first section of the act of Sep 30, 1850. 2-Thos Foster to be Sec to said Commission. 3-John H Rollins, Jesse Stem, & John A Rogers, to be special Agents for the Indian tribes in Texas, under the same act. 4-Ethelbert W Saunders, to be Register of the Land Ofc at Cahaba, Ala, vice Alanson Saltmarsh. 5-Hardy Herbert, to be Register of the Land Ofc at Montg, Ala, vice Duncan B Graham. 6-Edw A Taylor, to be Register of the Land Ofc at Demopolis, Ala, vice Lewis B McCarty. 7-Wm Judge, to be Register of the Land Ofc at Sparta, Ala, vice Wade H Greening. 8-Wm B Figures, to be Register of the Land Ofc at Huntsville, Ala, vice Jno J Coleman.

Dr Alex'r Y P Garrett, of Va, has resigned his position as Passed Assist Surgeon in the navy, & will devote himself to the practice of medicine & surgery in this city.

Mrd: on Nov 5, at the Wesley Chapel Parsonage, by Rev Wm B Edwards, Mr Robt C Stevens to Miss Christiana, daughter of Mr Benj E Gittings, of Wash City.

Mrd: on Nov 4, in Gtwn, D C, by Rev Dr Ryder, S J, Wm B Fitzgerald, U S Navy, to Clara, daughter of the late Raphael Semmes.

Died: on Mon, Mrs Mary H Wilcox, consort of the late Chas G Wilcox, in her 68th year. Her funeral is this evening at 4 o'clock, from the residence of her son, Chas G Wilcox, on 18th st.

THU NOV 7, 1850
Under arrest in Canada West for high crimes is Wm Walker, who a few days ago, at Hamilton, pleaded guilty of abstracting letters from the post ofc at Brantford, of which he was postmaster. Sentence of death was recorded against him. He had married the daughter of one of the most respectable residents of Brantford.

Wash Corp: 1-Ptn of Wm O Davis for remission of a fine: referred to the Cmte of Claims. 2-Ptn from N B Wilkerson for remission of a fine: referred to the Cmte of Claims. 3-Bill for the relief of Wm B Wilson: passed. 4-Ptn from Washington Adams for a flag footway across 8th st west: passed. 5-Bills referred to the Cmte of Claims: relief of W W McCreery; of W A Mulloy; of Thos Dant; & of Robt F Magee. 6-Act for the relief of Cornelius Brasnahan: rejected. 7-Ptn of Jas Riordan, praying to be refunded certain taxes paid on Corp stock: referred to the Cmte of Ways & Means. 8-Ptn of Philip Ennis for the remission of a fine incurred by his servant: referred to the Cmte of Claims. 9-Ptn of John McDevitt for remission of a fine: referred to the Cmte of Claims.

For rent: large 3 story brick house at 10th & H sts: entirely new. –Wm F Bayly, Stationer, Pa ave, Wash.

Marshal's sale by writ of venditioni exponas on judgment of condemnation: sale on Nov 16: of sundry household furniture & articles, to satisfy judicials 260, to Oct, 1850, Wm H Irwin vs John Connor. -Richd Wallach, Marshal Dist of Columbia

All persons indebted to Edmund Mitchell, late of Wash City, deceased, are notified that the undersigned is alone authorized to collect all debts or accounts due the said deceased. -Maria C Fulford, excx

FRI NOV 8, 1850
An 1,800 pound grindstone, in a knife grinding establishment in Buckland, Mass, exploded a week ago, & killed a workman, Apollus Perkins.

Postmaster Gen has est'd the following new Post Ofcs for the week ending Nov 2, 1850.

Ofc	County, State	Postmaster
East Northport	Waldo, Me	Henry Brown
Neelysville	Morgan, Ohio	S Neely
Ratcliff-burgh	Vinton, Ohio	John Dixon
Baker's Run	Hardy, Va	Jas D Boone
Butcher's Store	Randolph, Va	Ely B Butcher
Neill's Creek	Cumberland, N C	C H Colfield
Jenny Ling	Chatham, N C	Eli B Emmerson
Adolph	Chathan, N C	Wm G Harris
Cypress Creek	Bladen, N C	Wm J Parker
Sawyer's Mills	Lexington Dist, S C	Wm E Sawyer
Poplar Springs	Hall, Ga	Jas Hardage
Abe Spring	Calhoun, Fla	Thos Lann
Buckysville	Coosa, Ala	John McKenzie
Wrightsville	Pontotoc, Miss	Richd Wright
Fayetteville	Fayette, Texas	S S Munger

Names Changed:
Fancy View, Bedford Co, Va, changed to Peaksville.
Fireman's Hill, Polk Co, Texas, changed to Cold Spring.

Chancery sale of valuable improved real estate at the corner of Pa ave & 4½ st west: by decree of the Circuit Court of Wash Co, D C, wherein Virginia Semmes & others are cmplnts, & Clara Semmes & others are dfndnts: sale on Dec 9, lot 13 in reservation A, lying in Wash City, with all the bldgs & improvements thereon: a 3 story brick house & back bldgs, containing about 30 rooms. It is leased until Sep 1, 1851. –B L Semmes, jr, Walter D Davidge, trustees -Dyer & McGuire, aucts

$100 reward for runaway mulatto woman Judy, 27 years of age. –Wm Major, 9 miles south of Culpeper Court-house, Va.

Mrd: yesterday, at the Wesley Chapel Parsonage, by Rev Mr Edwards, Mr Edw Thomas, of Cornwall, England, to Miss Winifred J Lakin, of Wash City.

Mrd: on Nov 5, by Rev Wm B Edwards, R C Stevens, of Md, to Miss Christa Ann Gittings, of Wash City.

Mrd: on Nov 5, at *Spring Hill*, residence of Dr S T Taylor, Fauquier Co, Va, by Rev Milton Henry, David Hansborough to Virginia Learned, daughter of Gen J D Learned, late of St Louis, Mo.

Died: on Nov 7, Wm Devereux, Clerk in the ofc of Indian Affairs. His funeral is today at 4 o'clock, from his late residence, I & 13th sts.

Dissolution of the copartnership existing between Messrs Green & Tastet, by mutual consent. The business will be carried on at the old stand, Pa ave & 6th st, under the old name of A Green. –A Green, Jos M Tastet

$10 reward for return of a dark Sorrel Mare strayed or stolen from the Wagon yard of Mr P W Dorsey, on Oct 15. Information to Mr Dorsey, 7th st, Wash, or to the subscriber, Thos Owen, near Mechanicsville, Montg Co, Md.

$5 reward for return of a small brindle cow. –Jno C Fitzpatrick, B st, Capitol Hill

SAT NOV 9, 1850
A letter in the New Orleans Picayune, dated Indianola, Texas, Oct 25, announces the conviction & sentence of the murderer of Mr Tenant, of Gtwn. The jurors were for hanging the wretch Turner.

Died: on Nov 7, in Wash City, of water on the brain, in her 4th year, Jane Emilie, daughter of M J & Mary E Thomas. Her funeral is today at 12 o'clock, from the residence of her grandfather, J Thomas, on Pa ave, next to the Irving Hotel.

The Solemn High Mass of Requiem, announced on last Sunday at St Peter's Church, Capitol Hill, for the repose of the soul of the late Rev Jos Van Horsigh, is postponed until Nov 12, which it will be celebrated at 9 o'clock a m.

In reply to Mr Hazard's notice a few days since in regard to certain notes which I hold against him, I have only to say that I yet hold them, & expect to do so until they are taken up by him or his assigns; & I deny his having any just or legal offset against them.
-Danl Rowland

MON NOV 11, 1850
Phil Inquirer of Sat: explosion on board one of the Ericsson steamers, on the river Delaware, last evening, opposite Newcastle. Killed: Wm Stevens, cabin passenger; Mgt Diston, cook, & Chas Biddle, steward, both colored; John Miller, 1st engineer; Jos Morton, fireman; Jeremiah Paine, Michl Borden, Eugene Kinney, Jas Vourk, ___ Green & 4 children; Patrick Murphy, & Jas Headly. John Dennis, missing. Wounded: Capt Claypoole, John Meredith, Alice Green, Patrick Blandford, Jas Harley, Michl Sullivan, Danl McCarthy, & Patrick Tobin.

The report of the death of W H Tuck, one of the members of the Constitutional Convention from PG Co, Md, is incorrect. Mr Tuck is in good health. Mr W G Tuck, of Annapolis, who was said to have died on Thu, was alive yesterday. –Balt Patriot of Sat

Jas Webb, tried & convicted at Kingston, Canada, of the murder of Wm Brennan, & sentenced to be executed on Dec 10, has confessed his guilt. His only motive was to secure a note for L4.10s which Brennan held against him.

Mrd: on Nov 7, at St Paul's Lutheran Church, by Rev J G Butler, Mr Chas Schwartzkopt, of Norfolk, Va, to Miss Loretta Antonie Voss, of Wash City.

Mrd: on Nov 7, by Rev Mr Hodges, Mr John Truman Davis to Eliz Ann Whitemore, all of Wash City.

Mrd: on Nov 6, in Phil, by Rev H W Ducachet, D D, Paul Shirley, U S N, to Margaretta L, youngest daughter of the late Capt John Gwinn, U S N.

Died: on Oct 27, in Balt, at the residence of her father, M McBlair, Eliz C Lloyd, aged 32 years, wife of the late J Murray Lloyd.

Died: yesterday, after a short but severe illness, Mr Jas E W Thompson. For the last 10 years he has been an ardent & consistent total abstinence man.

TUE NOV 12, 1850
Valuable 3 story brick house & lot at public auction: belonging to & occupied by W T Steiger, on 8th, between E & F sts: repainted throughout in 1848. It also has an observatory on top. The bldg was erected in 1842. Title indisputable. –A Green, auct

Windfall: the Will proved at Liverpool, Eng: the testator, Col Daniels, was formerly a sojourner at New Haven, Conn. Clause in his will: And now, having no other near relatives or friends who need my bequest, I give to a certain bookseller in New Haven, Conn, U S A, all my shares in the Banks of Liverpool, Eng, & Dumfries, Scotland, amounting to four hundred thousand & sixty-two pounds, currency. The name of the aforesaid legatee I do not remember; but he kept a bookstore south of Tontine Hotel, & in a large 4 or 5 story block, make of brick, having a bank in one of its divisions. And my reason for this bequest is, that the said bookseller showed me many marks of kindness & courtesy, & visited me during a sickness of several days. He was a married man; a member of the English Church, &, if now living, is about 40 years of age, or more. The person alluded to is Mr Levi H Young, eldest son of Col Guilford D Young, of the 29th regt infty, U S army, in the war of 1812. Mr Young commenced life as editor of a newspaper at Norwich, Conn; was afterwards a bookseller at New Haven, Conn; & there, between 1833 & 1837, became acquainted with the above named Col Daniels. Mr Young has no doubt that he is the person indicated in the will, yet he thinks the amount bequeathed to him is far too great for his deservings in having rendered the services which seem to have so strongly influenced the testator of the will. Mr Young's attention was for the first time called to the fact of the will by Maj Gen Winfield Scott.

Public auction: by deed of trust from Isaac Young, dated Nov 16, 1849: sale on Dec 12 next, in front of the premises, the 3 story brick house in Gtwn, D C, on north side of Bridge st, between High & Congress sts, which was formerly occupied as a banking house by the Union Bank of Gtwn, with the lot of ground on which it stands. The ground story of this house is fitted up with bars, counters, & a vault; the upper part is a commodious dwlg-house. –John Marbury, trustee

Mrd: on Nov 10, by Rev Thos Myers, Mr Edw Biggs to Miss Anna Brooks, both of Wash City.

Died: yesterday, in Wash City, after a short but painful illness, Mrs Susan Minery Davis, wife of Geo T M Davis, late of St Louis, Mo, in her 41st year. A dutiful child, a devoted wife, a faultless mother, a generous neighbor, & a meek & consistent Christian. Her funeral is this afternoon, at 3:30 o'clock, from the residence of her husband, on 12th st between F & G sts.

Mrd: on Oct 31, at Holyesville, Gaston Co, N C, by Rev R N Davis, Mr E S Barrett, of Lincolnton, to Miss Mary A, daughter of the late Eli Hoyle, of the former place.

Died: yesterday, in Wash City, Mrs Catherine King, in her 83rd year. Her funeral will take place today at 3 o'clock, for the residence of her son-in-law, Mr Wm Wise, on 4½ st, near Md ave.

WED NOV 13, 1850
Balt, Nov 12. Thos Moody, Robt E Haslett, & Thos Hannegan, 3 of the parties charged with the murder of Mr Edmund Mitchell, [the Pres of the Vigilant Fire Co, who was shot dead while entering a public house on the late election night,] were yesterday released by Judge Nisbet on bail for their appearance at the next term of the Balt City Court to answer the charge against them. The bail demanded & given in each case was $6,000.

Household & kitchen furniture at auction: on Nov 14, at the residence of Lt De Haven, on N Y ave, near 17th st. –Green & Tastet, aucts [The house is also for rent. Apply to Chas DeSelding, Todd's Bldg, near Brown's Hotel, Wash.]

Shocking stage accident kills Dr Flanders, of Londonderry, N H, after leaving Lyndon on Tue week, when the coach fell down an embankment. Others were injured. Dr Flanders had his neck broken; he was between 50 & 60 years old.

John H T Jerome was inaugurated on Mon last as Mayor of the city of Baltimore.

Ex-Govn'r Ford, of Ill, died at his residence in Peoria on Nov 4.

Mrs Alice, another of the unfortunate victims of the explosion on board the steamboat **Telegraph**, died at the Phil hospital on Sunday.

Mrd: on Nov 10, in Wash City, by Rev Mr French, Warwick Evans to Miss Mary Mason Washington, youngest daughter of Lund Washington.

Died: on Oct 27, aged 57 years, Mrs Lucinda Willing, for many years a resident of Gtwn, D C.

Died: on Nov 7, after a few days' illness, at Fairmont, Marion Co, Va, John Strother, infant son of Jas Lingan & Emily Strother Randolph.

Distressing accident yesterday in the Chesapeake Bay, near Balt. Capt Grant, of the schnr **Caroline A Cook**, saw a canal boat drifted ashore on White Rocks, with men in it giving signals of distress. He sent a boat to their relief, & when coming back, the boat upset, & 7 men out of 8 in it were drowned, among whom were Mr Geo Smith, mate of the schnr, Capt Grant's brother, & others whose names are not yet ascertained.

Public sale of valuable real estate: about 230 acres in PG Co, Md. Persons wishing to purchase the property will be shown it by Geo A Digges. –Geo A Digges, Norah Digges

$10 reward for lost, from in front of the door of Geo W Stewart's Grocery Store, on 12th st, a small mare, attached to a carriage of small dimensions. –Geo W Stewart

THU NOV 14, 1850
From the Tuscaloosa, Ala, we learn that the Hon Marmaduke Williams has soon followed to the precincts of the tomb the partner of his long life, [80 years,] whose decease was lately announced. This worthy gentleman was a Rep in Congress nearly 50 years ago from the State of N C, of which he was a native.

Wash Corp: 1-Cmte of Claims: Act for the relief of Wm A Mulloy: passed. Same cmte: act for the relief of Robt F Magee: passed. Same cmte: bill for the relief of Thos Dant: rejected. Same cmte: bill for the relief of Perry Biggs: rejected. 2-Ptn from John Shreve for the remission of a fine: referred to the Cmte of Claims. 3-Cmte of Claims: asked to be discharged from the further consideration of the ptn of Anthony Addison: discharged accordingly. 4-Giles Dyer has leave to withdraw his ptn & papers. 5-Cmte of Claims: asked to be discharged from the further consideration of the ptn of P Ennis: discharged accordingly. 6-Act for the relief of Walter Linkens: referred to the Cmte on Improvements. 7-Bill for the relief of J C Donaven: referred to the Cmte of Claims. 8-Ptn from Alex'r Lee & 150 other citizens, complaining of the nuisance caused by certain ready-made clothing shops hanging out their goods on the pavements: Cmte on the Police to report on this 2 weeks hence what measures are necessary.

City Ordinances-Wash. 1-Act for the relief of Wm B Wilson: to pay him $550.13, being the balance due for work done in front of the City Hall. 2-Act for the relief of B L Jackson & Brother: sum of $60 be paid to them for a certificate issued to Patrick Crowley for paving done on 7th st, said certificate having been mislaid or lost. 3-Act for the relief of Morris Holloran: sum of $79.90 be paid to him, for the balance due on Moses Holloran's bill for grading & gravelling 4½ st, as per Surveyor & Register's certificates.

In Chancery. Thos Blagden against John F Callan, adm, & Marion B Hoban, widow, & Anna, Marion, Jas, Fred'k, & Lawrence Hoban, heirs at law of Jas Hoban, deceased. Circuit Court of Wash Co, D C: claims to be filed on or before Nov 25.
–W Redin, auditor

Died: on Nov 13, Mrs Sarah B Martin, widow of the late *____ Martin, in her 36th year. Her funeral is this day at 2 o'clock, from the residence of her mother, 10th & F st. [*Copied as written.]

Died: at the Washington Infirmary, in his 33rd year, Nathan S Engle, of Evesham, N J. He was upon his return home from the South, where he had been for the purpose of recruiting his health. [No death date given-current item.]

Died: on Nov 12, Mary Eliz, aged 2 years, daughter of Mathew & Sarah E Cook. Her funeral is this afternoon, at 2:30 o'clock, from the residence of the parents, corner of 3rd & H sts.

Household & kitchen furniture at auction: on Nov 19, at the residence of J F Kahl, on Pa ave, between 9th & 10th sts. –Dyer & McGuire, aucts

FRI NOV 15, 1850
The visit of Mr Custis, of Arlington, the aged adopted son of Washington, & M Edmond Lafayette, the youthful grandson of Gen Lafayette, to the Tomb of **Mouunt Vernon**, on Nov 6, was a pilgrimage to that venerated spot of peculiar interest & character. Mr Custis pointed out the spot of his first interview with the Marquis de Lafayette in 1784; although but a child he well remembered the arrival of the Maquis accompanied by Count deux Ponts & the Chevalier Coraman. Mr Custis presented a ring containing a lock of Washington's hair to the Nat'l Guest. M Edmond Lafayette was interested in all that was told him touching his estimable father, Geo Washington Lafayette, [lately deceased,] of his first arrival in Phil in 1796, & introduction to the Pres of the U S. –Alex Gaz

The Will of Gen Jas Taylor, who died about 2 years ago at Newport, Ky, has lately been before the Courts in that city. The Cincinnati Chronicle say: The estate in Ohio is estimated at from $500,000 to $1,000,000, situated principally in this city & county, & in the Va Military Dist in this State, in which there are some forty to fifty thousand acres of land belonging to the estate. Results of the decision: the court, denying the validity of the will in this State at this time, in effect denies its validity forever, because the time of 2 years from the death of the testator, limited for the recording of wills from other States, has elapsed. The decision is final. The heirs at law, to wit, Col Jas Taylor; Mrs Harris, wife of Maj H T Harris; Mrs Tibbats, wife of Col John W Tibbatts, & Mrs Williamson, wife of Geo I Williamson, of this city, take this large estate as heirs-at-law, without regard to the will. We congratulate the numerous citizens of Ohio who are interested in this matter at this result, which brings a large estate into the market, with a good title, untrammeled by the entailments & limitations endeavored to be imposed upon it by the will.

By writ of fieri facias, I have seized the right & title in & to one negro woman, Kitty Frances, seized & taken in execution as the property of Albert Greenleaf, to satisfy a debt due Balaam Burch, & shall expose the same to public sale on Nov 21. Terms of sale cash. –Jas M Busher, constable

Milliard Fillmore, Pres of the U S, recognizes Edw Smith Sayers, who has been appointed Vice Consul of Portugal for Pa, Dela, & West Jersey, to reside at Phil. -Nov 12, 1850

Mrd: on Oct 12, at the residence of the Rt Hon Lord Weymouth, by Rev Dr Wellesley, assisted by Rev J S Donaldson, the Rt Hon W L M Scarlett, of Leicester Park, Scotland, to Miss Kate Wilmot, only daughter of Col W Randolph, U S A.

Died: on Nov 14, in Wash City, Miss Eliz Nicholson, eldest daughter of the late Dr Wm H Nicholson, of Queen Anne's Co, Eastern Shore, Md. Her funeral will take place this day, at 2 o'clock, from Miss Briscoe's boarding-house, 7th & La ave.

Died: on Nov 14, Allen, youngest son of Danl & Jane Campbell, aged 11 months & 14 days. His funeral is this day at 3 p m.

By writ of fieri facias, on Dec 12, I shall expose to sale part of lot 18 in square 407, seized & levied upon as the property of Owen Connolly, & will be sold to satisfy judicials 114, to Oct term, 1850, in favor of Bartholomew McGowan. –Richd Wallach, Marshal Dist of Columbia

SAT NOV 16, 1850
On Oct 12 the Duke of Palmella died at Lisbon. –Boston Daily Advertiser

The late Judge Danl Smith, of Va, died at his residence in Harrisonburg, Rockingham Co, Va, on Nov 8, in his 73rd year.

Mrd: on Oct 17, at Mountville, in the Parish of St Landry, La, by Rev Mr Tiernan, Dr Edw J Heard to Sarah Jane, daughter of Maj Amos Webb, both of the Parish of St Landry.

Mrd: on Nov 12, in N Y, by Rev A E Campbell, Mr Jas A Brown, of Wash City, to Miss Eliz Penfield, of the former place.

Mrd: on Nov 12, by Rev Dr Johns, Clarence Pell, of N Y, to Annie, daughter of the Hon J F H Clairborne, of Mississippi.

Mrd: in Phil, Paul Shirley, U S Navy, to Margaretta J, youngest daughter of the late Capt John Gwin, U S Navy. [No marriage date-current item.]

Died: on Thu last, Mary Eliz Davis, daughter of Thos J Davis, in her 15th year.

Died: on Nov 14, Mrs Jane Fleming, in her 88th year, born in the County Armah, Ireland, but for the last 24 years a resident of Gtwn, D C. Her funeral is at 3 o'clock on Nov 17, from the residence of her son-in-law, Mr Saml Cunningham, High st, Gtwn.

The U S steamer **Fashion** arrived at New Orleans on Nov 4 from Tampa, & stopped at Pensacola to land Brevet Maj Grafton's company of artl, which company is to garrison **Fort Pickens**. There came passengers Maj Wise, Capt Jordan, Lt Hayes, Lt Hudson, Rev Mr Axtell, chaplain U S Army; Capt Forbes Britton, as also a party of Indians from Florida, consisting of the chief Saml Jones' family.

A domestic in the service of Maj Wm Wolf, of Westminster, Md, in arranging the affairs of the house one day this week, put a splendid gold watch & jewelry in a small box, & set them in an apartment of a stove. Forgetting to return them to their proper place, fire was made in the stove & the articles were destroyed.

Postmaster Gen has est'd the following new Post Ofcs for the week ending Nov 9, 1850.

Ofc	County, State	Postmaster
Phoenix	Windham, Conn	Clifford Thomas
Mine Kill Falls	Schoahrie, N Y	P V Mattice
Cush	Clearfield, Pa	Asa White
Susquehanna Depot	Susquehanna, Pa	Jas M Ward
Lake	Luzerne, Pa	Lewis Allen
Freland's	Muskingum, Ohio	Morgan Morgan
Scotch Ridge	Wood, Ohio	Chas Bowsprit
Alonquin	Houghton, Mich	Thos H Hogan
Shirleysville	Abbeville Dist, S C	John R Shirley
Planter's Stand	Madison, Ga	Henry White
Indian Key	Dade, Fla	Wm H Hilliard
Ancilla	Jefferson, Fla	Peter K Builler
Smut Eye	Coffee, Ala	Wm H Buzbee
Lawrence	Monroe, Miss	Wm Stott
Deer Creek	Issaquanna, Miss	Mordecai Powell
Carter's	Jackson Parish, La	Henry Carter
Union Point	Concordia, La	Jas Q Richards
Siam	Leon, Texas	Horatio Woodward
Troy	Freestone, Texas	W L Adams
Quincy	Washita, Ark	Junius H Rogers
Spring Creek	Randolph, Ark	Chas Hatcher
Hurricane Hill	Lafayette, Ark	G L Hudgins
Mount Pinson	Jackson, Ark	Harvey Blain
Pleasant Ridge	Hot Spring, Ark	John Guilt
Wilmot	Noble, Ind	David Bowman
Knox	Stark, Ind	Jacob Tilman
Sherburnville	Lake, Ind	David Britton
Dixonville	Lawrence, Ind	Jas P Park

Saltillo	Jasper, Ind	G L Moore
Fulton	Fulton, Ind	Robt Aikin
Anderson River	Spencer, Ind	Isaac Jennings
Big Barren	Claiborne, Tenn	J G Palmer
Quincy	Gibson, Tenn	Solomon Shaw
Tatesville	McNairy, Tenn	Jas Tate
Gibson Wells	Gibson, Tenn	Eason Jones
Nettle Carier	Overton, Tenn	Rawlings H Johnson
Deatsville	Nelson, Ky	Leand'r F Bradshaw
Swan Point	Knox, Ky	Spencer H Tuggle
Meadow Creek	Whitley, Ky	Thos N Berry
Senex	McLean, Ill	Jas Gray
New Maysville	Pike, Ill	Saml Laird
Avery	Joe Daviess, Ill	Wm Avery
Pleasant View	Schuyler, Ill	Ebenezer Dimick
Wales	Ogle, Ill	Flemming Welsh
Old Ripley	Bond, Ill	Henry C Zandt
Belle Prairie	Hamilton, Ill	Cloyd Cronch
Hager's Grove	Shelby, Mo	John Hager
Clay	St Clair, Mo	Wm H Small
Pleasant Valley	Wright, Mo	Abraham P Pool
Bremen	St Louis, Mo	Jas Huston
Elkhorn	Montgomery, Mo	David R Clarkson
Spring Fork	Pettis, Mo	J E Crawford
Old Mission	Winneshick, Iowa	John L Carson
Philadelphia	Van Buren, Iowa	Cyrus Bartoe
Cynthiann	Wapello, Iowa	Jno J Tinsley

Names Changed:
Collinsville, Blair Co, Pa, changed to Altoona.
Reedersville, Lawrence Co, Tenn, changed to Wayland's Springs.
Blythe's Ferry, Meigs Co, Tenn, changed to Mouth of Hiwassee.
Tylerville, Warren Co, Ill, changed to Utah.
Fremont, Richland Co, Ill, changed to Calhoun.
Eldridge, Dupage Co, Ill, changed to York Centre.
Navarre, Des Moines, Ill, changed to Dodgeville.
Plymouth, Washington Co, Oregon, changed to St Helen.
Albany, Linn Co, Oregon, changed to New Albany.

Fancy Furs: Gibson & Co, aucts, Balt, Md: 7, North Chas st.

Trustee's sale of dwlg-house: by virtue of 2 deeds of trust, dated Feb 21, 1844 & Sep 16, 1848: public sale on Dec 13, of lot 19 in square 28, with 2 story brick dwlg-house, recently occupied by Mr S E Scott. The lot fronts on north K st. –Jno Marbury, trustee

Sale of real estate, by order of the Circuit Court of Wash Co, D C, in the matter of the heirs of Edw Stabler, deceased, made on Jun 11, 1850: sale of a valuable brick house & lot in square 379, fronting on Pa ave, the store-room is now occupied by Miss Morley, & the dwlg part by Messrs Parmele & Malster. –Geo S Gideon, H T Weightman, Rob Keyworth, Eleazer Lindsley, Rob S Patterson, Com'rs

Furnished house for rent: corner of 13th & I sts. Inquire at the house, or to J T Cochrane, at Mrs Manning's, 13th st, below F.

Millard Fillmore, Pres of the U S, recognizes Signor Luigi B Biusse, who has been appointed Consul Gen of the Pontifical States, to reside in N Y. –Nov 15, 1850

MON NOV 18, 1850
Mrs Frances Jones, at East Cambridge, Mass, on Mon, was wounded so severely by the accidental discharge of a gun, that little hope is entertained for her recovery. It appears that her 14 year old son was amusing himself with a loaded gun and in taking it from him, the gun discharged its contents in her breast.

Diabolical murder Nov 15, at 51 Dey st, N Y, occupied by a Belgian named Chas Maria Rouseau & his family, who lived there but a short time. They were visited by their countryman Henry Carnal, who had ascertained that his friends had nearly $250 in ready money laid away for future use. Carnal arrived late one night & asked for lodging. The elder Rouseau objected but his 2 sons, Louis & Chas, consented. During the night Carnal stabbed Louis in the abdomen; Chas was struck in the neck; & the father was stabbed in the neck, severing the jugular vein. Dr Monson Jones, residing at 148 Chambers st, was called to the dreadful scene. He dressed the wounds of the 2 young men. The awful wretch who perpetrated the crime was arrested the next morning. -Express

Lost, or ran away from his home, Enoch Donnington, an indented apprentice, about 14 years of age. Information leading to his discovery will be thankfully received by his father, John Donnington, huckster, Centre Market, or at the subscriber's Hair Cutting Rooms, Pa ave, between 9th & 10th sts. –J H Gibbs

In Chancery: Circuit Court of Wash Co, D C. Edmund Hanley's excs, against Susan D Shepherd, widow, & admx of Alex'r Shepherd, deceased, & Alex'r R Shepherd, Anna P Shepherd, Mary E Shepherd, Thos M Shepherd, Wilmer J Shepherd, & Arthur S Shepherd, heirs at law of said Alex'r Shepherd. Trustee has reported the sale made by him of the real estate of the late Alex'r Shepherd, on Aug 16, 1849, the said Susan D Shepherd was the highest bidder & became the purchaser of the whole of lot 7 in reservation A, with improvements thereon, in Wash City, for $3,492.59; that she hath passed the notes of Peregrine W Browning, [to whom she had sold her interest in said premises,] for $3,250, & her own $250. –Jno A Smith, clerk

Orphans Court of Wash Co, D C. Letters of administration on the personal estate of John M Porter, late of said county, deceased. –J F Wollard, A Dixon, adms

City Ordinances-Wash. 1-Act for the relief of Robt F Magee: fine imposed for an alleged violation in regard to hackney carriages is remitted, provided Magee pay the cost of prosecution. 2-Act for relief of Wm A Mulloy: the sum of $79.13 be paid to him for cost of commitments & taking persons to the Workhouse for the 2 years ending Sep 7, 1850.

Orphans Court of Wash Co, D C. Letters of administration on the personal estate of Wm Levering, late of said county, deceased. –Maria G Devereux, admx

Orphans Court of Wash Co, D C. In the case of Thos C Daniel, adm of Alfred B Thruston, deceased, the court & administrator have appointed Dec 3 next for distribution of the assets in the hands of the administrator. –Ed N Roach, Reg/o wills

Anacostia Fire Co's Ball: Nov 27, at their Hall, Navy Yard. Managers:
Jas Burdine	T P Tench	J H Mead
John Simmons	Chas Eadlin	Jas Smith
J McKuen	J N Mitchell	T Harrison
Geo Brown	F Ober	
Wm Morgan	J B Ellis	

TUE NOV 19, 1850
Household & kitchen furniture at auction: on Nov 21, at the residence of J H Eberbach, on 8th st, corner of E st. –Dyer & McGuire, aucts

Fred'k [Md] Herald of Nov 16. On Wed last, the afflicting news reached the city that Dr Edw Y Goldsborough, one of our most respected citizens & physicians, was lying dead at the toll gate, on the turnpike leading to Emmitsburg. He was on his return home, & dismounted & entered the house, complaining of a pain above the eye. In one short half hour he breathed his last. His family circle mourn one so endeared to them.

Commission on Claims against Mexico: 1-Memorial of Benj D Lovell, claiming for an illegal penalty of $2,000 imposed on him at Alamos in 1829; for loss by consequent stoppage of his business there & at Jesus Maria; & for a forced loan at Guanajuato in 1833. 2-Memorial of Lewis M Dreyer, claiming for goods confiscated on board the schnr **Susannah**, bound from New Orleans to Corpus Christi, & driven by stress of weather into the Rio Grande, in Nov, 1845. 3-Memorial of Edw Hoffman, claiming for illegal confiscation of his property & imprisonment of his person by the Mexican authorities of the town of El Paso del Norte, in 1843 & 1844. 4-Memorial of A B Thompson, claim for supplies & moneys furnished from 1837 to 1846 to the Mexican Gov't in Calif; for a forced loan in 1837 from himself & partner, John C Jones. 5-Memorial of John F Bullock, claiming for expulsion & seizure of corn at Matamoros, & imprisonment at Monterey. 6-Memorial of Simeon Remer, claiming for expulsion from Matamoros. 7-Memorial of Sandforth Kidder, claiming for expulsion from Matamoros. 8-Memorial of J M Jarero, claiming for moneys loaned to the revolutionary Gov't of Mexico in 1816, & for interest & expenses, was examined & ordered to be suspended. The Board then adjourned.

The Warsaw [Ill] Whig says that Dr Wm C Morris was drowned in the Osage river, near that place a few days ago. He was thrown from his horse in attempting to ford the river. He was a surgeon in the British army & navy for 40 years, & was at the battle of Trafalgar under Lord Nelson.

On Tue an operation of some importance was performed at the Infirmary in Wash City by Dr J F May, assisted by Drs Miller, Johnston, Stone, & Garnet, of Wash City, & Drs Wetherspoon & Coolidge, of the U S Army. The patient was Richd Eaton, aged 37 years, who has for many years living in Wash City, & following huckstering, & ducking, as a means of support. Three years ago he was taken with white swelling or a scrofulous degeneration of the knee-joint, & for the past 7 months has been bed-ridden. His knee was as large as his head. Dr May disarticulated the hip joint, & removed the entire limb, in a lttle over 30 seconds, with the loss of more than half a pint of blood. Last evening the subject was found quite comfortable, & apparently doing well. –Nat Intel

Mrd: on Nov 5, in Christ Church, St Louis, by Rt Rev Dr Hawes, Hon Edw Carrington Cabell, of Florida, to Anna Maria Wilcox, daughter of Mrs Gen Ashley.

Mrd: on Nov 7, at Jefferson Barracks, by Rev Mr McCarty, Bvt Capt Mansfield Lovell, 4th Artl U S Army, to Emiliem, daughter of Col Jos Plympton, 7th Infty, U S A.

Mrd: on Oct 30, at Hanover, N H, Mr Theodore Hinsdale, of N Y C, to Miss Grace Webster Haddock, daughter of Prof Chas B Haddock, of Dartmouth College.

Died: on Nov 7, in the town of Delaware, Ohio, Mrs Martha McCabe, wife of Prof McCabe, of the Weslyan Univ, & niece of the late Dr Sewall of Wash City.

For sale: most elegant & commodious house in Wash, with large coach house, stable, & extensive garden. Title indisputable. Apply to Dr Chas S Frailey, Gen Land Ofc.

For rent: 2 story brick house on G, near 5th st. –Mary B Alexander, 12th & C sts.

WED NOV 20, 1850
Two weeks ago, near Mechanicsburg, about 14 miles from Springfield, Ill, Mr Thos Baker, a brother of the Hon E D Baker, was driving a spirited horse in the prairie. Mr Baker fell forward of the wheels, & his leg fastened between the springs & axle, his body on the ground. The horse took fright and carried him 4 miles when he stopped. Mr Baker had presence of mind to disengage his limb, while suffering intense pain. On the third day he was discovered by a drover, & relief secured. He lingered 6 days longer, when he died. He was about 32 years of age. His wife died a few months ago.

To let: a brick house containing 6 rooms, in the First Ward. The proprietor can be seen on 4½ st, near City Hall. –John E F L McConchie

Died: on Nov 14, in Murfreesborough, N C, of consumption, Mr Saml Polkinhorn, aged 44 years, formerly of Wash City.

Postmaster Gen established the following new Post Ofcs for week ending Nov 16, 1850.

Ofc	County, State	Postmaster
East Orange	Orange, Vt	Lathrop Fish
Decatur	Mifflin, Pa	Geo Sigler
Eden	McKean, Pa	Jonathan Marsh
Spring Run	Franklin, Pa	Wm A Mackey
Blair Furnace	Blair, Pa	Hugh McNeal
Hickerson's X Roads	Morgan, Ohio	Stephen Jones
North Ridge	Hancock, Ohio	Jonah Porter
Abrahamtown	Marion, Fla	Robt H Williams
Old Courthouse	Bryan, Ga	John Baley
Newtonsville	Attala, Miss	Thaddeus Wigley
Smithland	Cass, Texas	Hezekiah Horner
Myrtle Springs	Bowie, Texas	R J Battle
St Charles	Arkansas, Ark	Chas W Belknap
Lakeville	St Joseph, Ind	John Henderson
Sulphur Well	Shelby, Tenn	Wm Griffin
Miller's Creek	Estell, Ky	John W Lyle
Graves Ferry	Ohio, Ky	John H Graves
Good Springs	Mead, Ky	N Faulconer
Bear Creek	Montgomery, Ill	Wm Russell
Williamsonville	Macon, Mo	W H Rowland
Rushbottom	Holt, Mo	Danl David
Wyaconda	Scotland, Mo	Wm Troth
Lind	Winnebago, Wis	Geo W Taggart
Las Vegas	N Mexico	Levi Keithly

Names Changed:
Taylor Hall, Balt Co, Md, changed to Elengowan.
Summerville, Kent Co, Mich, changed to Sparta Centre.
Kennon's Landing, Chas City Co, Va, changed to Apperson's.
Rehobothville, Morgan Co, Ga, changed to Wellington.
Free Soil, Cherokee Co, Ga, changed to Freemansville.
Prairie Hill, Montg Co, Ala, changed to Hawthorn.
Dallas, Vermillion Co, Ill, changed to Indianola.

In Chancery. A T Yerby & others, creditors of Francis Lombardi, against Caroline Lombardi, widow & admx, & Chas G & Laura Lombard, heirs of said Francis Lombardi, Michl A Guista, & Nicholas Callan. Claims to be presented by Nov 30 next, at my ofc in the City Hall, Wash. –W Redin, auditor

In Chancery: Circuit Court of Wash Co, D C. Albert T Yerby & Adonis L Yerby, trading under the name, style, & firm of Yerby & Brother, vs Caroline Lombardi, widow & admx of Francis Lombardi, Chas G Lombardi, & Laura Lombardi, infants & heirs at law of said Francis Lombardi, Michl A Guista, & Nicholas Callan, trustee. Chas S Wallach, trustee, reported a sale made by him of the property named in the above cause on Jan 8, 1850, Geo Barber, being the purchaser thereof, for $900; & that the said Geo Barber, on Jan 8,

1850, granted, bargained & sold, assigned, transferred, & set over the said property, & all his right, title, interest, claim, & demand in & to the same to Chas B Clusky, & that Cluskey has complied with the terms of the sale. –Jno A Smith, clerk

Mrs Simpson, widow of the late A C Simpson, of Fayetteville, N C, who died suddenly several months ago from the effects of poison alleged to have been administered by her, has returned to Fayetteville & delivered herself up, & is now in jail to await her trial. [Nov 21st newspaper: Mrs Ann K Simpson, charged with having murdered her husband was found not guilty. The evidence showed that Mr Simpson had died from the effects of poison, but not that it was administered by his wife.]

L H Young, son of Col Young, U S Army, is the person to whom the lately deceased Englishman, Col Daniels, died leaving $2,000,000 to a certain bookseller, for kindness to him while sick in New Haven, Conn, some years ago. The New Haven register, which says it is Dr Uhlorn, now of Cincinnati, who is the proper claimant, says also that there was a firm of Young & Uhlorn, booksellers, in New Haven, & it is probable both gentlemen paid Col Daniels some kindley attention. –Balt Sun
+
There seems to some doubt as to the real legatee, we may state that L H Young occupied the store below the Tontine in New Haven from the time it was completed in 1833 till 1841. Col Daniels was in New Haven between 1833 & 1837, & a frequent visiter at Mr Young's. Dr Uhlorn was in New Orleans during Col Daniel's visit, & probably never knew or saw him. Mr Young well remembers Col Daniels. –Boston Atlas

Mrd: on Nov 13, in Wheeling, at the residence of Dr McElhenney, by Rev Mr Weed, Wm H Montgomery, of Lewisburg, Va, to Miss Ruth E Jacob, daughter of the late John J Jacob, of Ohio Co, Va.

Mrd: on Nov 14, at **Fanwood**, Douglas Robinson to Fanny Monroe, eldest daughter of the Hon Jas Monroe.

Mrd: on Nov 18, at Charles street Church, Balt, by Rev Mr Hirst, Wm Welmore Orndorff to Mary, daughter of Jas L Ridgely, of Balt Co.

Died: on Nov 18, in Wash City, Mary E, Wife of Henry Kuhl, after a somewhat protracted & painful illness, in her 23rd year. Her funeral is from the residence of her mother, Mrs Fowler, on E st, this afternoon, at 2 o'clock.

Died: on Nov 18, of consumption, John Walter, eldest son of Philip & Eliz A Boteler, aged 21 years, 3 months & 11 days. His funeral is this evening, at 3 o'clock, from the residence of his father, corner of 14th & D sts.

Died: on Nov 17, at Phil, Mrs Catharine Arnold, in her 77th year, relict of the late Thos Arnold.

THU NOV 21, 1850
Col Richd M Johnson, a brave soldier during the war of 1812, died at Frankfort, Ky, on Tue last, while in the discharge of his duties as a member of his State Legislature. His illness was brief, having been seized with a second attack of paralysis, under which he suffered but a few days, when, at a ripe age, he was relieved by death.

Saml Harker, for many years the editor of the Balt Republican, died in that city on Fri.

In Overton, Tenn, the census taker found a lady, named Stevens, whose age was 120 years. She was married at the time of Braddock's defeat. Her youngest son is a smart lad of 70 years.

The San Antonio Ledger says that the Odd Fellows of that place have erected a monument over the grave of the gallant Capt Saml Walker. He was a member of Central Lodge, #1, of this city.

By 2 writs of venditioni exponas, I will expose to public sale, on Nov 21, lot 6 in square 75, with the improvements, in Wash City, D C, the property of Thos Llewellin; seized & taken in execution at the suit of Michl Thompson. –H R Maryman, constable

Wash Corp: 1-Ptn of Jas Pilling, jr & others, for opening & grading the alley in square 222: referred to the Cmte on Improvements. 2-Ptn of Jas Maher, praying the remission of certain fines: referred to the Cmte of Claims. 3-Bill for the relief of J A Dunawin: passed. 4-Bill for the relief of the heirs of Francis Iardell: referred to the Cmte on Improvements. 5-Bill for the relief of W W McCreery: ordered to lie on the table. 6-Ptn of C J Henry, praying remission of a fine: referred to the Cmte of Claims.

In Chancery-Circuit Court of Wash Co, D C. Wm G W White et al, vs Edw N Roach, adm, et al. Saml S Williams, the Trustee in the above case, reported to the Court that he hath sold the real estate in said cause, & that Wm G W White became the purchaser of the same, namely: lots 26 & 27 in square 462, for $1,900, & he has complied with the terms of said sale. –Jno A Smith, clerk

In Chancery-Circuit Court of Wash Co, D C. Eliz Ford, et al, vs Peter Brady, adm et al. Saml S Williams, the Trustee in the above cause, reported that he sold the west part of lot 1 in square 121, to Geo McGlue for $2,275; & that the east part of lot 1 in said square was sold to Michl Shanks for $511.78; that part of lot 3 in square 8 was sold to Thos P Morgan, for $87.50; & the south half of lot 18 in square 143, was sold to Edw Cruso, for $167.36. –Jno A Smith, clerk

Cholera at Indianapolis, Ind. J S Johnson, a colored barber, died in 4 hours. Mr Van Ben Thuson, of Shelby Co, Ind, the oldest member of the Convention, died early on Thu. -Louisville Courier, 15th

Mrd: on Tue last, at St John's Church, in Wash City, by Rev Smith Pyne, Chas B Maury to Sally Fontaine, daughter of the late Richd B Maury, of Fredericksburg, Va.

The heirs of the Clement Wood, a native of the city of Lincoln, in England, & only son of Mgt & Cary Woods, of the parish of St Michl, in that city, emigrated to the U S about 1784. It is not known to what part he emigrated, nor has he been heard of since he left England. Should he or any of his descendants be now residing in the U S, he or they, by applying to Wm B Webb, Atty, of Wash City, or to Pishey Thompson, #5 Bank Chambers, Lothbury, London, will hear something very much to his or their advantage. An ancestor of the said Clement Wood was named Benoni Wood. This was a family name, & very likely to be continued among the descendants of the said Clement Wood. Isaac & Margaret are also names which frequently occur in the said family. All letters to London must be post-paid to England.

Mrd: on Oct 17, in Balt, by Rev Mr Burnap, Wm A Purdy, of Wash, to Miss Mary McNulty, of Balt.

Sale by order of the Orphans Court of Wash Co, D C: on Nov 25, at the late residence of Danl Homans, deceased, on Capitol Hill, between 1st & 2nd sts, near Pa ave, a part of his personal effects: theatre scenery, carpenter's tools, workbench, window frames & sash, & new washing machines. -A Green, auctioneer

FRI NOV 22, 1850
Messrs Saml Wethered, of Balt, Newton Williams, of Boonville, & Brevort, of Kansas, lately reached St Louis from Santa Fe. On their way a plan was laid to rob them of their means, which was happily prevented in good time. A young man named Fox had arranged to travel in their company, & while out on the prairie give alarm to some Indians to murder them & his servant, & take possession of their money. Kit Carson, living at Ryado, aware of this, obtained an escort of 12 dragoons, accompanied by Capt Ewall & servant, Johnson, & 128 soldiers, traveled 150 miles in 28 hours to apprize the party of their danger, & to take Fox a prisoner back to Santa Fe. This they did, much to the relief of Wethered & party.

Wingate's Md Law Reporter: the case of Thos D Hurt et al, vs John Stull, before the Md High Court of Chancery, Jul term, Chancellor Johnson decided that in a contract for the sale of land for a gross sum, in which by the introduction of the words <u>more or less</u> the representation of the quantitiy is qualified, the number of acres is to be considered as merely descriptive, & not of its essence, &, in the absence of fraud, deficiency or surplus in the quantitiy of land will not avail to vacate the contract. The dfndnt, John Stull, purchased of Thos D Hurt a farm, ***Mother's Care***, for $2,300-$500 cash & the balance in yearly payments. The farm was described as containing 173 acres, more or less, but by a subsequent survey it was found to contain but 145 acres, & the dfndnt asked that a proportionate deduction be made from the purchase money for the difference. The Chancellor decided unless a fraudulent representation of the quantitiy was proved, the contract must hold good. –Balt Sun

Orphans Court of Wash Co, D C. In the case of John H Bayne, adm de bonis non, with the will annexed of John B Kerby deceased: the adm & Court have appointed Dec 14 next for the final settlement of said estate. –Ed N Roach, Reg/o wills

Advices from Boston state that the U S ship-of-war **Yorktown** was lost, & the ofcrs & crew were on board the ship **Dale**, all safe. The **Yorktown** was under command of Capt Marsten, of Phil.

The Phil papers announce the death of Zachariah Poulson, one of the oldest printers & publishers in the U S..

The young wife of Mr Vizard, at New Orleans, was killed on Nov 7 by falling from her bed room window in her sleep.

Household & kitchen furniture at auction: on Nov 26, at the residence of H W Hunt, on Pa ave, between 3rd & 4½ st. -A Green, auctioneer

Danl C Webb, an aged & most respectable citizen of Charleston, S C, met a sudden death in that city last Sunday, while attending Divine worship in the Unitarian church. Mr Webb was observed to droop & all efforts to resuscitate him were ineffectual. -Mercury

Mrs M France has removed to 7th st, over the ofc of the Nat'l Era, where she can accommodate boarders by the day, week, or month. Reasonable rates.

Commission on Claims against Mexico: 1-Memorial of Simeon Remer & of Sanforth Kidder, severally claiming for expulsion from Matamoros, in Apr, 1846: Board came to the opinion that the claims are valid: amount to be awarded subject to the future action of the Board.

Appropriations: Statements: 1-Payment of a balance certified by the First Comptroller of the Treas to be due to Jas D Doty, as govn'r & superintendent of Indian affairs for the Territory of Wisconsin: $1,148.09. 2-Compensation due Lt Geo Thorn, U S corps of Topographical Engineers, while acting upon the northeastern boundary during 1843, 1844, & 1845, for his necessary traveling & other personal expenses, as authorized by the Sec of State: Commission on Claims against Mexico: 1-1,152. 3-Balance due Jose Yanardy, formerly Consul at Cadiz, Spain: $1,228.08. 4-Compensation to Dr Thos O Edwards, for his services as examiner into the practical operation of the law for the prevention of the importation of spurious & adulterated drugs & medicines, under appointment from the Sec of the Treasury, Oct 10, 1848: $250. 5-Payment to W J Duane, of Phil, exc of Danl Parker, deceased, late Paymaster Gen, & agent for paying salaries to his ofc, a balance found due the said Parker: $886.00. 6-Payment to Maj W H Chase, of the Corps of Engineers, in pursuance of the decision of the 2nd Comptroller of the Treasury of Nov 2, & 15, 1849: $1,119.68. 7-Payment to Richd Rush of a balance due for his salary as Atty Gen of the U S, & for the satisfaction of which there is no appropriation: $259.59. 8-Payment to Cpt Chas Hawke, ascertained as due him by the 4th Auditor of the Treasury: $176.38. 9-To defray the expenses of transporting the remains of Gen Taylor from the cemetery in Wash to Ky, to be expended under the direction of the Pres of the U S: $4,000. 10-Pay to Chas Stuart, late a private in Co K, of the 7th Regt of N Y volunteers, commanded by Col Stevenson, known as the Calif regt, such sum as he would have been entitled to receive for pay, rations, & clothing, from the time he enlisted to his return to Norfolk, on Oct 18, 1847, had he remained with said regt during that time: indefinite. 11-For pay of commission, warrant, & petty ofcrs & seamen, including the engineer corps of the navy; & that there be paid by the proper accounting ofcrs to Wm J McAlpine & Wm P S Sanger the same salary that was paid to their predecessors as engineers-in-chief, during the time they severally performed such service at the navy yard, Brooklyn, N Y; & that the same amount of salary as is provided for the said Wm J McAlphin & Wm P S Sanger be paid to Jas Herron, the Engineer-in-Chief at the navy yard at Pensacola, during the time he has been employed at said yard: $2,758,262.00. 12-For an advance to the Chippewas of Mississippi & Lake Superior of this amount retained by the late sub-agent, J P Hays; the same to be reimbursed to the U S when recovered from the late sub-agent or his sureties: $1,382.29. 13-Advancement to the Wyandot Indians of this sum retained by the late sub-agent, Richd Hewitt, the same to be reimbursed to the U S when received from said sub-agent or his sureties: $828.09. 14-Payment to S B Lowry, for services rendered as interpreter & assist conductor to a delegation of Winnebago Indians who visited the seat of gov't & concluded the treaty with that tribe of Oct 13, 1846: $305. 15-Payment to Henry M Rice for articles of outfit furnished to the Winnebago delegation who visited the seat of gov't & concluded the treaty of 1846 with that tribe: $762.10. 16-Payment to Henry M Rice for expenses as one of the delegates from the Winnebago Nation to Wash City in 1846, & compensation for valuable services rendered the Gov't in the negotiation of the treaty concluded at that time: $670. 17-For payment in full heretofore wrongfully paid by the Sec of War, out of the annuities of the Winnebago Indians to the legal reps of John McFarland, deceased: $12,000. 18-For redemption of the daughter of Mr & Mrs Jas M White, who was captured by the Indians on the borders of New Mexico: $1,500. 19-For payment to So-le Emarthla, a Seminole Indian, this amount stolen from him by U S soldiers at New Orleans: $125. 20-To pay the central Bank of Georgia, assignee of H W Jarnegan & Co, & others: $21,044. 21-For payment of the awards of Gen Wm B Mitchell, com'r under the treaty of Chicago of Sep 26, 1833, with the Potswamies, reported by him to the Sec of War on Jan 28, 1841, adjudicated & approved by the Sec, in his decision of Mar 3, 1841: $8,589.32. 22-To pay be paid by the Creek agent to the surviving chiefs of the McIntosh party of Creek Indians, to be divided among the chiefs & warriors, the friends & followers of the late Gen Wm McIntosh, who have not received their proportion of the sum of $100,000, stipulated by the 9th article of the treaty between the U S & the Creek nation, made at Wash City, on Jan 24, 1826, to be in full of all demands of said Indians under the said article: $39,901.67. 23-To audit & settle accounts of the companies of Texas Mounted Rangers, commanded by Capts B F Hill, J M Smith, J Roberts, J S Sutton, S P Ross, H E McCulloch, J W Johnson, & C Blackwell, who were retained in or called into service by the Gov't of said State: $72,000. 24-Act for the relief of Jesse Sutton: to pay him, for services rendered, & coal, iron, & steel furnished the Texas Indians, as public blacksmith, from Mar 20, 1846, to May 20, 1847: $1,000. 25-Act for the relief of Wm B Crews: accounting ofcrs are to ascertain whether he has been paid for all military services rendered by him from Aug 8, 1847, to Feb 14, 1848, & to be paid such money as may be found his due: provided the sum does not exceed $80.

Mrd: on Nov 18, at Wilmington, N C, by Rev Dr Drane, Gen Waddy Thompson, of S C, to Miss Cornelia A, daughter of Col John D Jones, of the former place.

Mrd: on Nov 5, in Gtwn, by Rev N Tillinghast, Edw B Powell, of Alexandria, to Cordelia S Armstrong, of the former place.

Mrd: on Sabbath last, by Rev T Myers, Francis Gates to Catharine A Hasel, both of Wash Co, D C.

Mrd: on Nov 19, by Rev T Myers, Thos Piles to Eliz, 2nd daughter of Mr John Walker, all of PG Co, Md.

Died: on Nov 20, in Wash City, Richd Key Watts, in his 83rd year. His funeral is Sat next, at 3 o'clock, from the residence of his daughter, Mrs M K Wallace, on F, between 6th & 7th sts, north side.

SAT NOV 23, 1850
Queen's Co, Long Island: Nov 18. Court of Oyer & Terminer, just held, Wm H Remson, about 40 years old, was found guilty of setting fire to his father's, Jacob Remson's barn, near Manhasset. He was sentenced to 7 years in the State prison.

Splendid estate at private sale, on the Potomac river, in Chas Co, Md, about 20 miles below Alexandria, containing 731 acres: commodious dwlg house built at a cost of nearly $6,000, located on an eminence; & all necessary out bldgs. Possession will be given on Jan 1, 1851. –Chas A Pye, near Port Tobacco, Md.

Orphans' Court at York, for York Co, Pa, on Nov 5, 1850, before Hon Danl Durkee, et al, Judges of the same Court, duly assigned: on motion of Messrs Evans & Mayer, atty, the Court award a rule upon the collateral heirs. The issue of his eldest son, Thos Gibson, deceased; Jacob Gibson, of ___ Co, Pa; Mary Ann, wife of Jos Brooks, of ___ Co, Indiana; Thos Nelson Gibson, of ___ Co, Ohio. The issue of another deceased brother, Geo Gibson, viz: Nancy Anne, wife of Nathl Wise, of Peachbottom Township, York Co; Jacob J Gibson, of same; Eliza M Gibson, of same; Paulina Gibson, of same; Patty Jane Gibson, of same; & Wm Thos Gibson, of same. Also, John Gibson, a surviving brother. The issue of another deceased brother, Hugh W Gibson, viz: Jacob Gibson, of ___, Ohio, Benj Gibson, of Cecil Co, Md; Anne Mitchel, widow of Geo Mitchel, of the same place; & Jane Gibson, who resided in Ohio when last heard from supposed in Richland Co. Also, a sister of said Jacob Gibson, viz: Anne, the wife of Geo Prall, of Lancaster Co. Another sister, Mary Gibson, widow of John Gibson, deceased, late of Peachbottom Township aforesaid; & also, another sister, Jane, the wife of Andrew Martin, of Lower Chanceford Township, York Co, aforesaid; & also Margaret, another sister, & one of these petitioners. All of the said persons are believed to be of age except Thos Nelson Gibson, who is a minor, under the guardianship of his mother, Susan Gibson, widow, of the same place, where he resides. Heirs & legal reps of Jacob Gibson, late of Peachbottom Township, York Co, deceased, to be & appear at an Orphans' Court, to be held for said York Co, on Jan 7, 1851, & then & there to accept or refuse to accept of the real estate marked & described as per the inquisition filed of the said Jacob Gibson, deceased, at the valuation, or show cause why the same should not be sold by order of the Court. –John A Wilson, Clerk

Letter from Lt Frailey on the loss of the U S sloop-of-war **Yorktown**, Capt Marston: U S ship **Dale**, Port Praya, Sep 30, 1850. On Sep 6, while endeavoring to pass between the island of Mayo & Buena Vista, the ship striking upon a ledge of rocks, extending from the northern point of the former island, 30 miles distant from this place, became an entire wreck in less than an hour after first striking. The ship fell over on to her side & everything was swept into the sea. Two men were saved by cutting a hole in the deck, the water having cut off their egress by the hatches.

Notice of Copartnership. J T Radcliff has associated with him his brother, Saml J Radcliff, under the firm of J T Radcliff & Co. Complete assortment of the very best goods, candles, sugar, tea, lard, starch, buckwheat, etc. –Odd Fellows Hall, 7th st

Millard Fillmore, Pres of the U S, recognizes Edw Frith, who has been appointed Vice Consul of the Pontifical States, to reside at Phil, Pa. -Nov 21, 1850

Commission on Claims against Mexico: 1-Memorial of Andrew Fenton, claiming for 30 days' detention of the brig **Ada Eliza**, & for other damages was ordered to be received.

Died: on Nov 14, at New Orleans, in his 47th year, Wm Henry Watkins, 2nd son of Dr T Watkins, of Wash City.

Appropriations: Statements: 1-For 15 days' services of Jos Bryan, as com'r to take testimony in pursuance of an inquiry by direction of the Sec of the Treas: $120. 2-For contingent expenses of the ofc of the Register of the Treasury, being an amount due to J C McGuire for printing, ruling, & binding books, etc, & for desks & other furniture: $3,546.25. 3-Refunding to John Jos Chance, Bishop of Natchez, the duties paid on a cathedral bell, presented to said Bishop by Prince Alexander Torlonia, of Rome: $250.

MON NOV 25, 1850
Fredericksurg News: the old establishment known as **Laneville**, in King & Queen, which has been in the family of the Corbins of **Laneville** for a century or more, & now the property of Maj Jas Parke Corbin of Moss' Neck, Caroline, who had within the last year put it in through repair, was entirely consumed by fire on Nov 13. The News says that this was the largest & oldest private dwlg in the State, built entirely of imported brick.

Explosion at N Y on Sat: the boiler of the propeller tow-boat **Resolute** exploded killing Wm Sheppard, engineer, & Saml T Cook, cook. It severely injured the capt, Woodhull Hartman; Jos Plummer, fireman; Thos Watts, deck hand; Chas Malony, boy; & Woodfield, assist fireman.

John R Stockman, Mayor of the City of Natchez, died there on Nov 11; a native of Pa; resided in Natchez for the last 16 years; elected Mayor in 1843, & retained the ofc by the popular vote to the hour of his death.

Household & kitchen furniture at auction: on Nov 26, at the residence of Rev S G Gassaway, on the corner of 1st & Market sts. –E S Wright, auct

Trustees sale of improved property on 14th st west: by deed of trust dated Jan 9, 1846, recorded in Liber W B, 123, folios 289, one of the land records for Wash Co, D C: sale on Dec 27, of half part of lot 12 in square 253, in Wash City, bounded by the house & lot owned by the heirs of John Poor, on the north by the house & lot owned by the heirs of Wm James, & on the west by 14th st, being the property conveyed unto Joshua Dawson by Thos H Gilliss, by his indenture, recorded in Liber A F 31, folios 107, of the land records of Wash Co, together with all & singular the bldgs & improvements thereon. –John W Maury, trustee -A Green, auctioneer

For sale, one of the most elegant houses in Gtwn, with coach house & stable attached, on the corner of Gay & Green sts, & was occupied for several years by the Hon R Barnwell Rhett. Apply to Otho L Manchester, Bridge st, Gtwn.

Sale of valuable property: by deed of trust from Richd G Briscoe to the subscribers, dated on the 22nd, & recorded on the 24th day of Feb, 1849, in Liber J A S 2, folios 304 to 310, of the land records of Wash Co, D C: sale of all that part of lot 9, in square 382, in said city, at 9th & La ave; improved with 8 three-story brick stores, with granite fronts & slate roofs. –John A Linton, Robt W Latham, Aug E Perry, trustees -C W Boteler, auct

On Sat the Paper Mill near the Chain Bridge, 4 miles above Gtwn, was destroyed by fire. It was the only mill of that description in this District. The mill was partly owned & worked by Mr Geo Hill, jr. The loss exceeds $2,000. Mr O M Linthicum, of Gtwn, also had an interest in the property.

Rev Stephen G Gassaway, having resigned his position as Rector of Christ Church, Gtwn, yesterday delivered his farewell sermon. He had been connected to the Church for some 8 years. We believe his new field of ministerial labor will be in St Louis.

The fine schnr **Rachel Jane**, was launched at N Y last Wed, from the ship-yard of Mr John E Darling. She is intended for the Washington trade, & to be commanded by Capt Saml N Smith, who is part owner.

Died: on Nov 24, after a protracted illness, Mr John Gaither, aged 38 years. His funeral is tomorrow at 9 o'clock, at his residence on 6th st, between G & H sts.

Died: Nov 12, at **Pleasant Hill**, St Mary's Co, Md, Mrs Ann A Carpenter, consort of Wm Carpenter, in her 68th year. She leaves a devoted family to mourn their irreparable loss.

Died: on Sat, in Wash City, A Sophia Edmondston, youngest daughter of Mr Franklin Edmonston, in her 15th year.

$50 reward: on Sat last the store of A & T A Richards, N & So Capitol sts, was entered, & $310 taken therefrom. Reward for the detection of the thief or recovery of the money. -A & T A Richards

Mrs Garret Anderson has just received a large supply of new & popular Music; superior guitars & violins. Pa ave, 2 doors east of the Irving House.

TUE NOV 26, 1850
Geo T Bigelow has been appointed a Judge of the Supreme Court of the State of Mass, to fill the vacancy occasioned by the decease of Judge Wilde.

Gen Garret D Wall, U S Senator from N J during Gen Jackson's term, died on Fri, at his residence in Burlington, N J. His disease was dropsy on the chest.

The model of the first steamboat [built by John Fitch] was discovered a few days ago in the garret of the late residence of Col Kilbourne, a brother-in-law of John Fitch, near the town of Columbus, Ohio. It has been in the possession of Col K more than 30 years. It is about 2 feet long, & set upon wheels.

Col Chas May, formerly in command of the Barracks at Carlisle, Pa, arrived at that place from Santa Fe on Tue. He look well, though somewhat reduced in flesh from sickness & the hardships of a campaign in New Mexico.

The Hon Seth Barton, while American Charge d'Affaires in Chili, married a lady of high standing in that country. She came with him to the U S, & took up residence at New Orleans. We regret to see from the papers that she died suddenly on Nov 14, at age 28 years, of cholera.

Trustee's premptory sale: by authority of a decree of the Circuit Court of Wash Co, D C, passed in a cause wherein Bronough M Daringer is cmplnt, & Wm Choppin & Archibald C Peachy are dfndnts: auction on Dec 26, of the following property, near Brentwood, on the limits of Wash City: land is in Wash Co, beginning at the end of the lands of Mary Y Walsh, held under an indenture of partition between John Farley & wife & Jos C Walsh & his wife & the late Clement Cox, dated Sep 29, 1838; line runs near a division line of Robt Y Brent; & near that of Fenwick: with a dwlg house & out bldgs. —W Redin, trustee -A Green, auctioneer

Commission on Claims against Mexico: 1-Memorial of John Patherson, claiming for demurrage of schnr **Fanny**, at Campeachy, in 1843, & for the loss of a chain cable, being taken up for consideration, together with the proofs & documents connected therewith, the Board came to an opinion that the claim was not a valid one against the Republic of Mexico: the same was not allowed. 2-Memorial of Charlotte B Hotz, adm of Peter Hotz, claiming for general average on schnr **Arete Ellis**, & for loss & damage of cargo & vessel, being taken up for consideration, together with proofs & documents connected therewith, the Board came to an opinion that the claim was not a valid one against the Republic of Mexico: the same was not allowed.

Balt, Nov 25. Mr Murdock, the tragedian, under mental alienation, wandered off from this city a few days ago, & got on the cars at Bladensburg, whither he had walked. His father has him in charge at Barnum's; his mind still effected.

Mrd: on Nov 20, at St Peter's Church, by Rev Mr Lanahan, J Alexander Simpson, of Gtwn, D C, to Julia C, 4th daughter of the late Guiseppe Franzoni.

Mrd: on Nov 7, at the residence of Jas W S Donnell, in Lawrence Co, Ala, by Rev Mr Bridinthat, Hon Truman Smith, of Litchfield, Conn, to Miss Mary A Dickinson, of the former place.

WED NOV 27, 1850
The funeral of the aged Hon Richd M Johnson, distinguished patriot, took place at Frankfort, on Nov 20. The places of private business in the city were closed in his honor.

Election in Calif on Oct 7 resulted in the election of Jas F Nooney, [Whig] as superintendent of public instruction; Jac A McDougal, [Dem] atty gen; E H Thorpe, [Dem] clerk of supreme court. Vallejo appears to have been selected as the seat of gov't.

Five of the men injured by the explosion of the two-boat **Resolute** have died: Woodhull Hartman, capt; Wm Shepard, engineer; S F Hall, cook-colored; Jos Plummer & Woodhull Kemble, two of the hands. Thos Watts was mortally wounded & not expected to live.

Postmaster Gen established the following new Post Ofcs for week ending Nov 23, 1850.

Ofc	County, State	Postmaster
Coila	Washington, N Y	Robt McNeil
N'th Tarrytown	West Chester, N Y	Wm P Lyon
Hamlet	Chautauque, N Y	Jesse M Tiffany
Bethlehem Centre	Albany, N Y	Lucius W Vider
Quiet Dell	Harrison, Val	Abel P Bond
Zion	Iredell, N C	Thos L Jennings
Sulphur Springs	St Clair, Ala	John McDaniel
Glencoe	Bolivar, Miss	Romulus Thistle
Tangapaha	St Helena P, La	Jas H George
Plenitude	Anderson, Texas	Jas S Hanks
Union Bridge	Titus, Texas	J W Dabbs
Oldenburg	Smith, Texas	C C Taylor
Armstrong Academy	Choctaw Nation, Ark	Philip P Brown
Martin's Landing	Perry, Ia	Job Hatfield
Hemlo	Whitesides, Ill	Asa M Abbott
Ohio	Andrew, Mo	Widow Henderson
Alanthus Grove	Gentry, Mo	Abraham Engart
Oak Grove	Linn, Iowa	Levi W Johnson
Delhi	Winnebago, Wis	Wm B Miller

Names Changed:
Cato Four Corners, Cayuga Co, N Y, changed to Meridian.
Foundry, Pulaski Co, Va, changed to Humility.
Windsor, Bureau Co, Ill, changed to Indiantown.
Keiths, Titus Co, Texas, changed to Lone Star.

A gentleman residing in Gtwn wishes to employ a tutor for his family. –O C Wight

Corp Ordinances-Wash. 1-Act for the relief of the heirs of Francis Iardella: damage, if any, to the property at the corner of N J ave & south B st, belonging to the above, by change in graduation, to be paid to the heirs: sum shall not exceed $150.

Commission on Claims against Mexico: 1-Memorial of Jos Bowles, withdrawn by leave on Jun 17 last in order to amend, was resubmitted, examined & ordered to be received. 2-Memorial of David Douglas, claiming for expulsion from Chihuahua on Sep 6, 1846, for 6 months' imprisonment, & for consequent damages, was submitted, examined, & suspended. 3-Memorial of Jas H Clay, claiming for seizure on Dec 14, 1845, of schnr **Susannah**, of which he was master & half owner, for her confiscation, & for his own fine & imprisonment at Matamoros, was submitted, examined, & ordered to be received. 4-Memorial of John Christian, a seaman, claiming for confiscation of property & imprisonment of person at Monterey, Calif, in 1840, was submitted, examined, & ordered to be received.

Orphans Court of Wash Co, D C. In the case of Susan K & Jeremiah Williams, adms of Ann Stewart, deceased, the Court & adms have appointed Dec 17 next, for the settlement of the estate, of the assets in the hands of the adms, so far as the same has been collected & turned into money. –Edw N Roach, Reg/o wills

THU NOV 28, 1850
Wash Corp: 1-Cmte of Claims: bill for the relief of John Shreeve: passed. 2-Bill for the relief of J E Dunavin: agreed to. 2-Cmte of Claims: asked to be discharged from the further consideration of the ptn of Jas Maher. 3-Cmte of Claims: bill for the relief of W H Barnaclo: passed. Same cmte: act for the relief of Fanny Buchanan: passed. Same cmte: asked to be discharged from the further consideration of the ptn of P Ennis: which was agreed to.

For sale: *Hygeian Hall*, a snug Farm in Va, containing 85 acres,: improvements are new & tastily built, barn, etc. City property would be taken in part. Address Richd B Lloyd, Alexandria, Va. I have a bright mulatto boy, aged 16 years, called John Clavoe, strolling about the city. To any one taking him up I will give $10.

Household & kitchen furniture at auction: on Dec 3, at the residence of Mr Montgomery Parks, on I st, between 9th & 10th sts. –C W Boteler

Desirable Farm in market: by decree rendered in the Circuit Superior Court of Law & Chancery for Berkeley Co, on Oct 2, 1850, in which Vincent M Butler, adm with the will annexed of Wm Shortt, is cmplnt, & Jacob Van Doren & others are dfndnts: public auction on Dec 30, before the court-house in Martinsburg, that desirable Farm belonging to Jacob Van Doren, & upon which his tenant, Wm Coffenberger, at this time resides. This farm embraces 330 acres: the dwlg house is one of the best in this section of the State, a large stone rough-cast bldg, recently erected. –Andrew M Vanarsdale, Spec Com'r

Hon Isaac R Douglass, Judge of the 13th Judicial Court of Va, died on Sat at Charlestown, in his 62nd year. He was attacked with apoplexy on Tue, on his return home from holding the fall term of his Court for Fred'k Co. [Dec 4th newspaper: in the obituary-Judge Douglass died on Nov 24, in his 61st year, leaving a wife & children to mourn their loss.]

Pension & Genr'l Agency: Geo C Ames, having resigned the ofc which he held in the Bureau of the Com'r of Pensions for the last 7 years, has associated with him Tully R Wise, in an Agency for the prosecution of claims. His connection with the Pension Bureau was 5 years. Address either at Wash, D C.

In Chancery: Circuit Court of Wash Co, D C. Jos L Shoemaker, vs Mary Shoemaker, Edw Jas Shoemaker, & others, widow & heirs of David Shoemaker. The late David P Shoemaker died seized of 17 acres of land in this county, on the New road, about 1 mile from Gtwn, & of a dwlg house on part of lot 163, in Beatty & Hawkins' Addition to Gtwn, & of parts of lots 163 & 164, in the same Addition, intestate, leaving the cmplnts & dfndnts above mentioned, & the other dfndnts [minors] in the bill named, his widow & children & heirs at law; that the said real estate is not susceptible of division among said heirs; & that it would be for the advantage of the adults as well as the minor heirs that the same should be sold for division; the object of said bill is to obtain a sale of the same pursuant to the act of Assemby of 1785, c 72 s 12; & it appearing that Edw Jas Shoemaker is now a resident of Calif: ordered that the non-resident dfndnt appear in this Court on or before the first Mon in April next. –Jno A Smith, clerk

By writ of 2 writs of fieri facias, I will expose to public auction, on Dec 28, of the south part of lot 3 in square 837, in Wash City, seized & taken as the property of Wm H Hamilton, & to satisfy debts due John M Young. –David Westerfield, Constable

Furnished rooms for rent: Mrs C M Fleury, Pa ave, between 9th & 10th sts.

Trustee's sale of household furniture: by deed of trust from Mrs E C B Thompson to the subscriber, dated Dec 8, 1849, recorded in Liber J A S 7, folios 400 thru 404: sale at the residence of the said Mrs Thompson, Pa ave, between 4½ & 6th sts. –J L Smith, trustee -C W Boteler, auct

For rent: the house on the corner of I & 13th st, lately occupied by Mr Devereaux, deceased. The house is nearly new, built in the most modern style. –W A Evans, at the Treas Bldg

Premptory sale of very valuable lots: by deed from all the heirs at law of the late Lewis Grant Davidson: the remaining lots in Wash City: Lots 13 thru 19 in square 126. Lot 2 in square 127. Lots 1 thru 9 in square 161. Lots 2, 4, 5, 11, 16, & 21, in square 163. Lots 10 thru 12, & 14 thru 16, in square 165. Lots 2 & 4 in square 168. Lots 1 thru 25 in square 183. Lots 1 thru 6, & lots 8 thru 16, & lot 18, in square 184. These lots are numbered according to Davidson's subdivision. Some are in the square immediately east of the residence of W W Corcoran. –W Redin -A Green, auctioneer

Household & kitchen furniture at auction: on Dec 3, at the late residence of M Devereaux, deceased, 13th & I sts. –Dyer & McGuire, aucts

SAT NOV 30, 1850
Capt Henry Johnson, of Lexington, Ky, now with his family at his plantation near Lake Washington, Miss, lost 28 of his negroes recently by cholera.

Friends' Asylum for the Insane: located about 5 miles north of Phil city: under the care of Dr Joshua H Worthington, Superintendent, & Wm & Mary D Birdsall, Steward & Matron. –Chas Ellis, Clerk of the Board of Managers, 56 Chestnut st, Phil; Wm Bettle, Sec of the Cmte on Adminissions, 14 south 3rd st, Phil, Pa.

Balt, Nov 29. The large steamer **Columbus**, which runs between Balt & Richmond as a freight & passenger boat, was totally destroyed by fire yesterday, while on her way to Richmond, in the Chesapeake Bay, off the mouth of the Potomac. All escaped in lightboats. She was commanded by Capt Hollingshead. The boat was valued at $60,000.

Mrd: on Nov 25, by Rev O B Brown, Mr Albert Buckley to Miss Britania A Smith, both of Prince Wm Co, Va.

Died: on Nov 28, at the residence of her son, in Montg Co, Md, Mrs Edw Stubbs, consort of Edw Stubbs, in her 63rd year. Her funeral will take place from St Patrick's Church, this day, at 12 o'clock.

Died: on Nov 28, Carvallo, infant son of Jas & Henrietta Tucker, aged 6 months & 2 weeks. His funeral is at 2 o'clock this afternoon, from the residence of the parents, N Y ave, between 9th & 10th sts.

House for rent: corner of 6th & G sts. Apply to Mrs A Allen, near the premises, or to Thos C Donn, J P, La ave, near 7th st.

MON DEC 2, 1850
The ship **Kate Hunter**, which arrived at N Y from Tampa Bay, brought the following passengers: S G DeCamp, Surgeon U S A; S C Ridgely, Brevet Major, 4th Artl, commanding battalion; G W Getty, Brevet Capt 4th Artl; G W Rains, Brevet Capt; J A Browne, 1st Lt; R M Howard, 1st Lt; J C Moore, 2nd Lt, 2nd Artl & lady; & 5 companies of 4th Artl, C F H S & M, numbering 225 men.

The steamer **Gipsey** arrived at New Orleans & brought down from Baton Rouge Co I, 4th Artl, under the command of Maj J B Scott & Lt J W Hazzard, A C S & Q M, & landed at the barracks below the city. They are enroute for ***Fort Washington***, on the Potomac river. –New Orleans Delta [No date-current item.]

The Cherokee Advocate of Nov 5 records the death of Saml Downing, a member of the Nat'l Council. [No death date given-current item.]

Jonathan Phillips, a boy of 12 years, has just been convicted of manslaughter at Phil, in killing another boy, with whom he was quarelling, with a pair of tongs, & sentenced to 2 years' imprisonment.

Mrd: on Nov 30, by Rev Mr Blox, Johnson Eliot, M D, to Miss Mary J Llewellyn, all of Wash City.

Mrd: on Nov 26, by Rev Mr Hodges, Mr Wm H Havenner to Miss Catharine Collins, both of the Dist of Columbia.

Died: on Nov 30, in Wash City, in his 45th year, John G Brown, late of N Y.

Orphans Court of Wash Co, D C. In the case of Moses Poor, adm of Ann W Benning, deceased, the adm & Court have appointed Dec 24 next, for the final settlement of said estate: of the assets in the hands of the administrator. –Ed N Roach, Reg/o wills –M Poor, adm

Millard Fillmore, Pres of the U S, recognizes J M Wright, who has been appointed Vice Consul of Austra, at Appalachicola, in Florida. Also: Andrew Low, who has been appointed Vice consul of Austria at Savannah, Georgia. Nov 23, 1850

Dr A Wislizenus, late of St Louis, having taken up his residence in Wash, tenders his services to the public in the various branches of his profession. Ofc & residence on Pa ave, south side, one square west of the Navy Dept.

Miss E B Scott will give music Lessons on Piano & Guitar at Miss Mary E Bronaugh's next door to the Hon Mr Holmes' on Missouri ave, between 3rd & 4½ sts.

Harper's new monthly magazine for Dec: this number commences the second volume. -Jos Shillington, Agent, Odeon Bldg, 4½ & Pa ave, Wash.

TUE DEC 3, 1850
31st Congress-2nd Session, commenced Dec 2, 1850. 1-Mr Joel B Danner, elected from the 15th Congressional district of Pa, to fill the vacancy occasioned by the death of the Hon Henry Nes. 2-Mr Geo W Morrison, elected from the 3rd Congressional district of N H, to fill the vacancy occasioned by the resignation of Mr Jas Wilson.

WED DEC 4, 1850
U S Patent Ofc: ptn of Dexter Pierce of Montague, Mass, praying for the extension of a patent granted to him Mar 11, 1837: for an impovement in scythe snaths. –Thos Ewbank, Com'r of Patents

Orphans Court of Wash Co, D C. Letters of administration on the personal estate of Adam Sweitzer, late of said county, deceased. –A E L Keese, adm

Mobile Register, Nov 27: dreadful steamboat explosion. The steamboat **Arkansas No 5** arrived at this port yesterday, with the painful intelligence that the steamboat **Antoinette Douglass**, Capt Montgomery, had burst her boilers yesterday, at Tait's Shoals, on the Alabama, killing a very large number of passengers. There were about 125 passengers aboard, besides the ofcrs & hands, who numbered some 40 more. The passengers were asleep at the time of the explosion. Among the killed we recognize Mr Montgomery, the brother of the Capt. Edw McCord, a son of Col McCord, of Lowndes, was dreadfully scalded, & died just as the **Arkansas** landed here. Of the number of ladies & children aboard, not one was hurt. [Dec 5th newspaper: names of the dead, so far as reported: J A Golson, of Antigua; Saml Montgomery, barkeeper; Edw McCorde, of Mobile; A G Tuttle, of Pike; Adolphus Carter, of Wilcox; N M King, of Ga; T H Lockett & John Cole, of Marion, Ala; S A Watts, of Dallas.]

Wash City Ordinance: 1-Act for the relief of J E Dunawin: $5 fine imposed for running a carryall without license is remitted, provided he pay the costs of prosecution.

Criminal Court Grand Jury:

Thos Carbery, Foreman	Henry Matthews	Shemuel Godwin
Geo Lowry	Henry Haw	Jas A Kennedy
W G W White	Thos Bates	Matthew St C Clarke
Ulysses Ward	O M Linthicum	Jos Walsh
Gregory Ennis	Selby Scaggs	John Mason
Wm Orme	Wm Easby	Wm C Bamberger
B B French	Walter Smoot	Wm Marshall
John Purdy	Jas A Gordon	Robt S Patterson

District Court: Monday: true bill found against Jas Matthews, Ecles Richend, & John Fitzpatrick, charged with mutiny on board of the brig **Ann Elizabeth** whilst on her passage from Gtwn to Boston, in Oct last. The prisoners will be tried for this offence.

Official: Gen Orders 41: War Dept, Adj Gen's Ofc, Wash, Dec 2, 1850. The Pres appoints the following ofcrs to constitute a Board, to assemble at Wash City, on Dec 2, 1850: to provide for additional grades of commissioned ofcrs in the U S Army, & if so, what grades in addition to the present organizations should be created.
Brvt Maj Gen T S Jesup, Pres of the Board
Brvt Maj Gen J E Wool
Brvt Maj Gen G Gibson
Brvt Brig Gen J G Totten
Brvt Brig Gen G Talcott
Col I B Crane, 1st Artl
Brvt Col E A Hitchcock, 3rd Infty
Brvt Maj J F Lee, Recorder
Report their opinions to this Dept: C M Conrad, Sec of War.

Mrd: on Nov 28, by Rev T Myers, Mr Wm Garner to Miss Mary Ann Gibson, all of Wash City.

Mrd: on Nov 28, in Poughkeepsie, N Y, Hon Robt L Rose, of Ontario Co, to Anna Macomb.

Died: on Dec 3, suddenly, Mr D E Dunscomb, of Wash City, aged 63 years. His funeral is this Thu evening, at 3 p m.

Died: on Nov 5, at the residence of Robt Swift, Island St Thos, W I, Anne Middleton, wife of Thos McEwen, of Phil, Pa, & daughter of the late Ralph Izard, of South Carolina.

Trustee's sale of real estate: on Dec 2, by deed of trust recorded in Liber W B 138, folios 188 thru 191: sale of all the lots, or parcels of ground owned or claimed by Thos Y Conley & Azariah Fuller, in square 60, & believed to be lot #1; that part of lot #2 which was conveyed by Scholfield to Evans on Jan 28, 1797; & lots 3, 5, & 6 in said square: with a large frame dwlg-house & stable. –H Naylor, trustee -A Green, auct

THU DEC 5, 1850
Senate: 1-Memorial of John R Presher, of Tioga Co, N Y, asking for a pension, in consideration of certain injuries received while in the naval service of the U S during the late war with Great Britain: referred to the Cmte on Pensions. 2-Memorial of Lt Wm D Porter, of the U S Navy, asking to be remunerated for expenses incurred in conveying from Genoa to the U S his excellency Amin Bey & suite, a Com'r from his serence highness the Sultan of Turkey: referred to the Cmte on Foreign Relations. 3-The case of Wm Wilkinson & others: referred to the Cmte on Revolutionary Claims. 4-Resolved, that the Sec of War be directed to lay before the Senate the proceedings of a court-martial holden at *Fort Constitution*, in Portsmouth, N H, on Sep 10 last, for the trial of ___ *Haniver, a private soldier, on the charges of mutiny & disobedience of orders. 5-Cmte of Claims: ptn of Jno Anderson, deceased: recommitted to the Cmte of Claims. 6-Cmte of Claims: ptn of John McAvoy: not entitled to relief. 7-Cmte on Pensions: adverse report on the memorial of Susannah Rose: discharged from the further consideration of the same. 8-Cmte of Claims; ptn of Martin Dubois: discharged from the further consideration of the same. 9-Cmte of Pensions: ptn of Wm C Sterrett: discharged from the further consideration of the same. 10-Cmte of Pensions: ptn of Garet Burns: discharged from the further consideration of the same. 11-Cmte of Claims: ptn of Thos B Winston: ought not to be granted. 12-Cmte on Naval Affairs: ptn of John J Glasson: memorial not be granted. 13-Cmte on Pensions: ptn of Wm Fergurson: ought not to be granted. 14-Cmte on Naval Affairs: ptn of Julius Meire: ought not to be granted. 15-Cmte of Claims: ptn of N B Hill, adm of Gilbert Stalker, deceased: praying payment for the use of the steamboat **James Adams**, be rejected. 16-Cmte on Pensions: ptn of certain citizens of Pa in behalf of Eliz Porter, widow of Jos Porter: discharged from the further consideration of the same. [*Dec 13th newspaper: Wm Hanniver, court martial case.]

Intemperance & Murder. Last week in Talbot Co, Md, Thos Grinnum was convicted of the murder of Thos Hemmons, in Vienna, on Oct 3 last. The sentence of death was pronounced by Judge Hooper.

House of Reps: 1-Intelligence received of the decease of the Hon Chester Butler, who died in Phil, on his way from this city to his own home, in Wilkesbarre, on Oct 5. He was seized by illness & died on the 3rd or 4th day after he was attacked. His last moments were cheered by the presence of her whose love & devotion could not fail to give, even to the house of a stranger, a character as benignant as that of the home of childhood. He was descended from Revolutionary ancestors. The Col Zebulon Butler who commanded the tragedy which happened in the valley of Wyoming, [his birthplace,] met their death by the hands of the savages.

Commission on Claims against Mexico: 1-Memorial of Lewis Polock, claiming for seizure of person & imprisonment, & for destruction of property, at San Francisco, in 1840: ordered to be received. 2-Memorial of Chas H Cooper, claiming for seizure of person & imprisonment, with consequent losses of property, at Santa Cruz, Calif, in 1840: ordered to be received. 3-Memorials of Jos Bolles & of John Christian, seaman, claiming for imprisonment of person & confiscation of property, in Calif, in 1840: claims are valid: amount to be awarded subject to the future action of the Board. 4-Memorial of Jas H Clay, claiming for seizure of schnr **Susannah**, at Matamoros, in 1845: same was allowed: amount to be awarded subject to the future action of the Board.

Mrd: on Dec 3, by Rev S A Roszell, Mr Quincy Page, of Wash, to Miss Mary Louisa Fitzhugh, formerly of Winchester, Va.

Died: on Dec 4, at Brentwood, near Wash, Mary Y, wife of Lt Jos C Walsh, U S Navy, & daughter of the late Hon Jos Pearson. Her funeral will take place at the residence of Mrs Pearson, on Fri, at half-past 2 p m.

Died: on Oct 10 last, at San Francisco, Calif, Thos Jefferson Smith, jr, in his 22nd year, son of Thos Jefferson Smith, of the same place, formerly judge of the Marine Court of N Y C. Mr Smith, jr, was a native of Wash, educated in N Y. The District & Superior Courts honored his memory by adjourning to attend his funeral

For sale or rent: my house near 10th & G sts. Apply to Jas Caden, on the premises.

Recently in St Mary's Co, Jas Gardner, a youth of 19 years, was killed by the accidental discharge of his own gun.

FRI DEC 6, 1850
Wash City: 1-Mr John Fill was elected as teacher of the Male Primary School to be established in the 2nd School Dist. 2-Miss E A King was elected as teacher of Primary School #3, 2nd Dist. 3-Miss Mary E Nevins was elected as assist teacher in Primary School #2, 1st Dist, in place of Miss E A King, promoted.

Criminal Court-Wash-Wed. Sarah Gordon was found guilty of petit larceny for stealing bed linen from the U S Hotel, the property of Edw Fuller. She was sentenced to 6 months' imprisonment in the county jail.

The late Sereno E Dwight, D C: the decease of this once distinguished man ought not to pass without a word of comment. He was minister of Park st Church, Boston, for many years; on his return from a visit to Europe, he became the Pres of Hamilton College, N Y, where he remained a few years, & then to New Haven, & opened a high school in the bldg now known as the Pavilion-his Lady, a daughter of the Hon David Daggett, of New Haven, co-operating. Since his wife's death, he has lived the life of a hermit in N Y C. -Journal of Commerce [No death date given-current item.]

Household & kitchen furniture at auction: on Dec 6, at the late residence of E L Childs, on Indiana ave, next door to the residence of the Rev Mr Cushman. -A Green, auctioneer

Postmaster Gen established the following new Post Ofcs for week ending Nov 30, 1850.

Ofc	County, State	Postmaster
Lenox Furnace	Berkshire, Mass	Wm A Phelps
Remington	Alleghany, Pa	Saml B Marks
Gordonsville	Lancaster, Pa	Hathorn Freeland
Riblet's	Richland, Ohio	Danl Riblet
Henley's Store	Franklin, Ga	John S Jenley
Thomas'	Marion, Fla	Spencer Thomas
Volusia	Marion, Fla	W Shepherd
Robinson's Springs	Autauga, Ala	A C Thomasson
Mandeville	St Tammany Parish, La	Lewis Coquillon
Mooresville	Union Parish, La	Thos T Moore
Pleasant Grove	Jefferson, Texas	John Houston
Narrows	Daviess, Ky	Wm A Oglesby
Durham	Hancock, Ill	Jehu Meguire
Pay Down	Osage, Mo	Thos Kinsey
Grand River	Caldwell, Mo	Wm Colvin
Slough	Clackeman, O Terr	John Switzler
Monticello	Lewis, O Terr	David Stone
Lexington	Clatsop, O Terr	David E Pease

Names Changed:
Quondock, Windham Co, Conn, changed to Sterling.
Sterling, Windham Co, Conn, changed to Sterling Hill.
Moon's Point, Lexington Co, Ill, changed to Reading.

Senate: 1-Memorial of the heir of Moses Elmer, deceased, a surgeon's mate in the Revolutionary army, asking to be allowed commutation pay: referred to the Cmte on Revolutionary Claims. The act of May 15, 1828, did not give him full pay for life, but only a pension from Mar 4, 1826, until his death, leaving 43 years of his life unprovided for. 2-Memorial of John Ashburn Hagan, a citizen of Ga, relative to a plan for preventing the overflow of the Mississippi & its tributaries: referred to the Cmte on Public Lands.

3-Ordered, that Jas M Marsh have leave to withdraw his papers. 4-Ordered that the papers relating to certain Creek Indians for losses sustained in the war of 1812, & the memorial of C M Hitchcock, exc of A R S Hunter, deceased, & the memorial of Amos & John E Kendall, & the ptn of Philip E Thomas & others, in behalf of the Seneca Indians: be recommitted to the Cmte on Indian Affairs. 5-Bill for the relief of John A McGaw, of N Y: referred to the Cmte of the Whole.

SAT DEC 7, 1850
Late from Mexico: Gen Thos Reguena died on Nov 30, at Gudalajara, & Gen Manuel Romero on Nov 31, at San Louis Potosi. Gen Joaquin Rea, living at a village called Minerva, was, about the same time, murdered by one Felipe Delgado, & a band of scoundrels under his command.

On Sat last, in Vanattenville, N Y, in raising the frame work of a Methodist Church, the temporary support fell killing Mr Reuben Barnes. –Elmira Republican

Alexander Wilson was killed by a collision of the Phil & Paterson trains on Dec 1. The collision was the result of carelessness on the part of the Paterson train.

The iron steamship **Helena Sloman**, Capt Paulson, was abandoned at sea on Nov 28 in a sinking condition. She was kept afloat until discovered by the packet-ship **Devonshire**, Capt Hovey, who took off nearly all her passengers & crew & brought them to N Y. Five passengers & 3 seamen, & the 3rd mate of the **Devonshire**, were lost by the staving of a boat in transferring the passengers from one vessel to the other.

Commission on Claims against Mexico: 1-Memorial of Chas H Cooper, of Conn, claiming for seizure of person, imprisonment, & loses of property, in Calif, in 1840: same was allowed: amount to be awarded subject to the future action of the Board. 2-Memorial of Anthony S Robinson, son of Gen John Hamilton Robinson, claiming for pay of his father as an ofcr in the Mexican service: rejected. 3-Memorial of David Douglas, examined on Nov 26: ordered not to be received. 4-Memorial of Lewis M Dreyer: allowed: amount to be awarded subject to the future action of the Board; but this claimant to make further proof of the extent of his interest.

The U S frig **Brandywine**, arrived yesterday at the Brooklyn navy yard. She sailed from Norfolk on Sep 8, 1847. List of her ofcrs: Capt, Chas Boarman; Lts, Luther Stoddard, Saml Larkin, J R M Mullany, J J Guthrie; Purser, Edw Fitzgerald; Fleet Surgeon, Benj F Bache; Assist Surgeon, Philip Lansdale; Chaplain, John L Lenhart; acting Master, Richd L Law; 1st Lt of Marines, John C Grayson; Cmdor's Sec, Jacob J Storer; Passed Midshipmen, John T Barraud, Theodorick L Walker; Midshipmen, John G Sproston, Randolph K Breese, John P Baker, Wm Gwin, Bayard E Hand, Robt T Chapman; Capt's Clerk, Jos Montobio; Purser's Clerk, Elijah Goodridge; Boatswain, Wm Smith; Gunner, Thos P Venable; Carpenter, Jos Cox.

A colored nurse wanted. A slave, who is competent to take charge of a child 18 months old. Apply immediately to C D Blanchard, at the Census Ofc, on 8th st.

The U S frig **Saranac**, [recently built at Portsmouth, N J, for Gov't service,] sailed from N Y on Wed. She will touch at Norfolk for Com Parker, & thence probably proceed to the West Indies. List of her ofcrs: Jos Tattnall, Capt; Thos L Brent, O J Carr, W May, & Geo Wells, Lts; A N Smith, Sailingmaster; N Pinkey, Surgeon; M Duvall, Passed Assist Surgeon; J J Jones, Purser; J T Doughty, Lt of Marines; J P Stall, Passed Midshipman; D L Braine, J Rowan, B Gheradi, T Ramey, Midshipmen; W W W Wood, Chief Engineer; M Quin, W L Lynch, D Mapes, J W Parks, & A C Jackson, Assistants; John Crosby, Boatswain; H Robinson, Gunner; Chas Boardman, Carpenter; J Fraser, Sailmaker.

Mrd: on Dec 2, by Rev John J Murray, Robt A Griffin to Miss Mgt A Norris, both of Gtwn, D C.

MON DEC 9, 1850

Ill State Register: Hon Wm H Bissell, now representing the 1st Congressional dist of Ill, being a candidate in the same dist at the election lately held for Reps to the next Congress, was elected without opposition, receiving every vote, to the number of 12,941!

From Calif: 1-Mr John Bates, of Wash City, died at Sacramento on Nov 28, & Andrew T Bull, of Gtwn, died at San Francisco on Nov 31, both of cholera. 2-Francis E Jones, 20 years of age, son of John C Jones, formerly U S consul at Honolulu, died at that place on Sep 21. 3-The city hospital of Dr Smith, at San Francisco, was destroyed by fire on Nov 1. The sick, 150, were removed in safety. The dwlg of Mrs Irene McCready, adjoining, was likewise burnt.

On Mon, in our Criminal Court, the first conviction took place of Chas Weideig for willful perjury in a fraud case. [Obtaining money & land warrants as the pretended reps of soldiers entitled, under the law, to such money & bounty land.]

Miss Fanny Wallace closed a very successful engagement at the Adelphi last Sat. Her impersonation of Hamlet was the best we ever witnessed on the Washington boards. Mrs Geo Mossop, late Mrs Hunt, makes her first appearance there this evening.

Ofc of the Board of Health, Wash, Dec 5, 1850. Interments during the month of Nov, 1850: 63 total. Thos Miller, M D, Pres.

Wash Corp: 1-Bill for the relief of John Cox: passed. 2-Bill for the relief of A C Kidwell: passed. 3-Ptn from Thos Brestman for the remission of a fine: referred to the Cmte of Claims. 4-Cmte of Claims: Bill for the relief of Richd Bollenger, for the remission of a fine: passed. 5-Act for the relief of the heirs of Jas Nairn: referred to the Cmte on Finance. 6-Ptn of J S Reese, praying remission of a fine: referred to the Cmte on Claims. 7-Ptn of Geo Page, respecting the wharf now erecting by him on the Potomac, in front of square 472: referred to the Cmte on Wharves. 8-Ptn of Jas Towles & others, for relaying a gutter on H st north: referred to the Cmte on Improvements. 9-Act for the relief of Christian F Henry; & act for the relief of John McDevitt: referred to the Cmte of Claims. 10-Ptn of Jas Maher: laid on the table.

The citizens of Westmoreland Co, Va, the birthplace of Washington, have furnished a block of marble from that county for the monument to be erected at Salem, Mass; the city where sat the first provincial Congress, & whose ancestors were the first to resist & drive back the British troops in arms.

Millard Fillmore, Pres of the U S, recognizes Mr Geo Aitz, who has been appointed Vice Consul of Sardinia, at Mobile, in Alabama. –Dec 5, 1850

Charleston [S C] Mercury of Dec 4. At auction yesterday by Z B Oakes, the slaves belonging to the estate of the late Wm Brockelbank brought the following handsome prices:

Cato, 28, a plasterer: $2,135.
Sam, 30, a plasterer: $1,805.
Isaac, 24, a plasterer: $1,775.
Paris, 24, a plasterer: $1,100.
Noble, 20, a plasterer: $730.
Minnie, 24, a laborer: $805.
Hardtimes, 20, a laborer: $660.

Boots for the Season: Henry Janney, 8th st, near the Genr'l Post Ofc.

Saml Butt, Druggist & Chemist, corner of Pa ave & 12th sts.

Furnished rooms for rent: P A DeSaules [Waverly House, Pa ave, between 4½ & 6th sts.]

Mrd: on Nov 28, at Newport, Ky, by Rev C H Page, Thos B Bryan, of Cincinnati, Ohio, to Miss Jennie Byrd Page, of the former city.

Died: on Nov 26, near New Orleans, on her passage from Louisville to that city, Mary Lee Whiting, wife of Lt Wm B Whiting, U S Navy, in her 33rd year.

Died: on Nov 26, in New Orleans, of cholera, whilst on a visit to his daughter, Townshend Waugh, in his 60th year, formerly & for several years an efficient clerk in the Indian Bureau.

Notice to Heirs. The will of Isaac S Sweringen, late of Franklin Co, Ind, deceased, provides that after the death of his widow, notice shall be given to his legal distributes to prove their right to share in the distribution of his personal estate, & that all who do not make such proof within 3 years from the giving of such notice shall be precluded from any share whatever in such distribution. Mrs Barbara Sweringen, the widow of said testator, died Jul 4, 1848. Notice was then given. Hitherto but a single claim, out of a number known to exist, has been proved. Distribution will probably be in 1851. The amount is about $5,000. The undersigned will give all information in his power, & afford every facility for making the necessary proof. –J D Howland, Brookville, Indiana

TUE DEC 10, 1850
Liberal reward for return of a Spanish Tree Saddle, stolen from the stable of the subscriber on Dec 9. –John Carroll Brent

Senate: 1-Memorial of John H Dhiel, proposing to establish a line of steamers between Phil & Liverpool, for carrying the mail between those places, once a month, upon certain conditions: referred to the Cmte on Naval Affairs. 2-Ptn of Anna Norton & Louisa Forkit, daughters & sole surviving heirs at law of Zephaniah Ross, asking to be allowed the pension said Ross would have been entitled to had his name not been striken from the pension roll: referred to the Cmte on Pensions. 3-Memorial of the executors of Henry Eckford, deceased, asking payment of an amount declared to be due them by a judgment of the U S Circuit Court for the southern district of N Y: referred to be Cmte of Claims. 4-Ptn from Chester Griswold, a soldier in the last war with Great Britain, asking to be allowed arrears of pension: referred to the Cmte on Pensions. 5-Memorial of the heirs of Gen Stephen Moylan, asking the passage of an act declaring that the non-settlement of the accounts of said Moylan may be no bar to his heirs receiving commutation pay: referred to the Cmte of Claims. 6-Additional documents submitted relating to the claim of Thos R Johnson, adm of Rinaldo Johnson & Sally Ann Nuttritt, admx of Anne E Johnson: referred to the Cmte of Claims. 7-Ptn of Eliza M Evans, asking to be allowed interest on a sum of money advanced by her father, Walton White, deceased, for the use of a regt commanded by him during the Revolutionary war: referred to the Cmte on Revolutionary Claims. 8-Ptn of Denton Offutt, professing to make known for a just & reasonable compensation of a system of taming & improving the breed of all domestic animals: referred to the Cmte on Agriculture. 9-Ptn of Michl Hanson, on the files of the Senate: referred to the Cmte on Pensions. 10-Ptn of Philip R Frieze, on the files of the Senate: referred to the Cmte on Commerce. 11-Ptn of Wm C Easton, on the files of the Senate: referred to the Cmte on Military Affairs. 12-Mr Pearce to ask leave to introduce a bill for the relief of Mrs Sarah McKay. 13-Resolved, that the Sgt-at-Arms be authorized to employ as page to the Senate Thos Reed, late page to the Vice-Pres. 14-Bill for the relief of John A McGaw, of N Y, reconsidered in Cmte of the Whole: engrossed for a 3rd reading.

Green B Samuels has been unanimously elected by the Gen Assembly to be Judge of the Rockingham District of Va, vice Judge Smith, deceased.

Mr B R Hardin, son of Ben Hardin, of Ky, disappeared suddenly from Panama, shortly after he had received there the revocation of his appointment of Sec of Legation to Chili. The Panama Star says: on Fri last, as a party of gentlemen were ascending the mountain in the rear of the city, they discovered the remains of a human being. Bare bones was all that was left, but there is sufficient evidence to render them those of Hardin. A letter was found in one of the pockets dated Havana, Dec, 1849, addressed to Hon Ben Hardin, Bardstown, Ky, commencing: My dear father, & ending with Your affectionate son, Rowan. From the appearance of the ground there is some suspicion that he was murdered.

Henry Douglass, Florist & Seedsman: corner of 15th & G sts, Wash. [Ad]

Died: on Dec 9, Dr Jas B Waugh, lately of Jefferson Co, Va. His funeral will take place at the residence of the family, on F st, today at 3 o'clock.

Died: on Dec 8, in Wash City, Wm Seymour, aged 6 years, 2 months & 14 days, son of Geo C & Mgt S Ames, of Wash City. His funeral will be from the Church of the Epiphany, at 11 o'clock this morning.

Died: on Dec 5, at *Prospect Hill*, PG Co, Md, [the residence of Mr John M Brown,] John Grover, son of Dr W A & R Caroline Manning, aged 2 years, 6 months & 24 days.

D Francisco de Menezes de Brito do Rio, for some years attached to the Legation of Portugal in Wash City, died from the effects of disease of the heart. He was found dead by his attendants in his carriage. He was journeying towards Lisbon. [No death date given-current item.

WED DEC 11, 1850
Wash City Ordinance: 1-Act for the relief of C Buckingham, for work done in the 5th Ward: sum of $37.33 be paid to him, to pay a deficiency due him for laying water pipes. 2-Act for the relief of Patrick Flynn: fine imposed for selling window shades without license is remitted: provided he pay the costs of prosecution. 3-Act for the relief of John Cox: to be paid $16.08, being the costs incurred in a suit instituted against the late Com'r of the 6th Ward & the said Cox, for carrying into effect an order of the Board of Health. 3-Act for the relief of W W McCreery: the sum of $500 be paid to him to compensate for pecuniary losses & personal injuries said to have been sustained by him in consequence of falling into an open sewer on the night of Feb 21, 1850.

Senate: 1-Ptn of Jas C Wilson, a clerk in the ofc of the chief engineer, asking to be allowed an increase of compensation: referred to the Cmte on Military Affairs. 2-Ptn of Clara M Williams, asking that provision may be made by law for satisfying a military land warrant issued to her father for his services as a midshipman during the war of the Revolution: referred to the Cmte of Claims. 3-Additional documents submitted in relation to the claim of Eleazer Williams for a pension: referred to the Cmte on Pensions. 4-Ordered that Gen Leslis Combs have leave to withdraw his memorial & papers relating to a claim against the State of Texas. 5-Bill for the relief of Sarah D McKay: referred to the Cmte on Pensions. 6-Bill for the relief of E Parenstedt & Schumacher: passed. 7-Bill for the relief of John McGaw, of N Y: passed. 8-Bill to pay Allen G Johnson, the sum of $137.23, the value of certain military stores which were turned over by him in 1840 as quartermaster, but for which he had not been duly credited: engrossed for a third reading. 9-Cmte of the Whole, bill 78 for the relief of Brevet Maj H L Kendrick: to credit him with the sum of $1,294.66 in the settlement of his accounts of the sale made by him at Puebla, Mexico, by order of Gen Worth, of certain ordnance stores, the same being the amount that was stolen from him at Jalapa while conveying it to Vera Cruz. 10-Cmte of the Whole: bill for the relief of the legal reps of John Rice Jones, deceased.

U S Patent Ofc, Dec 10, 1850. Ptn of Edson Fessenden, conservator of the person & property of Wm Crompton, a lunatic of Hartford, Conn, [late of Taunton, Mass,] for the extension of a patent granted to said Crompton for an improvement in figure power looms, for 7 years from expiration of said patent, which takes place on Nov 25, 1851. -Thos Ewbank, Com'r of Patents

House of Reps: 1-Bill for the relief of Isaac Hill & sons: referred. 2-Memorial of Jas C Wilson, praying for an increase of salary. 3-Ptn of Jacquelin Taylor, Thos Ellis, & others, of Richmond, Va, praying the return of certain duties exacted under circumstances of peculiar hardship. 4-Ptn of Clara McWilliams, of Fredericksburg, Va, for an appropriation to make good a land warrant heretofore issued on compensation of the Revolutionary services of his father. 5-Memorial of Saml W Skinker, adm of Dr John Julian, surgeon in the war of the Revolution, praying for 5 years full pay under the act of Congress, passed Mar 22, 1783. 6-Memorial of Fayette Mauzy & Robt G Ward, praying for relief from a judgment obtained by the U S against them. 7-Bill for the relief of Saml Raybourn, of Alabama. 7-Resolved, that it be referred to the Cmte on Military Affairs to report a bill conferring the rank of Lt Gen upon Maj Gen Winfield Scott, for his gallant service in the late war with Mexico.

Circuit Court of Wash Co, D C, Oct Term, 1850. Wm S Herriman vs the adms & heirs at law of Thos J Davis & others. John Marbury, the trustee appointed by the decree of this court in the above entitled cause, to sell the real estate of Thos J Davis, deceased, for the payment of his debts, reported he sold the whole of said real estate, so far as it has come to his knowledge, & that Wm M Boyce, Wm D Beall, & Vincent J Taylor were the purchasers of the mill & machinery therein, & of the wharf thereto attached, for the sum of $30,100; & the warehouse adjoining the said mill property, & lying between it & the warehouse & property of John Mason, deceased, to the same persons, for $890. The purchasers have complied with the terms of the sale. –Jno A Smith, clerk

Household & kitchen furniture at auction: on Dec 19, at the residence of Mr Haswell, on 16th st, one square north of St John's Church. –Dyer & McGuire, aucts

The dwlg of John Dick, an aged German, who has resided in Carlisle, Pa, for a number of years past, was destroyed by fire last night, Dec 7. Mr Dick, his wife, & daughter, aged 27 years, perished in the flames.

Thos Mitchell, postmaster at West Fowler, St Lawrence Co, Utica, was arrested for robbing the U S mail. He was required to give bail in the amount of $3,000.

Mrd: on Dec 9, at St Patrick's Church, by Rev Wm Matthews, J Pearce Miller, of Waterford, Pa, to Miss Rosina Johnson, of Fairfax Co, Va!.

Commission on Claims against Mexico: 1-Memorial of Edw Dwyer & of J J H Gimmont, passengers on board of schnr **Champion**, claiming severally for losses by her capture at Matamoros, Apr 1, 1837, & for imprisonment & other personal injuries, they being then citizens of Texas: memorials were rejected.

To let in Gtwn: a convenient 3 story brick dwlg house on west side of Jefferson st, between Canal & Water st, in complete order. Apply to Wm Calhoun, opposite Jos Brooks', Collector, Gtwn, or to Chas De Selding, Todd's Bldg, Pa ave, Wash.

Wash Co, D C: I certify that Thos Perkins, of said county, brought before me, as an estray, a Chickasaw Horse. —Jas Crandell, J P [Owner is to prove property, pay charges, & take him away. —Thos Perkins, south side of the Eastern Branch Bridge]

Postmaster Gen established the following new Post Ofcs for week ending Dec 7, 1850.

Ofc	County, State	Postmaster
Letter A, No 2	Oxford, Maine	Noah Townsend
East Haven	Essex, Vt	Elijah Avery
White River Junction	Windsor, Vt	Saml Nutt
Manhattanville	N Y, N Y	Benj Moore
Blink Bonny	St Lawrence, N Y	Wm H Cleghorn
Limerick Bridge	Montgomery, Pa	Benj Frick
North Springfield	Summit, Ohio	Jacob Thompson
Gladeville	Preston, Va	Clinton Brown
Morgan's Ridge	Marion, Va	John Conothers
Glenn Mills	Culpeper, Va	John W Luttrell
Oatlands	London, Va	Saml Heflebower
Leavenworth	Darlington dist, S C	Thos E Howle
Meadway	Burke, Ga	S H Littlefield
Walnut Grove	Walton, Ga	John C Brewer
Peoria	Franklin, Ind	Jonas Roberson
Winterville	Decatur, Ind	John W Ammerman
Christiansburg	Brown, Ind	Geo Roush
Happy Valley	Carter, Tenn	N G Taylor
Buck Horn	Brown, Ill	Henry Briggs, jr
Elba	Dodge, Wis	Ambrose Foster

Names Changed:
East Surgar Load, Luzerne Co, Pa, changed to Mount Surprise.
Southland, Harden Co, Ky, changed to Big Clifty.
Snow Hill, Jefferson Co, Ky, changed to Hay's Spring.
Judy's Gap, Hickory Co, Mo, changed to Quincy.

Jenny Lind's first concert in Washington is to take place on Monday next, at the Nat'l Theatre, where the improvements are nearly completed.

Criminal Court-Wash. On motion of P B Key, B B French was admitted as an atty.

THU DEC 12, 1850
Chancery sale of valuable improved real estate: by decree of the Circuit Court of Wash Co, D C, sitting in equity, in the cause wherein Beverly W Boteler, Ellen Amelia Boteler, & Rosanna Phillips, infant, by her next friend, the said Beverly W Botler, heirs-at-law of Overton C Phillips, deceased, are cmplnts, & Angenetta Phillips, Sarah J Phillips, & Emily V Phillips, infants, & heirs-at-law of said Overton C Phillips, deceased, are dfndnts: the trustree will sell at public auction, on Jan 13 next, that piece or parcel of ground on 9th st west, between I & N Y ave, being part of lot 12 in square 373, with a 2 two-story frame houses. —Chas S Wallach, trustee -C W Boteler, auct

Senate: 1-Memorial of Wm Baynton, asking to be indemnified for certain merchandise destroyed by the Creek Indians in 1836: referred to the Cmte on Indian Affairs. 2-Memorial of Calvin B Seymourn, asking indemnification for merchandise destroyed by the Creek Indians in 1836: referred to the Cmte on Indian Affairs. 3-Memorial of Augustus Steele, asking payment of his salary & the expenses incurred by him for the hire of boat-hands while inspector of the customs at St Mark's, in Fla: referred to the Cmte on Commerce. 4-Additional documents submitted in relation to the claim of Isaac Varus, senior: referred to the Cmte of Claims. 5-Bill for the relief of Chas D Arfredson, late Charge d'Affaires ad interim of the U S at the Court of Norway & Sweden. 6-Announcement of the death of the Hon Amos E Wood, one of the Reps in the House of Reps, from the State of Ohio. He was born in Jefferson Co, N Y. In 1825, when about 15 years old, he removed with his father to Portage Co, Ohio. He was afterwards, for nearly 2 years, a member of the family of his near relative, the present Govn'r of the State. In 1833 he settled permanently in Woodville, Sandusky Co. He died at **Fort Wayne**, Ind, whither he had gone for the purpose of placing 2 of his children at school, on Nov 19 just passed.

Public sale of valuable property: by deed of trust from Bernard Brien to Clement Cox, dated Oct 3, 1845, & of records, & of a subsequent decree of the Circuit Court of Wash Co, D C, sitting as a Court of Chancery, made in the cause of Pearson vs Brien & others: sale on Dec 27, on the premises, all that part of lot 43 in Old Gtwn, on the south line of Bridge st; to the Tobacco Warehouse alley; parallel with Market space to the ground conveyed by Anthony Reitzell to Catharine Kurtz, & now held & owned by Thos Bogue. -Walter S Cox, trustee -A Green, auctioneer

In Chancery. John Withers against Sarah Payne & others, heirs at law of Jas Long. By order of the Circuit Court of Wash Co, D C, I am directed to ascertain & state the debts due from the late Jas Long. All persons having claims are to file on or before Feb 1 next. -W Redin, Auditor, City Hall, Wash.

House of Reps: 1-Ptn of Jas M Davis, Register, & J T B Stapp, Receiver of Public Moneys at the Land Ofc in Vandalia, Ill, praying compensation for locating military bounty land warrants.

Teacher wanted to take charge of a small school in a private family. –Jas W Foster, "The Plains" Post Ofc, Fauquier Co, Va

Female teacher wanted to conduct a school of 5 pupils in my family, my own daughters, from 11 to 18 years. –Th Goode, Hot Springs, Bath Co, Va

Female Union Benevolent & Employment Society of Wash: the undersigned gentlemen to act as collecting cmtes in their respective wards:

Geo J Abbott	J B H Smith	Robt Farnham
Maj Geo Bender	J H McBlair	D F Howard
Rev C A Davis	Wm H Dove	Wm F Bayly
Dr Richmond Johnson	Dr Wm B Magruder	Wm B Todd

McClintock Young	Thos Parker	Wm H Bland
John A Blake	Mathew G Emory	C W Davis
Jas F Haliday	John C Whitwell	Wm M Ellis
Danl Ratcliffe	Hugh Sweeny	G H Fulmer
Silas H Hill	Dr John B Blake	Chas H Gordon
J A M Duncanson	Jas Adams	Thos Thornley
John C Harkness	John C Brent	Dr N Young
R S Patterson	Peter Brady	Col Wm B Randolph
Valentine Harbaug	B B French	Saml Byington
Chas F Wood	Chas R Gardiner	Craven Ashford
David Saunders	John Underwood	D Morgan
Wm R Riley	G Watterston	Wm Wise
Wm H Campbell	Wm J McDonald	Jonas B Ellis
Stanislaus Murray	General Henderson	Joel W Jones
Fitzhugh Coyle	Robt M Coombs	

–W W Seaton, John P Ingle, Walter Lenox, Cmte

Criminal Court-Wash, Wed. 1-Isaiah Contee, free negro, guilty of grand larceny: sentenced to 2 years in the penitentiary. 2-Saml Ford, free negro, not guilty of grand larceny. 3-Bable Seymour, freed negro, guilty of an assault & battery with an intent to commit a rape.

House & lots of ground in Alexandria for sale: by decree of the Circuit Court for Alexandria Co, Val, rendered at Nov term, 1850, in the case of Larmour, guardian, vs Larmour et al: public sale on Jan 7,1851, the following property, in & near the said town of Alexandria, belonging to & comprising a large portion of the real estate of which the late Saml B Larmour died seized. 1-Two story brick store & lot on King st, between Water & Union sts. 2-A lot of ground on Water st, beginning at Swift's alley. 3-A lot of ground on the west side of Water st, 60 feet south of King st. 4-A 2 story brick dwlg house on north side of King st, between Patrick & Henry sts, beginning at the western line of the house now owned & occupied by Louis A Cazenove. 5-A square of ground bounded by Columbus, Alfred, Franklin, & Jefferson sts, with a frame & brick dwlg, know as *"the Village,"* & now occupied by Turner Dixon. 6-A square of 3 acres of ground east of *"the Village."* 7-A square, or 2 acres of ground, east of #6, with a small frame tenement thereon. 8-One acre of ground, beginning at the s e corner of the lot granted by the excs of John Alexander to Andrew Wales, in 1784, in front on Fairfax st 100 feet. 9-One half a square of ground, bounded by Pitt, Royal, & Wythe sts. 10-One half square of ground, bounded by St Asaph, Gibbon, & Pitt sts. 11-One half square of ground, bounded by Madison, Alfred, & Columbus sts. 12-A lot on Princess st, fronting on Princess st. 13-A tract of land in Alexandria Co, the south half of the 50 acre lot lying on the west side of the Wash Turnpike, about a half mile from town. 14-A square of ground, immediately south of the Village, bounded on the north by Jefferson st. This square is immediately in the rear of the house & lot occupied by Turner Dixon. 15-Three acres in Fairfax Co, adjoining the above on the west. 16-Two acres of ground near the Great Hunting Creek Bridge, in Fairfax Co. 17-A ground rent of $17.50 on a frame tenement, on the s e part of lot 14. –Francis L Smith, Chas E Stuart, Com'rs

Mrd: on Dec 9, in Balt, by Rev Dr Wyatt, Wm H Ford to Miss Virginia L, daughter of Richd Patten, of Wash City.

Mrd: on Dec 4, at Mt Airy, Richmond Co, Va, by Rev Wm N Ward, Jas C Jenifer, of Chas Co, Md, to Miss Louisa Rebecca, eldest daughter of Wm H Taylor.

Died: on Nov 28, at *Twiford*, his residence in Westmoreland Co, Va, after an illness of 8 days of inflammation of the lungs, Col John W Hungerford, in his 63rd year. He was an ofcr in the war of 1812, & acted as volunteer aid to his uncle, Gen John P Hungerford. He represented his native county, Westmoreland, in the Legislature of Va. The sorrowing widow alone can know how devoted & kind he was as a husband. His 6 children can never cease to remember a fond & indulgent father. –M

Appointments by the Pres: 1-Richd H Bayard, of Delaware, to be Charge d'Affaires of the U S, in Belgium, in place of Thos G Clemson, recalled. 2-Chas B Hadduck, of N H, to be Charge d'Affaires of the U S, in Portugal, in place of Jas Brown Clay, recalled at his own request.

FRI DEC 13, 1850
Furnished rooms to let: one square north of the Capitol. Inquire of Thos Scrivener.

House of Reps: 1-Bill to make compensation to Walter Colton: committed. 2-Bill for the relief of Hyacinth Riopel & others, heirs & assignees of Ambrose Riopel, deceased: committed. 3-Cmte on the Judiciary: bill of the Senate for the relief of Gamaliel Taylor, [late marshal of Indiana,] & his sureties: reported the same back without amendment. 4-Ptn of Richd Nodine & 41 others, members of a company of sappers & miners at West Point, praying to be discharged or disbanded. 5-Ptn of Matthew Small, an invalid soldier of the war of 1812. Also, a like ptn of Oliver Brown.

Mrs Eliza W Farnham, formerly a matron of the Sing Sing Prison, & the projector of a partially successful scheme of female emigration to Calif, has become the proprietress of a fine farm near San Francisco, the crops of which this season are estimated to be worth $60,000. The Calif Courier gives an account of a judgment obtained by her in one the courts in San Francisco against Jos S Rucker, for $3,661.27. –N Y Courier

Senate: 1-Ptn of Nancy Whiting, widow of an ofcr of the army during the last war with Great Britain, asking a pension: referred to the Cmte on Pensions. 2-Ptn of Jas Dunning, asking interest on an amount due under a contract with an ofcr of the Gov't: referred to the Cmte of Claims. 3-Memorial of John A Rogers, asking compensation for his services as an examiner in the land ofcs in Alabama & Mississippi: referred to the Cmte of Claims. 4-Memorial of Mrs Martha Gray, of Boston, the widow of Capt Robt Gray, the discoverer of the Columbia river. He was in the naval service of the country during a part of the Revolutionary war. Being afterwards employed in the merchant service, he made a voyage, between 1787 & 1790, in the sloop **Washington**, & was the first to carry the flag of our Union at the masthead of a vessel bearing that august name in triumph round the world. In 1792 he discovered & entered the Columbia river, & gave to it the name of the ship which he then commanded. Here is the original sea-letter, signed by Geo Washington, & attested by Thos Jefferson, under which the Columbia sailed from Boston in 1790. Here is a similar paper, bearing the seal of the Commonwealth of Mass, & the signature of John Hancock, its then Govn'r. Here is the clearance certificate from the Boston custom-house, signed by Benj Lincoln, then collector of the port, but whose name is more familiar to history in its connexion with more than one of our great Revolutionary battlefields, both at the North & at the South. Here too are the original instructions of Jos Barrell, the owner of the **Columbia**, an emiment merchant of that day, showing the objects with which the voyage was undertaken. Capt Gray died in 1806 leaving a widow & 4 children, & very little property. Mrs Gray & her daughters, only one of whom has been married, have since supported themselves mainly by their own exertions & economy, the widow having never even enjoyed the benefit of a pension for her husband's Revolutionary services, owing in part to the date of her marriage, & in part to some technical defect in the evidence. Her ptn was referred to the Cmte of Revolutionary Pensions, who reported in favor of giving her an immediate pension of $500 per annum during the remainder of her life, & when surveys should have been made, a township of land in Oregon should be granted to her & her children. 5-Cmte on Revolutionary Claims: bill for the relief of Francis Nash, with a recommendation that it do not pass. Same cmte: memorial of Caroline L Eustis, widow of M Eustis, late a surgeon in the Revolutionary war, submitted an adverse report in writing. Same cmte: ptn of the reps of Wm Russworn, submitted an adverse report in writing. 6-Passed: bill for the relief of Allen E Johnson; bill for the relief of Brevet Maj H L Kendrick; & bill for the relief of the legal reps of John Rice Jones, deceased.

Mr Wm Hurd, formerly a paper-maker of Newton Lower Falls, Mass, was killed on Tue, near Framingham, on the Worcester railroad, by attempting to jump from the cars. He fell down, the train passed over him, & he lived but a short time.

Wm Coult & his wife, in Manchester, N H, lost their lives on Dec 3 by crossing a railroad track in a carriage while the cars were approaching. They were hit by the locomotive.

At Colebrook, N H, on Nov 30, two sons of Elijah Sawyer, & two of Chas Currier, were found near Morse pond, the bodies of all were taken from the water, having been drowned in the same spot. The youngest was 12 & the oldest 22 years of age.

Mr Jos P Wheeler, merchant, 42 Central wharf, Boston, was passing by the hold of his ship **Moses Wheeler**, loading at Lewis' wharf, when he was struck by the derrick, swinging 3 casks of nails, & knocked into the hold with great violence. He was killed instantly, his skull broken to pieces. He was about 45 and unmarried.

Mrd: on Dec 10, by Rev Mr Roszell, Mr Jas F Harvey to Miss Maria E Borland, all of Wash.

Died: on Dec 11, Sarah, wife of Simeon Matlock, in her 62nd year. Her funeral is this afternoon at 2 o'clock, from her late residence on 8th st, between G & H sts.

Died: on Dec 11, Mr Jas Williams, late mail contractor of Wash City, in his 57th year. His funeral is on Sunday at 2 o'clock, from his late residence, 5th & H sts.

Died: on Dec 7, near James' Creek, Fred'k Co, Md, Francis Asbury Davis, brother to the Hon John W Davis, aged 49 years. The deceased was an exemplary member of the Methodist Episcopal Church, a kind & indulgent parent & husband, an affectionate brother, & a good man.

Criminal Court: 1-Jas Butler, free negro, guilty for riot. 2-*Fred'k Strother, free negro, guilty for assault. 3-Saml Hall, alias Jas Hall, alias Jos Hall, a white youth about 16, guilty of forgery. 4-Frank Bell, free negro, not guilty of grand larceny. 5-Saml Hall, alias Jas Hall, guilty of forgery in another case. [Dec 14th newspaper: *Strother sentenced to 3 months in the county jail, & fined $1.]

SAT DEC 14, 1850
Abraham Van Auken, who died in Mount Morris, N Y, on Dec 1, aged 60, of paralysis, with which he was seized in Feb last, had subsisted for 60 days immediately preceding his death entirely without food. Nothing passed his lips but pure water. So says the Livingston Union.

Household & kitchen furniture at auction: on Dec 23, by order of the Orphans Court of Wash Co, D C: sale at the late residence of Mrs Sarah Hammond, on I st north, & 9th st east. -A R Frasier, Cmte -A Green, auctioneer

Criminal Court: 1-Geo Butler, free negro, charged with an assault upon Edw McCubbin: acquitted. 2-Walter Brest, Jas Pumphrey, Thos Simpson, John Usher, Jas A Gill, & A R Thomas, found guilty of riot. 3-Geo Bowen & Ellen Cowan found guilty of an assault: fined $5 each. 4-Babel Seymour, free negro, convicted of an assault upon a little white girl, sentenced to pay a fine of $1, & 3 months in the county jail. [Dec 16th newspaper: Pumphrey, Usher & Gill, to pay a fine of $10. Simpson & Thomas have not yet been arrested.]

An old Offender caught. Yesterday ofcrs Wm Cox & John E Little, of the Auxiliary Guard, seized a burglar, Chas Mahlon, as he was making his escape from the back premises of Messrs A Hoover & Son's, whose shoestore on Pa ave the fellow had entered with felonious intent, which he was prevented from carrying out by a sudden alarm.

Wash City Ordinances: 1-Act for the relief of A C Kidwell: the sum of $26.64 be paid him for taking up & relaying the gutter on B st. 2-Act for the relief of John McDevitt: fine imposed for an alleged violation of the law relative to gravel footwalks, is remitted: provided McDevitt pay the costs of prosecution. 3-Act for the relief of Christian F Henry: fine imposed for a violation of law in selling in the market-house without a license, is remitted: provided he pay the costs of prosecution.

The Harrisburg Union states that Jos Milliken, a young man of 17 years, recently found guilty in setting fire to the State bridge at Clark's Ferry, has been sentenced to 3 years in the penitentiary, the longest time under the law.

F A Whitescarver has invented an instrument for taking Horizontal & Vertical Angles without changing the position of the instrument, & at the same time getting distances to objects, heights, without the ordinary measurements or use of logarithms. In a word, it supersedes the necessity of having chain-carriers in any country.

Mrd: on Dec 10, at Thoroughfare, Prince Wm Co, Va, by Rev Mr Towles, Thos W Swann, of Alexandria Co, Va, to Helen Mary, daughter of the late Geo Chapman, of the former place.

Wanted: a gentleman of middle or advanced age to take charge of certinaly 2, & probably 4 boys, well advanced in their classical, English, & mathematical studies. Address the subscriber, postpaid, or a personal interview finally would be absolutely necessary, at Good Luck Post Ofc, PG Co, Md. My residence can be easily reached in 8 miles from either Bladensburg or Beltsville, on the Balt & Wash railroad. —Geo W Duvall

MON DEC 16, 1850
We learn that the Hon Danl E Miller, Whig member of Congress from Iowa, is reported to be laying at the point of death at the residence of his brother-in-law, in Pittsburg. [Dec 18th newspaper: Hon Danl F Miller is now convalescent.]

Criminal Court-Wash-Sat last. Anne McDonald, a white woman, charged with larceny, was tried & acquitted of the charge.

Wash Corp: 1-Ptn from Wm A Hughes, in relation to the taxes on a certain lot: referred to the Cmte on Finance. 2-Bill for the relief of John McDevitt: passed. 3-Bill of Richd Ballenger: referred to the Cmte of Claims.

Teacher wanted in the English dept connected with Wash College, on Jan 1, 1851: salary is $300 certain, & a portion of the tuition fees, which for several years averaged $200. -Jas F Gordon, Sec of the Board, Wash College, Chestertown, Kent Co, Md.

Circuit Court of Wash Co, D C, in Chancery. John Withers vs Jas Long's heirs. The trustees report they sold part thereof to Saml Caughy & Isaac N Winston for the sum of $48,500, the property mentioned in the said decree. —Jno A Smith, clerk

Jacob Straum, of Jacksonville, Ill, the wealthiest man in the State, has been taken to a lunatic asylum in Ohio. He has for some time suffered from an aberration of mind said to have its origin in an incessant desire to accumulate more wealth.

Mrd: on Thu last, by Rev Mr Lanahan, Saml F Clarke to Miss Josephine Mereman, all of Wash City.

Died: on Dec 13, Hannah Sandford, daughter of Geo M & Georgianna Davis, aged 4 years & 6 months.

Died: on Dec 15, Barton, son of Saml & Christina Duvall, aged 3 months. His funeral is today at 2 P M, from the residence of his parents, Pa ave, between 19th & 20th sts.

TUE DEC 17, 1850
Senate: 1-Ptn of Jos Bradley, deceased, asking to be allowed a pension: referred to the Cmte on Pensions. 2-Ptn from the children & heirs of R S Dix, deceased, late a paymaster in the army, asking to be allowed a pension: referred to the Cmte on Pensions. 3-Memorial of J D Pollock, in behalf of the heir of Wm Harper, asking to be allowed a quarter section of land in lieu of a like quantity of land granted said Harper for services in the last war with Great Britain, & forfeited for taxes: referred to the Cmte on the Public Lands. 4-Memorial of Clara M Williams, asking indemnity for French spoliations prior to 1800: referred to the Cmte on Finance. 5-Additional documents submitted in relation to the claim of the legal reps of Thos R Johnson & Anne E Johnson: referred to the Cmte of Claims. 6-Ordered, that the ptn & papers of Jos Byrd, on the files of the Senate, be referred to the Cmte on Military Affairs.

Trustee's sale of valuable land in PG Co, Md: by decree of the Court of Chancery, passed on Aug 19, 1850, wherein Thos C Worthington & others are cmplnts, & Sarah F Contee & others are dfndnts, the trustees will expose to public sale, on Jan 15, that valuable plantation called **Park Hall**, of which the late Mrs Sarah Slater died seized & possessed, containing about 270 acres, more or less: adjoins the estate of Jos K Roberts, [the dwlg plantation of the late Gov Kent,] & is about 6 miles from Bladensburg. The improvements consist of a large brick dwlg & tobacco houses.
–Alex Randall, Thos G Pratt, trustees

House of Reps: 1-Ptn of John S Galiwood, for pay for a horse lost in the war of 1812, 1813, & 1814. 2-Ptn of Wm W Dennis et al, for a light-house on Lake Michigan. 3-Ptn of Anthony Walker, Seneca W Ely, Thos J Winship, & John Hough, of Chillicothe, Ohio, praying compensation for locating military bounty land warrants. 4-Ptn of Wm Hicks, of Claiborne Co, Tenn, asking to be placed upon the invalid pension roll. 5-Memorial of W B & A M Lloyd, praying compensation for the use & occupation of lots of land at the harbor of Cleveland, Ohio.

New Orleans, Dec 13. The steamer **Anglo Norman**, while on a pleasure trip today, with 110 persons on board, blew up, & from 75 to 100 persons are killed, missing & wounded. Mr Perry, of the New Orleans Bulletin, is killed, & Mr Kidd, of the Daily Crescent, & Mr Bigna, of the Delta, wounded. Mr Nathan Jarvis, Mr Stillman, & Mr Storm, of the N Y Novelty Works, are mortally wounded. Capt Annibal & Capt Thompson, of the commercial marine, & others, are badly wounded. Mr Junius Bebee, a State Senator, is supposed to be killed.

Mrd: on Nov 27, in Brunswick, Va, by Rev Mr Johnson, Dr Wm B Price to Miss Ann Hicks, daughter of E B Hicks, of Lawrenceville.

Mrd: on Dec 15, by Rev Mr Hill, J W Bangs to Miss Adelphia Jenkins, both of Alexandria, Va.

Mrd: on Dec 11, by Rev Wm Evans, Zachariah Brown, of Wash, to Miss Susan E Carpenter, daughter of the late Wm & Ann A Carpenter, of *Pleasant Hill*, St Mary's Co, Md.

Died: on Dec 14, in Wash City, Louis, aged 7 years & 11 months, only son of John & Mary L Contee, of PG Co, Md.

Died: on Dec 3, in Pictou, N S, Helen Theresa, youngest daughter of B Hammatt Norton, American Consul at that port, in her 8th year.

Commission on Claims against Mexico: 1-Memorial of Danl Collins, claiming for damages by seizure & condemnation of the same brig: the same was allowed accordingly: the amount to be awarded subject to the future action of the Board.

$10 reward for return of a large dark bay horse stolen on Dec 12.
–Wm Pumphrey, near Bladensburg

The U S ship **Marion** was at Whampo_, China, on Sep 25 last. List of her ofcrs: Cmder, Wm M Glendy; Lts, A M Pennock, B S Gantt, R Aulick, [acting,] John Wilkes, [acting:] Surgeon, J A Lockwood; Assist Surgeon, E Shippen; Purser, N White; Acting Master, J P Jones; Passed Midshipman, W D Whiting; Midshipman, J J Laughlin; Capt's Clerk, Wm M Macauley; Boatswain, Burdett; Gunner, Stocken; Carpenter, Rusti; Sailmaker, Maule

WED DEC 18, 1850
Gen Orders #42. War Dept, Adj Genrl's Ofc, Wash, Dec 9, 1850.
I-Promotions
Regt of Mounted Riflement
2nd Lt Danl M Frost, to be 1st Lt, Nov 30, 1850, vice Denman, resigned.
Bvt 2nd Lt Caleb E Irvine, to be 2nd Lt, Nov 30, 1850, vice Frost, promoted.
Bvt 2nd Lt Wm E Jones, to be 2nd Lt, Nov 30, 1850, vice Addison, resigned.
1st Regt of Artl
Bvt 2nd Lt Powell T Wyman, of the 3rd Artl, to be 2nd Lt, Sep 16, 1850, vice Haynes, deceased.
4th Regt of Artl
1st Lt Thos Williams, to be Capt, Sep 12, 1850, vice Brent, Assist Quartermaster, who vacates his regimental commission.
1st Lt John C Pemberton, to be Capt, Sep 16, 1850, vice Bainbridge, deceased.
1st Lt Chas F Wooster, to be Capt, Sep 27, 1850, vice Shiras, appointed Commissary of Subsistence, who vacates his regimental commission.
2nd Lt Clermont L Best, to be 1st Lt, Sep 12, *1850, vice Williams, promoted.
2nd Lt Richd C Drum, to be 1st Lt, Sep 16, 1850, vice Pemberton, promoted.

2nd Lt Robt V W Howard, to be 1st Lt, Sep 27, 1850, vice Wooster, promoted.
Bvt 2nd Lt Edw McK Hudson, of the 3rd Artl, to be 2nd Lt, Sep 12, 1850, vice Best, promoted.
Bvt 2nd Lt Cuvier Grover, of the 1st Artl, to be 2nd Lt, Sep 16, 1850, vice Drum, promoted.
Bvt 2nd Lt Jos H Wheelock, of the 3rd Artl, to be 2nd Lt, Sep 27, 1850, vice Howard, promoted.

1st Regt of Infty
1st Lt Geo W F Wood, to be Capt, Jun 10, 1850, vice Backus, promoted to 3rd Infty.
1st Lt Geo W Wallace, to be Capt, Jun 10, 1850, vice Wood & Masten, Assist Quartermasters, who vacate their regimental commissions.
1st Lt Benj H Arthur, to be Capt, Jun 26, 1850, vice Gardenier, deceased.
1st Lt Theophilus d'Orremieulx, to be Capt, oct 27, 1850, vice Scott, deceased.
2nd Lt Eugene E McLean, to be 1st Lt, Jun 10, 1850, vice Wood, promoted.
2nd Lt Chas C Gilbert, to be 1st Lt, Jun 10, 1850, vice Masten, Assist Quartermaster, who vacates his regimental commission.
2nd Lt Parmence T Turnley, to be 1st Lt, Jun 26, 1850, vice Wallace, promoted.
2nd Lt Geo D Brewerton, to be 1st Lt, Jun 26, 1850, vice Arthur, promoted.
2nd Lt Egbert L Viele, to be 1st Lt, Oct 27, 1850, vice d'Oremieulx, promoted.
Bvt 2nd Lt Richd W Johnson, of the 6th Infty, to be 2nd Lt, Jun 10, 1850, vice McLean, promoted.
Bvt 2nd Lt Saml B Holabird, to be 2nd Lt, Jun 10, 1850, vice Gilbert, promoted.
Bvt 2nd Lt Thos G Williams, of the 2nd Infty, to be 2nd Lt, Jun 10, 1850, vice Turnley, promoted.
Bv 2nd Lt Thornton A Washington, of the 6th Infty, to be 2nd Lt, Jun 26, 1850, vice Brewerton, promoted.
Bvt 2nd Lt Chas B Alvord, of the 8th Infty, to be 2nd Lt, Oct 27, 1850, vice Viele, promoted.

2nd Regt of Infty
Bvt 2nd Lt John W Frazer, to be 2nd Lt, Jun 30, 1850, vice Hendershott, promoted.
Bvt 2nd Lt Jas P Roy, of the 8th Infty, to be 2nd Lt, Oct 27, 1850, vice Viele, promoted.

3rd Regt of Infty
Capt Electus Backus, of the 1st Infty, to be Major, Jun 10, 1850, vice McCall, appointed Inspec Gen, who resigns his regimental commission.

5th Regt of Infty
Bvt 2nd Lt Thos C English, to be 2nd Lt, Jul 31, 1850, vice Neill, promoted.
Bvt 2nd Lt Jos H McArthur, of the 2nd Infty, to be 2nd Lt, Aug 12, 1850, vice Burns, promoted.

7th Regt of Infty
Bvt 2nd Lt Alfred Cumming, of the 8th Infty, to be 2nd Lt, Jul 16, 1850, vice Van Bokkelen, promoted.

II-Appointment
Chas Devall, of Louisiana, to be Military Storekeeper in the Ordnance Dept, Nov 11, 1850, vice Thorpe, declined.

III-Casualties: Resignations
Col Geo A McCall, Inspec Gen, as Major in the 3rd Regt of Infty, [only] Jun 10, 1850.
1st Lt Chas L Denman, Mounted Riflemen, Nov 30, 1850.
2nd Lt John McL Addison, Mounted Riflemen, Nov 30, 1850.
Bvt 2nd Lt Danl McClure, Mounted Riflemen, Nov 30, 1850.
Bvt 2nd Lt Zetus S Searle, 8th Infty, Oct 31, 1850.
Assist Surgeon Washington M Ryer, ____
Commissions vacated under the provisions of the 7th section of the act of Jun 18, 1846.
Capt Thos L Brent, 4th Artl, *Sep 12, 1850, Assist Quartermaster.
Capt Geo W F Wood, 1st Infty, *Jun 10, 1850, Assist Quartermaster.
1st Lt Fred'k H Masten, 1st Infty, *Jun 10, 1850, Assist Quartermaster.
Deaths
Bvt Maj John M Scott, Capt 1st Infty, at Louisville, Ky, Oct 27, 1850.
1st Lt Thos B J Weld, 2nd Artl, at **Fort Moultrie**, S C, Sep 10, 1850.
2nd Lt Jas M Haynes, 1st Artl, in the city of Mexico, Sep 16, 1850.
IV-The vacancies of Major in the 3rd Infty, occasioned by the resignation of Maj G A McCall, appointed Inspec Gen, & of Capt, in the 4th Artl & 1st Infty, by Capts & Assist Quartermasters Brent, Wood, & Masten, electing to retain their staff commissions under the provisions of the 7th section of the act approved Jun 18, 1846, require corrections of certain dates of promotion, heretofore announced, as follows:
Correction of Dates.
4th Regt of Artl
Capt Thos Williams, to rank from Sep 12, 1850, [Co L,] instead of Sep 16, 1850.
Capt John C Pemberton, to rank Sep 16, 1850, [Co F,] in stead of Sep 27, 1850.
Capt Chas F Wooster, to rank from Sep 27, 1850, [Co M,] instead of Sep 29, 1850.
1st Lt Clermont L Best, to rank from Sep 12, 1950, instead of Sep 16, 1850.
1st Lt Richd C Drum, to rank from Sep 16, 1850, instead of Sep 27, 1850.
1st Lt Robt V W Howard, to rank from Sep 27, 1850, instead of Sep 29, 1850.
2nd Lt Edw McK Hudson, to rank from Sep 12, 1850, instead of Sep 16, 1850.
2nd Lt Cuvier Grover, to rank from Sep 16, 1850, instead of Sep 27, 1850.
1st Regt of Infty
Capt W F Wood, to rank from Jun 10, 1850, instead of Jun 26, 1850. [Vacated.]
Capt Geo W Wallace, to rank from Jun 10, 1850, [Co G,] instead of Oct 8, 1850.
Capt Benj H Arthur, to rank from Jun 26, 1850, [Co F,] instead of Oct 10, 1850.
1st Lt Eugene E McLean, to rank from Jun 10, 1850, instead of Jun 26, 1850.
1st Lt Chas C Gilbert, to rank from Jun 10, 1850, instead of Oct 8, 1850.
1st Lt Parmenus T Turnley, to rank from Jun 10, 1850, instead of Oct 10, 1850.
1st Lt Geo D Brewerton, to rank from Jun 10, 1850, instead of Oct 10, 1850.
2nd Lt Richd W Johnson, to rank from Jun 10, 1850, instead of Jun 26, 1850.
3rd Regt of Infty
Major Electus Backus, to rank from Jun 10, 1850, instead of Oct 10, 1850.
Transfers & Corrections of Dates
2nd Lt Saml B Holabird, from the 2nd Infty, with the date of Jun 30, to the 1st Infty, [Co C,] to date from Jun 10, 1850.
2nd Lt Thos G Williams, from the 7th Infty, with the dae of Jul 16, 1st Infty, [Co F,] to date from Jun 10, 1850.

2nd Lt Thornton A Washington, from the 5th Infty, with the date of Jul 31, to the 1st Infty, [Co B,] to date from Jun 26, 1850.
2nd Lt John W Frazer, from the 5th Infty, with the date of Aug 12, to the 2nd Infty, [Co F,] to date from Jun 30, 1850.
2nd Lt Alfred Cumming, from the 2nd Infty, with the date of Aug 31, to the 7th Infty, [Co A,] to date from Jul 16, 1850.
By order: R Jones, Adj Gen
*Regimental commission [only] vacated.

Millard Fillmore, Pres of the U S: recognizes Sr Don Henrique Francisco Fallon, who has been appointed Consul of the Republic of Chili at Boston, Mass. Dec 16, 1850

In Chancery: Circuit Court of Wash Co, D C. Law vs Law & others. Jas Adams, the trustee in this cause, reported to the Court, Apr 13 & on Nov 29, in 1850, that he had sold the particular squares, lots, & parts of lots, designated: same to be ratified. –Jno A Smith, clerk [No specifics as to amount or purchaser or purchasers.]

By order to distrain, on Dec 26, I shall offer for sale one frame bldg, seized & taken, to be sold for cash, to satisfy ground rent in arrears due from Thos Y & A Hurdle, to Wm W Corcoran. Sale of west half of lot 23 in square A, Pa ave, between 3rd & 4½ sts.
-J L Henshaw, D M

Senate: 1-Mr Berrien presented the memorial of Jacqueline Taylor, of Richmond, Va, of Thos Ellis & Chas Ellis, adms of Chas Ellis, sen, deceased, & of Andrew Low, sen, sole devisee of the effects of the late firm of Low, Taylor & Co, of Savannah, Ga, asking the return of duties paid on certain cloths, accompanied by a bill for the relief of Jaqueline Taylor & others: referred to the Cmte on Finance. 2-Cmte of Claims: bill for the relief of Solomon T Nichell & Jas Clinch, of N Y C: recommded its passage. 3-Obit-announcement of the death of John H Harmanson, who died in New Orleans in Oct last, where he had gone, accompanied by his wife, to his friend & relative, Dr Davezac, who might arrest his disease, with his medical skill. Mr Harmanson was born in 1803, in Norfolk, Va. His father removed with his family, while John was but 11 years of age, to the parish of Rapides, in La. His death a few years later, threw upon his son the care & responsibilities of a family. He read law for a time with Gen Downs. He located himself in the parish of Avoyelles, as a cotton planter, where he had a large family.

Ex-Govn'r Wm Plumer died at his residence in Epping, N H, last week, aged about 94. He was the last surviving member of the Convention which framed the present Constitution of N H, which he took a very active part in framing, & which he lived under for 58 years.

THU DEC 19, 1850
Hon E C Cabell, Rep in Congress from Florida, has been called from his duties in the Capitol to the bedside of his father, who lies in a critical condition at Richmond, Va.

Senate: 1-Ptn of the administrator of Gerard Wood, deceased, a surgeon's mate during the Revolutionary war, asking to be allowed commutation pay: referred to the Cmte on Pensions. 2-Claim of Lewis Ralston, with additional documents: referred to the Cmte on Indian Affairs. 3-Ptn of Robt Jamison & Benj Williamson, asking compensation for their services in carrying the mail: referred to the Cmte on the Post Ofc & Post Roads. 4-Memorial of David Butler, late military storekeeper, representing that injustice has been done him in the proceedings of a court-martial, & asking redress as Congress may think proper to grant: referred to the Cmte on Military Affairs. 5-The ptn of Dr Saml White, on the files of the Senate: referred to the Cmte on Pensions.

The U S sloop-of-war **Germantown** is now lying at the Brooklyn Navy Yard, ready for sea. Cmder J D Knight, of Charleston, has received orders from the Dept to take command of her.

In Chancery. John King against Mary A Webster, Eliz Webster, John W Webster, Eli Webster, & Geo Webster, heirs at law of Geo Webster, & Jas Marshall, his administrator. By order of the Circuit Court of Wash Co, D C, an account is required to be stated, showing to whom & in what proportion the proceeds of the sale of the real estate in the Trustee's report mentioned should be distributed; & notice is directed to be given of the taking of such account to the creditors & heirs at law of the said Geo Webster. Parties above named, & said creditors, are notified that on Jan 2 next, at my ofc, in City Hall, Wash, I shall state the account required by the order of the Court. –W Redin, auditor

Criminal Court-Wash-yesterday. 1-Harriet Johnson, free negress, found guilty with an assault with intent to kill Thos B Goddard. Mr Ratcliffe moved the Court to grant a new trial. 2-Danl Robinson, free negro, found guilty of mayhem, which consisted in biting off his brother's ear. 3-*Thos Harry, indicted for a violent assault & battery with intent to rob John Payne Toder & Robt S Wharton, was on trial when the Court adjourned. [*Dec 20th newspaper: Thos Harry was found guilty.]

Wash Corp: 1-Ptn of W C Choate & others, complaining of certain existing nuisances: referred to the Cmte on Police. 2-Act for the relief of Wm B Wilson: passed. 3-Ptn from Mrs Eliz Collison for remission of a fine: referred to the Cmte of Claims. 4-Ptn from Jas W Garner, in reference to an erroneous assessment: referred to the Cmte on Finance. 5-Ptn of Edw Chapman, praying to be refunded certain taxes erroneously paid for a lot in square 281: referred to the Cmte of Claims. 6-Ptn of H L Heiskell & others, for flag footways in the 2nd Ward: referred to the Cmte on Improvements. 7-Ptn of J F Callan, atty for Jos Hoban, praying to be refunded a certain amount erroneously paid for taxes on a lot in square 10: referred to the Cmte of Claims. 8-Ptn of J B Iardella, for himself & the other heirs, praying to be indemnified for certain damages incurred by changing the grade of N J ave: referred to the Cmte on Improvements. 9-Act of exempting the stock of the city from taxation, & for the relief of Jas Riorden & others: referred to the Cmte on Ways & Means. 10-Cmte of Claims: bill for the relief of Rachel Ballenger, reported the same without amendment.

The Rockville Journal states that all efforts to obtain bail for Wm L Chaplin have failed, & his trial will come on before the next session of the Howard District Court.

Jenny Lind Music for sale. Sold at our unvarying price of 4 cents per page.
–Wm Fischer, at the Music Store adjoining the Irving Hotel.

Commission on Claims against Mexico: 1-Memorial of Francisco del Hoys, atty of Cayetano Noguerra, administrator of Francisco Arenas, claiming for expulsion from Oajaca, in 1833, as a native of Spain, for consequent losses of property, & for imprisonment in 1838, was submitted & examined, & suspended. 2-Memorial of Edw Hoffman, claiming for confiscation of goods at El Paso in 1843, for imprisonment, & loss by sale of goods in 1844 under a Mexican decree prohibiting to foreigners the retail trade, being taken up for consideration, together with the proofs & documents connected therewith, the Board came to an opinion that so much of the claim as arises out of the confiscation at El Paso, in Sep, 1843, is one valid against the Republic of Mexico, & the same was allowed accordingly; the amount to be awarded subject to the future action of the Board.

Trustee's sale of dwlg house & lot: by deed of trust from Wm H English, dated Jun 14, 1850, recorded in Liber J A S #14, folios 278 thru 280, of the land records of Wash Co, D C: sale on Jan 8, of lot 1, according to subdivision of square 415, with a new 1 story frame dwlg house & back bldg, at G & 8th st, on the Island. –H C Spalding, trustee -Dyer & McGuire, aucts

Leesburg Academy is under the direction of Messrs S H Marsh, A M, & J W Marsh, A B. The terms commence on the 1st Mon of Sep, & on the 1st Mon of Feb: tuition fee is $16.66 per term. Trustees:

John Janney	Gen Lee	Chas L Powell
C G Eskridge	Wm B Tyler	H T Harrison
Wm H Gray	F W Luckett	A S Tebbs
Wm A Powell	Burr W Harrison	Jos Birkby
Thos P Knox	D G Smith	

Furnished rooms: Mrs Garret Anderson, over the Music & Stationery store, 2 doors east of the Irving Hotel.

Mrd: on Dec 17, by Rev Jas Laurie, D D, of Wash City, the Rev Isaac N Hays, of Hunterstown, to Miss Rebecca H King, of Adams Co, Pa.

Mrd: on Dec 17, in Wash City, by Rev Smith Pyne, Allan McLane, U S Navy, to Maria C, youngest daughter of the late Richd Bache.

Mrd: on Nov 19, at St Paul's Church, Balt, by Rev Dr Wyatt, Edw Plater to Mary A Penn, all of Md.

Died: on Dec 4, in Providence, R I, Mrs Lydia Knight, wife of Hon N R Knight, in her 70th year.

Died: on Dec 8, in Lexington, Ky, Nimrod L Finnell, lately Editor of the Lexington Daily Atlas, & father of John W Finnell, Sec of State.

Died: on Dec 18, William Theobold Mathew, infant son of Geo & Susanna A Savage. His funeral is this evening at 2 o'clock.

FRI DEC 20, 1850
Commission on Claims against Mexico: 1-Memorial of John Belden, claiming for damages by seizure & condemnation of merchandise, in Zacatecas, in 1841: ordered to be received.

House of Reps: 1-Ptn of Geo Taylor, asking indemnity for French spoliations prior to 1800. 2-Ptn of Saml Hilton, praying for indemnity for 2 horses lost in the war of 1812. 3-Memorial of Henry Dwight, W S Verplanck, G L Rose, Wm Young, & others, citizens of Geneva, N Y, in favor of stipulated arbitration between nations. 4-Ptn of Anthony Walke & others, of Chillicothe, Ohio, praying compensation for locating military bounty land warrants.

Criminal Court-Wash, Thu. 1-Horsed Mediperis, [a Mexican messenger in one of the public ofcs,] was put upon his trial for an assault with intent to kill Louisa V Parkhurst. Pending this trial the Court adjourned. [Dec 24th newspaper: Mediperis found guilty of assault & battery only. The trial of the same prisoner for another offence was next taken up, & not finished when the Court adjourned.]

Jenny Lind Head-dresses & Bonnets for sale: Mrs M A Hamilton, from Balt, at the corner of 12th & Pa ave, over Butt's drug store, has on a hand a beautiful assortment.

The estate of the late Lewis G Davidson. The children & heirs at law of the late Mr & Mrs Davidson, having authorized the sale of the remainder of their property, first, to pay any debts remaining unpaid of Mr or Mrs Davidson; next, such as may have been created for the joint benefit of the family to the period of her death; & 3rd, the residue to be divided among the heirs. All claims are to be presented to Saml G Davidson, in Wash, or to me: the trust will be closed on Jan 15 next. –W Redin

For sale: that elegant & commodious house on H st, between 17th & 18th sts, known as the ***Bush House***, & now leased by the Sec of the Navy. Apply to Dr Chas Frailey, Gen Land Ofc, or to John A Smith, City Hall.

Senate: 1-Memorial of Catharine Pearson, & heirs & legal reps of the late Jos Pearson, asking indemnity for injuries done to a certain mill & certain water privileges by the Com'r of the Public Bldgs in supplying water under an act of Congress: referred to the Cmte of Claims. 2-Ptn of Deborah Johnson, of Coventry, Kent Co, R I, in behalf of herself & other heir-at-law of Isaac Johnson, [who was an ofcr in the war of the

Revolution,] stating that he was paid in bills of credit which became greatly depreciated in value, & asking payment of a bill of credit issued under a resolution of Congress passed in Sep, 1778: referred to the Cmte on Revolutionary Claims. 3-Memorial of John Plumbe, asking the construction of a railroad from the Valley of the Mississippi to the Pacific ocean, & claiming for himself its paternity, being more than 7 years in advance of any other individual in memorializing Congress for a road to connect the Atlantic & Pacific, which had the special sanction of the late Senator Linn & Geo W Jones, a delegate from Iowa, & resulted in an appropriation for the first public survey ever made in reference to the route of this contemplated road: referred to the cmte on Roads & Canals.

The McDonogh Estate. On Dec 6, in New Orleans, excitement was created by an application through the Atty Gen to the 5th Dist Court for an order of sequestration of the real estate of the late John McDonogh. The ptn alleged that the seizing of the real estate of John McDonogh, deceased, was not by his will given to his executors, & that there is no one at this time, except the States of La & Md, having the legal right to the seizing thereof, or to take charge or administer the same. The executors have no such right, & if they assume any such right they are intermeddlers & trespassers. The said real estate belongs to the States of Md & La, & they alone have the right to the possession thereof. There is great danger, as the said real estate is now situated, that it will be dilapidated, & that the revenues & fruits produced by the property will be lost. This application was granted, & the Judge ordered the Sheriff, Gen Lewis, to take possession of all the said real estate. The process of sequestration is merely a mode, provided by the civil law, by which the sheriff takes possession of real estate in dispute, to save it from waste or injury until the title is settled. By this procedure, Gen Lewis becomes, for the present, the sole administrator of the will of McDonogh as to his vast real estate. The executors have merely the control of the personal property of the deceased. They have taken steps to have this order of a sequestration set aside, & have filed a motion to that effect. This is now pending before the Court. On Dec 10 a Bill in Chancery was filed in the U S Court, by J R Grymen, Benjamin & Miou, Mott & Frazier, & Reverdy Johnson, counsel for the heirs of John McDonogh, commanding the executors of the will of the deceased, as also the Mayor & Municipalities of New Orleans, to appear in Court on Jan 1 next, to show cause why the former should not abandon their trust, & the latter be shut our from all participation in the bequest made to the Mayor, Aldermen, & inhabitants of New Orleans & their successors forever.

Mrd: on Dec 17, in Wash City, by Rev C M Butler, D D, Richd B Keys, of Balt, to Miss Mary R, daughter of Jas N Barker.

SAT DEC 21, 1850
House of Reps: 1-Bill for the relief of the legal reps of Col John H Stone: laid on the table. 2-Bills for the relief of John G Wilkinson & Benj F Wesley: severally laid on the table. 3-Bill for the relief of Wm Slocum, of N Y: passed. 4-Cmte of the Whole: discharged from the further consideration of the bill for the relief of Charlotte Lynch.

Court-martial of Capt Thos Ap Catesby Jones, a captain in the U S Navy, to wit: Charge first-Fraud against the U S.
Specification first. The said Capt Jones, being in command of the U S naval forces in the Pacific ocean, on Oct 31, 1848, off Monterey, Upper Calif, unlawfully & fraudulently, & for his own private uses, specualtions, & gains, did withdraw, &, by color of his ofc & command aforesaid, cause & procure to be withdrawn from the public use, & from the custody of Edw D Reynolds, a purser in the U S navy, then & there charged with the custody thereof for public use, a large sum of money, to wit: $10,643.09,of the fund known as the military contribution fund; the said money then & there being of the public moneys of the U S.
Specification second: Capt Jones, then in command of the U S naval forces in the Pacific ocean, at San Francisco, Calif, on Nov 1, 1848, & on divers days & times between Nov 1, & Nov 26, unlawfully & fraudulently did convert to his own use, & by color of his ofc & command aforesaid, unlawfully & fraudulently did cause & procure to be converted to his own use, by adventuring & causing to be adventures the same in his own private speculations & adventures, & by dealing with the same as his own private funds & moneys, divers sums of money, amounting in the whole to $10,643.09; the same then & there being of the public moneys of the U S.
Specification third: Capt Jones, then in command of the U S naval forces in the Pacific ocean, at San Francisco, Calif, on or about Oct 31, 1848, fraudulently, by color of his ofc & command aforesaid, did cause & procure the sum of $10,643.09 of the public moneys of the U S, of a fund known as the military contribution fund, levied upon Mexico during the war between that Republic & the U S, to be transferred from the custody of Edw D Reynolds, a purser in the navy, then & there charged with the custody thereof for public use, to the custody of Jos Wilson, a purser in the navy, with intent to convert the said sum of money to his, the said Capt Jones' own use; & unlawfully & fraudently, & by color of his ofc & command aforesaid, & with the intent aforesaid, at Monterey bay, on Nov 1, 1848, did address & deliver, & cause to be delivered, to Purser Wilson, then being under his command, the order, to wit: Flag-ship **Ohio**, Monterey Bay, Nov 1, 1848.
Sir: There being an unexpended balance of several thousand dollars of the military war contribution sum collected at Mazatlan by the squadron during the late war with Mexico, ever & above any legitimate claim which I can now foresee as likely to arise against it, & as the inhabitants of Upper Calif, & especially the miners in the gold regions, are greatly embarrassed in their dealing & operations for want of a silver circulating medium, you will, on your arrival at San Francisco, exchange so much of the aforesaid fund as may then be in your hands for uncoined gold at the current market price, which gold you will hold subject to my further orders. –Thos Ap Jones, Cmder-in-Chief U S Naval Forces, Pacific ocean. To Purser Jos Wilson, U S ship **Lexington**.
Capt Jones did not receive the moneys aforesaid, or any part thereof, from Wilson, but received the uncoined gold, the same being of much greater value than the sum aforesaid, to & for his the said Capt Jones' own use, & for his own private traffic, speculation, & gain; thereby, & by means of the premises, fraudulently & unlawfully converting the public moneys of the U S to his own use, & committing a fraud against the U S.
[The plea of not guilty is received & entered to the remaining charges & specifications.]

Mrd: on Dec 19, by Rev J R Eckard, Mr Philip Hinkle, of Cincinnati, to Miss Martha Gaither, daughter of Mr Jas Gaither, of Wash City.

Mrd: on Dec 19, in Wash City, by Rev J E Weems, Mr Jos Harrison to Miss Mgt Redman, both of Prince Wm Co, Va.

Augusta [Ga] Chronicle of Dec 15. Jas Williams, of notoriously bad character, was today arrested in Hamburg, S C, at the instance of 2 citizens of Thos Co, Ga, McLendon & James, charged the murder, in that county, about Dec 1, of a young man & woman, supposed to be husband & wife, & from papers found, to be Durin Moore & Charity Gore, [probably her name before her marriage,] from Brunswick Co, N C, who were moving to Florida in a one-horse wagon. Williams was arrested & committed to jail. The couple were found in their night clothes in the wagon, murdered by blows on the head, probably inflicted with an axe. The motive is supposed to have been to rob them, which was done.

Mrd: on Dec 19, in Wash City, by Rev J E Weems, Mr John L McKney to Miss Matilda H Harrison, of said county & State.

Mrd: on Thu, by Rev Mr McElfresh, Mr Christopher C Clark, of PG Co, Md, to Miss Maria C Whitaker, of Wash.

Died: in Wash City, after an illness of 9 days, Mr Jas Mount, aged 42 years, formerly of N J, but for the last 13 years a resident of Wash City. His funeral is on Sunday at 2 o'clock, from his late residence, between H & I sts, on N J ave.
+
It is my painful duty to announce the death, on Fri, of Jas Mount. The ofcrs & members of Mount Vernon Tent I O of R, of which the deceased was a member, will take place tomorrow, at 12 o'clock, from his late residence near N J ave, south of the canal.
-Richd H Carver, R S

MON DEC 23, 1850
Mr Senator Winthrop was called home a few days since by the death of his sister, the wife of Dr John C Warren, of Boston.

Dissolution of co-partnership between Parker & Norris, by mutual consent. M P Parker will settle all business connected with the firm. –M T Parker, W G Norris

Telegraphic dispatch from Fredericton, received at the News Room, at St John's, New Brunswick, on Dec 12, announced that the house of Mr John Coulthard, in Queensbury, was consumed by fire with all his family, consisting of Mr Coulthard, wife & child. Cause of the fire unknown.

Mr Chaplin was, on Thurs, liberated from the jail of Montg Co, $19,000 bail having been entered for his appearance at Howard District court. Bail of $6,000 had been given in this District. He passed through Balt on Thursday on his return home. -Republic

Wash City Ordinance: 1-Act for the relief of John Shreve: fine imposed for violation of the law in relation to huckstering during market hours, is remitted: provided Shreve pay the costs of prosecution.

Criminal Court-Wash-Sat. 1-Ellen Lindsly, free negress, found guilty of grand larceny. 2-Harriet Johnson, free negress, sentenced to 2 years in the penitentiary, for an assault with intent to kill Thos B Goddard, by wounding him severely with an axe. 3-Geo McCallion guilty of resisting an ofcr in the discharge of his duty: sentenced to 1 month in jail. 4-David Robinson, free negro, found guilty for mayhem: sentenced to 1 year in jail.

New Orleans, Dec 14. Explosion of the steamboat **Anglo-Norman** on Dec 13. Of the killed & missing, there are, Junius Beebe, one of our most enterprising citizens; Chas Perry, reporter of the Bulletin, a worthy man; Alfred Stillman, of the Novelty Works at N Y; Mr McDowell, of Balt, & 4 colored persons. Wounded: Capt Annibal, J L Warner, Capt J P Barnett, Richd Nelson, Wm Elliott, John Taylor, Mr Whittemore, Mr Thayer, Mr Brady, mate, Mr Hill, 1st engineer, Capt Thompson, Mr Storm, Mr N Jarvis, Mr Stephen Jarvis, Mr J W Andrews, J O Pierson, Mr Bigney, Mr Kidd, J Wilson, deck hand, the cook, & 3 colored firemen.

I certify that Alex Maddox, of Wash Co, D C, brought before me as an estray trespassing upon his enclosures, a small red & white cow. –Jas Crandell, J P [Owner is to prove property, pay charges, & take her away. –Alex Maddox, near the Navy Yard]

Circuit Court of Wash Co, D C-in Chancery. Thos Kennersley et al, against John L Hammond et al. The trustee reported he sold the real estate mentioned in said cause on Jul 27, 1850, at public auction, to Augustus D Clemens, for $800. –Jno A Smith, clerk

Mrd: on Dec 19, by Rev Mr Blox, Mr Henry S Davis to Miss Mary E Galt, all of Wash City.

Mrd: on Dec 18, by Rev L F Morgan, Moses Copp to Margaretta A Hutchens, all of Wash City.

Mrd: on Dec 19, by Rev L F Morgan, Jos Gawler to Anne L Benner, of Wash.

Mrd: Dec 20, by Rev L F Morgan, Stephen King & Cordelia A V Cross, of Fairfax, Va.

Died: yesterday, after a short illness, Mr Alfred R Dowson, an old & respectable citizen of Wash City, aged 67 years. His funeral is this afternoon at 3 o'clock, from his late residence, Mrs Rice's, #2 ***Dowson's Row***, Capitol Hill.

TUE DEC 24, 1850
By virtue of 2 writs of fieri facias, I shall expose to public sale, on Dec 31, sundry goods & chattels, [furniture, etc,] seized & taken as the property of Wm McCormick, & will be sold to satisfy 2 judgments in favor of Wm B Lewis. –R R Burr, constable

Confectionary: Wm Emmert, Bridge st, Gtwn. P S. Balls, dinners, & other parties attended to with dispatch.

Senate: 1-Memorial of Ezekiel Lincoln, proposing to carry mail between Phil & Rio de Janeiro, touching at Pernambuco, once a month, asking that a contract with him for that purpose may be authorized by law: referred to the Cmte on Commerce. 2-Memorial of Chas McCormick, an assist surgeon in the army, asking compensation for extra services: referred to the Cmte on Military Affairs. 3-Ptn of Jas Robertson, asking redress for injuries suffered in consequence of his arrest & imprisonment Dec 6, 1849: referred to the Cmte of Claims. 4-Memorial of Amos M Johnson, representing that he had discovered a mode of preventing the potato rot, which he proposes to make known for a valuable consideration: referred to the Cmte on Agriculture. 5-Mr Clay: I have a memorial, signed by a respectable citizen, who is personally known to me, John Timberlake, of Monticello, Albemarle Co, Va. Subject-tariff. He has engaged near Monticello, [the former residence of the late Mr Jefferson] an extensive manufacture of cotton, having invested some $60,000 or $70,000 in the business; under the tariff of 1842 he received a fair profit upon his capital, sufficient to encourage the business; that under the tariff of 1846 he is in danger of utterly losing the whole amount of his capital: referred to the Cmte on Manufacture. 6-Memorial of Jos E Caro, praying compensation for his services as keeper of the Florida archives: referred to the Cmte on Public Lands. 7-Communication from Jas W Simmons, a military storekeeper, stating that he is about to be ordered to Oregon or Calif, & that the salary allowed is totally inadequate for his support: referred to the Cmte on Military Affairs.

Cost of the Mexican war: $217,175,575.81. Sec Corwin's Report

Household & kitchen furniture at auction: on Dec 27, at the residence of the late Danl E Dunscomb, deceased, on 11th st, between F & G sts. –Dyer & McGuire, auct

WED DEC 25, 1850
Postmaster Gen established the following new Post Ofcs for week ending Dec 21, 1850.

Ofc	County, State	Postmaster
West Danville	Cumberland, Me	Jos S Foster
Forest City	Tompkins, N Y	John F Burdick
Black Lake	St Lawrence, N Y	Wm H Davis
Pugsley's Depot	Tompkins, N Y	Abram B Pugsley
West Yorkshire	Cattaraugus, N Y	David H Wood
West Newstead	Erie, N Y	Jacob Wheeler
Rock Rift	Delaware, N Y	Peter M Hess
North Lawrence	St Lawrence, N Y	J H Conant
Trevorton	Northumberland, Pa	Wm Atwater
Amberson's Valley	Franklin, Pa	Benj Culbertson
Easton	Wayne, Ohio	Aug S Bruce
Duncan	Sheboygan, Mich	Alex McLeod
Potato Creek	Ashee, N C	John McMillan
Zeno	York District, S C	A A McKenzie

Willow Creek	Marion District, S C	Thos W Lane
Natural Grove	Williamsburg District, S C	Wm H Cockfield
Friendfield	Marion District, S C	Moses W Brown
Clay Hill	York District, S C	John Watson
Spread Oak	Jefferson, Geo	J J Brown
Warrington	Escambia, Fla	Aug W Nicholson
Park's Store	Jackson, Ala	Jas M Parks
Prune Hill	Montgomery, Ala	K Jones
Palmyra	Warren, Miss	Henry Turner
Branchtown	Cherokee, Texas	Green B Hardwick
Kickapoo	Anderson, Texas	John Mosely
Magnolia Spring	Jasper, Texas	K L Walker
Guadelupe	Victoria Texas	Wm M McGrew
Cypress Crossing	Newton, Texas	Oliver Mahaffey
Concord	Harrison, Texas	Jas R McCarty
Worthville	Johnson, Ind	Jas F McClelland
Moore's Vineyard	Bartholomew, Ind	Burris Moore
Prince William	Carroll, Ind	Abel Slayback
Standing Shore	Overton, Tenn	John Whitaker
Hawkerville	Franklin, Tenn	Jas N Carson
Duncan's Mills	Jasper, Tenn	Robt M Ward
High Spring	Green, Mo	R C Price
Shoal Creek	Newton, Mo	Matthew H Ritchey
Metomen	Fond du Lac, Wis	Giles Egleston
Genoa	Walworth, Wis	Jas S Stillson
Nevada City	Cal	Alex M Blanton

Names Changed:
Amboy, Oswego Co, N Y, changed to Cartersville.
Watkinsville, Goochland Co, Va, changed to Perkinsville.
Delaware Hill, Green Co, Ark, changed to Greensboro'.
Trask, Grant Co, Ind, changed to Bissell.
Nicklesonville, Hamilton Co, Ind, changed to Clarkesville.
Owen Hill, Williamson Co, Tenn, changed to Jordan's Store.
Cornett's, Letcher Co, Ky, changed to Boone Valley.
Theoiko, Lee Co, Ill, changed to China.
Harrisburg, Lafayette Co, Mo, changed to Chapel Hill.
Hallsville, Boone Co, Mo, changed to Middleburg.
Vancouver, Clarke Co, Oregon Territory, changed to Columbia City.

Mrd: on Dec 23, by Rev Mr Hodges, Mr John Adams to Eliza Ann Peake, all of Wash.

Mrd: on Thu last, by Rev J G Butler, Wm R Woodward to Adelaide Lavender.

Died: on Dec 18, in Emmittsburg, Md, Motter Eichelberger, eldest son of Jas W Eichelberger, M D, aged 18 years, 2 months & 24 days.

Cuban Invaders. The leading participants in the Cuban Expedition were arraigned before the U S Circuit Court at New Orleans on Dec 16. The following appeared to answer to their names:

Gen Narciso Lopez	Col W H Bell	L J Sigur
Col Theodore O'Hara	Capt A J Lewis	Gen D Augustin
Col John Picket	Col Robt Wheate	
Maj Thos J Hawkins	Gen John Henderson	

Those who did not appear:

A Gansyles	Sullivan	N D Haden
Governor Quitman	Maj Bunch	
John O	Peter Smith	

U S Patent Ofc: Dec 24, 1850. Ptn of J A Pitts, of Springfield, Ohio, & H A Pitts, of Alton, Ill, praying for the extension of a patent granted to them on Jun 29, 1837, for an improvement in thrashing & cleaning grain for 7 years from expiration of said patent, which takes place on Jun 29, 1851. Also, the ptn of O W Whittier, of Concord, N H, for the extension of a patent granted to him on May 30, 1837, for an improvement in fire-arms for 7 years from expiration of said patent, which takes place on May 30, 1851. –Thos Ewbank, Com'r of Patents

By writ of fieri facias, I have seized & taken all the right, title, interest, claim, & demand of Wm McCormick, in & to the unexpired term of a certain lease, made & executed by Dr Wm Jones to said McCormick & Matthew Valentine, bearing date of Jun 1, 1850, of the south half of lot 15 in square 348, & all the right, title, interest, claim, & demand of McCormick in & to the bldgs erected & built upon said lot, in Wash City, to pay & satisfy judgment in favor of Wm B Lewis. On Jan 3, in front of the premises, I shall proceed to sell the same. –R R Burr, constable

Real estate at auction: on Dec 30, by deed of trust to the undersigned, dated Jan 18, 1844, recorded in Liber W B 118, folios 288 & 289, of the land records of Wash Co, D C: sale of the house & lot on G st, near 5th st, being part of the original lot 4 in square 518. –J Hellen, trustee –A Green, auctioneer

Orphans Court of Wash Co, D C. Letters of administration on the personal estate of Danl E Dunscomb, late of Wash Co, deceased. –Jane E Dunscomb, admx [Claims to be presented to Nicholas Callan, at his ofc on F st.]

FRI DEC 27, 1850
Wash Corp: 1-Ptn from Chas Whitney, for remission of a fine: referred to the Cmte of Claims. 2-Ptn from Chas Petit: referred to the Cmte of Claims: 3-Ptn from Wm Hunter: referred to the Cmte on Improvements. 4-Bill for the relief of W H Barneclo: passed. 5-Cmte on Police: asked to be discharged from the further consideration of the ptn of Wm C Choate & others: discharged accordingly. 6-Cmte of Claims: bill for the relief of Wm Ross: laid on the table. 7-Ptn of John L Nelson, for remission of a fine: referred to the Cmte of Claims. 8-Relief of Reuben Brown: referred to the Cmte of Claims.

Senate: 1-Memorial of Saml L Boots, asking payment of a balance of salary due him as a clerk in the Treas' ofc: referred to the Cmte of Claims. 2-Ptn of Capt H Paulding, of the U S Navy. The papers show that for 30 years previous to 1848 there never had been a ship of war of the U S in the North Seas; that none had ever entered the Weiser; that it was thought by the Gov't of the U S at that time, considering the peculiar situation of Europe, to be expedient to dispatch a U S ship-of-war upon an independent cruise throughout the North of Europe. The frig **St Lawrence**, commanded by Capt Paulding, was dispatched on that service. The object of this petition is to have an appropriation made to indemnify him for expenses incurred in reciprocating for the hospitalities given in Southampton; at Bremer Haven; the Senate of Bremen; the Queen of Greece; deputations from Prussia, from Denmark, & from Sweden, to the cmder. They involved him in expenditures quite inconsiderable for the U S; but, inasmuch as no appriation was made for the purpose, too considerable for him. While it cannot make the claim any more just, that Capt Paulding, is a son of Paulding, one of the captors of Maj Andre, I move the ptn be referred to the Cmte on Naval Affairs. Ptn referred. 3-Memorial of Thos B Livingston, U S Consul at Halifax, in the province of Nova Scotia, asking to be allowed a salary: referred to the Cmte on Commerce.

House of Reps: 1-Ptn of the heirs of Anthony G Willis, deceased, asking for pay for the use of a wagon & team pressed into the service of the U S during the last war with Great Britain. 2-Ptn of John Philips, of Mercer Co, Ky, praying, on behalf of his son, a grant of bounty land & extra pay on account of the services of Jas Malay, a volunteer in the 2nd Regt of Ky volunteers in the war with Mexico. 3-Ptn of Sarah Wardel, praying for a pension.

The steam frig **Susquehanna** is now ready for sea, & will leave Phil for Norfolk on Thu. C W Copeland designed the engines, & his plans were executed by Messrs Murray & Hazlehurst, the builders. List of ofcrs attached to the **Susquehanna**: Wm Inman, Capt; S W Gordon, Lt; Thos T Hunter, Lt; John B Randolph, Lt; Israel Wait, Lt; Geo H Cooper, Master; E C Bittinger, Chaplain; Chas Eversfield, Passed Assist Surgeon; Garret R Barry, Purser; John H Hartzell, Purser's Clerk; J W Bennett, Passed Midshipman; Robt L May, Acting Midshipman; Hen A Adams, do; F A Boardman, do; Wm H Cheever, do; O F Stanton, do; Chas E Hawley, do; Richd Follins, Boatswain; Wm B Brown, Gunner, John Green, Carpenter; Wm Ryan, Sailmaker. Engineers' Dept: Wm P Williamson, Chief Engineer; Saml Archbold, 1st Assist Engineer; Wm H Schock, 1st do; Geo F Hebard, 2nd do; H H Stewart, 2nd do; Edwin Fithian, 3rd do; John C E Lawrence, 3rd do.

State of N Y: Supreme Court-in Equity. Henry Vail et al, excs of Larent Salles, dec's, vs John Tonnele et al. Pursuant to a decretal order of this Court, made in the above cause, will be sold, under the direction of the subscriber, the Referee in said order named, by Anthony J Bleecker, auctioneer, at the Rotundo in the Merchants' Exchange, N Y C, on Jan 9, all that certain lot of land, with dwlg-house & improvements thereon, on the south side of H st, in Wash City, D C, adjoining the residence of the late Mrs Jas Madison, being the lot known as lot 16 in square 221, containing 5,824 sqaure feet, more or less. Dated N Y, Dec 20, 1850. Thos Addis Emmet, Referee -G T Strong, Solicitor

An elegant classic Monument has, within a short time, been erected in St Peter's Church-yard, in Phil, over the remains of the late Cmdor Stephen Decatur. The remains were deposited in the church-yard on Oct 29, 1846, & the monument was erected during the present year. The eagle was sculptured by Mr Hargrave. The material was prepared under the direction of Mr S K Hoxie. The inscriptions on the four sides are:
STEPHEN DECATUR
Born January 5th, 1779,
Entered the Navy of the United States, as
Midshipman,
April 30th, 1798,
Made Captain
For Distinguished Merit,
Passing over the rank of Commander,
February 16th, 1804.
Died,
March 22nd, 1820.
Devoted to his Country by a
Patriot Father,
He cheirshed in his heart,
And sustained by his intrepid actions,
The inspiring sentiment,
"Our Country! Right or wrong!:
A Nation
Gave him in return
Its applause and gratitude.
This Gallant Officer,
Whose prompt & active valor,
Always on the watch,
Was guided by a wisdom
And supported by a firmness
Which never tired:
Whose exploits in arms
reflected
The daring fictions of
Romance & Chivalry.
A Name,
Brilliant from a series of
Heroic Deeds
On the Coast of Barbary,
And illustrious by achievements against
More disciplined enemies:
The Pride of the Navy,
The glory of the
Republic.
-Phil Inquirer

By order to distrain: for sale on Jan 4, 1851, one frame bldg, seized & taken, to be sold for cash, to satisfy ground rent in arrears due from Thos T & A Hurdle to Wm W Corcoran. Sale of the west half of lot 23 in Square A, Pa ave, between 3nd 4½ sts. –J L Henshaw, D M

Saml Ankney, at one time a man of affluence in Wash Co, Md, & quite a dashing gentleman, was found dead in a garden in Clearspring the other morning, having during the night crawled out of a stable, where he had laid down while intoxicated.

By 2 writs of fieri facias, I have levied on lots 9 & 10 in square 544, in Wash City, as the property of Jos Martini, to pay & satisfy judgments due Nathl Carusi, Wm McCormick, & Jas A Ratcliffe: sale on Jan 27, 1851, in front of the premises at 4½ & M sts, Island. -Wm Coale, Constable

Loss of the steamer **South America**, Capt Logan, from Cincinnati for New Orleans, with a full cargo & about 200 passengers, including 105 U S recruits, from Newport Barracks, took fire in the wood rack, along side of the boilers, on Dec 16, when near Morgan's Bend, about 15 miles above Bayou Sars. The pilot at once ran her into the bank, but the fire had enveloped her. Some 30 or 40 lives were lost. Mrs Logan, the engineer's wife, was lost. The U S recruits under the command of Lt Williamson, were on their way to San Antonio. Soldiers lost: Gildermester, Hunt, Frank, Reaser, Rosendale, Drury, Dumont, Daily, Dwyer, Girard, Hyer, Johnston, Kimbell, Loomis, Werther, Lindpainter, & Downie.

Judge Hallyburton on Mon passed sentence of death upon Clements & Reid, the two sailors recently convicted at Richmond of piracy & murder on board the schnr **J B Lindsay**. They are to be executed on Jan 31, 1851.

Natchez Courier of Dec 13. The highly respected townsman, J B Maxwell, had not been seen for some 3 weeks. The body of a drowned man was found 2½ miles below the city, on the bank of the river, which proved to be Mr Maxwell. His watch, chain, penknife, & pocket-book were identified. He was to go on board the boat **Belle Creole**, & probably missed his footing, or was seized with vertigo, & fell overboard.

Four persons named Toomy were held to bail on Tue for firing a pistol at a young man named Alex'r Dubant, on Pa ave, on Tue, near the Adelphia Theatre.

Mrd: on Dec 24, by Rev W T Eva, Mr Geo W Hodges to Miss Josephine C Crossfield, all of Wash City.

Mrd: on Tue last, by Rev Mr Remick, Jas A Allen to Julia Ann Hardt, both of Montg Co, Md.

Died: on Dec 25, at Alexandria, Val, after a short but painful illness, Catharine A, consort of Mr Jas Entwisle, jr, of that place, & eldest daughter of Jos Radcliff, of Wash City, in her 20th year.

Died: on Dec 25, in Wash City, after a severe & painful illness, Wm J Stewart, son of Ignatius & Mary Stewart, formerly of Alexandria, D C, in his 31st year, leaving a wife & 2 children to mourn his irreparable loss. His funeral is tomorrow, at 3 o'clock, from the residence of his mother, on E st, between 6th & 7th sts.

SAT DEC 28, 1850
The late Hon Marmaduke Williams: was born on Apr 6, 1772, in Caswell Co, N C, & there married on Dec 25, 1798, to Mrs Agnes Harris, whose maiden name was Payne. He was elected to Congress from the Caswell district in 1803, to succeed his brother, Robt Williams, who was appointed by Mr Jefferson Govn'r of the Mississippi Territory; & continued in Congress until Mar 3, 1809. He was a republican. In 1810 he removed with his family to Madison Co, Ala, which then formed a part of the Mississippi Territory, & from there to Tuscaloosa, in 1818, where he continued to reside until his death, which occurred on Oct 29, 1850. Thus ended the life of one who for nearly 79 years had been permitted to sojourn on earth. –Tuscaloosa Monitor

The late London papers announce the death of Mr Jeremiah Wombwell, at the age of 72 years. He was the owner of 3 large traveling menageries, embracing a large collection of rare & valuable wild animals & birds, by the exhibition of which he had acquired a handsome fortune.

The steamship **Ohio**, under the command of Lt Jas Finlay Schenck, of the U S Navy, arrived at Norfolk on Thu, & among the passengers were the Hon Reverdy Johnson, Brantz Mayer, Gen Benj C Howard, & Hon A G Penn, of La, successor in the House of Reps: to the late Mr Harmanson. She was bound for N Y & when about to leave Havana on Dec 18, the first evolution of her engines blew out the head of one of her cylinders. This detained her in the harbor until the 19th, when she departed with the perfect use of only one engine. She encountered a violent gale; she sprung a leak, the water in the hold increased some 10 feet; the passengers organized in bands to assist in freeing the vessel, by pumping & bailing with the coal buckets. She then bore up for Norfolk, reaching that port on Thu.

Appointments by the Pres: 1-J M Jones, of San Jose, Calif, to be Dist Judge of the U S for the Southern District of Calif. 2-J L Pettigru, of S C, to be Atty of the U S for the Dist of S C. 3-Hugh O'Neal, of Indiana, to be Atty of the U S for the Dist of Indiana.

Official: Dept of State, Wash, Dec 27, 1850. Information received from Amos B Corwine, U S Counsul at Panama, of the death within his Consular District of the following American citizens, viz: Mich Lowe, late of Wash, D C; John M Holt; Geo Ringgold, seaman of barque **Susan**; Chas Reed, seaman of barque **R A Everetts**; A Maxfield, of steamer **Tobaga**; Capt J J Wainwright, of the brig **Mary Stewart**.

Millard Fillmore, Pres of the U S, recognizes: Carl Friedrich Adax, who was appointed Consul of Hanover at Cincinnati, in Ohio. Dec 24, 1850

Railroad accident on Dec 24, on the Charlotte road, for Winnsboro, when the train was precipitated about 30 feet into Elkin's Mill pond. Mr Nicholas Gibson, the depot agent at Winsboro, & an infant of Mr & Mrs Powell, died from the injuries received. A servant girl of Mr Lyles was drowned. Gen Ewen had an arm dislocated, & a cut forehead.

Mrd: on Dec 26, at Normanstone, near Gtwn, by Rev John M P Atkinson, R S T Cissell to Mary C, daughter of Robt Barnard.

Mrd: on Dec 24, in Christ Church, Wash, by Rev Mr Hodges, Mr Hugh McCormick to Miss Frances A McCauley, all of Wash City.

Died: on Dec 24, Catherine T Quigley, only daughter of Wm Quigley, aged 1 year & 9 months.

MON DEC 30, 1850
Wash City Ordinance: 1-Act for the relief of Wm B Wilson: the sum of $11.48 be paid to him for the payment of the balance due him for the flag footway across B st, at 7th. 2-Act for the relief of W H Barnaclo: the sum of $23.09 be paid to him for a balance found to be due to him as fees for commitments & taking persons to the Workhouse. 3-Act for the relief of Wm Johnson: to pay to him $74.87, for removal of nuisances in the 3rd Ward.

Mrd: on Dec 29, by Rev Mr Morgan, Mr Wm H Kelly, of PG Co, Md, to Miss Margaret McCubbin, eldest daughter of Mr Edw McCubbin, of Wash City.

Mrd: on Dec 24, by Rev Mr T Murson, Mr Chas A Sengstack, of Wash City, to Miss Mary J Burgee, of PG Co, Md.

Died: on Dec 5, at her grandson's, Geo W Dunlop's, in Wash City, Ann Shanklin, at the advanced age of 116 years. Eighty years of her life was spent in the service of her God, as she was a consistent member of the Baptist Church.

Died: on Dec 29, after a short but painful illness, Mary Catherine Miller, aged 23 years. Her funeral is tomorrow at 2 o'clock, from the residence of her father, on Va ave, between 6th & 7th sts.

The funeral of Mrs Mary L Whiting, wife of Lt Wm B Whiting, U S N, whose death near New Orleans on Nov 26 was noticed, & whose remains have been brought to Wash City, will take place this afternoon at 2 o'clock, from St John's Church.

TUE DEC 31, 1850
The Eastern Mail brings us news of the decease of the Hon Saml Bell, of N H, formerly Govn'r of that State, & for a number of years one of its Senators in Congress, & in every station, public & private, one of the most upright & exemplary of men. He died at Chelsea, N H, on Dec 23. His age is not mentioned, but we think he has reached, or is near his 80th year.

Died: on Dec 26, at Carlisle, Pa, after a short illness, Mrs Virginia King, consort of Dr Benj King, U S Army. She leaves her husband & children to mourn her irreparable loss. Her funeral is today, at 12 o'clock, from *Colross*, Alexandria, the residence of her sister, Mrs Judge Mason.

Died: on Dec 30, Mrs Sarah Virginia, consort of Mr Wm S Darrell, of the Gen Post Ofc Dept. Her funeral is this day at 3 o'clock, from her late residence on Mass ave, between 6th & 7th sts.

Wash City property to be sold for taxes: on Mar 26 next, unless the said taxes be previously paid to the Collector. –A Rothwell, Collector
Alexander, Columbus: 1848-1850: $41.86
Ault, Henry: 48-50: $51.06
Anthony, Jos: 47-50: $4.76
Adams, Jas: 47-50: $77.09
Appleton, John: 46-50: $19.95
Acton, Osbourne: 48-50: $5.92
Allen, Thos D: 48-50: $28.65
Acken, Wm D: 48-50: $28.93
Burche, Benj & Saml: 48-50: $188.03
Bean, Benj: 47-50: $75.63
Bulfinch, Chas: 47-50: $35.26
Biddle, Clement: 47-50: $1.12
Bomford & Decatur: 46-50: $26.63
Barry, David: 47-50: $1.44
Barnes, Elias: 46-50: $14.50
Boothe, Edw: 47-50: $1.28
Buckey, Geo: 47-50: $8.79
Burns, Geo: 47-50: $113.50
Barnes, Hanson: 47-50: $33.28
Breckenridge, John: 47-50: $8.68
Barcroft, John: 47-50: $55.44
Butler, Jared: 48-50: $7.72
Brent, J F: 47-50: $5.40
Brown, John: 46-50: $14.67
Bowen, Jas A: 47-50: $3.44
Blondell, J D: 48-50: $4.56
Beck, Jos W: 46-50: $15.01
Burch, J C: 48-50: $38.52
Benning, Jas & Lucy: 46-50: $2.07
Brady, John: 48-50: $20.51
Bowen, John: 48-50: $5.81
Baltzer, John: 48-50: $18.17
Boardley, John B: 48-50: $2.16
Birch, Jas H: 44-50: $4.17
Bowyer, Matilda: 47-50: $21.26

Brown, Mary: 48-50: $26.18
Bowen, Martha A: 47-50: $6.88
Brown, Nathan: 47-50: $2.52
Brady, Nathl: 44-50: $17.38
Bias, Noah: 48-50: $8.19
Bradley, Phineas J: 47-50: $18.98
Boston, Robt: 47-50: $23.50
Briscoe, Richd G: 48-50: $152.40
Brown, Robt: 47-50: $7.85
Brent, Robt: 46-50: $54.10
Bayan, Sarah E: 47-50: $1.18
Burche, Saml: 47-50: $33.08
Boyd, Thos S W: 46-50: $37.48
Bulfinch, Thos: 48-50: $6.60
Brown, Wm: 44-50: $4.50
Billing, W W: 45-50: $7.86
Bird, W, jr: 47-50: $45.60
Bottemly, John: 49-50: $5.92
Bruning, John H; 48-50: $37.02
Bradley, Wm A: 48-50: $30.31
Cox, Clement: 46-50: $32.60
Carroll, Chas, jr: 47-50: $.48
Chester, Elijah: 47-50: $.64
Coombe, Griffith, interest: 45-50: $2.16
Craig, Henry: 47-50: $1.16
Colborn, Jas, & A Ward: 48-50: $19.90
Carrico, Jas: 48-50: $65.46
Clarke, Jos S & R S Briscoe: 43-50: $11.64
Callan, John F: 47-50: $51.82
Clarke, Jas T: 43-50: $7.47
Cull, Jas: 46-50: $5.62
Carroll, Mary: 46-50: $26.10
Callanan, Mary: 47-50: $105.47
Carter, Maria: on interest from Dec 6, 1848: $14.82
Culver, Mgt A: 47-50: $99.14
Craig, Maria: 47-50: $7.90
Clarke, Ruth Ann: 45-50: $85.09
Clements, Rachel: 46-50: $14.39
Coleman, S S: 45-50: $.44
Collins & Smith, & B C Smith: 47-50: $11.28
Cathcart, Thos J: 47-50: $13.52
Cranch, Wm G: 45-50: $513.83
Coxe, Eliza, improvements Chas Schusler: 46-50: $94.36
Carbery, Thos & W Jones, in trust for E Miller: 46-50: $48.36
Callahan, Thos: 48-50: $7.71
Carrico, Wm B: 45-50: $2.52

Corcoran, W W: 50: $4.20
Conley, Thos Y: 47-50: $620.50
Davis, Chas A: 47-50: $4.30
Douglass, Eliz: 48-50: $8.72
Densley, Hugh: 45-50: $1.68
Dines, Hanson: 47-50: $21.47
Dulaney, John: 47-50: $12.88
Davidson, L G: 47-50: $56.28
Dick, Mgt: 47-50: $42.82
Dick, Robt: 47-50: $5.58
Davis, Richd: 48-50: $33.01
Davis, Chas B: 43-50: $141.83
Dale, Richd: 48-50: $19.32
Dumphey, Thos E: 47-50: $25.08
Dant, Thos E: 48-50: $9.11
Donaphan, Thornton A: 46-50: $5.64
Douglass, Wm: 47-50: $14.68
Deitz, W H; 47-50: $82.00
Donelan, Wm C: 47-50: $.48
Doniphan, Wm: 48-50: $18.20
Enos, D C: 47-50: $5.40
Elliot, Jared L: 48-50: $9.63
Eschbach, John: 36-50: $31.12
Eberbach, John H: 47-50: $209.52
Eastburn, Martin, & others: 46-50: $8.28
Ennis, Philip: 46-50: $57.52
Elliot, S A: 47-50: $35.32
Eliot, Saml & J G McDonald: 48-50: $1.02
Evans, Wm: 47-50: $110.02
Favier, Agricol: 46-50: $117.75
Freedy, Christian: 47-50: $32.72
Fairfax, Ferdinand: 44-50: $2.07
Farrell, Harriet: 47-50: $16.28
Freeman, John: 46-50: $35.20
Fitzpatrick, John C: 42-50: $110.33
Farland, John: 47-50: $15.98
Forble, Mgt: 48-50: $12.33
Forest, Richd: 48-50: $13.86
Frazier, Thos? 48-50: $23.75
Fletcher, Thos: 47-50: $157.25
Fitnam, Thos: 48-50: $22.91
Fischer, W & L Johnson: 48-50: $59.43
Fowler, Abraham: 1850: $1.13
Graham, Aloysius: 48-50: $72.44
Gainor, Catharine W: 47-50: $.98
Grentrup, Fredinand: 48-50: $21.62

Grammer, G C: 37-50: $152.17
Gass, John G: 47-50: $9.76
Gadsby, John: 47-50: $36.40
Gardiner, John: 48-50: $31.95
Gideon, Jacob: 48-50: $39.46
Gibson, Joshua: 48-50: $18.60
Guista, Michl A: 49-50: $18.68
Gibson, Mary H: 47-50: $4.58
Gill, Priscilla: 48-50: $16.31
Gorsuch, Wm G: 45-50: $40.46
Gunnell, W H & S P Franklin: 48-50: $8.97
Gault, M & M G Emory: 46-50: $70.55
Gilles Groenweldt, Rudolph Mees, & Pieter V W Vollenhoven: 45-50: $350.00
Greenleaf, Jas: 48-50: $61.12
Higdon, Andrew, Francis, & C F: 47-50: $53.22
Harper, Alex'r: 47-50: $81.62
Hoover, Barbara: 47-50: $30.68
Headley, Eliza: 47-50: $15.04
Handy, Edw: 48-50: $32.79
Hall, Edw: 48-50: $32.34
Harkness, G W: 45-50: $55.84
Hinton, Geo: 44-50: $16.34
Jocks, Henry: 47-50: $2.44
Hager, John F: 46-50: $16.41
Hall, J C: 41-50: $222.49
Hall, Jos B: 46-50: $24.78
Hoffman, John: 47-50: $2.92
Hunter, John: 42-50: $6.07
Hoover, Michl: 47-50: $113.88
Herrity, Mgt: 44-50: $3.60
Hammond, M A B: 42-50: $26.18
Haswell, N B: 47-50: $7.56
Horsey, Outterbridge: 46-50: $1.40
Hoffman, Peter: 47-50: $6.96
Handy, Saml W: 47-50: $67.83
Hammond, Sarah: 47-50: $105.15
Hayman, Wm: 47-50: $136.60
Howe, John: 48-50: $16.96
Hall, David A: 45-50: $1,797.20
Jardin, Armand: 48-50: $25.38
Jackson, Chaney: 47-50: $7.30
Jones, Chas: 48-50: $4.80
Jones, David & B, minor: 47-50: $7.86
Johnson, John: 45-50: $30.51
Jones, Jas & Henry: 47-50: $7.00
Johnson, Polly & Thos Hammond: 48-50: $23.82

Johnson, Peter & Wm: 46-50: $.59
Kelly, Bernard: 48-50: $45.88
Kurtz, Danl: 45-50: $.60
Kane, Elias: 47-50: $10.64
Kirty, Francis: 47-50: $5.52
Kingman, Eliab: 46-50: $10.05
Keller, Eliz: 44-50: $120.18
King, Geo, of Chas: 47-50: $.72
Kendrick, Geo W: 47-50: $24.90
King, Martin: 49-50: $48.92
Kedglie, John: 47-50: $42.48
Kerr, Mary Ann: 48-50: $24.20
Kerr, Robt, in trust for the heirs of Henry: 48-50: $25.29
Kerr, Robt E: 47-50: $100.88
Knowles, Robt O: 47-50: $27.60
Kavanaugh, Thos: 48-50: $3.24
Lefevre, Ann M: 48-50: $62.90
Lucas, Bennett: 48-50: $19.20
Little, Franklin & T Law: 47-50: $77.44
Lombardi, Francis: 47-50: $25.35
Lee, John: 47-50: $12.30
Little, John: 47-50: $24.94
Little, John E: 47-50: $15.56
Luther, Sarah: 46-50: $18.00
Law, Thos: 46-50: $365.56
Lewis, Saunders: 45-50: $93.04
McElwee, Aaron: 47-50: $21.14
Milburn, Benedict: 48-50: $19.50
McWilliams, Clement: 47-50: $24.26
Moore, Danl S: 48-50: $10.86
Moore, Fred'k: 45-50: $.42
Miller, Geo: 47-50: $22.74
McKnight, Geo B & M H: 48-50: $12.34
Merryman, Horatio R: 47-50: $280.04
Moscrop, Henry: 41-50: $.54
Millard, Joshua: 47-50: $60.32
Marshall, John & Jas, & Jas H Causten & W W Corcoran: 48-50: $36.46
Madison, Jas: 48-50: $187.50
Marshall, Jas: 47-50: $33.30
Marshall, John: 47-50: $34.30
Maher, Jas: 48-50: $205.80
Morgan, John B: 45-50: $31.62
Moss, Julia A: 47-50: $31.04
Maury, J W: 46-50: $27.75
McCormick, Jas: 46-50: $246.09
McQuay, Mary: 48-50: $26.13

Maddox, Notley: 48-50: $1.08
Mauro, Philip: 46-50: $5.45
Marlborough, Rachael: 47-50: $24.72
Monroe, Thos: 47-50: $25.07
Morris, Thos: 48-50: $3.76
Morton, Wm: 48-50: $15.62
McLean, Wm: 47-50: $32.21
McCormick, W J: 38-50: $1.99
Mardes, Wm: 45-50: $6.36
Morris, John B: 48-50: $1,594.56
Nesmith, Ann: 26-50: $28.41
Neil, Eliz: 47-50: $2.20
Nourse, Jos: 47-50: $43.04
Nokes, Jas G: 48-50: $32.11
Newton, Isaac: 45-50: $1.87
Nicholson, Jos H: 47-50: $1.28
Narden, Mary: 48-50: $25.28
Noyes, Wm: 47-50: $6.53
Nailor, Allison: 47-50: $119.33
O'Leary, Jeremiah: 47-50: $37.66
O'Neale, Wm: 47-50: $122.68
Pennock & Ash: 48-50: $32.55
Parker, Albert: 47-50: $10.15
Peter, David: 46-50: $130.00
Pickrell, Esau & Adolphus: 45-50: $2.88
Peter, Geo: 48-50: $3.39
Peck, Jos: 48-50: $7.89
Pepper, J P: 42-50: $9.28
Phillips, Jas B: 46-50: $83.81
Patton, Jas; 46-50: $1.44
Pollock, John: 47-50: $2.24
Prout, Mary: 1848 & 1850: $2.37
Phillips, Overton C: 47-50: $48.02
Packard, Perez: 47-50: $4.84
Pearson, Peter M: 48-50: $5.97
Parrott, Richd: 45-50: $.72
Phillips, Saml: 48-50: $34.32
Prout, Wm: 47-50: $11.10
Parker, Wm H: 44-50: $143.98
Pratt, Henry: 46-50: $463.57
Reynoldson, Catherine: 46-50: $17.50
Redden, David & others in trust: 46-50: $3.32
Rosenstock, Geo: 46-50: $2.19
Robbins, Harriet: 47-50: $21.08
Randall, H K: 48-50: $6.93
Ricar, John G C: 48-50: $5.05

Randall, John: 47-50: $25.62
Rogers, Minerva: 45-50: $145.62
Roberts, Sarah: 47-50: $15.74
Rawlings, Washington: 47-50: $13.04
Rattrie, Wm: 35-50: $5.37
Shepherd, Alex'r: 47-50: $107.92
Smith, A T: 47-50: $28.63
St Clair, Arthur: 47-50: $54.68
Simms, Basil: 47-50: $149.69
Stewart, Chas: 47-50: $24.96
Simonda, Cornelia: 47-50: $20.07
Smith, Clement: 47-50: $29.78
Stephens, Edw: 47-50: $14.14
Smallwood, Enoch W: 47-50: $2.92
Selden, Francis: 46-50: $62.00
Shorter, Fanny: 46-50: $32.62
Scott, Geo: 48-50: $16.38
Simmons, Streshley: 1850: $.28
Sweeny, Hugh B: 45-50: $22.44
Smith, John S: 46-50: $59.72
Snowden, John, & others: 47-50: $3.92
Shekles, John; 47-50: $9.52
Smith, John T: 45-50: $12.08
Seymour, Jonathan: 48-50: $20.76
Simms, Mary Ann E: 47-50: $41.68
Sentis, Matthew: 47-50: $.90
Shine, Michl R: 47-50: $2.04
Smith, Paca: 47-50: $2.64
Sweet, Parker H: 40-50: $20.79
Stewart, Wm H: 46-50: $181.73
Smith, Wm: 48-50: $11.76
Stott, Saml: 45-50: $6.38
Thomas, Amelia: 47-50: $7.88
Tayloe, B O: 47-50: $8.14
Tucker, Enoch: 48-50: $58.77
Taylor, Emily: 47-50: $20.38
Tilghman, Frisby: 47-50: $4.32
Toughey, Hugh: 47-50: $3.52
Thomas, John H: 47-50: $13.80
Taylor, John jr: 47-50: $2.60
Thompson, Jos: 46-50: $22.29
Travers, Nicholas: 46-50: $1,721.24.
Voorhees, B M: 47-50: $24.12
Van Patten, C H: 47-50: $256.15
Van Ness, Cornelius P: 47-50: $440. 59
Vernon, Henry T: 46-50: $42.27

Vernon, Henry T: 46-50: $65.54
Van Ness, Matilda E: 48-50: $2.
Washburn, Ann: 46-50: $2.
Waller, A B: 45-50: $1.80
Waugh, Beverley: 47-50: $11.94
Wiltberger & Burche: 47-50: $11.94
Waters, Benj: 44-50: $.32
Winder, Chas H: 47-50: $68
Walker, Dorcas: 47-50: $7.74
Watterston, David A: 42-50: $41.75
Wailes, Dorothea: 40-50: $3.90
Wilson, David: $2.90
Wood, Ferdinand: 46-50: $68.02
Wharton, Franklin: 47-50: $44.64
Watterston, Geo & John Kedglie: 46-50: $5.06
Warring, Henry: 49-50: .72
Watkins, Julius: 40-50: $18.
Watson, Jas: 47-50: $18.
Woodside, John, use of J L Cathcart: 47-50: $5.28
Whitney, Jas: 47-50: $6.22
Ward, Jos D: 48-50: $6.36
Wilson, John A: 47-50: $95.16
Waller, J D, in trust: 47-50: $2.02
Wallace, Israel: 46-50: $.36
Williams, Lemuel: 44-50: $44.73
Winder, Levin H: 47-50: $22.72
Williams, Lloyd: 47-50: $27.42
Wertz, Mary E: 48-50: $190.51
Wall, Mary Ann: 46-50: $12.75
Wroe, Mary: 41-50: $7.19
Wigle, Richd: 48-50: $8.04
Waters, Robt A: 48-50: $.62
Wheatley, Wm J: 47-50: $25.38
Williams, S S: 47-50: $4.26
Welch, Thos: 46-50: $29.33
Young, Benj: 47-50: $79.56.
Young, Mary: 47-50: $3.13
Young, Mgt: 48-50: $.56
Young, Nicholas: 47-50: $8.16

A

Abbot, 103, 133, 201, 397, 429
Abbott, 50, 186, 198, 201, 209, 331, 393, 459, 475
Abell, 390
Abercrombie, 169, 231
Abernathy, 28
Abernethy, 426
Abert, 83, 185, 362, 370
Aborn, 357
Abrahams, 215
<u>Academy of the Visitation</u>, 302
Achard, 270
Acken, 34, 501
Acker, 142, 310, 394
Ackerman, 354
Ackley, 393
Acton, 359, 501
Adae, 97
Adair, 59, 163
Adam, 108
Adams, 7, 10, 38, 49, 51, 68, 69, 79, 85, 87, 97, 103, 110, 158, 164, 187, 196, 201, 226, 232, 251, 252, 267, 279, 297, 298, 330, 331, 344, 345, 355, 358, 359, 368, 375, 383, 393, 396, 404, 426, 429, 436, 444, 476, 485, 494, 496, 501
Adamson, 367
Adax, 499
Addison, 108, 121, 142, 211, 248, 255, 287, 291, 349, 359, 372, 393, 415, 441, 482, 484
Adhby, 57
Adkins, 57, 78, 294
Adler, 57, 156
Adolph, 362
Agassiz, 194
Agee, 314
Agnew, 294, 395
Aguero, 387
Ahern, 57
Ahrenfeldt, 38, 96, 117, 119, 383
Aigler, 108, 190

Aiglet, 108
Aiken, 81
Aikin, 445
Ailer, 110
Aimey, 108
Aisquith, 44
Aiton, 331
Aitz, 470
Akers, 352
Al loh-la, 335
Albagnac, 422
Albert, 58
Albertson, 57, 190, 316
Alcalda, 233
Alcott, 208
Alcoy, 387, 408
Alden, 77
Aldridge, 305
Alencon, 124
Alexander, 9, 15, 24, 28, 101, 143, 146, 185, 186, 217, 222, 342, 367, 370, 372, 448, 476, 501
Alford, 137, 138
Alga, 60
Alger, 68
Algoma, 260
Alice, 440
Alig, 4, 63, 71, 72, 403
Allcott, 37
Allen, 13, 25, 34, 51, 75, 85, 86, 94, 98, 108, 133, 144, 173, 183, 192, 199, 201, 202, 208, 219, 231, 240, 268, 296, 305, 323, 324, 336, 343, 359, 389, 406, 413, 414, 421, 435, 444, 462, 498, 501
Alley, 328, 331
Alliance, 69
Allison, 15, 342, 402
Allison's Park, 319
Allman, 118
Allmand, 376
Al-lo-lah, 396
Allyn, 5, 47
Almy, 187
Alston, 85, 340

Altemus, 61, 207
Alvey, 416
Alvord, 483
Alward, 222
Always, 252
Ames, 342, 461, 472
Ammen, 404
Ammerman, 474
Ampudia, 286
Amstiad, 120
Anderson, 20, 34, 37, 41, 81, 86, 105, 121, 130, 137, 163, 186, 205, 209, 221, 255, 258, 287, 288, 292, 313, 320, 322, 333, 339, 340, 342, 359, 362, 370, 373, 428, 458, 465, 487
Andony, 393
Andre, 496
Andrews, 84, 118, 133, 168, 216, 218, 261, 274, 278, 310, 327, 362, 394, 492
Ankney, 498
Annan, 198
Annibal, 481, 492
Anthony, 501
Antoine, 393
Applegate, 399
Appleton, 134, 501
Appointments by the Pres, 25, 27, 34, 99, 116, 134, 136, 142, 146, 167, 170, 180, 182, 187, 189, 196, 200, 217, 219, 234, 236, 245, 254, 259, 268, 269, 270, 275, 289, 305, 312, 314, 323, 340, 343, 354, 356, 375, 382, 384, 389, 393, 395, 397, 398, 402, 419, 424, 436, 477, 499
Arbogast, 391
Archbishop, 407
Archbold, 496
Archer, 35, 45, 63, 146, 230, 377
Archibald, 148
Ardinger, 273
Ardre, 42
Arenas, 54, 487
Arford, 271
Arfredson, 475
Arion, 342
Arista, 286

Arlee, 301
Arlege, 195
Armistead, 18, 110, 338
Armisted, 433
Armitage, 206
Armstead, 14, 388
Armstrong, 2, 3, 20, 30, 52, 73, 75, 90, 92, 146, 153, 163, 174, 187, 205, 224, 238, 253, 335, 455
Arndt, 341
Arnold, 1, 4, 72, 73, 84, 125, 132, 141, 323, 328, 339, 450
Arnow, 312
Arrington, 296
Arth, 362
Arthur, 299, 483, 484
Asbury, 296, 344
Ash, 127
Ashby, 102, 180
Ashcroft, 297
Ashdown, 203
Ashe, 232, 419
Ashford, 256, 476
Ashland, 44
Ashley, 57, 448
Ashmead, 254
Ashton, 57, 193, 247, 297, 358, 410
Ashworth, 157
Askew, 132
Asquith, 30
Astaburuaga, 308
Atchenson, 349
Atchison, 201, 229, 303
Atherton, 306, 315
Atkins, 8, 15, 103, 183, 366, 372
Atkinson, 122, 146, 176, 500
Atwater, 10, 493
Atwood, 80, 198, 204
Auchincloss, 22
Auguera, 355
August, 299
Augustin, 273, 495
Auld, 248
Aulick, 56, 482
Ault, 501
Austin, 70, 235, 341

Averill, 158, 162, 196, 390, 396
Averitt, 65
Avery, 29, 61, 155, 167, 370, 390, 445, 474
Avirett, 118
Axtell, 444
Aydelott, 206
Ayers, 294
Ayler, 103, 246, 359, 369
Aylmer, 110, 370
Ayton, 16

B

Babb, 153
Babcock, 29, 276, 290, 322, 349, 394, 425, 434
Baber, 235
Bache, 59, 147, 228, 229, 319, 362, 378, 468, 487
Bachman, 333
Backus, 142, 160, 394, 483, 484
Bacon, 78, 110, 296, 366, 389, 429
Baden, 80, 108, 153, 301, 332
Baget, 57
Bagge, 27
Baggett, 416
Bagley, 204
Bagnall, 26
Bagwell, 391
Bailey, 47, 146, 290, 310, 395
Baily, 141, 205, 389
Bain, 252
Bainbridge, 94, 380, 400, 482
Baird, 143, 299, 326, 422
Baker, 9, 24, 113, 125, 136, 149, 175, 224, 228, 232, 235, 253, 285, 287, 298, 299, 342, 355, 435, 448, 468
Balch, 295, 313, 404
Baldwin, 16, 42, 68, 71, 101, 133, 163, 244, 277, 295, 338, 429, 430, 431
Balentine, 189
Baley, 449
Ball, 84, 90, 114, 188, 209, 214, 222, 247, 362, 392, 416
Ball's Mill, 317
Ballad, 237

Ballamy, 156
Ballantine, 201, 311, 420
Ballard, 327, 328, 379
Ballenger, 369, 480, 486
Ballinger, 136, 369
Ballintine, 388
Ballou, 199
Balmain, 301, 337
Baltzer, 501
Bamberger, 464
Banagan, 347
Bancroft, 73, 85, 317, 321
Bandorim, 39
Bandouin, 75
Bangs, 69, 288, 482
Bank Lot, 185
Bank Property, 185
Bank Territory, 185
Banker, 342
Bankhead, 328
Banks, 318, 366
Banning, 283
Bannister, 429
Banter, 148
Bar, 19
Barbarin, 214
Barber, 72, 75, 89, 108, 121, 362, 369, 416, 449
Barbour, 253, 327, 328, 384, 397, 419
Barbydt, 12
Barclay, 55, 213, 269
Barcroft, 103, 501
Bardona, 366
Barhydt, 128
Barker, 47, 85, 238, 251, 263, 367, 391, 431, 489
Barkett, 57
Barkley, 278
Barley, 148
Barlow, 15, 198, 206, 278
Barnaclo, 267, 460, 500
Barnard, 22, 291, 310, 325, 341, 354, 382, 404, 416, 500
Barneclo, 495

511

Barnes, 2, 23, 66, 74, 108, 112, 135, 151, 267, 359, 362, 379, 381, 404, 468, 501
Barnett, 102, 404, 492
Barney, 6, 22, 177, 188, 193, 229, 232, 253, 358, 424
Barnhill, 362, 368
Barnhouse, 370
Barnitz, 127
Barns, 77, 172
Barnum, 89, 194, 199, 235, 458
Barny, 31
barque **Agnes**, 167
barque **Aristide Marie**, 353
barque **Bogota**, 298
barque **Chieftain**, 79
barque **Cornwallis**, 157
barque **Georgiana**, 408
barque **Israel Meade**, 404
barque **James Patton, jr**, 298
barque **John W Cater**, 236
barque **R A Everetts**, 499
barque **Sarah**, 44, 55, 168, 260
barque **Sherwood**, 162
barque **Susan**, 499
Barr, 22, 103, 111, 187, 336, 342, 359
Barrabino, 187
Barraud, 468
Barrell, 81, 386, 478
Barren, 75
Barret, 283
Barrett, 96, 119, 122, 235, 237, 267, 281, 293, 321, 359, 396, 440
Barrey, 301
Barringer, 397
Barrington, 314
Barron, 53, 215, 348, 362
Barronton, 183
Barrow, 51, 429
Barry, 60, 65, 96, 106, 119, 131, 190, 207, 237, 301, 395, 416, 496, 501
Barstow, 395
Barstown, 404
Barter, 398
Bartholomew, 410
Bartine, 193

Bartlett, 5, 37, 67, 86, 108, 254, 270, 372, 374
Bartley, 89
Bartoe, 445
Bartoll, 71
Barton, 107, 232, 244, 326, 336, 431, 458
Bascomb, 356
Bass, 205, 318
Bassett, 144, 307, 316
Bassham, 241
Bassigallope, 309
Bastianelli, 108, 411
Batchelder, 68
Bateman, 303, 435
Batemen, 57, 359
Bates, 30, 51, 52, 60, 82, 108, 136, 198, 200, 232, 256, 283, 296, 328, 358, 359, 369, 375, 376, 397, 404, 417, 464, 469
Batson, 184
Batston, 309
Battem, 278
Battle, 219, 449
Battles of the Revolution, 419
Battoni, 156
Battson, 279
Baudouin, 155
Baughn, 15
Baum, 419
Baumgardner, 239
Baury, 140
Bayan, 502
Bayard, 125, 145, 183, 477
Bayley, 390
Baylis, 315
Bayliss, 107, 111, 210, 359, 411
Baylor, 146, 382
Bayly, 108, 229, 288, 362, 436, 475
Bayne, 40, 50, 106, 114, 127, 452
Bayne's Burial Ground, 260
Baynham, 337
Baynton, 475
Beach, 3, 51, 126, 380, 392, 421
Beachey, 301
Beachlin, 103, 114

Beadle, 94
Beakey, 198
Beal, 28, 218
Beale, 129, 207, 313, 344, 388, 402, 404, 411, 412
Beall, 111, 231, 232, 271, 300, 346, 359, 364, 366, 416, 418, 473
Beals, 183
Bean, 8, 59, 108, 111, 189, 204, 266, 267, 311, 359, 362, 501
Beard, 100, 394, 416
Beardsley, 242
Bearwallow, 274
Beasley, 105, 362
Beatty, 1, 20, 65, 322, 377
Beaty, 261
Beaugrand, 54
Bebee, 481
Bechtel, 38, 278
Beck, 235, 243, 323, 501
Becker, 336
Beckert, 49
Becket, 416
Beckett, 103, 105, 227, 282, 362, 410
Beckwith, 187, 328
Bee, 187, 310
Beebe, 45, 492
Beebee, 132
Beecher, 36
Beeckman, 244
Beekmann, 91
Beelan, 430
Beelen, 170
Beeler, 343, 406
Beener, 177
Beers, 182
Beetley, 60
Begges, 128
Begley, 59
Begnam, 105
Behler, 187
Behn, 355
Beirne, 155
Bekert, 112
Belamy, 31
Belden, 2, 488

Belding, 65
Belfield, 61
Belger, 333
Belknap, 153, 449
Bell, 10, 19, 42, 43, 51, 53, 77, 90, 101, 103, 105, 111, 122, 151, 186, 201, 232, 235, 273, 290, 315, 317, 362, 376, 381, 387, 416, 421, 479, 495, 500
Bellamy, 222
Belle Air, 80
Bellevue, 247
Bellinger, 301, 302
Belt, 57, 99, 204, 232, 234, 375, 421
Beltzhoover, 376
Belzhoover, 50
Bender, 42, 85, 166, 214, 332, 475
Benedict, 84, 182, 186
Benezette, 134
Benham, 94, 397
Benjamin, 116, 234, 393, 397, 489
Benner, 46, 278, 362, 492
Bennet, 185
Bennett, 16, 57, 148, 198, 330, 416, 422, 496
Benning, 59, 74, 157, 323, 463, 501
Bensley, 82, 85, 90, 262
Benson, 79, 218, 234, 238, 298, 421
Bentalou, 22
Benter, 103, 113, 114, 268, 275, 368, 372
Bentley, 65
Benton, 161
Berckmann, 418
Berger, 171
Bergling, 72
Bergman, 106, 114
Berkeley, 33
Berkley, 103, 150, 372
Berlyn, 71, 378
Bernard, 146, 287
Bernhard, 330
Berret, 99, 213
Berrian, 352
Berrien, 151, 194, 485

Berry, 29, 79, 98, 108, 114, 118, 128, 145, 154, 168, 218, 234, 302, 351, 368, 404, 445
Bertrand, 343
Besore, 148
Besschlin, 359, 369
Besse, 81
Best, 261, 400, 482, 483, 484
Bestor, 103, 282
Bettle, 462
Bevan, 111
Bevans, 331
Beven, 108
Beverly, 245
Beyer, 421
Beyland, 136
Bias, 502
Bicknall, 117
Bicknell, 114, 325
Bicksler, 366
Biddle, 22, 351, 426, 438, 501
Bidlack, 134
Bierwith, 48, 396
Bieswirth, 18
Bigelow, 182, 382, 384, 421, 458
Biggs, 366, 440, 441
Bigna, 481
Bigney, 492
Bilby, 283
Bill, 269
Billing, 340, 502
Billings, 25, 100
Billups, 5
Bingham, 199, 217, 258, 327
Bingley, 30
Bingly, 192
Birch, 77, 108, 344, 426, 501
Birchett, 236
Bird, 108, 211, 232, 359, 502
Birdsall, 314, 462
Birge, 188
Birkby, 487
Birkhead, 76
Birth, 368
Biscoe, 113, 209
Biser, 69

Bishop, 15, 73, 84, 108, 125, 259, 339
Bispham, 84, 223
Bissell, 77, 257, 469
Bittinger, 210, 215, 404, 496
Biusse, 446
Bivings, 94
Bix, 75
Blache, 304
Black, 14, 75, 103, 132, 198, 297, 371, 375
Blackburn, 47, 90, 92, 189, 350, 354, 375
Blackford, 219
Blacklock, 120
Blackman, 184
Blackney, 150
Blackston, 232
Blackstone, 390
Blackwell, 401, 454
Bladen, 351
Blagden, 17, 79, 131, 256, 362, 369, 372, 442
Blague, 390
Blain, 444
Blair, 77, 176, 310, 317, 378, 381, 397, 400, 416
Blake, 49, 262, 296, 325, 376, 379, 389, 416, 418, 476
Blakely, 93, 378
Blanchard, 3, 11, 14, 30, 44, 72, 116, 156, 168, 468
Blanche, 232
Bland, 207, 476
Blandford, 438
Blannerhassett, 339
Blanton, 494
Bleart, 416
Bleck, 71
Bleecker, 496
Blenehim, 23
Blevins, 93
Blincoe, 317
Bliss, 102, 198, 289, 293, 299, 321, 425
Blizzard, 148
Blodget, 3, 202, 342
Blondell, 501

Bloomer, 181
Blount, 19, 177, 232, 384, 390
Blow, 246
Blox, 156, 463, 492
Bloxham, 57, 162
Blundell, 333
Blunt, 228
Board of Health, 62, 135, 155, 197, 316, 469
Boardley, 501
Boardman, 21, 73, 217, 469, 496
Boarman, 333, 468
boat **Belle Creole**, 498
boat **Doubloon**, 224
boat **Fashion**, 246
boat **James Rumsey**, 133
boat **Resolute**, 456, 459
boat **Southampton**, 395
Bock, 103
Boclanger, 112
Bode, 370
Bodey, 14
Bodisco, 59, 191, 195, 308
Bodley, 341
Bogakin, 45
Bogan, 103
Bogardus, 322
Bogart, 143
Boggess, 209
Boggs, 229, 234
Bogue, 166, 475
Bohlayer, 227, 369
Bohrer, 107, 113
Boislandry, 19
Bokkelen, 483
Bolen, 55
Bollenger, 469
Bolles, 59, 256, 376, 466
Bolling, 299
Bolster, 241, 271
Bolton, 65, 78
Boltzer, 114
Bomar, 195
Bomford, 52, 221, 501
Bond, 88, 116, 369, 372, 393, 420, 459
Bondall, 309

Bonifant, 339
Bonn, 57
Bonner, 303
Bonney, 132
Bonsall, 3
Bonton, 143
Booley, 14, 39, 60
Booly, 23, 75, 138, 155
Boomer, 310
Boone, 108, 325, 359, 437
Boos, 95
Boose, 73
Bootes, 37
Booth, 344, 357, 398, 406
Boothe, 501
Booton, 388
Boots, 356, 496
Borden, 438
Bordley, 33
Borland, 82, 83, 244, 403, 478
Borremans, 108, 302
Borrows, 47, 107
Boscoe, 110, 362
Boses, 411
Bosher, 147
Bostick, 387
Boston, 57, 232, 362, 502
Boswell, 47
Bosworth, 47, 57, 189, 350, 416
Boteler, 39, 76, 102, 105, 108, 186, 207, 229, 230, 239, 251, 263, 277, 287, 415, 419, 431, 450, 457, 460, 461, 474
Bothe, 57
Bottemly, 502
Boudinot, 121, 255
Bouer, 413
Boughton, 402
Bouic, 174, 231
Boulanger, 346
Boulanger's, 255
Boulden, 134
Bouldin, 262
Bourke, 391
Bourn, 197
Boutelle, 59
Bouton, 3, 90, 92

Boutwell, 415
Bowden, 15, 389
Bowdoin, 54
Bowdon, 22
Bowen, 30, 40, 66, 72, 75, 105, 141, 162, 209, 219, 281, 321, 328, 337, 341, 346, 355, 400, 427, 479, 501, 502
Bower, 103, 110, 114, 352, 379
Bowie, 57, 103, 147, 304, 318, 383, 395, 402, 408, 415, 419
Bowland, 73
Bowler, 65
Bowles, 41, 195, 284, 416, 460
Bowlin, 40
Bowling, 24, 57, 333
Bowman, 103, 208, 228, 294, 340, 444
Bowser, 232
Bowsprit, 444
Bowyer, 433, 501
Box, 394
Boyce, 300, 312, 473
Boyd, 5, 55, 111, 155, 170, 187, 189, 209, 234, 283, 285, 321, 335, 382, 392, 394, 502
Boye, 78
Boykin, 128
Boyle, 32, 105, 187, 193, 285, 344, 355, 362, 367, 374, 378, 385, 404, 406, 410, 412
Boynton, 57
Brackenridge, 385
Brackett, 354
Brackney, 197
Bradbury, 83
Braddock, 113, 276, 415, 451
Braden, 415
Bradford, 18, 62
Bradish, 12, 299
Bradley, 58, 103, 107, 108, 114, 136, 210, 213, 233, 270, 287, 290, 305, 340, 404, 414, 417, 426, 435, 481, 502
Bradley, Mary, 113
Bradshaw, 445
Brady, 67, 102, 103, 113, 189, 190, 320, 451, 476, 492, 501, 502
Bragden, 125

Bragg, 373
Braham, 31
Brainard, 201, 246
Braine, 55, 121, 255, 469
Brakelenkay, 156
Bramham, 428
Bramkall, 284
Bramlette, 241
Branch, 239, 302
Brand, 381
Brandon, 402
Brandt, 141
Brannan, 5, 234
Brannin, 421
Brannon, 57, 232
Brashear, 197
Brashears, 111, 114, 359, 362
Brasher, 235
Brasnahan, 111, 436
Brauns, 384
Brawley, 342
Brawner, 228, 302, 411, 412
Braxton, 105
Bray, 55
Breckenridge, 18, 501
Breek, 261
Breese, 255, 468
Breeze, 273
Bremmer, 77
Breneman, 88
Brennan, 439
Brenner, 108, 165, 234, 243, 321, 411
Brent, 95, 100, 134, 160, 171, 179, 217, 232, 303, 304, 359, 362, 370, 400, 401, 458, 469, 470, 476, 482, 484, 501, 502
Brenton, 394
Brereton, 108, 110, 359, 370, 411
Bresnehan, 372
Brest, 479
Brestman, 469
Brett, 261
Brevort, 452
Brewell, 198
Brewer, 247, 474
Brewerton, 483, 484

Brewster, 11, 72, 341
Brice, 26
Brick, 407
Brick Capitol, 301
Bridewell, 412
Bridges, 242
Bridget, 100, 359
Bridgman, 232
Bridinthat, 459
Briel, 103, 362
Brien, 475
brig **Ada Eliza**, 456
brig **Advance**, 234
brig **Andover**, 126
brig **Ann Elizabeth**, 464
brig **Arabian**, 228
brig **Bainbridge**, 14
brig **Emblem**, 246
brig **Excellent**, 265
brig **Frances Jane**, 265
brig **Frolic**, 315
brig **John**, 63
brig **John Hill**, 162
brig **Lincoln**, 196
brig **Mary Stewart**, 499
brig **Ophir**, 126
brig **Porpoise**, 9, 23, 153, 249
brig **Rescue**, 234
brig **Somers**, 378
brig **Splendid**, 82
brig **Washington**, 323, 378
brig **Wasp**, 315
Brigance, 336
brigantine **Ada Eliza**, 142
Briggs, 15, 41, 161, 177, 235, 430, 474
Bright, 108, 161, 332, 349, 429
Brightwell, 146
Brillhart, 118
Brindley, 430
Brinkley, 352
Brintmoele, 226
Brisbois, 168
Briscoe, 15, 39, 108, 277, 302, 304, 369, 377, 387, 443, 457, 502
Bristow, 177
Brite, 380

Britingham, 201
Brittingham, 126, 151, 322, 378, 381
Britton, 192, 238, 327, 328, 444
Broadbeck, 108, 362
Broadbent, 110, 151
Broadrup, 385
Broadus, 102, 274
Brobson, 86
Brobston, 99
Brocchus, 397
Brock, 333
Brockelbank, 470
Brockenbrough, 288
Brockway, 46
Brodhead, 212, 224
Brogan, 31
Broke, 77
Bromberg, 393
Bronaugh, 373, 463
Bronson, 257, 389
Brook, 355
Brooke, 33, 38, 59, 70, 232, 249, 297
Brooks, 26, 45, 57, 67, 80, 103, 168, 223, 224, 227, 232, 234, 287, 304, 305, 311, 339, 359, 362, 371, 416, 440, 455, 473
Broome, 56
Brosnahan, 380
Brotherton, 198
Brower, 108
Brown, 11, 28, 30, 40, 53, 57, 59, 65, 68, 81, 86, 88, 93, 96, 98, 103, 105, 106, 107, 108, 110, 112, 113, 114, 116, 117, 124, 126, 127, 129, 131, 141, 142, 147, 148, 153, 155, 158, 163, 170, 172, 179, 182, 187, 189, 196, 197, 209, 213, 214, 216, 225, 234, 249, 266, 267, 274, 275, 277, 282, 283, 288, 290, 298, 315, 319, 328, 331, 336, 349, 354, 358, 359, 362, 368, 369, 370, 376, 380, 385, 390, 391, 396, 399, 404, 405, 409, 410, 412, 414, 416, 437, 443, 447, 459, 462, 463, 472, 474, 477, 482, 494, 495, 496, 501, 502
Browne, 198, 209, 232, 462

Brownell, 272
Browning, 69, 79, 103, 108, 191, 228, 229, 322, 334, 349, 350, 375, 396, 446
Brownlee, 249
Brubaker, 148, 253
Bruce, 227, 234, 265, 372, 493
Brune, 18
Bruner, 411
Bruning, 502
Brunner, 267
Brush, 39, 41, 208, 274
Bry, 280
Bryan, 69, 76, 170, 208, 214, 224, 234, 275, 313, 333, 410, 456, 470
Bryant, 198, 359, 404
Bryen, 280
Buchanan, 165, 316, 414, 460
Buchanon, 57
Buchell, 38
Buck, 28, 389
Buckey, 501
Buckhart, 29
Buckhouse, 5
Buckingham, 231, 266, 472
Buckley, 24, 165, 263, 359, 412, 462
Buckly, 112, 256
Buckner, 8, 201, 359
Bucknor, 14, 39
Budd, 205
Buell, 187
Buete, 102, 105, 112, 362
Buffington, 59, 397, 401
Buford, 186
Builler, 444
Buist, 281
Buit, 13
Buiz, 333
Bulfinch, 501, 502
Bulger, 340
Bulkley, 349
Bull, 207, 469
Bulland, 40
Bulley, 112
Bullitt, 305
Bullock, 117, 341, 447
Bully, 103

Bulow, 8, 14, 39, 298
Bulwer, 308
Bumah, 60
Bunce, 167
Bunch, 75, 273, 312, 495
Buncombe, 47, 410
Bundy, 68
Bunker, 180
Bunnon, 234
Bunting, 131
Burall, 270
Burch, 88, 137, 208, 333, 357, 443, 501
Burchard, 355
Burche, 258, 288, 375, 425, 501, 502, 508
Burchell, 169
Burd, 172, 334
Burdear, 193
Burdett, 482
Burdick, 416, 493
Burdine, 203, 211, 222, 287, 300, 370, 421, 447
Burditt, 56
Burg'e, 419
Burge, 278
Burgee, 500
Burgess, 267, 312, 359, 370
Burgin, 127
Burke, 24, 213, 359
Burman, 416
Burn, 67
Burnap, 452
Burnes, 2, 57, 149
Burnet, 275, 379
Burnett, 20, 54, 63, 246, 362, 369, 383
Burnham, 330
Burns, 30, 69, 72, 107, 108, 195, 272, 362, 378, 400, 402, 465, 483, 501
Burr, 134, 203, 211, 234, 267, 289, 299, 342, 355, 358, 492, 495
Burrell, 362
Burrill, 105
Burroughs, 215, 267, 367
Burrows, 134, 265, 334, 346
Bursley, 198
Burt, 1, 14, 19

Burtles, 333
Burton, 198, 339, 342
Burwell, 429
Bush, 14, 82, 102, 105, 376
Bush House, 488
Busha, 105
Busher, 10, 256, 263, 267, 282, 443
Bussell, 9
Bute, 114
Buthmann, 111
Butler, 7, 10, 24, 30, 42, 46, 48, 50, 55, 57, 60, 61, 82, 85, 87, 91, 99, 103, 105, 113, 114, 137, 149, 151, 169, 180, 182, 193, 199, 204, 210, 217, 252, 258, 259, 275, 280, 283, 297, 298, 301, 310, 314, 327, 332, 339, 344, 346, 348, 351, 358, 359, 362, 369, 370, 372, 376, 388, 394, 395, 396, 399, 401, 402, 404, 405, 416, 418, 423, 439, 460, 466, 479, 486, 489, 494, 501
Butt, 4, 108, 156, 324, 470, 488
Butterfield, 44, 213, 301
Butterworth, 208, 377
Button, 298
Butts, 20, 337
Buxenstein, 237, 238
Buxton, 61
Buzbee, 444
Byersly, 143
Byington, 194, 375, 429
Byrd, 162, 377, 470, 481
Byrne, 11, 54, 87, 103, 170, 209, 219, 282, 357, 368, 378, 406, 424
Byron, 195

C

Cabell, 36, 100, 254, 328, 448, 485
Cabrera, 271
Caden, 82, 135, 363, 409, 466
Cadwalader, 186
Cadwell, 216
Caho, 360
Cain, 32, 266
Calderon, 308
Caldwell, 3, 84, 130, 202, 363, 426

Caley, 176
Calhoun, 49, 68, 150, 178, 186, 196, 298, 308, 319, 327, 394, 426, 433, 435, 473
Calisle, 124
Call, 340
Callaghan, 39, 232, 307
Callahan, 300, 502
Callan, 7, 38, 173, 194, 203, 211, 274, 299, 355, 384, 442, 449, 486, 495, 502
Callanan, 502
Callaway, 176
Callow, 47
Calney, 32
Calvert, 134, 151, 232, 260
Cambridge, 186
Cameron, 2, 16, 61, 160, 360, 369, 370, 372, 374
Cammack, 27, 34, 40, 70, 81, 82, 121, 302
Cammett, 371
Camp, 41, 85, 313
Campbell, 2, 19, 57, 77, 85, 90, 99, 136, 161, 167, 195, 209, 232, 252, 254, 309, 310, 312, 313, 325, 366, 399, 410, 415, 443, 476
Camper, 324
Canedo, 180
Canfield, 303, 352, 391
Caniell, 282
Cannon, 185
Canny, 92
Canter, 209
Caper, 271
Capers, 137, 290
Caperton, 62, 217
Capron, 186, 236
Caray, 89
Carbajah, 384
Carberry, 207
Carbery, 194, 204, 221, 347, 399, 464, 502
Carden, 305
Carder, 310
Cardoza, 339
Cardwell, 363

Carey, 68, 201, 254, 370
Carley, 124, 126, 138, 315
Carlin, 328
Carlisle, 148, 259, 266
Carlon, 416
Carlton, 48
Carman, 291, 343, 423
Carmichael, 34
Carmick, 30, 87, 98
Carnal, 446
Carnatz, 45
Carnes, 48, 162
Caro, 493
Carpender, 21
Carpenter, 2, 125, 457, 482
Carr, 5, 8, 18, 60, 68, 77, 198, 217, 288, 327, 342, 401, 414, 469
Carrico, 221, 345, 502
Carrigan, 159
Carroll, 26, 59, 66, 69, 118, 163, 209, 225, 291, 318, 341, 352, 407, 412, 416, 502
Carson, 120, 445, 452, 494
Carter, 21, 60, 76, 86, 96, 126, 140, 198, 223, 224, 226, 234, 235, 259, 268, 277, 282, 310, 371, 373, 444, 464, 502
Cartwright, 360
Carusi, 498
Caruther, 234
Carvallo, 308
Carver, 122, 125, 491
Carvers, 87
Cary, 120, 194
Casanave, 359
Casey, 21, 416
Casparis, 114, 362, 379
Cass, 76
Cassady, 96, 117, 119, 145
Cassell, 363
Cassiday, 51
Cassidy, 65, 283
Cassin, 311
Cast, 88
Castell, 331, 362
Castleman, 131, 433
Caswell, 252

Catchings, 296
Cathcart, 181, 250, 502, 508
Catlin, 340, 344
Cato, 470
Catoir, 307
Caughran, 128
Caughy, 480
Causin, 74
Causten, 45, 162, 505
Caustin, 14
Cavan, 268
Cavanaugh, 372
Cavener, 353
Cavileer, 399
Cayce, 294
Caze, 410
Cazeau, 95
Cazeneau, 60
Cazenova, 230
Cazenove, 404, 476
Ceare, 71
Cecil, 236
Cedar Grove, 141
Chabot, 125
Chafee, 314
Chaffee, 243
Chaler, 380
Chalfin, 329
Chalk, 205
Chalmers, 22, 191
Chamberlain, 41, 409
Chambers, 93, 357
Champ, 48, 74
Champagne, 35
Champlin, 342
Chance, 335, 456
Chandler, 43, 65, 132, 139, 148, 265, 314, 374
Chaney, 37, 504
Chapin, 47, 359, 360
Chaplin, 317, 324, 487, 491
Chapman, 8, 84, 91, 93, 143, 144, 209, 330, 347, 395, 401, 426, 468, 480, 486
Charles, 341
Charlotte Hall School, 300
Chartae, 60

Chase, 11, 49, 68, 82, 135, 152, 156, 183, 187, 226, 227, 319, 352, 453
Chatfield, 180, 255
Chauncey, 363
Cheatham, 257, 259
Cheever, 331, 496
Chenaulet, 26
Chenault, 394
Cheney, 176
Chenowith, 6
Cherry, 223
Cherry Hill, 376
Chesapeade & Ohio Canal, 434
Chesapeake & Ohio Canal, 392, 415
Cheseline, 57
Cheshire, 228, 264
Chesney, 335
Chess, 143
Chester, 502
Chew, 46, 359, 363, 390, 409
Chilcutt, 149
Child, 71
Childers, 380
Childress, 435
Childs, 160, 209, 257, 467
Chiles, 23, 428
Chill, 246
Chilson, 179, 222
Chinn, 47, 81
Chipman, 6, 142, 200
Chisum, 68
Chitty, 379
Choat, 68
Choate, 381, 486, 495
Choppin, 458
Chouteau, 140
Christell, 71
Christian, 5, 66, 194, 254, 301, 416, 460, 466
Christie, 305
Christopher, 198
Christophers, 8
Chubb, 154, 362, 425
Chum, 232
Chun, 136
Church, 29, 371

Churchill, 30, 52, 75, 338
Churchman, 52
Cicote, 163
Cicott, 6
Cisneros, 387
Cissell, 500
Claflin, 65, 125
Clagett, 17, 179, 282, 288
Claiborne, 38, 65, 131
Clairborne, 443
Clapdon, 321
Clapham, 207
Clapp, 309, 312, 344
Clare, 302
Clark, 3, 14, 26, 39, 51, 80, 92, 94, 107, 112, 124, 144, 148, 175, 193, 198, 215, 220, 254, 289, 305, 307, 314, 334, 339, 340, 341, 344, 362, 367, 371, 394, 403, 434, 435, 491
Clarke, 19, 26, 41, 51, 88, 102, 108, 154, 187, 209, 213, 225, 232, 247, 256, 261, 284, 310, 323, 342, 360, 362, 367, 369, 378, 387, 409, 424, 464, 480, 502
Clarkson, 445
Clarvoe, 165, 281, 360
Clary, 313
Claude, 297
Clavadatcher, 415
Claveleam, 4
Clavoe, 460
Claxton, 102
Clay, 44, 116, 118, 142, 188, 198, 256, 273, 423, 460, 466, 477, 493
Claypoole, 44, 73, 438
Clayton, 62, 170, 212, 286, 343
Cleary, 4
Cleghorn, 474
Clemants, 27
Clemens, 416, 492
Clements, 2, 165, 235, 303, 338, 355, 363, 367, 430, 498, 502
Clemmons, 232
Clemson, 477
Clendenin, 134, 153
Clephane, 363

Cleveland, 132
Cliborn, 216
Click, 125
Clifton, 125
Clinch, 96, 128, 164, 204, 208, 485
Clinton, 265, 315, 419
Closson, 391
Clough, 264
Clouse, 358
Clow, 7, 101
Clowes, 397
Cluskey, 450
Cluss, 24
Clutes, 351
Coad, 390
Coakley, 7, 146
Coale, 220, 498
Coates, 163
Coats, 125
Cobb, 84, 125, 163, 186, 202
Coburn, 182
Cochran, 213
Cochrane, 63, 395, 446
Cock, 336
Cocke, 152, 396
Cocken, 263
Cockerill, 24
Cockern, 73
Cockfield, 494
Cocknell, 369
Cockrell, 108, 131, 314, 330
Coe, 57, 248, 390
Coff, 45
Coffenberger, 460
Coffey, 254
Coffin, 215, 341
Coffroth, 99
Coil, 143
Coit, 155
Coke, 362
Cokern, 69
Colborn, 502
Colburn, 74, 81, 98
Colby, 88
Colcord, 328
Colden, 97

Cole, 2, 22, 74, 98, 170, 235, 302, 328, 384, 396, 401, 464
Colelaser, 57
Coleman, 78, 305, 306, 436, 502
Coles, 144, 147
Colet, 8
Coley, 179
Colfield, 437
Collamer, 286, 300, 311
Collard, 17, 79, 363
Collier, 3, 26, 69, 75, 155, 158, 179, 247
Collins, 28, 77, 82, 116, 155, 212, 256, 280, 294, 320, 323, 333, 335, 372, 412, 418, 463, 482, 502
Collison, 486
Collyer, 352
Colman, 51, 97
Colmarine, 163
Colross, 501
Colson, 57
Colt, 226, 238, 245, 362
Coltman, 14, 143, 203, 411
Colton, 25, 38, 89, 200, 349, 477
Coltson, 371
Columbian Foundry, 32
Colville, 33
Colvin, 241, 467
Colwell, 23, 143
Combs, 122, 274, 279, 362, 411, 472
Compton, 19, 57, 99, 156, 182, 392
Conant, 493
Concord Fight, 299
Condict, 191
Condit, 404
Condor, 4
Coners, 57
Congdon, 294
Congress Burying Ground, 287
Congressional Burial Ground, 234
Congressional Burying Ground, 426
Congressional Cemetery, 150
Conklin, 394
Conlan, 333, 360
Conlay, 57
Conley, 465, 503
Connell, 248, 360

Connelly, 2, 18, 433
Conner, 23, 45, 71, 227, 342, 411
Connolly, 93, 406, 443
Connor, 32, 190, 228, 363, 409, 437
Conolly, 237, 244
Conothers, 474
Conrad, 28, 147, 395, 414, 464
Conser, 177
Constable, 35
Contee, 363, 403, 476, 481, 482
Converse, 125
Conway, 78, 92, 98, 223
Conyers, 61
Coodery, 5
Coodey, 95
Coody, 266
Cook, 10, 16, 30, 31, 44, 54, 55, 78, 135, 202, 209, 215, 222, 252, 253, 260, 293, 314, 340, 360, 374, 415, 442, 456
Cooke, 46, 416
Cookern, 81, 98
Cooley, 74
Coolidge, 272, 376, 448
Cooly, 209
Coombe, 502
Coombs, 120, 213, 285, 351, 476
Coons, 242
Cooper, 9, 23, 24, 45, 51, 57, 96, 128, 137, 157, 166, 174, 191, 213, 236, 241, 340, 396, 466, 468, 496
Copeland, 123, 496
Copp, 492
Copperthwaite, 12, 26
Copway, 92, 116, 219
Coquillon, 467
Coraman, 442
Corbin, 167, 426
Corbins, 456
Corby, 14
Corcoran, 18, 70, 348, 363, 461, 485, 498, 503, 505
Cordell, 185
Cordery, 311
Core, 20
Corey, 3, 51, 252
Corkern, 343

Corley, 328
Cornelius, 131
Cornell, 41
Cornis, 404
Cornock, 319
Cornus, 330
Cornwall, 199
Cornwallis, 419
Cornwell, 413
Correll, 149
Corringham, 2
Corser, 345
Cortell, 89
corvette **St Louis**, 154
Corwin, 296, 493
Corwine, 80, 499
Coryell, 89
Cosby, 55
Cosgrove, 157
Cost, 399
Costen, 363
Coster, 234
Costin, 121
Cotterell, 259
Cotton, 278, 358
Coult, 478
Coulter, 117, 225, 422
Coulthard, 491
Courtney, 47
Couser, 422
Covanhovan, 261
Covington, 227
Cowan, 189, 347, 391, 479
Cowden, 190
Cowder, 310
Cowen, 48, 61, 155
Cowling, 366
Cowman, 432
Cox, 3, 7, 24, 31, 34, 57, 76, 118, 174, 192, 204, 224, 267, 278, 285, 294, 295, 363, 385, 408, 432, 458, 468, 469, 472, 475, 479, 502
Coxe, 22, 45, 162, 163, 323, 375, 502
Coy, 31, 160
Coyle, 99, 189, 201, 288, 432, 476
Cozart, 358

Cozby, 318
Cozens, 24
Crabb, 14, 91, 227
Crabtree, 159
Crady, 404
Craig, 69, 77, 369, 502
Crain, 265, 340
Cramer, 330
Crampton, 72, 159
Cranch, 124, 130, 420, 502
Crandall, 139, 284
Crandell, 142, 152, 204, 222, 359, 384, 474, 492
Crane, 154, 170, 259, 386, 464
Crannin, 416
Crapster, 169
Crassin, 378
Cratty, 406
Craven, 147
Cravens, 241
Crawford, 1, 93, 119, 159, 176, 178, 198, 220, 272, 286, 293, 309, 315, 317, 399, 445
Creecy, 47, 200
Creighton, 209, 232
Cressy, 163
Crew, 45
Crews, 38, 96, 117, 119, 223, 454
Cringley, 225
Criswell, 83
Crittenden, 296, 306, 312
Crocker, 268
Croft, 28
Crogan, 209
Croggin, 411
Croghan, 407
Crome, 82
Crompton, 472
Cronch, 445
Cronin, 238, 245
Crooks, 416
Cropley, 367
Crosby, 46, 173, 226, 313, 316, 433, 469
Croskey, 393
Cross, 16, 266, 287, 310, 332, 359, 362, 369, 370, 371, 424, 492

Crossfield, 405, 498
Crowell, 96
Crowley, 40, 360, 366, 441
Crown, 163, 309
Croxall, 172, 354
Cruit, 73, 82, 222, 249, 334, 363, 366, 367, 411
Crump, 156
Cruse, 25
Cruso, 451
Crutchett, 40, 66, 266, 362, 368
Cruttenden, 99, 359
Cruyal, 215
Cryer, 357, 373
Culbertson, 328, 493
Cull, 502
Cullum, 335
Culp, 143
Culver, 164, 313, 502
Cumming, 329, 400, 483, 485
Cummings, 187, 223, 236, 318
Cummins, 130, 261, 274
Cunningham, 12, 40, 49, 94, 128, 141, 312, 444
Cuott, 136
Curcton, 347
Curley, 57
Curran, 207
Currier, 478
Curry, 426
Cursen, 380
Curson, 267, 362, 416, 423
Curtis, 41, 76, 77, 141, 205, 235, 291, 434
Curtiss, 198
Cushing, 86
Cushman, 45, 56, 341, 390, 467
Cusing, 397
Custis, 276, 442
Cutchen, 283
Cuthbert, 416, 421
Cutter, 172
cutter **Hamilton**, 37, 273
cutter **Morris**, 435
Cutts, 83, 209

D

d'Oremieulx, 483
d'Orremieulx, 483
D'Orsoli, 298
D'Ouville, 334
Dabbs, 459
Dade, 22, 57, 137, 344, 386
Daggett, 467
Daily, 28, 205, 498
Daisy, 246
Dakin, 383
Dale, 503
Daley, 56, 367
Dallam, 21
Dallas, 56
Dalton, 416, 434
Daly, 30, 134, 234
Dameron, 202
Dana, 90, 120, 131, 418
Danforth, 376, 421
Daniel, 198, 206, 242, 254, 360, 447
Daniels, 77, 127, 223, 439, 450
Dankworth, 363
Danner, 463
Dant, 371, 379, 436, 441, 503
Daphna, 234
Darby, 204
Dare, 46
Daringer, 458
Darling, 19, 25, 190, 192, 279, 432, 457
Darnall, 171, 433
Darrell, 29, 501
Darrington, 85
Dart, 259, 391, 402
Dashiell, 22, 46
Davall, 109
Davant, 198
Davenport, 47, 91, 143, 189, 283, 326, 328
Davey, 185
Davezac, 485
David, 449
Davidge, 69, 218, 288, 425, 437
Davids, 352
Davidson, 69, 75, 83, 86, 102, 130, 241, 296, 336, 366, 369, 379, 393, 461, 488, 503
Davie, 179
Davies, 35
Davis, 17, 39, 45, 51, 57, 66, 73, 76, 88, 90, 92, 114, 131, 136, 147, 148, 149, 156, 163, 171, 184, 185, 190, 191, 195, 199, 203, 207, 208, 209, 213, 215, 218, 222, 234, 240, 256, 258, 259, 264, 267, 269, 281, 289, 292, 300, 301, 305, 310, 322, 343, 344, 345, 360, 363, 367, 378, 380, 383, 395, 404, 411, 416, 435, 436, 439, 440, 443, 473, 475, 476, 479, 481, 492, 493, 503
Davis Farm, 126
Davis' Farm, 250
Davis' Mill, 218
Davison, 130, 296
Dawes, 57, 411
Dawson, 8, 12, 18, 55, 60, 133, 139, 156, 209, 227, 356, 402, 432, 457
Dawson's tavern, 415
Day, 52, 98, 132, 243, 288
Dayton, 147, 212, 342, 416
de Armas, 343
de Arrieta, 387
de Balzac, 353
de Bouboulon, 308
de Bouillon, 344
De Ferriet, 3
De Forrest, 433
de Hass, 167
De Haven, 224, 234, 371, 440
De Kalb, 143
De Kay, 65
De Krafft, 264
de la Figaniere, 9
De la Roche, 48
De La Roche, 315
De Lano, 325
De Leon, 255
De Lirac, 298
de Lomagne, 197
De Merritt, 385

de Montesqion, 89
de Montesquiou, 194
De Mott, 198
De Mun, 140
de Neufville, 258, 342
de Rochambeau, 276
de Russe, 143
De Russy, 33, 326, 329
de Saint Vital, 169
De Saules, 284
De Selding, 367, 473
De Treville, 301
Deakin, 185
Deakins, 232
Deal, 131
Deale, 267
Deamit, 125
Dean, 30, 57, 186, 206
Deany, 263, 310
Dearborn, 152
Deaton, 205
DeBellerne, 33
Deblois, 340
DeButts, 211
DeCamp, 462
Decatur, 65, 217, 335, 404, 497
Decker, 63, 124
Decover, 134
Deeble, 60
Deeven, 360
Deevers, 360, 410
Defly, 383
Degrand, 92
DeHaven, 138
Deitz, 144, 503
DeKalb, 158
DeKay, 25
del Hoys, 487
Delano, 234
Delany, 31, 57, 360
Delgado, 468
Dellaway, 217
Delony, 4
Demain, 340
Dement, 182, 291, 387
Deming, 8, 144

Demoss, 94
Dempsey, 17, 261
DeNeale, 114
Dengler, 310
Denham, 252, 371
Denholn, 40
Denison, 16, 38, 143
Denman, 326, 482, 484
Dennesson, 4
Dennett, 90, 95, 170
Dennis, 11, 14, 102, 243, 316, 396, 438, 481
Dennison, 190, 293
Denormandie, 64
Densley, 503
Dent, 20, 358, 360, 363, 373
Depew, 127
Deplaigne, 332
Derbis, 240
Derby, 92, 221, 372
Dermott, 221
Derode, 234
Derrick, 212
Derrington, 310
Desabaye, 240
DeSaules, 470
DeSelding, 440
Deshler, 199
Deshong, 427
Desmond, 369, 372
Detchmendy, 145
Detter, 363
Devall, 483
DeVaughan, 414
Devaughn, 416
Devaughn's subdivision, 207
Devaul, 416
Develin, 8, 158
Devens, 187
Devereaux, 461, 462
Devereux, 438, 447
Devers, 388
Devies, 381
Devina, 387
Devine, 258
Devitt, 298

Devlin, 6, 228, 339
Dewdney, 10, 100, 211, 234, 281, 325, 349, 385
Dewdny, 135
Dewees, 317, 333
Dewey, 26, 38, 45, 56, 65, 117, 119
Dewitt, 53, 62
Dexter, 53, 70, 100, 125, 377
Dhiel, 471
Diaz, 347
Dibble, 52
Dick, 198, 473, 503
Dickel, 77
Dickerson, 71, 326
Dickey, 395
Dickins, 45
Dickinson, 54, 313, 351, 377, 425, 459
Dickson, 65, 96, 128, 155, 158, 170, 206, 216, 255, 256
Digges, 298, 303, 441
Diggle, 363
Diggs, 209, 363
Dillard, 131
Diller, 251
Dillinger, 68
Dillon, 220, 230, 242, 341
Dillow, 363
Dillworth, 176
Dilworth, 340
Dimick, 325, 445
Dimmick, 15
Dimond, 85
Dinah, 210
Dines, 57, 434, 503
Dinkgrave, 343
Dinnies, 210
Dinsby, 209
Diomatari, 196
Dishony, 391
Diston, 438
Dix, 57, 149, 268, 277, 377, 481
Dixon, 24, 59, 67, 75, 98, 132, 143, 155, 180, 207, 232, 255, 406, 437, 446, 476
Doane, 17, 75, 155
Dobbin, 18, 185, 186, 208, 374
Dobbins, 175, 318

Dobney, 338
Dobson, 405
Dobyns, 310, 336
Dodd, 44
Dodge, 157, 212, 287, 382
Dodson, 261, 363, 371, 383
Doiscroux, 57
Dole, 393
Doloughrey, 227
Domkee, 283
Donaldson, 202, 411, 443
Donaphan, 503
Donathien, 57
Donaven, 441
Donelan, 45, 75, 76, 182, 274, 292, 309, 315, 373, 403, 404, 406, 416, 419, 432, 503
Donelly, 10
Doniphan, 19, 240, 503
Donn, 66, 93, 110, 202, 260, 462
Donnell, 459
Donnington, 446
Donohaugh, 203, 287
Donoho, 232, 323, 363, 429
Donohoo, 363
Donohugh, 300
Donovan, 369, 372, 412
Dooley, 89
Dorr, 232
Dorrey, 288
Dorsett, 22, 69, 75, 119, 199
Dorsey, 38, 146, 395, 409, 438
Dortch, 131
Doswell, 101
Doty, 453
Dougherty, 15, 67, 357, 401
Doughty, 217, 469
Douglas, 3, 93, 172, 213, 221, 460, 468
Douglass, 85, 92, 156, 201, 346, 369, 371, 390, 397, 421, 461, 471, 503
Dove, 31, 267, 288, 360, 388, 475
Dovilliers, 156
Dow, 99, 314, 426
Dowd, 15, 32
Dowell, 360

Dowling, 57, 76, 78, 90, 93, 266, 287, 360, 366
Downer, 65, 96, 117, 119, 363
Downey, 10, 32, 275, 333
Downie, 498
Downing, 7, 50, 55, 76, 168, 291, 403, 462
Downs, 5, 25, 87, 120, 202, 223, 267, 363, 485
Dowson, 227, 492
Dowson's Row, 492
Doxey, 171, 298
Doyle, 270
Dozier, 294, 363
Drake, 99, 117, 177, 222, 294, 333, 343
Drane, 454
Draper, 354, 404
Drenner, 394
Drew, 5, 72, 294
Dreyer, 447, 468
Drill, 241
Drinker, 38, 42
Drinkhouse, 38, 75, 155
Drinkwater, 79
Driscoll, 190
Drudy, 38
Drugnan, 26
Drum, 123, 199, 400, 482, 483, 484
Drummond, 253
Drury, 10, 72, 99, 204, 359, 363, 372, 419, 426, 427, 498
Drysdale, 80
Du Barry, 143, 329
Du Bernard, 333
Du Bose, 220
Duane, 431, 453
Dubant, 86, 498
Dubarry, 55, 119
Dubois, 8, 333, 378, 465
Ducachet, 439
Duchachet, 306
Duckworth, 7
Dudley, 402
Duel, 55
Duer, 52, 93, 304, 404
Duerson, 125

Duff, 10, 28
Duffy, 53, 114
Dufief, 345
Dugan, 294
Duhamel, 240
Duke of Palmella, 443
Dulaney, 503
Dulany, 363, 373
Dumbolton, 362
Dumester, 22
Dumont, 332, 392, 498
Dumphey, 503
Dumphrey, 70
Dunavin, 460
Dunawin, 426, 451, 464
Dunbar, 237, 241, 406
Duncan, 11, 45, 64, 91, 96, 143, 215, 216, 225, 241, 326, 327, 329, 423
Duncanson, 476
Duncome, 186
Dundas, 185, 212, 276, 280
Dundass, 245
Dungan, 328
Dunham, 15, 98, 206, 342, 407
Dunlap, 57, 184
Dunlop, 11, 219, 232, 369, 416, 500
Dunn, 34, 80, 109, 160, 191, 209, 231, 395
Dunning, 234, 477
Dunnington, 363, 370, 371
Dunscomb, 85, 465, 493, 495
Dunton, 315
Dupee, 232
Duperu, 247
Dupont, 186
Dupree, 266
Duralde, 423
Durand, 156
Durant, 5, 19
Durbin, 336
Durfee, 285
Durham, 131
Durham, 209
Durkee, 455
Durnell, 330
Durrine, 39

Durrive, 143
Dustin, 102
Dutton, 274
Duty, 273
Duval, 222
Duvall, 21, 57, 217, 337, 339, 346, 360, 401, 420, 435, 469, 480, 481
Dwight, 341, 467, 488
Dwinnell, 43
Dwyer, 255, 473, 498
Dyas, 206
Dye, 352
Dyer, 19, 64, 106, 109, 134, 165, 194, 201, 202, 203, 253, 333, 348, 359, 362, 363, 387, 441
Dyess, 261
Dygert, 181
Dyson, 287, 321, 360, 427
Dyvernois, 113

E

E kins, 76
Eaches, 389
Eadlin, 447
Eager, 342
Eagerton, 77
Eaker, 198
Earl, 103, 108, 224
Earlanger, 96
Earle, 105, 241
Early, 113, 323
Earner, 192
Ears, 232
Easby, 256, 381, 464
East, 31, 216, 258, 273
Eastburn, 503
Easter, 120
Easterlin, 347
Eastin, 48
Eastland, 422
Easton, 346, 389, 471
Eaton, 62, 87, 103, 203, 281, 357, 448
Eberbach, 46, 416, 427, 447, 503
Eberback, 413
Eberle, 322
Eberley, 363

Eberling, 108
Ebert, 114
Eccleston, 308
Eckard, 491
Eckardt, 232
Eckford, 471
Ecklof, 240
Eckloff, 76, 141, 291, 403, 423
Eddins, 189
Eddy, 39, 50, 86, 108, 114, 151, 155, 227, 305, 363
Edelen, 63, 403, 410
Edelin, 74, 103, 137, 209, 304, 411
Edes, 287, 360
Edgar, 393
Edmonds, 5, 341
Edmonson, 168, 416
Edmonston, 108, 168, 217, 315, 457
Edney, 289
Edwards, 39, 57, 76, 118, 131, 146, 202, 206, 212, 213, 230, 263, 309, 321, 331, 337, 341, 368, 376, 395, 399, 436, 437, 438, 453
Egan, 106, 108
Egbert, 67
Egleston, 494
Ehlen, 103
Ehrmanntrant, 112
Ehrmantrout, 411
Eichelberger, 200, 494
Eichorn, 103, 107
Eld, 187, 189
Elder, 33
Eldred, 362, 370
Eldridge, 117, 249, 422
Elgin, 24, 132
Eliason, 99
Eliot, 108, 195, 411, 418, 463
Elisha, 107
Elkins, 76
Ellerslie, 228
Elliot, 16, 26, 170, 283, 332, 363, 385, 503
Elliott, 47, 149, 187, 217, 281, 352, 401, 492

Ellis, 30, 84, 108, 111, 207, 231, 273, 274, 341, 357, 403, 447, 462, 473, 476, 485
Ellison, 147
Ellmaker, 393
Ellsworth, 183, 335
Ellwood, 231, 250
Elmer, 467
Elmore, 196, 230, 234
Elsey, 275
Elson, 216
Elwell, 385
Ely, 2, 62, 75, 80, 290, 343, 437, 481
Elzey, 360
Emarthla, 454
Emathla, 401
Embree, 177
Emendrout, 368
Emerick, 106
Emerson, 2, 71, 162, 211, 228, 274, 369
Emery, 345, 360, 369
Emick, 408
Emmerman, 368
Emmerson, 437
Emmert, 103, 493
Emmet, 496
Emmons, 19, 320
Emory, 312, 476, 504
Emott, 164
Empson, 97
Enfield Chase, 20
Engart, 459
Engelbrecht, 84
England, 288
Engle, 442
English, 101, 140, 142, 252, 340, 483, 487
Ennis, 52, 73, 90, 103, 147, 173, 203, 215, 222, 242, 267, 273, 316, 317, 321, 360, 395, 406, 420, 432, 436, 441, 460, 464, 503
Enos, 503
Entrisell, 53
Entwisle, 345, 413, 498
Ergood, 363
Erskine, 200

Erwin, 160
Eschbach, 239, 503
Eshelman, 222
Eskridge, 352, 487
Espey, 66
Esputua, 77
Espy, 232, 237, 363
Essex, 238
Estes, 422
Etchison, 343
Etheridge, 212, 287
Etter, 344
Eude, 240
Euen, 318
Euleck, 65
Eustis, 1, 325, 337, 478
Eva, 174, 207, 309, 322, 498
Evan, 132
Evans, 4, 16, 18, 40, 52, 65, 76, 78, 96, 100, 102, 103, 111, 117, 119, 143, 145, 179, 190, 203, 225, 232, 258, 279, 290, 312, 325, 334, 342, 363, 371, 388, 391, 392, 398, 403, 410, 441, 455, 461, 465, 471, 482, 503
Everest, 77, 168
Everett, 6, 75, 87, 155, 158, 213, 258, 260, 297, 339, 363
Evermay, 86
Eversfield, 113, 496
Ewall, 452
Ewbank, 83, 136, 213, 242, 243, 354, 463, 472, 495
Ewell, 325
Ewen, 500
Ewing, 15, 172, 193, 286
Exler, 47
Eyre, 4, 416

F

Faber, 18, 396
Fabricus, 156
Face, 341
Fah, 409
Fahey, 321
Fahnestock, 326, 328
Fair, 402

Fairall, 57
Fairchild, 372
Fairfax, 237, 249, 405, 503
Fairservice, 134, 197
Falch, 99
Falconer, 29
Faley, 35
Falkner, 190
Fallis, 184
Fallon, 485
Fanning, 51, 108
Fant, 97, 310
Fanwood, 450
Fapp, 183
Farland, 503
Farley, 458
Farnham, 7, 108, 256, 325, 413, 429, 475, 477
Farnsworth, 163, 241
Farquhar, 103, 279
Farr, 102
Farragut, 38
Farrall, 31, 363
Farrant, 80
Farrar, 114, 218, 274
Farrel, 413
Farrell, 503
Farrelly, 213
Farrer, 18
Farrington, 36, 65, 90, 143, 262
Farroll, 31
Farrow, 22, 125
Farwell, 55
Fatio, 332
Fauble, 396
Faulconer, 449
Faulk, 116
Faulkner, 167, 367
Fauntleroy, 3, 59, 325
Faussett, 57
Faver, 48
Favier, 175, 369, 503
Fawz, 14
Faxon, 141
Fay, 160, 264
Fearson, 103, 107

Feaster, 330
Feeney, 108, 363
Fell, 279
Fellows, 399
Felton, 66, 155, 158, 348, 396
Fendall, 389
Fenders, 283
Fennall, 189
Fennelly, 232
Fenner, 304
Fenton, 142, 172, 391, 393, 456
Fenwick, 30, 292, 367, 412, 416, 458
Ferguson, 465
Ferguson, 7, 9, 16, 81, 96, 103, 117, 119, 122, 123, 132, 209, 252, 253, 267, 311, 398
Fergusson, 307
Fernstein, 411
Ferral, 411
Ferrell, 399
Ferris, 74, 310, 332
Ferritor, 307
Ferrity, 360
Fess, 57
Fessenden, 355, 395, 472
Fester, 103
Fetterman, 282, 302
Fetts, 341
Fetzer, 253
Fickey, 426
Field, 154, 252
Fields, 209, 357, 370
Fienfrutch, 4
Figley, 352
Figures, 436
Fill, 340, 466
Fillens, 114
Fillmore, 286, 292, 293, 313, 320, 345, 373, 383, 384, 406, 409, 421, 433, 443, 446, 456, 463, 470, 485, 499
Filman, 149
Finch, 246, 319
Finckel, 122
Findlay, 23, 95, 380
Findley, 216
Fink, 103, 410

Finkle, 240
Finkman, 113
Finley, 15, 149, 173
Finnall, 65, 377
Finnegan, 31
Finnell, 488
Finney, 319
Fiorentino, 270
Fischer, 77, 108, 487, 503
Fish, 68, 102, 113, 123, 449
Fishback, 310
Fisher, 4, 26, 50, 56, 68, 97, 102, 105, 112, 128, 143, 209, 255, 275, 286, 288, 360, 363, 368, 369, 373
Fiske, 341
Fister, 369
Fitch, 18, 28, 60, 112, 390, 458
Fithian, 217, 496
Fitman, 239
Fitnam, 108, 113, 200, 213, 503
Fitton, 103
Fitz, 25, 343, 344
Fitzgerald, 6, 46, 112, 113, 163, 213, 232, 355, 358, 363, 369, 436, 468
Fitzhugh, 99, 232, 405, 424, 466
Fitzpatrick, 26, 220, 224, 397, 416, 438, 464, 503
flag ship **Plymouth**, 413
Flaget, 89
Flagg, 259, 351
Flag-ship **Ohio**, 490
Flaherty, 192
Flanagan, 14, 64, 164
Flanders, 440
Flannagan, 9, 168
Flannegan, 120
Fleet, 363
Fleischmann, 80
Fleming, 363, 371, 428, 444
Flemming, 105
Flenner, 108
Fletch, 209
Fletcher, 2, 57, 94, 103, 105, 111, 135, 242, 332, 360, 363, 370, 380, 418, 503
Fleury, 19, 79, 461
Flewellen, 328

Flint, 372
Flood, 31
Flourney, 273
Floyd, 247
Flusser, 376
Flynn, 416, 432, 472
Foertsch, 17
Foley, 42, 202, 232
Follansbee, 37, 51, 96, 103, 119, 152, 367
Foller, 111
Follett, 328
Follins, 496
Folsom, 217, 276
Fonda, 198
Fontaine, 219, 451
Fooley, 31
Foot, 34, 170
Foote, 105, 134, 152, 190, 302, 401
Forbes, 257, 408, 416
Forble, 503
Force, 76, 256, 296
Ford, 3, 43, 75, 103, 108, 113, 150, 189, 200, 209, 214, 282, 283, 302, 341, 342, 360, 440, 451, 476, 477
Fordyce, 210
Foreman, 198
Forest, 209, 503
Forkit, 471
Forman, 13, 171
Forney, 249
Forrest, 66, 98, 103, 147, 169, 187, 216, 249, 263, 323, 373, 426
Forrester, 36
Forsyth, 293
Fort Atkinson, 29
Fort Constitution, 83, 329, 465
Fort Croghan, 329
Fort Du Quesne, 276
Fort Gaines, 95
Fort Gallion, 75
Fort George, 227
Fort Gibson, 14
Fort Hamer, 269
Fort Harrison, 286
Fort Independence, 257

Fort Kearny, 338, 400
Fort Laramie, 149
Fort Leavenworth, 293, 329, 394
Fort Macomb, 351
Fort Madison, 37
Fort McHenry, 50
Fort McIntosh, 153, 329
Fort Meade, 269
Fort Meigs, 431
Fort Monroe, 329
Fort Moultrie, 316, 484
Fort Pickens, 444
Fort Smith, 191
Fort Snelling, 193
Fort Washington, 260, 462
Fort Wayne, 12, 64, 74, 394, 396, 475
Fort Winnebago, 260
Fosbee, 369
Fosdick, 10, 389
Foskey, 371
Foss, 88, 390
Foster, 53, 68, 132, 186, 187, 207, 299, 310, 338, 352, 367, 436, 474, 475, 493
Foulke, 310
Fowkes, 248
Fowle, 123
Fowler, 5, 13, 37, 57, 59, 107, 108, 113, 114, 205, 209, 300, 323, 325, 360, 375, 409, 414, 422, 450, 503
Fox, 68, 103, 128, 273, 413, 452
Foxwell, 76
Foy, 113, 183, 296, 393
Frailer, 111
Frailes, 363
Frailey, 315, 448, 456, 488
Fraim, 86
France, 33, 138, 257, 291, 409, 453
Frances, 443
Francis, 16, 65, 83, 99, 182, 346, 363, 371, 419
Francisco, 163, 472
Frank, 107, 111, 247, 285, 498
Franklin, 4, 82, 89, 108, 138, 154, 182, 193, 220, 224
Franklin Row, 200
Franks, 209

Franz, 409
Franzoni, 459
Fraser, 17, 28, 103, 307, 357, 469
Frasier, 211, 229, 294, 479
Frazer, 134, 197, 217, 304, 329, 400, 483, 485
Frazier, 109, 174, 253, 489, 503
Fraziers, 285
Fream, 6
Freedy, 503
Freeland, 294, 411, 467
Freeman, 9, 50, 78, 95, 111, 143, 149, 163, 183, 185, 273, 290, 303, 355, 372, 422, 503
Frees, 103
Fremont, 54, 63, 304, 310
French, 33, 77, 78, 84, 138, 139, 144, 199, 205, 210, 290, 296, 297, 313, 359, 363, 399, 418, 441, 464, 474, 476
Frenckall, 355
Freret, 398
Fribourg, 368
Frick, 56, 474
Fridley, 88, 243
Fried, 28
Frieze, 471
frig **Brandywine**, 152, 468
frig **Congress**, 237
frig **Cumberland**, 381
frig **Dean**, 21
frig **Philadelphia**, 65, 96, 128, 155, 335, 382
frig **Raritan**, 323
frig **Saranac**, 120, 217, 469
frig **Savannah**, 414
frig **St Lawrence**, 87, 496
frig **Susquehanna**, 496
Frisbee, 337
Frisby, 230, 371
Friss, 429
Frith, 456
Frost, 117, 164, 222, 433, 482
Frothingham, 339
Fry, 125
Frye, 135, 181, 214, 288
Fugett, 111, 426

533

Fugitt, 108, 251, 360, 363, 369
Fulford, 437
Fuller, 15, 46, 91, 113, 141, 260, 287, 298, 333, 369, 382, 465, 466
Fullmore, 178
Fullock, 341
Fullwood, 327, 329
Fulmer, 99, 267, 476
Fulph, 336
Fulwood, 188
Funk, 108
Furguson, 17, 173
Furr, 33
Furtner, 332
Fusting, 333
Futnam, 108

G

Gadsby, 504
Gage, 176
Gaines, 44, 53, 248, 249, 250, 268, 339, 356
Gainor, 503
Gaiones, 57
Gaither, 124, 457, 491
Gale, 45, 213, 243, 398, 431
Gales, 61, 375, 416
Galiger, 76
Galiwood, 481
Gallaer, 399
Gallagan, 30, 32
Gallagher, 306, 340
Gallaher, 99, 212, 354
Gallant, 49, 76, 291, 322
Galligan, 35, 108, 355
Galloway, 313, 406, 416
Galphin, 159
Galt, 108, 363, 367, 386, 492
Galvin, 351, 374, 395
Gambel, 209
Gamble, 14, 57, 75, 342
Gamwel, 232
Gansevort, 265
Gansyles, 495
Gantt, 56, 168, 363, 427, 482
Garcia, 214, 314

Garde, 26
Gardener, 176, 193
Gardenhire, 28
Gardenier, 326, 329, 483
Gardere, 24
Gardiner, 13, 37, 123, 196, 207, 213, 214, 219, 265, 333, 386, 417, 476, 504
Gardner, 23, 85, 103, 108, 125, 143, 165, 175, 220, 304, 311, 329, 350, 466
Garfield, 187
Garland, 61, 317, 324, 331, 344
Garlock, 163
Garner, 103, 108, 464, 486
Garnet, 268, 448
Garnett, 18, 37, 182, 248, 337, 389
Garnsey, 37, 133
Garrand, 194
Garrard, 336
Garrason, 43
Garratt, 247
Garret, 366
Garretson, 220
Garrett, 72, 94, 371, 426, 427, 436
Garrison, 253
Garrretson, 108
Gaskins, 57, 150
Gass, 504
Gassaway, 101, 159, 215, 276, 282, 297, 363, 456, 457
Gast, 330
Gasy, 190
Gatchell, 349
Gates, 68, 118, 412, 419, 455
Gatewood, 341
Gatton, 173
Gattrell, 200
Gault, 504
Gautier, 103, 108
Gawler, 492
Gay, 198
Gayle, 209
Gaylor, 284
Gaylord, 17
Gear, 193
Gearhart, 277
Geer, 223

Geisenger, 146
Geisinger, 255
Geldermeister, 360, 369
Gemmill, 278
Generee, 273
Gengenbach, 129
Gensler, 412
Gent, 430
Gentry, 375
Geoghan, 416
Geore, 371
George, 459
Geren, 321
German, 77, 363
Gerry, 178
Getty, 269, 462
Geyer, 6, 85
Gheradi, 401, 469
Gherardi, 217
Gibble, 340
Gibbon, 400
Gibbons, 61, 84, 333, 416
Gibbs, 11, 108, 180, 340, 363, 446
Gibson, 19, 28, 41, 160, 261, 268, 269, 302, 319, 343, 360, 363, 366, 394, 445, 455, 464, 500, 504
Giddings, 264, 266, 283
Gideon, 446, 504
Giffin, 19, 75, 155, 158
Gifford, 162
Giger, 77
Gilbert, 20, 136, 235, 246, 383, 424, 483, 484
Gildermeister, 371
Gildermester, 498
Gill, 60, 140, 226, 316, 360, 479, 504
Gillard, 209
Gillet, 347
Gillett, 213
Gilley, 118
Gillis, 166, 212, 237
Gillispie, 369
Gilliss, 72, 151, 250, 277, 457
Gilman, 50, 108, 129, 146, 164, 342
Gilmer, 422
Gilpin, 313, 345

Gimmont, 473
Ginity, 232
Ginn, 56
Ginnalty, 396
Ginnatty, 384
Ginnaty, 381
Ginnetty, 369
Girard, 498
Gisner, 273
Gittings, 231, 281, 298, 436, 438
Givens, 325
Giveny, 363
Givins, 198
Gladman, 363
Glandon, 78
Glanton, 288
Glascock, 366
Glasgow, 209
Glassell, 11
Glasson, 388, 465
Glavarry, 136
Gleason, 80
Glendenin, 197
Glendy, 56, 482
Glenn, 65, 96, 119, 209
Glick, 76, 103, 369
Glisan, 327
Glover, 188, 237, 301, 354
Goatherd, 105, 106
Goble, 242
Godard, 76
Godbee, 28
Goddard, 38, 74, 103, 111, 212, 216, 244, 267, 275, 280, 287, 289, 291, 382, 408, 486, 492
Godeffroy, 129
Godfrey, 302
Godley, 320
Godman, 377
Godwin, 241, 464
Goff, 48, 284
Gohan, 32
Goherns, 102
Goings, 371
Gold, 393
Golden, 105, 113, 190

Goldin, 57, 107, 165
Golding, 105
Goldsborough, 121, 211, 229, 376, 447
Goldsmith, 222, 340
Golson, 464
Golstein, 273
Gomph, 315
Gonzalez, 273, 387
Gooch, 353, 367
Good, 84, 241
Goodall, 363
Goode, 259, 337, 475
Gooden, 68
Goodenow, 28
Goodrich, 249, 257, 343, 363
Goodridge, 468
Goodsell, 390
Goodwin, 3, 15, 22, 161, 310
Goodyear, 164
Goolsach, 103
Gordon, 9, 23, 34, 107, 123, 161, 199, 207, 242, 280, 295, 304, 363, 371, 397, 407, 464, 466, 476, 480, 496
Gore, 315, 491
Gorge, 127
Gorman, 232
Gorsuch, 131, 160, 504
Goss, 122, 432
Gossage, 357
Goszler, 304
Gott, 214
Gough, 63
Gould, 183
Goundie, 355
Gove, 163
Governeur, 264
Gozmere, 337
Grace, 32, 232
Graeme, 344
Grafton, 408, 444
Graham, 57, 65, 130, 142, 147, 189, 198, 213, 252, 267, 296, 316, 338, 348, 363, 377, 402, 426, 436, 503
Grammer, 168, 197, 296, 504
Granberry, 183
Grandstaff, 278

Granger, 275, 363
Grannin, 404
Grannis, 404
Grant, 141, 176, 186, 193, 237, 377, 441
Gratiot, 17, 85, 383
Graves, 51, 75, 155, 266, 449
Gray, 7, 15, 81, 103, 105, 106, 108, 145, 153, 155, 160, 181, 198, 210, 237, 310, 335, 350, 363, 391, 445, 477, 487
Grayson, 8, 94, 228, 340, 344, 434, 468
Greason, 103, 112, 363, 429
Great Mills, 27
Greaves, 267
Greble, 198
Greely, 389
Green, 3, 6, 27, 34, 49, 57, 64, 87, 88, 102, 103, 108, 111, 114, 118, 127, 129, 131, 183, 196, 198, 202, 203, 207, 209, 211, 217, 230, 232, 242, 291, 293, 310, 326, 335, 347, 360, 361, 363, 365, 367, 369, 390, 413, 416, 438, 496
Green Mount Cemetery, 237, 248, 315
Greene, 57, 60, 139, 162, 274, 297, 304, 391, 417, 419
Greenfield, 111
Greenhow, 83, 303
Greening, 436
Greenleaf, 97, 122, 228, 245, 248, 297, 443, 504
Greenleaf's Point, 63, 120, 316
Greenwell, 53, 132, 189, 287, 363, 368
Greenwood, 149, 426
Greer, 44, 108, 164, 217, 296, 360, 363, 382
Gregg, 169, 205, 243, 287, 300
Gregory, 389
Grennell, 138
Grensel, 136
Grentrup, 503
Grey, 154, 322, 363, 390
Grier, 183, 379
Grieve, 426
Griffin, 61, 108, 138, 163, 195, 224, 234, 255, 265, 290, 330, 341, 390, 435, 449, 469

Griffith, 2, 26, 29, 47, 52, 103, 319, 330, 354, 375, 394, 424
Griffiths, 350
Grigg, 314
Griggs, 136, 333
Grignon, 146, 157, 189, 197, 382
Grigsby, 136
Grimes, 73, 103, 105, 106, 108, 111, 126, 171, 360, 377, 416
Grimshaw, 334
Grimsley, 170
Grinalds, 393
Grindage, 409
Grinder, 53, 108
Grindle, 77
Grinnell, 82, 154, 182, 224, 294
Grinnum, 465
Grisby, 393
Grisham, 237
Grissell, 320
Griswold, 62, 471
Grobe, 334
Groenweldt, 504
Gross, 1, 113, 212, 303, 367, 372, 412
Grover, 49, 219, 274, 328, 400, 472, 483, 484
Grubb, 70, 118, 242
Grummond, 253
Grunebaum, 108
Grupe, 103, 108, 369
Grymen, 489
Grymes, 25, 301
Guerry, 330
Guest, 131
Guilbeau, 215
Guild, 25
Guilt, 444
Guinard, 310
Guion, 1, 198
Guista, 449
Guiton, 108
Gulick, 176
Gunn, 198, 288
Gunnell, 71, 100, 113, 156, 165, 213, 272, 504
Gunnison, 390
Gunter, 17, 44, 200
Gunton, 368
Gurley, 45, 56, 234, 262, 290
Guthrie, 116, 468
Guttenshu, 108
Guy, 45, 387
Guyer, 363, 369
Guzenback, 111
Gwaltney, 217
Gwin, 63, 303, 443, 468
Gwinn, 341, 348, 439
Gwynn, 254

H

Hachette, 199
Hackett, 428
Hackley, 216
Hackney, 5, 415
Haddock, 186, 448
Haddock's Hills, 265
Hadduck, 73, 477
Haden, 216, 495
Hadley, 235
Hagan, 304, 407, 467
Hagar, 229
Hager, 14, 363, 367, 369, 385, 422, 445, 504
Hagerty, 320, 357, 360
Haggard, 25, 73, 143
Haggerty, 90, 106, 111, 131
Hagner, 212, 292, 327
Hagy, 41
Haight, 283
Hail, 375
Haile, 328
Hailstock, 417
Haines, 38, 213
Hainline, 15, 185
Haislep, 109
Haislip, 360
Haitchen, 16
Haite, 363
Hale, 10, 208, 348
Haley, 120
Haliday, 267, 293, 411, 429, 476

Hall, 35, 41, 63, 65, 67, 82, 85, 94, 96, 106, 109, 111, 114, 119, 120, 127, 135, 163, 176, 187, 194, 196, 206, 212, 217, 223, 232, 254, 264, 279, 281, 287, 296, 307, 313, 323, 363, 364, 366, 384, 391, 401, 408, 422, 459, 479, 504
Hallaran, 430
Hallett, 5, 21
Halley, 379
Halliday, 394
Halloway, 198
Hallowell, 379
Hallyburton, 498
Halstead, 66
Halsted, 254
Ham, 11, 219, 220
Hamersley, 103, 109, 333, 369
Hamersly, 219
Hamilton, 3, 20, 55, 57, 74, 93, 98, 109, 131, 147, 148, 178, 189, 282, 326, 329, 333, 337, 340, 341, 364, 376, 461, 468, 488
Hamlet, 469
Hammack, 108
Hammer, 396
Hammersley, 82, 372
Hammersly, 165, 203, 211
Hammet, 389
Hammett, 128, 223
Hammon, 379
Hammond, 3, 55, 108, 118, 218, 258, 309, 405, 413, 479, 492, 504
Hamner, 146
Hampton, 84, 133, 261, 322
Hancock, 15, 113, 363, 422, 426, 478
Hand, 468
Handley, 109, 211, 307
Handly, 383
Handy, 111, 128, 259, 267, 324, 364, 371, 380, 416, 427, 504
Haniver, 465
Hanks, 275, 459
Hanley, 103, 446
Hann, 11
Hannegan, 79, 440

Hanniver, 465
Hannon, 398
Hansborough, 438
Hanscom, 84
Hansell, 268, 354, 381
Hanson, 131, 317, 360, 471
Hantch, 194
Haralson, 255
Harbam, 76
Harbaug, 476
Harbaugh, 109, 222, 363, 429
Hardage, 437
Harden, 232
Hardenbrook, 47
Harder, 28
Hardin, 42, 132, 133, 209, 336, 350, 375, 471
Harding, 33, 48, 57, 75, 113, 154, 155, 171, 240, 343, 354, 396
Hardt, 498
Hardtimes, 470
Hardwick, 494
Hardy, 126, 129, 187, 239, 254
Hargrave, 36, 497
Hargrove, 199
Harken, 32
Harker, 451
Harkins, 269
Harkley, 340
Harkness, 267, 287, 476, 504
Harley, 232, 438
Harlin, 288
Harlowe, 79
Harman, 370
Harmanson, 232, 429, 485, 499
Harmony, 3, 19, 75, 155
Harnick, 54
Harper, 92, 109, 111, 183, 207, 420, 423, 481
Harr, 205
Harra, 18
Harrell, 323
Harriman, 183
Harrington, 72, 93, 113, 198, 212, 288, 366, 397

Harris, 22, 28, 46, 49, 79, 103, 106, 125, 132, 190, 206, 209, 232, 295, 303, 323, 363, 364, 366, 376, 397, 437, 442, 499
Harrison, 85, 102, 112, 136, 138, 144, 153, 231, 243, 286, 299, 310, 329, 368, 371, 397, 410, 414, 447, 487, 491
Harrover, 109
Harry, 287, 486
Harshman, 360
Hart, 69, 91, 187, 301, 351, 363, 390
Hartman, 209, 456, 459
Harton, 183
Hartsfield, 127
Hartshoren, 48
Hartshorn, 106, 115
Hartsook, 435
Hartung, 88
Hartwick, 14, 65
Hartzell, 422, 496
Harvey, 48, 106, 109, 111, 157, 163, 170, 180, 190, 205, 259, 274, 331, 360, 478
Harwood, 57
Hasam, 131
Hasbrouck, 293
Hascall, 6, 96, 128, 374
Hasel, 455
Haseltine, 206
Haskell, 29, 45, 241, 313, 354, 389, 397
Haskill, 421
Haskins, 344
Haslett, 440
Haslitt, 422
Haslup, 289
Hassler, 254
Hastings, 1, 65, 96, 117, 119, 232
Haswell, 473, 504
Hatch, 1, 65, 108, 116, 212, 399
Hatcher, 444
Hatfield, 459
Hathaway, 2, 268
Haughton, 67, 309
Hauley, 149
Hauptman, 222, 376
Haust, 417

Havenner, 21, 222, 369, 463
Haverstick, 159
Havest, 67
Haviland, 76, 222, 424
Haw, 129, 256, 464
Haward, 372
Hawes, 68, 186, 325, 448
Hawk, 28
Hawke, 134, 453
Hawkins, 20, 78, 107, 203, 222, 225, 227, 273, 366, 372, 495
Hawks, 384
Hawley, 67, 390, 496
Hayden, 197, 326
Haye, 318
Hayes, 35, 40, 354, 417, 444
Hayman, 149, 193, 504
Haymes, 360
Hayn, 45
Hayne, 364
Haynes, 107, 148, 199, 294, 482, 484
Hays, 85, 94, 118, 134, 185, 190, 253, 264, 308, 331, 417, 454, 487
Hayward, 14, 38
Haywood, 397
Hazard, 21, 70, 108, 267, 432, 438
Hazel, 155, 363, 371
Hazelfield, 269
Hazell's row, 418
Hazen, 252
Hazle, 331
Hazlefield, 289
Hazlehurst, 496
Hazleton, 186
Hazzard, 326, 462
Head, 336
Headley, 435, 504
Headly, 438
Headren, 296
Healey, 397
Heany, 209
Heap, 178, 209
Heard, 191, 265, 412, 443
Hearn, 15
Heart, 184
Heaston, 227

Heath, 87, 140, 149, 255
Heatherby, 253
Hebard, 496
Hebb, 298
Heck, 326, 328
Hederick, 295
Hedge, 280
Hedgeman, 193
Hedges, 132
Hedgman, 411
Hedrick, 418
Heflebower, 474
Heger, 367
Heilsman, 249
Heimberger, 251
Heiskell, 486
Heisler, 112
Heisley, 11
Heiss, 306
Heitmiller, 360, 369
Heitmuller, 103
Hekroth, 56
Hellen, 196, 296, 353, 414, 495
Hellriggle, 322
Heminger, 82
Hemmons, 465
Hemphill, 223
Hempstead, 343
Hemtress, 8
Hendebert, 180
Henderick, 33
Hendershott, 236, 326, 483
Henderson, 1, 10, 57, 68, 232, 273, 449, 459, 476, 495
Hendley, 113, 115
Hendricks, 163, 224, 294
Hendrickson, 273
Hening, 86
Henke, 413
Henkle, 305
Henning, 33, 109, 111, 202
Henow, 143
Henry, 14, 41, 50, 206, 232, 266, 268, 276, 419, 438, 451, 469, 479
Henshaw, 13, 26, 91, 287, 312, 340, 377, 485, 498

Henson, 41
Hepburn, 214, 281, 339, 353
Herbert, 232, 405, 436
Herbst, 233
Hercus, 111
Hereford, 307
Herman, 261
Hermitage, 408
Herndon, 279, 310
Herold, 103, 207, 364
Herreman, 235
Herrick, 11, 42, 82, 285
Herriess, 127
Herriman, 218, 240, 473
Herrity, 103, 504
Herron, 454
Hersey, 75, 155, 162, 342, 396
Herst, 107
Herty, 302
Hervey, 5, 87
Hesler, 232
Heslip, 67
Hess, 103, 312, 411, 422, 493
Hester, 6, 27, 148, 392
Hestor, 194
Hetzel, 60, 90, 256, 297
Heustis, 404
Heveningham, 7
Heverin, 148
Hewett, 50
Hewitt, 454
Heydon, 109
Heylman, 117
Heymann, 97
Heywood, 391
Hibbs, 297
Hickerson, 106
Hickey, 31
Hickman, 75, 103, 122, 177, 364
Hicks, 7, 117, 340, 360, 374, 481
Hiers, 379
Higginbotham, 40, 84, 198
Higgins, 148, 330
Highlands, 124
Higley, 149

Hill, 4, 11, 33, 43, 55, 61, 68, 75, 91, 92, 107, 109, 124, 125, 149, 180, 202, 215, 240, 259, 280, 301, 302, 330, 341, 349, 360, 390, 401, 410, 454, 457, 465, 473, 476, 482, 492
Hillery, Sarah, 209
Hilliard, 123, 175, 178, 199, 273, 296, 444
Hilliary, 143
Hills, 38
Hillsman, 232
Hillyard, 111, 163, 225
Hillyer, 77
Hilton, 202, 229, 252, 292, 488
Hinchell, 2
Hindman, 28
Hinds, 86, 155, 227
Hines, 109, 111
Hinge, 111
Hinkle, 252, 491
Hinsdale, 448
Hinson, 232
Hinton, 160, 222, 303, 340, 345, 504
Hipkins, 19
Hirst, 450
Hise, 134
Hisey, 28
Hiss, 103
Hitchcock, 136, 252, 317, 337, 383, 464, 468
Hite, 244
Hits, 267
Hitz, 103, 109, 111
Hixt, 142
Hoagland, 192
Hoban, 442, 486
Hobart, 147, 177
Hobbie, 103, 213, 287
Hobbs, 87, 106, 125
Hobson, 241
Hoburg, 322
Hock, 232
Hocker, 214
Hocking, 380
Hodge, 111, 183, 354

Hodges, 45, 48, 69, 72, 74, 86, 120, 137, 183, 203, 292, 298, 373, 414, 421, 439, 463, 494, 498, 500
Hodgkins, 412
Hodgman, 283
Hodgskins, 372
Hodgson, 4, 344, 383
Hodson, 77
Hoffman, 112, 167, 363, 447, 487, 504
Hoffmeister, 241
Hogan, 43, 69, 83, 271, 299, 444
Hoge, 142
Hogmire, 285
Hogue, 177
Holabird, 326, 483, 484
Holand, 30
Holbrook, 2, 311, 389
Holcomb, 160, 237
Holcombe, 347
Holden, 25, 94, 163, 379
Holford, 153
Holiday, 327
Holladay, 209
Hollahan, 154
Holland, 31, 183, 184, 364
Holliday, 113, 232
Hollidge, 103, 267
Hollingshead, 462
Hollingsworth, 146
Hollins, 403
Hollister, 78, 202
Hollohan, 47, 373
Holloran, 441
Holman, 269
Holmead, 109, 111, 147, 215, 220, 316, 395, 431
Holmes, 19, 21, 198, 234, 237, 271, 280, 415, 422, 423, 463
Holohan, 274
Holohon, 230
Holroyd, 363
Holt, 8, 11, 223, 499
Holton, 297
Holtzman, 351, 368, 434
Holyneaux, 41
Homan, 36

Homans, 335, 356, 452
Home, 170
Homestead, 126, 250
Homestead Farm, 126
Homiller, 187
Hone, 18, 390
Honeycut, 379
Honsthamp, 103
Hood, 314
Hooe, 109, 136, 337
Hook, 183, 354
Hooker, 26, 51, 55
Hoon, 330
Hooper, 63, 368, 465
Hootman, 224
Hoover, 57, 106, 114, 183, 201, 287, 360, 363, 479, 504
Hope, 422
Hopeton, 122
Hopkins, 143, 146, 215, 351, 360, 422
Horgon, 190
Horn, 181, 182, 197
Hornblower, 408
Horner, 101, 106, 449
Horning, 103, 109, 369
Hornkeith, 7
Hornor, 172
Horobert, 261
Horsey, 504
Horst, 161
Horsthamp, 360
Horton, 55, 82, 215, 221, 422
Hosler, 117
Hotchkiss, 241, 390
Hotz, 458
Houck, 77
Hough, 107, 481
Houghton, 421
Houn, 112
Hourch, 334
House, 29, 174, 201
Houston, 70, 163, 278, 296, 344, 356, 377, 467
Houtz, 206
Hovey, 15, 468
How, 57, 280

Howard, 103, 109, 113, 127, 190, 198, 222, 232, 240, 252, 266, 294, 304, 316, 331, 342, 364, 369, 370, 371, 417, 462, 475, 483, 484, 499
Howe, 15, 65, 70, 141, 205, 261, 267, 287, 327, 329, 419, 504
Howell, 45, 66, 73, 81, 84, 111, 114, 115, 163, 237, 322, 344, 366, 367, 376
Howison, 113, 129, 142, 202, 409
Howland, 25, 470
Howle, 103, 474
Hows, 115
Hoxie, 10, 497
Hoye, 258, 359
Hoyle, 440
Hoyt, 14, 65, 102, 132, 301, 346
Hubbard, 148, 196, 290, 291, 402
Hubbs, 241
Hubgh, 144
Huddleston, 252
Hudgins, 444
Hudry, 8
Hudson, 65, 153, 236, 326, 329, 338, 400, 413, 444, 483, 484
Hues, 118
Huggins, 108, 109
Hughes, 35, 63, 92, 107, 111, 188, 190, 218, 229, 247, 285, 310, 343, 352, 369, 371, 384, 412, 413, 420, 480
Hughs, 120
Huginin, 109
Huici, 308
Hull, 40, 67, 177
Hulme, 379
Hulse, 350, 352
Humber, 327
Humbert, 397
Humble, 279
Hume, 57, 364, 417
Humes, 77
Humeston, 148
Humphrel, 209
Humphrey, 174, 188, 216
Humphreys, 12, 62, 133, 209, 232, 262, 265, 295
Humphries, 95, 300, 338

Hungerford, 12, 368, 477
Hunk, 241
Hunnicutt, 287
Hunt, 92, 146, 162, 194, 310, 368, 417, 421, 430, 453, 469, 498
Hunter, 124, 190, 229, 236, 237, 248, 322, 331, 337, 352, 383, 386, 391, 398, 428, 429, 468, 495, 496, 504
Huntington, 13, 270, 274
Huntley, 132
Huntsman, 252
Hurd, 478
Hurdle, 128, 170, 260, 303, 485, 498
Hurless, 295
Hurley, 57, 106, 232, 432
Hurst, 291, 356, 377
Hurt, 69, 452
Huscamp, 111
Hussey, 60
Husted, 340
Huston, 290, 445
Hutchens, 492
Hutchins, 47, 92, 163, 252, 427
Hutchinson, 60, 72, 141, 305, 310, 385, 423, 426
Hutchison, 8, 88, 222
Hutter, 168
Hutton, 117, 357, 364
Huysey, 291, 298
Hyatt, 76, 109, 294, 411, 412
Hyde, 40, 56, 67, 108, 161, 195, 198, 323, 360, 393
Hyer, 498
Hygeian Hall, 460

I

Iardell, 451
Iardella, 367, 460, 486
Iddins, 364
Ijams, 126, 250
Ijamsville Property, 250
Imbrecht, 364
Inch, 268, 332
Indermaner, 364
Ingalls, 92
Ingersoll, 157
Ingham, 336
Ingle, 17, 93, 99, 209, 267, 288, 301, 371, 476
Inglis, 333
Inglish, 93
Ingraham, 388
Inman, 346, 422, 496
Insinore, 188
invalid, 153
Ireland, 174, 214, 232, 313, 340
Iron Business, 193
Irons, 185, 193, 313, 402
Irvin, 25, 354
Irvine, 482
Irwin, 141, 152, 434, 437
Isaac, 360, 470
Iseminger, 304
Isherwood, 37, 51, 96, 119
Izard, 465

J

Jackson, 7, 17, 27, 40, 73, 86, 91, 102, 104, 109, 111, 161, 164, 165, 176, 187, 209, 232, 252, 263, 287, 288, 340, 350, 352, 360, 366, 368, 369, 370, 371, 375, 397, 401, 410, 441, 458, 469, 504
Jacob, 103, 450
Jacobs, 14, 56, 193, 431
James, 19, 28, 51, 91, 174, 334, 432, 457, 491
Jameson, 56, 104, 106, 333, 402, 411
Jamesville, 87
Jamieson, 106
Jamison, 430, 486
Janes, 215
Janney, 73, 74, 308, 359, 470, 487
Jarboe, 360
Jardin, 504
Jardine, 125
Jarero, 447
Jarnegan, 401, 454
Jarnigan, 308
Jarrett, 65
Jarvis, 118, 346, 371, 481, 492
Jasper, 106, 366, 410

543

Jaudon, 40
Jay, 57, 136
Jeffers, 106, 111, 364
Jefferson, 226, 240, 286, 298, 335, 364, 478, 493, 499
Jeffery, 24
Jeffrey, 95, 97
Jeffries, 176
Jellard, 203
Jenifer, 364, 477
Jenkins, 90, 238, 323, 364, 482
Jenley, 467
Jenness, 82
Jenney, 132
Jennings, 115, 232, 352, 445, 459
Jernigan, 62, 339
Jerome, 134, 440
Jesse, 82
Jesup, 104, 123, 199, 305, 386, 407, 464
Jesurun, 146
Jett, 45, 96, 119
Jewell, 13
Jewett, 303, 389
Jillard, 109, 288
Jimeson, 122
Jobson, 54
Jocks, 504
John, 28
Johns, 33, 69, 76, 274, 326, 419, 443
Johnson, 2, 3, 6, 7, 12, 17, 20, 21, 22, 38, 40, 48, 50, 51, 57, 60, 63, 66, 71, 72, 73, 75, 81, 89, 104, 106, 107, 109, 111, 121, 125, 138, 146, 150, 160, 173, 177, 184, 187, 197, 201, 209, 214, 219, 225, 227, 228, 232, 234, 237, 244, 246, 254, 261, 267, 270, 274, 275, 277, 278, 286, 288, 296, 304, 314, 331, 341, 342, 343, 351, 354, 355, 356, 358, 360, 364, 367, 369, 371, 373, 375, 376, 388, 401, 402, 407, 411, 417, 424, 428, 433, 435, 445, 451, 452, 454, 459, 462, 471, 472, 473, 475, 478, 481, 483, 484, 486, 488, 489, 492, 493, 499, 500, 503, 504, 505
Johnstan, 138

Johnston, 85, 143, 153, 198, 232, 237, 247, 269, 307, 309, 316, 324, 327, 448, 498
Jolly, 109, 360
Jones, 3, 5, 8, 13, 21, 22, 25, 26, 28, 35, 38, 48, 50, 56, 57, 60, 66, 68, 70, 77, 81, 83, 85, 86, 89, 91, 100, 104, 107, 109, 111, 113, 121, 145, 148, 156, 161, 163, 164, 173, 182, 187, 192, 200, 203, 209, 212, 215, 217, 226, 227, 232, 237, 240, 241, 247, 254, 255, 283, 296, 299, 302, 305, 311, 315, 316, 317, 329, 330, 335, 336, 339, 340, 341, 342, 345, 346, 347, 351, 354, 356, 359, 360, 364, 369, 371, 375, 397, 399, 400, 401, 402, 403, 411, 417, 418, 422, 426, 429, 444, 445, 446, 447, 449, 454, 469, 472, 476, 478, 482, 485, 489, 490, 494, 495, 499, 502, 504
Jopling, 435
Jordan, 78, 156, 177, 198, 342, 364, 417, 430, 444
Jordon, 368
Jose, 266, 427
Jost, 113, 114, 115, 321, 332, 349, 364
Jouett, 326
Journegin, 261
Joy, 122
Joyce, 10, 70, 111, 211
Joynes, 93, 389
Judd, 326
Judge, 436
Judson, 353
Juilan, 209
Julian, 473

K

Kah-ge-ga-gah-baugh, 92
Kahl, 91, 442
Kahoe, 409
Kain, 39
Kale, 101, 367
Kane, 111, 224, 234, 388, 389, 505
Karl, 57, 393
Karnes, 78

Karr, 120, 190
Kasson, 195
Kauffman, 364
Kaufman, 76, 353, 371, 386
Kavanaugh, 505
Kaxton, 313
Kearhan, 190
Kearly, 206
Kearney, 160
Kearny, 147
Kearsley, 22, 351
Keatley, 25
Kedglie, 505, 508
Keech, 20
Keechey, 20
Keefe, 178, 364, 368
Keeler, 30
Keen, 347
Keene, 12, 235, 378
Keep, 294
Keese, 119, 129, 225, 289, 383, 411, 463
Keesling, 278
Keister, 380
Keith, 56, 76
Keithly, 333, 449
Kelcher, 411
Keleher, 375
Keller, 119, 125, 202, 322, 505
Kellet, 334
Kellett, 354, 375
Kelley, 1, 5, 199, 271, 314
Kellogg, 29, 390, 393, 399, 430
Kelly, 62, 76, 87, 90, 111, 256, 261, 340, 364, 500, 505
Kelsey, 67
Kemberly, 139
Kemble, 284, 459
Kemle, 397
Kemper, 140
Kenan, 198
Kendall, 7, 213, 246, 305, 410, 468
Kendrick, 6, 48, 102, 106, 364, 388, 472, 478, 505
Kengla, 187
Kennard, 22
Kennaugh, 287

Kennedy, 5, 57, 64, 74, 136, 149, 166, 183, 234, 272, 288, 464
Kennehan, 27
Kennell, 330
Kennersley, 492
Kenney, 133
Kennimore, 402
Kennon, 187
Kenny, 333
Kent, 187, 354, 403, 481
Kenyon, 241
Keobel, 98, 111
Kepler, 104
Ker, 182
Kerby, 452
Kercheval, 279, 340
Kerfoot, 21, 53, 170
Kern, 99, 232
Kernan, 31
Kerr, 57, 505
Kersey, 364
Kervand, 211
Kessinger, 219, 220
Kesting, 427
Keswick, 238
Ketcham, 8, 162
Ketchum, 389
Key, 305, 369, 431, 474
Keyes, 28
Keys, 109, 489
Keyser, 87
Keyworth, 104, 109, 165, 446
Kiaking, 214
Kibbal, 364
Kibball, 360, 369
Kibbey, 109, 364, 366
Kibby, 111, 259
Kibly, 389
Kidd, 31, 397, 481, 492
Kiddal, 13
Kidder, 142, 447, 453
Kidwell, 57, 90, 192, 349, 353, 364, 379, 411, 417, 427, 469, 479
Kieckhoefer, 295
Kiger, 106
Kilbourn, 222

Kilbourne, 458
Kilgour, 163
Killiam, 228
Killian, 104, 106
Killmon, 111
Kilman, 267
Kilroy, 54
Kimball, 102, 258
Kimbell, 498
Kimberly, 61
Kimmell, 106, 108, 186
King, 8, 19, 41, 47, 51, 65, 67, 85, 86, 106, 111, 113, 116, 125, 130, 154, 171, 191, 192, 199, 217, 232, 250, 255, 256, 261, 262, 270, 287, 340, 341, 344, 354, 364, 386, 398, 401, 412, 413, 414, 417, 424, 435, 440, 464, 466, 486, 487, 492, 501, 505
Kingman, 104, 505
Kingsbury, 8, 64, 79, 201
Kingsland, 85
Kinnard, 206
Kinnell, 29
Kinnersley, 218
Kinney, 38, 180, 291, 438
Kinsey, 198, 223, 467
Kinslay, 416
Kinsley, 106, 423
Kinsloe, 337
Kinsman, 389, 396
Kintzing, 376, 399
Kinzie, 343
Kirby, 99, 104, 153, 253, 310, 411
Kirk, 21, 27, 143, 144, 156, 193, 265, 335
Kirkland, 318
Kirkpatrick, 13
Kirkwood, 287
Kirty, 505
Kiser, 330
Kissick, 417
Kitchen, 192
Kitcher, 106
Kittson, 235
Klauser, 67
Kleiber, 162, 266

Klein, 75, 263
Kleindeinst, 364
Kleindenst, 50
Kleindienst, 412
Kliendenst, 27, 40
Kline, 263
Klingler, 77
Kloman, 77, 190, 364, 411
Klomann, 113
Klopfer, 222, 364
Knal, 22
Knapp, 5, 91, 141, 310, 347
Knaup, 234
Kneller, 343
Knickerbocker, 116
Knight, 102, 104, 136, 139, 141, 310, 360, 364, 486, 488
Knoblock, 413
Knoffenberger, 143
Knott, 109, 111, 165, 291, 364
Know, 198
Knowles, 62, 505
Knowlton, 4, 5, 77, 358
Knowman, 115
Knox, 22, 29, 33, 121, 217, 396, 402, 487
Korff, 4
Korns, 218
Kosciusko, 43, 52, 191
Kounig, 81
Kouns, 169
Kounslar, 6
Krafft, 104, 109, 124, 157, 369
Kretschmar, 269
Krober, 104
Krofft, 404
Kuhl, 104, 112, 412, 450
Kuhn, 232, 239
Kuhns, 239
Kummer, 364
Kumner, 367
Kunkle, 379
Kurner, 234
Kurtz, 291, 316, 475, 505
Kutzenberger, 412
Kuykendall, 13, 54, 65, 127, 347

Kyan, 17

L

La Croix, 128
La Grange, 118
La Reintree, 102
La Reintrie, 386
Labbe, 318
Lacey, 241
Lachance, 66, 142, 201
Lacoste, 9, 233
Lacroix, 125
Lacy, 107
Ladd, 48, 77, 352, 377
Ladew, 198
Lafayette, 20, 276, 432, 442
Lagrange, 20
Lahin, 340
Lair, 309
Laird, 219, 445
Lake, 67
Lakin, 437
Lallum, 232
Lamar, 166
Lamb, 39, 117, 253, 261
Lambell, 104
Lambert, 65, 72, 96, 128, 155, 158, 196
Lambkin, 166
Lamble, 360
Lamborn, 162
Lameke, 2
Lamer, 92
Lamerre, 279
Lanaghan, 154
Lanaham, 261
Lanahan, 29, 131, 173, 280, 331, 459, 480
Lancaster, 282, 284
Landre, 233
Landrick, 104
Landstreet, 131
Lane, 37, 99, 102, 109, 195, 213, 218, 279, 345, 367, 407, 494
Laneville, 456
Lang, 41, 204, 224, 236, 377, 409
Langdon, 198, 367

Lange, 355, 382
Langford, 294
Langworthy, 327
Lanham, 312
Lann, 437
Lannahan, 96
Lansdale, 48, 468
Laplace, 343
Larabbe, 95
Larabee, 95
Lardner, 249
Larkin, 271, 468
Larmour, 476
Larned, 212
Larner, 417
Larrabee, 87, 274
Larring, 24
Laskbroke, 198
Laskey, 202, 358, 367, 434
Lasportas, 6
Latham, 53, 94, 104, 280, 315, 364, 367, 375, 381, 398, 457
Lathrop, 206, 213, 342, 350, 398
Latimer, 196
Latta, 253
Laub, 111, 125, 272, 303, 364, 411
Lauck, 107, 236
Laughlin, 56, 213, 229, 239, 392, 482
Laurel Farm, 186
Laurie, 350, 352, 487
Lauxman, 364
Lavalette, 331
Lavender, 104, 107, 494
Lavy, 190
Law, 104, 468, 485, 505
Lawler, 62
Lawrence, 53, 57, 71, 75, 94, 109, 183, 211, 213, 232, 269, 288, 294, 298, 344, 358, 389, 434, 496
Lawrenson, 49
Lawson, 13, 104, 211, 242, 257, 299, 364
Lawton, 50, 389
Layton, 310
Lazell, 198
Le Blanc, 278

Le Leon, 52
Le Roy, 80, 356, 375
Lea, 61, 275, 394
Leach, 30, 278, 432
Leahy, 95
Learned, 438
Leasus, 77
Leatherbury, 305
Leathers, 184
Leavenworth, 221
Lecaze, 8
Leckie, 163
Leddy, 111, 364, 367
Lederer, 369
Ledever, 104
Lee, 14, 51, 57, 75, 104, 106, 115, 123,
    154, 171, 198, 199, 215, 244, 245,
    274, 353, 360, 364, 369, 372, 395,
    411, 430, 441, 464, 487, 505
Lee, 232
Leech, 198, 417
Leeds, 96
Leef, 84, 155
Lees, 177
Leet, 8, 78
Lefavour, 341
Lefevre, 505
Lehey, 190
Lehmah, 112
Lehman, 115, 321, 364, 372, 412
Lehmann, 266
Lehr, 176
Leighton, 358
Leisintzer, 364
Leitch, 391
LeLamogne, 208
Lemist, 341
Lemmon, 77
Lemon, 334
Lendorff, 124
Lendrum, 75
Lenhart, 468
Lenman, 66, 109, 369
Lennahan, 314
Lenox, 293, 340, 408, 415, 433, 476
Lentz, 132, 148

Leonard, 130, 204, 245, 307, 424
Lepretre, 304
Lepreux, 111, 364
Lerch, 195
Leroy, 1, 130
Leslie, 11
Lester, 406
Letcher, 234
Letmate, 109
Letting, 21
Levell, 293
Levering, 447
Levings, 421
Levy, 142
Lewellyn, 185
Lewis, 4, 7, 18, 34, 53, 54, 63, 73, 76,
    81, 82, 84, 101, 104, 106, 107, 109,
    121, 122, 135, 140, 148, 167, 173,
    174, 183, 203, 222, 223, 242, 245,
    267, 283, 288, 291, 296, 305, 306,
    312, 323, 329, 336, 356, 360, 364,
    367, 371, 382, 413, 417, 429, 432,
    489, 492, 495, 505
Libbey, 122, 210, 385
Liedberg, 136
Liesberger, 367
Light, 193
Lightelle, 17
Lightfoot, 171, 364, 371
Ligon, 340
Likens, 191
Likins, 12
Lilburne, 351
Lilly, 48
Lincoln, 288, 341, 478, 493
Lincon, 234
Lind, 374, 474, 487, 488
Lindenberger, 243
Lindlay, 134
Lindle, 241
Lindley, 197
Lindpainter, 498
Lindsay, 74, 120, 420
Lindsey, 222
Lindsley, 109, 360, 364, 384, 446
Lindsly, 104, 115, 340, 492

Link, 125
Linkens, 441
Linkins, 80, 360, 364
Linn, 182, 253, 489
Linthicum, 46, 77, 99, 287, 457, 464
Linton, 39, 287, 457
Liomin, 104
Liphard, 109, 368
Lippett, 331
Lippitt, 373
Lipscomb, 278
Lisle, 224
Littell, 9
Little, 1, 35, 58, 104, 135, 145, 155, 165, 167, 173, 187, 241, 260, 267, 274, 357, 360, 364, 371, 479, 505
Littlefield, 149, 474
Littleton, 33
Litton, 232
Livingston, 60, 154, 264, 401, 432, 496
Llangollen, 160
Llewellin, 416, 451
Llewellyn, 21, 463
Lloyd, 4, 92, 109, 132, 170, 177, 412, 439, 460, 481
Locke, 233
Lockett, 464
Lockling, 71
Lockney, 111
Lockwood, 24, 30, 56, 67, 155, 168, 320, 374, 404, 482
Locust Grove, 46, 227
Lodge, 187, 426
Logan, 28, 96, 340, 422, 498
Lokey, 372
Loman, 418
Lomax, 5, 212, 226
Lombard, 78, 95, 449
Lombardi, 449, 505
London, 161
Long, 25, 101, 199, 295, 305, 328, 394, 435, 475, 480
Longbottom, 423
Longdon, 417
Longlois, 25
Longworth, 351

Longworthy, 422
Looby, 106, 112
Looker, 237
Loomis, 121, 246, 360, 498
Lopez, 247, 273, 408, 495
Lord, 18, 104, 111, 166, 181, 201, 263, 411
Loring, 157, 295
Loudon, 193, 364, 371
Loughery, 213
Loury, 117
Love, 191, 341
Lovejoy, 427
Loveless, 73, 360
Lovell, 25, 224, 234, 394, 447, 448
Lovenstine, 148
Loventy, 124
Lovett, 430
Lovocat, 233
Low, 65, 215, 216, 246, 260, 393, 463, 485
Lowd, 269
Lowe, 79, 107, 154, 247, 253, 364, 395, 418, 431, 499
Lowman, 299
Lowrey, 256
Lowrie, 299, 417
Lowry, 176, 350, 401, 454, 464
Loyall, 426
Lozier, 187
Luby, 97
Lucas, 55, 78, 381, 417, 505
Luce, 278
Luckett, 70, 215, 487
Ludington, 421
Ludwick, 183
Lulborough, 219
Lund, 177, 222
Lundy, 109
Luney, 6
Lunt, 1, 382
Lusby, 57, 109, 320, 356, 411, 412
Lusk, 202, 391
Luther, 505
Luttrell, 474
Lutz, 69, 222, 288, 412

Lyle, 449
Lyles, 57, 325, 500
Lyman, 341, 430
Lynch, 16, 26, 32, 62, 202, 217, 221, 234, 237, 307, 322, 335, 349, 350, 354, 358, 368, 375, 399, 401, 469, 489
Lyndsley, 370
Lynes, 147, 300
Lynn, 246
Lyon, 15, 25, 41, 232, 256, 303, 459
Lyons, 147, 261, 360

M

Maack, 413
Mabry, 422
Mabson, 252
Macaulay, 146
Macauley, 5, 56, 482
Macdaniel, 353
MacDaniel, 107
Macfeely, 328
Macias, 387
Mack, 328
Mackaboy, 202
Mackall, 6, 230, 265, 277
Mackay, 236, 325, 329, 348, 349, 356
Mackey, 111, 115, 361, 412, 449
Macklin, 209
Macleaven, 190
Maclurg, 430
Macomb, 83, 152, 186, 201, 465
MacPherson, 204
Macrae, 233, 319
MacRae, 30
Mactier, 21
Mactire, 48
Madan, 387
Madden, 145
Maddox, 107, 146, 149, 219, 261, 265, 418, 492, 506
Madella, 417
Madigan, 376
Madison, 36, 101, 229, 286, 360, 361, 496, 505
Madlam, 91
Madlan, 81

Maffit, 238
Magar, 267, 300, 364
Magee, 106, 111, 293, 334, 369, 436, 441, 447
Magers, 220
Magill, 373
Maginnis, 404
Magle, 109
Magnetic Telegraph Co, 407
Magnus, 308, 368
Magruder, 58, 104, 106, 109, 201, 287, 302, 303, 323, 327, 334, 360, 367, 411, 426, 431, 475
Maguire, 90, 101, 106, 115, 135, 321, 349, 388
Maguirek, 365
Magyer, 233
Mahaffey, 494
Mahar, 104, 216
Maharney, 320
Maher, 113, 129, 233, 372, 451, 460, 469, 505
Mahlon, 479
Mahon, 173, 287, 321, 388
Mahurin, 118
Mains, 202
Major, 25, 86, 316, 437
Malay, 198, 496
Mallet, 8, 410
Mallicote, 340
Mallion, 181
Mallory, 123, 296, 358
Malone, 115, 367
Maloney, 402
Malony, 456
Malster, 446
Malthy, 163
Managin, 275
Manahan, 141
Manchester, 62, 457
Mandeville, 38
Mangum, 352
Mankin, 104, 289, 358, 367
Mankins, 412
Manley, 344
Manly, 136, 302, 314

Mann, 106, 246, 364
Manning, 207, 345, 446, 472
Mannon, 235
Mansfield, 25, 60, 140, 162, 322, 364, 380, 381, 392, 396
Mansion House, 335
Mantz, 173
Mapes, 217, 352, 469
Mar, 58
Marbury, 211, 218, 258, 282, 440, 445, 473
Marceron, 111, 159, 196, 207, 368
Marchand, 255
Marche, 159
Marcus, 132, 333
Marcy, 191
Marden, 365
Mardes, 506
Marie, 308, 345
Mariott, 233
Markle, 330
Marks, 67, 82, 104, 123, 155, 251, 259, 299, 331, 383, 467
Markward, 403
Marlborough, 506
Marlow, 143, 279
Marrast, 1
Marriott, 11, 298
Marron, 191, 213
Marsh, 15, 23, 78, 122, 168, 175, 212, 221, 226, 269, 278, 449, 468, 487
Marshal Hall, 282
Marshall, 36, 50, 54, 79, 106, 165, 179, 209, 233, 282, 297, 328, 333, 364, 365, 367, 371, 389, 418, 464, 486, 505
Marshall Hall, 179
Marsolette, 308
Marsten, 453
Marsters, 393
Marston, 9, 456
Martin, 29, 33, 58, 101, 106, 109, 148, 190, 217, 233, 252, 256, 259, 265, 267, 323, 333, 340, 364, 365, 368, 369, 387, 391, 404, 417, 434, 435, 442, 455
Martinas, 131

Martini, 498
Marvin, 60, 270
Maryman, 27, 53, 203, 293, 387, 416, 451
Mash, 149
Masi, 109, 126, 364
Mason, 13, 32, 37, 47, 58, 104, 106, 115, 185, 194, 200, 216, 218, 233, 305, 325, 326, 329, 340, 360, 369, 391, 397, 399, 413, 418, 441, 464, 473, 501
Massa, 191
Massey, 163, 365
Massoletti, 22, 124
Masten, 483, 484
Masters, 424
Mather, 28, 67
Mathew, 246
Mathews, 165
Mathieu, 386, 398
Matlock, 198, 478
Matthews, 9, 24, 27, 38, 65, 76, 163, 177, 218, 279, 341, 347, 432, 464, 473
Matthieu, 408
Mattice, 444
Mattingly, 19, 58, 106, 113, 263, 348, 371, 387
Matzanbaugh, 310
Maughan, 219
Maul, 56
Maule, 268, 482
Maulsby, 137, 138, 327
Maupin, 49
Maurice, 417
Mauro, 506
Maury, 124, 376, 451, 457, 505
Mauzy, 473
Maw'd, 419
Maxell, 390
Maxfield, 499
Maxon, 176
Maxwell, 34, 109, 140, 235, 310, 311, 328, 344, 364, 391, 393, 396, 435, 498
May, 132, 134, 140, 174, 217, 228, 262, 303, 401, 448, 458, 469, 496
Mayer, 455, 499
Maynard, 144, 253, 295, 301, 430

Mayo, 392
Mayor, 209
McAbee, 233
McAdams, 69, 148, 301
McAdow, 294
McAfee, 427
McAlaster, 31
McAlpine, 454
McAlwee, 292, 353
McArann, 386
McArthur, 86, 428, 483
McAtee, 304
McAvoy, 43, 319, 465
McBlair, 19, 111, 122, 147, 162, 229, 287, 439, 475
McBride, 149
McCabe, 76, 448
McCafferty, 367
McCaffray, 401
McCaffrey, 132
McCain, 120
McCall, 226, 327, 483, 484
McCalla, 212
McCallem, 370
McCallen, 394
McCallion, 233, 492
McCallister, 393
McCallum, 116
McCane, 136
McCann, 35
McCarter, 178
McCarthy, 109, 136, 214, 365, 417, 438
McCartney, 300
McCarty, 421, 436, 448, 494
McCaslin, 241
McCathran, 207
McCauley, 11, 207, 281, 312, 500
McChesney, 250
McChesny, 111
McCheyne, 190
McClain, 235
McCleary, 199
McClellan, 6, 58, 98
McClelland, 51, 209, 376, 494
McClery, 104, 109
McClintock, 11, 33, 60, 140, 226, 341

McClung, 134, 380, 388
McClure, 269, 294, 484
McCodding, 294
McColgan, 133, 392
McCollam, 76, 291
McCollum, 347, 362
McComas, 78
McComb, 207
McCombs, 55
McConchie, 448
McConnell, 117, 305, 433
McCook, 29
McCord, 464
McCorde, 464
McCorkle, 116
McCormick, 29, 91, 115, 223, 340, 492, 493, 495, 498, 500, 505, 506
McCoun, 187
McCoy, 233, 296, 364, 406
McCranie, 154
McCraw, 88
McCready, 469
McCreary, 376
McCreery, 135, 187, 203, 266, 287, 432, 436, 451, 472
McCubbin, 479, 500
McCue, 164
McCullen, 32
McCulloch, 132, 212, 389, 401, 454
McCulloh, 185, 276
McCullough, 305
McCully, 5, 341
McCurdy, 386, 393
McCutchan, 347
McCutchen, 109, 206, 278, 323
McDaniel, 126, 314, 333, 459
McDanolds, 148
McDermot, 395
McDermott, 9, 158, 180, 258, 260, 364
McDevitt, 106, 109, 369, 436, 469, 479, 480
McDills, 290
McDonald, 86, 104, 118, 143, 237, 279, 309, 326, 476, 480, 503
McDonnell, 58
McDonogh, 429, 489

McDonoghville, 429
McDonough, 190, 429
McDougal, 14, 75, 382, 459
McDougall, 20, 70
McDowel, 85
McDowell, 234, 271, 421, 492
McDuell, 379
McDuffie, 2, 30, 242
McEleyett, 403
McElfresh, 27, 131, 170, 201, 260, 388, 413, 432, 491
McElhany, 75
McElhenney, 450
McElwee, 418, 505
McEnally, 184
McEnery, 344
McEntire, 270
McEwen, 465
McEwing, 311
McFadden, 280
McFaddin, 240
McFaden, 227
McFarland, 41, 78, 352, 454
McFarlin, 206
McGaha, 402
McGan, 185
McGanley, 111
McGarvey, 10, 90, 97, 111, 114, 181, 197, 208, 250, 369
McGaw, 60, 468, 471, 472
McGeary, 175
McGee, 131, 184
McGhee, 143
McGill, 183, 309
McGinn, 32
McGinnis, 212
McGlaughon, 341
McGlover, 404
McGlue, 267, 361, 451
McGowan, 406, 434, 443
McGrann, 112
McGraw, 341
McGregor, 58, 83, 100, 109, 127, 364, 369, 372
McGrew, 341, 494

McGuire, 222, 229, 256, 293, 387, 392, 456
McHatton, 223
McIlhaney, 121
McIlhany, 376, 382, 423
McIlvain, 85
McIlvaine, 351
McInerney, 361
McIntire, 21, 104
McIntosh, 2, 22, 26, 54, 81, 160, 209, 217, 237, 347, 350, 351, 375, 401, 454
McIntyre, 85
McJilton, 125, 221
McKaig, 395
McKay, 28, 91, 471, 472
McKean, 109, 235, 364, 367
McKeavie, 143
McKee, 67, 84, 123, 155, 199, 397, 419
McKeen, 397
McKeever, 237, 326
McKelden, 40, 360, 369
McKelway, 399
McKennan, 374
McKenney, 25, 77, 95, 256
McKenzie, 437, 493
McKibben, 330
McKibber, 32
McKiernan, 332
McKim, 42, 429
McKin, 364
McKinly, 209
McKinne, 166
McKinney, 159, 310, 382
McKinny, 75
McKinsley, 369
McKinstree, 372
McKissic, 279
Mckluskey, 279
McKney, 491
McKnight, 184, 297, 348, 394, 505
McKown, 40
McKuen, 447
McLain, 49, 287
McLane, 58, 224, 283, 487
McLaughlin, 58, 217, 239, 335

McLean, 22, 101, 106, 109, 177, 198, 326, 333, 344, 483, 484, 506
McLenahan, 240
McLendon, 491
Mcleod, 187
McLeod, 35, 100, 223, 493
McManus, 50, 228, 282, 292
McMaster, 72, 388
McMechan, 209
McMillan, 313, 493
McMillen, 148
McMillon, 295
McMonegle, 135
McMullen, 24, 135, 324
McNair, 163
McNamara, 106
McNamee, 288
McNeal, 111, 449
McNeil, 85, 89, 99, 116, 145, 255, 281, 459
McNeill, 115, 121
McNeir, 269, 289
McNier, 412
McNorton, 104
McNulty, 70, 452
McNutt, 310
McPeak, 321, 364
McPherson, 10, 104, 109, 111, 123, 230, 233, 273, 409
McQuade, 31
McQuay, 505
McQuay, B, 104, 107
McQueen, 344, 381
McQuigley, 413
McQuiston, 217
McRae, 162, 164, 404
McRea, 293
McRee, 41
McSpadden, 58
McVeigh, 202
McWilliams, 144, 151, 281, 335, 473, 505
McWillie, 375
Meacham, 20
Mead, 68, 78, 86, 205, 257, 379, 447
Meade, 92, 116, 140, 373, 426

Meadows, 235, 269
Meaher, 120
Means, 72
Mears, 117, 195
Mebane, 328
Mechlin, 104, 130, 212, 364
Medill, 213
Mediperis, 488
Meehan, 104
Meeker, 389
Mees, 504
Meffert, 386
Megee, 64
Megill, 172
Meguire, 467
Meier, 125
Meiere, 91, 388
Meire, 465
Melcher, 5, 263
Melillton, 17
Melinx, 251
Melling, 209
Melville, 215
Melvin, 299, 435
Mendenhall, 271
Menell, 141
Mercer, 98, 106, 115, 193, 198, 203, 296
Merchant, 163
Meredith, 187, 286, 289, 412, 438
Mereman, 480
Mering, 176
Merino, 233
Merret, 235
Merriam, 128
Merrick, 334
Merrifield, 252
Merrill, 85, 341, 375
Merrit, 391
Merritt, 254
Merriwether, 343
Merryman, 505
Merullat, 364
Messer, 313
Messervey, 119, 131, 142
Mester, 361
Metcalf, 402

Metcalfe, 288
Mexican war, 493
Meyer, 256
Michael, 102
Michie, 428
Michum, 364
Mickey, 320
Mickum, 120
Middleton, 104, 111, 113, 137, 229, 231, 265, 288, 290, 303, 360, 364, 366, 385, 414, 417, 465
Midherst, 412
Mil, 113
Milan, 163
Milburn, 8, 17, 64, 102, 323, 340, 365, 433, 505
Miles, 20, 68, 99, 177, 417
Milhado, 117
Milhardo, 96, 119
Milhau, 272
Milholland, 26
Mill, 250
Mill property, 126
Mill Seat, 245, 385
Millar, 5
Millard, 341, 505
Miller, 5, 12, 20, 21, 45, 58, 62, 69, 82, 102, 104, 109, 117, 141, 145, 149, 155, 175, 176, 183, 187, 203, 206, 209, 212, 218, 242, 264, 273, 278, 285, 287, 288, 311, 316, 319, 330, 334, 336, 361, 364, 368, 369, 371, 372, 379, 383, 400, 417, 420, 421, 431, 432, 434, 438, 448, 459, 469, 473, 480, 500, 502, 505
Milligan, 58, 153, 157
Milliken, 480
Millikin, 5, 186
Mills, 24, 41, 46, 78, 106, 111, 119, 121, 138, 150, 183, 195, 220, 229, 233, 276, 297, 314, 322, 338, 351, 354, 358, 365, 369, 375, 421, 425
Milne, 371
Milnes, 176
Milstead, 111
Milton, 393

Milwee, 118
Mina, 256
Miner, 56, 379
Mines, 219, 261
Minifield, 202
Minnie, 470
Minor, 124, 351, 353, 389
Minton, 336
Miou, 489
Mirick, 388
Miss, 26
Misses Rooker's Academy, 337
Mitchel, 5, 455
Mitchell, 9, 41, 42, 60, 70, 77, 80, 99, 108, 109, 115, 187, 198, 209, 224, 226, 241, 243, 261, 295, 306, 309, 360, 365, 367, 385, 390, 393, 394, 396, 401, 437, 440, 447, 454, 473
Mizner, 51, 394
Mobley, 394
Moenster, 371
Moffat, 396
Moffett, 267, 284
Mohon, 58
Mohum, 17
Mohun, 34, 211, 360, 380, 423
Monaghan, 191
Mondawmin, 146
Monday, 58, 209
Money, 264
Monroe, 36, 58, 173, 222, 264, 450, 506
Montange, 80
Montesquieu, 427
Montesquiou, 194
Montgomery, 3, 24, 126, 129, 199, 310, 311, 315, 435, 450, 464
Montobio, 468
Moody, 135, 168, 341, 353, 383, 429, 440
Mooers, 350
Mooney, 344
Moore, 6, 7, 15, 20, 29, 41, 45, 58, 73, 77, 82, 88, 96, 104, 107, 109, 115, 123, 125, 128, 133, 141, 171, 174, 175, 177, 186, 193, 201, 209, 219, 225, 233, 246, 252, 291, 295, 301,

310, 354, 357, 368, 369, 374, 376, 380, 389, 398, 399, 404, 405, 410, 420, 433, 445, 462, 467, 474, 491, 494, 505
Moorehouse, 307
Moorhead, 355
Moosley, 37
Moran, 77, 115, 147, 165, 202, 316, 361, 395
Morao, 308
Morass, 192
Morehead, 33
Morey, 205
Morfit, 100
Morfitt, 357
Morford, 175
Morgan, 1, 4, 31, 45, 47, 56, 58, 72, 73, 81, 84, 88, 97, 98, 102, 117, 123, 130, 131, 152, 162, 176, 184, 199, 229, 243, 262, 316, 318, 320, 334, 339, 344, 367, 375, 382, 395, 418, 419, 444, 447, 451, 476, 492, 500, 505
Morley, 109, 446
Mormons, 1
Morrill, 92
Morris, 4, 27, 48, 64, 66, 109, 133, 153, 248, 269, 326, 345, 394, 402, 417, 448, 506
Morrison, 15, 25, 35, 58, 109, 163, 209, 228, 252, 271, 332, 341, 412, 463
Morrow, 42, 379, 409
Morse, 102, 124, 127, 192, 226, 238, 241, 245, 372, 407, 421
Morsel, 408
Morsell, 111, 204, 260, 414
Morson, 34, 36
Mortimer, 109, 179, 255, 341
Morton, 58, 72, 183, 234, 240, 308, 392, 417, 438, 506
Morum, 361
Moscrop, 505
Moseley, 336
Mosely, 206, 494
Moses, 376
Mosier, 355
Moss, 183, 340, 379, 505

Mossop, 469
Mother's Care, 452
Mothershead, 109, 360
Mott, 67, 163, 208, 290, 489
Moughon, 418
Moulton, 243, 422
Mount, 104, 255, 332, 334, 491
Mount Auburn, 426
Mount Hebron, 395
Mount Hope, 426
Mount Olivet, 38
Mount Pisgah, 185
Mount Pleasant, 23, 419
Mount Vernon, 44, 89, 161, 248, 276, 410, 426, 491
Mount Zephyr, 410
Mounts, 98
Mouton, 304, 328, 400
Mouunt Vernon, 442
Mower, 386, 394
Moyers, 132
Moylan, 471
Mt Pleasant, 219
Mubriney, 211
Mudd, 201, 209, 213, 267, 305, 410
Mulford, 333
Mullany, 203, 468
Mullegan, 85
Mullen, 60, 87, 104, 106, 256, 379, 427
Muller, 319
Mulligan, 209
Mullikin, 58, 220, 221, 367
Mullin, 84, 145, 233, 294
Mulloy, 10, 243, 257, 267, 304, 416, 436, 441, 447
Mulreny, 135
Mulvey, 31
Munch, 104, 367, 412
Muncy, 358
Munger, 437
Munroe, 44, 60, 403
Murdaugh, 224, 234
Murdock, 243, 256, 458
Mure, 104
Murillo, 156

Murphy, 31, 58, 71, 104, 115, 180, 278, 320, 343, 369, 372, 379, 406, 438
Murray, 4, 58, 68, 102, 104, 107, 111, 141, 157, 196, 205, 209, 215, 223, 229, 233, 247, 256, 268, 303, 304, 364, 368, 414, 469, 476, 496
Murson, 500
Murtagh, 109
Muschett, 205
Muse, 33, 404
Musgrave, 241
Mussey, 14
Mussi, 13
Musson, 182
Mustin, 104, 213, 299, 418
Myer, 176
Myeres, 193
Myerle, 143
Myers, 21, 26, 53, 111, 131, 137, 159, 181, 191, 209, 319, 320, 373, 378, 422, 440, 455, 464
Myrick, 132, 136

N

Nace, 68
Nadal, 292
Nadel, 88
Naff, 398
Nagle, 421
Nail, 118
Nailor, 10, 34, 40, 50, 70, 106, 108, 109, 113, 165, 175, 287, 355, 506
Nairin, 181
Nairn, 109, 266, 321, 469
Nalley, 361, 371, 372
Nally, 58, 152, 210, 246
Nance, 28
Narden, 411, 506
Naser, 411
Nash, 78, 242, 261, 390, 478
Naylor, 38, 109, 116, 129, 142, 204, 217, 267, 271, 365, 415, 417, 465
Naysmith, 156
Neal, 45, 143, 155, 379
Neale, 169, 302, 361, 365, 426
Nealey, 67

Needhan, 390
Neel, 253
Neely, 437
Neff, 271
Neil, 409, 417, 506
Neill, 15, 46, 327, 329, 483
Nelson, 3, 64, 86, 92, 113, 210, 233, 237, 265, 278, 301, 417, 429, 430, 432, 448, 492, 495
Neosho, 63
Nepp, 361, 365
Nes, 323, 358, 463
Nesbit, 2
Nesmith, 506
Ness, 323
Netcke, 282
Neville, 58
Nevin, 133
Neving, 46
Nevins, 77, 142, 466
New Haven Cemetery, 178
Newcomer, 278
Newell, 138, 215, 262, 369
Newman, 58, 285, 322
Newmeyer, 367
Newmyer, 94
Newspapers edited by ladies, 181
Newton, 54, 58, 102, 104, 176, 185, 268, 281, 321, 356, 361, 369, 412, 413, 420, 506
Nichell, 485
Nicholas, 59, 389
Nicholls, 37, 190, 355, 411
Nichols, 33, 43, 181, 218, 229, 233, 310, 322, 358, 404
Nicholson, 107, 123, 199, 229, 306, 310, 312, 443, 494, 506
Nickels, 21
Nickerson, 391
Nicoll, 96, 128, 164, 204, 208
Nicols, 271
Niell, 330
Niles, 427
Nimmo, 326
Nims, 295
Nippes, 74, 301

557

Nisbet, 440
Nixon, 56, 189, 197, 198
Noble, 25, 60, 104, 112, 344, 361, 376, 417, 470
Nock, 359
Nodine, 477
Noe, 55
Noell, 109, 194
Noerr, 361, 369
Noguerra, 487
Nokes, 34, 104, 222, 506
Noland, 113, 136, 247, 275, 412
Nones, 17, 52, 399
Nooney, 459
Norbeck, 77, 109
Norcross, 176
Noriego, 397
Norman, 2, 411
Norris, 3, 14, 18, 71, 124, 247, 268, 269, 469, 491
North, 62, 123
Northrup, 177
Northup, 127
Norton, 53, 141, 160, 343, 354, 471, 482
Norvell, 182, 383, 400
Norwood, 208, 432
Nottingham, 109, 365
Nourse, 19, 35, 42, 85, 124, 142, 147, 185, 213, 367, 506
Noxen, 16
Noyes, 109, 137, 385, 421, 422, 506
Nugent, 104, 131, 177
Nunamaker, 392
Nunnelley, 88
Nuthall, 292
Nuthill, 12
Nutinack, 310
Nutt, 94, 152, 236, 474
Nutter, 241
Nuttritt, 471
Nye, 95, 125

O

O'Bannon, 88, 140
O'Brien, 11, 182, 193, 210, 215, 326, 366

O'Bryan, 417
O'Bryen, 406
O'Bryon, 433
O'Connell, 31
O'Conner, 210
O'Dell, 109
O'Donald, 243
O'Donnell, 110, 233
O'Donnoghue, 302, 303
O'Donoghue, 106, 365
O'Donohue, 361, 369
O'Dwyer, 210
O'Ferrall, 265
O'Flaherty, 7
O'Flannagan, 247
O'Grady, 391
O'Hara, 273, 407, 495
O'Hare, 111, 225, 361
O'Leary, 111, 506
O'Mara, 411
O'Mear, 175
O'Meara, 367
O'Neal, 29, 419, 499
O'Neil, 32, 58
O'Sullivan, 273
Oak Hill, 169, 264, 424
Oak Springs, 358
Oakes, 470
Oaks, 94
Ober, 111, 366, 447
O'Brien, 120, 169, 329
O'Bryon, 274
Och, 412
Ochiltree, 121, 255
Odbert, 94
Odell, 340
Oden, 210
Odenheimer, 45
O'Donnell, 385
Oelricks, 197
Oerlenschlager, 133
O'Fallan, 85
Ofenstein, 365
Offley, 147
Offutt, 37, 47, 72, 306, 375, 471
Ogden, 64, 121, 138, 340, 396

Ogelthorpe, 153
Ogle, 322, 325
Oglesby, 467
Ohr, 70
Old Fields, 317
Old Whitey, 289
Oldham, 357
Oldom, 417
Olds, 70
Olive, 78, 412
Oliver, 197, 198, 341
Olmstead, 235, 259, 271
Olstine, 337
Onderdock, 117
O'Neale, 83, 104, 506
O'Neill, 285
Oothoudt, 310
Ord, 399
Orem, 107, 365
Orendorf, 301
Orme, 99, 111, 210, 231, 267, 464
Ormsby, 237
Orndorff, 450
Osborn, 38, 218, 271, 302, 417
Osborne, 51, 129, 294, 303, 398
Osbourn, 376
Osburn, 211
Oslia, 379
Osteller, 290
Otis, 198
Ott, 192, 234
Otterback, 104, 361
Ourand, 365
Overman, 16
Owen, 109, 148, 310, 420, 438
Owens, 24, 104, 251, 361, 418
Owings, 37
Owner, 365, 371
Oyster, 107, 152, 367
Ozias, 163

P

Pace, 248
Packard, 506
Packer, 202
packet-ship **Caleb Grinshaw**, 31

Pacquette, 168
Paddock, 310, 390
Paddy, 45, 96, 117, 119, 145, 407
Paden, 336
Padgett, 69, 207
Padjet, 76
Paez, 307
Page, 12, 22, 47, 56, 104, 106, 146, 147, 163, 190, 213, 228, 237, 238, 244, 252, 272, 281, 285, 287, 312, 323, 348, 367, 369, 394, 396, 413, 414, 417, 435, 466, 469, 470
Paillet, 81
Paillett, 229
Paine, 107, 168, 187, 361, 369, 438
Pairo, 39, 125, 193, 200, 367, 370
Pakenham, 159
Palen, 216, 425
Palermo, 171
Palfrey, 303
Pallet, 378
Palmer, 27, 72, 107, 127, 149, 172, 198, 249, 252, 283, 292, 310, 314, 445
Panchard, 352
Pane, 58
Pannill, 26
Papendick, 164
Papin, 49
Pardonnes, 370
Paredes, 286
Parenstedt, 472
Paris, 470
Park, 117, 444
Park Hall, 403, 481
Parke, 104, 109, 112
Parker, 8, 22, 23, 70, 81, 86, 109, 110, 111, 112, 130, 147, 153, 171, 195, 197, 202, 203, 205, 210, 214, 220, 221, 256, 257, 263, 272, 284, 287, 293, 330, 344, 349, 351, 365, 366, 369, 386, 391, 404, 432, 437, 453, 469, 476, 491, 506
Parkers, 357
Parkeson, 200
Parkhurst, 488
Parkinson, 161

Parkman, 138, 279, 310
Parks, 142, 150, 157, 169, 183, 271, 460, 469, 494
Parmegiano, 156
Parmele, 393, 446
Parris, 97, 212, 365
Parrot, 27
Parrott, 64, 214, 238, 506
Parson, 13, 365
Parsons, 8, 33, 94, 111, 124, 133, 200, 289
Partridge, 261
Patch, 122
Patchell, 222
Patchin, 196, 330
Pate, 149
Paterson, 417
Patherson, 458
Patrick, 253, 326, 328, 353
Pattee, 294
Patten, 70, 477, 507
Patterson, 27, 41, 50, 72, 110, 112, 344, 375, 446, 464, 476
Patteson, 435
Pattison, 275
Patton, 278, 334, 506
Patty, 241
Paul, 67, 95, 134, 212
Paulding, 496
Paulina, 298
Paulson, 468
Pavenstadt, 119
Pavenstedt, 44, 117
Paxton, 367
Payne, 21, 143, 150, 162, 170, 215, 221, 275, 303, 475, 499
Payson, 49
Peabody, 194, 302
Peachy, 458
Peaco, 401
Peacock, 235
Peacocke, 380
Peak, 284
Peake, 207, 320, 365, 494
Peaks, 354
Peale, 73, 84, 213, 324

Pearce, 1, 44, 88, 98, 296, 301, 328, 471
Pearl, 225, 312
Pearle, 58, 411
Pearsall, 171
Pearse, 395
Pearson, 109, 112, 256, 264, 306, 369, 429, 466, 475, 488, 506
Pearson's mill, 230
Pearsons, 127
Pease, 204, 223, 467
Peay, 278
Peck, 104, 139, 292, 361, 506
Peddicord, 107
Peel, 104
Peerce, 111
Peete, 340
Pegg, 111, 211, 287, 371
Pegram, 198
Pell, 414, 443
Peltier, 66, 142
Pemberton, 284, 400, 482, 484
Pemerton, 235
Pena, 49, 59
Pence, 107
Pender, 198
Pendleton, 210, 276, 411
Penfield, 443
Penman, 204
Penn, 154, 302, 487, 499
Pennock, 56, 482, 506
Penny, 53, 210, 422
Pentz, 198
Peoples, 228
Pepper, 121, 128, 374, 395, 506
Perkins, 106, 109, 112, 175, 241, 320, 326, 338, 365, 367, 437, 474
Perpignon, 425
Perrie, 285
Perrin, 245, 342
Perrine, 26, 79, 346
Perrit, 288
Perry, 38, 63, 66, 109, 112, 118, 136, 176, 290, 324, 338, 397, 457, 481, 492
Persons, 271
Peter, 120, 219, 245, 506
Peternell, 94

560

Peters, 111, 179, 215, 268, 306, 368, 371, 389, 411, 417
Peterson, 20, 104, 130, 361, 411
Petit, 393, 495
Pettengill, 187
Pettibone, 9, 104, 110, 112, 181, 253, 300, 361, 365, 369
Petticord, 233
Pettigru, 499
Petting, 168
Pettingal, 15
Pettit, 9, 38, 218, 353, 365
Pettitt, 58
Pettus, 75, 155, 158
Petty, 176, 338
Peugh, 266
Peyton, 56, 85, 169, 198, 269, 306, 346
Phagan, 198
Pharoah, 403
Pharr, 222
Phelps, 53, 117, 125, 175, 192, 252, 305, 311, 318, 326, 467
Phenix, 198
Philharmonic Society, 295
Philibert, 308
Philippe, 356
Philips, 391, 496
Phillip, 14, 193
Phillipe, 383
Phillippi, 261
Phillips, 28, 85, 99, 109, 112, 121, 174, 198, 232, 241, 251, 253, 288, 332, 341, 348, 406, 463, 474, 506
Phoenix, 270
Piatt, 3, 383
Pickering, 97, 176
Picket, 495
Pickett, 94, 170, 273, 278, 309
Pickrell, 122, 134, 201, 255, 506
Piedmont Farm, 196
Pierce, 74, 81, 82, 85, 142, 202, 204, 226, 306, 325, 329, 385, 392, 463
Piercy, 75
Pierson, 181, 349, 492
Pigg, 402
Pigott, 419

Pike, 102, 227
Pilcher, 164
Piler, 204
Piles, 254, 455
Piling, 7
Pilling, 111, 367, 451
Pillings, 372
Pinckney, 401
Piney Point, 263, 292
Pinkerton, 95
Pinkey, 469
Pinkney, 217, 233, 313, 387
Pinnell, 28
Piper, 413
Piscataway Academy, 254
Pitcher, 85
Pitkins, 395
Pitman, 252
Pitts, 495
Pius IX, 420
Pix, 155
Pizarro, 233
Place, 336
Plant, 104, 193, 350, 365
Plater, 487
Platt, 122, 164, 397
Pleasant Hill, 457, 482
Pleasant Ridge, 185
Pleasanton, 325
Pleasants, 58, 104, 213
Pleasonton, 212
Plowden, 93
Plowman, 16, 267
Plumb, 310
Plumbe, 184, 489
Plumer, 35, 485
Plummer, 126, 222, 310, 456, 459
Plunkett, 69, 75, 155, 158, 179, 278
Plympton, 448
Poage, 59
Poe, 125, 237, 302, 303
Poindexter, 2, 146, 200, 256, 297, 428
Poisal, 131
Poletti, 365, 371
Polk, 2, 23, 99, 159, 212, 396
Polkinhorn, 325, 448

Polland, 31
Pollard, 296
Pollard Row, 406
Pollard's row, 186
Pollock, 406, 481, 506
Polock, 466
Pomeroy, 198, 221
Pomnietezritzky, 292
Pomonkey Farm, 93
Pond, 342, 393
Ponderock, 365
Ponts, 442
Pool, 19, 41, 163, 164, 445
Poole, 210
Poor, 74, 214, 240, 385, 457, 463
Pope, 53, 58, 74, 116, 117, 407, 417
Popham, 271
Porche, 304
Porter, 6, 12, 45, 48, 102, 134, 176, 183, 206, 231, 233, 262, 270, 294, 316, 331, 335, 344, 368, 378, 383, 417, 431, 446, 449, 465
Porterfield, 154, 246
Posey, 417
Post, 141
Post Ofcs, 15, 28, 40, 55, 67, 77, 88, 94, 117, 127, 132, 148, 160, 183, 216, 222, 235, 271, 278, 294, 304, 313, 318, 330, 336, 347, 352, 358, 379, 391, 402, 421, 430, 433, 437, 444, 449, 459, 467, 474, 493
Poston, 104, 267, 365
Potter, 150, 186, 214, 251, 348, 355, 417
Potts, 49, 217
Pouder, 110
Poulson, 405, 453
Poussieloue, 308
Powell, 5, 106, 109, 111, 160, 193, 199, 235, 241, 344, 352, 379, 380, 410, 435, 444, 455, 482, 487, 500
Power, 210
Power's statue, 298
Powers, 30, 242, 243, 292, 341, 361
Pragoff, 141
Prall, 58, 455

Prather, 16, 132, 136, 314, 361, 369, 370, 385, 411
Pratt, 73, 190, 215, 243, 403, 481, 506
Prentis, 45
Prentiss, 148, 163, 174, 290, 365
Prescott, 92
Presher, 465
Preston, 98, 109, 112, 120, 182, 229, 249, 286, 297, 306, 412
Prettymen, 131
Prevost, 261, 419
Prewett, 130, 181, 266
Prewitt, 266
Price, 23, 78, 102, 120, 123, 125, 145, 155, 233, 237, 481, 494
Prichard, 358
Prickett, 56, 227
Prine, 327
Pritchard, 26, 274
Pritchett, 159
Proctor, 205
propeller **Secretary Walker**, 171
Prospect Hill, 248, 472
Prosperi, 312
Prout, 365, 506
Provest, 420
Pruitt, 198
Pryor, 235
Puckner, 253
Pugsley, 493
Pulizzi, 104, 361
Pullin, 366
Pulte, 180
Pulvermaker, 110, 112
Pumphrey, 76, 102, 108, 111, 199, 361, 365, 368, 411, 479, 482
Punchard, 164
Purcell, 7, 39, 130, 143, 236
Purdy, 54, 110, 112, 141, 217, 343, 361, 369, 452, 464
Purkett, 198
Purnell, 146
Pursell, 104, 109, 112
Purviance, 99
Pusey, 148, 376
Putnam, 390, 394, 419

Pye, 333, 455
Pyle, 117
Pyne, 46, 152, 154, 162, 195, 247, 249, 287, 451, 487
Pyper, 317
Pywell, 106, 114, 369

Q

Quackenboss, 39, 84
Quail, 252
Quarles, 53
Queen, 222, 267, 303, 413
Queen of Portugal, 97
Quenandon, 73
Ques, 156
Quick, 15
Quigley, 112, 368, 412, 500
Quin, 469
Quincy, 349
Quinn, 31, 32, 217
Quinton, 202
Quitman, 273, 495

R

Rabbit, 165, 367, 370
Radcliff, 207, 266, 281, 310, 367, 456, 498
Radcliffe, 216
Rady, 275, 282, 361
Ragan, 321, 324, 361
Raggan, 417
Raggio, 417
Ragsdale, 16
Rahl, 419
Raiford, 394
Railey, 361, 365, 390
Rainey, 9, 15, 217, 401, 412
Rains, 269, 462
Rainy, 304
Ralls, 336
Ralph, 206
Ralston, 48, 49, 342, 486
Ramage, 286
Ramey, 28, 469
Ramsay, 133, 245, 302, 436
Ramsburg, 114

Ramsdell, 352
Ramsey, 27, 198, 310, 320, 390
Rand, 358
Randall, 106, 112, 121, 235, 252, 365, 390, 403, 424, 481, 506
Randolph, 152, 173, 174, 213, 287, 340, 341, 429, 441, 443, 476, 496
Randon, 151, 365
Randou, 240
Raney, 313, 422
Rankin, 18, 49, 77, 101, 390, 402
Ransom, 77, 327
Ranson, 196
Rappahannock Academy, 297
Rappetti, 365
Ratcliff, 124, 417
Ratcliffe, 233, 476, 486, 498
Ratliff, 15
Rattrie, 507
Raub, 203, 211, 242, 361, 365, 411, 417
Rawlings, 254, 361, 365, 372, 507
Rawson, 143
Ray, 104, 257, 323
Raybourn, 473
Raymond, 14, 30, 66, 125, 365
Rea, 67, 310, 468
Read, 2, 130, 169, 247, 254, 285, 316, 327, 328
Reader, 210
Ready, 112
Reardon, 41
Reaser, 498
Reaves, 176
Reber, 318
Reddall, 287
Redden, 506
Reddick, 96, 399
Redding, 271, 398
Redfern, 104, 361
Redin, 38, 147, 231, 395, 442, 458
Redman, 491
Redmond, 148
Redmun, 203
Redstrate, 112
Redstreak, 359
Redwin, 330

Reece, 217
Reed, 38, 50, 67, 99, 110, 112, 118, 122, 125, 141, 187, 191, 198, 210, 233, 256, 361, 365, 471, 499
Reeder, 22, 233, 351, 354, 356, 375
Reese, 45, 84, 85, 469
Reeside, 287, 298, 368, 412
Reeve, 182, 336, 367, 370
Reeves, 326, 412
Regan, 128
Reglin, 239
Regnault, 135
Reguena, 468
Rehren, 427
Reichenbach, 332
Reid, 21, 152, 174, 247, 365, 410, 498
Reider, 365
Reill, 136
Reilly, 85, 370
Reily, 371
Reinback, 253
Reitzell, 475
<u>Remains of the Pres</u>, 286
Remer, 447, 453
Remick, 340, 498
Remington, 1, 408
Remson, 455
Renick, 176
Renner, 377
Rennoe, 376, 382
Renny, 372
Renwick, 98, 213
Repass, 330
Ressequire, 195
Reswick, 101, 110
Revere, 343
Revolutionary Soldier's Lot, 185
Reynes, 181
Reynolds, 6, 195, 206, 421, 490
Reynoldson, 506
Rhea, 15
Rhett, 457
Rhind, 255
Rhinelander, 237
Rhoads, 28, 341

Rhodes, 37, 69, 104, 172, 235, 264, 313, 361
Ribber, 2
Riblet, 467
Ricar, 506
Ricard, 46, 411
Rice, 104, 112, 120, 123, 252, 282, 301, 311, 362, 370, 401, 417, 421, 422, 454
Rich, 78
Richards, 32, 69, 75, 150, 155, 158, 165, 179, 233, 271, 361, 365, 429, 444, 457
Richardson, 9, 41, 58, 107, 205, 215, 281, 296, 315, 330, 341, 359, 361, 365, 393
Richend, 464
Richmond, 242
Ricker, 104
Rickets, 330
Ricketts, 331, 365
Riddell, 289
Riddells, 245
Riddick, 65
Riddle, 429
Rider, 345
Ridgely, 7, 110, 214, 240, 269, 272, 450, 462
Ridgeway, 157, 240
Ridgway, 113, 222
Riell, 139
Rigdon, 110, 112, 372
Riggle, 123
Riggles, 368
Riggs, 74, 202, 348, 385, 411
Rignal, 143
Riley, 15, 24, 32, 69, 74, 102, 110, 112, 113, 126, 198, 322, 326, 361, 365, 370, 372, 382, 411, 431, 476
Rillman, 58
Rind, 9, 65
Ring, 65
Ringgold, 195, 201, 354, 373, 499
Ringo, 245, 343
Riopel, 477
Riordan, 104, 436
Riorden, 486
Ripley, 13, 242, 257, 299

Risdon, 252
Risin, 361
Rising, 100, 233
Rissity, 32
Ritchey, 494
Ritchie, 55, 198, 308, 351, 375
Ritter, 102, 110, 112, 118, 371
Rives, 134
Roach, 45, 73, 130, 231, 236, 250, 281, 288, 302, 321, 356, 365, 396, 447, 451, 452, 460, 463
Roan, 225
Robards, 158
Robb, 58, 213, 371, 380
Robbins, 9, 506
Roberson, 474
Roberts, 14, 39, 41, 65, 75, 104, 112, 117, 155, 186, 217, 220, 221, 269, 276, 341, 347, 401, 403, 454, 481, 507
Robertson, 13, 19, 49, 58, 85, 87, 145, 154, 170, 198, 216, 228, 254, 259, 262, 267, 279, 325, 337, 342, 374, 378, 493
Robeson, 149
Robey, 371
Robinson, 24, 31, 58, 66, 76, 82, 91, 110, 115, 118, 119, 130, 131, 157, 202, 210, 233, 250, 252, 267, 284, 302, 310, 342, 354, 362, 365, 370, 371, 399, 400, 413, 417, 450, 468, 469, 486, 492
Robison, 163
Roby, 260, 417
Rock Creek Church, 124
Rockefeller, 222
Rockett, 16
Rockwell, 41, 131, 148, 213, 268, 354, 381
Rodgers, 32, 67, 91, 131, 152, 154, 237, 244, 298, 401, 404
Rodier, 58, 308, 340
Rodman, 35, 55, 237, 375, 421
Rodney, 355
Roe Down, 199
Roemmly, 112
Roenne, 86

Roger, 36, 128
Rogers, 14, 30, 33, 34, 36, 37, 48, 68, 75, 80, 85, 164, 170, 176, 183, 198, 251, 272, 301, 311, 314, 336, 352, 389, 421, 436, 444, 477, 507
Roland, 302
Rolando, 404
Rollins, 77, 110, 112, 186, 368, 436
Rolls, 19, 254
Romero, 468
Ron, 164
Rone, 365
Roney, 217
Rood, 187
Rooker, 361
Root, 173, 235, 242, 344
Ropelle, 249
Roper, 121, 169
Ropes, 393
Rorer, 206
Rosa du Tivoli, 156
Rose, 42, 61, 190, 378, 412, 465, 488
Rosebury, 125
Rosedale, 88
Rosenbaum, 216
Rosendale, 498
Rosenstock, 107, 506
Rosevelt, 394
Rosher, 233
Roshier, 271
Rosier, 233, 417
Ross, 1, 12, 47, 63, 77, 106, 148, 177, 184, 223, 233, 265, 282, 290, 318, 338, 354, 365, 393, 399, 401, 406, 431, 454, 471, 495
Rosser, 433
Rosset, 11
Rosston, 370
Roszel, 131
Roszell, 49, 466, 478
Rotch, 25, 192
Roth, 104, 367
Rotham, 384
Rothwell, 33, 166, 501
Round, 305
Rous, 365

Rouse, 73, 150, 301
Rouse's Point, 216
Rouseau, 446
Roush, 474
Routzahn, 239
Roux, 370
Rowan, 58, 255, 469, 471
Rowe, 31, 299
Rowell, 252
Rowland, 115, 222, 432, 438, 449
Rowles, 291
Roy, 146, 483
Roys, 338, 400
Royston, 417
Ruark, 294
Rucker, 477
Rudd, 207
Ruff, 107, 365, 366
Rugby Academy, 332
Ruger, 199
Ruggles, 33
Rumsey, 2
Rundle, 402
Runkle, 261
Runner, 219, 220
Rupell, 85
Rupp, 104, 113
Ruppell, 112, 115
Rupple, 413
Rural Hill, 188
Rush, 100, 134, 192, 198, 404, 453
Rusk, 301
Russel, 146
Russell, 24, 55, 70, 117, 177, 197, 233, 235, 295, 326, 329, 341, 379, 393, 394, 400, 418, 449
Russworm, 13
Russworn, 478
Rust, 146, 177
Rusti, 482
Rustic, 56
Rutherford, 380
Rutledge, 295, 323
Rutter, 104, 404, 411
Ryan, 226, 425, 496
Rydal Mount, 205, 207

Ryden, 29
Ryder, 102, 193, 227, 436
Rye, 403
Ryer, 327, 484
Ryerson, 314
Ryland, 131, 132
Rynders, 36
Rynex, 420
Ryon, 112, 366
Rythers, 113

S

S sloop-of-war **St Mary's**, 426
Sacket, 389
Saeville, 233
Saffell, 423
Saffler, 361
Sage, 255
Sager, 344
Sagethy, 51
Sain, 308
Salles, 496
Salmens, 278
Salmon, 49, 175
Salomon, 72
Salsbury, 361
Saltmarsh, 436
Saltonstall, 233
Salubria, 274
Salvage, 318
Sam, 470
Sampson, 217, 278, 361
Samson, 7, 78, 79, 126, 136, 139, 162, 174, 202, 311, 373, 381
Samuel, 118
Samuels, 471
Sanborn, 15
Sanchez, 387
Sanders, 85, 107, 202, 226, 354, 399, 402, 421
Sanderson, 105, 367
Sandford, 134, 481
Sands, 153, 323
Sandwich Islands, 121
Sanford, 70
Sanger, 73, 454

Santer, 370
Santmeyer, 413
Sappington, 278
Sargent, 213, 328
Sarti, 386
Sartori, 140
Sasscer, 288, 303, 333
Sasserne, 355
Saubnier, 256
Sauer, 432
Saunders, 11, 39, 69, 105, 125, 135, 144, 164, 167, 222, 233, 323, 361, 397, 430, 436, 476
Saur, 104, 307
Sausser, 58
Sauter, 411
Savage, 5, 110, 143, 391, 405, 488
Savell, 347
Savery, 341
Sawtelle, 198
Sawyer, 233, 304, 437, 478
Saxon, 230
Saxton, 169, 400
Sayers, 443
Saylor, 223
Sayre, 132, 205
Sayres, 149
Sayward, 3
Scaggs, 351, 402
Scarborough, 94
Scarlett, 443
Schad, 412
Schadd, 368, 372
Schank, 210
Scharr, 310
Schatzell, 273
Schaub, 129
Schenck, 303, 425, 499
Schenig, 210
Schermerhorn, 383
Schley, 255, 268
Schliecker, 14
Schmaling, 193
Schneider, 72
schnr **Abel**, 117
schnr **Arete Ellis**, 458
schnr **Bravo**, 131
schnr **Carnelion**, 71
schnr **Caroline A Cook**, 441
schnr **Champion**, 40, 257, 259, 473
schnr **Consolation**, 63
schnr **Dream**, 140
schnr **Elmira**, 190
schnr **Essex**, 259
schnr **Eufaula**, 39
schnr **Falcon**, 388
schnr **Fanny**, 458
schnr **Gardiner**, 50
schnr **Hannah Elizabeth**, 131
schnr **Julius Caesar**, 46, 137, 259
schnr **Marcia M Briggs**, 353
schnr **Mary Elizabeth**, 30
schnr **Orient**, 101, 123
schnr **Rachel Jane**, 457
schnr **Rebecca Eliza**, 90
schnr **Robert Rennie**, 14
schnr **Savannah**, 51
schnr **St Croix**, 138
schnr **Susannah**, 447, 460, 466
schnr **Taney**, 153
schnr **Tippecanoe**, 144
schnr **William**, 7, 51
schnr **William A Turner**, 7
Schock, 148, 496
Schofield, 92
Scholfield, 465
Schoolcraft, 81, 84, 324
Schott, 8, 12
Schreck, 222
Schreiner, 343
Schrieber, 377
Schriver, 150
Schroeder, 77
Schucking, 319
Schultz, 27, 421
Schumacher, 96, 117, 119, 472
Schumacker, 44
Schurmann, 164
Schusler, 502
Schuyler, 3, 94
Schwartz, 110, 412
Schwartze, 365

Schwartzkopt, 439
Schwarzman, 36, 179
Schwearing, 413
Schwenck, 41
Schwitzer, 105
Schwrar, 152
Scoffin, 409
Scofield, 15, 41
Scott, 28, 34, 36, 61, 68, 94, 97, 105,
    113, 123, 129, 134, 139, 141, 153,
    163, 164, 171, 198, 203, 205, 206,
    213, 235, 246, 271, 298, 300, 315,
    333, 344, 358, 361, 365, 370, 371,
    376, 381, 386, 396, 412, 439, 445,
    462, 463, 473, 483, 484, 507
Scribner, 435
Scrivener, 181, 477
Scudder, 50
Seaman, 212
Searing, 38
Searle, 275, 328, 345, 381, 395, 484
Sears, 109
Seaton, 375, 476
Seaver, 99
Seawell, 153
Sebastine, 113
Secor, 141, 246, 383
Sedwick, 151
Seeley, 19
Seely, 26, 116, 200, 410, 430
Seewald, 313
Seider, 77
Seifferle, 105, 110
Seigle, 30
Seitz, 367, 371, 372
Selby, 9, 361, 464
Selden, 56, 115, 213, 227, 373, 433, 507
Seldner, 104, 107
Selfridge, 3, 75, 155
Sellhausen, 110
Seman, 365
Semmes, 29, 104, 105, 111, 112, 165,
    259, 268, 303, 366, 370, 371, 425,
    436, 437
Semoice, 143
Sems, 98

Sengstack, 24, 105, 107, 112, 213, 500
Sennot, 367
Senseney, 99
Sentis, 507
Sentrell, 313
Sertwell, 141
Servant, 25
Servin, 291
Sessford, 182, 346
Session, 295
Seuzeneau, 258, 273
Severance, 243
Sevier, 252
Sewall, 105, 134, 283, 361, 376, 448
Sewell, 177, 415
Sexton, 252
Seybolt, 86
Seymour, 4, 193, 310, 311, 348, 365,
    396, 476, 479, 507
Seymourn, 475
Shackelford, 223, 302
Shackleford, 229, 244, 396
Shad, 365
Shadd, 110, 112, 113, 114, 282, 368, 372
Shade, 30
Shaefer, 164
Shafer, 84, 301
Shaffer, 110, 314
Shaine, 411
Shaler, 49, 87
Shallcross, 297
Shanklin, 500
Shanks, 81, 102, 107, 110, 256, 413, 451
Shannon, 106
Shannondale Springs, 211
Share, 26
Sharkey, 146
Sharp, 301
Sharp's Patent Rifle, 301
Sharpe, 241
Sharpless, 403
Sharrell, 361
Shatts, 382
Shaw, 6, 8, 14, 18, 65, 105, 113, 273,
    283, 323, 340, 445
Sheafe, 33

Sheahan, 197, 208, 222, 250
Shearman, 384
Sheckles, 316
Shedd, 105, 370
Sheekels, 233
Sheele, 225
Sheen, 1
Sheets, 106
Sheffield, 343
Sheid, 107
Shekell, 405
Shekells, 112
Shekles, 507
Shelby, 170
Shellady, 187
Shelter, 231
Shelton, 330
Shepard, 459
Sheperd, 12
Shepherd, 169, 347, 446, 467, 507
Shepley, 11
Sheppard, 456
Shepperd, 198
Sheridan, 210
Sheriff, 138
Sherman, 59, 167, 193, 196, 198, 295, 340, 400
Sherrard, 204
Sherrer, 310
Sherrick, 219, 220
Sherwood, 58, 315, 367
Sherwood Forest, 293
Shields, 104, 384, 415
Shiles, 293
Shillington, 110, 463
Shinault, 198
Shine, 507
Shinn, 54
ship **Albany**, 152
ship **Alleghany**, 315
ship **Atlantic**, 246
ship **Brandywine**, 227
ship **Caleb Grimshaw**, 10, 44, 135, 168, 260
ship **Caledonia**, 63
ship **Canada**, 381

ship **Catharine**, 26
ship **Chandler Price**, 142
ship **Columbia**, 142
ship **Crescent City**, 421
ship **Dale**, 453, 456
ship **Devonshire**, 468
ship **Dolphin**, 413
ship **Elizabeth**, 298, 308, 319
ship **Erie**, 50
ship **Essex**, 18
ship **Henry Thompson**, 18, 48
ship **James Mitchell**, 5, 87, 180
ship **John**, 2
ship **John Adams**, 153, 265, 410
ship **Kate Hunter**, 462
ship **Lexington**, 226, 490
ship **Maria Christina**, 196
ship **Marion**, 227, 413, 482
ship **Massachusetts**, 255
ship **Meteor**, 82
ship **Monterey**, 50
ship **Moses Wheeler**, 478
ship of the line **Ohio**, 174
ship **Ohio**, 167, 189, 216, 490
ship **Pennsylvania**, 246
ship **Portsmouth**, 153
ship **Sarah**, 30, 135
ship **St Lawrence**, 13
ship **St Mary's**, 69, 255, 323
ship **Supply**, 249
ship **Tartar**, 136
ship **Yarmouth**, 10
ship **Yorkshire**, 237
Shipley, 20, 195, 218, 257, 361
ship-of-the-line **Ohio**, 187
ship-of-war **Yorktown**, 453
Shipp, 26
Shippen, 56, 482
Shiras, 297, 400, 482
Shirley, 439, 443, 444
Shirtleff, 331
Shively, 21
Shoemaker, 84, 155, 158, 183, 200, 417, 461
Short, 359
Shorter, 105, 106, 507

Shortt, 460
Shotherd, 100
Shover, 373, 399, 400
Shreeve, 53, 460
Shreeves, 287
Shreve, 105, 107, 108, 151, 163, 367, 441, 492
Shreves, 81, 193
Shriver, 218
Shrum, 143
Shubrick, 275, 386
Shull, 118
Shultz, 166
Shumway, 55
Shuster, 110, 221, 277, 410
Shuter, 216
Shutter, 304
Sibbald, 60, 137, 272, 275, 350
Sibley, 98, 225, 233, 361, 367, 370, 391
Siddall, 183
Sidney, 265, 290
Sigler, 394, 449
Sigur, 273, 495
Sill, 341
Silliman, 56, 341
Silsbee, 317
Silvey, 329
Simkins, 5
Simmes, 112, 361, 365
Simmons, 28, 29, 58, 123, 193, 203, 255, 294, 327, 361, 370, 379, 411, 413, 447, 493, 507
Simms, 27, 58, 73, 79, 105, 112, 115, 265, 267, 275, 361, 365, 411, 412, 413, 415, 507
Simon, 332
Simonda, 507
Simons, 202
Simonton, 17, 76, 140, 254, 280, 289
Simpers, 356
Simpkins, 2, 19
Simpson, 7, 11, 40, 49, 80, 100, 206, 225, 237, 259, 278, 318, 365, 385, 391, 450, 459, 479
Simpton, 298
Sims, 17, 121, 372, 413

Sinclair, 213, 287
Sing Sing Prison, 477
Sinon, 181, 365, 412
Sinsheimer, 107
Sioussa, 105
Sirani, 156
Sis, 107
Sisters of Charity, 7
Sizer, 141
Skeel, 222
Skidmore, 107, 386, 398, 408
Skiff, 15
Skinker, 473
Skinner, 29, 162, 228, 268, 274, 399
Skipwith, 95, 136
Skipworth, 154
Skirving, 228, 345, 413
Skriving, 110
Skyrin, 42
Slacum, 13, 81, 140
Slade, 27, 313, 370
Slater, 481
Slatery, 357
Slattery, 49, 72, 205, 383
Slaughter, 253, 394
slave trade, 384
Slaven, 434
Slavin, 66, 125
Slayback, 494
Slaymaker, 140
Sleight, 73
Slemmer, 319, 328
Slemons, 269, 355
Slicer, 22, 45, 142, 292, 298
Slight, 105
Slingerland, 202, 311
Sloan, 74
Sloat, 92
Slocum, 65, 91, 155, 183, 489
sloop of war **Albany**, 174
sloop of war **Marion**, 56
sloop of war **Saratoga**, 376
sloop of war **Washington**, 30
sloop **Washington**, 477
sloop-of-war **Epervier**, 83
sloop-of-war **Germantown**, 486

570

sloop-of-war **St Louis**, 152
sloop-of-war **Yorktown**, 456
Sloss, 278
Slosson, 341
Small, 64, 141, 241, 346, 445, 477
Smalley, 198
Smallwood, 4, 106, 165, 361, 365, 366, 394, 507
Smead, 123, 198, 199
Smiley, 375, 397
Smith, 1, 5, 9, 13, 18, 19, 23, 27, 32, 34, 36, 38, 42, 52, 53, 55, 56, 58, 65, 71, 75, 78, 80, 86, 88, 90, 92, 96, 102, 105, 106, 108, 109, 112, 115, 117, 118, 119, 120, 124, 128, 130, 131, 132, 139, 140, 142, 143, 144, 147, 155, 156, 157, 160, 161, 162, 163, 178, 184, 185, 187, 188, 199, 201, 202, 210, 211, 212, 218, 219, 220, 221, 222, 225, 227, 231, 233, 234, 235, 237, 239, 242, 245, 246, 249, 253, 257, 258, 261, 264, 273, 274, 276, 288, 293, 294, 299, 305, 307, 308, 309, 310, 311, 313, 314, 316, 318, 322, 332, 333, 336, 338, 340, 341, 342, 344, 345, 355, 356, 361, 365, 367, 368, 369, 371, 372, 376, 381, 388, 390, 396, 397, 398, 399, 401, 403, 404, 414, 417, 418, 433, 441, 443, 446, 447, 450, 451, 454, 457, 459, 461, 462, 466, 468, 469, 471, 473, 475, 476, 480, 485, 487, 488, 492, 495, 502, 507
Smith's Row, 425
Smithia, 108, 324
Smithson, 106
Smoot, 89, 142, 201, 259, 303, 361, 365, 371, 419, 464
Smull, 300, 382
Smyly, 195
Sneden, 23
Snider, 25, 119, 249, 279, 336, 352
Sniffin, 331
Snodgrass, 22, 28, 208
Snow, 13, 118, 176, 397
Snow Hill, 259

Snowden, 196, 507
Snyder, 126, 151, 208, 278, 320, 379, 432
Solomon, 296, 319
Somby, 365
Somers, 19
Somerville, 233, 280, 308, 361
Sommers, 76
Sontag, 48
Sothern, 112
Sothoron, 256, 277
Southall, 124
Southard, 396
Southerland, 253, 374
<u>Southern Press</u>, 255
Southey, 207
Southmayde, 26
Spalding, 49, 65, 70, 86, 119, 233, 252, 253, 302, 318, 374, 425, 487
Spall, 150
Sparkman, 128, 130
Sparks, 86, 125
Sparrow, 9
Spaulding, 29, 88, 136, 268, 394
Speake, 174
Speaks, 365
Spear, 144
Spears, 279
Specht, 148
Speed, 146, 187
Speiden, 24, 182, 296, 371
Spelman, 32
Spencer, 12, 74, 76, 210, 308, 390, 414
Sperry, 15, 136
Spicer, 69, 365
Spignall, 105, 107
Spirling, 203
<u>spitting in churches</u>, 36
Splane, 199
Sprague, 310, 405
Sprigg, 105, 196, 291, 414
Spring Hill, 438
Springman, 365, 367
Springsteen, 358
Sproston, 468
Sprowl, 294

571

Squier, 134
Sr Mary Loyola, 351
Sriver, 380
St Clair, 113, 507
St George's island, 21
St Patrick's burial yard, 245
Stabler, 324, 420, 446
Stackpole, 226
Stadt, 96
Staffan, 107
Stafford, 66, 130, 301
Staley, 261
Stalker, 280, 375, 465
Stall, 469
Stamp, 390
Stamps, 179
Stan, 102
Standiford, 340
Stang, 383
Stanley, 130, 144, 175
Stansbury, 69, 102, 385
Stanton, 134, 155, 496
Staplefoot, 241
Staples, 16, 63, 75, 155, 162, 354
Stapleton, 127
Stapp, 343, 475
Starbuck, 277, 417
Stark, 139, 208, 274, 419
Starks, 49
steamboat **Anglo-Norman**, 492
steamboat **Antoinette Douglass**, 464
steamboat **Arkansas No 5**, 464
Steamboat Hotel, 433
steamboat **James Adams**, 465
steamboat **Phenix**, 54
steamboat **Telegraph**, 440
Steamboat Wharf, 280
steamer **Admiral**, 197
steamer **Alleghany**, 124
steamer **Anglo Norman**, 481
steamer **Anthony Wayne**, 190
steamer **Atlantic**, 305
steamer **Baltimore**, 263
steamer **Bay State**, 264
steamer **Bellona**, alias **Hidalgo**, 63
steamer **Cincinnati**, 126

steamer **City of Toronto**, 427
steamer **Columbia**, 323
steamer **Columbus**, 462
steamer **Crescent City**, 243
steamer **Dove**, 135
steamer **Empire State**, 357
steamer **Europe**, 427
steamer **Fashion**, 444
steamer **Gipsey**, 462
steamer **Griffith**, 260, 264
steamer **H S Smith**, 152
steamer **Henlopen**, 384
steamer **Hermann**, 159
steamer **Hope**, 23
steamer **Jefferson**, 221, 323, 349
steamer **Kate Fleming**, 407
steamer **Louisiana**, 23
steamer **Marshall Ney**, 102
steamer **Missouri**, 249
steamer **North River**, 59
steamer **Princeton**, 5, 14
steamer **Robert Collins**, 79
steamer **Saranac**, 401
steamer **Senator**, 382
steamer **South America**, 498
steamer **St John's**, 120
steamer **Tobaga**, 499
steamer **Troy**, 141, 167
steamer **United States**, 18
steamer **Virginia**, 356
steamer **Walker**, 353
steamer **Wayne**, 197
steamer **Wilson G Hunt**, 150
steamer **Yuba**, 423
steamship **Baltic**, 101
steamship **Constitution**, 257
steamship **Helena Sloman**, 468
steamship **Ohio**, 499
steamship **Republic**, 424
steamship **Southerner**, 404
steamship **United States**, 48
Stedham, 54
Stedman, 278
Steele, 63, 94, 193, 235, 269, 376, 475
Steen, 75, 208, 308
Steenrod, 75, 155

Steer, 110
Steiger, 105, 396, 439
Stella, 156
Stem, 436
Stendabecker, 314
Stengere, 222
Stephen, 295
Stephens, 120, 122, 507
Stephenson, 347, 398
Stepney, 58
Stepper, 365, 370
Steptoe, 238, 269
Sterling, 313
Sterman, 344
Sterret, 378
Sterrett, 75, 275, 298, 465
Stetson, 42
Stettinius, 408, 414
Stevens, 107, 110, 137, 143, 197, 205, 323, 330, 331, 399, 401, 436, 438, 451
Stevenson, 23, 89, 192, 258, 324, 343, 361, 366, 370, 385, 453
Stevinson, 273
Steward, 97, 198, 202
Stewart, 3, 19, 22, 34, 54, 67, 76, 77, 110, 112, 114, 124, 135, 182, 184, 195, 210, 223, 234, 300, 310, 321, 322, 333, 361, 365, 371, 373, 378, 395, 412, 413, 416, 417, 419, 423, 441, 460, 496, 499, 507
Stickney, 340
Stiens, 28
Stiles, 41, 330
Stille, 391
Stillman, 481, 492
Stillson, 494
Stillwell, 87, 226
Stilwell, 49, 164, 422
Stimson, 98
Stipes, 280
Stith, 174, 328
Stock, 365
Stockdale, 46
Stocken, 482
Stocker, 376
Stocking, 56

Stockman, 456
Stockton, 13, 87, 98, 162, 310, 326, 329
Stoddard, 321, 367, 468
Stoeckl, 308
Stokely, 223
Stokes, 26, 163, 233, 240, 271, 396, 407, 433
Stone, 15, 47, 65, 96, 137, 141, 146, 202, 206, 333, 336, 361, 362, 370, 411, 419, 424, 448, 467, 489
Stoneall, 237
Stonestreet, 247, 280, 411
Stoodley, 235
Stoops, 62, 110, 112, 302, 355
Stophlet, 396
Storer, 5, 95, 468
Stores, 144
storeship **Relief**, 159
storeship **Supply**, 250
Storey, 346
Storm, 73, 112, 166, 267, 481, 492
Story, 6, 65
Stott, 10, 110, 361, 444, 507
Stowe, 245
Stowell, 392
Strain, 404
Straine, 41
Strang, 251
Stratton, 237
Straub, 370
Straum, 480
Street, 421
Stribling, 187, 245
Strickland, 183
Stroble, 130
Strong, 156, 250, 354, 496
Strother, 273, 338, 441, 479
Stryker, 393
Strykins, 25
Stuart, 9, 141, 155, 156, 158, 161, 193, 198, 261, 325, 357, 374, 390, 396, 404, 453, 476
Stubb, 379
Stubbs, 462
Stuckle, 355
Studds, 107

Stull, 452
Stultz, 115
Stunt, 107
Sturgeon, 5, 61
Sturgis, 37, 49, 60, 74, 215, 273, 293
Stutz, 104, 112, 113, 173, 365, 372
Sugar Land Farm, 215
Suissman, 99
Suit, 99
Suite, 77
Sulano, 74
Sulger, 331
Sullivan, 49, 177, 198, 210, 238, 287, 319, 343, 374, 412, 417, 419, 438, 495
Summer, 15
Summers, 241
Summerville, 317
Sumner, 241
Sumter, 65, 96, 139
Suter, 159, 357
Sutherland, 38, 272, 284, 295, 306, 371
Sutler, 50
Sutter, 324
Sutton, 51, 53, 96, 105, 106, 117, 119, 122, 226, 396, 401, 454
Swafford, 127
Swagert, 40, 53, 70
Swaggard, 121
Swaggart, 73
Swaggert, 17, 27, 82
Swain, 45, 407
Swan, 313, 317
Swann, 54, 120, 190, 205, 244, 265, 303, 480
Swartwout, 39, 52
Swartz, 371
Swearing, 112
Swearingen, 86
Swearinger, 314
Sweat, 261
Sweeney, 288
Sweeny, 90, 105, 259, 432, 476, 507
Sweet, 507
Sweeting, 113, 365
Sweitzer, 463
Sweringen, 470

Swift, 20, 24, 242, 465
Swigart, 370
Swinners, 379
Swisshelm, 181
Switzler, 467
Sykes, 15, 198
Sylvester, 213, 415
Symington, 146

T

Tabb, 146
Tabbs, 21, 27
Taber, 252
Tackett, 297
Taft, 127, 167, 278
Taggart, 18, 105, 449
Tait, 266
Talbot, 112, 365, 366
Talburt, 411
Talburtt, 273
Talcott, 133, 168, 336, 464
Talfair, 301
Talleson, 60
Talley, 365
Tallmadge, 217
Talmage, 136
Talman, 92
Talty, 114
Tanner, 105
Tarbox, 96, 189
Tarle'n, 419
Tarlton, 105, 402
Tarn, 86, 310
Tasker, 411
Tastet, 64, 102, 205, 418, 438
Tastett, 105
Tate, 78, 110, 323, 392, 445
Tatham, 98, 142
Tatnall, 120, 217, 401
Tattnal, 301
Tattnall, 217, 469
Tatum, 428
Taukwang, 214
Taverring, 115
Tayloe, 129, 507

Taylor, 8, 9, 11, 13, 17, 28, 38, 43, 51, 53, 58, 59, 67, 73, 81, 82, 95, 97, 100, 101, 105, 110, 112, 118, 121, 125, 126, 129, 133, 140, 141, 146, 147, 153, 154, 162, 164, 165, 168, 172, 186, 188, 192, 193, 194, 197, 199, 201, 204, 205, 210, 224, 230, 233, 235, 237, 246, 249, 251, 252, 261, 264, 272, 274, 284, 285, 286, 287, 288, 289, 293, 299, 300, 303, 305, 310, 314, 324, 334, 361, 371, 373, 390, 391, 396, 401, 404, 420, 425, 434, 436, 438, 442, 453, 459, 473, 474, 477, 485, 488, 492, 507
Taylor Furnace, 204
Tayloy, 118
Tebbs, 487
Tee, 73
Tehan, 277, 280, 282
Temple, 78, 419, 420
Templeman, 185, 276
Ten Broeck, 147
Ten Brook, 318
Ten Eyck, 74, 198
Tenant, 438
Tench, 105, 112, 287, 366, 447
Tenney, 34, 53, 99, 136, 225, 418
Tenny, 118, 293
Terceiro, 308
Terrell, 261
Terrill, 371
Tettermay, 30
Tevis, 328
Thacker, 11
Tharp, 70
Thaxter, 340, 389
Thayer, 302, 492
The Refuge, 334
the Village, 476
Thistle, 459
Thocmorton, 58
Thom, 195
Thoma, 368
Thomas, 17, 48, 74, 96, 105, 112, 114, 130, 149, 168, 176, 196, 198, 202, 206, 237, 248, 265, 272, 282, 288, 318, 324, 325, 336, 354, 361, 365, 366, 367, 370, 371, 382, 401, 411, 437, 438, 444, 467, 468, 479, 507
Thomasson, 467
Thompson, 8, 10, 45, 50, 58, 62, 63, 78, 81, 88, 96, 107, 110, 112, 113, 127, 148, 157, 161, 162, 163, 176, 179, 181, 184, 189, 199, 206, 210, 212, 214, 224, 233, 235, 238, 265, 293, 298, 306, 309, 313, 322, 332, 333, 340, 345, 349, 352, 361, 365, 366, 368, 371, 377, 384, 391, 393, 394, 413, 416, 417, 436, 439, 447, 451, 452, 454, 461, 474, 481, 492, 507
Thoms, 340, 370
Thomson, 204, 276, 367
Thorn, 110, 273, 367, 370, 453
Thornley, 99, 112, 476
Thornton, 97, 210, 216, 233, 296, 306, 417
Thorp, 327
Thorpe, 459, 483
Threft, 351
Thrift, 233, 353
Throckmorton, 136, 206, 417
Thruston, 7, 125, 207, 394, 424, 447
Thumb, 405
Thuson, 451
Thwing, 49
Thyson, 103, 110, 359, 369
Tibbats, 442
Tibbett, 358
Tibbitts, 411
Tibbs, 87
Tidball, 125, 327, 418
Tiernan, 443
Tiffany, 459
Tilghman, 119, 302, 365, 366, 507
Tilley, 41, 223, 331
Tillinghast, 134, 151, 229, 291, 455
Tillman, 174
Tilman, 444
Tilton, 245
Timberlake, 493
Tims, 323, 324, 421
Tindale, 67

Tingley, 272
Tinney, 105, 370
Tinsley, 189, 445
Tirado, 308
Tittermary, 30
Tobey, 261
Tobin, 438
Toby, 133
Tochman, 43, 52, 191
Todd, 85, 107, 125, 166, 341, 344, 402, 419, 475
Toder, 486
Todschinder, 370
Todschnider, 105
Todshinder, 115
Toley, 291
Tolman, 235
Tomlinson, 309
Tompkins, 90, 370
Tomtillott, 175
Tonge, 300
Tonnele, 496
Tool, 34, 315
Toomy, 498
Tooney, 31
Topham, 114, 366
Tophman, 365
Topping, 12, 298
Torlonia, 335, 456
Torre, 3
Torrence, 146
Torrey, 131
Totchinder, 321
Totchnider, 112
Tottchender, 81
Tottchinder, 73, 135, 300, 427
Totten, 159, 201, 237, 431, 464
Touey, 330
Toughey, 507
Touhy, 321
Tourtelotte, 132
Tousey, 304
Tower, 41, 218
Towers, 288, 291
Towle, 413, 432
Towles, 35, 469, 480

Townsend, 347, 474
Tracey, 383
Tracy, 17, 285
Traham, 132
Trainer, 31
Trainor, 190
Trantham, 177
Trapnell, 373
Trapp, 84
Travers, 110, 112, 187, 361, 365, 507
Treadwell, 198
Treakle, 76
Tredwell, 233
Tree, 78, 289
Trenchard, 22
Trepagnier, 33
Trevit, 252
Trigg, 248, 389
Trimble, 112
Trinnel, 168
Triplet, 417
Triplett, 107, 233
Tromma, 384
Trook, 97
Trosklamski, 73
Troth, 449
Trousdale, 2, 244
Trowbridge, 21
Troxel, 42
Troxil, 252
True, 361
True, Miss, 210
Trug, 378
Trumbull, 295
Trummer, 366
Trunnel, 168, 368
Trunnell, 233
Truxtun, 344
Tschiffely, 200, 366
Tsing, 214
Tuck, 202, 297, 439
Tucker, 48, 54, 77, 109, 110, 128, 135, 198, 207, 252, 259, 265, 269, 287, 289, 292, 320, 335, 338, 345, 365, 371, 391, 407, 412, 462, 507
Tuggle, 445

Tuner, 384
Tunstall, 342, 426
Tuomey, 307, 412
Turner, 28, 51, 58, 61, 63, 80, 92, 106, 113, 116, 131, 149, 175, 176, 181, 182, 223, 237, 252, 280, 289, 298, 303, 317, 340, 349, 354, 365, 366, 373, 431, 438, 494
Turnley, 483, 484
Turpin, 105, 365, 367
Turt, 149
Turton, 72
Tuston, 366
Tuttle, 464
Tuxton, 361
Tweedy, 102, 115, 395
Twichell, 187
Twiford, 477
Twiggs, 51, 65, 173, 269, 335
Twine, 105, 106
twin-sisters, 192
Twomey, 403
Tyler, 191, 233, 245, 261, 293, 298, 361, 380, 417, 487
Tynes, 186
Tyree, 296
Tyrell, 241
Tyson, 19, 110, 345

U

Udall, 48, 273
Uhlorn, 450
Ulzley, 150
Umphrey, 372
Umstead, 283
Underwood, 56, 145, 170, 201, 233, 251, 268, 350, 354, 376, 381, 476
Union Row, 59, 280
Updegraff, 393
Upp, 295
Upperman, 112, 426
Upshur, 245
Upton, 203, 421
Usher, 112, 361, 412, 479

V

Vail, 175, 496
Valentine, 23, 106, 221, 495
Vallandingham, 279
Valle, 84, 225
Vallego, 177
Vallejo, 459
Van Alen, 323
Van Auken, 479
Van Benthuysen, 87
Van Bokkelen, 327
Van Brunt, 14, 39, 121
Van Campen, 3
Van Doren, 460
Van Duzen, 310
Van Dyke, 72, 91
Van Horsigh, 438
Van Ingen, 301
Van Kloeck, 195
Van Ness, 11, 39, 176, 208, 409, 507, 508
Van Patten, 179
Van Patton, 415
Van Rensselaer, 9, 13, 23, 30, 143, 404
Van Renwick, 370
Van Reswick, 115
Van Riswick, 285
Van Stavoren, 256, 270
Van Valdenburg, 14
Van Valkenbrugh, 45
Van Valkenburgh, 19
Van Vleit, 330
Van Vorbes, 344
Van Winkle, 20, 138
Vanarsdale, 460
Vance, 261, 417
Vancoble, 398
Vanderford, 242
Vanderhorst, 226, 231
Vandervoort, 29
Vanderwerken, 298, 368, 412
Vandevort, 278
Vandyke, 45
Vangevar, 14
Vanhooser, 311
Vanmeter, 78

Vann, 223, 354
Vanness, 274
Vannuxen, 11
Vansant, 110, 178
Vanuxen, 19, 20
Varden, 113, 384
Varn, 379
Varus, 475
Vasques, 331
Vasquez, 189
Vasse, 11
Vaudricourt, 304, 366
Vaughan, 119, 120, 162, 205, 234, 249
Vawters, 12, 44
Veasy, 148
Veich, 421
Veirs, 431
Venable, 110, 414, 468
Verbeyest, 16
Verbeyst, 6
Vermillion, 190, 202, 320
Vermot, 320
Vernon, 42, 507
Verplanck, 488
Vertu, 313
Vesey, 141
vessel **Advance**, 224
vessel **Alex Scott**, 24
vessel **Kensington**, 40
vessel **Legare**, 353
vessel **Niagara**, 50
vessel **Rescue**, 224
vessel **Tepeyac**, 40
vessels **Advance** & the **Rescue**, 138
Vethake, 310
Vibbard, 294
Victor, 48, 396
Vider, 459
Viele, 153, 253, 483
Vigo, 30, 80
Villard, 169
Villaverde, 387
Villipigue, 198
Vinal, 37, 318
Vincent, 8, 410
Violett, 169

Viper's Sting, 145
Visser, 105, 107, 110, 370, 413
Vivan, 130
Vivans, 119, 419
Vizard, 453
Vodges, 269
Vogel, 210
Voght, 96, 117, 119
Vogt, 38, 383
Vollenhoven, 504
Volucia, 319
Von Essen, 106
Von Kapff, 18
Von Racknitz, 265
Von Witzleben, 284
Vonderlick, 366
Voorhees, 121, 507
Vorment, 314
Voss, 196, 282, 439
Vourk, 438
Vowell, 8
Vreeland, 224, 234

W

W, 399
Waddell, 344, 355
Wade, 83, 198, 294, 326, 329, 338, 342
Wadsworth, 105, 205, 222, 259
Waggaman, 340
Waggoner, 370
Wagner, 105, 367
Wail, 133
Wailes, 508
Wainwright, 404, 410, 499
Wait, 404, 496
Waite, 173, 386, 390
Wakefield, 307
Wakeling, 412
Walbach, 163, 329, 334, 426
Waldimar, 195
Waldridge, 206
Waldron, 163, 435
Waldrop, 205
Wales, 19, 48, 95, 127, 476
Walke, 344, 488

Walker, 41, 42, 51, 56, 62, 96, 99, 100, 105, 106, 108, 117, 119, 132, 139, 141, 149, 186, 189, 190, 195, 264, 278, 291, 304, 309, 314, 315, 318, 322, 327, 330, 361, 372, 376, 379, 380, 382, 418, 423, 436, 451, 455, 468, 481, 494, 508
Wall, 45, 83, 93, 102, 107, 110, 413, 458, 508
Wallace, 88, 107, 213, 227, 240, 252, 280, 283, 296, 309, 330, 366, 367, 394, 417, 455, 469, 483, 484, 508
Wallach, 133, 166, 187, 201, 202, 213, 229, 230, 239, 263, 272, 287, 288, 366, 374, 378, 385, 406, 435, 437, 443, 449, 474
Wallack, 319
Walleinstein, 370
Wallen, 326
Waller, 37, 218, 245, 371, 508
Wallingsford, 39, 107, 264
Wallis, 152, 197
Walls, 377
Waln, 215, 352
Walnut Grange, 405
Walsh, 53, 100, 110, 127, 135, 139, 303, 429, 458, 464, 466
Walter, 2, 39, 77, 94, 289, 352
Walters, 309
Walthall, 399
Waly, 304
Wampole, 389
Wand, 132
Wankowicz, 43
Wankowitz, 191
Wannall, 110, 166
Wantland, 376
Wanton, 39
Waples, 301
Warburton, 269
Ward, 41, 58, 63, 66, 76, 86, 102, 107, 110, 114, 138, 141, 155, 179, 187, 191, 288, 291, 294, 302, 361, 403, 417, 426, 444, 464, 473, 477, 494, 508
Wardel, 496
Warden, 395

Warder, 110, 361
Ware, 341, 375
Warfield, 11, 14, 69, 75, 282, 395
Warfield Academy, 169
Waring, 303, 304
Warley, 249
Warner, 105, 146, 216, 362, 366, 379, 492
Warnock, 65
Warren, 213, 237, 327, 419, 491
Warrenton, 70
Warriner, 110
Warring, 508
Warrington, 2, 83, 143, 147, 154, 187, 375
Warters, 237
Warwick, 132
Washburn, 277, 386, 508
Washingto Nat'l Monument, 347
Washington, 43, 44, 70, 73, 89, 92, 130, 213, 247, 248, 256, 272, 276, 295, 298, 311, 327, 340, 371, 407, 410, 419, 470, 483, 485
Waterloo, 418
Waters, 55, 110, 118, 198, 264, 267, 353, 361, 368, 405, 508
Watkins, 118, 159, 257, 302, 340, 456, 508
Watmough, 85
Watson, 2, 6, 12, 25, 46, 58, 62, 84, 105, 110, 118, 125, 155, 184, 237, 342, 366, 389, 494, 508
Watt, 61, 313
Watterson, 396
Watterston, 40, 99, 105, 154, 292, 476, 508
Wattles, 13
Watts, 61, 371, 455, 456, 459, 464
Waugh, 68, 347, 470, 471, 508
Wayman, 233
Wayne, 6, 376, 419
Weast, 234
Weatherhead, 53
Weaver, 133, 310, 313, 422

Webb, 69, 73, 81, 98, 112, 141, 161, 198, 299, 323, 347, 366, 367, 370, 412, 439, 443, 452, 453
Weber, 105, 224, 310
Webster, 7, 21, 55, 58, 99, 138, 146, 152, 161, 176, 208, 249, 254, 257, 259, 275, 279, 288, 296, 330, 342, 346, 361, 388, 394, 398, 408, 414, 448, 486
Weed, 6, 158, 198, 367, 450
Weeden, 289
Weeks, 41, 68, 148, 177, 344
Weems, 3, 134, 203, 320, 491
Wehnert, 91
Weideig, 469
Weidman, 175
Weightman, 446
Weir, 56, 249, 404
Weissinger, 93
Weister, 233
Welch, 32, 223, 283, 508
Welchmann, 110
Weld, 388, 392, 399, 484
Wellbaum, 336
Weller, 176
Welles, 213
Wellesley, 443
Wellford, 138, 144
Welling, 337
Wells, 72, 118, 142, 217, 233, 234, 271, 301, 330, 340, 341, 401, 407, 413, 469
Welmore, 170
Welsh, 31, 106, 112, 119, 413, 445
Wendell, 87
Wentsril, 100
Wentworth, 263, 284, 324, 342
Wentworths, 432
Werdon, 61
Werner, 366
Werther, 498
Wertz, 148, 508
Wesley, 65, 96, 489
West, 58, 79, 84, 91, 106, 113, 114, 115, 153, 155, 158, 169, 236, 255, 350, 366, 373, 396, 414
Westcott, 107, 110, 353

Westerfield, 110, 366, 368, 461
Western Connexion, 185
Weston, 151, 163
Wethered, 452
Wetherford, 279
Wetherspoon, 448
Wetmore, 22, 74, 192
Weymouth, 252, 443
Whalen, 230
Whaling, 421
Wharton, 196, 486, 508
Wheat, 105
Wheate, 273, 495
Wheatley, 107, 112, 115, 260, 372, 405, 508
Wheatly, 150
Wheeler, 72, 99, 105, 110, 264, 267, 305, 478, 493
Wheelock, 81, 218, 328, 483
Whelan, 406
Wherrett, 246
Whetmore, 34
Whicher, 155, 158, 340, 396
Whicker, 255
Whieher, 75
Whinery, 68
Whipple, 49, 195, 227, 435
Whitacre, 380
Whitaker, 491, 494
Whitcomb, 68, 205, 430
White, 14, 17, 19, 28, 34, 49, 56, 61, 70, 77, 78, 83, 89, 92, 97, 110, 123, 125, 146, 186, 199, 204, 231, 234, 250, 252, 253, 256, 277, 287, 302, 303, 313, 327, 342, 366, 370, 371, 391, 393, 401, 411, 426, 444, 451, 454, 464, 471, 482, 486
Whiteford, 330
Whitemore, 439
Whitescarver, 480
Whitfield, 384
Whitford, 340
Whiting, 56, 67, 137, 325, 470, 477, 482, 500
Whitlock, 105
Whitman, 176, 245, 251, 268

Whitmore, 362
Whitney, 8, 12, 190, 241, 246, 280, 304, 341, 417, 495, 508
Whiton, 434
Whittemberg, 336
Whittemore, 492
Whittier, 56, 495
Whittlesey, 110, 212, 220, 397
Whitwell, 366, 420, 476
Wickes, 167
Wickham, 137, 430
Wickliffe, 98, 348
Wickmine, 154
Wickware, 35
Widener, 218
Widup, 199
Wier, 181
Wiggeman, 366
Wight, 460
Wigle, 508
Wigley, 449
Wigton, 101
Wilberforce, 225, 239
Wilbor, 355
Wilbur, 129, 341
Wilcox, 15, 58, 210, 294, 326, 343, 366, 387, 398, 412, 436, 448
Wilde, 458
Wilder, 13, 81
Wiley, 41, 187, 321
Wilkerson, 58, 267, 366, 436
Wilkes, 56, 97, 148, 189, 482
Wilkins, 3, 110, 141, 163, 233, 305
Wilkinson, 24, 65, 96, 163, 227, 233, 247, 321, 465, 489
Willard, 114, 127, 222
Willer, 197
Willet, 366, 419
Willett, 210
William, 368
Williams, 2, 5, 12, 14, 16, 18, 22, 23, 24, 28, 33, 44, 49, 54, 62, 64, 73, 75, 78, 81, 94, 102, 105, 106, 107, 108, 110, 113, 117, 121, 142, 147, 154, 155, 156, 162, 164, 171, 186, 189, 210, 214, 226, 227, 229, 234, 244, 250, 251, 272, 273, 279, 294, 303, 311, 313, 327, 332, 340, 341, 343, 350, 351, 361, 362, 379, 380, 387, 396, 398, 399, 400, 408, 417, 426, 427, 432, 441, 449, 451, 452, 460, 472, 479, 481, 482, 483, 484, 491, 499, 508
Williamson, 53, 196, 237, 322, 417, 442, 486, 496, 498
Willing, 441
Willink, 11
Willis, 81, 85, 141, 151, 262, 428, 496
Willisma, 226
Willitz, 14
Wills, 33, 282
Willson, 77, 107, 319
Wilmer, 9, 356
Wilmot, 443
Wilner, 110
Wilson, 8, 10, 17, 21, 27, 28, 40, 48, 56, 58, 62, 66, 68, 82, 87, 92, 99, 100, 103, 105, 107, 110, 111, 112, 115, 118, 122, 131, 158, 162, 164, 165, 180, 181, 183, 184, 188, 189, 198, 213, 217, 230, 233, 234, 236, 241, 267, 278, 288, 294, 304, 310, 325, 328, 356, 361, 362, 366, 367, 370, 374, 376, 384, 388, 389, 393, 394, 412, 417, 418, 425, 431, 434, 436, 441, 455, 463, 468, 472, 473, 486, 490, 492, 500, 508
Wiltberger, 101, 204, 266, 508
Wimsatt, 81, 112, 222, 267, 323
Winchester, 318, 366, 411
Winden, 434
Winder, 130, 307, 328, 403, 404, 414, 508
Wineman, 118
Winfield, 51, 386
Winfrey, 198
Wingenroth, 114
Winn, 192, 240
Winneford, 241
Winpenny, 149
Winship, 481
Winslow, 65, 157, 164, 233
Winsor, 126

581

Winston, 62, 381, 428, 465, 480
Winter, 105, 110, 287, 366
Winthrop, 395, 491
Wintinger, 375
Wirick, 78
Wirt, 121, 186, 288, 366
Wise, 27, 53, 82, 101, 102, 105, 127, 193, 252, 266, 339, 347, 362, 366, 368, 371, 427, 440, 444, 455, 461, 476
Wishart, 143
Wislizenus, 463
Wister, 413
Witcher, 186
Withers, 329, 391, 435, 475, 480
Witt, 78, 296
Wittick, 313
WmWheat, 287
Wold, 380
Wolf, 372, 399, 444
Wollard, 267, 338, 412, 431, 446
Wollcott, 341
Womble, 336
Wombwell, 499
Wonderlich, 370
Wonderlick, 110
Wood, 22, 26, 42, 47, 55, 79, 123, 143, 161, 163, 177, 182, 187, 195, 199, 237, 261, 278, 289, 293, 296, 312, 314, 322, 326, 352, 362, 366, 370, 391, 401, 410, 422, 452, 469, 475, 476, 483, 484, 486, 493, 508
Woodbridge, 6, 142, 269
Woodburn, 28, 145, 181
Woodbury, 186, 201, 270, 381
Woodcock, 73
Woodfield, 456
Woodford, 210
Woodhull, 319
Woodland, 362, 382
Woodruff, 313
Woods, 27, 51, 193, 254, 324, 362, 378, 390
Woodside, 508
Woodward, 27, 40, 46, 53, 110, 202, 204, 207, 222, 342, 352, 444, 494
Woodworth, 13, 43, 116, 129, 137, 177

Wool, 200, 244, 383, 386, 464
Woolery, 279
Woolley, 6, 22, 42, 85, 124, 153, 249
Woolsey, 36, 58, 227
Woolworth, 133
Wooster, 482, 483, 484
Worden, 136, 187, 362
Wordsworth, 205, 207
Wormley, 106, 284, 310
Wormly, 115
Wormsley, 17
Worrall, 67
Worth, 3, 43, 45, 83, 137, 164, 204, 281, 310, 472
Wortham, 128
Worthen, 297, 301
Worthington, 176, 180, 221, 236, 367, 374, 403, 412, 462, 481
Wotherspoon, 272
Wozencraft, 397, 419
Wren, 25, 115, 233, 368
Wright, 20, 33, 41, 42, 58, 64, 65, 69, 72, 93, 96, 106, 115, 120, 141, 143, 167, 181, 184, 196, 199, 202, 218, 238, 249, 276, 277, 294, 318, 329, 362, 403, 415, 437, 463
Wroe, 112, 508
Wyatt, 477, 487
Wyche, 375
Wylie, 71
Wyman, 328, 426
Wymbs, 32
Wynan, 404
Wynnes, 347

Y

yacht **Twilight**, 433
Yanardy, 453
Yarbrough, 422
Yarrington, 424
Yates, 66, 100, 106, 161, 211, 310
Yeates, 115, 336
Yeatman, 107, 359
Yerby, 110, 216, 302, 367, 449
York, 341
Yost, 94

Young, 44, 58, 69, 77, 87, 106, 107, 113, 115, 128, 135, 138, 154, 156, 158, 161, 163, 184, 187, 201, 202, 210, 212, 213, 254, 256, 261, 278, 302, 330, 331, 333, 334, 343, 359, 362, 366, 370, 397, 398, 399, 413, 417, 426, 435, 439, 440, 450, 461, 476, 488, 508
Youngs, 341
Yulee, 180
Yuob, 313
Yznardy, 337

Z

Zandt, 445
Zantzinger, 120
Zekind, 233
Zelinger, 210
Zell, 156
Zerbee, 148
Zimmerman, 75, 155, 158, 176, 255, 396
Zolkowski, 52
Zueile, 67

Other Heritage Books by the author:

National Intelligencer *Newspaper Abstracts*
Special Edition: The Civil War Years
Volume 1: January 1, 1861-June 30, 1863

National Intelligencer *Newspaper Abstracts*
Special Edition: The Civil War Years
Volume 2: July 1, 1863-December 31, 1865

National Intelligencer *Newspaper Abstracts 1850*

National Intelligencer *Newspaper Abstracts 1849*

National Intelligencer *Newspaper Abstracts 1848*

National Intelligencer *Newspaper Abstracts 1847*

National Intelligencer *Newspaper Abstracts 1846*

National Intelligencer *Newspaper Abstracts 1845*

National Intelligencer *Newspaper Abstracts 1844*

National Intelligencer *Newspaper Abstracts 1843*

National Intelligencer *Newspaper Abstracts 1842*

National Intelligencer *Newspaper Abstracts 1841*

National Intelligencer *Newspaper Abstracts 1840*

National Intelligencer *Newspaper Abstracts, 1838-1839*

National Intelligencer *Newspaper Abstracts, 1836-1837*

National Intelligencer *Newspaper Abstracts, 1834-1835*

National Intelligencer *Newspaper Abstracts, 1832-1833*

National Intelligencer *Newspaper Abstracts, 1830-1831*

National Intelligencer *Newspaper Abstracts, 1827-1829*

National Intelligencer *Newspaper Abstracts, 1824-1826*

National Intelligencer *Newspaper Abstracts, 1821-1823*

National Intelligencer *Newspaper Abstracts, 1818-1820*

National Intelligencer *Newspaper Abstracts, 1814-1817*

National Intelligencer *Newspaper Abstracts, 1811-1813*

National Intelligencer *Newspaper Abstracts, 1806-1810*

National Intelligencer *Newspaper Abstracts, 1800-1805*

www.ingramcontent.com/pod-product-compliance
Lightning Source LLC
Chambersburg PA
CBHW070004010526
44117CB00011B/1425